Get It Together

Readings About African American Life

AKUA DUKU ANOKYE
Arizona State University West

JACQUELINE BRICE-FINCH
Benedict College

Longman

New York San Francisco Boston
London Toronto Sydney Tokyo Singapore Madrid
Mexico City Munich Paris Cape Town Hong Kong Montreal

Senior Vice President and Publisher: Joseph Opiela
Acquisitions Editor: Lynn M. Huddon
Executive Marketing Manager: Ann Stypuloski
Production Manager: Donna DeBenedictis
Project Coordination, Text Design, and Electronic Page Makeup: The Clarinda Company
Cover Designer/Manager: John Callahan
Cover Image: Jacob Lawrence (1917–2000). *The Library*, 1960. Tempera on fiberboard, 24 ×
   29-⅞ʺ (60.9 × 75.9 cm). Smithsonian American Art Museum, Washington,
   DC/U.S.A./Art Resource, NY.
Manufacturing Buyer: Roy Pickering
Printer and Binder: The Maple-Vail Book Manufacturing Group
Cover Printer: Phoenix Color Corporation

Library of Congress Cataloging-in-Publication Data

Get it together: readings about African American life/[compiled] by Akua Duku Anokye,
Jacqueline Brice-Finch.
        p. cm.
     Includes bibliographical references and index.
     ISBN 0-321-09268-6 (pbk.)
        1. African Americans—Social conditions. 2. African Americans—History. 3. African
Americans—Intellectual life. 4. United States—Social conditions. 5. United States—
Race relations. I. Anokye, Akua Duku. II. Brice-Finch, Jacqueline.

E185.86 .G44 2003
305.896′073—dc21

                                                                              2002030161

Please visit our website at http://www.ablongman.com

ISBN 0-321-09268-6

1 2 3 4 5 6 7 8 9 10—MA—05 04 03 02

For our parents,

Bernard Edward Brice and Elaine LaNear Hopkins Brice
Finus Melvin Harris and Helen Marie Hatchett Mitchell

and
our loving children,

Nataki Finch Richards
Yao Nmanu Opare Dinizulu

CONTENTS

Preface xi

1 The Color Line: Racism 1

W. E. B. DuBois ■ "Of Our Spiritual Strivings" 2

Ralph Bunche ■ "What Is Race?" 8

Richard Wright ■ "The Ethics of Living Jim Crow:
An Autobiographical Sketch" 12

Langston Hughes ■ "Who's Passing for Who?" 16

James McBride ■ "Black Power" 19

Toi Derricotte ■ from *The Black Notebooks* 22

Kathy Russell, Midge Wilson, and Ronald E. Hall ■ "Black Identity:
Shades of Beauty and Pride" 24

Shelby Steele ■ "Race-Holding" 27

Stanley Fish ■ "Reverse Racism, or How the Pot Got to Call the Kettle
Black" 30

George F. Will ■ "Dropping the 'One Drop' Rule" 37

Media Resources 40

2 Talk That Talk 41

Geneva Smitherman ■ "From African to African American" 43

W. F. Allen ■ "The Negro Dialect" 47

Literary Digest ■ "Objecting to the Negro Dialect" 52

Zora Neale Hurston ■ "Pa Henry's Prayer"   54

Countee Cullen ■ "Incident"   56

Amiri Baraka ■ "Primitive Blues and Primitive Jazz"   56

Keith Gilyard ■ "A Legacy of Healing: Words, African Americans, and Power"   59

Linguistic Society of America ■ "Linguistic Society of America Resolution on the Oakland 'Ebonics' Issue"   69

Jacqueline Brice-Finch ■ "Ebonics: When Is Dialect Acceptable English?"   70

Akua Duku Anokye ■ "A Case for Orality in the Classroom"   72

Robert W. Reising ■ "Do We Need a National Language Policy?"   75

Emma D. Jackson ■ "The N-Word"   76

Gwen Pough ■ "Confronting and Changing Images and Representations of Black Womanhood in Rap Music"   81

Media Resources   85

3 Warriors on the Trading Block   87

William Wells Brown ■ "The Narrative of William W. Brown: From Slave to Abolitionist"   90

James Weldon Johnson ■ "Black Manhattan"   91

Charles Aikens ■ "The Struggle of Curt Flood"   94

Mark Conrad ■ "Blue-Collar Law and Basketball"   100

Dennis A. Williams ■ "Robbing the Cradle"   109

Susan Cahn ■ "'Cinderellas' of Sport: Black Women in Track and Field"   111

Peter King ■ "The NFL's Black Eye"   114

Jon Entine ■ "More Brains or More . . ."   115

Harry Edwards ■ "Crisis of Black Athletes on the Eve of the 21st Century"   119

John Edgar Wideman ■ "Hoop Roots"   125

Media Resources   129

4 Justice/Just-Us? 131

David Walker ■ "David Walker's Appeal in Four Articles: Preamble" 132

Scott L. Malcomson ■ "We Can Be as Separate as the Fingers: Segregation from the American Revolution to the Gilded Age" 135

Ida B. Wells-Barnett ■ "A Red Record: The Case Stated" 142

Derrick Bell ■ "Neither Separate Schools Nor Mixed Schools: The Chronicle of the Sacrificed Black Schoolchildren" 148

Sonia Sanchez ■ "elegy" 163

Kenneth Meeks ■ "Shopping in a Group While Black: A Coach's Story" 165

Lieutenant Arthur Doyle ■ "From the Inside Looking Out: Twenty-Nine Years in the New York Police Department" 168

Johnnie Cochran ■ "My Brother's Keeper" 173

Mary Fisher ■ "The Witch-Hunt" 181

Carl Rowan ■ "The Clarence Thomas Fiasco" 193

Media Resources 204

5 The Mirror Has Many Faces 205

Donald Bogle ■ "Black Beginnings: From *Uncle Tom's Cabin* to *The Birth of a Nation*" 206

James Baldwin ■ "My Dungeon Shook: Letter to My Nephew on the One Hundredth Anniversary of the Emancipation" 216

Ted Joans ■ "Je suis un homme" 219

Mari Evans ■ "I Am a Black Woman" 221

John Langston Gwaltney ■ "The Many Shades of Black: Angela McArthur and Celia Delaney" 223

Johnetta B. Cole ■ "Culture: Negro, Black, and Nigger" 231

Michael Eric Dyson ■ "Bill Cosby and the Politics of Race" 237

Jewelle Gomez ■ "Black Lesbians: Passing, Stereotypes, and Transformation" 244

Media Resources 250

6 One Family, One Blood   253

John W. Blassingame ■ "The Slave Family" 254

Frank D. Banks ■ "Plantation Courtship" 269

Guy Bailey, Natalie Maynor, and Patricia Cukor-Avila ■ "Laura Smalley" 270

Etheridge Knight ■ "The Idea of Ancestry" 273

Joseph Beam ■ "Color Him Father: An Interview" 275

Elizabeth Clark-Lewis ■ "A Woman Just Wouldn't" 277

Farai Chideya ■ "The Myth of the Welfare Queen" 282

Anna Mulrine ■ "In Praise of Black Family Reunions" 286

Marian Wright Edelman ■ "A Family Legacy" 287

Morehouse Research Institute ■ "Turning the Corner on Father Absence in Black America: About the Morehouse Conference" 289

Media Resources 307

7 We Come This Far by Faith   309

Stacey K. Close ■ "Sending Up Some Timber: Elderly Slaves and Religious Leadership in the Antebellum Slave Community" 311

Gwendolyn Sims Warren ■ "Steal Away: Traditional Spiritual" 319

Jarena Lee ■ "The Subject of My Call to Preach Renewed" 321

Frederick Douglass ■ "Black Churches and Segregation" 327

Cheryl Townsend Gilkes ■ "Together and in Harness: Women's Traditions in the Sanctified Church" 329

Malcolm X and Alex Haley ■ "Mecca" 333

Alice Walker ■ "Roselily" 336

James S. Tinney ■ "Why a Black Gay Church?" 340

Mikelle Smith Omari-Tunkara ■ "Completing the Circle: Notes on African Art, Society, and Religion in Oyotunji, South Carolina" 342

Monica Rhor ■ "For U.S. Blacks, an Ancient Faith, a Renewed Hope"   346

Susan Taylor ■ "Coming to Faith"   348

Media Resources   352

Credits   355

Index   359

PREFACE

Get it together. Such a simple sentence, as in, "You better . . ."; the threat of punishment hanging over a child's head—"When you . . ."; the promise of enrichment (a reward, reconciliation after an argument). The "it," that elusive indeterminate pronoun which embodies one's intellect, one's physicality, one's spirit; the "it" that embraces family, community, nation, planet—if we earthlings don't get it together, nurturing each other as ourselves, will "it" matter?

In the African American community, the admonishment, "You better get yourself together," has societal implications. Given the privilege of whiteness that permeates all aspects of American society still, many African Americans grow up under the pressure to be twice as good while both acquiring book learning and relying on common sense. "Get it together" is a reminder to be thoughtful, aware, concerned, involved in order to survive and thrive. Minds, hearts, souls always have to be "in the game" of life. Hence, in response to this call, many folks have worked hard to "get it together." The title of this collection, therefore, has a long tradition in the African American community. It recognizes and embraces the need to obtain the necessary information in order to be a productive, conscientious member of the community.

The urge to "get it together" is seen not only in issues of racism, language, or even sports but also in issues of justice, images, family, and spirituality—all clearly issues, concerns, problems, and achievements of African Americans that have contributed to the history and making of America. *Get It Together: Readings About African American Life* underscores the spirit of holistic interdisciplinary education and provides exposure to the problems that have made African Americans both unique to and, at the same time, representative of American culture. The seven topics are examined in successive chapters. Each chapter includes a wide variety of readings—primarily nonfiction—that illustrate the experiences of African Americans. The selections contextualize or historicize the topic, foregrounding contemporary writings by including selections from the nineteenth century or early to mid-twentieth century that lay the groundwork for pieces found in current periodicals and literary sources. In this way the chapters present the continuity of problems and concerns of black America.

This collection aims to bring together topics that will help readers "get it together" by providing historically connected essays and articles about a multiplicity of subjects in one text. These selections provoke and promote critical thinking about how the issues impact the lives of all Americans. The author note preceding each reading provides a means for understanding the author's engagement with the topic and his or her contribution to the struggle to "get it together." In truth, an underlying notion of this book is that some issues for African Americans have not substantially changed. Throughout, the authors support this idea.

The focus of Chapter 1, "The Color Line," is on racism. How does a parent teach a child that the color of one's skin matters? That it can affect the way the child learns the mannerisms and mores that the child absorbs? The opportunities and privileges accorded? How does a child internalize the concept white and black when these colors are applied to skin hues ranging from alabaster to midnight? How does an adult explain rationally and logically why color matters in these United States today, yesterday, yesteryear?

One drop of so-called black blood or being at least one-sixteenth black was believed to define a person as African American in the past. Now many persons of mixed parentage are demanding that they not be forced to choose white or black on government documents, such as the U.S. Census, or on employment applications. They check both categories, European American and African American. Some choose the "Other" category; still others fill in "Human" when asked about their "race."

Chapter 2, "Talk That Talk," points out the problems of African Americans talking that talk over several centuries in America. It also celebrates African American linguistic ingenuity. "Nommo," belief in the magical power of the word, frames this experience and spans social, political, musical, spiritual, emotional, even psychological boundaries. If African American language begins and ends with the recognition of the power of words, then what's in a name? The writers in "Talk That Talk" examine naming practices, names, history, and trends, including the age-old controversy of a hated name used in reference to the African American.

One of the ugliest ongoing controversies in America revolves around Black English. In spite of documented evidence of Black English use, there is still today denial that it either exists or that it should be classified as a bona fide language form. Interestingly enough, not only are features of Black English used in some form by a substantial number of African Americans, but also black style has been co-opted by mainstream television, advertising, and the media. The popular Budweiser beer commercial that uses the phrase "Whatzup?" is an easy example. The chapter also explores African American traditions in music and the powerful oral language practices that connect them, traditions that span the field hollers of the eighteenth and nineteenth centuries and the present-day hip-hop revolution. Reading the historical insights about the use and description of African American language should provide readers with evidence that will assist them in the evaluation of their own beliefs, values, and expectations about those who "talk that talk."

The African American's experience in sports has been a rocky road, including untold stories of heroism, dedication, abuse, misrepresentation, discrimination, and heartache. No matter the gender, there have been harsh lessons. The purpose of Chapter 3, "Warriors on the Trading Block," is to illustrate not just the tremendous achievements and glorious records but also the examples of racism, discrimination, barriers, and stereotypes that men and women in sports have had to overcome. It attempts to show that many of these struggles are similar to those surrounding the slave auction. It can be argued that the militant rebellions and slave revolts are in some ways reflected in the trailblazing actions of today's gladiators. The title of the chapter, "Warriors on the Trading Block," aptly reflects this notion.

There are many troubling questions regarding the athlete. What about free agency is not free? How can contracts (athletes) be bought and sold without consultation, using the "reserve clause" as bait? What about the millions of dollars earned in revenues by athletic departments in colleges and universities across this nation? Why can't the athletes reap those monetary benefits? Do athletes really get an education while playing "the game"? Writers in this section express opinions regarding these questions and more, including the horribly persistent stereotypes and the continued use of mascots that caricature blacks and other minorities. Why are so many Americans oblivious to the racism embedded in these behaviors? This chapter gives students an opportunity to read about some of the ongoing struggles of the African American athlete as a microcosm of the struggles of African Americans. It ends with a moving description by John Edgar Wideman that creates a moment of reflection on sports figures as "warriors on the trading block."

The writings in Chapter 4, "Justice/Just-Us?", trace the great strides of a people to secure legal remedies even when the laws themselves were promulgated to deprive them of all rights as human beings. It is no wonder that the African American community has a wary relationship with law enforcement. Justice for African Americans during the Colonial Period was grounded in laws designed to deny them basic civil and human rights. The liberators of colonial America, so-called traitors from the British perspective, could not relinquish their economic windfall resulting from slavery in order to extend their inalienable rights to blacks and Native Americans. White colonists welcomed the support of blacks during the Revolutionary War to free this nation from the tyranny of Great Britain. Yet when blacks acted to end the tyranny of slavery, freedom fighters such as Nat Turner, Gabriel Vesey, Frederick Douglass, and Harriet Tubman were labeled contraband, runaway slaves with bounties on their heads, or killed as insurgents. The free men and women of color saw over this same period a steady deterioration of rights, culminating in the Fugitive Slave Act of 1850. Following the Civil War, Jim Crow laws plagued the country well into the last third of the twentieth century.

Yet, this same U.S. legal system has been used to redress judicial ills. With the passage of the Thirteenth, Fourteenth, and Fifteenth Amendments to the Constitution after the Civil War, it appeared that full redress was a consideration. However, the circumvention of the intent of these amendments through states' rights initiatives created another, brutal servitude for African Americans—segregation. The Civil Rights Movement of the 1950s and 1960s sparked the legislative, executive, and judicial branches of the federal government to enact laws, programs, and enforcement mechanisms to establish a more equitable republic. However, the toll on the United States, especially the African American community, has been great. All facets of life for the African American have been affected by unfair laws: housing; education—public and private schools and universities; private, municipal, state, and federal employment; health; human services; the military; and property.

The judicial system is still inequitable, with many African Americans feeling that some laws are for "just us." Crime remains a racial divide, whether the issue is drugs, theft, robbery, murder, or white-collar infractions. Statistically, African Americans are disproportionately arrested and imprisoned. This chapter contains writings of fiction and fact that address the above-mentioned issues from many perspectives. The problems are many; the solutions few.

Chapter 5, "The Mirror Has Many Faces," addresses the myths and stereotypes associated with African Americans. How does one develop a healthy self-image when the dominant culture of one's nation chooses to celebrate the features of only one cultural group? This conundrum Africans faced when they arrived in the United States. The people who claimed to be their masters looked nothing like the Ibos and Yorubas and Fan and other African peoples. The Africans were told that they were physically ugly because of their skin color and Negroid features, that their mannerisms were beastly and their mores heathen. Some were cowed by these assessments, but others stubbornly maintained their pride in all aspects of their personhood and culture.

The concept of the melting pot through assimilation and integration had become an intrinsic part of American life by the eighteenth century. Conformity in dress, language, and cultural and social habits were the American way. Deviation from these rules of orderliness resulted in ostracism, or worse. People of African descent learned quickly that they had to praise their own people, promote their own role models, because the European Americans who controlled the press, the media, and other means of communication were intent on celebrating whiteness and often ignored or denigrated blackness. African Americans used their creativity in the arts to celebrate their cultural heritage, which they enriched by absorbing and often transforming mores from the dominant European American culture.

The stereotypes and myths associated with African Americans abound. Sadly, African Americans believe many of these false assumptions. Many were propagated to justify the enslavement of Africans. Biblical scripture was distorted to condone slavery. Slaves were property and had no rights. They could be made to breed and their offspring sold or raised by others. Although they were not allowed to have monogamous relationships without the consent of the slave master, the men and women in bondage were nevertheless labeled licentious even though they were forced to mate with many partners. A hierarchy within the slave community developed as the house slaves learned trades and garnered opportunities for a better life usually denied to the field slaves. House slaves were often the progeny of the slave master, and another myth arose that the whiter the skin, the more intelligent the slave. However, the mulatto was also thought to be discontented because of the racial mixing. Intraracial prejudice or colorism arose from this preferential treatment and mixing of the races. The legacy of this propaganda and conditioning is still apparent in American life. The very words used to describe African Americans of certain skin tones are qualitative: *light-skinned, clear, fair, dark*. This chapter explores some of the issues that still persist today.

Readings in Chapter 6, "One Family, One Blood," explore wide-ranging topics related to the family. The African American family has been under siege ever since the first slave was brought to these shores. Yet there is a tenacity and resiliency that refuses to allow its complete destruction. Conditions of courtship, love, marriage, child rearing, work, and economic and political pressures have had an impact on the African American family. Are fathers really absent from the family? What are the repercussions of "broken families"? What role did slavery play in the shaping of the African American family? How have proud men and women conveyed pride while facilitating survival in a hostile climate? How important is the extended family, and how is it maintained in American society? Why are single mothers portrayed as immoral and loose, or masculine and virile, or elderly mammies, or man-eating shrews?

The African American family survived slavery because the community uncles, aunts, and neighbors took responsibility for rearing the children. With the threat of selling, maiming, and raping ever present during that period, the community was left to pick up the pieces. Even though men were unable to protect their wives, mothers, or children, they did what they could to contribute to everyone's survival. Today, the absence of the father—whether imposed through such conditions as imprisonment, war, or economic hardships—adds to the assortment of problems in the African American family. Nevertheless, black women have persevered, reared remarkable children, and have been the mainstay of religious and social institutions.

Positive forces are at work to strengthen the African American family. Using their own families as models, some writers in this chapter discuss the benefits of service to their community and the strengthening of African American families through such organized practices as family reunions. These instructions give hope for positive growth through extended family support and community involvement, building on the tradition of "one family, one blood."

Faith is the trust, confidence, and complete acceptance of a truth that cannot be demonstrated or proved by the process of logical thought. The concluding chapter, "We Come This Far by Faith," fittingly demonstrates the glue that has held the African American community together in spite of its many hardships and troubles: faith, the will to remain loyal, steadfast, and conscientious. The spirituality of the African American extends from African roots. This faith in the spirit has been the mainstay of African Americans and has long been a source of wonder, praise, and stability.

The indisputable continuity with the African worldview shows itself in the interesting admixture of sacred and secular in music, language, art, and community that reinforces and affirms the importance of spiritual experience in daily life. Regardless of the many attempts to deny African American cultural or religious traditions predating the slave experience, numerous practices did survive the Middle Passage, and these are nowhere more apparent than in the African American religious experience. The call and response pattern between the minister and the congregation and the powerful place spiritual leaders hold in African American society are only two of many examples of the profound effect of Africa. The church, temple, and shrine has been the center of social and political power and change from Nat Turner to Jesse Jackson, from Sojourner Truth to Minister Ava Muhammad. Time and again, as readers study the revolts, the movements, and the civil actions embraced by the African American, they find religious leaders at the apex. Whether one investigates films, music, poetry, or short stories, the spiritual experience is at the core.

Chapter 7 invokes not one religious experience but many. Writers examine the Christian, Muslim, and traditional African religious experiences of African Americans that continue to flourish into the twenty-first century. Added to these experiences is the "new age" affirmation of faith in self and a higher spiritual, divine force. Thus, the readings in this chapter express the collective spiritual search in the past and in the present. They also share the intention of establishing a framework for continued activism, positivism, change, and stability in the African American community. After reading this chapter, the reader cannot help but see that the African American has "Come This Far by Faith."

Our hope is that *Get It Together* will engage readers through its inclusion of contextual and real-life situations. The readings, preceded by biographical author notes, show African American life in action. Whether celebrations of double consciousness, language dexterity, physical excellence, justice, family, or spiritual connection, the readings reflect African American experiences past and present. Teachers and students may choose from several selections in this text that aptly illuminate the issues. Some will want to use other works with this anthology. Thus, we have tried to keep this book fairly brief to allow room in a course for use of other texts and readings.

Included at the end of each chapter are titles of suggested films and other media selections that supplement the readings. The films help sensitize the reader to the issues in a visual manner and reinforce the development of the themes. They help readers visualize the issues as they are played out in society. In fact, with the growing focus on visual literacy and students' responsiveness to visual stimuli, recent research has strongly supported multimedia approaches to learning and pedagogy. The films help readers to "get it together," to understand and interact with the readings, and to conduct further research. All of the media resources are readily available through college and university resources or local bookstores, libraries, and video stores.

Finally, *Get It Together: Readings about African American Life* is the outgrowth of conversations we have had about the classes we taught, the papers we presented, and the seminars and workshops we conducted about African American culture, its literature, language, mores, and faith. We often talked about the supplementary materials that we had to prepare, for all too often our students, colleagues, and audiences expressed a need for additional information to widen their perception and perspectives. We decided to "get ourselves together" and edit this collection.

▓ Acknowledgments

We wish to thank first and foremost our families for their support and encouragement during the past several years of this project. We especially thank our sisters—Kandaky Meriama Ashby, for her generosity in sharing her library files on African American culture as soon as she heard about the project, and Rebecca Hankins, whose archivist skills and resources have gotten us through several sleepless nights. We can't forget Kenneth Payton, who had the patience of Job. He didn't know what he was getting into.

We also owe a debt of gratitude to our colleagues and staff at our respective universities: University of Toledo—Jamie Barlowe and Joan Mullin; Arizona State University West—Dottie Broaddus, Millie Garcia, and Gloria Cuadraz; and James Madison University—Sandra Eagle, Karen Evans, Joan Frederick, and Kamau Kemayo. We were blessed with enthusiastic and relentless research assistants Traci Knapper, Camille Cain, Kim Nottingham, and Cat Lollis, and caring administrative assistants Stacey Kimbell and Dodie Peart at ASUW, along with JMU English Department secretaries Rose Gray and Judy Good and Benedict College administrative assistants Connie Outen and Dorothy Richardson, who willingly ignored our fits of inconsistency. Jamise Liddell's knowledgeable input and research on films was an immense help as was student worker Tawnte Garcia's tenacious Web search skills and Thomas Adkins' unrelenting cheer along with Liza Bacerra, Jessica Clark, Catherine Cornachio, David Gwin, Sarita Hartz, Marissa Johnson, Corinna Quinn, Travis Rountree, Kristin Sadler, Emily Setzer, Don Steele, and Torrey Templer.

For their feedback and long discussions about our work, we would also like to thank our fellow ETS/College Board consultants, particularly Pat Gantt and Roxanne Hannon Odum, as well as members of the NCTE and CCCC, especially Jacqueline Jones Royster and Keith Gilyard.

We appreciate the gracious support and assistance from librarians at Carrier Library at JMU, as well as Alderman and other libraries at the University of Virginia. We are especially grateful to Rebecca Feind, librarian extraordinaire at JMU's Carrier Library, Jennifer Glasscock at Broadway High School, and Dennis Isbell at ASU West's Fletcher Library for their cheerful assistance and expertise in finding elusive material, especially authors' notes.

We are surely grateful to the reviewers who gave of their time, expertise, and goodwill providing helpful comments and consistent encouragement for this project: Lisa Albrecht, University of Minnesota; Lena Ampadu, Towson University; Deborah Ayer, Emory University; Jonathan Bass, Samford University; Samantha Blackmon, Purdue University; Jane L. Donawerth, University of Maryland; Anthonia Kalu, University of Northern Colorado; Valerie F. Kinloch, University of Houston, Twin Cities; and Kathy Walsh, Central Oregon Community College.

Last, but not least, we wish to thank our editor at Longman Publishers, Lynn Huddon, for her unswerving support throughout the project; editorial assistant Kristi Olson; permissions editor Melanie M. Becker; and the many other staff persons who made this project a reality.

AKUA DUKU ANOKYE
JACQUELINE BRICE-FINCH

Get It Together

*Readings About
African American Life*

CHAPTER 1

The Color Line: Racism

The United States was founded by immigrants seeking new fortune, others searching for relief from persecution, and still others indentured to serve. Once it became profitable to enslave humans, an ideology was created in an attempt to sanction the atrocity. Although slavery was outlawed in the 1860s, the effects of this peculiar institution linger. The leaders of this nation continue to seek solutions to this endemic problem, which ravages all people.

How racism has affected America, and particularly the African American, is the focus of this chapter. The selections have been chosen and ordered to present various perspectives on race since the founding of the Republic. Within the African American community, the effects of racism have been pervasive, particularly psychologically and economically. Double consciousness, recognizing that one's color affects one's citizenry, remains a matter of survival.

The first selection is the first chapter of W. E. B. Du Bois's *The Souls of Black Folk,* published in 1903, in which Du Bois gives the historical context of race relations in America. He calls the major problem of the twentieth century the color line, the differentiation among people according to the color of their skin. At mid-century, Ralph Bunche researches the anthropological, historical, and social determinants for classifications of race. Richard Wright graphically delineates the harsh treatment he experienced as an African American teen during the 1930s and 1940s while being forced to adhere to Jim Crow laws and mores.

Langston Hughes, James McBride, and Toi Derricotte discuss the implications of passing, relying on physical features to blend into a community or majority culture. Hughes humorously satirizes the concept of race when people fail to determine whether a couple is black or white in a Harlem club during the 1950s. James McBride's mother, a white Jew, declares that she is a light-skinned black to deflect criticism for marrying a black man. And Toi Derricotte, presenting yet a third view, describes how she, an African American, deals with the mistaken assumption that she is white.

Kathy Russell, Midge Wilson, and Ronald Hall address the issue of biracial adoption in contemporary times. In their selection, the parents are white and their adopted daughter black. The daughter explains her confusion about her racial identity while growing up. Shelby Steele, Stanley Fish, and George Will offer commentary on more contemporary hot topics about race. Steele questions the use of the "race card" to excuse deficiencies. Fish exhorts Americans opposed to affirmative action to consider its historical context and the moral imperative to right a wrong. Will returns to a centuries-old belief that African American status is determined by the presence of any admixture of black ancestry. He endorses a California initiative to end government classification by race.

These selections provide a framework for discussion of racism and its causes, effects, and possible remedies.

W. E. B. Du Bois

W. E. B. Du Bois (1868–1963) was one of the great thinkers of the twentieth century. As one of the founders of the National Association for the Advancement of Colored People (NAACP), he served as the first editor of *Crisis,* its journal publication. Du Bois was also the first African American to earn a doctorate at Harvard University in 1895. His dissertation, *The Suppression of the African Slave Trade to the United States of America 1638–1870,* became the first volume in the Harvard Historical Studies series. His sociological studies include *The Philadelphia Negro* (1899), *The Gift of Black Folk: The Negroes in the Making of America* (1924), *Black Reconstruction: An Essay Toward a History of the Part Which Black Folk Played in the Attempt to Reconstruct Democracy in America, 1860–1880* (1935), and *Black Folk, Then and Now: An Essay in the History and Sociology of the Negro Race* (1939). His awards include the Spingarn Medal (1932), election to the National Institute of Arts and Letters (1943), and the Lenin International Peace Prize (1958).

The following is Chapter 1 from DuBois's 1903 ground-breaking study *The Souls of Black Folk,* in which he discusses double consciousness, the two-ness of being African American and American.

Of Our Spiritual Strivings

O water, voice of my heart, crying in the sand,
　　All night long crying with a mournful cry,
As I lie and listen, and cannot understand
　　　The voice of my heart in my side or the voice of the sea,
　　O water, crying for rest, is it I, is it I?
　　All night long the water is crying to me.

Unresting water, there shall never be rest
   Till the last moon droop and the last tide fail,
And the fire of the end begin to burn in the west;
      And the heart shall be weary and wonder and cry like the sea,
   All life long crying without avail,
      As the water all night long is crying to me.

ARTHUR SYMONS

Between me and the other world there is ever an unasked question: unasked by some through feelings of delicacy; by others through the difficulty of rightly framing it. All, nevertheless, flutter round it. They approach me in a half-hesitant sort of way, eye me curiously or compassionately, and then, instead of saying directly, How does it feel to be a problem? they say, I know an excellent colored man in my town; or, I fought at Mechanicsville; or, Do not these Southern outrages make your blood boil? At these I smile, or am interested, or reduce the boiling to a simmer, as the occasion may require. To the real question, How does it feel to be a problem? I answer seldom a word.

And yet, being a problem is a strange experience,—peculiar even for one who has never been anything else, save perhaps in babyhood and in Europe. It is in the early days of rollicking boyhood that the revelation first bursts upon one, all in a day, as it were. I remember well when the shadow swept across me. I was a little thing, away up in the hills of New England, where the dark Housatonic winds between Hoosac and Taghkanic to the sea. In a wee wooden schoolhouse, something put it into the boys' and girls' heads to buy gorgeous visiting-cards—ten cents a package—and exchange. The exchange was merry, till one girl, a tall newcomer, refused my card,—refused it peremptorily, with a glance. Then it dawned upon me with a certain suddenness that I was different from the others; or like, mayhap, in heart and life and longing, but shut out from their world by a vast veil. I had thereafter no desire to tear down that veil, to creep through; I held all beyond it in common contempt and lived above it in a region of blue sky and great wandering shadows. That sky was bluest when I could beat my mates at examination-time, or beat them at a foot-race, or even beat their stringy heads. Alas, with the years all this fine contempt began to fade; for the worlds I longed for, and all their dazzling opportunities, were theirs, not mine. But they should not keep these prizes, I said; some, all, I would wrest from them. Just how I would do it I could never decide: by reading law, by healing the sick, by telling the wonderful tales that swam in my head,—some way. With other black boys the strife was not so fiercely sunny: their youth shrunk into tasteless sycophancy, or into silent hatred of the pale world about them and mocking distrust of everything white; or wasted itself in a bitter cry, Why did God make me an outcast and a stranger in mine own house? The shades of the prison-house closed round about us all: walls strait and stubborn to the whitest, but relentlessly narrow, tall, and unscalable to sons of night who must plod darkly on in resignation, or beat unavailing palms against the stone, or steadily, half hopelessly, watch the streak of blue above.

After the Egyptian and Indian, the Greek and Roman, the Teuton and Mongolian, the Negro is a sort of seventh son, born with a veil, and gifted with second-sight in this American world,—a world which yields him no true self-consciousness, but only lets him see himself through the revelation of the other world. It is a peculiar sensation, this double-consciousness, this sense of always looking at one's self through the eyes of others, of measuring one's soul by the tape of a world that looks on in amused contempt and pity. One ever feels his two-ness,—an American, a Negro; two souls, two thoughts, two unreconciled strivings; two warring ideals in one dark body, whose dogged strength alone keeps it from being torn asunder.

The history of the American Negro is the history of this strife,—this longing to attain self-conscious manhood, to merge his double self into a better and truer self. In this merging he wishes neither of the older selves to be lost. He would not Africanize America, for America has too much to teach the world and Africa. He would not bleach his Negro soul in a flood of white Americanism, for he knows that Negro blood has a message for the world. He simply wishes to make it possible for a man to be both a Negro and an American, without being cursed and spit upon by his fellows, without having the doors of Opportunity closed roughly in his face.

This, then, is the end of his striving: to be a co-worker in the kingdom of culture, to escape both death and isolation, to husband and use his best powers and his latent genius. These powers of body and mind have in the past been strangely wasted, dispersed, or forgotten. The shadow of a mighty Negro past flits through the tale of Ethiopia the Shadowy and of Egypt the Sphinx. Throughout history, the powers of single black men flash here and there like falling stars, and die sometimes before the world has rightly gauged their brightness. Here in America, in the few days since Emancipation, the black man's turning hither and thither in hesitant and doubtful striving has often made his very strength to lose effectiveness, to seem like absence of power, like weakness. And yet it is not weakness,—it is the contradiction of double aims. The double-aimed struggle of the black artisan—on the one hand to escape white contempt for a nation of mere hewers of wood and drawers of water, and on the other hand to plough and nail and dig for a poverty-stricken horde—could only result in making him a poor craftsman, for he had but half a heart in either cause. By the poverty and ignorance of his people, the Negro minister or doctor was tempted toward quackery and demagogy; and by the criticism of the other world, toward ideals that made him ashamed of his lowly tasks. The would-be black *savant* was confronted by the paradox that the knowledge his people needed was a twice-told tale to his white neighbors, while the knowledge which would teach the white world was Greek to his own flesh and blood. The innate love of harmony and beauty that set the ruder souls of his people a-dancing and a-singing raised but confusion and doubt in the soul of the black artist; for the beauty revealed to him was the soul-beauty of a race which his larger audience despised, and he could not articulate the message of another people. This waste of double aims, this seeking to satisfy two unreconciled ideals, has wrought sad havoc with the courage and faith and deeds of ten thousand thousand people,—has sent them often wooing false gods and invoking false means of salvation, and at times has even seemed about to make them ashamed of themselves.

Away back in the days of bondage they thought to see in one divine event the end of all doubt and disappointment; few men ever worshipped Freedom with half such unquestioning faith as did the American Negro for two centuries. To him, so far as he thought and dreamed, slavery was indeed the sum of all villainies, the cause of all sorrow, the root of all prejudice; Emancipation was the key to a promised land of sweeter beauty than ever stretched before the eyes of wearied Israelites. In song and exhortation swelled one refrain—Liberty; in his tears and curses the God he implored had Freedom in his right hand. At last it came,—suddenly, fearfully, like a dream. With one wild carnival of blood and passion came the message in his own plaintive cadences:—

> "Shout, O children!
> Shout, you're free!
> For God has bought your liberty!"

Years have passed away since then,—ten, twenty, forty; forty years of national life, forty years of renewal and development, and yet the swarthy spectre sits in its accustomed seat at the Nation's feast. In vain do we cry to this our vastest social problem:—

> "Take any shape but that, and my firm nerves
> Shall never tremble!"

The Nation has not yet found peace from its sins; the freedman has not yet found in freedom his promised land. Whatever of good may have come in these years of change, the shadow of a deep disappointment rests upon the Negro people,—a disappointment all the more bitter because the unattained ideal was unbounded save by the simple ignorance of a lowly people.

The first decade was merely a prolongation of the vain search for freedom, the boon that seemed ever barely to elude their grasp,—like a tantalizing will-o'-the-wisp, maddening and misleading the headless host. The holocaust of war, the terrors of the Ku-Klux Klan, the lies of carpet-baggers, the disorganization of industry, and the contradictory advice of friends and foes, left the bewildered serf with no new watchword beyond the old cry for freedom. As the time flew, however, he began to grasp a new idea. The ideal of liberty demanded for its attainment powerful means, and these the Fifteenth Amendment gave him. The ballot, which before he had looked upon as a visible sign of freedom, he now regarded as the chief means of gaining and perfecting the liberty with which war had partially endowed him. And why not? Had not votes made war and emancipated millions? Had not votes enfranchised the freedmen? Was anything impossible to a power that had done all this? A million black men started with renewed zeal to vote themselves into the kingdom. So the decade flew away, the revolution of 1876 came, and left the half-free serf weary, wondering, but still inspired. Slowly but steadily, in the following years, a new vision began gradually to replace the dream of political power,—a powerful movement, the rise of another ideal to guide the unguided, another pillar of fire by night after a clouded day. It was the ideal of "book-learning"; the curiosity, born of compulsory ignorance, to know and test the power of the cabalistic letters of the white man, the longing to know. Here at last seemed to have been discovered the mountain path to Canaan; longer than the highway of Emancipation and law, steep and rugged, but straight, leading to heights high enough to overlook life.

Up the new path the advance guard toiled, slowly, heavily, doggedly; only those who have watched and guided the faltering feet, the misty minds, the dull understandings, of the dark pupils of these schools know how faithfully, how piteously, this people strove to learn. It was weary work. The cold statistician wrote down the inches of progress here and there, noted also where here and there a foot had slipped or some one had fallen. To the tired climbers, the horizon was ever dark, the mists were often cold, the Canaan was always dim and far away. If, however, the vistas disclosed as yet no goal, no resting-place, little but flattery and criticism, the journey at least gave leisure for reflection and self-examination; it changed the child of Emancipation to the youth with dawning self-conciousness, self-realization, self-respect. In those sombre forests of his striving his own soul rose before him, and he saw himself,—darkly as through a veil; and yet he saw in himself some faint revelation of his power, of his mission. He began to have a dim feeling that, to attain his place in the world, he must be himself, and not another. For the first time he sought to analyze the burden he bore upon his back, that dead-weight of social degradation partially masked behind a half-named Negro problem. He felt his poverty; without a cent, without a home, without land, tools, or savings, he had entered into competition with rich, landed, skilled neighbors. To be a poor man is hard, but to be a poor race in a land of dollars is the very bottom of hardships. He felt the weight of his ignorance,—not simply of letters, but of life, of business, of the humanities; the accumulated sloth and shirking and awkwardness of decades and centuries shackled his hands and feet. Nor was his burden all poverty and ignorance. The red stain of bastardy, which two centuries of systematic legal defilement of Negro women had stamped upon his race, meant not only the loss of ancient African chastity, but also the hereditary weight of a mass of corruption from white adulterers, threatening almost the obliteration of the Negro home.

A people thus handicapped ought not to be asked to race with the world, but rather allowed to give all its time and thought to its own social problems. But alas! while sociologists gleefully count his bastards and his prostitutes, the very soul of the toiling, sweating black man is darkened by the shadow of a vast despair. Men call the shadow prejudice, and learnedly explain it as the natural defence of culture against barbarism, learning against ignorance, purity against crime, the "higher" against the "lower" races. To which the Negro cries Amen! and swears that to so much of this strange prejudice as is founded on just homage to civilization, culture, righteousness, and progress, he humbly bows and meekly does obeisance. But before that nameless prejudice that leaps beyond all this he stands helpless, dismayed, and well-nigh speechless; before that personal disrespect and mockery, the ridicule and systematic humiliation, the distortion of fact and wanton license of fancy, the cynical ignoring of the better and the boisterous welcoming of the worse, the all-pervading desire to inculcate disdain for everything black, from Toussaint to the devil,—before this there rises a sickening despair that would disarm and discourage any nation save that black host to whom "discouragement" is an unwritten word.

But the facing of so vast a prejudice could not but bring the inevitable self-questioning, self-disparagement, and lowering of ideals which ever accompany repression and breed in an atmosphere of contempt and hate. Whisperings and portents came borne upon the four winds: Lo! we are diseased and dying, cried the dark hosts; we cannot write, our voting is vain; what need of education, since we must always cook and serve? And the Nation echoed and enforced this self-criticism, saying: Be content to be servants, and nothing more; what need of higher culture for half-men? Away with the black man's ballot, by force or fraud,—and behold the suicide of a race! Nevertheless, out of the evil came something of good,—the more careful adjustment of education to real life, the clearer perception of the Negroes' social responsibilities, and the sobering realization of the meaning of progress.

So dawned the time of *Sturm und Drang:* storm and stress to-day rocks our little boat on the mad waters of the world-sea; there is within and without the sound of conflict, the burning of body and rending of soul; inspiration strives with doubt, and faith with vain questionings. The bright ideals of the past,—physical freedom, political power, the training of brains and the training of hands,—all these in turn have waxed and waned, until even the last grows dim and overcast. Are they all wrong,—all false? No, not that, but each alone was over-simple and incomplete,—the dreams of a credulous race-childhood, or the fond imaginings of the other world which does not know and does not want to know our power. To be really true, all these ideals must be melted and welded into one. The training of the schools we need to-day more than ever,—the training of deft hands, quick eyes and ears, and above all the broader, deeper, higher culture of gifted minds and pure hearts. The power of the ballot we need in sheer self-defence,—else what shall save us from a second slavery? Freedom, too, the long-sought, we still seek,—the freedom of life and limb, the freedom to work and think, the freedom to love and aspire. Work, culture, liberty,—all these we need, not singly but together, not successively but together, each growing and aiding each, and all striving toward that vaster ideal that swims before the Negro people, the ideal of human brotherhood, gained through the unifying ideal of Race; the ideal of fostering and developing the traits and talents of the Negro, not in opposition to or contempt for other races, but rather in large conformity to the greater ideals of the American Republic, in order that some day on American soil two world-races may give each to each those characteristics both so sadly lack. We the darker ones come even now not altogether empty-handed: there are to-day no truer exponents of the pure human spirit of the Declaration of Independence than the American Negroes; there is no true American music but the wild sweet melodies of the Negro slave; the American fairy tales and folk-lore are Indian and African; and, all in all, we black men seem the sole oasis of simple faith and reverence in a dusty desert of dollars and smartness. Will America be poorer if she replace her brutal dyspeptic blundering with light-hearted but determined Negro humility? or her coarse and cruel wit with loving jovial good-humor? or her vulgar music with the soul of the Sorrow Songs?

Merely a concrete test of the underlying principles of the great republic is the Negro Problem, and the spiritual striving of the freedmen's sons is the travail of souls whose burden is almost beyond the measure of their strength, but who bear it in the name of an historic race, in the name of this the land of their fathers' fathers, and in the name of human opportunity.

And now what I have briefly sketched in large outline let me on coming pages tell again in many ways, with loving emphasis and deeper detail, that men may listen to the striving in the souls of black folk.

Ralph Bunche

Ralph Bunche (1904–1971) had an extraordinary career as a diplomat. He effectively negotiated difficult agreements and policies regarding race and culture globally while serving in the U.S. Department of State. The first black to hold a desk job there, Bunche became the associate chief of the Division of Dependent Area Affairs. While heading the Palestine Commission in the United Nations Secretariat, he was awarded the 1950 Nobel Peace Prize and the 1949 NAACP Spingarn Award for his extraordinary negotiation of the 1949 armistice between Israel and Arab states. He was also Department Chair and Professor of Political Science at Howard University (1928–1942). He is the author of *Peace and the United Nations* (1952), *The Political Status of the Negro in the Age of FDR* (1973), and *An African American in South Africa: The Travel Notes of Ralph J. Bunche, September 27, 1937–January 1, 1938* (1992).

The following selection is excerpted from Chapter 1, "What Is Race?," in *A World View of Race* (1936), which he wrote following his postdoctoral work in anthropology and colonial policy, which involved fieldwork in several African countries.

What Is Race?

O ur concept of race is a comparatively recent one. The term "race" is one employed, however, with a looseness and inaccuracy matched only by its frequency in our literature. Even the social scientists, the sociologists and anthropologists, have great difficulty in explaining what is meant by "race," and often disagree in their conclusions. The average man in the street, however, will demonstrate an ability to expound at length on the term at the slightest provocation. That is because race is so intimately related to the social and national doctrines with which the layman is familiar, superficially, and to which he gives unreasoning loyalty.

For dominant groups and powerful industrial nations the definition of race is usually cut to suit the pattern of their economic and political policy. The subtle fallacy and the power of emotional stimulation inherent in the idea of race serve to make it a perfect instrument of politics. People, blindly, and often contrary to their own interests, find it a compelling sort of social voodoo. In the passionate embrace of race they are led to bloody slaughters and barbaric orgies of human torture and lynching. Yet, as employed in the world today, it is a not very consistent myth.

■ Origin and Meaning of Race

The origin of the word "race" is uncertain. It is said to have first appeared in the English language in the sixteenth century. In usage, however, the term soon acquired a vague and confused meaning which has persisted to the present day. At present it is used in several very different ways. In our early geography lessons we were taught that there were five divisions of the human family according to color:—white, black, yellow, brown and red. These peoples were supposed to be distributed geographically with no direct relation to existing national lines.

However, this classification is much too broad to permit race to be used as an effective instrument of national policy. The term often has been employed, therefore, to denote what is asserted to be the physically homogeneous population of a particular country, group or nation, which, supposedly, is distinguishable by its hereditary characteristics,—as the "British race" or the "French race." Again, it is used to indicate a non-existent "pure race," which is said to have existed historically, though subsequently it was contaminated by "foreign or alien blood." This is the basis of the current racial theory in Germany which pays tribute to and thrives on the doctrine of the "Germanic race." Sometimes, also, the concept is mistakenly used to identify peoples who happen to speak the same language, as in references to the "Latin races." Herbert Spencer adopted an explanation of race which tickled the ego-palates of many peoples. He explained races by evolution, on a sort of "stepladder" basis, and the idea developed that races represented distinct levels of advancement which were determined by nature. Thus there were "superior" and "inferior," "advanced" and "backward" races—which became the basis for the moral justifications and the grand rationalizations of modern imperialistic tutelage of millions of peoples. Since color was the simplest means of identifying "races," race traits were usually definitely associated with color.

On one point in all these conceptions of "race" there seems to be general agreement: there must be certain physical characteristics which are determined by heredity, and which are handed on from one generation to another. But even on this point there is great disagreement among those who advance theories of race as to what *type* of physical characteristics should be employed to detect and measure race.

Classifications of Race

In the attempt to establish rigid racial classifications for particular groups the scientist encounters the greatest difficulty. If two groups of peoples are said to be racially differentiated by distinct physical characteristics, then, strictly speaking, every member of one group should be different from every member of the other group in respect to these physical features. This would be more certain if there were any such thing as "pure" racial groups. However, if short stature and tall stature are supposed to be characteristic of two different racial groups such as Japanese and Norwegians, not even the most ardent racial theorists would contend that all Norwegians would be taller than all Japanese. There is great variety in the stature of the members of both groups and much overlapping. Thus there would be many Japanese who would be found to be taller than many Norwegians. The same condition prevails in respect to all other physical traits of human groups. That is, there is great variability among the members of any particular group to which a racial label is given.

Since there is no homogeneity within any given "race" it follows that there can be no clear line of distinction between one race and another. This variability makes it impossible to compare accurately one race with another. Because of the great overlapping in biological features among groups of peoples, it is clear also that general descriptions of so-called racial groups need have no application to individual members of a group. And often do not. It cannot be assumed that because a man is a Japanese he must be short, or that a particular North European will be tall. It may be true that "all Negroes look alike" to some white men who are socially conditioned to regard Negroes in this light. But it is equally true that all Negroes are *not* alike, that the particular set of physical characteristics ascribed to the Negro "race" by the particular racial theorist are subject to great variability among the members of the group, that all Negroes do not behave similarly in the presence of similar conditions, and that these same physical traits, called "Negroid" traits, will be found in varying degree among many whites.

The plain fact is that the selection of any specific physical trait or set of traits as a basis for identifying racial groups is a purely arbitrary process. On the basis of anthropological studies now existent, it would be difficult to say whether there are a few races or several hundred. It may be admitted that physical differences exist among peoples and also that these differences can be discerned and are significant. Yet, a brief survey of the classifications of races will demonstrate convincingly that no satisfactory method of classification has yet been devised, and that in all probability, none can be devised. In consequence, on the basis of any scientific standards, we are forced to conclude that existing racial divisions are *arbitrary, subjective and devoid of scientific meaning.*

The earliest efforts toward a systematic arrangement of human groups were made in the eighteenth century. These early classifications took skin color, the most obvious physical trait, as their basis. The Dutch Linnaeus (Carol Linné), with little detailed information concerning the distribution of human types, listed four "races," representing the types of human beings inhabiting the four large continents. The German J. F. Blumenbach later worked out a system of anthropological classification based on physical measurement. He distinguished five races of man based on distinctions of color, hair and descriptive features of skull and face. They were Caucasian (European), Mongolian, Ethiopian, American and Malayan. According to Blumenbach, however, these various types of men differ from each other in degree, and not in kind, and are connected by innumerable gradations. Later, F. Müller based his classification on hair texture and reached results quite different from the earlier systems. According to Müller, human groups could be divided into the Woolly-haired (including the Tuft-haired and Fleecy-haired) and the Straight-haired (including the Stiff-haired and Wavy-haired).

Thus, color, hair texture, form of nose and shape of skull became in modern science the primary bases for distinguishing human races. The extreme diversity in methods and results of classification of human types is illustrated excellently in a comparison of the systems of J. Deniker and G. Sergi. Deniker adopted a combination of skin color, hair texture, eye color and shape of nose as his test of race. As a result he established seventeen main races and twenty-nine sub-races. Sergi, on the other hand, was interested in head and face shape and measurements, and arrived at only two divisions or species, the long-headed (dolichocephalic) and round-headed (brachycephalic). In Sergi's system the long-headed category included the African, Mediterranean and Nordic peoples, who were held to be closely related. The differences in skin color among these "races" were explained by him as being due to differences in temperature, climate and food. The round-headed species included the Slavs, Celts, Germans and Asiatics.

One of the classifications which receives qualified acceptance today among many anthropologists is that which postulates three main racial types: the Negroid, or black, the Mongoloid or yellow-brown, and the Caucasian or white. The *Negroid* race is characterized by dark pigmentation, frizzly hair, full lips, broad nose, long arms and legs, and comparatively little bodily hairiness. The *Mongoloid* race is described as yellow or brown in color, with straight hair, short arms and legs, thin lips, slight bodily hairiness, and slanting eyes. The *Caucasian* or white race, divided into a number of sub-classifications such as the Nordic, Alpine and Mediterranean, is held to be characterized by light pigmentation, blond, wavy hair, and narrower nose. Among these sub-varieties of the white race there is admitted to be considerable differentiation, however. The Nordic or North European type is described as long-headed, with tall stature, blue eyes, blond hair and light pigmentation. The Alpine or Central European is round-headed, shorter and more swarthy. The Mediterranean or South European type is even more short and dark, but is long-headed.

Such wide divergence in theories of racial classification inevitably leads to great confusion and contradiction. For example, if head shape is used as the distinguishing feature, the African and North European peoples, differing in respect to other physical characteristics such as skin color, hair texture and nose form, are classified together. Again, if skin color is employed, the North and Central Europeans who show marked difference in head shape, are lumped together. Such inconsistencies, particularly in the popular understanding of race classifications, can be multiplied endlessly. In fact, the more scientific we become in attempts to designate specific race categories for human groups, the more glaring and shocking are these discrepancies and contradictions. The mongrelization of *Homo sapiens* frustrates at some point every possible scheme of racial classification.

All this difficulty arises from the tendency to view races as clearly defined units. The problem has been oversimplified by picturing the race as an individual who embodies all of the most pronounced (or the most desirable) traits of the particular group considered. However, few individuals in the group can be found who possess all of these so-called typical traits.

There is, accordingly, much reason for contending that the term "race," when applied in the biological sense to groups, has no scientific validity today. It is a convenient tool for the anthropologist, who employs it as a more or less artificial and arbitrary means of classifying peoples. On the other hand it is an increasingly vicious weapon in the hands of fanatical rulers and irresponsible demagogues who wield it ruthlessly to flatter national egos and to carry out sinister political and economic policies. . . .

There is much historical evidence of constant human migration and the resultant intermingling of all human groups. Even in earliest prehistoric times human migrations must have occurred. Consequently it would seem clear that any differentiations in the fundamental physical forms of man that are now said to exist must have developed during periods of complete isolation of small groups of men. But obviously such periods must be extremely remote; so remote, in fact, that they could have little significance to present classifications of racial groups. For, keeping in mind the unusual fertility of even extreme cases of physically differentiated types of man and man's history of constant migration, it must be concluded that human groups have been cross-breeding for tens of thousands of years. For example, the invasions of Mongolian peoples from the east have left their physical marks upon the peoples of Eastern Europe. Even the great majority of the natives of Africa, who are popularly thought to have lived in comparative isolation and to be "racially pure," have inherited Caucasian genes as a result of historical crossing with Hamitic stocks. As a result, with rare exception, *all existing human groups are of definitely mixed origin.* In the vast majority of cases it is impossible to refer to the population of any region as belonging to any definite "race," since every such group inevitably includes a great number of types and their various combinations, as a result of group migrations and cross-breeding. It is for this reason that some scientific writers now suggest that we drop the term "race" with reference to existing groups and substitute some more accurate description such as "ethnic groups" or "peoples." Such designations are non-committal and realistic, taking into consideration the fact that present groupings of men are the product of migration and crossing, thus making clear-cut biological definition in terms of "race" impossible. . . .

It follows that the idea of a German, Italian, French or American "race" is a meaningless but dangerous political fiction. Similarly, the idea that a particular "race" must be kept pure by protecting it against race-mixture becomes not a matter of race, but rather a matter of nationality, class or social status. Thus when political leaders and their handy-men, the official propagandists, attempt to make a case for race purity and against a particular racial minority group in the population, it can be safely concluded that this is merely a ruse to promote group antagonisms as a smoke-screen for some ulterior and ill-conceived political or economic policy. The real root of such theories will always be found in some social condition such as economic fear, nationalist ambition, class hatred, religious conflict or misguided cultural pride. . . .

So finally we may conclude that though racial antagonisms constitute a serious world problem, they have no scientific basis in biology, nor can they be accepted as the inevitable result of group differences. Such antagonisms must be analyzed and understood in their social and historical setting. *Group antagonisms are social, political and economic conflicts, not racial,* though they are frequently given a racial label and seek a racial justification.

Richard Wright

Richard Wright (1908–1960) garnered international acclaim with the publication of his first novel, *Native Son* (1940), and his autobiography, *Black Boy* (1945). These two works are powerful social documents, as well as indictments of racism, of American life mid-twentieth century. Wright became an expatriate in 1947, choosing to live in France until his untimely death of a heart attack November 28, 1960, in Paris. His other works, many of which were published posthumously, include *Twelve Million Black Voices: A Folk History of the Negro in the U.S.* (1941), *The Outsider* (1953), *White Man, Listen!* (1957), *Eight Men* (1961), *Lawd Today* (1963), *The Man Who Lived Underground* (1971), *American Hunger* (1977), *Rite of Passage* (1994), and *Haiku: This Other World* (1998).

The following essay about learning the strictures of race in Jim Crow society is the first selection of *Uncle Tom's Children: Four Nouvellas* (1938).

The Ethics of Living Jim Crow
An Autobiographical Sketch

My first lesson in how to live as a Negro came when I was quite small. We were living in Arkansas. Our house stood behind the railroad tracks. Its skimpy yard was paved with black cinders. Nothing green ever grew in that yard. The only touch of green we could see was far away, beyond the tracks, over where the white folks lived. But cinders were good enough for me and I never missed the green growing things. And anyhow cinders were fine weapons. You could always have a nice hot war with huge black cinders. All you had to do was crouch behind the brick pillars of a house with your hands full of gritty ammunition. And the first woolly black head you saw pop out from behind another row of pillars was your target. You tried your very best to knock it off. It was great fun.

I never fully realized the appalling disadvantages of a cinder environment till one day the gang to which I belonged found itself engaged in a war with the white boys who lived beyond the tracks. As usual we laid down our cinder barrage, thinking that this would wipe the white boys out. But they replied with a steady bombardment of broken bottles. We doubled our cinder barrage, but they hid behind trees, hedges, and the sloping embankments of their lawns. Having no such fortifications, we retreated to the brick pillars of our homes. During the retreat a broken milk bottle caught me behind the ear, opening a deep gash which bled profusely. The sight of blood pouring over my face completely demoralized our ranks. My fellow-combatants left me standing paralyzed in the center of the yard and scurried for their homes. A kind neighbor saw me and rushed me to a doctor, who took three stitches in my neck.

I sat brooding on my front steps, nursing my wound and waiting for my mother to come from work. I felt that a grave injustice had been done me. It was all right to throw cinders. The greatest harm a cinder could do was leave a bruise. But broken bottles were dangerous; they left you cut, bleeding, and helpless.

When night fell, my mother came from the white folks' kitchen. I raced down the street to meet her. I could just feel in my bones that she would understand. I knew she would tell me exactly what to do next time. I grabbed her hand and babbled out the whole story. She examined my wound, then slapped me.

"How come yuh didn't hide?" she asked me. "How come yuh awways fightin'?"   5

I was outraged, and bawled. Between sobs I told her that I didn't have any trees or hedges to hide behind. There wasn't a thing I could have used as a trench. And you couldn't throw very far when you were hiding behind the brick pillars of a house. She grabbed a barrel stave, dragged me home, stripped me naked, and beat me till I had a fever of one hundred and two. She would smack my rump with the stave, and, while the skin was still smarting, impart to me gems of Jim Crow wisdom. I was never to throw cinders any more. I was never to fight any more wars. I was never, never, under any conditions, to fight *white* folks again. And they were absolutely right in clouting me with the broken milk bottle. Didn't I know she was working hard every day in the hot kitchens of the white folks to make money to take care of me? When was I ever going to learn to be a good boy? She couldn't be bothered with my fights. She finished by telling me that I ought to be thankful to God as long as I lived that they didn't kill me.

All that night I was delirious and could not sleep. Each time I closed my eyes I saw monstrous white faces suspended from the ceiling, leering at me.

From that time on, the charm of my cinder yard was gone. The green trees, the trimmed hedges, the cropped lawns grew very meaningful, became a symbol. Even today when I think of white folks, the hard, sharp outlines of white houses surrounded by trees, lawns, and hedges are present somewhere in the background of my mind. Through the years they grew into an overreaching symbol of fear.

It was a long time before I came in close contact with white folks again. We moved from Arkansas to Mississippi. Here we had the good fortune not to live behind the railroad tracks, or close to white neighborhoods. We lived in the very heart of the local Black Belt. There were black churches and black preachers; there were black schools and black teachers; black groceries and black clerks. In fact, everything was so solidly black that for a long time I did not even think of white folks, save in remote and vague terms. But this could not last forever. As one grows older one eats more. One's clothing costs more. When I finished grammar school I had to go to work. My mother could no longer feed and clothe me on her cooking job.

There is but one place where a black boy who knows no trade can get a job,   10
and that's where the houses and faces are white, where the trees, lawns, and hedges are green. My first job was with an optical company in Jackson, Mississippi. The morning I applied I stood straight and neat before the boss, answering all his questions with sharp yessirs and nosirs. I was very careful to pronounce my *sirs* distinctly, in order that he might know that I was polite, that I knew where I was, and that I knew he was a *white* man. I wanted that job badly.

He looked me over as though he were examining a prize poodle. He questioned me closely about my schooling, being particularly insistent about how much mathematics I had had. He seemed very pleased when I told him I had had two years of algebra.

"Boy, how would you like to try to learn something around here?" he asked me.

"I'd like it fine, sir," I said, happy. I had visions of "working my way up." Even Negroes have those visions.

"All right," he said. "Come on."

I followed him to the small factory.   15

"Pease," he said to a white man of about thirty-five, "this is Richard. He's going to work for us."

Pease looked at me and nodded.

I was then taken to a white boy of about seventeen.

"Morrie, this is Richard, who's going to work for us."

"Whut yuh sayin' there, boy!" Morrie boomed at me.   20

"Fine!" I answered.

The boss instructed these two to help me, teach me, give me jobs to do, and let me learn what I could in my spare time.

My wages were five dollars a week.

I worked hard, trying to please. For the first month I got along O.K. Both Pease and Morrie seemed to like me. But one thing was missing. And I kept thinking about it. I was not learning anything and nobody was volunteering to help me. Thinking they had forgotten that I was to learn something about the mechanics of grinding lenses, I asked Morrie one day to tell me about the work. He grew red.

"Whut yuh tryin' t' do, nigger, get smart?" he asked.   25

"Naw; I ain' tryin' t' git smart," I said.

"Well, don't, if yuh know whut's good for yuh!"

I was puzzled. Maybe he just doesn't want to help me, I thought. I went to Pease.

"Say, are yuh crazy, you black bastard?" Pease asked me, his gray eyes growing hard.

I spoke out, reminding him that the boss had said I was to be given a chance   30
to learn something.

"Nigger, you think you're *white,* don't you?"

"Naw, sir!"

"Well, you're acting mighty like it!"

"But, Mr. Pease, the boss said . . . "

Pease shook his fist in my face.   35

"This is a *white* man's work around here, and you better watch yourself!"

From then on they changed toward me. They said good-morning no more. When I was just a bit slow in performing some duty, I was called a lazy black son-of-a-bitch.

Once I thought of reporting all this to the boss. But the mere idea of what would happen to me if Pease and Morrie should learn that I had "snitched" stopped me. And after all the boss was a white man, too. What was the use?

The climax came at noon one summer day. Pease called me to his work-bench. To get to him I had to go between two narrow benches and stand with my back against a wall.

"Yes, sir," I said.   40

"Richard, I want to ask you something," Pease began pleasantly, not looking up from his work.

"Yes, sir," I said again.

Morrie came over, blocking the narrow passage between the benches. He folded his arms, staring at me solemnly.

I looked from one to the other, sensing that something was coming.

"Yes, sir," I said for the third time.   45

Pease looked up and spoke very slowly.

"Richard, *Mr.* Morrie here tells me you called me *Pease.*"

I stiffened. A void seemed to open up in me. I knew this was the show-down.

He meant that I had failed to call him Mr. Pease. I looked at Morrie. He was gripping a steel bar in his hands. I opened my mouth to speak, to protest, to assure Pease that I had never called him simply *Pease,* and that I had never had any intentions of doing so, when Morrie grabbed me by the collar, ramming my head against the wall.

"Now, be careful, nigger!" snarled Morrie, baring his teeth. "*I* heard yuh call   50
'im *Pease!* 'N' if yuh say yuh didn't, yuh're callin' me a *lie,* see?" He waved the steel bar threateningly.

If I had said: No, sir, Mr. Pease, I never called you *Pease,* I would have been automatically calling Morrie a liar. And if I had said: Yes, sir, Mr. Pease, I called you *Pease,* I would have been pleading guilty to having uttered the worst insult that a Negro can utter to a southern white man. I stood hesitating, trying to frame a neutral reply.

"Richard, I asked you a question!" said Pease. Anger was creeping into his voice.

"I don't remember calling you *Pease,* Mr. Pease," I said cautiously. "And if I did, I sure didn't mean . . . "

"You black son-of-a-bitch! You called me *Pease,* then!" he spat, slapping me till I bent sideways over a bench. Morrie was on top of me, demanding:

"Didn't yuh call 'im *Pease?* If yuh say yuh didn't, I'll rip yo' gut string loose   55
with this bar, yuh black granny dodger! Yuh can't call a white man a lie 'n' git erway with it, you black son-of-a-bitch!"

I wilted. I begged them not to bother me. I knew what they wanted. They wanted me to leave.

"I'll leave," I promised. "I'll leave right *now.*"

They gave me a minute to get out of the factory. I was warned not to show up again, or tell the boss.

I went.

When I told the folks at home what had happened, they called me a fool.   60
They told me that I must never again attempt to exceed my boundaries. When you are working for white folks, they said, you got to "stay in your place" if you want to keep working.

Langston Hughes

Langston Hughes (1902–1967), one of the most prolific writers and editors of the twentieth century, had an abiding love for his culture. He is the author of "The Negro and the Racial Mountain," an essay in which he states his resistance, as an African American writer, to pressure from white and black critics who wish to set standards for him. In his short story collections, many based on the fictitious Jesse B. Semple, a Harlem character, Hughes offers opinions, often satirical, on American life. He wrote two autobiographies: *The Big Sea* (1940) and *I Wonder As I Wander* (1955). His poetry volumes include *The Weary Blues* (1926), *Fine Clothes to the Jew* (1927), *The Dream Keeper and Other Poems* (1932), *Ask Your Mama: Twelve Moods for Jazz* (1947), and *The Panther and the Lash: Poems of Our Times* (1967).

The following selection is a short story from *Laughing to Keep from Crying* (1952), in which characters fail to determine the race of a couple.

Who's Passing for Who?

One of the great difficulties about being a member of a minority race is that so many kindhearted, well-meaning bores gather around to help. Usually, to tell the truth, they have nothing to help with, except their company—which is often appallingly dull.

Some members of the Negro race seem very well able to put up with it, though, in these uplifting years. Such was Caleb Johnson, colored social worker, who was always dragging around with him some nondescript white person or two, inviting them to dinner, showing them Harlem, ending up at the Savoy—much to the displeasure of whatever friends of his might be out that evening for fun, not sociology.

Friends are friends and, unfortunately, overearnest uplifters are uplifters—no matter what color they may be. If it were the white race that was ground down instead of Negroes, Caleb Johnson would be one of the first to offer Nordics the sympathy of his utterly inane society, under the impression that somehow he would be doing them a great deal of good.

You see, Caleb, and his white friends, too, were all bores. Or so we, who lived in Harlem's literary bohemia during the "Negro Renaissance" thought. We literary ones considered ourselves too broad-minded to be bothered with questions of color. We liked people of any race who smoked incessantly, drank liberally, wore complexion and morality as loose garments, and made fun of anyone who didn't do likewise. We snubbed and high-hatted any Negro or white luckless enough not to understand Gertrude Stein, Ulysses, Man Ray, the theremin, Jean Toomer, or George Antheil. By the end of the 1920's Caleb was just catching up to Dos Passos. He thought H. G. Wells good.

We met Caleb one night in Small's. He had three assorted white folks in tow.   5
We would have passed him by with but a nod had he not hailed us enthusiastically, risen, and introduced us with great acclaim to his friends who turned out to be schoolteachers from Iowa, a woman and two men. They appeared amazed and delighted to meet all at once two Negro writers and a black painter in the flesh. They invited us to have a drink with them. Money being scarce with us, we deigned to sit down at their table.

The white lady said, "I've never met a Negro writer before."

The two men added, "Neither have we."

"Why, we know any number of *white* writers," we three dark bohemians declared with bored nonchalance.

"But Negro writers are much more rare," said the lady.

"There are plenty in Harlem," we said.   10

"But not in Iowa," said one of the men, shaking his mop of red hair.

"There are no good *white* writers in Iowa either, are there?" we asked superciliously.

"Oh, yes, Ruth Suckow came from there."

Whereupon we proceeded to light in upon Ruth Suckow as old hat and to annihilate her in favor of Kay Boyle. The way we flung names around seemed to impress both Caleb and his white guests. This, of course, delighted us, though we were too young and too proud to admit it.

The drinks came and everything was going well, all of us drinking, and we   15
three showing off in a high-brow manner, when suddenly at the table just behind us a man got up and knocked down a woman. He was a brown-skinned man. The woman was blonde. As she rose he knocked her down again. Then the red-haired man from Iowa got up and knocked the colored man down.

He said, "Keep your hands off that white woman."

The man got up and said, "She's not a white woman. She's my wife."

One of the waiters added, "She's not white, sir, she's colored."

Whereupon the man from Iowa looked puzzled, dropped his fists, and said, "I'm sorry."

The colored man said, "What are you doing up here in Harlem anyway, inter-   20
fering with my family affairs?"

The white man said, "I thought she was a white woman."

The woman who had been on the floor rose and said, "Well, I'm not a white woman, I'm colored, and you leave my husband alone."

Then they both lit in on the gentleman from Iowa. It took all of us and several waiters, too, to separate them. When it was over the manager requested us to kindly pay our bill and get out. He said we were disturbing the peace. So we all left. We went to a fish restaurant down the street. Caleb was terribly apologetic to his white friends. We artists were both mad and amused.

"Why did you say you were sorry," said the colored painter to the visitor from Iowa, "after you'd hit that man—and then found out it wasn't a white woman you were defending, but merely a light-colored woman who looked white?"

"Well," answered the red-haired Iowan, "I didn't mean to be butting in if they   25
were all the same race."

"Don't you think a woman needs defending from a brute, no matter what race she may be?" asked the painter.

"Yes, but I think it's up to you to defend your own women."

"Oh, so you'd divide up a brawl according to races, no matter who was right?"

"Well, I wouldn't say that."

"You mean you wouldn't defend a colored woman whose husband was knock-   30
ing her down?" asked the poet.

Before the visitor had time to answer, the painter said, "No! You just got mad because you thought a black man was hitting a *white* woman."

"But she *looked* like a white woman," countered the man.

"Maybe she was just passing for colored," I said.

"Like some Negroes pass for white," Caleb interposed.

"Anyhow, I don't like it," said the colored painter, "the way you stopped de-   35
fending her when you found out she wasn't white."

"No, we don't like it," we all agreed except Caleb.

Caleb said in extenuation, "But Mr. Stubblefield is new to Harlem."

The red-haired white man said, "Yes, it's my first time here."

"Maybe Mr. Stubblefield ought to stay out of Harlem," we observed.

"I agree," Mr. Stubblefield said. "Good night."   40

He got up then and there and left the café. He stalked as he walked. His red head disappeared into the night.

"Oh, that's too bad," said the white couple who remained. "Stubby's temper just got the best of him. But explain to us, are many colored folks really as fair as that woman?"

"Sure, lots of them have more white blood than colored, and pass for white."

"Do they?" said the lady and gentleman from Iowa.

"You never read Nella Larsen?" we asked.   45

"She writes novels," Caleb explained. "She's part white herself."

"Read her," we advised. "Also read the *Autobiography of an Ex-colored Man*." Not that we had read it ourselves—because we paid but little attention to the older colored writers—but we knew it was about passing for white.

We all ordered fish and settled down comfortably to shocking our white friends with tales about how many Negroes there were passing for white all over America.

We were determined to *épater le bourgeois* real good via this white couple we had cornered, when the woman leaned over the table in the midst of our dissertations and said, "Listen, gentlemen, you needn't spread the word, but me and my husband aren't white either. We've just been *passing* for white for the last fifteen years."

"What?"

"We're colored, too, just like you," said the husband. "But it's better passing   50
for white because we make more money."

Well, that took the wind out of us. It took the wind out of Caleb, too. He thought all the time he was showing some fine white folks Harlem—and they were as colored as he was!

Caleb almost never cursed. But this time he said, "I'll be damned!"

Then everybody laughed. And laughed! We almost had hysterics. All at once we dropped our professionally self-conscious "Negro" manners, became natural, ate fish, and talked and kidded freely like colored folks do when there are no white folks around. We really had fun then, joking about that red-haired guy who mistook a fair colored woman for white. After the fish we went to two or three more night spots and drank until five o'clock in the morning.

Finally we put the light-colored people in a taxi heading downtown. They turned to shout a last good-by. The cab was just about to move off, when the woman called to the driver to stop.

She leaned out the window and said with a grin, "Listen, boys! I hate to con-   55
fuse you again. But, to tell the truth, my husband and I aren't really colored at all. We're white. We just thought we'd kid you by passing for colored a little while—just as you said Negroes sometimes pass for white."

She laughed as they sped off toward Central Park, waving, "Good-by!"

We didn't say a thing. We just stood there on the corner in Harlem dumbfounded—not knowing now *which* way we'd been fooled. Were they really white—passing for colored? Or colored—passing for white?

Whatever race they were, they had had too much fun at our expense—even if they did pay for the drinks.

James McBride

James McBride (1957–), journalist, musician, and freelance writer, wrote his autobiography, *The Color of Water: A Black Man's Tribute to His White Mother* (1996), after receiving favorable reviews regarding a Mother's Day essay that appeared in the *Boston Globe*. A former staff writer for *The Washington Post, People Magazine,* and *Boston Globe,* McBride has also written for *Essence, Rolling Stone,* and *The New York Times.* He is the recipient of the 1997 Anisfeld Wolf Book Award for Literary Excellence and was awarded an Honorary Doctorate of Humane Letters from Whitman College. He is also the recipient of several awards for his work as a composer in musical theater, including the 1996 American Arts and Letters Richard Rodgers Award, the 1996 ASCAP Richard Rodgers Horizons Award, and the American Music Festival's 1993 Stephen Sondheim Award.

In the following excerpt from Chapter 4 of the autobiography,
McBride's mother, the daughter of a rabbi, acknowledges that she
wants to pass for black.

Black Power

When I was a boy, I used to wonder where my mother came from, how she got on this earth. When I asked her where she was from, she would say, "God made me," and change the subject. When I asked her if she was white, she'd say, "No. I'm light-skinned," and change the subject again. Answering questions about her personal history did not jibe with Mommy's view of parenting twelve curious, wild, brown-skinned children. She issued orders and her rule was law. Since she refused to divulge details about herself or her past, and because my stepfather was largely unavailable to deal with questions about himself or Ma, what I learned of Mommy's past I learned from my siblings. We traded information on Mommy the way people trade baseball cards at trade shows, offering bits and pieces fraught with gossip, nonsense, wisdom, and sometimes just plain foolishness. "What does it matter to you?" my older brother Richie scoffed when I asked him if we had any grandparents. "You're adopted anyway."

My siblings and I spent hours playing tricks and teasing one another. It was our way of dealing with realities over which we had no control. I told Richie I didn't believe him.

"I don't care if you believe me or not," he sniffed. "Mommy's not your real mother. Your real mother's in jail."

"You're lying!"

"You'll see when Mommy takes you back to your real mother next week. Why do you think she's been so nice to you all week?"   5

Suddenly it occurred to me that Mommy *had* been nice to me all week. But wasn't she nice to me all the time? I couldn't remember, partly because within my confused eight-year-old reasoning was a growing fear that maybe Richie was right. Mommy, after all, did not really look like me. In fact, she didn't look like Richie, or David—or any of her children for that matter. We were all clearly black, of various shades of brown, some light brown, some medium brown, some very light-skinned, and all of us had curly hair. Mommy was, by her own definition, "light-skinned," a statement which I had initially accepted as fact but at some point later decided was not true. My best friend Billy Smith's mother was as light as Mommy was and had red hair to boot, but there was no question in my mind that Billy's mother was black and my mother was not. There was something inside me, an ache I had, like a constant itch that got bigger and bigger as I grew, that told me. It was in my blood, you might say, and however the notion got there, it bothered me greatly. Yet Mommy refused to acknowledge her whiteness. Why she did so was not clear, but even my teachers seemed to know she was white and I wasn't. On open school nights, the question most often asked by my schoolteachers was: "Is James adopted?" which always prompted an outraged response from Mommy.

I told Richie: "If I'm adopted, you're adopted too."

"Nope," Richie replied. "Just you, and you're going back to your real mother in jail."

"I'll run away first."

"You can't do that. Mommy will get in trouble if you do that. You don't want to see Ma get in trouble, do you? It's not her fault that you're adopted, is it?"

He had me then. Panic set in. "But I don't want to go to my real mother. I want to stay here with Ma . . . "

"You gotta go. I'm sorry, man."

This went on until I was in tears. I remember pacing about nervously all day while Richie, knowing he had ruined my life, cackled himself to sleep. That night I lay wide awake in bed waiting for Mommy to get home from work at two A.M., whereupon she laid the ruse out as I sat at the kitchen table in my tattered Fruit of the Loom underwear. "You're not adopted," she laughed.

"So you're my real mother?"

"Of course I am." Big kiss.

"Then who's my grandparents?"

"Your grandpa Nash died and so did your grandma Etta."

"Who were they?"

"They were your father's parents."

"Where were they from?"

"From down south. You remember them?"

I had a faint recollection of my grandmother Etta, an ancient black woman with a beautiful face who seemed very confused, walking around with a blue dress and a fishing pole, the bait, tackle, and line dragging down around her ankles. She didn't seem real to me.

"Did you know them, Ma?"

"I knew them very, very well."

"Did they love you?"

"Why do you ask so many questions?"

"I just want to know. Did they love you? Because your own parents didn't love you, did they?"

"My own parents loved me."

"Then where are they?"

A short silence. "My mother died many, many years ago," she said. "My father, he was a fox. No more questions tonight. You want some coffee cake?" Enough said. If getting Mommy's undivided attention for more than five minutes was a great feat in a family of twelve kids, then getting a midnight snack in my house was a greater thrill. I cut the questions and ate the cake, though it never stopped me from wondering, partly because of my own growing sense of self, and partly because of fear for her safety, because even as a child I had a clear sense that black and white folks did not get along, which put her, and us, in a pretty tight space. . . .

As a boy, I often found Mommy's ease among black people surprising. Most white folks I knew seemed to have a great fear of blacks. Even as a young child, I was aware of that. I'd read it in the paper, between the lines of my favorite sport columnists in the *New York Post* and the old *Long Island Press,* in their refusal to call Cassius Clay Muhammad Ali, in their portrayal of Floyd Patterson as a "good Negro Catholic," and in their burning criticism of black athletes like Bob Gibson of the

St. Louis Cardinals, whom I idolized. In fact I didn't even have to open the paper to see it. I could see it in the faces of the white people who stared at me and Mommy and my siblings when we rode the subway, sometimes laughing at us, pointing, muttering things like, "Look at her with those little niggers." I remember when a white man shoved her angrily as she led a group of us onto an escalator, but Mommy simply ignored him. I remember two black women pointing at us, saying, "Look at that white bitch," and a white man screaming at Mommy somewhere in Manhattan, calling her a "nigger lover." Mommy ignored them all, unless the insults threatened her children, at which time she would turn and fight back like an alley cat, hissing, angry, and fearless. She had a casual way of ignoring affronts, slipping past insults to her whiteness like a seasoned boxer slips punches. When Malcolm X, the supposed demon of the white man, was killed, I asked her who he was and she said, "He was a man ahead of his time." She actually liked Malcolm X. She put him in nearly the same category as her other civil rights heroes, Paul Robeson, Jackie Robinson, Eleanor Roosevelt, A. Philip Randolph, Martin Luther King, Jr., and the Kennedys—any Kennedy. When Malcolm X talked about "the white devil" Mommy simply felt those references didn't apply to her. She viewed the civil rights achievements of black Americans with pride, as if they were her own. And she herself occasionally talked about "the white man" in the third person, as if she had nothing to do with him, and in fact she didn't, since most of her friends and social circle were black women from church. . . .

Toi Derricotte

Toi Derricotte (1941–), Professor of English at the University of Pittsburgh, has written extensively on the issue of color as it impacts self-identity. She has garnered several awards, including creative writing fellowships in poetry, the Lucille Medwick Memorial Award for 1985 by the Poetry Society of America, and fellowships from the National Endowment for the Arts in 1985 and 1990. In 1989 she was a nominee for the Pushcart Prize. Her poetry books include *The Empress of the Death House* (1978), *Natural Birth* (1983), *Captivity* (1989), and *Tender* (1997).

The following excerpt is from *The Black Notebooks* (1997), a prose autobiography.

from *The Black Notebooks*

I'm sure most people don't go around all the time thinking about what race they are. When you look like what you are, the external world mirrors back to you an identity consistent with your idea of yourself. However, for someone like me, who does not look like what I am, those mirrors are broken, and my consciousness or lack of consciousness takes on serious implications. Am I not conscious because, like others, I am just thinking of something else? Or is it because I don't want to be conscious? Am I mentally "passing"?

All my life I have passed invisibly into the white world, and all my life I have felt that sudden and alarming moment of consciousness when I remember I am black. It may feel like I'm emerging too quickly from deep in the ocean, or touching an electric fence, or like I'm a deer stuck in the headlights of an oncoming car. Sometimes in conversation with a white person who doesn't know I'm black, suddenly a feeling comes over me, a precursor—though nothing at all has been said about race—and I either wait helplessly for the other shoe to drop, try desperately to veer the conversation in another direction, or prepare myself for painful distinctions. My desire to escape is indistinguishable from my desire to escape from my "blackness," my race, and I am filled with shame and fury. I think the first time I became conscious of this internal state was when I was fifteen, on my way cross-country on a train, the California Zephyr.

The first day out, a young white man sat in the seat beside me. We had had a very pleasant conversation, but at night, when I grew tired, I asked him if he would go back to his seat so that I could stretch out. He said, "If you saw what's sitting in the seat beside me, you'd know why I can't go back." Of course, I knew without looking back what he meant, and as I stood up and turned around to see, I felt that now familiar combination of sickening emotions: hope that my sense of the situation was incorrect—in effect preferring to distrust my own perceptions—and fear that it wasn't, that my tender feelings for this man, and his feelings for me, were in mortal danger. If I spoke, I would make myself vulnerable. At the very least, he might categorize me in the same way he had categorized the other black person. If I didn't, I would be a coward, a betrayer of my people.

It seemed to me that even deeper than laws, than institutional practices, it was his invisible thoughts that hurt me. In fact, it seemed that, in a way, it is the combined thoughts, conscious and unconscious, of all of us that hold the machinery of racism in place, and in small remarks such as these, I am able to grasp, because I am allowed entry into it, a world of hatred so deep and hidden that it is impossible to address. This juncture in communication may seem so small an event in the history of racism, and of such indeterminate origins, that it is hardly worthy of speech. But it is precisely in such moments that I sense the local and engendering impulse, the twisted heart that keeps us locked in separate worlds of hate. It makes me despair of any real intimacy between blacks and whites.

I turned around and, sure enough, there was a young black man, a soldier, sitting in the seat. I said, very softly, "If you don't want to sit next to him, you don't want to sit next to me." I had hoped he'd be too stupid or deaf to understand. But he grew very quiet and said, after a few minutes, in an even softer voice than mine, "You're kidding." "No," I said. "You're kidding," he said again. "No," I said. "You're kidding." Each time he said it, he grew quieter. He excused himself. He may have slept in the bathroom. Every other seat was taken, and when I looked back to see if he was sleeping beside the soldier, the seat was empty.

The next morning, he found me on the way to breakfast and profusely apologized. "Please let me buy you breakfast," he said. I was lonely and wanted company, but I felt I had to punish him. I thought punishment was the only way he would gain respect for black people, and I felt the most effective kind of punishment was not verbal confrontation—which would probably only confirm his stereotypes of hostile blacks—but cool withdrawal. I had to punish myself, too, for I didn't want

5

the pain of loneliness and alienation. I wanted and needed company, I liked him. But I felt in order to cut myself off from him, I had to cut off my feelings of tenderness and trust.

The last night on board, just before we were to arrive, I looked back and saw him sleeping beside the soldier. Perhaps he had gotten sick of sleeping in the bathroom, or perhaps my suffering had done some good.

Kathy Russell, Midge Wilson, and Ronald E. Hall

Kathy Russell is a scriptwriter and poet and worked as a researcher for Fox TV's *Bertice Berry Show,* based in Chicago. She is the author of *A Discussion with Kathy Russell about the Politics of Skin Color Among African Americans* (1992).

Midge Wilson is a Professor of Psychology and Director of First Year Programs at DePaul University. Her research centers on the impact of first impressions on African American and European American women in regard to perceptions about attractiveness, body size, skin color, and facial features. Wilson and Russell are co-authors of *Divided Sisters: Bridging the Gap Between Black Women and White Women* (1996).

Ronald E. Hall is a Scholar at the David Walker Research Institute, College of Human Medicine, at Michigan State University whose research focuses on human behavior, race and ethnicity, and the social implications of skin color. His "Clowns, Buffoons, and Gladiators: Media Portrayals of the African-American Man" in *The Journal of Men's Studies* (February 1993) describes how the media portrays African American males.

The following is an excerpt from the chapter entitled "Black Identity: Shades of Beauty and Pride" of *Color Complex: The Politics of Skin Color Among African Americans,* in which an African American adopted by a white couple explains her confusion as a child about race.

Black Identity
Shades of Beauty and Pride

A child's awareness and appreciation of the value of different skin colors occurs some time after racial awareness has developed. Some psychologists believe that Black children rarely use skin color as a criterion for racial grouping, but instead rely on facial features, eye color, and hair texture as indicators of Blackness. Other researchers think that children become more sensitive to skin-color variations as they become better able to extrapolate from information they have acquired about the world. For example, if a Black child gleans from fairy tales that only bad people and witches wear black and that heroes and fairy princesses are always dressed in white, the child may begin to reject other things that are black and dark, including himself. Some children are able to apply this kind of reasoning as early as age four, others around six or seven. In yet another replication of the doll test, psychologists George Gitter, David Mostofsky, and Yoichi Satow found in 1972 that dark-skinned Black children between the ages of four and six were more likely than those who were lighter to select White dolls when asked, "Which doll looks most like you?"

By the time they enter elementary school most children have learned to recognize certain subtleties of racial identity. Even so, some stumble over the word "Black." To young children, "black" is foremost a color, not an abstract racial category—and to be told that they are Black when they can see for themselves that they are not can be quite puzzling.

Katie K., the daughter of a Black man and a White woman in a predominantly White town in Minnesota, recalls having felt an intense confusion about race during her childhood. From the age of ten months, she was raised by a White family, who formally adopted her when she was two. These White parents tried to instill in her a strong sense of pride and self-esteem, and they told her at an early age not only that she was adopted but also, in the jargon of the early sixties, that she was a Negro. Just when Katie was starting to understand what it meant to be a Negro, the lexicon changed, and her parents told her she was Black. That made little sense to the five-year-old Katie, as she could see for herself that she was light-skinned. One day when she was around seven she asked her mother, "Am I a nigger?" She had heard the word at school. Shocked, her mother exclaimed, "Don't ever say that again, Katie," leading Katie to conclude that she was not Black after all. For the next four or five years Katie was aware that she was different, but she was not sure how. It took her until she was eleven to figure it out, and some years more to reassess and accept her past confusion.

By the time they are teenagers, African-American children have well-defined stereotypes about skin color. Charles H. Parrish was one of the first to explore the nature of skin-color stereotyping in Black teenagers. He discovered in the 1940s that junior-high students used as many as 145 different terms to describe skin color, including "half-white," "yaller," "high yellow," "fair," "bright," "light," "redbone," "light brown," "medium brown," "brown," "brownskin," "dark brown," "chocolate," "dark," "black," "ink spot," "blue black," and "tar baby." Each term was associated with a particular personality type: in general, light to medium skin tones were linked to intelligence and refinement, while dark skin tones suggested toughness, meanness, and physical strength.

Although Parrish's study is fifty years old, similar attitudes about skin color 5 prevail among today's Black youth. Many believe that light skin is feminine and dark skin is masculine, and very light-skinned boys and very dark-skinned girls often suffer from being at odds with this cultural stereotype.

Some light-skinned Black males learn to compensate by exaggerating their masculinity, acting tough and streetwise. In an article in *Essence* entitled "Who Is Black," writer Itabari Njeri describes the plight of her cousin Jeffrey, who looked like singer Ricky Nelson but wanted to be "the baddest nigger on the block." Jeffrey died young on the streets trying to prove that he was not the enemy. And Michel Marriott, a reporter for the *New York Times*, recollects how, as a light-skinned Black youth coming of age during the sixties, "black cool dictated [his] every rhythm." Marriott's large Afro, his bodacious swagger, his white high-top Converse All-Stars, his obsession with knowing the latest Black music and dance moves, and his ability to cite Malcolm X flawlessly—all these traits articulated what his light skin never could, that he was a "bro-ske." As he wrote:

> A light-skinned teenager could not afford to get caught slipping when it came to the required black behavior [and] if you did you were very likely to get stoned with the hardest rock in a black teenager's rhetorical arsenal: Someone might call you a *whiteboy*.

Yet, says one brown-skinned corporate manager, a man named Ron Holt, once they outgrow adolescence light-skinned Black men are quick to realize the enormous advantages of their color. They discover that they have better job prospects, appear less threatening to Whites, and are more popular with women, who teasingly call them "pretty boys" or "run-round men." Many of these men, having fought harder to establish their Black identity, have a clearer sense of who they are as a result. Holt claims that it is the darker-skinned Black man, not his lighter-skinned brother, who is "Stepin Fetchitized" out of his masculinity. (Stepin Fetchit was an early Black film actor who always portrayed shuffling, laconic characters.)

For Black women, skin color is even more central to identity. Despite more than twenty years of "Black Is Beautiful" rhetoric, negative attitudes about women with dark skin persist. In a recent study at DePaul University in Chicago, Midge Wilson and two of her students, Lisa Razzano and Sherry Salmons, selected almost eighty people, evenly divided between males and females, Blacks and Whites, and asked them to look at photographs of twelve Black women and characterize their impressions of each. Regardless of the individual woman's attractiveness (prejudged to be high or low), the study participants nearly always rated the dark-skinned women as less successful, less happy in love, less popular, less physically attractive, less physically and emotionally healthy, and less intelligent than their light-skinned counterparts. The only quality in which the dark-skinned females were *not* rated lower was sense of humor, a phenomenon they labeled the "Whoopi Goldberg effect."

Certainly, the extent to which one can generalize from this research may be limited; everyone knows that first impressions, especially those formed from a photograph, are subject to change. Nonetheless, the halo that surrounds the light-skinned Black female may make it easier for her to form friendships and develop a positive sense of self, while dark-skinned females must work to overcome the negative stereotype. In fact, recent research by psychologist Cornelia Porter indicates that girls as young as six are twice as likely as boys to be sensitive to the social importance of skin color.

Black psychologist Maisha Bennett, who heads Maisha Bennett and Associates/Hamilton Behavioral Health Care in Chicago, conducts workshops for African-American women on self-esteem, relationships, and career development. She has found that in the safe atmosphere of a workshop Black women will discuss—often for the first time—their deepest fears about being "too light" or "too dark" or not having the "right" features. Some workshop participants may even discover that they have been using their skin color to distance themselves psychologically from others, in the same way that obese people sometimes use their weight to keep others at bay. While many Blacks can sympathize with those who are "too" dark-skinned, fewer are willing to acknowledge the pain of those who are very light-

10

skinned, like the green-eyed, light-skinned Chicago woman who says that she has had people accuse her of being phony or of having a superiority complex simply because her skin is light and her eyes are not brown.

Dr. Tracy L. Robinson of North Carolina State University and Dr. Janie Victoria Ward of Simmons College have done studies showing that adolescents who are satisfied with their skin color are happiest with themselves and that those who believe that their skin is either too dark or too light are most likely to feel discontent. Robinson and Ward emphasize, however, that 80 percent of the adolescents they studied had high self-esteem. In fact, Ward found in another study that Black girls tend to have much higher self-esteem than White girls, perhaps because Black culture emphasizes independence and assertiveness in females. . . .

Shelby Steele

Shelby Steele (1946–) has published extensively and lectured widely on the subject of race relations, debunking attitudes of oppression that lead to a psychology of victimization and rejecting affirmative action initiatives as no longer necessary. His documentary *Frontline* (1990) delves into the racial climate that resulted in the murder of Yusuf K. Hawkins, a young black teenager, by four white teenagers. Other works include *Essay Collection* (1993) and *A Dream Deferred: The Second Betrayal of Black Freedom in America* (1998).

The following excerpt about a middle-class African American's attitude about race is from Chapter 2 of *The Content of Our Character: A New Vision of Race* (1990), which won the 1990 National Book Critics Circle Award for nonfiction.

Race-Holding

I am a fortyish, middle-class, black American male with a teaching position at a large state university in California. I have owned my own home for more than ten years, as well as the two cars that are the minimal requirement for life in California. And I will confess to a moderate strain of yuppie hedonism. Year after year my two children are the sole representatives of their race in their classrooms, a fact they sometimes have difficulty remembering. We are the only black family in our suburban neighborhood, and even this claim to specialness is diminished by the fact that my wife is white. I think we are called an "integrated" family, though no one has ever used the term with me. For me to be among large numbers of blacks requires conscientiousness and a long car ride, and in truth, I have not been very conscientious lately. Though I was raised in an all-black community just south of Chicago, I only occasionally feel nostalgia for such places. Trips to the barbershop now and then usually satisfy this need, though recently, in the interest of convenience, I've taken to letting my wife cut my hair.

I see in people's eyes from time to time, and hear often in the media, what amounts to a judgment of people like myself: You have moved into the great amorphous middle class and lost your connection to your people and your cultural roots. You have become a genuine invisible man. This is a judgment with many obvious dimensions, many arrows of guilt. But, in essence, it charges me with selfishness and inauthenticity.

At one point I romanticized my situation, thought of myself as a marginal man. The seductive imagery of alienation supported me in this. But in America today racial marginality is hard to sell as the stuff of tragedy. The position brings with it an ugly note of self-insistence that annoys people in a society that is, at least officially, desegregated.

For better or worse, I'm not very marginal. In my middle-American world I see people like myself everywhere. We nod coolly at stoplights, our eyes connect for an awkward instant in shopping malls, we hear about one another from our white friends. "Have you met the new doctor at the hospital . . . the engineer at IBM . . . the new professor in history?" The black middle class is growing. We are often said to be sneaking or slipping or creeping unnoticed into the middle class, as though images of stealth best characterized our movement. I picture a kind of underground railroad, delivering us in the dead of night from the inner city to the suburbs.

But even if we aren't very marginal, we are very shy with one another, at least until we've had a chance to meet privately and take our readings. When we first meet, we experience a trapped feeling, as if we had walked into a cage of racial expectations that would rob us of our individuality by reducing us to an exclusively racial dimension. We are a threat, at first, to one another's uniqueness. I have seen the same well-dressed black woman in the supermarket for more than a year now. We do not speak, and we usually pretend not to see each other. But, when we turn a corner suddenly and find ourselves staring squarely into each other's eyes, her face freezes and she moves on. I believe she is insisting that both of us be more than black—that we interact only when we have a reason other than the mere fact of our race. Her chilliness enforces a priority I agree with—individuality over group identity.

But I believe I see something else in this woman that I also see in myself and in many other middle-class blacks. It is a kind of race fatigue, a deep weariness with things racial, which comes from the fact that our lives are more integrated than they have ever been before. Race does not determine our fates as powerfully as it once did, which means it is not the vital personal concern it once was. Before the sixties, race set the boundaries of black life. Now, especially for middle-class blacks, it is far less a factor, though we don't always like to admit it. Blacks still suffer from racism, so we must be concerned, but this need to be concerned with what is not so personally urgent makes for race fatigue.

I have a friend who did poorly in the insurance business for years. "People won't buy insurance from a black man," he always said. Two years ago another black man and a black woman joined his office. Almost immediately both did twice the business my friend was doing, with the same largely white client base.

Integration shock is essentially the shock of being suddenly accountable on strictly personal terms. It occurs in situations that disallow race as an excuse for personal shortcomings and it therefore exposes vulnerabilities that previously were hidden. One response to such shock is to face up to the self-confrontation it brings and then to act on the basis of what we learn about ourselves. After some struggle, my friend was able to do this. He completely revised his sales technique, asked himself some hard questions about his motivation, and resolved to work harder.

But when one lacks the courage to face oneself fully, a fear of hidden vulnerabilities triggers a fright-flight response to integration shock. Instead of admitting that racism has declined, we argue all the harder that it is still alive and more insidious than ever. We hold race up to shield us from what we do not want to see in ourselves. My friend did this at first, saying that the two blacks in this office were doing better than he was because they knew how to "kiss white ass." Here he was *race-holding*, using race to keep from looking at himself.

Recently I read an article in the local paper that explored the question of whether blacks could feel comfortable living in the largely white Silicon Valley. The article focused on a black family that had been living for more than a decade in Saratoga, a very well-to-do white community. Their neighborhood, their children's schools, their places of employment, their shopping areas and parks—their entire physical environment—were populated by affluent whites. Yet during the interview the wife said they had made two firm rules for their children: that they go to all-black colleges back east and that they do "no dating outside the race, period." 10

I have pushed enough black history and culture on my own children to be able to identify with the impulse behind the first of these rules. Black children in largely white situations must understand and appreciate their cultural background. But the rigidity of these rules, not to mention the rules themselves, points to more than a concern with transmitting heritage or gaining experience with other blacks. Rigidity arises from fear and self-doubt. These people, I believe, were afraid of something.

What was striking to me about their rules, especially the one prohibiting interracial dating, was their tone of rejection. The black parents seemed as determined to reject the white world as to embrace the black one. Why? I would say because of integration shock. Their integrated lives have opened up vulnerabilities they do not wish to face. But what vulnerabilities? In this case, I think, a particularly embarrassing one. On some level, I suspect, they doubt whether they are as good as the white people who live around them. You cannot be raised in a culture that was for centuries committed to the notion of your inferiority and not have some doubt in this regard—doubt that is likely to be aggravated most in integrated situations. So the rejecting tone of their rules is self-protective: *I will reject you before you have a chance to reject me.* But all of this is covered over by race. The high value of racial pride is invoked to shield them from a doubt that they are afraid to acknowledge. Unacknowledged, this doubt gains a negative power inside the personality that expresses itself in the rigidity and absolutism of their rules. Repressed fears tend always to escalate their campaign for our attention by pushing us further and further into irrationality and rigidity.

The refusal to see something unflattering in ourselves always triggers the snap from race fatigue to race-holding. And once that happens, we are caught, like this family, in a jumble of racial ironies. The parents in Saratoga, who have chosen to live integrated lives, impose a kind of segregation on their children. Rules that would be racist in the mouth of any white person are created and enforced with pride. Their unexamined self-doubt also leaves them unable to exploit fully the freedom they have attained. Race fatigue makes them run to a place like Saratoga, but integration shock makes them hold race protectively. They end up clinging to what they've run from.

Once race-holding is triggered by fear, it ensnares us in a web of self-defeating attitudes that end up circumventing the new freedoms we've won over the past several decades. I have seen its corrosive effects in my own life and in the lives of virtually every black person I've known. Some are only mildly touched by it, while others seem incapacitated by it. But race-holding is as unavoidable as defensiveness itself, and I am convinced that it is one of the most debilitating, yet unrecognized, forces in black life today.

I define a *holding* as any self-description that serves to justify or camouflage a 15 person's fears, weaknesses, and inadequacies. Holdings are the little and big exaggerations, distortions, and lies about ourselves that prop us up and let us move along the compromised paths we follow. They develop to defend against threats to our self-esteem, threats that make us feel vulnerable and that plant a seed of fear. This fear can work like wind on a brushfire, spreading self-doubt far beyond what the initial threat would warrant, so that we become even more weakened and more needy of holdings. Since holdings justify our reticence and cowardice, they are usually expressed in the form of high belief or earthy wisdom. A man whose business fails from his own indifference holds an image of himself as a man too honest to be a good businessman—a self-description that draws a veil over his weakness.

For some years I have noticed that I can walk into any of my classes on the first day of the semester, identify the black students, and be sadly confident that on the last day of the semester a disproportionate number of them will be at the bottom of the class, far behind any number of white students of equal or even lesser native ability. More to the point, they will have performed far beneath their own native ability. Self-fulfilling prophesy theory says that their schools have always expected them to do poorly, and that they have internalized this message and *done* poorly. But this deterministic theory sees blacks only as victims, without any margin of choice. It cannot fully explain the poor performances of these black students because it identifies only the forces that *pressure* them to do poorly. By overlooking the margin of choice open to them, this theory fails to recognize the degree to which they are responsible for their own poor showing. (The irony of this oversight is that it takes the power for positive change away from the students and puts it in the hands of the very institutions that failed them in the first place.)

The theory of race-holding is based on the assumption that a margin of choice is always open to blacks (even slaves had some choice). And it tries to make clear the mechanisms by which we relinquish that choice in the name of race. With the decline in racism the margin of black choice has greatly expanded, which is probably why race-holding is so much more visible today than ever before. But anything that prevents us from exploiting our new freedom to the fullest is now as serious a barrier to us as racism once was. . . .

Stanley Fish ▪

Stanley Fish (1938–) is a distinguished lawyer and academician who served as Kenan Professor of English at Johns Hopkins University (1974–1985), Distinguished Professor of English and Law at Duke University (1985–1998), and Dean of the College of Liberal Arts and Sciences at the University of Illinois at Chicago (1999). His interest in contemporary social policy is evident in works such as *There's No Such Thing as Free Speech, and It's a Good Thing* (1994), *Professional Correctness: Literary Studies and Political Change* (1995), and *The Trouble with Principle* (1999). His awards for scholarship in English literature, law, and literary theory include the PEN/ Spielvogel-Diamonstein Award for *There's No Such Thing as Free Speech, and It's a Good Thing* (1994) and the Hanford Book Award for the second edition of *Surprised by Sin: The Reader in Paradise Lost* (1998).

In the following article published in the November 1993 issue of *Atlantic Monthly,* Fish discusses affirmative action and reverse racism.

Reverse Racism, or How the Pot Got to Call the Kettle Black

I take my text from George Bush, who, in an address to the United Nations on September 23, 1991, said this of the UN resolution equating Zionism with racism: "Zionism . . . is the idea that led to the creation of a home for the Jewish people. . . . And to equate Zionism with the intolerable sin of racism is to twist history and forget the terrible plight of Jews in World War II and indeed throughout history." What happened in the Second World War was that six million Jews were exterminated by people who regarded them as racially inferior and a danger to Aryan purity. What happened after the Second World War was that the survivors of that Holocaust established a Jewish state—that is, a state centered on Jewish history, Jewish values, and Jewish traditions: in short, a Jewocentric state. What President Bush objected to was the logical sleight of hand by which these two actions were declared equivalent because they were both expressions of racial exclusiveness. Ignored, as Bush said, was the *historical* difference between them—the difference between a program of genocide and the determination of those who escaped it to establish a community in which they would be the makers, not the victims, of the laws.

Only if racism is thought of as something that occurs principally in the mind, a falling-away from proper notions of universal equality, can the desire of a victimized and terrorized people to band together be declared morally identical to the actions of their would-be executioners. Only when the actions of the two groups are detached from the historical conditions of their emergence and given a purely abstract description can they be made interchangeable. Bush was saying to the United Nations, "Look, the Nazis' conviction of racial superiority generated a policy of systematic genocide; the Jews' experience of centuries of persecution in almost every country on earth generated a desire for a homeland of their own. If you manage somehow to convince yourself that these are the same, it is you, not the Zionists, who are morally confused, and the reason you are morally confused is that you have forgotten history."

◼ A Key Distinction

What I want to say, following Bush's reasoning, is that a similar forgetting of history has in recent years allowed some people to argue, and argue persuasively, that affirmative action is reverse racism. The very phrase "reverse racism" contains the argument in exactly the form to which Bush objected: In this country whites once set themselves apart from blacks and claimed privileges for themselves while denying them to others. Now, on the basis of race, blacks are claiming special status and reserving for themselves privileges they deny to others. Isn't one as bad as the other? The answer is no. One can see why by imagining that it is not 1993 but 1955, and that we are in a town in the South with two more or less distinct communities, one white and one black. No doubt each community would have a ready store of dismissive epithets, ridiculing stories, self-serving folk myths, and expressions of plain hatred, all directed at the other community, and all based in racial hostility. Yet to regard their respective racism—if that is the word—as equivalent would be bizarre, for the hostility of one group stems not from any wrong done to it but from its wish to protect its ability to deprive citizens of their voting rights, to limit access to educational institutions, to prevent entry into the economy except at the lowest and most menial levels, and to force members of the stigmatized group to ride in the back of the bus. The hostility of the other group is the result of these actions, and whereas hostility and racial anger are unhappy facts wherever they are found, a distinction must surely be made between the ideological hostility of the oppressors and the experience-based hostility of those who have been oppressed.

Not to make that distinction is, adapting George Bush's words, to twist history and forget the terrible plight of African-Americans in the more than 200 years of this country's existence. Moreover, to equate the efforts to remedy that plight with the actions that produced it is to twist history even further. Those efforts, designed to redress the imbalances caused by long-standing discrimination, are called affirmative action; to argue that affirmative action, which gives preferential treatment to disadvantaged minorities as part of a plan to achieve social equality, is no different from the policies that created the disadvantages in the first place is a travesty of reasoning. "Reverse racism" is a cogent description of affirmative action only if one considers the cancer of racism to be morally and medically indistinguishable from the therapy we apply to it. A cancer is an invasion of the body's equilibrium, and so is chemotherapy; but we do not decline to fight the disease because the medicine we employ is also disruptive of normal functioning. Strong illness, strong remedy: the formula is as appropriate to the health of the body politic as it is to that of the body proper.

At this point someone will always say, "But two wrongs don't make a right; if it was wrong to treat blacks unfairly, it is wrong to give blacks preference and thereby treat whites unfairly." This objection is just another version of the forgetting and rewriting of history. The work is done by the adverb "unfairly," which suggests two more or less equal parties, one of whom has been unjustly penalized by an incompetent umpire. But blacks have not simply been treated unfairly; they have been subjected first to decades of slavery, and then to decades of second-class citizenship, widespread legalized discrimination, economic persecution, educational deprivation, and cultural stigmatization. They have been bought, sold, killed, beaten, raped, excluded, exploited, shamed, and scorned for a very long time. The word "unfair" is hardly an adequate description of their experience, and the belated gift of "fairness" in the form of a resolution no longer to discriminate against them legally is hardly an adequate remedy for the deep disadvantages that the prior discrimination has produced. When the deck is stacked against you in more ways than you can even count, it is small consolation to hear that you are now free to enter the game and take your chances.

A Tilted Field

The same insincerity and hollowness of promise infect another formula that is popular with the anti-affirmative-action crowd: the formula of the level playing field. Here the argument usually takes the form of saying "It is undemocratic to give one class of citizens advantages at the expense of other citizens; the truly democratic way is to have a level playing field to which everyone has access and where everyone has a fair and equal chance to succeed on the basis of his or her merit." Fine words—but they conceal the facts of the situation as it has been given to us by history: the playing field is already tilted in favor of those by whom and for whom it was constructed in the first place. If mastery of the requirements for entry depends upon immersion in the cultural experiences of the mainstream majority, if the skills that make for success are nurtured by institutions and cultural practices from which the disadvantaged minority has been systematically excluded, if the language and ways of comporting oneself that identify a player as "one of us" are alien to the lives minorities are forced to live, then words like "fair" and "equal" are cruel jokes, for what they promote and celebrate is an institutionalized unfairness and a perpetuated inequality. The playing field is already tilted, and the resistance to altering it by the mechanisms of affirmative action is in fact a determination to make sure that the present imbalances persist as long as possible.

One way of tilting the field is the Scholastic Aptitude Test. This test figures prominently in Dinesh D'Souza's book *Illiberal Education* (1991), in which one finds many examples of white or Asian students denied admission to colleges and universities even though their SAT scores were higher than the scores of some others—often African-Americans—who were admitted to the same institution. This, D'Souza says, is evidence that as a result of affirmative-action policies colleges and universities tend "to depreciate the importance of merit criteria in admissions." D'Souza's assumption—and it is one that many would share—is that the test does in fact measure *merit*, with merit understood as a quality objectively determined in the same way that body temperature can be objectively determined.

In fact, however, the test is nothing of the kind. Statistical studies have suggested that test scores reflect income and socioeconomic status. It has been demonstrated again and again that scores vary in relation to cultural background; the test's questions assume a certain uniformity in educational experience and lifestyle and penalize those who, for whatever reason, have had a different experience and lived different kinds of lives. In short, what is being measured by the SAT is not absolutes like native ability and merit but accidents like birth, social position, access to libraries, and the opportunity to take vacations or to take SAT prep courses.

Furthermore, as David Owen notes in *None of the Above: Behind the Myth of Scholastic Aptitude* (1985), the "correlation between SAT scores and college grades . . . is lower than the correlation between weight and height; in other words you would have a better chance of predicting a person's height by looking at his weight than you would of predicting his freshman grades by looking only at his SAT scores." Everywhere you look in the SAT story, the claims of fairness, objectivity, and neutrality fail away, to be replaced by suspicions of specialized measures and unfair advantages.

Against this background a point that in isolation might have a questionable   10
force takes on a special and even explanatory resonance: the principal deviser of the test was an out-and-out racist. In 1923 Carl Campbell Brigham published a book called *A Study of American Intelligence,* in which, as Owen notes, he declared, among other things, that we faced in America "a possibility of racial admixture . . . infinitely worse than that faced by any European country today, for we are incorporating the Negro into our racial stock, while all of Europe is comparatively free of this taint." Brigham had earlier analyzed the Army Mental Tests using classifications drawn from another racist text, Madison Grant's *The Passing of the Great Race,* which divided American society into four distinct racial strains, with Nordic, blue-eyed, blond people at the pinnacle and the American Negro at the bottom. Nevertheless, in 1925 Brigham became a director of testing for the College Board, and developed the SAT. So here is the great SAT test, devised by a racist in order to confirm racist assumptions, measuring not native ability but cultural advantage, an uncertain indicator of performance, an indicator of very little except what money and social privilege can buy. And it is in the name of this mechanism that we are asked to reject affirmative action and reaffirm "the importance of merit criteria in admissions."

■ The Reality of Discrimination

Nevertheless, there is at least one more card to play against affirmative action, and it is a strong one. Granted that the playing field is not level and that access to it is reserved for an already advantaged elite, the disadvantages suffered by others are less racial—at least in 1993—than socioeconomic. Therefore shouldn't, as D'Souza urges, "universities . . . retain their policies of preferential treatment, but alter their criteria of application from race to socioeconomic disadvantage," and thus avoid the unfairness of current policies that reward middle-class or affluent blacks at the expense of poor whites? One answer to this question is given by D'Souza himself when he acknowledges that the overlap between minority groups and the poor is very large—a point underscored by the former Secretary of Education Lamar Alexander, who said, in response to a question about funds targeted for black students, "Ninety-eight percent of race-specific scholarships do not involve constitutional problems." He meant, I take it, that 98 percent of race-specific scholarships were also scholarships to the economically disadvantaged.

Still, the other two percent—nonpoor, middle-class, economically favored blacks—are receiving special attention on the basis of disadvantages they do not experience. What about them? The force of the question depends on the assumption that in this day and age race could not possibly be a serious disadvantage to those who are otherwise well positioned in the society. But the lie was given dramatically to this assumption in a 1991 broadcast of the ABC program *PrimeTime Live.* In a stunning fifteen-minute segment reporters and a camera crew followed two young men of equal education, cultural sophistication, level of apparent affluence, and so forth around St. Louis, a city where neither was known. The two differed in only a single respect: one was white, the other black. But that small difference turned out to mean everything. In a series of encounters with shoe salesmen, record-store employees, rental agents, landlords, employment agencies, taxicab drivers, and ordinary citizens, the black member of the pair was either ignored or given a special and suspicious attention. He was asked to pay more for the same goods or come up with a larger down payment for the same car, was turned away as a prospective tenant, was rejected as a prospective taxicab fare, was treated with contempt and irritation by clerks and bureaucrats, and in every way possible was made to feel inferior and unwanted.

The inescapable conclusion was that alike though they may have been in almost all respects, one of these young men, because he was black, would lead a significantly lesser life than his white counterpart: he would be housed less well and at greater expense; he would pay more for services and products when and if he was given the opportunity to buy them; he would have difficulty establishing credit; the first emotions he would inspire on the part of many people he met would be distrust and fear; his abilities would be discounted even before he had a chance to display them; and, above all, the treatment he received from minute to minute would chip away at his self-esteem and self-confidence with consequences that most of us could not even imagine. As the young man in question said at the conclusion of the broadcast, "You walk down the street with a suit and tie and it doesn't matter. Someone will make determinations about you, determinations that affect the quality of your life."

Of course, the same determinations are being made quite early on by kindergarten teachers, grade school principals, high school guidance counselors, and the like, with results that cut across socioeconomic lines and place young black men and women in the ranks of the disadvantaged no matter what the bank accounts of their parents happen to show. Racism is a cultural fact, and although its effects may to some extent be diminished by socioeconomic variables, those effects will still be sufficiently great to warrant the nation's attention and thus the continuation of affirmative-action policies. This is true even of the field thought to be dominated by blacks and often cited as evidence of the equal opportunities society now affords them. I refer, of course, to professional athletics. But national self-congratulation on this score might pause in the face of a few facts: A minuscule number of African-Americans ever receive a paycheck from a professional team. Even though nearly 1,600 daily newspapers report on the exploits of black athletes, they employ only seven full-time black sports columnists. Despite repeated pledges and resolutions, major-league teams have managed to put only a handful of blacks and Hispanics in executive positions.

■ Why Me?

When all is said and done, however, one objection to affirmative action is unanswerable on its own terms, and that is the objection of the individual who says, "Why me? Sure, discrimination has persisted for many years, and I acknowledge that the damage done has not been removed by changes in the law. But why me? I didn't own   15 slaves; I didn't vote to keep people on the back of the bus; I didn't turn water hoses on civil-rights marchers. Why, then, should I be the one who doesn't get the job or who doesn't get the scholarship or who gets bumped back to the waiting list?"

I sympathize with this feeling, if only because in a small way I have had the experience that produces it. I was recently nominated for an administrative post at a large university. Early signs were encouraging, but after an interval I received official notice that I would not be included at the next level of consideration, and subsequently I was told unofficially that at some point a decision had been made to look only in the direction of women and minorities. Although I was disappointed, I did not conclude that the situation was "unfair," because the policy was obviously not directed at me—at no point in the proceedings did someone say, "Let's find a way to rule out Stanley Fish." Nor was it directed even at persons of my race and sex—the policy was not intended to disenfranchise white males. Rather, the policy was driven by other considerations, and it was only as a by-product of those considerations— not as the main goal—that white males like me were rejected. Given that the institution in question has a high percentage of minority students, a very low percentage of minority faculty, and an even lower percentage of minority administrators, it made perfect sense to focus on women and minority candidates, and within that sense, not as the result of prejudice, my whiteness and maleness became disqualifications.

I can hear the objection in advance: "What's the difference? Unfair is unfair: you didn't get the job; you didn't even get on the short list." The difference is not in the outcome but in the ways of thinking that led up to the outcome. It is the difference between an unfairness that befalls one as the unintended effect of a policy rationally conceived and an unfairness that is pursued as an end in itself. It is the difference between the awful unfairness of Nazi extermination camps and the unfairness to Palestinian Arabs that arose from, but was not the chief purpose of, the founding of a Jewish state.

■ The New Bigotry

The point is not a difficult one, but it is difficult to see when the unfairness scenarios are presented as simple contrasts between two decontextualized persons who emerge from nowhere to contend for a job or a place in a freshman class. Here is student A; he has a board score of 1,300. And here is student B; her board score is only 1,200, yet she is admitted and A is rejected. Is that fair? Given the minimal information provided, the answer is of course no. But if we expand our horizons and consider fairness in relation to the cultural and institutional histories that have brought the two students to this point, histories that weigh on them even if they are not the histories' authors, then both the question and the answer suddenly grow more complicated.

The sleight-of-hand logic that first abstracts events from history and then assesses them from behind a veil of willed ignorance gains some of its plausibility from another key word in the anti-affirmative-action lexicon. That word is "individual," as in "The American way is to focus on the rights of individuals rather than groups." Now, "individual" and "individualism" have been honorable words in the American political vocabulary, and they have often been well employed in the fight against various tyrannies. But like any other word or concept, individualism can be perverted to serve ends the opposite of those it originally served, and this is what has happened when in the name of individual rights, millions of individuals are enjoined from redressing historically documented wrongs. How is this managed? Largely in the same way that the invocation of fairness is used to legitimize an institutionalized inequality. First one says, in the most solemn of tones, that the protection of individual rights is the chief obligation of society. Then one defines individuals as souls sent into the world with equal entitlements as guaranteed either by their Creator or by the Constitution. Then one pretends that nothing has happened to them since they stepped onto the world's stage. And then one says of these carefully denatured souls that they will all be treated in the same way, irrespective of any of the differences that history has produced. Bizarre as it may seem, individualism in this argument turns out to mean that everyone is or should be the *same*. This dismissal of individual difference in the name of the individual would be funny were its consequences not so serious: it is the mechanism by which imbalances and inequities suffered by millions of people through no fault of their own can be sanitized and even celebrated as the natural workings of unfettered democracy.

"Individualism," "fairness," "merit"—these three words are continually misappropriated by bigots who have learned that they need not put on a white hood or bar access to the ballot box in order to secure their ends. Rather, they need only clothe themselves in a vocabulary plucked from its historical context and made into the justification for attitudes and policies they would not acknowledge if frankly named.   20

George F. Will

George F. Will (1941–), well known for his biting satire on the decline of American society, is a political commentator for *The Washington Post* and *Newsweek* magazine. He also appears regularly on the ABC-TV programs *This Week* and *World News Tonight*. His publications include *The Pursuit of Happiness, and Other Sobering Thoughts* (1978), *The Morning After: American Successes and Excesses, 1981–1986* (1986), *Suddenly: The American Idea Abroad and at Home, 1986–1990* (1990), *The Leveling Wind: Politics, the Culture, and Other News, 1990–1994* (1994), and *The Woven Figure: Conservatism and America's Fabric, 1994–1997* (1997). His honors include a Pulitzer Prize in 1977 for distinguished commentary.

In the following essay, Will analyzes the Racial Privacy Initiative on the 2002 California ballot and its impact on the historical classification of an African American as a person who has any admixture of black ancestry.

Dropping the "One Drop" Rule

It is probably the most pernicious idea ever to gain general acceptance in America. No idea has done more, and more lasting, damage than the "one drop" rule, according to which if you have *any* admixture of black ancestry, you are black, period. This idea imparted an artificial clarity to the idea of race, and became the basis of the laws, conventions and etiquette of slavery, then of segregation and subsequently of today's identity politics, in which one's civic identity is a function of one's race (or ethnicity, or gender, or sexual preference).

Today nothing more scaldingly reveals the intellectual bankruptcy and retrograde agenda of the institutionalized—fossilized, really—remnants of the Civil Rights Movement than this: those remnants constitute a social faction clinging desperately to the "one drop" rule, or some inchoate and unarticulated version of that old buttress of slavery and segregation. However, in California, where much of modern America has taken shape, a revolt is brewing—a revolt against the malignant legacy of that rule, and against identity politics generally, and in favor of a colorblind society. The revolt is gathering strength—and signatures.

The signatures—1.1 million of them, by April 10—are required to put the Racial Privacy Initiative on California's November ballot. If enacted, the RPI will prevent government agencies in California from classifying individuals by race, ethnicity, color or national origin for any purpose pertaining to public education, public contracting or public employment.

Who can object to the RPI 50 years after Ralph Ellison, in *Invisible Man,* his great novel about black experience in America, wrote, "Our task is that of making ourselves individuals"? Who can object to the RPI 48 years after Thurgood Marshall, then an attorney representing the NAACP in *Brown v. Board of Education,* said, "Distinctions by race are so evil, so arbitrary and invidious that a state bound to defend the equal protection of the laws must not involve them in any public sphere"? Who can object to the RPI 34 years after Martin Luther King died struggling for a society in which Americans "will not be judged by the color of their skin but by the content of their character"?

Who? Here is who: People who make their living by Balkanizing America into 5 elbow-throwing grievance groups clamoring for government preferment. Such people include blacks in the civil rights industry who administer today's racial spoils system of college admissions and contract set-asides, and white liberals who have a political stake in blacks forever thinking of themselves as permanently crippled by history and hence permanent wards of government.

But Ward Connerly says: Enough—actually, much too much—already. Connerly, the prime mover behind the RPI, is a successful businessman, a member of the University of California Board of Regents, and the man responsible for California voters enacting in 1996 Proposition 209 to eliminate government-administered racial preferences. He is black.

At least, he is according to the "one drop" rule. Never mind that one of his grandparents was of African descent, another was Irish, another was Irish and American Indian, another was French Canadian. Furthermore, by the "one drop" rule, the children he and his Irish wife have had are black. And his grandchildren are black, even the two whose mother is half-Vietnamese.

A modest proposal: Instead of calling them, or grandfather Ward, blacks, why not call them Californians? In California today more children are born to parents of different races than are born to two black parents. In a recent 15-year span (1982–97) multiracial births in California increased 40 percent. There has been a sharp increase in the number of applicants to the University of California who refuse to stipulate their race.

The RPI follows the logic of the 2000 U.S. Census. The 1790 census classified Americans into five categories—white males 16 years and older, white males less than 16 years, white females, other white persons and slaves. In 1860 Chinese and American Indian were added as distinct races. By 1990 the census offered five major categories: white, black, Asian/Pacific Islander, American Indian/Native Alaskan and other. But births to black-white interracial parents nearly tripled in the 1990s. It is morally offensive and, the "one drop" rule notwithstanding, preposterous for a child of such a marriage to be required to choose to "be" the race of just one parent. And why should the alternative be "other"?

So in 2000 the census expanded the available choices from five to 63. The 63 did not include the category Tiger Woods concocted for himself—"Cablinasian," meaning Caucasian, black, Indian and Asian. But the 63 threatened those race-and-ethnicity entrepreneurs who toil to maximize their power and profits by maximizing the numbers they purport to speak for—the numbers of people who supposedly are clearly this or that race or ethnicity. Hence the hysteria against the RPI. 10

The American Civil Liberties Union's chapter in Berkeley—of course—says the RPI would effectively return California to "pre-1964" status. That is, to before the law that guaranteed blacks access to voting booths and public accommodations. Orwellian language multiplies: Professional racemongers denounce the RPI's ban on racial preferences as "racist," and people whose livelihood depends on dividing Americans into irritable clumps denounce the RPI as "divisive."

The RPI is sound social policy for a nation in which racial and ethnic boundaries are becoming wonderfully blurry. This accelerating development should please Americans regardless of whether they accept, reject or are agnostic about the idea that the very concept of race is scientifically dubious, or is a mere convention—a "social construct."

By enacting the RPI, the one eighth of Americans who are Californians can help the other seven eighths put the "one drop" rule where it belongs—in a far corner of the mental attic where the nation puts embarrassments from its immaturity.

Media Resources

Pinky. [1949] Directed by Elia Kazan. 100 minutes. 20th Century Fox. Young woman passing for white returns to her Southern home.

Imitation of Life. [1959] Directed by Douglas Serk. 124 minutes. Universal. Dramatization of Fannie Hurst's novel about a mulatto who tries to pass for white.

Dutchman. [1966] Directed by Anthony Harvey. 55 minutes. Image Entertainment. In this adaptation of Amiri Baraka's riveting 1964 play, the encounter between a taunting white woman and a black man on the New York subway erupts into violence.

The Eyes on the Prize. [1986] Directed by Judith Vecchione, Orlando Bagwell, James DeVinney, Callie Crossley. 60 minutes. Blackside Inc. This six-part drama of African America's civil rights victories from 1954 to 1965 covers issues such as the Jim Crow practices of the South from the 1880s to 1963, the student movement of 1960–61, the Emmett Till murder, compliance with *Brown v. Board of Education,* and clashes with the police.

True Colors. [1991] Produced by Mark Lucasiewicz. Performer is Diane Sawyer. 19 minutes. MTI/Fil & Video. The ABC *PrimeTime* host follows two men—one black, one white—as they test levels of prejudice.

Ghost of Mississippi. [1996] Directed by Rob Reiner. 130 minutes. Castle Rock. This movie is about the murderers of noted Mississippi civil rights leader Medgar Evers, who were twice acquitted in spite of clear incriminating evidence against them.

Rosewood. [1997] Directed by John Singleton. 140 minutes. Warner Brothers. The film is an adaptation of a true story of an African American town destroyed in 1923 by an angry mob after a white woman falsely reports that a black man beat and raped her.

CHAPTER 2

Talk That Talk

A universal human struggle is finding and exerting one's voice, breaking the patterns of silence and voicing opinions and beliefs about one's society. In 1966, Maulana Ron Karenga initiated the first Kwanzaa celebration (a seven-day festival celebrated by African Americans during the Christmas season). Part of the ritual involves the reciting of principles, among them Kujichagulia, self-determination. This was not the beginning of the struggle by African Americans for self-determination, but a modern verbalization of the need to exert one's self to speak for oneself. The focus of this chapter is self-determination, speaking for and naming oneself. The title of the chapter, "Talk That Talk," is celebratory in recognition and praise of the long struggle African Americans have experienced in order to speak and name themselves.

The ability to speak "well" is a very important component in the African American experience. Tied to performance, the use of language is the means by which many African Americans achieve recognition in the community. The widespread phenomenon, used to earn the community's respect, has its roots in African verbal art. "Nommo," belief in the magical power of the word, frames the African American experience. This power spans social, political, musical, spiritual, emotional, even psychological boundaries.

An excerpt from the introduction to Geneva Smitherman's 1994 *Black Talk*, a dictionary of African American terms, serves to illustrate that naming is an appropriate analogy for understanding the relationship between oppression and self-identity through language. She uses a variety of historical examples of African American discourses from music, slang, church, and popular culture to demonstrate the analogy.

Language use by African Americans has led to one of the ugliest ongoing controversies in America. From the early description of Negro dialect by W. F. Allen as phonetic decay and debasement of language on the isolated St. Helena Island in the Georgia Sea Islands in 1865 to the patronizing 1916 *Literary Digest* editorial that describes plantation songs as full of warm-blooded sentimentality, we see the negative depiction of African Americans through analysis of their language. Even when Zora Neale Hurston published her seminal work on Negro folklore in 1935, which represented the language, culture, and discourse style as accomplishments of pride, she was deeply criticized for exposing Negroes in a distasteful light. The excerpt from *Mules and Men,* "Pa Henry's Prayer," is an example of Negro dialect and discourse style. It demonstrates a personal approach to the "Father," uses spellings that represent speech, and provides testimonial.

In spite of documented evidence, there is still today denial either that Black English exists or that it should be classified as bona fide even though features of it are used in some form by a substantial number of African Americans and they are often co-opted by television, advertising, and the media. Over one hundred years after the Allen description of Negro dialect, at the height of the Oakland School Board controversy naming Ebonics as a language, the Linguistic Society of America announced a resolution affirming that, whatever the name used, the language variety was rule-governed, systematic, and distinct. A trilogy of short essays by Jacqueline Brice-Finch, Akua Duku Anokye, and Robert Reising in 1997 makes a plea for tolerance, respect, evaluation, understanding, and a new language policy.

Countee Cullen's 1928 poem "Incident" depicts the pain inflicted upon an impressionable child when called out of his name. In the 1994 essay by Keith Gilyard, we become acquainted with more contemporary methods of critiquing the impact of words. He is interested in the master narrative and the need to "flip the script," an adaptive response to victimization via language—the counterstory. Gilyard sets up a dialogue among opposites—between expression and repression, debilitating and therapeutic, African American literature and African American rumor—to illustrate language issues. Emma Jackson's 1999 article is an analysis of the same pejorative name that created havoc in Countee Cullen's poem. Based on interviews with African Americans from various backgrounds and experiences, this article attempts to examine changing definitions and perspectives. In 2002, Randall Kennedy makes a thorough examination of the use of this racial epithet in his book *Nigger: The Strange Career of a Troublesome Word.*

While W. F. Allen in 1865 misunderstood the spirituals of slavery as the only form of music produced by the Negro, Amiri Baraka's 1963 work illustrates the historical development of the blues out of the shouts and spirituals resulting from a better acquaintance with English, as well as greater isolation following emancipation. Gwen Pough, in a speech delivered at the 2001 American Studies Association Conference, explains that rappers speak for the people and voice their concerns. Like their earlier counterparts (the poets and the lyricists, the blues men and women, the workers, the slaves), their mission is to use language and style to "represent" the world, the complex cultural practices, styles, and innovation. As attention turns to women's language and use, we learn that black women rappers seek to confront and change their representations, to challenge the double standard, and to claim space for themselves.

Throughout this chapter we see that African American language begins and ends with the recognition of the power of words. What's in a name?—the inalienable choice at the core of selfhood. As early as the seventeenth century, questions about the names used to represent African slaves or indentured servants arose, and to this day similar battles are being fought by, for example, African American women in the hip-hop revolution. Who will "represent"? The writers in "Talk That Talk" "represent" the shifts in speaking for one's self over the past 300 years.

Geneva Smitherman

Geneva Smitherman (1940–) is a University Distinguished Professor of English and Director of the African American Language and Literacy Program at Michigan State University. Also known as "Dr. G," Dr. Smitherman is a highly respected authority on African American language. Internationally recognized as a scholar in this subject, she has lectured and conducted workshops the world over. She has also authored or coauthored 12 books, including the seminal work *Talkin' and Testifyin',* and over 100 articles and publications on language and education.

This excerpt comes from the Introduction to *Black Talk: Words and Phrases from the Hood to the Amen Corner* (1994), in which she discusses the many names used historically to identify African Americans, from *African* to *colored* and beyond.

From African to African American

Just as we were called colored, but were not that . . . and then Negro, but not that . . . to be called Black is just as baseless . . . Black tells you about skin color and what side of town you live on. African American evokes discussion of the world.

Names for the race have been a continuing issue since JUMPSTREET, 1619, when the first slave ship landed at Jamestown. From AFRICAN to COLORED to "negro" to NEGRO with the capital to BLACK to AFRICAN AMERICAN, with side trips to AFROAMERICAN, AFRIAMERICAN, AFRAAMERICAN, and AFRIKAN, what are we Africans in America, today thirty-five million strong, "we people who are darker than blue," as Curtis Mayfield once sang, to call ourselves?

Debates rage. The topic is discussed at conferences. Among leaders and intellectuals, as well as among everyday people, the issue is sometimes argued so hotly that folk stop speaking to one another! In 1904, the *A.M.E. Church Review* sponsored a symposium of Black leaders to debate whether the "n" of "negro" should be capitalized. However, participants in that symposium went beyond the mere question of capitalization to debate whether "negro" was the right name for the race in the first place. In 1967, during the shift from "Negro" to "Black," and again in 1989, during the shift from "Black" to "African American," *Ebony* magazine devoted several pages to the question "What's in a Name?" And the beat goes on . . . . The status of Blacks remains unsettled. Name changes and debates over names reflect our uncertain status and come to the forefront during crises and upheavals in the Black condition.

Although African Americans are linked to Africans on the Continent and in the DIASPORA, the Black American, as James Baldwin once put it, is a unique creation. For one thing, other Diasporic Africans claim citizenship in countries that are virtually all-Black—Jamaicans, Bajans, Nigerians, Ghanaians, for example, are not minorities in their native lands. For another, not only are Blacks a distinct minority in America, but our status as first-class citizens is debatable, even at this late hour in U.S. history. As the SISTA said about Rodney King's beating in Los Angeles, the torching of a Black man by whites in Florida, and Malice Green's death in Detroit, "After all we done been through, here it is [the 1990s], and we still ain free." Some activists and AFRICAN-CENTERED Blacks have coined the term NEO-SLAVERY to capture the view that the present Black condition, with whites still powerful and Blacks still powerless, is just enslavement in another form.

Blacks are a minority amid a population who look distinctly different physically and who promote racial supremacist standards of physical attractiveness. This state of affairs has created a set of negative attitudes about skin color, hair, and other physical features that are reflected in the U.S. Ebonics Lexicon, in terms such as GOOD HAIR (which Zora Neale Hurston once described as "nearer my God to thee"), BAD HAIR, HIGH YELLA, LIVER-LIPS, and NAPPY. Because black skin color was so devalued at one time, to call an African person "black" was to CALL HIM or HER OUTA THEY NAME. It was: "If you white, you all right; if you brown, stick around; if you black, git back." Thus the necessity, during the Black Freedom Struggle of the 1960s and 1970s, of purging the racial label "Black" and adopting it as a name for the race in symbolic celebration of the changed status of Africans in America.

Back to GIDDAYUP. The British colonists, who would become Americans in 1776, called the Africans "free" (a few were, but most were not), "slave," or, following fifteenth-century Portuguese slave traders, *negro* (an adjective meaning "black" in Portuguese and Spanish). But the Africans called themselves "African" and so designated their churches and organizations as in the names African Educational and Benevolent Society, African Episcopal Church, and African Masonic Lodge No. 459. In those early years, the thought was Africa on my mind and in my MIND'S EYE. Enslaved Africans kept thinking and hoping, all the way up until the nineteenth century, that they would one day return to Mother Africa. Some hummed the tune "I'll Fly Away," believing that, like the legendary hero Solomon, they would be able to fly back to Africa. And especially after fighting at Lexington, Concord, and Bunker Hill in the Revolutionary War, they just knew they would be free to return home. Instead, the thirteen British colonies that became the United States tightened the reins on their African slaves, passing laws abolishing temporary enslavement and indentured servitude for Africans and making them slaves for life.

By 1800, several generations of Africans had been born on American soil, thousands had been transported from Africa, and the Black population numbered more than one million. Both the vision and the possibility of returning to Africa had become impractical and remote. Further, a movement had begun to abolish slavery and to make the Africans citizens. And both free and enslaved Africans were becoming critically aware of their contributions to the development of American wealth. In light of this new reality and in preparation for citizenship and what they thought would be opportunities to enjoy the national wealth they had helped create through two hundred years of free labor, enslaved Africans began to call themselves "Colored" (often spelled "Coloured" in those days), and the designation "African" declined in use.

"Colored" was used throughout much of the nineteenth century until the white backlash began. The year 1877 marked the end of Reconstruction and set the stage for "the Coloreds" to be put back in their place. The political deal cut in D.C. led to the withdrawal of the federal/Union troops that had been stationed in the South to ensure justice for the ex-enslaved Africans. Power and home rule were returned to the Old Confederacy. The "freedmen" (as they were called by the federal government and by whites) lost the small gains in education, citizenship, and political power that the Civil War and the Emancipation Proclamation had made possible. New forms of repression and torture began—lynch mobs, Ku Klux Klan, loss of voting rights, and the beginning of separate but (*un*)equal. By 1900, the quest was on for a new name to capture the new reality of being neither "slave nor free," as one ex-enslaved African put it.

Although some Colored had begun using and rallying for the label "negro," when the National Association for the Advancement of Colored People (NAACP) was founded in 1909, the COMMUNITY had not yet reached a consensus. The push for "negro" and for its capitalization hit its full stride during the period between the two world wars. With the U.S. campaign to "make the world safe for democracy," and with Colored soldiers shedding their blood for America, the community thought surely that the contradictory status of Africans in America would be resolved on the side of first-class citizenship and economic equity. Leaders such as Dr. W.E.B. Du Bois, editor of the NAACP journal, *Crisis,* launched a massive nationwide effort to capitalize and to elevate the Portuguese-derived adjective "negro" to a level of dignity and respect. The NAACP mailed out more than seven hundred letters to publishers and editors. Community newsletters addressed the issue, both sides debated it, and talks and sermons in the Traditional Black Church focused on it. By 1930, the major European American media were using "Negro" and capitalizing it. (The two glaring exceptions were *Forum* magazine and the U.S. Government Printing Office.) The *New York Times* put it this way: "[This] is not merely a typographical change, it is an act in recognition of racial self-respect for those who have been for generations in the 'lower case.'"

"Negro" was the name until the 1960s when Africans in America struggled to throw off the shackles of Jim Crow and embraced Black Culture, the Black Experience, and black skin color. Again, conferences were held, many under the rubric of "Black Power," debates ensued, and yes, folk had hot arguments and DISsed one another about abandoning the name "Negro" for "Black," which was "only an adjective," as those who favored "Negro" often put it. However, the motion of history could not be stopped. The name change to "Black" and the profound significance of this change in the language and life of Blacks was captured in a 1968 hit song by James Brown: "Say It Loud (I'm Black, and I'm Proud)."

The final period in the name debate (for now, at least) began in late 1988 10 with a proposal from Dr. Ramona Edelin, president of the National Urban Coalition, to call the upcoming 1989 summit the African American, rather than the Black, Summit. She asserted that this name change "would establish a cultural context for the new agenda." Her view was that present-day Africans in America were facing a new reality—the erosion, since the late 1970s, of hard-won progress; high unemployment; the rise of racism; the growth of urban youth violence; the proliferation of crack (introduced, it continues to be widely argued in the Black community, by the CIA); and the general deterioration of the community. The situation called for a reassessment within the framework of a global identity, linking Africans in North America with those on the Continent and throughout the Diaspora.

As in previous eras, the name issue, this time the shift from "Black" to "African American," has been debated at community forums and conferences. It has been the topic of conversation and heated arguments at the barber and BEAUTY SHOP, at family reunions, social gatherings, and at Church events. The change has not been as cataclysmic, though, as the shift from "Negro" to "Black" in the 1960s, because "African American" lacks the negative history of "Black." Further, "African American" returns us to the source, the "African" of early years, but with a significant dimension added: "American." This addition calls attention to four hundred years of building wealth in America and legitimates the demand for political and economic equity, or at least FORTY ACRES AND A MULE. This line of argument was put forth as long ago as 1829 by David Walker, one of the first RED, BLACK, AND GREEN BROTHAS, in his *Appeal, in four Articles: Together with a Preamble to the Coloured Citizens of the World, but in particular, and very Expressly, to those of the United States of America.* His *Appeal* was published during the era of "Colored." Calling for open rebellion against enslavement, and opposing the American Colonization Society's plan to re-settle enslaved Africans in Africa, Walker wrote:

> Men who are resolved to keep us in eternal wretchedness are also bent on sending us to Liberia . . . America is more our country than it is the whites'—we have enriched it with our BLOOD AND TEARS.

To date, "African American" appears to have caught on throughout the community, although "Black" continues to be used also (and, to a lesser extent, the name "African"/"Afrikan"). In opinion polls about the name issue, Black youth are the strongest supporters of "African American," which is not surprising, given the African-Centered consciousness that has emerged in HIP HOP Culture. However, there are those—generally the parents and older siblings of youth—who still favor "Black" because this name generated an intense, long-overdue struggle around old, past scripts of racial self-hatred and because the eventual adoption of the name "Black" symbolized a victorious shift to the positive in the African American psyche.

The historical motion to reconfigure Black identity and Black Language, a movement launched in the 1960s and 1970s, can be viewed as the quest for Re-Africanization. The shift from "Black" to "African American" was inevitable as Black Americans have now come full circle, back to where they had been from the JUMP in 1619: "African." The process of linguistic Re-Africanization continues today and is most evident in HIP HOP Culture and in the works of Black women writers such as Alice Walker, Toni Morrison, and Terry McMillan. Simultaneously, there is an emerging sense of a bilingual consciousness among middle-class Blacks (particularly those who are not yet middle-aged), who value both U.S. Ebonics and the Language of Wider Communication ("standard English"); this linguistic consciousness has set the stage for a developing level of linguistic experimentation as they incorporate the FLAVA of Black Talk into dialogue and discourse. The linguistic efforts of Black women writers and the HIP HOP NATION, in concert with the linguistic experimentation of young Black professionals, will eventuate in a new language, reflecting a dynamic blend of traditional and innovative linguistic patterns, as U.S. Ebonics enters the twenty-first century. Stay tuned.

W. F. Allen

W. F. Allen wrote this letter to the editor of *The Nation* in 1865. Having spent several months in Port Royal, he had faith in his ability to describe the features of the dialect spoken on one of the Sea Island plantations in this letter.

The Negro Dialect

TO THE EDITOR OF THE NATION:

During a residence of some months upon one of the Sea Island plantations of Port Royal I gave considerable attention to the analysis of the negro dialect, and made some observations which I think possess interest and even philological value. I have hoped that some person with a wider experience than myself—for instance, Col. Higginson, who I know was interested in this subject—would treat it with more fulness than I can do. Fearing, however, that in the progress of civilization among these people those curious features will vanish, I wish to put them on record before they fade from my own memory.

Ordinary negro-talk, such as we find in books, has very little resemblance to that of the negroes of Port Royal, who were so isolated that they seem to have formed a dialect of their own. Indeed, the different plantations have their own peculiarities, and adepts profess to be able to determine by the speech of a negro what part of an island he belongs to, or even, in some cases, his plantation. My observations were confined to a few plantations at the northern end of St. Helena Island.

With these people the process of "Phonetic Decay" appears to have gone as far, perhaps, as is possible, and with it the extremest simplification of etymology and syntax. The usual softening of *th* and *v* into *d* and *b* is observed among them; likewise a frequent interchange of *v* and *w*: as *veeds* and *vell* for *weeds* and *well*; "De wile' sinner may return" (for *vilest*). This last illustrates also the habit of clipping syllables, which they do constantly: as *lee'* for *little; plant'shun* for *plantation*. The lengthening of short vowels is illustrated in both these words—*a*, for instance, never has our short sound, but always the European sound. The following hymn illustrates these points:

> "Meet, O Lord, on de milk-white horse,
>   An' de nineteen wile [viol] in his han',
> Drop on, drop on de crown on my head,
>   An' rolly in my Jesus' arm.
> E'en [in] dat mornin' all day,
>   When Jesus de Chris' bin born."

The same hymn, particularly the second verse,

> "Moon wont into de poplar tree,
>   An star went into blood."

(the figures evidently taken from the book of Revelations), is a fair specimen of the turn which Scriptural ideas and phraseology receive in their untutored minds. It should be observed, by the way, that the songs do not show the full extent of the de-basement of the language. Being generally taken, in phrases, from Scripture, or from the hymns which they have heard sung by the whites, they retain words and grammatical forms which one rarely hears in conversation. The common speech, in its strange words and pronunciation, abbreviations, and rhythmical modulation, sounds to a stranger like a foreign language.

These strange words are, however, less numerous than one would imagine.   5
There is *yedde* for *hear,* as in that sweetest of their songs:

> "O my sin is forgiben and my soul set free,
> An' I yedde from heaben to-day."

There is *sh' um,* a corruption of *see 'em,* applied to all genders and both numbers. There is "huddy" (how-do?), pronounced "how-dy" by the purists among them. It is not irreverence, but affectionate devotion, that is expressed in the simple song:

> "In de mornin' when I rise,
> Tell my Jesus huddy O,
> Wash my han' in de mornin' glory," etc.

Studdy (steady) is used to denote any continued or customary action. "He studdy 'buse an' cuss me," complained one of the school-children of another. This word *cuss,* by the way, is used by them with great latitude, to denote any offensive lan-guage. "He cuss me, 'git out,'" was the charge of one adult against another. "Ahvy [Abby: in this case the b had become v] do cuss me," was the serious-sounding but trifling accusation made by one little girl against her seat-mate. *Both* they seldom use: generally "all-two," or emphatically, "all two hoff togedder." *One* for alone. "Me one an' God," was the answer of an old man in Charleston when I asked him whether he escaped alone from his plantation. "Heaben 'nuff for me one" [*i.e.,* I suppose, "for my part"], says one of their songs. *Talk* is one of their most common words, where we should use *speak* or *mean.* "Talk me, sir?" asks a boy who is not sure whether you mean him or his comrade. "Talk lick, sir! nuffin but lick," was the an-swer to the question whether a particular master used to whip his slaves.

The letters *n* and *y* are often thrown in euphonically. I can only remember at this moment *n* before a long *u* as n'Europe, n'United States, no n'use; but I think it is used with other vowels. Of *y* also I can only recall one instance, which I will give presently. The most curious, however, of all their linguistic peculiarities is, I think, the following: It is well known that the negroes all through the South speak of their elders as "uncle" and "aunt;" from a feeling of politeness, I do not doubt—it seemed disrespectful to use the bare name, and from *Mr.* and *Mrs.* they were de-barred. On the Sea Islands similar feeling has led to the use of *cousin* towards their equals. Abbreviating this after their fashion, they get co'n or co' (the vowel sound u of *cousin*) as the common title when they speak of one another. C' Abram, Co' Robin, Co'n Emma, C' Isaac, Co' Bob, are specimens of what one hears every day. I have heard Bro' (brother) used in the same way, but seldom; as in the song,

> "Bro' Bill, you ought to know my name,
> My name is written in de book ob life."

I come now to the subject of grammar, upon which I might almost be entitled to repeat a very old joke, and say that there is no grammar; for there probably is no speech that has less inflection than that of these negroes. There is no distinction of case, number, tense, or voice—hardly of gender. Perhaps I am wrong in saying that there is no number, for this distinction is made in pronouns, and some of the most intelligent will, perhaps, occasionally make it in nouns. But "Sandy hat" would generally mean indifferently Sandy's hat or hats; "dem cow" is plural, "dat cow" singular; "nigger house" means the collection of negro houses, and is, I suppose, really plural. As to cases, I do not know that I ever heard a regular possessive, but they have begun to develop one of their own, which is a very curious illustration of the way inflectional forms have probably grown up in other languages. If they wish to make the fact of possession at all emphatic or distinct, they use the whole word "own." Thus, they will say "Mosey house;" but if asked whose house that is, the answer is "Mosey own." "Co' Molsy y'own," was the odd reply made by a little girl to the question whose child she was carrying; *Co'* is title; *y* euphonic.

Nearly all the pronouns exist. Perhaps *us* does not, *we* being generally in its place. *She* and *her* being rare, *him* is the usual pronoun of the third person singular, for all genders and cases. "Him lick we" was the complaint of some small children against a large girl. *Um* is still more common, as objective case, for all genders and numbers; as *Sh'um (see 'em)*.

It is too much to say that the verbs have no inflections; but it is true that these have nearly disappeared. Ask a boy where he is going, and the answer is "gwine crick for ketch crab,"—"going into the creek to catch crabs" (*for* being generally used instead of *to*, to denote purpose); ask another where the missing boy is, and the answer is the same, with *gone* instead of *gwine*. Present time is made definite by the auxiliary *do* or *da*, as in the refrains "Bell da ring," "Jericho da worry me." Past time is expressed by *done*, as in other parts of the South. The passive is rarely, if ever indicated. "Ole man call John," is the answer when you ask who is such and such a person. "Him mix wid him own fat," was the description given of a paste made of bruised groundnuts—the oil of the nut furnishing moisture.

I have not by any means exhausted the subject, but have given the chief part   10
of what I remember, and hope this may stimulate others to make a note of what I overlooked or have forgotten.

Many of my illustrations are taken from the songs of the colored people, and perhaps a few words upon this very interesting topic may not be out of place. The people of the Sea Islands have hardly any secular music. I heard, to be sure, one day, a verse beginning "Dog-flea da bite me"—profane enough one would say, but I think very likely it brought in the Jordan before the end. Even their boat music is chiefly religious; almost all the rowing tunes I recognized as having heard in the praise-meetings and "shouts." The only song that I am acquainted with which is purely a boat song, is the fine lyric:

> "Michael, row the boat ashore—Hallelujah,"

and here I have no doubt that it is the archangel Michael that is alluded to.

For the rest, the songs may be divided into *hymns* and *shouts;* or, as they class them themselves, *spirituals* and *running spirituals*. The first class contains many sweet and touching tunes, and many which bear strongly the impress of their peculiar religious ideas. For instance, to "fin' dat ting" means to find religion; and I suppose this is referred to in the favorite song, some of the verses of which are:

> "O where d' ye tink I fin' 'em?
> I fin' 'em, Lord, in de grave-yard.
> I fin' 'em in de boggy mire."

(For a verse is often only a single line, repeated with the refrain.) This last verse alludes also to their custom, when under religious excitement, of wandering through the woods and marshes, like the ancient Bacchantes. The following song, to a very beautiful tune, alludes to this still more distinctly:

> "I wait upon the Lord my God,
> Who took away the sins of the world.
> You want to be a Christian,—Go in the wilderness,
> To wait upon the Lord.
> Oh, come back, come back, etc.,
> Oh, half-done Christian," etc.

The following will, perhaps, give as good a notion as any of the character of these hymns. It is often sung in the church on St. Helena Island:

> "De talles' tree in Paradise
> De Christian call de tree ob life,
> An' I hope dis trumpet blow me home
> To de new Jerusalem.
>   Blow your trumpet, Gabriel,
>   Blow your trumpet, louder!
>   An' I hope, etc.
> "Paul an' Silas bound in jail
> Sing God's praise both night and day,
>   An' I hope," etc.

The greatest peculiarities are, however, found in the "shouting tunes," as, indeed, the "shout" is the most peculiar institution of these people. It is a kind of shuffling dance, accompanied by a measured movement of the arms and clapping of the hands, and a sort of ducking motion of the body at the turns of the tune, performed by a line of persons moving about in a circle. I am told that they sometimes move backward, but I do not think I ever saw this. The singing is usually done by a sort of choir of bystanders. One leading singer carries on the song, stringing verse after verse of the most absurd stuff, which he often makes up as he goes along. The others "base" him, as it is called; that is, sing the chorus or refrain. The "base" almost always overlaps the tune, striking in before the line is finished, when the singer at once stops without completing the line, taking up his part again in his time before the base is quite through. The whole is accompanied by clapping of hands. The tune is often preceded by an introduction, in chanting style, during which the "shouters" (that is, the dancers, not the singers) move quickly round in the circle, not beginning the "shout" proper until the turn in the tune. The following is a great favorite for "shouting," and is used also for rowing:

> "I know member, know Lord,
>   I know I yedde [hear] de bell da ring.
>   [*Repeated several lines.*]
>   I want to go to meetin'—[Base] Bell da ring.
>   I want to go to 'ciety (lecter),
>   De heaven-bell a-heaven-bell,
>   De road so stormy (boggy),
>   Brudder, hain't you a member?"

And so on to any extent. Every verse is repeated, and the refrain, "Bell da ring," repeated each time. The refrain in the "shouts" is usually some short phrase like the above, *e. g.,* "Hallelujah," "O Lord," "Yes, my Lord," "My army cross over," "Join the angel band." Sometimes it is a little longer, as "Turn, sinner, turn O!" (the most beautiful and dramatic of all the shouts), "O Lord, de rock o' jubilee," and "Archangel open de door." Sometimes the whole tune is more elaborate, as in the following, perhaps the finest of all:

> "I can't stay behind my Lord,
>   I can't stay behind.
>   There's room enough—[Base] Room enough,
>   Room enough in heaven for you (repeated),
>   I can't stay behind.
>   I binny all aroun'—I binny all aroun',
>   My fader call—An' I mus' go.
>   O stoback member—stoback member."

"Stoback" is "shout backwards."

Most of the music of these people has a quite civilized sound, and much of it might no doubt be traced to tunes which they have heard from the whites, and transformed for their own use. They have so much native musical capacity that it is a real obstacle to their learning tunes by heart—as soon as they have one partly learned they begin to sing it and soon change it into something quite different. At any rate, there is no doubt that their music as a whole has been influenced by their civilization, and is rather European than African in its character. It is probable, however, that the "shout" is the direct descendant of some African dance, as the Romaika is of the Pyrrhic; and I have thought that in a few tunes I observed a peculiar character, that might point to an African origin. For instance, there is a strange, wild, minor "shout:"

15

> "Jesus die—shall I die?
>   Die on de cross.
>   Jesus da comin',
>   Run for to meet him," etc.

Comparatively few of the tunes, however, are minor; some of them are even merry, and the prevailing character is that of sweetness and cheerfulness.

I append two of the most peculiar and characteristic of their "shouts:"

> "Pray a little longer—[Base] O Lord—Yes, my Lord.
> Pray, true believer.
> Jericho da worry me,
> Jericho—Jericho.
> Went to de meetin',
> Met brudder Haclers [Hercules],
> Wha' d' ye tink 'e tell me?
> Tell me for to turn back,
> Patrol around me.
> Tank God he no ketch me."

The two last lines point to the days of slavery. The other song has an incomprehensible introduction, followed by a very distinct allusion to the most prevalent form of illness—"pain in head an' feber":

> "Way my brudder, better true belieb,
>   Better true be long time get ober crosses;
> Way my sister, better true belieb,
>   An' 'e get up to heaben at las',
> My body rock' long feber [Base] O, wid a pain in 'e head,
>   I wish I bin to de kingdom,
> To set along side o' my Lord."

Literary Digest

"Objecting to the Negro Dialect" (November 11, 1916) is a defense of "Negro dialect" published in public school songbooks, but there is a patronizing underlying tone symptomatic of the era leading up to the Harlem Renaissance. The piece also raises questions of assimilation of all Americans.

Objecting to the Negro Dialect

High-school music-teachers of New York are reported to have exprest their disapproval of the "negro dialect in songs published in public-school text-books." Dr. Frank Rix is credited with saying the children should be taught a "pure English, not a dialect." But to this comes a vigorous protest from the South, where the Atlanta *Constitution* declares that if you "expurgate from our American song-books our good old Southern melodies, you rob them of their best, real, warm-blooded sentimentality." The Asheville *Times* also enters its voice of disapproval, saying that "such a change would be a loss to the literature of music in the world, and especially in the South." The director of music in the Asheville schools points out that "there are thousands of folk-songs and dialect songs that will have to be thrown away if they are to be pruned of the words that have helped to preserve their melodies throughout the centuries." *The Constitution* knows good English when it sees it, and also a good folk-song. It declares:

> "True, our Southern melodies may not be grammatically perfect as to English!—but they know 'no North, no South, no East, no West' in their popularity. They are sung by the girls and boys in the schoolhouses out in Oregon; sung round the camp-fire out in the heart of the Rockies; by the timber folk of New England; by prima donnas in the metropolis—and everywhere enjoyed with the same true, downright American spirit.
>
> "'Go to Sleep, My Little Pickaninny,' has lulled as many little babes of the Great Lakes States into the Land of Nod, comparatively, as in the Cotton Belt. It is known and sung and loved everywhere on the continent. Some consider 'Yankee Doodle'—because of the wording of it—sectional: 'Dixie' is universal. Yet those precise New York teacher-folk propose, in 'Dixie,' to 'change the words "de" and "nebber" to "the" and "never!"'
>
> "Good English? Who ever claimed those good old Southern songs— or any of the old favorites, for that matter—are pure English? Of course they're not. They wouldn't be characteristic; they wouldn't be half so sweet, half so popular, if they were.
>
> "Neither is 'Annie Laurie' good English; nor 'Bonnie Doon,' nor 'Hi'lan' Mary.' Yet we like them, not for their rhetoric, but for their sentiment, their melody, and themselves.
>
> "Let the school children of the land vote on what selections should remain uninterfered with in their song-books, and it is safe to say that the 'negro-dialect' songs would be among the very last to go.
>
> "At the Fulton County High School commencement exercises in Taft Hall last June the sweetest and most liberally applauded number on the whole program was Frank Stanton's 'Mighty Lak a Rose,' sung by one of the young girl graduates. The audience—seven-eighths of it school children— compelled her to 'sing it over again.'
>
> "No, the youngsters get enough grammar, English, correct-composition drill during class periods. Let them get 'back to earth' betimes and indulge in a bit of real sentiment, real Americanism, when it comes time to sing.
>
> "And don't censor the plantation melodies from the song-books; for when you do you spoil them."

The negro, of course, is absolved from any further responsibility for these songs than the furnishing of the dialect by which they are exprest. Curiously the negro, aside from Paul Laurence Dunbar, has written none of them. So far as ragtime is concerned, Mr. David Mannes asserts in the New York *Evening Post* that "the negro is most sorrowful that he is thought the producer of vulgar ragtime." Mr. Mannes adds:

> "To my knowledge no negro has ever written to his music words to which any one could take exception. Where vulgarity occurs in songs attributed to colored men, it is invariably some white man who has superimposed it. Furthermore, you must acknowledge the negro's sense of poetry.
>
> "To be sure, he is not now developed, but I would set no limit to his future growth. Recognizing his human qualities, who would deny him divine

right? If you deny these human qualities, then, of course, you deny the divine attributes. I combat most earnestly the theory that the negro's capacity for development is limited.

"Not having had the opportunity to develop a musical art-tradition of their own, our colored citizens must become acquainted with ours. There the difficulty lies because they must retain their natural genius and make their own music. Having no framework of their own upon which to build, their faith must rest on Bach and Beethoven and Brahms."

Mr. Mannes, among his other activities, teaches in the Music-School Settlement for Colored People in Harlem. He speaks from his own knowledge, then, when he says of the negro's abilities in musical performance:

"As the negro lends his own inflection to any tongue he learns, so his touch on the piano differs from the white man's. Here, too, his natural potentialities must expand. Negroes either pick on instruments or play on instruments of percussion; to my knowledge they have never turned to bowed instruments. So it is that the difficulty for the negro in playing on the violin lies in the bow. In their management of it they may approach the fine and natural legato of their own voices. . . .

"Their musical inspiration as a rule has as its initial force an intense spiritual feeling so common in the black race, literate and illiterate. True preparedness means the stimulating of the poetical, musical, and dramatic qualities of the child of to-day so that the man and the woman of to-morrow shall resist the onslaughts of material aggression. . . .

"As Theodore Thomas once said, familiar music is popular music. My whole idea, therefore, is to make Beethoven, Bach, Brahms, and César Franck familiar and popular with the colored people and raise them, through these masters, to the plane of intelligent appreciation of, and participation in, the best traditions which we have."

Zora Neale Hurston

Zora Neale Hurston (1891–1961) is regarded as one of the greatest writers of the twentieth century and among contemporary women authors. Hurston was born on January 7, 1891. She grew up in Eatonville, Florida, and went on to attend Howard University in 1920, where she began her writing. Her first publication was in a Howard University literary magazine in 1921. She attended Barnard College, where she studied anthropology and folklore with Franz Boas. Though often associated with the Harlem Renaissance in New York City during the twenties, Hurston found much of her subject matter in Florida and the American South. Included among her works are *Jonah's Gourd Vine* (1934), *Their Eyes Were Watching God* (1937), and her autobiography, *Dust Tracks on a Road* (1942). The folklore collection *Mules and Men* (1935) established a methodology for collection still pursued today. Unlike some of her contemporaries of the Harlem Renaissance, she felt no need to apologize for African American language style. In fact, she felt it should be celebrated.

The following piece, "Pa Henry's Prayer," from *Mules and Men* demonstrates a respect for the manner in which African Americans worship using creative language.

Pa Henry's Prayer

. . . You have been with me from the earliest rocking of
   my cradle up until this present moment.
You know our hearts, our Father,
And all de range of our deceitful minds,
And if you find anything like sin lurking
In and around our hearts,   5
Ah ast you, My Father, and my Wonder-workin' God
To pluck it out
And cast it into de sea of Fuhgitfulness
Where it will never rise to harm us in dis world
Nor condemn us in de judgment.   10
You heard me when Ah laid at hell's dark door
With no weapon in my hand
And no God in my heart,
And cried for three long days and nights.
You heard me, Lawd,   15
And stooped so low
And snatched me from the hell
Of eternal death and damnation.
You cut loose my stammerin' tongue;
You established my feet on de rock of Salvation   20
And yo' voice was heard in rumblin' judgment.
I thank Thee that my last night's sleepin' couch
Was not my coolin' board
And my cover
Was not my windin' sheet.   25
Speak to de sinner-man and bless 'im.
Touch all those
Who have been down to de doors of degradation.
Ketch de man dat's layin' in danger of consumin' fire;
And Lawd,   30
When Ah kin pray no mo';
When Ah done drunk down de last cup of sorrow
Look on me, yo' weak servant who feels de least of all;
'Point my soul a restin' place
Where Ah kin set down and praise yo' name forever   35
Is my prayer for Jesus sake
Amen and thank God.

Countee Cullen

Countee Cullen (1903–1946), noted poet of the Harlem Renaissance, was born in New York City and began writing poetry at the age of fourteen. Early on, his poems were published in *The Crisis* and *Opportunity*, and he won several awards for the poem "Ballad of the Brown Girl." In 1923, he graduated from NYU, and in 1925, his first volume of verse, *Color*, was published by Harper. This first volume explored experiences with color.

The classic poem "Incident," about a young African American child's experience with racial epithet, depicts the lasting effects and power of a word.

Incident

(For Eric Walrond)*

Once riding in old Baltimore,
    Heart-filled, head-filled with glee,
I saw a Baltimorean
    Keep looking straight at me.
Now I was eight and very small,   5
    And he was no whit bigger,
And so I smiled, but he poked out
    His tongue, and called me, "Nigger."
I saw the whole of Baltimore
    From May until December;   10
Of all the things that happened there
    That's all that I remember.

Amiri Baraka

Amiri Baraka (1934–), formerly known as Leroi Jones, was born in Newark, New Jersey. He is a respected playwright, poet, novelist, and essayist known for his intense exploration and examination of African American life. Baraka, who attended Howard University, published his first collection of poetry, *Preface to a Twenty Volume Suicide Note,* in 1961; founded the Black Arts Repertory Theater in Harlem in 1965; won critical acclaim for the Obie Award–winning play *Dutchman* in 1964; and is known for his active leadership in the African American struggle for political power. His more recent works include *Transbluesency: The Selected Poetry of Amiri Baraka/LeRoi Jones* (1995), *Wise Why's Y's: The Griots*

---

*Eric Walrond (1898–1966) was one of the touted young West Indian writers of the Harlem Renaissance. His collection of stories *Tropic Death* is uneven but contains good work. He worked for Garvey's publications on and off in the twenties and the thirties. He was impressed with Cullen's *Color* and gave it a very favorable review in *The New Republic*. Walrond won a Guggenheim in the same year as Cullen (1928).

Tale (1995), *Funk Lore: New Poems (1984–1995)* (1996) and *The LeRoi Jones/Amiri Baraka Reader* (1999). In addition to his writing and political activism, Baraka is a respected lecturer on the African American experience.

This excerpt from "Primitive Blues and Primitive Jazz" comes from Baraka's 1963 collection *Blues People*. In it he provides a historical connection between the blues, shouts, hollers, and work songs and the growing acquaintance with each other that African Americans experienced following the Civil War.

Primitive Blues and Primitive Jazz

The work songs and later blues forms differ very profoundly not only in their form but in their lyrics and *intent*.

> Oh, Lawd, I'm tired, uuh
> Oh, Lawd, I'm tired, uuh
> Oh, Lawd, I'm tired, uuh
> Oh, Lawd, I'm tired, a dis mess.
>
> (*repeated*)

Primitive blues-singing actually came into being because of the Civil War, in one sense. The emancipation of the slaves proposed for them a normal human existence, a humanity impossible under slavery. Of course, even after slavery the average Negro's life in America was, using the more ebullient standards of the average American white man, a shabby, barren existence. But still this was the black man's first experience of time when he could be alone. The leisure that could be extracted from even the most desolate sharecropper's shack in Mississippi was a novelty, and it served as an important catalyst for the next form blues took.

Many Negroes who were sharecroppers, or who managed to purchase one of the tiny farms that dotted the less fertile lands of the South, worked in their fields alone or with their families. The old shouts and hollers were still their accompaniment for the arduous work of clearing land, planting, or harvesting crops. But there was a solitude to this work that had never been present in the old slave times. The huge plantation fields had many slaves, and they sang together. On the smaller farms with fewer slaves where the older African forms died out quicker, the eight- and sixteen-bar "ballits," imitations of the songs of the white masters, were heard along with the shouts. Of course, there must have been lyrics to some of the songs that the slave could not wisely sing in front of his master. But the small farms and sharecroppers' plots produced not only what I think must have been a less self-conscious work song but a form of song or shout that did not necessarily have to be concerned with, or inspired by, *labor*. Each man had his own voice and his own way of shouting—his own life to sing about. The tenders of those thousands of small farms became almost identified by their individual shouts. "That's George Jones, down in Hartsville, shoutin' like that."

Along with this leisure there was also that personal freedom to conduct or ruin one's life as one saw fit. In the 1870s there were thousands of black migrant workers moving all through the South. There were also men who just moved around from place to place, not really migratory laborers, just footloose wanderers. There could come now to these ex-slaves a much fuller idea of what exactly America was. A slave on a Georgia plantation, unless he was sold or escaped, usually was born, grew to manhood, and died right in Georgia. To him, the whole of America would be Georgia, and it would have to conform strictly to what he had experienced. St. Louis, Houston, Shreveport, New Orleans, simply did not exist (and certainly not New York). But now for many Negroes there was a life of movement from farm to farm, or town to town. The limited social and emotional alternatives of the work song could no longer contain the growing experience of this country that Negroes began to respond to. Also, the entrance of Negroes into the more complicated social situation of self-reliance proposed multitudes of social and cultural problems that they never had to deal with as slaves. The music of the Negro began to reflect these social and cultural complexities and change.

Very early blues did not have the "classic" twelve-bar, three-line, AAB structure. For a while, as I mentioned before, blues-type songs utilized the structure of the early English ballad, and sometimes these songs were eight, ten, or sixteen bars. The shout as much as the African call-and-response singing dictated the form blues took. Blues issued directly out of the shout and, of course, the spiritual. The three-line structure of blues was a feature of the shout. The first two lines of the song were repeated, it would seem, while the singer was waiting for the next line to come. Or, as was characteristic of the hollers and shouts, the single line could be repeated again and again, either because the singer especially liked it, or because he could not think of another line. The repeated phrase also carries into instrumental jazz as the *riff*.

Another reason for the changes in musical form was the change of speech patterns among a great many Negroes. By now the language of America was mastered for casual use by most Negroes. While the work song or shout had only a few English words, or was composed of Africanized English words or some patois-like language that seemed more a separate language than an attempt at mastering English, early blues had already moved toward pure American lyrics (with the intent that the song be understood by other Americans). The endlessly repeated line of the shout or holler might also have been due to the relative paucity of American words the average field Negro possessed, the rhyme line being much more difficult to supply because of the actual limitation singing in American imposed. The lines came more easily as the language was mastered more completely. Blues was a kind of singing that utilized a language that was almost strictly American. It was not until the ex-slaves had mastered this language in whatever appropriation of it they made that blues began to be more evident than shouts and hollers.

The end of the almost exclusive hold of the Christian Church on the black man's leisure also resulted in a great many changes of emphasis in his music. The blues is formed out of the same social and musical fabric that the spiritual issued from, but with blues the social emphasis becomes more personal, the "Jordan" of the song much more intensely a *human* accomplishment. The end of slavery could be regarded as a Jordan, and not a metaphysical one either, although the analogy of the deliverance of the Jews and the Emancipation must have been much too cogent

5

a point for proselytizing to be lost on the local black minister. There was a definite change of *direction* in the primitive blues. The metaphysical Jordan of life after death was beginning to be replaced by the more pragmatic Jordan of the American master: the Jordan of what the ex-slave could see vaguely as self-determination. Not that that idea or emotion hadn't been with the very first Africans who had been brought here; the difference was that the American Negro wanted some degree of self-determination where he was living. The desperation to return to Africa had begun to be replaced by another even more hopeless one. The Negro began to feel a desire to be more in this country, America, than chattel. "The sun's gonna shine in my back door someday!"

The leisure and movement allowed to Negroes after the Civil War helped to standardize the new blues form as well as spread the best verses that were made up. Although there were regional differences in the way blues began to be sung, there were also certain recurring, soon "classical," blues verses and techniques that turned up in a great many places simply because a man had been there from Georgia or Louisiana or South Carolina and shown the locals what his town or region produced. . . .

Even with the relative formalization of secular Negro music, blues was still an extremely personal music. There were the songs extolling the merits and adventures of heroes or heroic archetypes, John Henry, Stagger Lee, Dupree, etc., but even as the blues began to expand its references it still remained a kind of singing that told about the exploits of the singer. Heroic archetypes or cowardly archetypes were used to point up some part of the singer's life.

> In come a nigger named Billy Go-helf
> Coon was so mean was skeered of hisself;
> Loaded wid razors an' guns, so they say,
> Cause he killed a coon most every day.

And this intensely personal nature of blues-singing is also the result of what can be called the Negro's "American experience." . . .

Keith Gilyard

Keith Gilyard (1952–) is known for his versatile writings, poetry, and scholarship, which draw upon personal experience, studies, and observations. His first book, *Voices of the Self: A Study of Language Competence* (1991), for which he received an American Book Award, set the standard for this genre of writing. He is Professor of English at Pennsylvania State University and former Chair of the Conference on College Composition and Communication of the National Council of Teachers of English.

"A Legacy of Healing: Words, African Americans, and Power" comes from *Let's Flip the Script* (1996). Gilyard makes his contribution to the notion of the power of words by examining literature and rumor.

A Legacy of Healing
Words, African Americans, and Power*

To claim that "words will never hurt me" is the all-time number one act of denial. Only a person profoundly hurt by words would attempt this psychological maneuver. I have, in fact, been rather adept at the sticks-and-stones competition but have been nicked quite a bit, along with others of my ethnic group, by the master narrative in which inferiority is ascribed to those of darker hues. I plead no special case here. African Americans aren't the only ones who don't fare well in the American script of exploitation—just a prominent example. My aim, therefore, is not merely to highlight the victimization of African Americans but to explore adaptive responses to that victimization along the axis of language. In other words, I am considering the healing qualities contained in the counterstory about language that has been central to the African American intellectual and expressive traditions. I don't argue that language alone oppresses, or that a magic combination of syllables could alone secure full empowerment. I simply choose to pay particular attention to the Word, even as I acknowledge that Word and Deed inevitably interact to shape destiny.

Imagine the first African slaves ever captured by Europeans. As soon as they were called *totally out they names,* they had to know they were up against a different game. They weren't losers in a mundane intracontinental conflict; they were to be subjected to the largest program of dehumanization ever seen in the western hemisphere, complete with tales and labels, sanctioned by respected intellects, that rationalized enslavement. *Nigger,* because of the variety of powerful reactions it can spur, and because of the particular history and present it inscribes, remains to this day the most potent word in the American vocabulary.

Although captured Africans were suffering huge losses in the skirmish about self-definition (we did call ourselves Negroes well into the twentieth century), they managed some impressive gains along other verbal fronts. Patricia Turner points out in *I Heard It through the Grapevine,* her fascinating study of rumor in African American culture, that the 1839 mutiny aboard the *Amistad* probably began because Cinque and other Africans believed the rumor that they were about to be literally eaten by their captors. That slavers were cannibals, in more than the obvious metaphoric sense, was an idea widely held by Africans. When Cinque and company made their move, therefore, they were propelled toward their eventual freedom by a specific linguistic form. So, while rumor generally connotes negativity, it has functioned systematically in the African American community, as Turner carefully and brilliantly documents, as a method of protection and resistance. Recent and popular rumors suggesting that there is an ingredient in certain fast-food chicken to sterilize Black males, or alleging Ku Klux Klan ownership of clothing companies like Troop, or asserting that Reebok sneakers were manufactured and/or distributed in South Africa circulate as sites of teaching and survival.

---

*Presented November 4, 1994, at the Third Annual Conference on African American Language and Communication at Teachers College, Columbia University.

The Reebok rumor even convinced supposed empiricists like my wife and me. The Boston-based manufacturer was, in fact, the first major U.S. shoe company to pull its products *out* of South Africa. But when some folks told us about the South Africa angle, and when we pondered how South African the word *Reebok* sounded, we soon vowed never to buy a pair of Reebok sneakers as long as South African apartheid existed. This really bothered our children. It was:

"Mommy, Daddy, but the sneakers is phat!"
"Yeah, but you not gittin em."

Through dialogue about sneakers, a very powerful channel, we taught our   5
children much about colonialism, the Mandelas, and boycott. And to communicate this most effectively, all we had to do was not purchase a few pairs of sneakers, which cost too much anyway. In fact, when one considers that every other major sneaker company has been hit by a rumor connecting it to the predemocracy South African government or the Ku Klux Klan, one understands that some folk are doing fine cultural work in trying to discourage African American youth, an audience specifically targeted by these manufacturers, from so intently, and sometimes perilously, accumulating so many pieces of overpriced leather and rubber. Health is one of the issues here, and not all the rhetoric can be pretty. As Turner concludes, "like a scab that forms over a sore, the rumors are an unattractive but vital mechanism by which the cultural body attempts to protect itself from subsequent infection" (220).

I'm not trying to start any trouble, but Crooked I, a company that produces malt liquor and fruit drinks, may easily be hit by a rumor. Some brother or sister may notice that the company's juices, whatever the flavor, are packaged in black cans and are available almost exclusively in the African American community. Someone else may notice that the product is produced in North Carolina and then associate it with the Ku Klux Klan. Another may discover the ultimately damning scoop, that is, if you dissect the company logo, the Crooked I, vertically, which you can do, say, by covering half of it with your finger, you will clearly see three K's. Opinion then spreads that in KKK-owned Crooked I products there is a chemical (beyond, but clearly connected to, the alcohol in the malt liquor our youth drink too much of) designed to destroy African Americans.

The grapevine also extends to literature. In his 1967 novel, *The Man Who Cried I Am,* John A. Williams has a character discover a document describing the King Alfred Plan, a "final solution" for African Americans in case of continued racial unrest. Agencies such as the FBI, CIA, National Security Council, Department of Defense, and local police forces are to coordinate their efforts in order to neutralize Black leadership and then "terminate, once and for all, the Minority threat to the whole of the American society, and, indeed, the Free World" (372). This conspiracy theory grabbed hold of the mass Black imagination. Black folk skipped past the first twenty-seven chapters to get to this King Alfred Plan they had heard about. They didn't care anything about Harry Ames or Max Reddick or Marion Dawes. The Black Topographical Society based a three-hour political awareness session, one I sat through in the early 1970s, on a version of the proposal. Speakers would explain, for example, that superhighways like the Dan Ryan Expressway in Chicago were always routed through Black ghettos to facilitate eventual military operations against those communities. I told one of the presenters that the King Alfred Plan came out of a novel. He replied that the novel was just telling the truth. And it is certainly easy to comprehend why it could ring true for anyone who had witnessed the suspicious assassinations of Martin Luther King, Jr., Malcolm X, and a long list of others, and who had seen or been a part of the post-Watts wave of inner-city uprisings.

Although it provided ample grist for the rumor mill, Williams's novel is, in addition, firmly linked to texts in the African American literary tradition. The Wright-like figure Harry Ames asserts, "I'm the way I am, the kind of writer I am, and you may be too, because I'm a black man; therefore, we're in rebellion; we've got to be. We have no other function as valid as that one" (49). The story is—as most stories in the tradition are—largely about the tension between expression and repression of the Black voice. This dynamic is manifest, for example, in the very first novel by an African American published in the United States, Harriet Wilson's *Our Nig; or, Sketches from the Life of a Free Black* (1859).

After being abandoned by her mother at the age of six, Frado begins a period of indenture in the New England home of the Bellmonts. She quickly becomes a favorite of men working around the farm, who "were always glad to hear her prattle" (37). However, Frado is soon silenced. When young Mary Bellmont accuses Frado of pushing her into a stream, Frado's true account of events is ignored. Mrs. Bellmont, with the aid of her daughter, beats Frado, props her mouth open with a piece of wood, and locks her in a dark room. Frado cannot even talk things over with herself, as many of us are wont to do in times of extreme distress.

As Frado grows older, the Bellmonts' son James, Aunt Abby, and Mr. Bellmont himself all try to shield her somewhat from Mrs. Bellmont's cruelty. But her mistress only becomes more selective and clandestine about the beatings, never failing to warn Frado that she wouldn't hesitate to "cut her tongue out" if she exposed her (72), threatening to do physically to Frado what she has been accomplishing symbolically all along. Frado tells anyway as her voice, encouraged by her advocates, is gaining in strength, which prompts a desperate Mrs. Bellmont to resort to one of her favorite techniques. She forces a wooden block into Frado's mouth and whips her with a rawhide strap. 10

Frado is undeterred. She reads and continues to converse with those willing to entertain her. And in the novel's climactic scene, when Mrs. Bellmont raises a stick to strike Frado because she feels Frado is taking too long with her chores, Frado loudly declares that if she is struck, she will never work again. Mrs. Bellmont, amazed at the direct verbal challenge, declines to test Frado's resolve. Frado, her period of indenture nearing its conclusion, becomes intensely interested in a wide range of reading material and pursues literacy with vigor. She keeps a book nearby even as she toils.

Charles W. Chesnutt explores nineteenth-century expression/repression conflict against a Southern backdrop, particularly in his Uncle Julius tales. He illustrates how tightly the voices and literate behaviors of slaves were monitored by slave owners. Dave, the central character in "Dave's Neckliss," hardworking and obedient, encounters no special problem with his master until he is found reading the

Bible. Dave uses his wit, however, to escape trouble. Mars Dugal, in contrast, cunningly attempts to reinforce control. As Julius narrates:

> "'Dis yer is a se'ious matter,' sezee; 'it's 'g'in de law ter l'arn niggers how ter read, er 'low 'em ter hab books. But w'at yer l'arn out'n dat Bible, Dave?"
>
> "Dave w'an't no fool, ef he wuz a nigger, en sezee: "Marster, I l'arns dat it's a sin fer ter steal, er ter lie, er fer ter want w'at doan b'long ter yer; en I l'arns fer ter love de Lawd en ter 'bey my marster.'
>
> "Mars Dugal' sorter smile' en laf' ter hisse'f, like he 'uz might'ly tickle' 'bout sump'n, en sezee: "'Doan 'pear ter me lack readin' de Bible done yer much harm, Dave. Dat's w'at I wants all my niggers fer ter know. Yer keep right on readin', en tell de yuther han's w'at yer be'n tellin' me. How would yer lack fer ter preach ter de niggers on Sunday?'" (134)

When Dave later is framed for a theft, his Bible is taken away and burned by the overseer.

African American writers have never lost sight of the language problematics posed by Wilson and Chesnutt. Toni Morrison, for one, always foregrounds, perhaps most notably in *Beloved,* the dialectic of expression/repression. Sixo, one of the Garner slaves, a bit more fiery than Dave, decides to stop speaking English because he sees no future in doing so. One can sympathize with Sixo's position after witnessing the conversation, a thoroughly postmodern one, between him and Schoolteacher when Sixo is accused of stealing a pig:

> "You stole that shoat didn't you?"
> "No, sir. I didn't steal it."
> Schoolteacher smiled. "Did you kill it?"
> "Yes, sir. I killed it."
> "Did you butcher it?"
> "Yes, sir."
> "Did you cook it?"
> "Yes, sir."
> "Well, then. Did you eat it?"
> "Yes, sir. I sure did."
> "And you telling me that's not stealing?"
> "No, sir. It ain't."
> "What is it then?"
> "Improving your property, sir."
> "What?"
> "Sixo plant rye to give the high piece a better chance. Sixo take and feed the soil, give you more crop. Sixo take and feed Sixo give you more work."(190)

Schoolteacher beats Sixo anyway to show him that, as the authorial voice puts it, "definitions belonged to the definers—not the defined" (190). Of course, Sixo knows this by then, and he seeks to become a definer. So he leaves the masters their language, only resorting to English again while formulating plans to escape. His plan is defeated, but he goes to his death singing his own song, laughing, and calling out, because his Thirty-Mile Woman (not her master's label) is pregnant, "Seven-O! Seven-O!" (226).

Baby Suggs also practices self-definition. After her freedom is purchased by   15
her son and she is escorted out of bondage by Mr. Garner, she asks why she was always referred to as Jenny. Garner informs her, naturally, that the name on her in-
voice is Jenny Whitlow. She bitterly rejects it. Another of the story's free elders has
cast aside his given name of Joshua and renamed himself Stamp Paid because he
feels he has settled any debt he might have owed in this world.

If Zora Neale Hurston and Ralph Ellison have written the most artistic "discovery of voice" books in the African American literary tradition, then *Beloved* will
probably go down as the most accomplished "claim your name" book. It is *The
Bluest Eye,* though, that conveys most powerfully Morrison's concern with both the
debilitating and therapeutic aspects of overall language practices.

The story opens with a paragraph that could have been excerpted from a typical primer: "Here is the house. It is green and white. It has a red door. It is very
pretty. Here is the family. Mother, Father, Dick, and Jane live in the green-and-white
house. They are very happy" (7).

The major trouble with primers is that characteristically they have depicted
the happy, white, suburban, nuclear family, which discounts the reality of most of
the nation including, of course, African American children like Pecola Breedlove,
who wishes for, above all things, a set of blue eyes.

In the second paragraph of the novel, Morrison repeats the wording of the
first, only she removes standard punctuation marks. The spaces between the lines
of type are smaller. In the third paragraph, she removes the spaces between the
words and even ignores conventional syllabification.

The reader soon realizes, even more so as similar phrases are repeated at the   20
outset of later chapters, that a narrative of domination contributes directly to
Pecola's plight and eventual insanity. Undeniably, there are other crucial factors:
neglect, abuse, incest, rape. But the fact that no voice is stronger to Pecola than the
one that encourages self-loathing is an essential element. So is the fact that her father, Cholly Breedlove, who eventually passes the sickness of his life to her, hasn't
grabbed hold of an enabling tale. In describing Cholly's relationship with his wife,
Morrison pens a line reminiscent of the description of *Native Son's* Bigger Thomas:
"He poured out on her the sum of all his *inarticulate fury and aborted desires*" (emphasis mine) (37).

Contradistinct to the inadequate language system most available to Pecola are
the rich verbal experiences shared by Claudia and Frieda MacTeer, who habitually
tune in to the vibrant verbal interplay of their mother and her friends. As Claudia
narrates:

> Their conversation is like a gently wicked dance: sound meets sound, curt-
> sies, shimmies, and retires. Another sound enters but is upstaged by still an-
> other: the two circle each other and stop. Sometimes their words move in
> lofty spirals; other times they take strident leaps, and all of it is punctuated
> with warm-pulsed laughter—like the throb of a heart made of jelly. The
> edge, the curl, the thrust of their emotions is always clear to Frieda and me.
> We do not, cannot, know the meaning of all her words, for we are nine and
> ten years old. So we watch their faces, their hands, their feet, and listen for
> truth in timbre. (16)

With ready access to a collaborative, self-affirming language community, the MacTeer girls have a shield against the dominant narrative.

Morrison's work advances significantly the African American literary project. Although not all characters in the tradition successfully counteract repression, many do achieve autonomy, expressive and otherwise. African American literature as a whole, much like protective African American rumor mechanisms, has been a grand gesture toward healing.

Rap, at its best, is on the same mission. A blend of urgent beats and reinvigorating Black orality, rap is recent testimony that the contesting Black voice in every generation will somehow force itself upon a broad audience. Ready or not, brand new flava will be kicked in your ear. Referring to the Stop the Violence Movement and HEAL (Human Education Against Lies), and to stars like KRS-One and Chuck D, Houston Baker argues that "these positive sites of rap are as energetically productive as those manned by our most celebrated black critics and award winning writers" (59–60). Baker, one of those celebrated critics, sees the connection between "this DJ be Warren G" and "this PHD be Houston B." He adds that "rap is the form of audition in our present era that utterly refuses to sing anthems of, say, STATE homogeneity." (96–97).

Tricia Rose, one of the most informed people on the planet about rap, amplifies Baker's comments:

> Rap music is, in many ways, a hidden transcript. Among other things, it uses cloaked speech and disguised cultural codes to comment on and challenge aspects of current power inequalities. Not all rap transcripts directly critique all forms of domination; nonetheless, a large and significant element in rap's discursive territory is engaged in symbolic and ideological warfare with institutions and groups that symbolically, ideologically, and materially oppress African Americans. (100–101)

Obscenity trials, widespread media attention, and the multibillion scramble over rap revenues indicate the power and importance of this verbal form. Also interesting is the elbowing over who gets to tell the most persuasive academic story about rap. The participation of Skip Gates in the 2 Live Crew trial is called careerism by Baker, who sees Gates as an uninformed outsider pimping the music for publicity. Baker, in turn, is criticized by Rose for marginalizing the female voice in his version of rap's origin and development. And Tricia, just beware. I don't know who is right on these questions, but it's amusing and gratifying to see rap on the agendas of professors at Harvard, Penn, and NYU.

General African American literacy initiatives have run parallel to folkloric and artistic concerns with language power. Immediately after the Civil War, Black folk took the lead on the issue of literacy and schooling for the newly freed population. Black illiteracy had been state-sanctioned, so it is little wonder that a widespread Black literacy project was conceived primarily as a self-help endeavor. These educational pioneers understood that to be literate was to be able to construct textual knowledge for oneself. They didn't want former slaves to be tricked by the textual interpretations of others, as was often the case during slavery when a literate ruling class would lie to slaves about the contents of abolitionist writing. It is common nowadays to hear the slogan "knowledge is power" associated with African American educational campaigns, but Thomas Holt reveals that the phrase has been in use at least since 1865, when the South Carolina Black Men's Convention used it in the preamble to a resolution to establish schools.

Holt also demonstrates quite clearly that there has been no greater dedication to the ideal of popular education in this nation's history than that made by the African American community in the South. The secret schools that operated during slavery, the free schools that were founded shortly after the war, contributions of money that were an amazingly high percentage of contributors' incomes, abundant in-kind resources made available, even the institution of voluntary tax collection systems to support schools when federal and state monies were withheld all constitute remarkable commitment.

The African American literacy project even survived, though barely, both the postreconstruction white backlash and the subsequent attempts of philanthropists like Rosenwald and Rockefeller to gain control of the agenda and ensure that Blacks received only the type of education that kept them "in place," so to speak, in Southern society—a sort of Booker T. Washington deal. W. E. B. Du Bois, as one probably would suppose, was prominent among the African American leadership who countered this idea. But, as Holt writes, opposition came also, and perhaps more importantly in terms of history, from another formidable source:

> Resistance also came from students at Tuskeegee, Fisk, Howard, and Hampton who, during the 1920s, went on strike against their school administrations and in many cases succeeded in getting new leadership. In the long run, all those struggles laid the basis for the student warriors during the civil rights movement in the late 1950s and early 1960s, because, next to the church, southern colleges were the most critical to the success of that movement. (p. 99)

One thing that now has to happen is that we tap into the fundamental valuation of education that exists to this day in the African American community. Although African Americans have become highly skeptical about certain educational practices and remain dismayed because even institutional certification ensures equal opportunity for them only sporadically, they still view effective schooling to be a key aspect of communal healing. It still represents great possibility.

Language professionals can help to improve educational practice by bringing clarity to discussions of language-related matters. They can share state-of-the-art knowledge about language acquisition and verbal processing and assess how instructional designs are consonant or inconsistent with this information. In addition, they can indicate some of the social variables that affect language instruction and stress, above all, the importance of honoring the language varieties that students bring to school. The teacherly impulse to eradicate specific dialects, for example, is wrong, as Peter Trudgill cogently argues, on grounds of psychology, sociology, and practicality (80–81). Such corrective attempts usually send the message that students are inherently deficient and fail to facilitate expansion of students' verbal repertoires. Students may, in turn, understanding the message clearly, make language a site of resistance and thus reject Standard English so as to solidify their rebellious identities. Some think that these concerns, particularly as they relate to African American students, were laid to rest back in the 1970s. However, that is not the case.

On November 28, 1992, the *New York Times* ran a front-page story entitled "Caribbean Pupils' English Seems Barrier, Not Bridge." The article dealt with the poor performance of students from the English-speaking Caribbean, who were en-rolling by the thousands in New York City public schools. To some extent, dialect was cited as the cause of failure, and I was reminded of the Black English debates of pre-vious decades (which continue today, though more quietly). Wary about the impact this article could have, I was eager to author a response and shake things up a bit.

Fortuitously, a reporter from the *Carib News* visited me to solicit my opinion. I told him that if folks are committed to discrimination, they can almost always use language as a pretext. I further expressed that the problem was one of method, not language. It has been demonstrated repeatedly, especially during the celebrated King case (or Black English trial) in 1979, that inappropriate *responses* to language diversity, not language diversity per se, are a major educational problem. I defi-nitely favored committing as much support as possible to helping the students in question; linking dialect with deficiency is what I was mainly arguing against.

I am fully aware of, and do not want to minimize, differences among Black English and a variety of Caribbean dialects. On the other hand, I feel a diasporic view with regard to African-derived language forms yields the most compelling analysis. Only diaspora aesthetics can properly explain rap, for instance, which could not have started as it did without Kool DJ Herc and other Jamaicans. And both Black English and Black Caribbean dialects are examples of what linguist John Holm terms *Atlantic Creoles*. The *Times* article, in fact, describing the language patterns of Caribbean students, reported that "Many forgo the past tense, drop the verb to be (he tall; she a princess) and switch subject and object pronouns (I tell she; him say). They express plurals and possessives differently (two house, or de house-dem; this is mines). Their words often carry different meanings, pronuncia-tion varies greatly and sentence stresses fall in different places" (p. 22). Every item mentioned here, with the possible exception of "de house-dem," is familiar to any-one who knows Black English.

Unfortunately, the reporter lumped my response with those of several other interviewees, not all of whom shared my views or academic background, in a piece entitled "American English Experts Respond!" As a group, we sounded as if there were no real problem at all. I wasn't surprised, then, when "Caribbean English Specialists Respond" appeared in a subsequent issue of the paper. A Caribbean scholar took us to task for being unqualified to address the matter; buying into West-Indians-as-cream-of-the-crop mythology; failing to properly understand the re-alities of bilingualism and bidialectalism; and ignoring the fact that the children were doing abysmally in school, scoring very low on standardized tests, and sitting in special education classes in disproportionate numbers.

I responded with a letter to the editor, which was graciously printed. I high-lighted again that I objected to any belief that dialect differences alone can account for the rate of so-called failure in our schools. I conceded the fact of bilingualism, as there is the issue of mutual unintelligibility between English and certain varieties of Caribbean creoles. But I warned that we must not conflate bilingualism with bidialectalism.

35

I remain supportive of serious attempts to enhance academic performances of Caribbean students both in class and on standardized tests. Programs that recognize the uniqueness of the Caribbean immigrant experience and build upon strengths in that experience make sense to me. But a reassessment of standardized tests is also required, as is the deconstruction of special education. It's easy to wind up there if you're Black, no matter which sounds come out of your mouth.

I don't pretend that my analysis has drastically effected change. It's merely illustrative of the insight that language professionals can offer. To fully implement correct, not simply corrective, language pedagogy, a varied action agenda is needed along with participation from many types of individuals and groups. Schools ultimately are sensitive to occurrences in the larger society. Anyone working toward positive social change is to some extent helping to strengthen language instruction.

One more flashback as we move forward. Arna Bontemps explains that during the eighteenth century, when even greater than usual pressure was being applied to repress the literacy of slaves, the beautiful, gorgeously double-voiced spirituals were born. As noted earlier, the contesting Black voice will find a way. Marveling at that achievement, James Weldon Johnson paid homage to those artists in "O Black and Unknown Bards," some of which goes:

> There is a wide, wide wonder in it all,
> That from degraded rest and servile toil
> The fiery spirit of the seer should call
> These simple children of the sun and soil.

It's a beautiful poem, but it's also a script we want to flip. We want to bring all the righteousness of African American expressive and intellectual output to bear full force upon the creation of more Black *known* bards whose production will be wide and wonderful as well.

WORKS CITED

Baker, Houston A. *Black Studies, Rap, and the Academy.* Chicago: The U of Chicago P, 1993.

Chesnutt, Charles W. "Dave's Neckliss" (1889). In Sylvia L. Render, ed., *The Short Fiction of Charles Chesnutt.* Washington, D.C.: Howard UP, 1981. 132–41.

Gilyard, Keith. "Disappointed with Dr. Irish." *Carib News,* June 9, 1993, p. 19.

Gutman, Herbert G. "Schools for Freedom: The Post-Emancipation Origins of Afro-American Education." In Ira Berlin, ed., *Power and Culture: Essays on the American Working Class.* New York: Pantheon, 1987. 260–97.

Holm, John A. *Pidgins and Creoles: Reference Survey.* Cambridge: Cambridge UP, 1989.

———. *Pidgins and Creoles: Theory and Structure.* Cambridge: Cambridge UP, 1988.

Holt, Thomas. "'Knowledge is Power': The Black Struggle for Literacy." In Andrea A. Lunsford, Helene Moglen, and James Slevin, eds., *The Right to Literacy.* New York: Modern Language Association, 1990. 91–102.

Ien, Seymour. "American English Experts Respond!" *Carib News,* Feb. 2, 1993, p. 6.

Irish, George. "Caribbean English Specialists Respond." *Carib News,* Feb. 16, 1993, p. 38.

Johnson, James Weldon. "O Black and Unknown Bards." In James Weldon Johnson, ed., *The Book of American Negro Poetry* (1931). New York: Harcourt Brace, 1969. 123–24.

Morrison, Toni. *Beloved.* New York: Knopf, 1987.

———. *The Bluest Eye* (1970). New York: Washington Square Press, 1972.

Rose, Tricia. *Black Noise: Rap Music and Black Culture in Contemporary America.* Hanover, NH: Wesleyan UP, 1994.

Sontag, Deborah. "Caribbean Pupils' English Seems Barrier, Not Bridge." *New York Times,* Nov. 28, 1992, pp. 1, 22.

Trudgill, Peter. *Sociolinguistics: An Introduction.* Harmondsworth: Penguin, 1974.

Turner, Patricia A. *I Heard It through the Grapevine: Rumor in African American Culture.* Berkeley: U of California P, 1993.

Williams, John A. *The Man Who Cried I Am* (1967). New York: Thunder's Mouth Press, 1985.

Wilson, Harriet E. *Our Nig; or, Sketches from the Life of a Free Black* (1859). New York: Random House, 1983.

Wright, Richard. *Native Son.* New York: Harper, 1940.

Linguistic Society of America

The Linguistic Society of America was founded in 1925 with the objective of the advancement and scientific study of language. Members of the LSA study numerous fields, including writing, language and the brain, diversity, linguistics and literature, and computer languages.

The following resolution, in which these language professionals explain and embrace linguistic diversity, was released at the height of the Oakland Ebonics controversy in 1997.

Linguistic Society of America Resolution on the Oakland "Ebonics" Issue

Whereas there has been a great deal of discussion in the media and among the American public about the 18 December 1996 decision of the Oakland School Board to recognize the language variety spoken by many African American students and to take it into account in teaching Standard English, the Linguistic Society of America, as a society of scholars engaged in the scientific study of language, hereby resolves to make it known that:

a. The variety known as "Ebonics," "African American Vernacular English" (AAVE), and "Vernacular Black English" and by other names is systematic and rule-governed like all natural speech varieties. In fact all human linguistic systems—spoken, signed, and written—are fundamentally regular. The systematic and expressive nature of the grammar and pronunciation patterns of the African American vernacular has been established by numerous scientific studies over the past thirty years. Characterizations of Ebonics as "slang," "mutant," "lazy," "defective," "ungrammatical," or "broken English" are incorrect and demeaning.

b. The distinction between "languages" and "dialects" is usually made more on social and political grounds than on purely linguistic ones. For example, different varieties of Chinese are popularly regarded as "dialects," though their speakers cannot understand each other, but speakers of Swedish and Norwegian, which are regarded as separate "languages," generally understand each other. What is important from a linguistic and educational point of view is not whether AAVE is called a "language" or a "dialect" but rather that its systematicity be recognized.

c. As affirmed in the LSA Statement of Language Rights (June 1996), there are individual and group benefits to maintaining vernacular speech varieties and there are scientific and human advantages to linguistic diversity. For those living in the United States there are also benefits in acquiring Standard English and resources should be made available to all who aspire to mastery of Standard English. The Oakland School Board's commitment to helping students master Standard English is commendable.

d. There is evidence from Sweden, the U.S. and other countries that speakers of other varieties can be aided in their learning of the standard variety by pedagogical approaches which recognize the legitimacy of the other varieties of a language. From this perspective, the Oakland School Board's decision to recognize the vernacular of African American students in teaching them Standard English is linguistically and pedagogically sound.

CHICAGO, ILLINOIS
JANUARY 1997

Jacqueline Brice-Finch

Jacqueline Brice-Finch (1946–) is Associate Dean, School of Humanities, Arts, and Social Sciences at Benedict College in Columbia, South Carolina. She is the founding Editor of *MaComère,* the journal of the Association of Caribbean Women Writers and Scholars, which is devoted to scholarly studies and creative works by and about Caribbean women in the Americas, Europe, and the Caribbean diaspora. Dr. Brice-Finch has written articles and reviews and made numerous professional presentations on Africana writers such as Paule Marshall, Edwidge Danticat, Derek Walcott, Ernest Gaines, and Toni Morrison.

In "Ebonics: When Is Dialect Acceptable English?," Brice-Finch asserts that we live in a bidialectal society.

Ebonics
When Is Dialect Acceptable English?

As a teacher who has taught students from diverse cultural and ethnic backgrounds, I have always told my classes that we are all bi-dialectal. We speak a dialect or vernacular that reflects a culture (Black English, for example). Or our English may reflect a region (Boston or Brooklyn) or a multicultural influence ("Spanglish," or Puerto Rican English). As an English professor, I must be able to teach language to the students, to communicate with them. If I can't understand what they say, it is my problem, not theirs. I have to learn what their words mean, to learn their vernacular, in order to get them to understand the necessity of their learning educated English, the lingua franca of the United States.

When I first heard reports that the Oakland Public School System was teaching children something called Ebonics, I, like many educators, was incensed that language that was community-based was being imported into the classroom, supplanting educated English, what is called standard English. Then, the media had to modify their inflammatory headlines once the Oakland superintendent publicized the correct information. It is my understanding that the program is designed to help teachers understand the local English spoken by many of their students. At that point, my opposition to the program ceased.

Much of the controversy is fueled by the frustration that educators experience when they try to find appropriate teaching methods to educate students who are deficient in their command of educated English. A similar discussion arose over bilingual education: whether students who were non-native speakers benefited more from total immersion in English-only classes or from bilingual classes. For the teacher who now has a mix of those students, how to teach is a daunting task.

Familiarity with the language of the students—and especially awareness of the features of their languages that make acquisition of educated English difficult—enables the teacher to use a variety of techniques. An affirmation of the student's orality is essential to ensure student cooperation. Denigrating a student's speech in the classroom can have adverse repercussions, especially if the student's attempt to practice the newly acquired language structures is also ridiculed or dismissed in the home environment. Sometimes, parents will view their children's use of educated English as pretentious or, more problematic, as an indirect criticism of their own speech and will forbid the children to use such language in the house. The same effect may occur on the playground or in other peer-related situations.

Students need to know that educated English is a norm for all speakers of 5 English, developed as a means of ensuring effective communication. The rules of grammar and diction serve to minimize ambiguity. Language is fluid, however, constantly expanding and contracting as new words and new meanings are added while others become archaic. The words *rap, hip hop,* and *dissing* have been absorbed into the language of the nineties as part of our multicultural popular culture. (Even an American president has dared to use what some would label substandard speech: Former President George Bush once began a national speech with "Yo!") The teacher should also explain the importance of learning and using educated English in formal situations, such as the classroom, the workplace, and the business environment.

What about the plaint that many teachers voice, that they have not been trained in linguistics, which is a feature in innovative teaching in a diverse classroom? Well, think about how we approached the varieties of English we encountered in high school. We all read Shakespeare, right? Elizabethan English was spelled funny and sounded weird too. Yet our teachers assured us that the literature was worth reading and speaking about in order for us to learn certain truths about the human condition. By the time we got to Chaucer in twelfth grade, we were used to tackling different versions of the language. We tried saying, "Whan that Aprille with its shoures soote." The teacher coaxed us to pronounce the words correctly and to pay attention to rhyme. We suffered through repeated glances at footnotes to glean meaning about pilgrims of another age.

Our teachers acted as if they knew exactly how to pronounce words that had become archaic, whose definitions and spelling may have changed. Yet, to the best of my knowledge, there were no classes in Pronouncing Old English, Middle English, and Elizabethan English. Our teachers relied on their exposure to oral recordings or presentations of the material—and passed on the skill as they understood it.

The same can be said about the English spoken in the United States. Some teachers are reluctant to use multicultural readings in their classrooms because they do not know how to pronounce dialect. However, if we look at some standard "classics," we find ample inclusion of dialect. In spite of ongoing censorship challenges, *The Adventures of Huckleberry Finn* is still read and enjoyed in American classrooms. Yet, the dialect that was roundly criticized in Mark Twain's time as being unsuitable for inclusion in a novel is still vibrant and essential in the Mississippi Valley. Another perennially popular text, Eugene O'Neill's *The Hairy Ape,* is a celebration of linguistically diverse voices emanating from the boiler room of an early-twentieth-century steamer.

On television, we view popular sitcoms in which variations of English are often quite marked. *All in the Family, Head of the Class, Good Times,* even the recent show *Pearl,* include characters who speak a vernacular that is not educated English. Likewise, the film industry has embraced dialects as a reflection of the varieties of English. The film *Secrets and Lies* recently garnered a Best Actress Award for an actress who spoke in a Cockney accent throughout the film. If we Americans initially had a little difficulty understanding her, our decision that she must be comprehensible or the producers would have given us subtitles was sufficient to get us to listen more intently to hear what language features we shared with the actress so that the undecipherable parts did not interfere with our understanding. We were willing to work hard to achieve success in the oral exercise. Likewise, for the recent film adaptation of *Romeo and Juliet,* which has a modern setting but maintains the original language of Elizabethan England, the producers expected the movie audience to make the effort to understand what the actors say.

English is no longer just the primary language of Americans and the British. 10 Increasingly, it is a national language that is taught in conjunction with the primary tongue of countries as diverse and multilingual as South Africa, Japan, and India. The term *international English* is increasingly becoming a replacement for *standard English.* As CNN, the Internet, and multinational trade and political agreements bring us closer to the concept of a global village, tolerance and acceptance of a panoply of dialects is a must, not a choice.

Akua Duku Anokye

Akua Duku Anokye (1948–) is Associate Professor of English and Co-Chair for the Department of American Studies at Arizona State University West. Her research and study include sociolinguistics, African American folklore, orality and literacy, and rhetoric and composition. Dr. Anokye is currently working on an analysis of the songs, dances, and festivals of a Ghanaian female ancestress/goddess as an archetype for Africana women's literature.

In "A Case for Orality in the Classroom," Anokye suggests ways that diverse language style can be used to facilitate learning.

A Case for Orality in the Classroom

Language and culture are inextricably connected. Society's attitudes toward a particular language variety affect the users' perceptions of self and their performance in the classroom as well as the marketplace. African Americans historically have been recipients of negative language attitudes in education and society. Over the years they have been mislabeled as culturally deprived and culturally disadvantaged, based on their language use. However, African American Vernacular English (AAVE) is a valid language that is not the result of deprivation or disadvantage but instead is simply linguistically different, just as other dialects of a language differ from one another. That fact is yet to be accepted widely by educators. Be that as it may, it is important to understand that AAVE runs much deeper than grammatical, syntactic, and morphological differences; it personifies different cultural expectations and norms for performance as well. Teachers of African American students have an obligation to familiarize themselves with some of the important differences in their students' language and culture that affect their learning in the classroom.

■ A Rich Oral Tradition

African Americans come from a rich oral tradition. The ability of a person to use active and copious verbal performance to achieve recognition within his or her group is widespread in the African American community, having its roots in African verbal art. Among the Limba of Sierra Leone, for example, individuals are not identified as Limba unless they learn to speak Limba well. The ability to speak well, to "have mouth," is often equated with intelligence and success among the Igbo of southeastern Nigeria. In Central Africa, one of the most important personal qualities of the Burundi people is *ubgenge* (successful cleverness), which is demonstrated by "intellectual-verbal management of significant life-situations" (Albert 1964, 44). Among the Fang of Gabon, individuals achieve highly respected positions as a result of their oratorical powers.

Here in America one need only observe those who are most admired by African Americans. They are those who are known as skillful practitioners of language whatever the content—Martin Luther King, Jesse Jackson, Barbara Jordan, L L Cool J, Malcolm X, Mohammed Ali. Each of those speakers has in common the ability to manipulate language orally, to use the oral tradition to convey the message.

Aspects of the African American oral tradition are observable in African American student behavior. For instance, in story telling, African Americans render abstract observations about life, love, and people in the form of concrete narrative sequences that may seem to meander from the point and take on episodic frames. That is a linguistic style that causes problems with Anglo-American speakers who want to get to the point and be direct. In African American communication style we find the following: overt demonstration of sympathetic involvement through movement and sounds; a prescribed method for how the performer acts and how the audience reacts; total involvement of the participants; the tendency to personalize by incorporating personal pronouns and references to self (African American students tend to use first-person-singular pronouns more frequently than Anglo-American students to focus attention on themselves); and use of active verbs coupled with adjectives and adverbs with potential for intensification (which are called features of elongation and variable stress). Prosodic structure of speech often reflects the way information is organized for presentation. All of those observable aspects of the African American communication style provide leads for teaching innovations.

Where writing is concerned, African Americans make use of features associated with oral language. However they are often penalized because those features depend for their effect on interpersonal involvement or the sense of identification between the writer or the characters and the reader. For example, rhetorical devices found in oral language (such as figures of speech, repetition, and parallelism in the grammatical system) may be transferred in writing, but the paralinguistics, such as pacing and vocal inflection, that must be translated into paragraphing, punctuation, and other conventions are often lost. African American communication emphasizes shared knowledge and the interpersonal relationship between communicator and audience. According to Deborah Tannen (1986), people coming from an oral tradition elaborate the metacommunicative function where words are used to convey something about the relationship between communicator and audience. This shows up as a deficit in writing if not properly enhanced. Teachers who are aware of those features can help their students transfer from an oral modality to a literate one (in appropriate situations) by enhancing the oral rhetorical skills in which the students take pride.

■ A Group-Centered Ethos

Shirley Heath's 1983 study of the African American community of Trackton, North Carolina, provides us with more insights. She identified members of the community as literate who were able to read printed and written material and on occasion produce written messages. Using the literacy event as a conceptual tool, she found that in a majority of cases adults showed their knowledge of written materials only through oral means. Furthermore they used a group-centered ethos, where the written materials only came to have meaning when interpreted through the experiences of the group, which turned them into occasions for public discussion. This heavy influence of an expressive performance style incorporating orality and group cohesiveness takes its toll when the interaction with audience is distanced and the call-and-response nature of the African American discourse style is impeded. Stating and counterstating, acting and reacting, testing the performance as it progresses are habitual dynamics in African American communication that writing often does not permit and traditional class dynamics may hinder. Armed with this kind of fundamental understanding of how the African American community functions orally, a teacher can use creative methods to lead to deeper, more profound learning.

Michele Foster (1989) conducted ethnographic research in the classroom of an African American woman teacher in an urban community college. Her study revealed two distinct but culturally appropriate styles of speaking and evaluated the styles in terms of success in the classroom. She concluded that the African American sermonic style—following the preacher-as-teacher model—lessened the social distance and created an identification with indigenous African American cultural norms. That style tended to promote a group-centered ethos toward learning and achievement and thereby reinforced group-sanctioned norms. This research, along with Heath's, highlights the impact that a group-centered ethos has on literacy activities.

While I am not advocating that teachers adopt the black sermonic style, I do encourage educators to promote achievement among African American students by using a group-centered approach to learning. Even students coming from varying socioeconomic backgrounds have benefited from the collective ethos. According to Foster, "By adopting cooperative learning activities congruent with the group ethos of the African American community, institutions can and do actually build on its strength" (27). Those are the strategies educators can exploit in order to improve their teaching styles and maximize African American learning.

Language learning is complicated. When compounded by teachers' unfamiliarity and, sometimes, disdain, the fundamental tool through which the majority of us learn is lost to a large population of African American children. We owe it to ourselves as well as to our children to learn as much as we can about their methods of knowing and taking in information.

REFERENCES

Albert, E. 1964. "Rhetoric," "logic," and "poetics" in Burundi cultural patterning of speech behavior. *American Anthropology* 66(6) pt. 2: 35–54.
Foster, M. 1989. "It's cooking now": A performance analysis of the speech events of a black teacher in an urban community college. *Language in Society* 18: 1–29.
Heath, S. B. 1983. *Ways with words: Language, life and work in communities and classrooms.* Cambridge: Cambridge University Press.
Tannen, D. 1986. Introducing constructed dialogue in Greek and American conversational and literary narrative. In *Direct and indirect speech,* edited by F. Coulmas. Berlin: Mouton.

Robert W. Reising

Robert W. Reising (1933–) is Professor of English, Theatre and Language at the University of North Carolina–Pembroke. Dr. Reising specializes in Native American and African American literatures and linguistics, especially dialectology and language acquisition development, as well as assessment and English education.

In "Do We Need a National Language Policy?," Reising suggests the need for a national language policy.

Do We Need a National Language Policy?

Dr. William Cartwright, former chair of education at Duke University, was well known for his often-uttered and elaborately explained belief that "If one will stand still long enough in education, the world will catch up with him or her." The wisdom of the retired professor's contention is illustrated in the current "flap" over Ebonics, which is but a continuation or rekindling of the controversy accompanying "The Students' Right to Their Own Language," the resolution proclaimed in 1974 by the Conference on College Composition and Communication (CCCC), an institutional arm of the National Council of Teachers of English (NCTE). The storm of the moment features the Oakland, California, school system; that of the 1970s, the Ann Arbor, Michigan, school system. Within five years of the publication of "The Students' Right," the U.S. District Court validated its claim concerning the linguistic legitimacy of "Black English," roughly the equivalent of Ebonics. In July 1979, Judge Charles W. Joiner ruled against the school system and for the plaintiffs, the parents of eleven children at Martin Luther King Elementary School who were in command not of standard English but Black English. The ruling demanded that Ann Arbor educators cease stigmatizing the speech of the eleven, all from a low-income housing project, and find ways to teach them to read. The ball, so to speak, was placed in the school system's court; after listening to expert witnesses for days on end, Joiner declared that the children should not be labeled educationally handicapped or learning disabled because they spoke Black English.

Identical issues have bubbled to the surface in Oakland and everywhere else the Oakland decision has been discussed in America. The legitimacy of Black English (however labeled), students' rights to their own speech, and success in reading remain the "hot buttons" that invariably get pushed when Ebonics enters a discussion or editorial. Every educated citizen, every legislator, and every columnist has an opinion. It might appear that this time a Supreme Court ruling, not simply one from a district court, is needed to allow the nation peace of mind, or at least resolution, concerning Ebonics.

But an alternative exists. On the eve of a new millennium, the nation may well want to entertain a National Language Policy, a supplement to the National Education Goals and to the national standards that have appeared in recent years. Such a policy would provide recommendations and suggestions helpful not merely to educators but to all citizens in the land—parents, industrialists, elected officials, school board members—everyone anxious to determine how languages and language-users can most constructively function in the twenty-first century.

Emma D. Jackson

Emma D. Jackson (1976–) graduated from the University of Toledo and became a staff writer for the *Sandusky Register.* Her interest in language use in the African American community led her to research on the racial epithet.

This article, "The N-Word: A History of Pain, a New Generation Converge Over a Painful Word," appeared in the *Sandusky Register* on December 15, 1999, and examines the reactions of young and old to the use of a derogatory word.

The N-Word

"Nigger."

Its been more than 20 years since Sandusky's Mary Newell heard the word and first felt the pain.

"It just cut so deep, and it still does," she said. Newell, 66, overheard a white man utter "Nigger" while referring to her.

"It made me feel unclean and uncomfortable. I was very sad, and I felt really bad about it."

But depending on who's saying it and how it's pronounced, the connotations   5
and implications vary in regard to the terms "nigger," and its slang form, "nigga."

In Sandusky High School, the casual exchange of "nigga" between many black students, as in "what's up, my nigga?" and "that nigga . . . " has an unfazing effect on most students.

A similar phenomenon occurs in the black community when "nigga" is used by blacks without causing a painful residue.

"It's a slang. It's not offensive," said black student Issian Redding, 15. "It's a way to address friends."

Sandusky's Maya Watkins, 27, said, "When a black person uses it, it's not vindictive. When a white person uses it, it's a put-down."

Many users of the word cite "nigga" as positive, which is how many black users   10
pronounce the word. But adding the "-er" ending is negative, which is how many white users say the word.

The double standard baffles many.

■ Why It's Used

"I am very distressed in some ways that the 'n-word' is used so freely especially by young people," said Akua Duku Anokye, a professor at Arizona State University who specializes in folklore. "They are not aware of, nor do they care about, the history from which the name was derived."

"It's amazing to me. It's extremely prevalent. It's said in a conversational tone," said Al Peugeot, assistant principal at Sandusky High School. "The (black) kids need to understand that it creates a question—you call yourself that word, why can't (white people)?"

There are many explanations for the contradictory use of the word "nigger," stemming from the legacy of slavery to changing the definition to take the hurt out of the word.

Manning Marable, a Columbia University professor of history and political   15
science, said black people using "nigga" is no different from other disenfranchised groups in society.

"As many oppressed people have done, blacks appropriated the term that had been used against them and turned its meaning into a neutral or even positive term. This isn't unusual—homosexuals proudly call themselves queers today," said Marable, who is also Columbia's director of the Institute for Research in African American Studies.

The Rev. Rufus Sanders of Emmanuel Temple Church in Sandusky said "nigga" is a vestige of slavery. It was ingrained in the minds of blacks as a result of that institution, and that's why many black Americans of all generations say the word.

"We lost just about all our values and historical heritage and religious principle when we were taken out of Africa against our will. What we call ourselves and the way we view ourselves has a direct linkage to the way we were socialized by our slave masters and other white people," he said. "They called us derogatory terms as a means of humiliation and control, but we began to call each other these terms. They have become part of our internal psyche and our culture."

The History of the 'N-Word'

"Nigger" is derived from words in the romance languages meaning "black."

"It was a term used to describe African people taken against their will as slaves   20
into the Americas in the 16th century and afterwards. (It) was widely used in colonial America by the middle of the 18th century," Marable said.

At that time, it had a neutral definition, said Geneva Smitherman, director of Michigan State University's African American Language Program and author of several books on black speech. Smitherman said that "nigger" didn't apparently have a negative connotation, either.

The term "nigger" in the U.S. was often synonymous with slave—not that being called slave is positive. For instance, in Mark Twain's classic novel, 'Huckleberry Finn,' the runaway slave was called 'Nigger Jim' by everybody, including other slaves. It amounted to calling him the slave Jim, rather than the way we think of 'nigger' today, Smitherman said.

However, after the Civil War and the beginning of segregation, "nigger" became a derision.

Abdul Alkalimat, director of the University of Toledo's Africana Studies program, said "nigger" was used then and is used now by whites to remind blacks of past injustices and to reiterate who has the power in America today.

When "nigga" bounces off the walls of Sandusky High School, Sandusky   25
Police Officer Lonnie Newell, 44, is taken back to the racism of the segregated South. Newell is also the school's resource officer, and he doesn't tolerate students using "nigga." As a child, Newell spent his summers in Meridian, Miss.

"I hate it," he said. I always ask (students) not to say the word. They usually stop. It's not allowed in my office and when I'm around in the halls."

"I remember the past, when it was used by whites to degrade us. Every time I hear it, it brings back the past—the segregated restrooms and water fountains down South."

"Nigger" is explosive when uttered in public by whites. "It's fighting words when a white person says it," said Mary Newell, who is not related to Lonnie Newell.

■ A Black Hypocrisy?

But "nigga" doesn't always have a positive or neutral meaning when a black person uses it, either.

According to Smitherman's "Black Talk," a dictionary of black speech, defini- 30 tions of "nigga" run the gamut from endearing to unproductive. The word is usually used to refer to black males and blacks as a whole.

"The intonation, the inflection, the body language can often make the most derogatory term an endearment," Anokye said. "For example, 'he's my n-' with a sway of the hips could mean that this is a very special man in the woman's life."

Frances Amison, president of the Sandusky chapter of the NAACP, said "nigga," used by a black person, should have the same resonance for blacks as when a white person says "nigger."

"It should be degrading. That word is associated with a low image and it depreciates your value," Amison said. "If you don't want a white person to call you that, it should not be right for a black person to call you that."

"We are sending a mixed signal if we insist that we are properly addressed by one segment of the society yet take liberties ourselves," Anokye said.

Alkalimat said there are a lot of people within the black community who say 35 "nigga" once in a while for effect, but the number of people who say it as part of everyday speech is very small. He sees a strong correlation between a lack of education and ambition and the individuals who frequently use "nigga."

White people say "nigger" amongst themselves more than blacks say "nigga" among themselves because "there is more hatred of black people than there is self-hatred of black people," he said.

■ Music Prompts Usage

But from listening to certain music and watching certain movies, it seems like "nigga" is a staple in the vocabulary of many blacks.

Although the word is tossed around in many films, "nigga" is most prevalent in the lyrics of hip-hop music.

"Jigga, My Nigga" was the title of a very successful song released by rapper Jay-Z in the summer. In September, rapper Ol' Dirty Bastard released an album entitled Nigga Please.

During the recent opening of the Rock and Roll Hall of Fame and Museum's 40 hip-hop exhibit, hip-hop legend Slick Rick said "nigga" was popularized in music by the group Niggaz With Attitude (NWA) about a decade ago.

And from then on, "nigga" had a home in hip-hop.

But Alkalimat believes entertainment executives are sustaining the usage.

"If you dig deeper into where you hear the word the most—it's very, very uneducated people who are driven by that kind of rap (music) that is corporate-based. So suddenly, you realize that this is not coming from blacks themselves. (Corporation executives) have got us acting like it's something we are doing. When in fact, we are being guided in that direction by this corporate environment," said Alkalimat, noting that in hip-hop's infancy, before corporate control, its lyrics were not littered as they are now with "nigga."

But Slick Rick said "nigga" was used by hip-hop pioneers, long before recorded music took it into the mainstream.

Layzie Bone, a member of the hip-hop group Bone Thugs-n-Harmony, said 45 "nigga" is very intertwined with hip-hop because it reflects reality.

"The word was popular before hip-hop. I heard it growing up. It started out as negative, but we changed it. Like the nigga Tupac (Shakur) said, N.I.G.G.A. means Never Ignorant Getting Goals Accomplished, and that's how we all look at it," Layzie Bone said.

■ So Can Whites Say It?

A report in *Time* says at least 70 percent of hip-hop music is purchased by whites.

Despite this, Smitherman said it's questionable if it will be acceptable for whites to utter "nigga" with the meaning hip-hop artists intended.

"The word is still out on whether or not black people are ready for whites to use it. It would seem that if a white person . . . identifies with hip-hop and . . . with the black cause . . . that he or she should be able to use the term. But that kind of logic flies in the face of emotion and history, so I'd just stay tuned," she said.

But 15-year-old Heidi Grohe of Sandusky High School is not waiting for offi- 50 cial approval.

The teen-ager buys CDs, watches videos and listens to the radio to get doses of her favorite type of music—hip-hop. She said she uses "nigga" among her peers— white and black—who are familiar with hip-hop culture. For her and her friends, it has no racial connotation.

"I say it to people of different colors if we are real good friends. But if I don't know you, and you don't like the music, I won't say it."

Melissa Wobser, 16, and Zack Moots, 14, also enjoy the music, but refrain from saying "nigga" because they fear what the response from blacks might be.

"It's weird, you don't know who you can say it to without them being of-fended, so I just don't say it," Wobser said.

Redding said he has many white friends who say "nigga," and he is not both- 55 ered. However, he doesn't want a non-hip-hop lover who is white to use it because then it has racial overtones.

■ Moving Away from Using It

Big Tigger, 26, host of Black Entertainment Television's "Rap City: Tha Bassment," said hip-hop artists aren't necessarily cognizant of who their listeners are, and the music is generally recorded for young black people, and not whites.

"It's not all right for whites to say 'nigga.' We were brought up with that stigma," he said.

In general, Big Tigger said "nigga" shouldn't be used by anybody and he is try-ing to curb his habit. He said hip-hop artists use of the word can be excessive.

Many Sanduskians also object to anyone saying the word.

"People who say it don't know any better. They are ignorant. That word does 60 not depict a race, it's just derogatory," said Sandusky's Perlette Watkins, mother of Maya Watkins.

Sandusky High's Peugeot agreed.

"It's a word that should be left unsaid. Then you don't have to deal with these issues. I wish nobody would use it," Peugeot said.

Smitherman said over the decades, most black people have ceased using "colored" and "Negro" to refer to other black people.

The same process would have to be employed with getting rid of "nigga."

Because the word hasn't succumbed to time, it serves a social and linguistic 65 purpose, she added.

Amison said, "It's a bad habit. I hope we can get to the point where we don't use it. We've come a long way (as black people), but we've got a long way to go."

Gwen Pough

Gwen Pough (1970–) is Assistant Professor of Women's Studies at the University of Minnesota, Twin Cities Campus. She completed her B.A. in English at William Paterson University–New Jersey, her M.A. in English at Northeastern University–Boston, and her Ph.D. in English at Miami University–Ohio. Currently a member of the Executive Committee of the Conference on College Composition and Communication, she is working on a book-length project that investigates black womanhood, hip-hop culture, and the public sphere.

This essay, "Confronting and Changing Images and Representations of Black Womanhood in Rap Music," comes from a talk given at the American Studies Association Conference in 2001. Pough examines women's effort to combat the double standard in hip-hop culture.

Confronting and Changing Images and Representations of Black Womanhood in Rap Music

You're like a hip-hop song ya know. Bonita Applebum, you gotta put me on.
TRIBE CALLED QUEST, "BONITA APPLEBUM"

Rappers, with their bold use of language and dress, use image and spectacle as their initial entry into the public sphere. They view representation or "representin'" as their role to speak for the people and voice their concerns. Michael Eric Dyson described the hip-hop generation's use of representation in a talk given at Brown University titled "Material Witness: Race, Identity and the Politics of Gangsta Rap":

> Within hip-hop culture, representation signifies privileged persons speaking for less visible or vocal peers. At their best rappers shape the torturous twist of urban fate into lyrical elegies. The act of representing that is much ballyhooed in hip-hop is the witness of those left to tell the afflicted's story.

Although Dyson's view that rappers speak for their "less visible or vocal peers" may sound a bit naïve to some, he no doubt arrives at this stance by taking into consideration the numerous rappers that have gone on record in interviews saying that they are the voice of their respective "hoods." Whether they actually perform this task or not can be argued, but suffice it to say here, rappers do bring issues and concerns, via their lyrics, to public attention that might not otherwise be heard. As S. Craig Watkins notes in *Representing: Hip-Hop Culture and the Production of Black Cinema:*

> The recognition by Black youth that representational practices are an important and necessary mode of politics and pleasure is a response to a world saturated with various forms of communications media. For Black youth, representing the world and how they experience it has evolved into a complex set of cultural practices, styles, and innovation. (Watkins 6)

For rappers, speaking for the people means representing the people. They are self-designated tellers of the people's suffering. The public spectacle is the first step—the first part of getting heard. For a historically marginalized and invisible group the spectacle is what allows them a point of entry in the public space that has proved to be violent and exclusionary. As Watkins notes, "For many Black youth, the sphere of popular culture has become a crucial location for expressing their ideas and viewpoints about the contradictory world in which they live." (Watkins 2)

Much of the representation that goes on in hip-hop is men rappers representing black women. This representing plays out in a variety of ways: The most often noted is the representation of black women as bitches, hoes, stunts, skeezers, hoochies, and chickenheads. Derogatory representations such as the ones listed above have been the subject of much of the feminist criticism on rap. Likewise, there has been a significant focus on rap's representations of black women as strong black mothers/"Dear Mamas"—not to be confused with baby mamas and their drama—and black queens. These are the more "positive" representations that serve as the flip-side to the bitches, hoes, etc. These representations remix the classic Madonna/Whore split in hip-hop terms. These are also the representations that black women rappers seek to confront and change.

Another representation that can be read as at the same time positive and negative is hip-hop being represented as a woman. The epigraph at the beginning of this essay helps highlight the dynamic of women being used as symbols in rap music and hip-hop culture. Perhaps the most widely recognized version of this particular form of woman as symbol is found in Common's "I Used to Love H.E.R." The song breaks down the history of rap music and hip-hop culture and in the song hip-hop is represented as a woman that Common loves/loved. He remembers when he first met her, when "slim was fresh yo/when she was underground/original, pure untampered and down." He takes us through hip-hop's afrocentric and pro-black stages and is quite upset when she goes to Los Angeles and becomes commodified. He mourns:

> But once the man got you well he altered her native
> Told her if she got an image and a gimmick
> That she could make money, and she did it like a dummy
> Now I see her in commercials, she's universal
> She used to only swing it with the inner city circle
> Now she be in the burbs lickin rock and dressing hip and on some dumb shit

5

He blames commercialization and a wave of gangsta rap for ruining the pure hip-hop he used to know but he vows to save her: "I see niggaz slammin' her, and takin' her to the sewer/but I'ma take her back hoping that the shit stop/cause who I'm talking bout y'all is hip-hop." Common's use of woman as a symbol for hip-hop can be compared to historical uses of woman as symbols of nation and symbols of virtues. These kinds of representations of black women in rap can be compared to early American representations of the woman's place in public. Mary P. Ryan writes:

> The "ladies" were toasted at public dinners and honored at civic celebrations . . . Female symbols, like the goddess of liberty and Columbia, were favored emblems of civic virtue carried in procession by merchants, artisans, and students alike. As a symbol or goddess, as a consort of the elite on ceremonial days, or as a sexual pariah in public houses, women bore the mark of either ornament or outcast in public life." (Ryan 266)

These national symbols and virtues can be compared to the "pure, untampered" hip-hop that Common raps about. Like the early American women, women rappers are used to represent the music and the culture symbolically. However, they are given a hard time or discouraged from claiming a public voice and representing the music and the culture via their own public voices. The struggle to claim a space in the masculine space of hip-hop leaves women not only fighting the historical stereotypes that plague black women, but also the negative images and misconceptions attributed to black women in hip-hop culture. In an effort to claim a space for themselves black women rappers must continuously confront and challenge the representations of black womanhood existing in hip-hop culture.

Black women rappers, not content to just be a symbol of hip-hop—and in acts of resisting and renegotiating the images that men rappers have used to represent women in rap music—have sought to confront and change the images. The most widely quoted and recognized example of this kind of confrontation comes from Queen Latifah with songs such as "UNITY" and "Ladies First." Women rappers such as Queen Latifah, Salt-N-Pepa, Yo-Yo, Missy Elliot, Roxanne Shante, Eve and others challenge the misrepresentations of black womanhood in hip-hop culture and rap music by their very presence in the counter public sphere that is rap. Their physical presence as real women, not symbols, helps to shake up notions of "a woman's place." The fact that they use their lyrics to bring women's issues to the forefront of rap music and hip-hop culture further disrupts the commonly held misconceptions and misrepresentations of black women in rap music. This disruption takes place on a variety of levels.

I will focus on one rapper that most would not credit with combating stereotypes. Foxy Brown, with her hypersexual personae, at first glance would appear to highlight the hoes and bitches that the men rap about. She in fact often claims these labels for herself. While the reclamation of terms once considered derogatory is widely debated, I will not enter that debate at the present time. I will offer, however, that rappers such as Foxy Brown and Lil Kim highlight the double standards that have plagued women throughout the ages. For example, in "My Life," Foxy Brown's forceful rap challenges age-old double standards and claims a space for herself as a woman in the sphere of rap. She also claims her right to be who she wants to be in that sphere—whether she is considered rude or sexually promiscuous. She also notably addresses the misconception that men are involved with rap for the love of it. Examples such as Common's "I Used to Love Her" and The Root's "Hip-Hop You the Love of My Life" highlight widely held beliefs that only men can have "real" love for hip-hop or only men can have "real" rapping skills. All others are in it for the money. Foxy challenges claims that she is in it for the money by asking, "what the fuck he in it for?" Foxy Brown's "My Life" offers but one example of the kind of changes that black women bring to the counter public sphere of rap. Eve's "Love is Blind" which addresses domestic violence and thereby brings women's issues with abuse into the public sphere is another. Missy "Misdemeanor" Elliot's celebration of her right to an attitude in "I'ma Bitch" is yet another. The list of black women confronting, changing, and thereby controlling their own representations in the counter public sphere of rap and the larger society is long and continues to grow each time a woman picks up a microphone.

10

WORKS CITED

A Tribe Called Quest. *People's Instinctive Travels and the Paths of Rhythm.* Jive, 1990.

Common (Sense). *Resurrection.* Loud, 1994.

Dyson, Michael Eric. perf. "Material Witness: Race, Identity, and the Politics of Gangsta Rap." Dir. Sut Jhalley. Videocassette. The Media Education Foundation, 1995.

Foxy Brown. *Chyna Doll.* Def Jam, 1999.

Ryan, Mary P. "Gender and Public Access: Women's Politics in Nineteenth-Century America." *Habermas and the Public Sphere.* ed. Craig Calhoun. Cambridge: MIT Press, 1996.

Watkins, S. Craig. *Representing: Hip-Hop Culture and the Production of Black Cinema.* Chicago: U of Chicago Press, 1998.

Media Resources

Cabin in the Sky [1943]. Directed by Vincent Minnelli. 98 minutes. MGM. A film depicting the power of prayer, faith, and love with language patterns to match.

Carmen Jones [1954]. Directed by Otto Preminger. 105 minutes. A version of the Bizet opera, with an African American cast that replicates the discourse and music styles of the late '40's and early '50's.

Cotton Comes to Harlem [1970]. Directed by Ossie Davis. 97 minutes. United Artists. The verbal exchanges between two Harlem detectives are representative of the best African American language and style.

Shaft [1971]. Directed by Gordon Parks. 98 minutes. MGM. A private eye is hired to find the kidnapped daughter of an underworld boss. Captures the discourse style of the early '70s.

Leadbelly [1976]. Directed by Gordon Parks. 126 minutes. Paramount. This film is a period piece that dramatizes the life of blues guitarist Huddie Ledbetter, better known as Leadbelly. The relationship between the blues and African American language style is clear.

Barbara Jordan—Keynote Address [1976]. 21 minutes and 30 seconds. Johnson/Rudolph Video Production. Bowling Green, KY © 1988. VHS format. The first keynote address given at a Democratic National Convention by a black woman, this speech demonstrates the language style of African American power and prestige.

Beat Street [1984]. Directed by Stan Lathan. 105 minutes. MGM Studios. Urban ghetto kids find creative outlets in painting graffiti, breakdancing, rapping, and developing new disco DJ routines.

Breakin' [1984]. Directed by Joel Silberg. 90 minutes. Cannon Group. A girl is a waitress by day, a breakdancer by night, giving vivid depictions of the life, language, and music of young people.

Breakin' 2: Electric Boogaloo [1984]. Directed by Sam Firstenberg. 94 minutes. Cannon Pictures. A developer tries to bulldoze a community recreation center. The local breakdancers try to stop it. This movie is a vivid depiction of the life, language, and music of young people in the early '80s.

Rappin' [1985]. Directed by Joel Silberg. 92 minutes. Cannon Pictures. This film chronicles the plight of a breakdancer/ex-con and his conflicts with a street gangster.

Yo! MTV Raps [1988–1995]. MTV networks. TV series focuses on the world of rap videos and entertainers including the style and methods of rap.

House Party [1990]. Directed by Ellen Brown and Reginald Hudlin. 100 minutes. New Line Cinema. Comedy about urban black teenagers and the events leading up to (and following) a house party one night.

Daughters of the Dust [1991]. Written and directed by Julie Dash. 12 minutes. American Playhouse. Dash examines the Gullah culture of the Sea Islands off the coast of South Carolina and Georgia in 1902 where African folkways were maintained well into the twentieth century.

House Party 2 [1991]. Directed by George Jackson and Doug McHenry. 94 minutes. New Line Cinema. Sequel has Kid (Reid) heading off to college—if he can just hold onto the money his church congregation has raised to send him there. The characters depict the language within African American families, churches, and communities.

Family Across the Sea [1991]. 58 minutes. South Carolina ETV Network. San Francisco: California Newsreel, VHS format [NTSC]. A delegation of Gullah people travels from the United States to Sierra Leone to trace the roots of their heritage. Taped mainly in English, some in Gullah.

Malcolm X. [1992]. Directed by Spike Lee. 194 minutes. Warner Bros. Screen version of the life of civil rights leader Malcolm X. Examples of African American language use and style over several decades.

House Party 3 [1994]. Directed by Eric Meza. 100 minutes. New Line Cinema. Kid, amid jitters over his impending marriage, is trying to make it in music management by signing a feisty female rap group and dodging a vindictive tour promoter. This film demonstrates the change in language use over a period of years by the same character.

AUDIO RESOURCES

I Have a Dream [1963]. 28 minutes. [Oak Forest, Ill.]: MPI Home Video, © 1986. Martin Luther King's speech at the Lincoln Memorial, August 28, 1963.

Slave Narratives [1981]. Washington, D.C.: Library of Congress, Archive of Folk Songs. The audio recordings of slave narratives and related material are in the Archive of Folk Songs. These recordings are noted for the insights of former slaves about their lives prior to emancipation.

The Revolution Will Not Be Televised [1988]. Gil Scott-Heron. [Sound recording] New York: Bluebird. This recording is representative of the predecessors to later rappers and hip-hop artists.

The Best of the Prime Time Rhyme of the Last Poets. vol. 2 [1996]. [Sound recording] Paris, France: On the One, Compact disc. Consists of previously released material. On the One: SP31CD. EFA: CD 18702-2. Contents: E pluribus unum—Tranquility—African slave—Beyonder—Oh my people—What will you do?—Tough enough—Unholy alliance. These politically and socially astute poets captured the imagination of the Black Arts movement.

Recordings by Tupac Shakur, The Notorious B.I.G., Sean Combs, Aaliyah, Queen Latifa, Erika Badu, B. B. King, Mahalia Jackson, Billie Holiday, etc. are examples of language and music that convey the African American experience.

CHAPTER 3

Warriors on the Trading Block

Sports figures hold places of importance in the social life of a community. They have been the source of pride and prejudice. African American athletes have often been the gladiators, fighting racism or other social ills in the sports arenas and in public life. They have experienced barriers and overcome pernicious stereotypes to achieve overwhelming success that frequently precedes improvements in African American life in general. Along the way, these rebels have made contributions to the social, economic, and political lives of African Americans while withstanding treatment that often resonated the slave experience.

Even in the twenty-first century team mascots caricature minorities. A colleague shared a story about his horrifying experience in an NBA chat room when he raised the issue of mascots, the Phoenix Suns' gorilla, in particular. Not only was he accused of being racist because he saw the gorilla as a mockery of the African American ball players but he was tagged with homophobic insults as well. Why is society so oblivious to racist caricatures such as the "Redskins," the buffoonery of the Cleveland Indians' red-faced mascot, or the Suns' gorilla? The tradition of the trading block and negative stereotypes have not yet been erased. Thus, the African American athlete's life remains a microcosm of the African American community, regardless of income or social acceptance.

Numerous cases abound of venom directed at prominent African American athletes. Note the callous statement made by Fuzzy Zoeller about Tiger Woods eating chicken following Tiger's first Masters win in Augusta, Georgia, in 1997. Or the angry boos and hisses heaped on Serena Williams in 2001 during her first title of the year at Indian Wells, California, amid the controversy over her sister Venus's withdrawal from their match in the semifinals. These sports figures could pursue stellar careers because of trailblazers like Arthur Ashe, Althea Gibson, and Lee Elder, who were often denied access to facilities and/or relegated to second-class citizenry in spite of their talents. The trailblazers—the famous and other athletes simply determined to play—have been the warriors on the trading block.

It is an excerpt from the 1847 autobiography of William Wells Brown that sets the tone for this chapter. Gambling, the sport of gentlemen on the steamboats, was often the cause for trading during slavery. In this selection, a young mulatto slave is used as collateral for a gambling debt.

By the turn of the next century, three professional sports had emerged in New York social life, according to James Weldon Johnson in *Black Manhattan* (1930). Johnson examines the role of the African American jockey, baseball player, and prizefighter. With the country moving rapidly toward segregation in all aspects of life, baseball was less of an option for the black athlete because it was a "team" sport. On the other hand, because prizefighting compelled one to organize for oneself, there were fighters with spectacular careers, such as Jack Johnson, a taunter of his opponents, who foreshadowed the emergence of Muhammad Ali later in the century. Both Johnson and Ali made sacrifices to ply their trade, and their successes had a huge impact on the lives of Americans.

Baseball, America's favorite pastime, was also the site of battles over labor and trade. In Charles Aikens's 1971 essay in *The Black Scholar,* we learn that, nearly a century after black men were allowed to play baseball, Curt Flood tackled baseball's "reserve clause," suing for $4.1 million to end that practice because he felt like a "chattel slave." Thus, Flood, another militant black athlete, confronted the antitrust laws of America. Nearly 30 years later in 1997, several years after his death, the Curt Flood Act was passed to amend the antitrust laws regarding baseball.

Basketball, not to be outdone by baseball, has had its share of labor disputes also. In 2000, Mark Conrad explored "Blue-Collar Law and Basketball" labor relations. He explains that the framers of the National Labor Relations Act of 1935 had no idea that someday the act would be used by multimillionaires to secure their own positions in collective bargaining and to fight such issues as the "reserve clause." Dennis Williams proposed in 1995 that college basketball students be permitted to be drafted by the professional teams and still remain eligible for college play. Thus, the college athlete could receive monies for his work on the court. This move would be opposed to the current NCAA rulings that favor large revenues for college programs and little in compensation for the athletes themselves, many of whom do not graduate. Williams describes the current situation as exploitation.

Football also has its share of discrimination, reserve clauses, and the like. Peter King's brief entry for *Sports Illustrated* in 2000 only suggests the depth of the problems. Here he examines the case of black football coaches in the NFL.

Other writers turn to issues such as the racializing of physical and intellectual capacities. In the excerpt from *Coming on Strong: Gender and Sexuality in Twentieth-Century Women's Sport* (1994), Susan Cahn comments on the negative stereotype emerging from slavery regarding African American women's "masculinity." By the mid-twentieth century, African American educators and journalists began to express their acceptance of women's sports, paving the way for more competition. Nevertheless, racialized notions of sexual virtue and feminine beauty still play a role in maintaining the virile or mannish black female stereotype.

In 2000, Jon Entine wrote *Taboo: Why Black Athletes Dominate Sports and Why We Are Afraid to Talk About It*. He recounts that the issues are filtered through the post-modernist cultural prism and concludes that, while some evidence of overrepresentation in sports by blacks can be explained by sociological factors, mounting genetic and physiological evidence of natural superiority needs to be considered. "Crisis of Black Athletes on the Eve of the 21st Century" was written by Harry Edwards, noted sociologist and activist, who decries the critical problems for black society created by black sports involvement. Edwards is concerned about the black student athletes whose parents and coaches push them toward sports careers relentlessly, often to the exclusion of other, critically important avenues to the athletes' personal and cultural development, adding to the problems of black athletic superiority and intellectual deficiency.

From another perspective, novelist John Edgar Wideman wrote *Hoop Roots* (2001), about his ongoing love of basketball. He played college ball at the University of Pennsylvania and his daughter played in the WNBA. Wideman shares memories that not only convey excitement about but also emphasize the importance of basketball to black men in a racist society. He compares the body type and color of a playground legend to the stigma of 500 years of racialized stereotypes about physique and color in America. His poignant remark concludes the chapter— "Though chattel slavery is a thing of the past, black bodies still occupy the auction block."

William Wells Brown

William Wells Brown (ca. 1814–1884) was born in Lexington, Kentucky, the son of Elizabeth, a slave woman, and a white relative of his owner. After 20 years in slavery, Brown escaped to freedom in January 1834. He worked on a Lake Erie steamboat running fugitive slaves to Canada. As a member of the Western New York Anti-Slavery Society, he investigated emigration possibilities to Cuba and Haiti. Fearing for his safety, British abolitionists "purchased" his freedom in 1854. His literary works include *Clotel: Or, The President's Daughter* (1853), the first novel published by an African American; *The American Fugitive in Europe: Sketches of Places and People Abroad* (1855); *The Escape or a Leap for Freedom: A Drama in Five Acts* (1858); and *My Southern Home: Or, the South and Its People* (1880). He also wrote three major volumes of black history: *The Black Man, His Antecedents, His Genius, and His Achievements* (1863), *The Negro in the American Rebellion: His Heroism and His Fidelity* (1867), and *The Rising Son, Or the Antecedents and Advancement of the Colored Race* (1873).

The following excerpt was adapted from *The Narrative of William W. Brown*, published by the Boston Anti-Slavery Society in 1847 and appears in *Slave to Abolitionist: The Life of William Wells Brown* (1976). It highlights the practice of using slaves as collateral for gambling debts.

The Narrative of William W. Brown
From Slave to Abolitionist

It was half past twelve and the passengers, instead of going to their berths, gathered at the gambling tables. To see five or six tables in the saloon of a steamer with half a dozen men playing cards at each, and money, pistols and bowie knives spread around in splendid confusion is an ordinary thing on the Mississippi River. The practice of gambling on the river has long been annoying to more moral people who travel by steamboat. Thousands of dollars in cash and merchandise often change owners during a trip from St. Louis, or Louisville, to New Orleans on a Mississippi steamer. Many men are completely wiped out, and duels are often fought.

"Go call my boy, steward," said Mr. Jones on this particular occasion as he took his cards one by one from the table.

In a few minutes a fine-looking bright-eyed mulatto boy, about sixteen years old, was standing by his master's side at the table.

"I am broke, all but my boy, Joe," said Jones as he ran his fingers through his cards, "but he is worth a thousand dollars and I will bet the half of him."

"I will call you," said Thompson as he laid five hundred dollars at the feet of   5
the boy who was now standing on the table. At the same time he threw his cards down.

"You have beaten me," said Jones. The other gentlemen laughed as poor Joe stepped down from the table.

"Well, I suppose I owe you half the nigger," said Thompson as he took hold of Joe and started to examine his arms and legs.

"Yes," said Jones, "he is half yours. Let me have five hundred dollars and I will give you a bill of sale for him."

"Go back to your bed," said Thompson to his chattel, "and remember that you now belong to me."

The poor slave wiped the tears from his eyes as he turned obediently to leave.   10

"My father gave me that boy," said Jones as he took the money. "I hope, Mr. Thompson, that you will allow me to redeem him."

"Most certainly, sir," said Thompson, "whenever you hand over the cool thousand, the Negro is yours."

Next morning, as the passengers were coming into the lounge and on deck and the slaves were running around waiting on or looking for their masters, poor Joe was seen entering his new master's stateroom, boots in hand.

Such is the uncertainty of a slave's life. He goes to bed at night the pampered servant of the young master who played with him as a child and would not let his slave be abused for anything, and gets up in the morning the property of a man he has never seen before.

James Weldon Johnson

James Weldon Johnson (1871–1938), born in Jacksonville, Florida, had an extraordinary career as writer, musician, civil rights activist, and diplomat. After graduating from Atlanta University, he taught at his high school alma mater, becoming principal. In 1898, he passed the Florida bar. He was a contributing editor to *The New York Age,* 1914–1916; NAACP field secretary from 1916 to 1920 and secretary from 1920 to 1930; Consul to Cabello, Venezuela, from 1906 to 1909 and to Nicaragua from 1909 to 1912; and Professor of Creative Writing at Fisk, 1930–1938. He and his brother Rosamund wrote in 1900 the Negro National Anthem, "Lift Ev'ry Voice and Sing"; he catalogued African American music and wrote musical scores. His literary works include *Autobiography of an Ex-Colored Man* (1912), *Fifty Years and Other Poems* (1917), *God's Trombone: Seven Negro Sermons in Verse* (1926), *Black Manhattan* (1930), and *Along This Way* (1933).

In this 1930 excerpt from Chapter 7 of *Black Manhattan,* Johnson reviews professional sports in early twentieth-century New York.

Black Manhattan

I have indicated that during the fourth quarter of the last century there was a pause in the racial activities of the Negroes in the North. It would be more strictly true to say that there was a change in activities. In New York the Negro now began to function and express himself on a different plane, in a different sphere; and in a different way he effectively impressed himself upon the city and the country. Within this period, roughly speaking, the Negro in the North emerged and gained national notice in three great professional sports: horse-racing, baseball, and prize-fighting. He also made a beginning and headway on the theatrical stage. And New York, the New York of the upper Twenties and lower Thirties west of Sixth Avenue became the nucleus of these changed activities.

Horse-racing as an American sport reached development first in the South. The Southern landowners and aristocrats had taken up from the English gentry both riding to hounds and racing early in the last century. By the middle of the century there was local racing on tracks at New Orleans, Mobile, Charleston, Richmond, Nashville, Lexington (Kentucky), and Louisville. The Civil War interrupted the sport; but immediately after the war it was resumed on a grander scale; associations were organized and race-meets were scheduled. This tendency culminated in the building of a great track at Louisville and the offering of large prizes. Then was established the Kentucky Derby, the first American racing classic, an event which each year drew the fancy from all over the country. The Southern horse-owners, naturally—in fact, of necessity—made use of Negro jockeys, trainers, and stable-boys; so there grew up a class of Negro horsemen unequalled by any in the land. When the first Kentucky Derby was run, out of the fourteen jockeys who rode in the race thirteen were coloured. Therefore when the center of horse-racing was shifted to the East and became, somewhat in the English sense, a national sport, Negro jockeys constituted the very first ranks of the profession. When racing shifted to the East and became also a profitable business venture, with the book-maker as a recognized factor, the great jockeys jumped into national popularity. In the hey-day of racing the name of the winner of the Futurity, the Suburban, the Realization, the Brooklyn Handicap, the Metropolitan Handicap, or the Saratoga Cup was as widely heralded and almost as widely known as the name of the winner of a present-day championship prize-fight. In the days when jockeys were popular idols, none were more popular than the best of the coloured ones. No American jockey was ever more popular than Isaac Murphy. All in all, Murphy was the most finished American horseman who ever rode a race. . . .

The Negro jockey has today almost entirely passed. But it may be said that horse-racing itself as a popular American sport has greatly declined. It has fallen into ill repute and under the heels of the reformers. Today not even the names of white jockeys are widely known. There were several factors in the passing of the Negro jockey, not the least of which was the economic one. When jockeys began to earn ten to twenty thousand dollars a year and even more, forces against the Negro were set in motion and kept at work until he was excluded. . . .

The record of the Negro in professional baseball makes not so full a page. He did not have so much of a chance in baseball as he had in racing and pugilism. He never gets so fair a chance in those forms of sport or athletics where he must be a member of a team as in those where he may stand upon his own ability as an indi-vidual. The difficulty starts with prejudice against his becoming a team member. In baseball, as in racing, the Negro gained his first experience in the South. By 1880 nearly every city and town in the South had its coloured baseball club. For a period of years the best teams in the South were the coloured teams. For some reasons the whites were tardy about taking up the game and becoming proficient at it. In many places, however, they were fierce partisans and strong supporters of the black team of their town. . . .

But the Negro player could not front the forces against him in organized   5
baseball; so he was compelled to organize for himself. The first professional Negro team to be formed was the Gorhams of New York. From the Gorhams came the fa-mous Cuban Giants. Following the success of the Cuban Giants, coloured profes-sional and semi-professional clubs called Giants of some kind were organized in a dozen or more cities. These professional clubs have become better organized and now play a regularly scheduled series of games. They play very good ball and are quite popular, especially when they are pitted against white teams—and they are quite frequently in New York. . . .

The Negro's fairest chance in the professional sports came in the prize-ring. Here was brought into play more fully than in any other sport the advantageous factor of sole dependence upon his own individual skill and stamina. The prize-fighter had an advantage over even the jockey, who might be handicapped by hope-less mounts. The Negro prize-fighter, of course, often ran up against the hostility of the crowd, an intangible but, nevertheless, very real handicap. This very antago-nism, however, according to the stout-heartedness of the fighter, might serve as a spur to victory. This is what actually happened when George Dixon defended his ti-tle of featherweight champion of the world and defeated Jack Skelly at New Orleans in 1892. This was more truly the case when Jack Johnson held his title of heavyweight champion of the world by knocking out Jim Jeffries at Reno, July 4, 1910. Johnson has said that not only did he have to fight Jeffries, but that psychologically he also had to fight the majority of the thousands of spectators, many of whom were howling and praying for Jeffries to "kill the nigger." In truth, Johnson had to do more; on that day he had to fight psychologically the majority of the population of the United States. Jeffries had been brought forth as "the hope of the white race." Indeed, during Johnson's term of championship and up to his defeat by Willard at Havana in 1915, every white fighter who was being groomed as a heavyweight contender was known as a "white hope." A good part of the press and some literary fellows were industrious in fomenting the sentiment that the security of white civilization and white supremacy depended upon the defeat of Jack Johnson. One of these writers assumed the role of both prophet and comforter and before the Reno battle wrote in the red-blooded style of the day that Jeffries was bound to win because, while he had Runnymede and Agincourt behind him, the Negro had nothing but the jungle; that the Negro would be licked the moment the white man looked him in the eye. This psychic manifestation of white superiority did not materialize, but that sort of thing did help to create a tenseness of feeling that constituted something real for Jack Johnson to contend with, and, furthermore, immediately after the fight, expended itself in the beating up of numerous individual Negroes in various parts of the country as a sort of vicarious obliteration of the blot of Jeffries's defeat, and in a manner not at all in accordance with the Marquis of Queensberry rules. In fact, the reaction was so great that pressure was brought which forced Congress to pass a law prohibiting the inter-state exhibition of moving pictures of prize-fights—a law which still stands to plague and limit the magnates of pugilism and of the movies. Perhaps it was Jack Johnson's sense of humor almost as much as his skill and courage that enabled him to overcome this thing in the air. All through the fight he kept up a running banter with James J. Corbett, who was in Jeffries's corner. He would say to Corbett: "Watch this one, Jim. . . . How did you like that?" He relates that once in the midst of the fight he looked at Corbett's face and had to laugh. He says: "Jim's face reminded me of a man who had tasted his first green olive."

The story of the Negro in the prize-ring goes back much further than one would think; and, curiously, the beginning of the story is laid in New York City. The earliest acknowledgment of any man as champion of America was made about 1809; and that man was Thomas Molineaux (sometimes written Molyneaux). Tom Molineaux was born in 1784, a black slave belonging to a Molineaux (or Molyneaux) family of Virginia. When he was about twenty years old, he came to New York as a freeman and got a job as porter in the old Catherine Street market. The precise manner in which he procured his freedom does not seem to be known, but it appears that it was not by running away. Catherine market was headquarters for Negro boxers, and the new-comer soon proved himself the best of them all. It is more than probable that he did not reach New York a raw novice. There is a tradition that his father and grandfather before him had been boxers down in Virginia. For tradition also had it that boxing as a sport in this country began in Virginia; that in Virginia, more than in any other colony or state, it was the custom for the scions of aristocratic families to be sent to England as a part of their education, to rub shoulders with the gentry of the mother country and get the final polish that was deemed necessary for a Southern gentleman; that these young bloods witnessed prize-fights in England—where it was then and is now good form for the gentry not only to attend fights, but also to take lessons in the manly art—and brought the sport back home. Then, of course, the only way in which they could continue to enjoy it was to train likely young slaves as boxers and hold contests between the champions of different plantations. It can easily be imagined how much excitement and sport this would afford the rich planters. . . .

Within the United States the Negro has made a high record in pugilism. In every important division of the sport since its organized establishment a Negro has held the championship of the world. . . .

Charles Aikens

Charles Aikens, a former professional baseball player with the Baltimore Orioles from 1958 to 1964, graduated from California State College at Hayward and was a Frederick Douglass Fellow for Journalism in 1969–1970.

The following article from *The Black Scholar* was written in November 1971. Aikens empathizes with Curt Flood in his battle with baseball management over antitrust and the reserve clause, likening it to the plantation experience.

The Struggle of Curt Flood

"I personally feel bad that he's gone," remarked Washington Senators' manager Ted Williams, after outfielder Curt Flood abruptly left his team and a $110,000 baseball salary.

I looked at the paper, angrily tossing it to the floor. I could not eat dinner that evening following work. Flood felt the same way I'd felt seven years earlier after finding I was an indentured servant bound by the reserve clause of professional baseball. It is a contract that binds a player to the organization that signs him until he is released, traded or returned. I was a $400 a month baseball player in 1962, and had been angered by the Baltimore Orioles' refusal to give me a raise after I'd hit .325 during the 1962 Appalachian league season. I made the league All-Star team that year, helping my team to win the title. Now, in 1969, brave little Curt was attempting to bowl over the monstrous reserve clause, just as he had bowled doubters of his ability (because of his small size) as a high school player from the ghetto of west Oakland.

Less than two years before Curt left the Senators, he tackled baseball's reserve clause, sueing for $4.1 million because he felt like a "chattel slave" after being traded against his will from the St. Louis Cardinals to the Philadelphia Phillies.[1]

It was fitting for Curt to be the one to attack the reserve clause. Said a former schoolmate of Curt's: "He was a warm and sensitive person with a lot of intelligence; he was so conscientious nearly the whole student body at Technical High School admired his athletic ability and artistic skills. He had so much pride in himself."

Washington Senators' manager Ted Williams abused this man's pride by 5
benching him for a pinch fielder five days before his departure. Although Flood
was the only living player to play a whole season without making an error, Williams
replaced him with Dal Unser, who hit .220, .230 and .231 in order to reach the major leagues. A player of that caliber had no business replacing Flood, or anyone. He
should not have been in the major leagues with those minor league figures. Flood
hit .340, .299 and .333 in the minors.[2] Flood was always a relatively slow starter and
usually picked up a major bundle of his hits as the season got progressively tougher.
He functioned on pride and desire, and Williams must have destroyed all of it on
that particular day.

The substitution also followed Judge Ben Cooper's August 12, 1970, ruling
which said that the reserve clause Curt Flood was fighting should be modified by
the players and owners.

This was like telling the slavemasters that they should modify slavery. The
slaves and any fool knew that couldn't happen. Williams' benching of Flood put
him in the position of the slave overseer who flogged the rebellious slave by the
embarrassment of a benching as he ran toward the outfield for the next inning.
Anyone who has ever played baseball knows this is the lowest blow a manager can
strike—allowing a player to leave the dugout and then calling him back in front of
a huge throng of fans. Following the benching, a May 1, 1971, news headline added
to the insult saying:

Flood Hit Famine
Just One of Nats Many Headaches

This was a blatantly racist headline, in that Flood had not yet been up 30 times during the first weeks of the season. Luis Aparicio went 0 for 41 and still managed to
make the American League All-Star Team. This indicates how writers can place the
blame for a team's failure on a particular ballplayer who isn't liked because he is a
rebel. Another example of racism was exhibited during the earlier parts of the 1971
season when Alex Johnson of the California Angels was branded the California
Angels' biggest problem, though he was the leading hitter on the Angels team at
that time. Too often, white players on a team will point the accusing finger at a
black star in order to keep attention away from their low batting averages.

An intelligent black baseball manager would probably be able to read between these lines, but that is probably why there are none of major league status at
this writing. In concluding his ruling in federal court upholding baseball's reserve
system, Judge Cooper said he was convinced that the reserve clause system could be
changed so as to be acceptable by the club and the players. The Judge said this was
the first time in 50 years that both the antis and pros of the reserve system had to
make their case on the merits and support it with truth in a court of law. Flood
brought the suit in October of 1969, charging that the reserve system was unlawful
and in violation of the anti-trust laws. He contended he was being sold as "chattel"
and being made to work as a "slave." His salary then was $90,000 a year. Flood claimed
further in the suit, that during his career he could not choose his own employer. Yet,
at anytime, that employer could dump him on an unconditional release.

Flood's suit is mindful of the Dred Scott decision in 1857, (the same year or-   10
ganized baseball clubs started). Chief Justice Roger B. Taney ruled against Scott, a
slave, saying that blacks could not be citizens of the United States because they
formed no part of "the people" referred to in the Declaration of Independence
and the Constitution, and had "no rights which white men were bound to respect."[3]

Curt had been an early inspiration to me as a youngster, although I had not
met him personally. He was a tenth grade player for the McClymonds High School
team along with Frank Robinson and Jess Gonder, who later went to the major
leagues by way of Cincinnati's minor league clubs. The first time I saw Flood play, I
remember hearing a loud voice yell, "he shor hit that one way out the park!"

I was approaching Raimondi Park in the factory filled area in (what we called)
deep West Oakland, making my first unescorted venture at 12 years of age to the
other side of town. The area around Raimondi was called the other side of town
because it was a glass littered, factory-filled, slum where all the rough dudes supposedly stayed. Before this particular afternoon walk and exploration, I'd been forcefully confined, by the threat of a whipping, to the vicinity between Linden and
Market Streets by my watchful parents. Frank Robinson told my older brother that
McClymonds was having a game that evening, so I went to see him play. Frank was
often a visitor at my home, then a three-car garage that my father converted into a
dwelling shortly after our second migration from Mississippi to California in the
early 1950's.

"Why does that boy (Frank) come over so much," my mother asked, "doesn't
he have a home?"

"Yea, he has a home," my brother, Wilbert answered, "but he's visiting his
brother who stays across the street because his father doesn't live with his mother."

Wilbert and Frank were high school running buddies. Curt Flood was a base-   15
ball player they often said was good, but I didn't know who he was until I saw him
rounding Raimondi's bases after hitting the long 367-foot homerun out of the park.

"That little joker ain't no bigger than me," I said while walking behind the
backstop that kept balls from being lost across 18th Street into the yard of the
Southern Pacific Railroad Station. As Flood touched homeplate, cheers rang out
from the small crowd and a thinly dressed lady reached her half nude bosom out of
a project window behind the third base dugout saying: "Thas thee way ta go . . .
honey. You kin come up to mah house anytime you want to."

Flood looked toward the window, smiled, then went into the dugout after having his backside slapped by happy teammates who were saying things like: "Little
man where did you get all that power—way to go rook." His coach George Powles
said, "Nice goin' Curt."

Then a gravel voiced man standing behind the backstop said, "Them scouts
up there in the stands are watching that boy. He's going to be another Jackie
Robinson."

"What's a scout?" said a small kid who was sucking on his thumb.

"They're guys who come from teams like the Dodgers and pick players that   20
they want to give a chance to play professional baseball. Sometimes they get a lot of
money."

I looked across to the stands behind the first base side of the dugout and saw
two well-tanned men who looked different from the usual pale-faced whites who

lived in West Oakland or came there to work. They reminded me of plantation owners coming to buy slaves at a slave auction. I saw them jotting down information in the small notebooks they had, so I curiously went over to see what they were up to. One told the other, "That kid Flood can do everything."

"I'll ask George Powles his age," said the other, who had a cigar in his mouth.

"He's 15," said the small youth who was sucking his thumb. "Thank you sonny," the heaviest of the two men said. He marked his notebook as Flood returned to the dugout following the next inning.

"I'm gonna watch this kid one more inning and if he gets another hit I'm gonna try to sign him right now."

"We really don't have to worry about him now," said the heavy scout. "He's too young now and will probably want to finish high school."   25

The thumb sucking kid said, "He's a tenth grader."

The youth smiled, showing a big gap where a tooth was broken and got even closer to the scouts who paid him a compliment for being intelligent. One of the scouts became irritated with the kid's ever-presence and gave him a dime to go buy some ice cream from a man who rode his freezer around on the front end of a three-wheel bike.

"You want a dime too, sonny," the fat one said as I got closer.

"No, my mama don't like me to take no money from strangers," I said in my still existing Mississippi accent. "But I'd like ta know whut you is doin?"

"We're watching players on this team to see if they have enough ability and hustle to play professional baseball with Cincinnati."

"Do you see anyone who might make some money?" I said.   30

"Yea," the cigar smoking one said, "that kid Robinson might make some dough one day if he keeps his nose clean."

"You mean a player has to keep his nose clean to play baseball?"

"Yea kid, if a player stays out of trouble with the law and is a nice boy and don't ask too many questions, he might be able to get a chance to go out and play for money."

"Flood is also a good-looking player along with that catcher (Gonder). But you can't tell what might happen to a youngster who grows up in this area."

"Whut you mean."   35

"I mean, if a player chases women all the time he might not be able to play ball like we want him to. He also has to stay in at night and keep out of night clubs at late hours."

"Um gonna be a ballplayer one day," I said.

"Ok—Ok kid, be anything you want to be but would you leave us alone so we can watch Flood hit."

I wondered why they paid more attention to Flood than to anyone else, but I learned the reason after hearing one say, "He can run, hit and throw. He also hustles on and off the field like a future pro should." I took mental notes on what they were looking for and vowed that I, too, would be like that little fellow named Flood, who had just got another hit that sent the scouts away smiling. . . .

I became another of the many McClymonds athletes to go into professional   40
baseball. I signed a 1962 contract with the Baltimore Orioles after being a vicious high school and college baseball player, grabbing attention by breaking infielders'

ribs while sliding into bases and doing everything well that the scouts said they wanted that summer day when I was a youngster watching Curt Flood.

My desire to make the professionals was so strong that I became known as "demolition" to my teammates, trying to destroy everything that got between me and success.

During my last season at Merritt College, I made up my mind that I too could be a star like Flood. I was only a few pounds heavier, but I had a stronger arm and was probably as fast.

While at Merritt, I began to get a picture of the selection process that takes place when a scout looks for a potential big league ballplayer. Many of the fellows were beginning to fail their trials in professional baseball, and some returned to the Oakland sandlots. They were bitter because they felt that the white people in control of professional baseball clubs eliminated any black who did not fit into the humble role of a dumb, stupid, know nothing ballplayer who would go out and break his neck, sweating like a slave in a cotton field, in order to get an advancement to the majors. I realized that I could not be my usual arrogant self if I ever got the opportunity to play professional baseball because scouts usually frowned when you talked to them like you had sense or knew the value you would be to the club.

I scoffed at being told by scouts that I was too small to be a professional baseball player. I was bigger than Curt Flood and many of the other players I'd seen on television. I could also run, hit and throw and I felt I should get a bonus for the talents I had.

Word also came around in the area that black players were not getting the bonuses that white players were getting. Take Frank Robinson, for example. J. W. Porter, a white player from Oakland, had gotten well over $50,000 for signing, while Robinson, who played in the same area had received a small bonus of less than $5,000 upon his initial contract. He'd hit as good or better than Porter in American Legion baseball. The same thing happened in the signing of blacks such as Curt Flood, Vada Pinson, Jess Gonder, Tommy Harper, Charlie Beamon and Curt Motton who all received small bonuses. For white stars who left the area, the case was just the opposite. Rich Berry, a Berkeley High star got a reported $60–80,000 bonus; Ernie Fazio got a reported $75,000; Lenny Gabrielson got a reported bonus of nearly $100,000; Frank Bertaina got an estimated $75,000. All these players were of lesser ability than the black players who went on to outstanding performances in major league baseball.

I became frustrated with baseball after seeing that kind of exploitation. I had decided to play my last game at Lincoln Park in Alameda when I was approached by a Baltimore scout. He came to my home the next evening and made an embarrassing offer of $1,000 to sign me to a professional contract. I was so angry I walked out of the room. He said I was too small to command a large bonus. I pointed out that I was as big as Flood and could run and throw as well. He replied, "Flood is something special."

"Yea," I said, "then why didn't he get a bonus like some of the other players from this area."

"He was so small," the scout said.

"Then why did a small player like Ernie Fazio get $75,000. He was smaller than Curt or me."

"Some organizations have more money to give out than others," he said.　　50

It didn't make sense to me how a young organization such as Houston could give a player $75,000 as opposed to a long-standing organization such as Cincinnati giving players Frank Robinson, Vada Pinson, Jess Gonder and Curt Flood a trifling $5,000 or less. Besides, Fazio was only five feet six or seven inches.

"College helps too," the scout had said. But Curt Motten was a student at the University of California when he signed. Tommy Harper was a student at San Francisco State when he signed. Both of them were very intelligent.

However, when it came to negotiating, they were all unprepared to deal with the racist white man who was in control of the dollar bills and could not bargain on an equal level as white players could.

The con game of the scouts came more clearly in focus when I heard a college coach of mine telling a white player that he would keep Aikens on the bench because some scouts might come around to sign him.

I became the victim of my first benching, and realized that a conspiracy existed　　55
among whites to provide opportunities for their financial existence, that did not take the black man into consideration. From that time on I knew why many black athletes were systematically eliminated from opportunities—because white coaches showed an interest only in their own kind, while exploiting blacks. I just wondered why blacks did not have the opportunities to manage their own black athletes.

I was awakened to the facts of life about the intelligent black athlete in professional baseball. Poor, racist, white baseball managers and scouts despised the intelligent black, and he was the first to be put on the release roster, no matter how good his ability. Other intelligent blacks from the Oakland area like Curt Motton and Tommy Harper were able to remain in uniform because they managed to act humble. Motten acted as if he didn't know A from Z when he was coming up in the minor leagues. Serious black guys like Alex Johnson always got labeled strange, distant, or as of late, rebellious.

From my own personal career, I noticed, white players of equal ability to blacks usually got raises twice as big during contract time. Many blatant instances of racism are exhibited by white sports writers, managers, scouts, front office men and umpires.

White reporters often write adversely about black players they don't like by describing them as lazy, strange, unaggressive or nonchalant, yet these adjectives are seldom used to describe the white player.

The manager usually gets his racist pokes by benching a good black player in the minor leagues when important scouts come to games to view major league prospects for advancement to the majors. Scouts do their racist deeds by giving talented black players smaller sums than whites of equal or less talent. Front office men get their racist wads off by looking the other way when a black player makes an outstanding play and by cheering a routine play of a white. Umpires get their demagogic kicks by calling a strike on a black player one to three feet outside the strike zone.

Today, Curt Flood and other black athletes are hip to the white sports estab-　　60
lishment's game. Black athletes are no longer willing to play by the racists' rules.

Flood's suit is among many events in the black struggle that have heightened awareness of a brutal system where people are still treated as "chattel," although slavery was supposed to have ended over 100 years ago. The Curt Floods, Alex Johnsons and Duane Thomases form the vanguard of the recent emergence of the militant black athlete who is striving to attain human rights and equal opportunities in the sports world.

ENDNOTES

1. See *Baseball Guide,* Spink Publishers: 1971, pp. 272–278.
2. See Del Unser, *Who's Who in Baseball,* 1971, p. 73.
3. Eric Forner, *America's Black Past,* Harper & Row: New York, p. 143.

Mark Conrad

Mark Conrad is an Associate Professor of Legal and Ethical Studies in the School of Business at Fordham University. Since 1987, he has been teaching sports media and Internet law. He writes and comments frequently on sports law issues, such as sports league governance, contract, labor, antitrust, and Internet issues in sports. Conrad serves as a columnist for the *New York Law Journal* and is the editor of the Internet publication *Mark's Sports Law News.*

In the chapter "Blue-Collar Law and Basketball" in *Basketball Jones: America Above the Rim,* Conrad analyzes the impact of the National Labor Relations Act of 1935 on the current experiences of the National Basketball Association.

Blue-Collar Law and Basketball

Maybe you don't see a connection between those men and women who risked everything they had to ask for minimum wage, overtime, and safe working conditions, and . . . basketball players . . . especially given the rather substantial wages some of them receive. The connection is there, however, and it is as real as the . . . NBA finals . . . what is at stake when professional athletes strike is a principle, and a protection for every working man and woman, a protection once fought for in the streets of our nation, with fists and guns, and lynching and mass arrests.

—COMMENTATOR HOWARD COSELL

The June 1998 decision of the NBA owners to impose a lockout of the players and jeopardize the basketball season brought the issue of labor relations and basketball into public view—with all its accompanying distrust and divisions. Giving the basketball fan a taste of the often acrimonious and high-stakes posturing also demonstrated how a sixty-year-old series of laws has applied, rightly or wrongly, to a professional sport comprised of wealthy (even superwealthy) employers and, at times, almost equally wealthy players.

Of course, basketball is not the first sport to be affected by labor–management disputes. Baseball, football, and hockey have seen their share of strikes and lockouts. But the NBA lockout and its results gave basketball fans a strong education in American labor laws, notably the National Labor Relations Act of 1935.[1]

These days, the basketball news forms an adjunct to the labor and financial pages of the local newspaper. In the "good old days" when sports was sports and news was news, the two rarely met. Now they engage in a tango of conflicting goals, resulting in frequent arguments.

The Labor Law Model

American labor law concepts—conceived to protect blue-collar workers in their quest to improve working conditions—have been injected into the world of professional basketball as well as other sports, over the last quarter of the twentieth century. Although basketball fans may hate to admit it, labor law in sports is here to stay.

In one sense, it is incongruous. Professional basketball employs personnel to represent elite, skilled practitioners of a sport barely a century old. Their working conditions (about six or seven months per year, arguably less than thirty-five hours per week) and their compensation scales are beyond the hopes and aspirations of the ordinary or even not-so-ordinary American worker. With an average salary of $1.5 million per season in 1998, players in the National Basketball Association surpassed the averages for partners in the nation's largest law firms and all but the very top surgeons; some salaries even exceeded those of many CEOs of Fortune 500 corporations.

Also, unlike the automobile and steel industries, professional basketball is a relatively new business, which came to fruition well after New York Senator Robert Wagner drafted the National Labor Relations Act in 1935. At the time of the law, Senator Wagner most likely did not consider it applicable to the weak professional basketball leagues of his day, which could not compete with the successful college basketball game of the 1930s. At Wagner's death in 1951, the modern NBA—conceived from the merger of the Basketball Association of America and the National Basketball League—was just two years old.

The passage of the National Labor Relations Act (NLRA) in 1935 marked a milestone in American labor. Called the "Magna Carta of Labor," the NLRA was intended to protect auto workers, printers, and clerical employees in their quest to unionize and bargain collectively with management without the fear of retaliation. The enactment of this law changed the nature of labor–management relations.

Before 1935, "workplace democracy" often collided with the mantra of laissez-faire capitalism. Unionization, a difficult process confronted with subtle and not-so-subtle threats of employee harassment or dismissal, was a legally unprotected act. Legal attempts to give workers greater rights previously had been incremental. But the New Deal period marked the emancipation of American labor. Senator Wagner, an ally of President Franklin Roosevelt, shepherded the NLRA through the Congress. Wagner firmly believed in the government's duty to take an active role in promoting the public good.

The NLRA guarantees workers the right to be represented by a union and provides for specific methods to attain union representation and employer recognition of a particular "collective-bargaining unit" to negotiate on behalf of a group of workers.[2] Elections are held, and if the National Labor Relations Board certifies the results, the union is recognized. Usually, if union recognition is granted, individual employees lose their right to negotiate on such subjects as "wages, hours or working conditions."

The NLRA also gives employees the right to strike.[3] Most strikes occur when a satisfactory collective-bargaining agreement, usually an attempt to secure better wages, hours, or working conditions, cannot be reached. This pits the collective economic power of the unionized workers against the employer's attempts to go on without the aid of their labor. Employers may replace striking workers with temporary or permanent replacements or get by with managerial employees who are not part of the collective-bargaining unit.[4] (This was done in the 1987 National Football League strike.)

The flip side of the strike is the lockout, a tactical measure taken by employers to prevent the union members from working. Just as the strike is an economic pressure tactic taken by the union, the lockout is a similar strategy for management. With the expiration of a collective-bargaining agreement, management may prefer to "call the shots" in determining the shutdown of an operation, rather than wait for the union to seize the opportunity. This tactic was employed by the National Hockey League (NHL) in 1994, resulting in a disruption of almost half the season. In 1998 the NBA owners, possibly taking their cue from the NHL outcome, declared a lockout in basketball.

One of the central components to the NLRA involves a series of actions known as "unfair labor practices."[5] Both employers and employees may be liable for these violations, which include interference with the unionization process, discriminatory treatment against employees for union-related activities, and most important, the refusal by either side to bargain in good faith. The last condition requires both sides to negotiate on the "mandatory" subjects—wages, hours, and working conditions. The law also established the National Labor Relations Board as the administrative agency to enforce the mandates of the NLRA.

Senator Wagner's goals for industrial justice centered on the steelworker, auto assembly-line employee, and sandhog, not the professional basketball player. Probably the farthest thing from his mind was the idea of the likes of Michael Jordan, Patrick Ewing, and Shaquille O'Neal as unionized workers.

Although Wagner's labor ideals did not center on labor in relation to sports, his one connection with sports was a case involving the suspension of baseball player Carl Mays, who had been traded to the New York Yankees. The Yankees wanted the suspension lifted, but American League president and baseball's de facto leader Bancroft "Ban" Johnson refused to reconsider. The case went to court and was heard by then New York Supreme Court justice Wagner. Wagner ruled in favor of the Yankees, enjoining Johnson from interfering with the player's performing for the Yankees. A quotation from the decision is quite prophetic:

> The commercialization of baseball is a highly-profitable undertaking, rendering lucrative returns to the member clubs, to their stockholders and to

their players. . . . The suspension of a player not only interferes with his individual contract; it may also interfere with the reputation and collective ability of the club.[6]

In limiting Johnson's power, this decision served to weaken his authority over the game and was one factor in his fall from grace. Just a few years later, baseball reorganized and created a commissioner's office to govern the sport. The commissioner system came to be used in every other professional sport, including basketball. The quotation is timeless in its applicability and could describe the sports environment today. This language could have been included in the recent arbitration involving Latrell Sprewell, where arbitrator John Feerick ruled that the NBA was unjustified in terminating Sprewell's contract after the player assaulted his coach.[7]

After the passage of the NLRA (which the Supreme Court subsequently upheld as a legitimate exercise of congressional power[8]), the blue-collar workers of the nation's central industries took advantage of the act and unionized. The resulting improvements in wages, hours, and general working conditions are a testament to the success of the law. In fact, many felt that the law was too pro-union, and in 1947, the so-called Taft-Hartley Amendments were passed to ensure that unions themselves do not engage in unfair labor practices.[9]

■ Application to Basketball

To keep operating costs down, the NBA originally copied the system employed in professional baseball and football to restrain player salaries. That device, the use of a "reserve" system to hitch players to their respective teams, severely restricted players' right to test their talents on the open market. This de facto monopolization achieved its effect and resulted in considerably lower player salaries, due to the lack of a free market for the players. The use of a contractual limitation on the right to secure employment remains a unique element of sports law and one of the most hotly contested issues in labor–management relations to this very day.

Yet trade unionism in the NBA came slowly. The National Basketball Players Association (NBPA) was formed in 1954, with Boston Celtics great Bob Cousy as its leader. Taking a cue from the nineteenth-century captains of industry, the NBA at first refused to recognize the association. In 1957, Commissioner Maurice Podoloff reluctantly conceded its validity, in part because he feared the NBPA would affiliate itself with a larger and stronger union, such as the steelworkers or teamsters. But the union's mettle was not seriously tested until 1964, when the NBPA threatened a strike at the 1964 All-Star Game.

In the 1950s, most professional sports "unions" were more like medieval guilds than modern labor organizations. The idea of collective bargaining between the union representatives and basketball owners did not begin in earnest until the 1960s, at just about the time that the percentage of unionized American workers began to shrink. Union membership in the United States peaked in 1953 to 37 percent of non-agricultural workers and has dropped steadily since. By 1991, the figure was 16 percent.[10] Though sports unions, including the NBPA, were late bloomers, in recent years they have crafted a singular position among American labor.

It was during the regime of union executive director Larry Fleisher that the NBPA began to think of itself in the same mold as other trade unions. Fleisher, called "the most successful labor leader of the 20th century" by former New Jersey senator Bill Bradley,[11] served as the head of the union until 1988 and negotiated the groundbreaking 1983 and 1988 collective bargaining agreements (CBAs), which created the salary-cap structure but also guaranteed the players a percentage of league revenues in either salary or benefits. In 1967, the average salary of an NBA player was $9,400; when Fleisher retired, it was $600,000. Not as well known as his compatriots Marvin Miller in baseball and Ed Garvey in football, Fleisher ably guided his players gradually, without protracted litigation and strikes.

In those days, the NBPA's representation dovetailed some of their experiences with those of other unions. Some thought their labor battles were a central component to trade unionism, as was stated by the late sports commentator Howard Cosell, in the epigraph to this chapter.[12] In the 1960s, Cosell's assessment accurately reflected the kinship between sports unions and unions at large. Today it serves as cant, glossing over major differences between the American labor experience on the one hand and the NBA and its players on the other. The differences far outweigh the similarities, legally, economically, and practically.

The Peculiarities of Basketball Labor Law

As *New York Times* sportswriter Murray Chass has noted, collective bargaining in professional sports has been described less as negotiating over working conditions than as "two mega-corporations talking to each other about mergers or splits or sales."[13] In the recently expired 1995 NBA collective bargaining agreement are sections that would be unheard of in a typical CBA.

First, much space was devoted to revenue sharing between the employer teams and the players. Players shared 59 percent of "gross defined revenues" and were guaranteed 48 percent of all NBA revenues—a staggering $700 million in 1994–95. Such revenues included fees from arena signage, sponsorships, parking, concessions, and luxury boxes. Players were entitled to share in the moneys generated from licensing and merchandising. True, some indications of a traditional labor contract exist, such as the minimum salary. But that amount, which began at $225,000 per season and rose to $272,500, towers over the $500-per-week minimum one frequently finds in the general labor force. And we are not even considering the complicated salary-cap structure.

The very nature of this agreement is more akin to a European Social Democratic partnership between labor and management than to the typical American model. It is both an irony and a success story that such sharing of the wealth has the potential to make both the employers and the employees very rich.

This brings us to the nature of the services and the public loyalty to the services provided. Brand loyalty occupies a sacred place in the dreams of a marketer. If a company's brand name exudes stature and quality, it will retain a following among consumers of that type of product. And that will be the case even if the actual quality of the brand suffers. To paraphrase that often-stated theme from the 1992 presidential campaign: "It's the perception, stupid."

Most buyers do not care who makes the cars they drive, as long as the vehicles run dependably, are well designed, and have reasonable comfort and performance. Even in a service industry, one doesn't care about who the individual employees are but rather about the service itself. So, while the employee is a cog in the overall scheme, the replacement of that person with another will not necessarily cause consumer discomfort (unless the service declines in quality).

Contrast this with professional basketball players. The fan loyalty to a star player may be of incalculable value. Only a very small number of athletes play professional basketball in the United States; they make up an elite group by definition, especially considering the millions who play the game. Only a select few make the cut through high school, college, and the draft to get in and stay in the NBA and to occupy an exalted place there. And unlike other industries, where a choice of products abounds, the NBA has one—basketball. Without any rival, the NBA is the ultimate brand, and its employees are the ultimate makers of that brand.

The athletes' clout is a function not only of their unique skills but also of the unique relationship consumers have with the service they deliver. The players' agents and their union leaders know this all too well. With the value of the individual players far from being equal, basketball stars such as Michael Jordan, Patrick Ewing, Kevin Garnett, and Shaquille O'Neal can command huge salaries, bonuses, and other contractual perks negotiated through a position of tremendous strength. They and the other elites who dominate their franchise get the top marquee billing. The less-talented players, good enough to play but not to star in the NBA, do the job but are not irreplaceable. The wide disparity in value of the talent makes the NBA players a widely diverse union, a group of employees with great differences of wages. Consequently, it is a union that is very hard to hold together. Fleisher could do so; things have become more difficult since.

In the 1980s, the union and the NBA negotiated novel CBAs that dramatically changed the landscape of professional sports. In 1981, sixteen of the then twenty-three teams lost money. Rumors of rampant drug use and escalating salaries resulted in declines in game attendance, television ratings, and league revenues.[14] Sensing the desperate situation, both the NBA and NBPA concluded the 1983 CBA, the first to include revenue sharing (53 percent of gross revenues, including the national TV contract, local gate profits, playoff profits) in return for a team cap on salaries. This CBA was further refined in 1988.

The league and the union became victims of their success. As professional basketball attained new heights of popularity both in the United States and worldwide, the marquee value of teams and players increased. Today, a great disparity in salaries exists. In 1998, 40 players made over $5 million per season and 120 made the league minimum. Free-agency rights apply only to certain veteran players. The salary-cap structure is porous, permitting the elites to command whatever the market will bear as long as they stay with their teams. While the union negotiates many working conditions on behalf of all the players, it does not mandate the actual money individual players make. The resulting disparity adversely affects union solidarity—difficult in many situations but far more challenging for the leader of the NBPA.

◼ Union Rules?

Tensions exist in many unions. But the kinds of tension that now exist at the NBPA reflect the huge differences between castes of players. For the best and the brightest, the union may be a hindrance and can put them in a weaker position than if they were "on their own." As the CBA does not involve individual salary negotiation, the impact that player agents have on the process is not insignificant. The major agents representing the big-time players do not have any built-in loyalty to the NBPA or to its continued existence. Indeed, attempts at decertification of the NBPA were seriously considered in 1995, during a period of contentious negotiations. Michael Jordan, Patrick Ewing, and Reggie Miller signed decertification notices because they were dissatisfied with the leadership of the union. They feared that the union would capitulate into accepting a "harder" salary cap. A tentative agreement exacerbated the issue. Ultimately, the union prevailed by a 226–134 vote, or 63 percent against decertification. The union accepted a final collective bargaining agreement the next year. Yet the issue of player "haves" versus player "have-nots" will not go away, and decertification may be revisited. The following statement by Tom Heinsohn, a former NBPA president who retired from playing in 1965, illustrates the dilemma:

> The players today take everything for granted. . . . Players all travel first-class, have plenty of meal money and they stay in separate rooms. The players have a very cavalier attitude about the union itself. Now, I'm fearful that if they decertify the union, all of the players are going to have to fight for those things individually in their contract.[15]

These problems represent an inner weakness in a union of such disparate members and a systematic weakness of individual (both in the performance sense and in the negotiating sense) employees attempting to band together. The greater the salary disparities, the more untenable the NBPA is. The structure of these labor–management relations also has led to use of a legal tactic that has probably done as much or more to accomplish union goals than collective bargaining: invocation of antitrust laws.

◼ The Antitrust Tango

As every law student knows, antitrust law ranks as one of those subjects full of theorists, long on explanation, and brimming with complex judicial determinations. Most unions do not partake of antitrust theory in their dealings with employers. The NBPA (along with the National Football League Players Association) has made antitrust application a virtual art form.

The basic antitrust laws—the Sherman Antitrust Act[16] and the Clayton Act[17]—date from 1890 and 1914 respectively and apply to concerted activities that restrain trade in interstate commerce. The intentions of these laws were to stop monopolistic activities that often resulted in large "trusts" in such industries as oil, sugar, and tobacco. To avoid the argument that union activity may constitute restraint of trade, section 6 of the Clayton Act states that "the labor or commerce of a human being is not subject to antitrust laws."[18] The scope of that provision has been a matter of considerable academic debate and practical application in the field of sports law.

Ostensibly, section 6 protects unions and employers from engaging in con-   35
certed activities such as strikes and lockouts. But what if there are sections in a collective bargaining agreement that may have antitrust implications? For example, does a salary cap or a limitation of free agency become a restraint of trade under antitrust laws? Because of the history of free-agency limitations and salary restrictions in all professional sports, including basketball, this issue has occupied the time of a number of courts over the last two decades of the twentieth century.

In the NBA, the issue has been the continuing validity of the exemption during and after the expiration of a collective bargaining agreement. In the case of *Wood v. NBA*,[19] Leon Wood, a point guard on the 1984 gold-medal U.S. Olympic team, was picked by the Philadelphia 76ers in the first round. Because of salary-cap constraints, Wood was offered a $75,000 one-year contract, well below his true market value. Ultimately, when cap room became available, his contract was amended to a four-year $1 million deal. Nevertheless, he sued the NBA, claiming that the cap violated antitrust laws. Wood was still in college at the ratification of the 1983 CBA that created the system and alleged that he should be a party to its provisions. The court rejected his claims, as the agreement was subject to the labor exemption. Otherwise, the court noted, federal labor policy would be subverted.

Also in 1987, a lower federal court, ruling in *Bridgeman v. NBA*,[20] concluded that the labor exemption continues to apply after the conclusion of a CBA during an impasse stage, if the employer "reasonably believes that the practice or a close variant of it will be incorporated in the next collective bargaining agreement." Junior Bridgeman challenged the cap rules but also lost. Shortly afterward, the 1988 CBA was concluded. In 1995, a similar ruling occurred in *National Basketball Association v. Williams*.[21]

The results of the *Bridgeman* case demonstrate how the NBPA turned a defeat into a victory. Even though the NBA won, the union, in a daring and ingenious move, threatened to decertify itself—meaning that no collective bargaining process would be in place and the owners would be wide open to antitrust suits. The plan worked; the NBA capitulated, not wanting anything to do with negotiating individual contracts with players in a free market, subject to antitrust laws. Shortly afterward, the parties concluded the 1988 agreement.

The ingenious tête-à-tête between labor and antitrust has benefited the NBPA. It is difficult to conceive of a non-sports union working the legal realm in such a way. Given the recent vintage of the NBPA, the disparity of talents and of payments made to its members, and the power of the player agents, it is ironic that the basketball players union could utilize the labor laws—especially the decertification threat—as a negotiating tactic to get its way. Or maybe, because of these attributes, the decertification sword had to be utilized to make the union's point.

In fact, a strong possibility for decertification exists in the not-too-distant fu-   40
ture. The elite twenty-five players who help establish the worldwide recognition of the NBA don't need a union. They could thrive in a non-union market because their services are in demand. But the lesser stars and journeymen would suffer in an environment where the gulf among the players may be as wide as the disparities between the players and the owners.

■ A Few Last Words

Despite the fissures in the union, the disparate interests, the pressures from the agents, and the difficulties of bargaining with a league composed of twenty-nine separate entities, the NBA players have done exceedingly well. And for most of the 1980s and 1990s, management has also done well in this fascinating industrial partnership. But the events of 1998 could turn out to be a watershed, signaling a rocky road for both sides.

For any basketball fan, the 1998 owners' lockout represented a sad state of affairs; a situation of prior union–management cooperation had become a victim of its own success. The grand scheme turned the NBA into a marquee product worldwide, with multibillion-dollar television contracts and a cadre of $100 million ballplayers who could do just as well without a union as with one. And even if a prolonged lockout occurred in 1998 or sometime in the future, a setup including matches between teams composed of the likes of Scottie Pippen, Kevin Garnett, Shaquille O'Neal, Juwan Howard, Allen Iverson, and Patrick Ewing would attract fan and television coverage. A group of striking coal miners cannot do the same.

The worst-case scenario for the NBA and the NBPA would have been a season-long shutdown of operations. As hard as that would have been for the players and the owners, they could rest assured that the league would not easily go out of business. Major League Baseball is testament to a sport that has come back, attendancewise, after the 1994 strike. Boosted by the home-run exploits of Mark McGwire and Sammy Sosa, baseball in 1998 and 1999 experienced a wave of popular goodwill not seen in many years. Attendance at games increased by 12 percent.[22]

But when all is said and done, the fact remains that in a splintered union of six-figure employees, millionaires, and multimillionaires using the labor and antitrust laws to win concessions from multiparty employers who are multimillionaires or billionaires themselves, something is askew. Is this what Robert Wagner had in mind when he drafted the landmark National Labor Relations Act?

That's hard to believe.   45

ENDNOTES

1. 29 U.S.C. sec. 151 *et seq.*
2. Ibid.
3. 29 U.S.C. secs. 157, 163 (1982).
4. See *NLRB v. MacKay Radio and Telephone Co.,* 304 U.S. 333 (1938).
5. 29 U.S.C. secs. 157, 158(a)(1)–(a)(5); 158(b)(1)–(b)(7) (1982).
6. See Harold Seymour, *Baseball—The Golden Age* (New York: Oxford University Press, 1971), 268.
7. See Dean John Feerick, "Arbitration Opinion and Award in the Matter of National Basketball Players Association on Behalf of Player Latrell Sprewell and Warriors Basketball Club and National Basketball Association," March 4, 1998.
8. See *NLRB v. Jones and Laughlin Steel Corp.,* 301 U.S. 1 (1937).
9. 61 *Statutes at Large* 136 (1947).
10. See also Melvyn Dubofsky, *The State and Labor in Modern America* (Chapel Hill, University of North Carolina Press, 1994), 130, cited in Deborah A. Ballam, "The Law as a

Constitutive Force for Change, Part II: The Impact of the National Labor Relations Act on the U.S. Labor Movement," *American Business Law Journal* 123, 126 (1995).

11. "Fleisher Is Eulogized," *New York Times,* May 9, 1989. D30, col. 1.

12. Howard Cosell, *What's Wrong with Sports* (New York: Pocketbooks, 1991).

13. See Murray Chass, "As Trade Unions Struggle, Their Sports Cousins Thrive," *New York Times,* September 5, 1994, 1; Kenneth A. Kovach, Patrizia Ricci, and Aladino Robles, "Is Nothing Sacred? Labor Strife in Professional Sports," *Business Horizons* (January 11, 1998): 34.

14. Martin Greenberg, *Sports Law Practice* (Charlottesville, Va.: Michie, 1993), vol. 1, 210.

15. See *Akron Beacon Journal,* August 23, 1998, cited in *Sports Business Daily,* vol. 4, no. 220 (August 24, 1998).

16. 26 *Statutes at Large* 209 (1890), as amended; 15 U.S.C. secs. 1 *et seq.*

17. 38 *Statutes at Large* 730 (1914), as amended; 15 U.S.C. sec. 12 *et seq.*

18. 15 U.S.C. at sec. 17.

19. 809 F. 2d 954 (2d Cir. 1987).

20. 675 F. Supp. 960 (D.N.J. 1987).

21. 45 F. 3d 684, 689 (2d Cir. 1995).

22. Major League Baseball's total attendance of 70,589,505 in 1998 is a 12 percent increase over 1997's 63,016,136. See *Sports Business Daily,* vol. 5, no. 18 (October 15, 1998).

Dennis A. Williams

Dennis A. Williams, formerly the director of the Learning Skills Center at Cornell University, currently directs the Center for Minority Educational Affairs and teaches English at Georgetown University. He is a frequent contributor to *Newsweek* magazine.

In this July 3, 1995, *Newsweek* article, Williams proposes a solution to the current problems with keeping top athletes in school rather than having them turn professional too early, before they have completed their education.

Robbing the Cradle

The first four picks in this week's NBA draft are expected to be underclassmen. Three of them have been in school for only two years. While the competitive wisdom of this baby boom may be questionable—some of the players are considered not quite ready for pro stardom—in educational terms the cradle-robbing trend is a disaster. More than ever, this year's draft exposes the poisonous relationship between college and professional sports.

As an educator, I often see the destructive power of the Hoop Dream. Granted, what I see in the nonscholarship Ivy League isn't the real thing; almost no one harbors serious NBA ambitions. Yet even here it is difficult for some recruited athletes to make up their minds about why they're really in school and what they will do when the ball stops bouncing.

But the young men who cashed in their books in the draft are not starry-eyed wanna-bes; they are highly talented players who will surely earn millions anyway when they get to the pros. So why the rush? The main reason may be that NBA owners, staggered by the multimillion-dollar contracts they are bestowing on untested players, are threatening to impose a rookie salary cap. In response students who've gone far enough in school to count to eight digits are opting to get theirs now.

There was a time when such premature gold-digging was not an option. The NBA declined to draft students whose college class had not graduated. That system demanded that collegiate stars wait their turn for pro careers. In the early 1970s, as paydays grew fatter, the NBA began allowing "hardship" exemptions to the draft rules so that financially strapped students could turn pro early.

By the 1980s, so many players were routinely claiming hardship status that the league dropped the pretense and simply allowed athletes to renounce their remaining college eligibility and grab the bucks. As a result, this year's draft crop is unusual only in the number of prominent youngsters and the brevity of their college tenure. The last three No. 1 picks in the NBA draft—Shaquille O'Neal, Chris Webber and Glenn Robinson—were all underclassmen. They've all been successful as pros, as the top pick should be. And their very success has helped to shatter the expectation that an outstanding college player should take school seriously.

The NCAA has been complicit in the dropout phenomenon by doggedly upholding the tradition, honored by time and not much else, of amateur purity. This quaint ideal predates the modern condition of colleges' serving as unabashed minor leagues for the pros. It also ignores the fact that basketball as well as football players generate enormous revenue for their schools. But in seeking to preserve college athletics from the taint of professionalism, the NCAA has devised a system guaranteed to make "student athletes" permanent nonstudents.

Unlike athletes, real college students frequently hold paying jobs. Many receiving financial aid are required to do so. Those who condone athletic dropouts often claim that some students are in effect majoring in basketball—that is the career they are going to school to prepare for. True enough, and college students regularly accept jobs in their industry of choice from paid summer internships to co-op work programs, without relinquishing their student status. (I worked for NEWSWEEK in college while practicing "amateur" journalism on collegiate publications.)

The solution is simple. Allow student prospects to be drafted by the pros—and remain eligible for college play. Let them negotiate a contract that will bind them to their future team for a standard three-year hitch. An insurance policy (paid by the pro team) could guard against income lost to injury. As with ROTC, the pro team could pick up the remainder of a player's college scholarship and pay a minimum living allowance, a minuscule investment for a multi-million-dollar asset. Even more radically, such an arrangement might stipulate that the draftee couldn't join the NBA until he actually graduated—reinforcing the idea that college is something more than a highly organized tryout camp.

Where is the conflict of interest if a player already committed to the New York Knicks competes against a future San Antonio Spur in an NCAA game? And how is that different from a student who has interned with IBM competing in class against a student who has a job offer from Apple? Because the primary beneficiary is the player, not the program, no school would have a recruiting advantage beyond what many now enjoy with promises of starting assignments, TV exposure and tournament appearances. Coaches would be assured that a recruited player who catches the pros' eyes would be around for four years instead of jumping ship as soon as he makes the cover of Sports Illustrated.

The "curse" of professionalism in this case is a self-serving illusion compared with the real problem of exploitation: students in school only to play ball, generating millions for their colleges and all too often leaving without their only tangible payment, a college degree. On the other hand, there may be some who don't want the degree—who don't really want to be in school in the first place. Let them try their luck landing NBA jobs directly, like Kevin Garnett, the high-school star who figures to be a high draft pick this week. Or they can work on their games in Rapid City or some other lower-level professional outpost. Colleges, meanwhile, can save their scholarships for students, including student athletes, as they should have been doing all along.   10

In order for any of this to work, the NCAA and its member institutions would have to pull their heads out of the sand and acknowledge that what's best for the athletic establishment is not necessarily what's best for students who play ball. And the NBA would have to agree, as it did in the past, to allow colleges to educate student athletes in return for developing their talent pool. It would be a tough sell, but worth the effort. Encouraging students to stay in school, as the NBA proclaims in its public-relations campaign, would be everyone's best move.

Susan Cahn

Susan Cahn is an Associate Professor of American History at the State University of New York–Buffalo. Her primary research focus has been twentieth-century U.S. history, specializing in gender and sexuality. Her most recent work looks at teenage sexuality in southern life for whites and blacks from the era of the New South to the Civil Rights period.

"'Cinderellas' of Sport: Black Women in Track and Field," comes from *Coming on Strong: Gender and Sexuality in 20th Century Women's Sports* (1994). In Chapter 5, Cahn discusses the black woman athlete's experience in track and field, with the attendant gender and racial stereotyping.

"Cinderellas" of Sport
Black Women in Track and Field

After World War II forced the cancellation of the 1940 and 1944 Olympic Games, Olympic competition resumed in 1948, hosted by London. Although England remained in a state of grim disrepair, the performance of three female track-and-field athletes shone through the bleakness of the postwar European setting. . . . The third athlete was Alice Coachman, a high jumper from Albany, Georgia. As a track and basketball star for Tuskegee Institute, Coachman had established a reputation as the premier black woman athlete of the 1940s. Her single gold medal in the high jump could not match the totals of Blankers-Koen or Ostermeyer. Nevertheless, it was historically significant, both as the only individual track-and-field medal won by U.S. women and, more important, as the first medal ever received by a woman of African descent. . . .

By mid-century the sport had a reputation as a "masculine" endeavor unsuited to feminine athletes. Few American women participated, and those who did endured caricatures as amazons and muscle molls. . . .

Among the athletes who withstood this kind of ridicule and continued to compete were African American women, who by mid-century had come to occupy a central position in the sport of track and field. Beginning in the late 1930s, black women stepped into an arena largely abandoned by middle-class white women, who deemed the sport unsuitable, and began to blaze a remarkable trail of national and international excellence. But their preeminent position in the sport had a double edge. On a personal level success meant opportunities for education, travel, upward mobility, and national or even international recognition. The accomplishments of such Olympians as Alice Coachman, Mae Faggs, or Wilma Rudolph also demonstrated to the public that African American women could excel in a nontraditional yet valued arena of American culture. However, viewed through the lens of commonplace racial prejudices, African American women's achievements in a "mannish" sport also reinforced disparaging stereotypes of black women as less womanly or feminine than white women.

. . . Along with basketball, boxing, football, and baseball, track was one of the most popular sports in black communities during the interwar years. African American men first gained fame as sprinters in the 1920s. Their reputation grew when Jesse Owens soundly defeated Hitler's vaunted Aryan superathletes in an astonishing triple-medal performance at the 1936 Berlin Olympics. The success of Owens and other black Olympians, including Ralph Metcalfe, Archie Williams, and Cornelius Johnson, challenged assumptions of white superiority and further popularized track and field among black sport fans and young athletes, including girls.

Although women's sport had clearly played second fiddle to men's in black communities, a significant sector of the population demonstrated interest in women's athletics, whether as fans, recreation leaders, or athletic sponsors. Additional encouragement came from African American educators and journalists, who expressed an acceptance of women's sport rare for their day. In 1939 prominent black physical educator E. B. Henderson agreed with others in his profession that the first priority of girls athletics should be health, not competition. But he went on to criticize "the narrowed limits prescribed for girls and women," arguing: "There are girls who ought to display their skill and national characteristic sport to a wider extent. These national exponents of women's sport are therefore to be commended for the prominence they have attained . . . The race of man needs the inspiration of strong virile womanhood."

Black women's own conception of womanhood, while it may not actively have encouraged sport, did not preclude it. A heritage of resistance to racial and sexual oppression found African American women occupying multiple roles as wageworkers, homemakers, mothers, and community leaders. In these capacities women earned respect for domestic talents, physical and emotional strengths, and public activism. Denied access to full-time homemaking and sexual protection, African American women did not tie femininity to a specific, limited set of activities and attributes defined as separate and opposite from masculinity. Rather, they created an ideal of womanhood rooted in the positive qualities they cultivated under adverse conditions: struggle, strength, family commitment, community involvement, and moral integrity.

Although these values were most often publicly articulated by women in positions of political and intellectual leadership, they were expressed in more mundane fashion by countless other women who helped build the infrastructure of black churches, community centers, club life, and entertainment—the institutions that sponsored athletic activities for girls and women. The work of earning a living and raising a family, often in near-poverty conditions, prevented the great majority of black women from participating in sport or any other time-consuming leisure activity. Yet by the 1930s and 1940s, as sport became a central component of African American college life and urban community recreation, women were included as minor but nevertheless significant players . . . .

. . . Tuskegee Institute formed the first highly competitive collegiate women's track team in 1929. . . .

Tuskegee was not alone among black colleges in encouraging women's track and field. Prairie View A & M of Texas added women's events to its annual relays in 1936, followed by Alabama State College. Florida A & M, Alcorn College in Mississippi, and Fort Valley State College of Georgia were among the schools attending early Tuskegee meets. . . .

African American track women compiled their record of excellence while suffering the constraints of racial and gender discrimination. In the late 1940s and early 1950s, efforts to end racial segregation in major league sports like baseball and basketball had made little impact on the extensive segregation in school, municipal, semipro, and minor league sport. The white press gave minimal coverage to black sports and seldom printed photographs of African American athletes. Black women found that sex discrimination, in the form of small athletic budgets, half-hearted backing from black school administrators, and the general absence of support from white-dominated sport organizations, further impeded their development.

The AAU policy of sponsoring white-only meets, where southern state laws permitted, posed another barrier. Southern black women's teams, excluded from regional competitions, were limited to black intercollegiate meets and the AAU national championships. . . .

Paradoxically, while black communities understood the athletic success of African American women to be a measure of black cultural achievement, it held a very different meaning when interpreted through the lens of white America's prevailing racial and sexual beliefs. . . .

Racialized notions of sexual virtue and feminine beauty were underpinned by another concept, that of the virile or mannish black female. African American women's work history as slaves, tenant farmers, domestics, and wageworkers disqualified them from standards of femininity defined around the frail or inactive female body. Their very public presence in the labor force exempted African

10

Americans from ideals of womanhood that rested on the presumed refinement and femininity of a privatized domestic arena. Failing to meet these standards, black women were often represented in the dominant culture as masculine females lacking in feminine grace, delicacy, and refinement.

The silence surrounding black athletes reflects the power of these stereotypes to restrict African American women to the margins of cultural life, occupying a status as distant "others." . . .

. . . While racism was only one factor contributing to the poor reputation of   15
women's track and field, the confluence of powerful racial and athletic stereotypes could only reinforce the stigmatized status of track women in general, and African American athletes in particular.

Peter King

Peter King has long been a journalist for *Sports Illustrated,* where he writes the popular column "Inside the NFL." He is also an analyst and reporter for CNN. A graduate of Ohio State University with a B.A. in journalism, King has also written five books on the NFL and the professional football player lifestyle.

In this February 7, 2000, *Sports Illustrated* article, King bemoans the lack of black coaches in the National Football League.

The NFL's Black Eye

Ted Cottrell has a dream. Since joining the NFL coaching fraternity as a linebackers coach with Kansas City in 1981, he has envisioned himself as boss of a team. Certainly he has the credentials. Cottrell, 52, has coached the linebackers and/or defensive line of the Chiefs, the USFL's New Jersey Generals, the Cardinals and the Bills. In '98 Buffalo promoted him to defensive coordinator; this season the Bills finished first in the NFL in team defense, allowing just 14.3 points and 252.8 yards per game. "I'm ready," Cottrell says. "I've learned from some of the best coaches in the game."

Ted Cottrell is black. His phone didn't ring in January, when the six teams with coaching vacancies conducted at least 15 interviews, only two of which were believed to have been with black candidates, new Kansas City linebackers coach Willie Shaw and Atlanta offensive line coach Art Shell. Unless the Saints hire a black coach (the front-runners are Dom Capers and Jim Haslett, both white), the NFL will continue its lily-white string of hires: Of the past 30 new head coaches, only one—Ray Rhodes in Green Bay last year—was black.

Commissioner Paul Tagliabue said last week that African Americans are "in the pipeline" for head coaching jobs. Really? What kind of pipeline excludes the coordinator of the league's best defense? Dave Wannstedt and Bill Belichick, both of whom had losing records in their previous head coaching stints, have taken over the Dolphins and the Patriots, respectively. Shell, who had a 54–38 record in six seasons as the Raiders' coach, has gone more than five years without a second shot. Rams offensive coordinator Mike Martz builds a potent unit and pops up on everyone's short list before re-upping with St. Louis in a deal that gives him the head job when Dick Vermeil retires. Cottrell builds a potent unit and makes no one's short list.

"I don't think it's overt racism," says Buccaneers coach Tony Dungy, one of two black NFL head coaches, along with the Vikings' Dennis Green, "but for some reason, Ted Cottrell isn't a household name and Mike Martz is. Very few of our owners would know who Ted Cottrell is."

Tagliabue says he can't force the 31 NFL owners—all white—to hire anybody. 5
But he offers no fresh ideas, nor does he do anything symbolic such as publicly chastising the owners. Meanwhile, Cottrell waits. "I guess we're just going to have to duplicate what we did with this year's defense next year," he says. "You can't get too discouraged. My father taught me never to give up my dreams."

Jon Entine

Jon Entine is an Emmy Award–winning news reporter and producer who frequently writes on sports. He produced the NBC documentary *Black Athletes: Fact and Fiction* [1989] and went on to publish *Taboo: Why Black Athletes Dominate Sports and Why We Are Afraid to Talk About It* (2000).

In "More Brains or More . . .," Entine debates whether cultural and environmental forces or genetic forces determine the success of the African American athlete.

More Brains or More . . .

Science on Trial

Despite intriguing scientific evidence and overwhelming on-the-field results, some academicians and journalists go through contortions to have us believe that tens of thousands of years of fighting for survival in radically differing climates in vastly different terrain has left no genetic footprint on Europeans, Africans, or Asians. This postmodernist ethic holds that human differences are for the most part "not in our genes," the title of a well-known polemic against linking behavior to biology. Even though group differences within species abound naturally in the animal kingdom and selective breeding may explain fleet-footed thoroughbreds and rats that can solve the most complicated of mazes, these critics contend that evolution cannot account for meaningful variations between human populations.

Postmodernist reasoning places science itself on trial. With all knowledge filtered through a cultural prism, relativity threatens to reign. In the extreme, race, ethnicity, religion, or even gender are reduced to mere linguistic or social constructs. Although people accept the role of genetics in individual differences—not many of us would expect to survive a one-on-one game of hoops with Allen Iverson—any evidence that innate differences exist between races or the sexes is considered inflammatory and inadmissible by the prevailing intellectual zeitgeist.

It is no surprise that the negative associations attached to the stereotype of black athletic success can sometimes overwhelm reason. In the United States, where the binding religion is a belief in equality, discussions of race take on metaphysical significance. For many, the concept of "equal in opportunity" has come to mean "identical in capacity": everyone is born with equal potential, with what amounts to a *tabula rasa* or empty slate on which life experiences write our biography. There are no differences, or at least none that can be traced to such ephemeral concepts as race, ethnicity, or nationality. A country nurtured on the myth that all people are created equal is understandably uncomfortable talking about innate differences, particularly when it comes to race.

So when blacks are referred to as physically superior or natural athletes, hackles are raised. What's the *real* and *underlying* agenda? If blacks are better at sports, are they better "sexual athletes"? Are they more brutish? Is black physical superiority inextricably connected to intellectual inferiority, like a seesaw—"more brains or more penis"?*

The belief that blacks rest at the bottom of an intellectual totem pole has merged with another stereotype, that of the "dumb jock." That's a somewhat recent and very North American belief. For much of modern history, physical and mental activity were inextricably linked but with a positive bias. The Greeks believed that physical fitness was essential to achieve a proper balance of mind and body, a tradition advocated during the Renaissance by Jean Jacques Rousseau in *Emile,* published in 1762. . . . Moreover, a great deal of evidence suggests that in fact there is a positive relationship between physical and mental fitness.

But the stereotype of the dumb jock, often tinged with racism, is far more pervasive, at least in the United States. In the 1960s, after the sports establishment finally opened its doors to young blacks, their immediate success triggered a reflexive backlash grounded in the lingering racist belief that blacks were not "smart enough" to handle the demands of "thinking" positions in sports, most notably quarterbacking in football. Whether consciously or as the result of deep-seated prejudices, it was believed that blacks could not cope in situations that placed a premium on strategy.

"Nobody had ever believed that a black man could handle the planning and pacing that it took to run any distance over the 800 meters," remembers John Velzian, a white Kenyan who directed the country's national track team for more than thirty years. That kind of presumptive prejudice hung heavily in the smoggy Mexico City air in the summer of 1968, when Jim Ryun faced off against Kip Keino, in the Olympic finals of the 1,500-meters. Of course, Keino annihilated the field.

5

---

* The phrase "more brains or more penis" has been attributed to J. Philippe Rushton, a controversial Canadian scientist who is convinced that a racial hierarchy in intelligence exists, with Asians at the top, whites in the middle, and blacks on the bottom. He supposedly uttered the phrase to summarize his scholarly work on race differences in an interview with Geraldo Rivera on the "Geraldo" show in 1989.

Such racial assumptions continue to haunt the sports world, and not only in the United States. Not too long ago it was the common wisdom in England that blacks would never become great soccer players because they lacked the "mental capacities." From Wales to South Africa, rugby is played almost exclusively by whites—except in New Zealand where an influx of Maori and Pacific Islanders has led to the kind of backroom whispers long familiar to black North Americans. According to some, they don't have "the discipline for physical conditioning. They lack the right kind of mental attitude. They just turn up and play."

In Australia, the outsized success of athletes with aboriginal genes in running, tennis, boxing, rugby, and Australian-rules football—Cathy Freeman, Tony Mundine, Lionel Rose, the Ella and Kracker brothers, Dale Shearer, and Evonne Goolagong Cawley—has led to under-the-breath comments about their supposed mental limitations. There is a widespread belief that their success can be explained away by their genetic advantage.

▓ Beyond "Racial Intelligence"

Rightly or wrongly, "racial intelligence" has become the subtext for all discussions   10
about athleticism. "The obsession with the natural superiority of the black male athlete is an attempt to demean all of us," charges sportswriter Ralph Wiley. Beneath expressions of admiration, he avers, public fascination serves a less noble fixation. "The search for genetic explanations would deny black athletes the right to dream, to aspire, to strive. It suggests that black men cannot set goals, which implies the struggle to survive, to triumph. That is the crux of the question. Our answer should be obvious."

"[Blacks] didn't [become stars] because they were smart," adds Brooks Johnson sarcastically. "They're just naturally good . . . they're just naturally fast." His eyes, usually inviting and friendly, focus into narrow brown darts. "That's the racist attitude that blacks are naturally lazy, so anything they get they don't get from hard work, they get because God just gave 'em the right gene."

Johnson is disturbed that even many blacks are seduced by what he believes is the pabulum of the belief in black physical superiority. "You have to understand that the whole secret of racism and sexism and all these other 'isms' is that the people who are oppressed end up spouting the party line of the oppressor. The whole idea is to convince black people that they're superior in some areas—sports—and therefore by definition must be inferior in other areas. It's interesting that the white people always have the best talent in the areas that pay the best money."

Most politically liberal white sociologists are equally adamant. "Isn't it strange," writes Richard Lapchick, founder of Northeastern University's Center for the Study of Sport in Society, "that no one feels very compelled to look for physical reasons for white dominance in sports?" University of Texas sociologist John Hoberman, who has written a number of cogent books on race and sports, dismisses genetic theories as "Euro-American white racialist thinking . . . quasi-scientific . . . irresponsible . . . sensational . . . scientifically invalid" and "tabloid science." Feminist sports sociologist Laurel Davis, an assistant professor of sociology at

Springfield College in Massachusetts, contends that "reports that purport to show black genetic advantages in sports [are] built upon racist assumptions" and reinforce "white power structures."

Neither blacks nor whites have totally clean hands in this matter of racializing intelligence. Consider black racial romanticism and Afrocentrism, which have turned athletic accomplishment into a symbol of black superiority. At the furthest extreme, so-called melanin scholars, including Leonard Jeffries at City College in New York, Wade Nobles at San Francisco State University, Asa Hilliard at Georgia State University, and retired professor Yosef A. A. ben-Jochannan, promote the notion that the pigment responsible for skin color acts as an energy sponge, endowing dark-skinned peoples with everything from superior intelligence to musical ability to superior speed. According to these scholars, black is a marker of all things advanced. Africa is home to the "Sun People" and Europe the "Ice People." Extreme Afrocentrists go so far as to claim that the ripest fruits of Western civilization, from philosophy to science, art and literature, originated in Africa, not Greece and Rome. Hundreds of years of Anglo-Saxon arrogance may make these ruminations understandable but no less bizarre and historically unsupportable.

The quest to understand intelligence has probably inspired more bad science than any other intellectual quest of modern times. "All of this has a connection with a very disagreeable history," acknowledged George Will, political analyst, long-suffering Chicago Cubs fan, and author of two best-selling books on baseball. "The decent, democratic American impulse is to say we have a lot of pluralism in this country but none in the chromosomes." 15

Politics threatens to overwhelm the science. It is striking that so many hardened critics of the study of human biodiversity are themselves so willing to play the race card. "The danger that interracial comparisons will be inhibited by considerations of political correctness," writes *Nature* in an article questioning the propriety of pursuing the issue of racial differences in sports, "is less serious than that interracial studies will be wrongly used."

Is it necessary to walk the edge of censorship to protect us against ourselves? Over reaction may be as dangerous as recklessness. The fear of even sounding racist has conspired to stifle debate and suppress legitimate scientific inquiry. Anyone who attempts to breach this taboo to study or even discuss what might be behind the growing performance gap between black and white athletes must be prepared to run a gauntlet of public scorn, survival not guaranteed.

"When you say you want to look at [differences between black and white athletes], you get labeled a redneck," notes Ken McFadden, a retired professor of anatomy from the University of Alabama. "But it's nothing to do with racial discrimination. Studying athletes will tell us what bodies are capable of, and I don't think people should get upset just because you are comparing different racial groups. . . ."

The controversy has put some of the most thoughtful black intellectuals on the spot. "The phenomenon of African Americans performing better than whites in certain areas does exist, and it is worth studying," comments David Hunter, head of the department of health and physical education at Hampton University in Virginia. Although he remains convinced that much of the over representation in sports by blacks can be explained by sociological factors, mounting genetic and physiological evidence has seeded his curiosity. "If we say, 'This might cause problems, let's not study it,' we simply perpetuate whatever thoughts we've had."

Arthur Ashe, Jr., the first black man to win the U.S. Open, Australian Open, and Wimbledon singles tennis titles, wrestled with this conundrum for much of the last decade of his life while writing his groundbreaking *A Hard Road to Glory,* which catalogues the history of black accomplishment in sports. He accumulated thousands of anecdotes of how cultural and environmental forces had shaped black success in sports. Still, Ashe couldn't put the genetic issue to rest. When asked about what he had come to believe after years of research, whether blacks had a physical advantage, Ashe responded deliberately: "The results are outstanding, nothing short of stellar. Sociology can't explain it. I want to hear from the scientists. Until I see some numbers [to the contrary], I have to believe that we blacks have something that gives us an edge.

"Damn it," he sighed, frustrated at the political incorrectness of his own beliefs. "My heart says 'no,' but my head says 'yes.' " So which is right—Ashe's head or his heart?

Harry Edwards

Harry Edwards is a Professor of Sociology at the University of California-Berkeley, and a consultant for the San Francisco 49ers. He has been a sports activist for over 30 years and played an instrumental role in organizing the revolt of African American athletes at the Mexico City Olympics in 1968. Dr. Edwards has written extensively on sports and society and lectured on the role of athletics in the black community. Author of *The Revolt of the Black Athlete* (1970) and *The Struggle That Must Be* (1980), he is a teacher with unparalleled involvement with what he teaches inside and outside the classroom.

In the following essay, Edwards recommends community and sports programs as means by which we can provide reconnections to alienated black youths.

Crisis of Black Athletes on the Eve of the 21st Century

For more than two decades I have been adamant in my contention that the dynamics of black sports involvement, and the blind faith of black youths and their families in sport as a prime vehicle of self-realization and social-economic advancement, have combined to generate a complex of critical problems for black society. At the root of these problems is the fact that black families have been inclined to push their children toward sports career aspirations, often to the neglect and detriment of other critically important areas of personal and cultural development.

Those circumstances have developed largely because of: (1) a long-standing, widely held, racist, and ill-informed presumption of innate, race-linked black athletic superiority and intellectual deficiency; (2) media propaganda portraying sports as a broadly accessible route to black social and economic mobility; and (3) a lack of comparably visible, high-prestige black role models beyond the sports arena. The result is a single-minded pursuit of sports fame and fortune that has spawned an institutionalized triple tragedy in black society: the tragedy of thousands upon thousands of black youths in obsessive pursuit of sports goals that the overwhelming majority of them will never attain; the tragedy of the personal and cultural underdevelopment that afflicts so many successful and unsuccessful black sports aspirants; and the tragedy of cultural and institutional underdevelopment throughout black society at least in some part as a consequence of the drain in talent potential toward sports and away from other vital areas of occupational and career emphasis, such as medicine, law, economics, politics, education, and technical fields.

Today there has developed a serious decline not only in the fact, but in the perception and even the hope of mainstream life choices and life chances for an increasing number of black youths. One-way integration and the resulting exit of the black middle-class from the traditional black community has contributed to a spiraling deterioration in institutional viability in many black communities—a deterioration encompassing the functionality of the family, education, the economy, the political infrastructure, and even the black church. This unfortunate situation has combined with the ongoing legacies of anti-black racism and discrimination in America, the erosion or elimination of civil rights gains such as affirmative action, and structural economic shifts in the broader society to generate the epidemics of crime, drugs, violence, gangs and gang warfare, and a pervasive despair, malaise, and hopelessness that now afflict broad sectors of black society.

In that environment, literally thousands of young black people have institutionally, culturally, and interpersonally disconnected: they attend school only infrequently, if at all; they have given up any hope of ever holding a legitimate job or of being otherwise productively involved in the mainstream economy; they respect only their closest peers and seek only their peers' respect; and, in many instances, they see no future for themselves or their generation and have little expectation of living beyond their teens or twenties. Some go so far as to pick out the coffin and the clothes in which they expect to be buried.

Predictably sports participation opportunities for those youths have also deteriorated. Playgrounds, sandlots, parks, and even backyard recreational sites in many instances have been taken over by drug dealers, or they have become battlegrounds in gang disputes, or they have simply become too dangerously exposed to eruptions of violence to be safely used. Cutbacks in educational budgets and shifts in funds from school athletic, physical education, and recreation programs to concerns deemed more vital in these fiscally strapped, troubled communities (including campus and classroom security) have further narrowed sports participation opportunities. Even where interscholastic sports participation opportunities have survived, security problems and fears of violence and other disruptions in an increasing number of cases have restricted both the scheduling of events and spectator attendance.

In the face of such discouraging circumstances, many black youths have opted to go with the flow, exchanging team colors for gang colors or simply dropping out of everything and chillin'. They move utterly beyond the reach and scope of established institutional involvements and contacts—save the criminal justice system, hospital emergency services, and the mortuary services industry.

The social circumstances facing young black males are particularly germane here. Nationally at least a quarter of all black males aged 16 to 29 are under the control of the courts; in some states (such as California) this figure is approaching one-third of the black males in this age range. One-third of all the deaths in this group nationally are homicides (usually perpetrated by other black males), and suicide ranks only behind homicides and accidents as a cause of death. Moreover, since the age range 16 to 29 represents the prime years of self-development and career establishment, it should be no surprise that black males are declining as a proportion of the population in virtually every institutional setting (e.g., higher education, the workforce, the church) save the prison system.

Predictably, black sports involvement is threatened as well. As alluded to earlier, developments at the intersection of race, sports, and education have over the years generated a situation wherein increasing numbers of black youths have focused their efforts on athletic achievement only to find themselves underdeveloped academically and unable to compete in the classroom.

Nonetheless, their talents were so critical to the success of revenue producing sports programs—most notably basketball and football—at major colleges and universities competing at the Division I level that those athletes were typically recruited out of high school or junior college notwithstanding their educational deficiencies, with the predictable result of widespread black athlete academic underachievement and outright failure. It was this tragedy and the attention it generated from sports activists and the media from the late 1960s into the 1980s that ultimately prompted the most far-reaching reform efforts in modern collegiate sports history.

But because black athletes' academic problems are in large part rooted in 10 and intertwined with black youths' societal circumstances more generally there can be no effective resolution of the educational circumstances of black athletes at any academic level except in coordination with commensurate efforts in society. In fact, to the extent that remedial efforts neglect such a coordinated dual approach, they are virtually guaranteed to exacerbate rather than better the situation of the black athletes that they impact.

Indeed, that has been the impact of much recent activity aimed at academic reform in athletics. At the high school level, the institution of more demanding academic requirements for athletic participation prompted many black athletes who subsequently have been declared academically ineligible to drop out of high school altogether.

At the collegiate level the establishment of Proposition 48, officially National Collegiate Athletic Association (N.C.A.A.) Bylaw 14.3, has had even more negative consequences. Proposition 48 required that before he could participate in Division I college varsity sports, a student had to have a minimum grade point average (GPA) of 2.0 in at least 11 courses in core subjects in high school and a minimum SAT score of 700 (ACT score of 17). The rule was instituted to counteract academically lenient recruitment practices, and though the specific requirements mandated under the regulation have been adjusted to accommodate various sliding scales of eligibility over the last decade, the essential thrust and intent of regulatory efforts remains the same today—as does their disparate impact on black athletes.

In the first two years of Proposition 48 enforcement (1984–1986), 92 percent of all academically ineligible basketball players and 84 percent of academically ineligible football players were black athletes. As late as 1996, the overwhelming majority of Proposition 48 casualties were still black student-athlete prospects. Despite attempts to the contrary such horrifically disproportionate numbers cannot be justified on grounds that ineligible athletes would not have graduated anyway. Richard Lapchick, director of the Center for the Study of Sports in Society, reports that if Proposition 48 had been in use in 1981, 69 percent of black male scholarship athletes would have been ineligible to participate in sports as freshmen, but 54 percent of those athletes eventually graduated.

Complicating the effects of Proposition 48 is Proposition 42, which was passed by the N.C.A.A. in 1989 and was designed to strengthen Proposition 48 by denying athletes who failed to meet Proposition 48 eligibility requirements all financial aid during the freshman year. Proposition 42 effectively prevented prospective scholarship athletes who did not qualify under Proposition 48 and who could not pay their own college expenses from attending college at all. Of course, this regulation disproportionately affected black athletes, since they numbered disproportionately among Proposition 48 casualties.

In 1990, following widespread objections to the draconian nature of Proposition 42 (most notably the protest efforts of Georgetown basketball coach John Thompson), Proposition 42 was modified to allow student-athletes who were "partially qualified" (i.e., who met either minimum grade point average or test score requirements) to receive non-athletic, need-based financial aid during the freshman year. Those who did not qualify under either test score or grade point average requirements still could not receive any type of financial aid. Still, black athlete prospects, always among the poorest and neediest of athlete recruits, continued to bear the brunt of the measure's negative impact. 15

It is now clear that the greatest consequence of Proposition 42, and similar regulations has been to limit the opportunities—both educational and athletic— that would otherwise be available to black youths. Those measures were neither conceived nor instituted with due consideration of black youths' circumstances beyond the academy and the sports arena. In consequence, while there has been some minor improvement in such concerns as black athlete college graduation rates (an increase estimated to be about 8 percent and possibly due as much to improved academic support services for black student-athletes after they arrive on college campuses as to any pre-recruitment screening function of propositions 48 or 42), those results must be weighed against the profoundly negative cost of lost opportunities and more subtle consequences such as the stigmatizing of black youths as Proposition 48 cases or casualties.

The diminution of opportunities for black youths to succeed at the high school and collegiate levels must inevitably register and be manifest in all sports and at all levels traditionally accessible to black athletes in numbers. Already many high schools are unable to field teams or schedule dependable competition. Beyond the high school ranks, in recent years there has been disturbing evidence of a downward trend in the statistics of virtually every skill category in Division I collegiate basketball: team and individual points per game averages; individual and team field goal percentages; individual and team free throw percentages; and assists.

Both college coaches and officials, and the media, tend to assume that such declining performance figures are due mostly to early entry into the professional ranks by star collegiate players. Many star players leave college after only one or two years of collegiate competition, and, in some instances, talented high school players skip college altogether and go directly into the National Basketball Association (NBA). But the NBA itself appears to be slumping statistically and, in any event, the league shows no evidence of having benefited from any would-be talent windfall.

In 1997, the average NBA team scored only 96.7 points, the lowest regular season league average since the 24-second shot clock was instituted. Moreover, in the 1996–1997 season the average age of players in the NBA was the highest in league history—older players are apparently able to hold on to their jobs and stay around longer because younger players are not able to displace them. Thus, regardless of how many collegiate basketball players are leaving or skipping college for the professional ranks, they are having no discernible impact as basketball talents at the professional level.

Other trends that individually would seem of little significance appear more troubling when considered within the context of emerging trends in black sports involvement. For example, black attendance at sporting events other than basketball and football games is virtually nonexistent. As ticket prices continue to increase and more leagues and teams choose "pay per view" and cable television broadcast options, ever fewer numbers of blacks will be watching even basketball and football either in person or on television. Those trends are likely to affect most severely people abiding in the lower and working-class strata of black society that have traditionally produced the greater proportion of black athlete talent. With school and community sports and recreation programs and opportunities on the decline, declining personal access and exposure to elite athletic performances virtually guarantees that both the interest and the involvement of that population in sport are likely to wane. [20]

In this regard, the character of black involvement in baseball may be a harbinger of the future of black involvement in sports overall. Though major league baseball teams claim not to keep track of the race of their players and other personnel, it is estimated that approximately 18 percent of major league players are black. (In 1996, in a team by team count, I arrived at figures of 14 to 17 percent, depending on how some players of Caribbean or black Latino heritage counted themselves.) Eighteen percent is approximately the same black player representation in the major leagues as ten years ago.

Relatively speaking, this stagnation in the proportion of black players in the major leagues may be the good news. It has been fairly well established that, for the most part, in urban areas (where over 80 percent of the black population lives) black adolescents and teenagers no longer either follow baseball or play it. Few black adults take their children to baseball games; in fact only about one percent of all major league baseball tickets sold are bought by blacks. Indeed, on opening day of the 1997 baseball season—a day which marked the fiftieth anniversary of Jackie Robinson breaking the color barrier against black participation in the major leagues—Jackie Robinson's former team had the same number of black players on its roster as it did the day that he first stepped on the field in a Dodger uniform—ONE!

All considered, unless steps are taken to reverse present trends in both sport and society, we could be witnessing the end of what in retrospect might well come to be regarded as the golden age of black sports participation. We are, quite simply disqualifying, jailing, and burying an increasing number of our potential black football players, basketball players, baseball players, and other prospective athletes—right along with our potential black lawyers, doctors, and teachers.

In the past I have resoundingly rejected the priority of playbooks over textbooks because of the triple tragedy scenario outlined above. So long as the traditional black community and the larger society—particularly in the wake of hard-won civil rights advances and opportunities—effectively created and sustained some realistic broad spectrum access to legitimate means of personal and career development for the black youths in question (that is, access beyond the dream of sports stardom), criticisms and admonitions warning of a black overemphasis on sports participation and achievement not only were justified but necessary and even obligatory correctives to misguided attitudes and dispositions toward sports in black society. But today there is no option but to recognize that for increasing legions of black youths, the issue is neither textbooks nor playbooks—the issue is survival, finding a source of hope, encouragement, and support in developing lives and building legitimate careers and futures.

Without question, the ultimate resolution to this situation must be the overall institutional development of black communities and the creation of greater opportunity for black youths in the broader society. In the meantime, however, if community and school sports programs can provide a means of reconnecting with at least some of those black youths who we have already lost and strengthening our ties with those who, by whatever miracle of faith and tenacity, have managed to hold on to hope and to stay the course, then those programs and the youths involved deserve our strongest support and endorsement. 25

Therefore, I now say that we must reconstitute and broaden access to school sports programs. We must create secure and supervised playgrounds, park recreation areas, and community sports facilities; open school sports facilities for supervised weekend community use and midnight basketball, volleyball, tennis, bowling, badminton, swimming, and other sports opportunities; recruit counselors, teachers, people trained in the trades, health care professionals, and religious leaders to advise, mentor, and tutor young people at those sports sites; network with corporate and government agencies to establish apprenticeship and job opportunities; and bring in students of sport and society who understand and can articulate the applicability of the great lessons and dynamics of black youths' sports success and achievement to their life circumstances and goals more generally.

Far from de-emphasizing or abandoning sport, or simply allowing our involvement to wane, black people must now more than ever intelligently, constructively, and proactively pursue sports involvement. We cannot afford to wait passively for better times or allow ourselves to be swept and herded along in the flow of events and developments at the interface of race, sports, and society. We must understand the forces threatening black sports participation while also recognizing that black sports participation need not become an obsession or preoccupation.

Today it is desirable, even necessary that black youths and black society as a whole continue to harbor dreams of achieving excellence in sports—there is much to be learned and gained from both the challenges of sports competition and the experiences of meeting those challenges. But all involved must learn to dream with their eyes open, always remaining fully cognizant of participation's pitfalls no less than its positive possibilities, of its potential as a dead end trap no less than its promise as a vehicle for outreach and advancement. As in the past, the responsibility for perpetually mapping the sports terrain and for the ongoing acculturation and education of black youths as they seek to productively navigate the possibilities of athletic achievement fall most heavily upon black people themselves.

In the final analysis, exploiting black youths' overemphasis on sports participation and achievement may be our only remaining avenue for guiding increasing numbers of them out of circumstances that today lead to even more devastating destructiveness and a greater waste of human potential than that which I, and others, have long decried in connection with unrealistic black sports aspirations. Not at all coincidentally it could also salvage the golden age of black sports participation.

John Edgar Wideman

John Edgar Wideman, born in Washington, D.C., but raised in Pittsburgh, is one of this century's best writers. He was captain of his University of Pennsylvania basketball team and graduated Phi Beta Kappa with a degree in English in 1963. The second African American to become a Rhodes Scholar, Wideman studied eighteenth-century philosophy at Oxford University. He currently teaches at the University of Massachusetts, Amherst. His daughter, Jamila, played as a point guard in the WNBA. Wideman has written several novels, including *Glance Away* (1967), *Hurry Home* (1969), *The Lynchers* (1973), *Sent for You Yesterday* (1983), *Philadelphia Fire* (1990), *The Cattle Killing* (1996), and *Two Cities* (1998); nonfiction, including *Brothers and Keepers* (1984) and *Fatheralong* (1994); and the short-story collections *Damballah* (1981), *Fever* (1989), *The Stories of John Edgar Wideman* (1992), and *All Stories Are True* (1992). His awards include the PEN/Faulkner Award in 1984 for *Sent for You Yesterday,* a National Book Award nomination in 1984 for *Brothers and Keepers,* the Lannan Award in 1991, the PEN/Faulkner Award and the American Book Award in 1991 for *Philadelphia Fire,* and the MacArthur Foundation Award in 1993.

In this excerpt from his latest publication, *Hoop Roots* (2001), Wideman recalls the skill of a playground legend as well as the stigma connected to his body type and color.

Hoop Roots

See. Didn't I tell you, man. Brother can jump to the moon but can't play a lick. Never could, never will. A hard head, you hear what I'm saying . . . hardheaded like you used to be till we schooled your youngblood ass . . . and I find myself back in the middle of a sentence that hasn't ended since the last time I blew into town, kicking back on Saturday morning with Cato and Gary and Craig and Jay and all the absent others summoned by the talk, in the bleachers, in Westinghouse Park or Mellon or East Liberty, gearing up, taping up ankles, bracing knees, binding hamstrings, Ace bandages, spandex, Ben Gay, Advil, eyeglasses secured by Croakies, waiting our turn to trot out for winners, our turn to hobble back after absorbing a beating, winners again on the sidelines as we fire up healing patter right where we left it simmering.

Nothing changes except not long ago I ran into Ed Fleming not on the playground but in a funeral parlor. How long since I'd seen him last the first question in my mind after I almost didn't recognize the broad-shouldered man in a dark suit surrounded by a cluster of mourners just inside the entrance of a viewing parlor down the hall from the one in which my brother's son Omar, victim of a gang killing, was laid out in Warden's. Ed Fleming a wee bit heavier, thicker than I remembered, but sure enough him, the big eyes, round face, dark skin, small, trim mustache, the intimidating poise and quiet reserve of his expression, a stern mask that disappears in a second when he recognizes an old acquaintance and beams. Bigger, yes, but definitely Ed Fleming. Solid, compact, that gliding, effortless go and flow in his movements. Cat quick. Cat eyes mobile, always scanning his surroundings. Sounding his options. Alert for whatever might be required next, fighting through a pick, planting an elbow in somebody's chest, tensing himself for a collision with a two-hundred-fifty-pound body hurtling toward him full speed. Hand fighting, chest bumping. Punishing in his own swift, sure way the beefy, six-foot-seven opposing forward, a cheap-shot bully who's been hissing nigger this and nigger that just loud enough to be heard above his bad kielbasa breath the whole first half.

Ed Fleming's body type and color a stigma, a danger to the bearer for five hundred years in racist America. Convict body, field hand body, too unadulterated African, too raw, too black, too powerful and quick and assertive for most whites and some colored folks to feel comfortable around until Michael Jordan arrived and legitimated Ed Fleming's complexion and physique, mainstreaming them, blunting the threatening edge, commodifying the Jordan look, as if the physical, sexual potency of a dark, streamlined, muscular body could be purchased, as if anybody, everybody—Swede, Korean, Peruvian, Croat, New Englander—could be like Mike.

Before Renoir painted them, Marcel Proust said, there were no Renoir women in Paris. But after Renoir painted them, you saw them everywhere. In his novel *Remembrance of Things Past,* Proust goes on to compare the great artist to an oculist who teaches his patients to see in a new fashion. Until a ubiquitous, saturating ad campaign established Michael Jordan as a paragon of male beauty, male style, male potency and achievement, a dark body like his was not deemed particularly attractive by most Americans. If acknowledged at all by either blacks or whites, Jordan's physical type usually was cast in a negative light, served as a sort of grown-up Sambo caricature or a dark blot on a mug shot. Like a stealth bomber, a body like Jordan's carried out its business below the cultural radar. Then, thanks to Nike among others, you began to see MJ everywhere. Suddenly everybody wanted to look like him. Ad after ad cashed in on the paradox of white fascination with blackness: the obdurate otherness, invisibility, and mandated inaccessibility of blackness versus its transparency, seductiveness, and omnipresence.

Though chattel slavery is a thing of the past, black bodies still occupy the auction block. And not just any old negro body, but bionic miracle machines like Michael Jordan's. This news brought customers from across the globe running. Anybody with the price of the ticket could become a shareholder. Buy the pleasure of watching the value of your stock and yourself in your MJ cap or sneakers or sweatsuit skyrocket as MJ leads the Chicago Bulls to another NBA world championship. This modern, media-driven, vicarious, virtual possession of a black body is better than buying a slave, with all the attendant burdens of ownership. By simply copping certain trademarked booty, you could choose if and when you wished to be like Mike. Or, to be more precise, you could choose to appropriate and identify with only those black body parts you desired (dismember and reconfigure the black body) and leave the rest, the negative, bad parts, alone. Unless you found a little touch of the gangster rap, drug, hoodlum deviancy nice; then you could turn your cap backward, droop your baggy, hip-hop trousers below the crack of your ass, represent some of that outlaw stuff too. Represent "bad" without worrying about paying dues bad black boys pay—poverty, jail, apartheid, early graves. Or so the deal seemed to promise.

Then somebody noticed that the black body's power to stir desire and sell things transcended any individual black pitchperson. If even the historically despised, abused black male body, the threatening, agile stereotype of rapist, runaway slave, athlete, criminal, could exert a fatal attraction, let's see what we can sell with other black bodies, light and dark, male and female, fat and slim, the beige ones you have to look at twice to decide their *race*. Highlighted and showcased in the Africanized entertainment subculture of contemporary American popular music, dance, fashion, and sport, where black body pleasure, black body performance, black body perfection are deployed to stand for those magical transformations certain products promise their consumers, it's no wonder the black body is irresistible, unforgettable.

Just as centuries ago the commerce in black bodies fostered a new worldwide economic order, the commerce in images of blackness during the last decade has accelerated globalization of the marketplace. Nike, to cite one obvious example, piled up enormous profits by building an international network of factories and outlets to exploit the allure of blackness, its status as contraband, as a primal site of guilt and pleasure, of longing and dread. In spite of or perhaps because of the shameful history of what we call "race relations," our collective imagination carries forward both the empathetic image of the long-suffering black Christ on the cross of white oppression and the black body as a field of dreams where whites can play out erotic fantasies. Again, is it in spite of or because of a reigning Christian ethos proclaiming such oppression, such desires, to be unacceptable? Today, given its proven track record as a desired commodity spawning other desirable commodities, the black body is too hot to touch, too hot not to touch. Perhaps the old African American folk saying is as relevant for cultures as for individuals: *Go black and you never go back.*

Ed Fleming's wide, sloping shoulders are exaggerated by a fashionable suit jacket tailored so any wearer of the style appears constructed the way Ed Fleming actually is under the rich fabric. He's a bit more rounded now, his shoulders thick from years of keeping opponents boxed out beneath the backboards, years of tensing his upper torso, especially the ridge of muscle across the top of his back, to receive blows, weight, or coiled for a leap—quick, high, balanced—when the basketball rebounds off the glass. Head held high, long arms poised comfortably at his sides, he appears taller than he is. With what would be in today's NBA a guard-size body, Ed Fleming in the fifties had mastered a big man's game. Three inches shorter, less elongated than Michael Jordan, Ed Fleming at about six-foot-three was a forward, an inside player his entire college and professional career. The sort of smart banger, hustler, who contests every free ball. Persistent, fearless, he picks up the loose change most players treat as below their notice, chump change floating around at unspectacular moments in a game. He earns small victories in pitched skirmishes peripheral to the main action, battles unrecorded on stat sheets or in scorebooks, relentless because he understands that the little stuff accumulates and determines who wins or loses close games, who winds up winning championships.

He played for very white teams in very white cities—Niagara University, Rochester Royals, Syracuse Nats—in very white leagues during an era when color as much as any other physical attribute decided the position—guard, forward, center— you'd play, determined, in most cases, if you were dark and not seven feet tall, that you wouldn't play at all in college or the pros.

How long. How long had it been since we'd seen each other last the question 10 I decided not to ask Ed Fleming in Warden's because Warden's Funeral Home already steeped in lost chances, lost causes, lost time, time nobody gets back, those heartrending, thuggish truths about time you don't need to waste more precious time bemoaning in Warden's. Warden's where everybody winds up when time's up. So I told myself, Forget about how long. Go on and enjoy your little chat with this man while there's still time. Leave time alone and maybe it will leave you alone a bit longer till you get past this season of dying. Sons dying before their fathers. Nephews gone before their uncles. A country dying before it grows past its adolescent bluster, selfishness, callousness, and cruelty.

Media Resources

The Jackie Robinson Story [1950]. Directed by Alfred E. Green. 76 minutes. Eagle-Lion Studios. This film stars Jackie Robinson himself.

The Great White Hope [1970]. Directed by Martin Ritt. 103 minutes. 20th Century Fox. This is the story of Jack Jefferson Johnson's bout with the racism and hatred of mid-century white America. He is not only the first black heavyweight contender, he is also in love with a white woman.

The Bingo Long Traveling All Stars and Motor Kings [1976]. Directed by John Bedham. 110 minutes. Universal Studio. This film is about the life of players in the Negro Baseball League.

The Greatest [1977]. Directed by Tom Gries, Monte Hellman. 103 minutes. Columbia Pictures. Muhammad Ali plays himself impressively in this biography of his remarkable boxing career.

The Hitter [1979]. Directed by Christopher Leitch. 90 minutes. USA. In this film about a man making his fortune by hustling one way or another, he does bare-knuckles fighting, a game he had quit after killing an opponent years before.

Cool Runnings [1993]. Directed by Ferd Sebastien. 109 minutes. Paramount Home Video. This comedy is about the Jamaican bobsledding team that competed in the 1992 Olympics.

Hoop Dreams [1994]. Directed by Steve James II. 170 minutes. This documentary follows the development of two African American boys playing basketball from high school through college and on the road to going professional.

When We Were Kings [1996]. Directed by Leon Gast. This documentary details the 1974 heavyweight championship bout in Zaire between champion George Foreman and underdog challenger Muhammad Ali.

The Great White Hype [1996]. Directed by Reginald Hudlin. 109 minutes. 20th Century Fox. Hudlin presents a satire on the fight game.

He Got Game [1998]. Directed by Spike Lee. 131 minutes. Buena Vista Studios. This movie is about the pressures on a star high school basketball player.

Any Given Sunday [2000]. Directed by Oliver Stone. 157 minutes. Warner Bros. Football players talk about their careers and their lives in this film.

The Legend of Bagger Vance [2000]. Directed by Robert Redford. 127 minutes. Dreamworks Studio. This movie is about the relationship between a golfer and a caddy with hints of extrasensory wisdom.

Love and Basketball [2000]. Directed by Gina Prince-Bythewood. 124 minutes. In this movie, two young basketball stars become lovers but also face the travails of high school and beyond in their sport.

Remember the Titans [2000]. Directed by Boaz Yakin. 113 minutes. Walt Disney Studios. This film is based on a true story about the integration of a high school football team.

Ali [2001]. Directed by Michael Mann. 158 minutes. Columbia Pictures. Based on the period from 1964 to 1974, this film depicts the most tumultuous decade of Muhammad Ali's life.

CHAPTER 4

Justice/Just-Us?

T he legal system of the United States is built upon a history of laws, the majority of which protect the rights of the individual. However, in order to protect the institution of slavery during the seventeenth, eighteenth, and nineteenth centuries, laws were promulgated that directly abridged the rights of Africans forced to become chattel. Repealing these laws was a monumental struggle for civic-minded Americans. From the local and state laws that restricted the rights of free blacks and slaves to national policy, such as the Fugitive Slave Act of 1850, and to the miscegenation laws that endured until the 1970s, readers will learn the complexities that race imposes on due process.

How to negotiate justice in a fair and equitable manner (justice for all) is the focus of Chapter 4, "Justice/Just-Us." The writers in the first three selections give a historical perspective of the issue. David Walker provokes the reader with his assessment of the proponents of slavery (representatives of church and state) during the eighteenth century. Scott Malcomson analyzes the development of segregation in American life in the eighteenth and nineteenth centuries. Ida B. Wells-Barnett reports on the local, state, and federal governments' tolerance for lynching well into the twentieth century.

Next, Derrick Bell creates a parable to delineate the benefits derived from the desegregation of public schools and to expose the many tactics used to thwart the implementation. Sonia Sanchez, Keith Meeks, and Lt. Arthur Doyle describe abuses of power by law enforcement officials on the local level. In a poem, Sanchez mourns the fiery death of people and destruction of a city block when citizens and the police clash. Keith Meeks describes the impact of racial profiling on a college basketball team when they go to a shopping mall. A retired police officer, Lt. Doyle, discusses police brutality in the New York Police Department.

Johnnie Cochran and Mary Fisher in their selections discuss abuses by federal law enforcement agents. In 1970, Cochran defended a Black Panther, Geronimo

131

Pratt, falsely convicted of murder. Pratt was imprisoned for almost 27 years before evidence was made available that FBI agents and city police framed him. Fisher investigates the preponderance of political corruption probes by federal agencies between 1981 and 1993 that targeted black elected officials.

Finally, Carl Rowan discusses the role that race played in the appointment of Clarence Thomas to the Supreme Court. In spite of contentious hearings and lukewarm endorsements, the Senate Judiciary Committee in 1991 confirmed the nomination. Rowan concludes with an assessment of Thomas's voting record in regard to individual rights.

Although the authors of these selections often take a definitive position on controversial topics, they nevertheless include the perspectives of others.

David Walker

David Walker (1785–1830), considered one of the first African American freedom fighters, exhorted his people to revolt against oppression. A bounty of $10,000 was placed on his head following his publication of *David Walker's Appeal in Four Articles: Together with a Preamble, to the Coloured Citizens of the World, but in Particular and Very Expressly, to Those of the United States of America* (1829). He died of poisoning after the third edition was printed.

This selection is the preamble to his *Appeal,* in which he lambastes American slaveowners as the worst oppressors in human history.

David Walker's Appeal in Four Articles
Preamble

My dearly beloved Brethren and Fellow Citizens.

Having travelled over a considerable portion of these United States, and having, in the course of my travels, taken the most accurate observations of things as they exist—the result of my observations has warranted the full and unshaken conviction, that we, (coloured people of these United States,) are the most degraded, wretched, and abject set of beings that ever lived since the world began; and I pray God that none like us ever may live again until time shall be no more. They tell us of the Israelites in Egypt, the Helots in Sparta, and of the Roman Slaves, which last were made up from almost every nation under Heaven, whose sufferings under those ancient and heathen nations, were, in comparison with ours, under this enlightened and Christian nation, no more than a cypher—or, in other words, those heathen nations of antiquity, had but little more among them than the name and form of slavery; while wretchedness and endless miseries were reserved, apparently in a phial, to be poured out upon our fathers, ourselves and our children, by *Christian* Americans!

These positions I shall endeavour, by the help of the Lord, to demonstrate in the course of this *Appeal,* to the satisfaction of the most incredulous mind—and may God Almighty, who is the Father of our Lord Jesus Christ, open your hearts to understand and believe the truth.

The *causes,* my brethren, which produce our wretchedness and miseries, are so very numerous and aggravating, that I believe the pen only of a Josephus or a Plutarch, can well enumerate and explain them. Upon subjects, then, of such incomprehensible magnitude, so impenetrable, and so notorious, I shall be obliged to omit a large class of, and content myself with giving you an exposition of a few of those, which do indeed rage to such an alarming pitch, that they cannot but be a perpetual source of terror and dismay to every reflecting mind.

I am fully aware, in making this appeal to my much afflicted and suffering brethren, that I shall not only be assailed by those whose greatest earthly desires are, to keep us in abject ignorance and wretchedness, and who are of the firm conviction that Heaven has designed us and our children to be slaves and *beasts of burden* to them and their children. I say, I do not only expect to be held up to the public as an ignorant, impudent and restless disturber of the public peace, by such avaricious creatures, as well as a mover of insubordination—and perhaps put in prison or to death, for giving a superficial exposition of our miseries, and exposing tyrants. But I am persuaded, that many of my brethren, particularly those who are ignorantly in league with slave-holders or tyrants, who acquire their daily bread by the blood and sweat of their more ignorant brethren—and not a few of those too, who are too ignorant to see an inch beyond their noses, will rise up and call me cursed—Yea, the jealous ones among us will perhaps use more abject subtlety, by affirming that this work is not worth perusing, that we are well situated, and there is no use in trying to better our condition, for we cannot. I will ask one question here.—Can our condition be any worse?—Can it be more mean and abject? If there are any changes, will they not be for the better, though they may appear for the worst at first? Can they get us any lower? Where can they get us? They are afraid to treat us worse, for they know well, the day they do it they are gone. But against all accusations which may or can be preferred against me, I appeal to Heaven for my motive in writing—who knows that my object is, if possible, to awaken in the breasts of my afflicted, degraded and slumbering brethren, a spirit of inquiry and investigation respecting our miseries and wretchedness in this *Republican Land of Liberty!!!!!!*

The sources from which our miseries are derived, and on which I shall comment, I shall not combine in one, but shall put them under distinct heads and expose them in their turn; in doing which, keeping truth on my side, and not departing from the strictest rules of morality, I shall endeavour to penetrate, search out, and lay them open for your inspection. If you cannot or will not profit by them, I shall have done *my* duty to you, my country and my God.

And as the inhuman system of *slavery,* is the *source* from which most of our miseries proceed, I shall begin with that *curse to nations,* which has spread terror and devastation through so many nations of antiquity, and which is raging to such a pitch at the present day in Spain and in Portugal. It had one tug in England, in France, and in the United States of America; yet the inhabitants thereof, do not learn wisdom, and erase it entirely from their dwellings and from all with whom they have to do. The fact is, the labour of slaves comes so cheap to the avaricious usurpers, and is (as they think) of such great utility to the country where it exists, that those who are actuated by sordid avarice only, overlook the evils, which will as sure as the Lord lives, follow after the good. In fact, they are so happy to keep in ignorance and degradation, and to receive the homage and the labour of the slaves, they forget that God rules in the armies of Heaven and among the inhabitants of the earth, having his ears continually open to the cries, tears and groans of his oppressed people; and being a just and holy Being will at one day appear fully in behalf of the oppressed, and arrest the progress of the avaricious oppressors; for although the destruction of the oppressors God may not effect by the oppressed, yet the Lord our God will bring other destructions upon them—for not unfrequently will he cause them to rise up one against another, to be split and divided, and to oppress each other, and sometimes to open hostilities with sword in hand. Some may ask, what is the matter with this united and happy people?—Some say it is the cause of political usurpers, tyrants, oppressors, &c. But has not the Lord an oppressed and suffering people among them? Does the Lord condescend to hear their cries and see their tears in consequence of oppression? Will he let the oppressors rest comfortably and happy always? Will he not cause the very children of the oppressors to rise up against them, and oftimes put them to death? "God works in many ways his wonders to perform."

I will not here speak of the destructions which the Lord brought upon Egypt, in consequence of the oppression and consequent groans of the oppressed—of the hundreds and thousands of Egyptians whom God hurled into the Red Sea for afflicting his people in their land—of the Lord's suffering people in Sparta or Lacedaemon, the land of the truly famous Lycurgus—nor have I time to comment upon the cause which produced the fierceness with which Sylla usurped the title, and absolutely acted as dictator of the Roman people—the conspiracy of Cataline—the conspiracy against, and murder of Cæsar in the Senate house—the spirit with which Marc Antony made himself master of the commonwealth—his associating Octavius and Lepidus with himself in power—their dividing the provinces of Rome among themselves—their attack and defeat, on the plains of Phillippi, of the last defenders of their liberty, (Brutus and Cassius)—the tyranny of Tiberius, and from him to the final overthrow of Constantinople by the Turkish Sultan, Mahomed II A.D. 1453. I say, I shall not take up time to speak of the *causes* which produced so much wretchedness and massacre among those heathen nations, for I am aware that you know too well, that God is just, as well as merciful!—I shall call your attention a few moments to that *Christian* nation, the Spaniards—while I shall leave almost unnoticed, that avaricious and cruel people, the Portuguese, among whom all true-hearted Christians and lovers of Jesus Christ, must evidently see the judgments of God displayed. To show the judgments of God upon the Spaniards, I shall occupy but a little time, leaving a plenty of room for the candid and unprejudiced to reflect.

All persons who are acquainted with history, and particularly the Bible, who are not blinded by the God of this world, and are not actuated solely by avarice—who are able to lay aside prejudice long enough to view candidly and impartially, things as they were, are, and probably will be—who are willing to admit that God made man to serve Him *alone*, and that man should have no other Lord or Lords but Himself—that God Almighty is the *sole proprietor* or *master* of the WHOLE human family, and will not on any consideration admit of a colleague, being unwilling to divide his glory with another—and who can dispense with prejudice long enough to admit that we are *men,* notwithstanding our *improminent noses* and *woolly heads,* and believe that we feel for our fathers, mothers, wives and children, as well as the whites do for theirs.—I say, all who are permitted to see and believe these things, can easily recognize the judgments of God among the Spaniards. Though others may lay the cause of the fierceness with which they cut each other's throats, to some other circumstance, yet they who believe that God is a God of justice, will believe that SLAVERY *is the principal cause.*

While the Spaniards are running about upon the field of battle cutting each other's throats, has not the Lord an afflicted and suffering people in the midst of them, whose cries and groans in consequence of oppression are continually pouring into the ears of the God of justice? Would they not cease to cut each other's throats, if they could? But how can they? The very support which they draw from government to aid them in perpetrating such enormities, does it not arise in a great degree from the wretched victims of oppression among them? And yet they are calling for *Peace!—Peace!!* Will any peace be given unto them? Their destruction may indeed be procrastinated awhile, but can it continue long, while they are oppressing the Lord's people? Has He not the hearts of all men in His hand? Will he suffer one part of his creatures to go on oppressing another like brutes always, with impunity? And yet, those avaricious wretches are calling for *Peace!!!!* I declare, it does appear to me, as though some nations think God is asleep, or that he made the Africans for nothing else but to dig their mines and work their farms, or they cannot believe history, sacred or profane. I ask every man who has a heart, and is blessed with the privilege of believing—Is not God a God of justice to *all* his creatures? Do you say he is? Then if he gives peace and tranquillity to tyrants, and permits them to keep our fathers, our mothers, ourselves and our children in eternal ignorance and wretchedness, to support them and their families, would he be to us a God of *justice?* I ask, O ye *Christians!!!* who hold us and our children in the most abject ignorance and degradation, that ever a people were afflicted with since the world began—I say, if God gives you peace and tranquillity, and suffers you thus to go on afflicting us, and our children, who have never given you the least provocation—would he be to us *a God of justice?* If you will allow that we are MEN, who feel for each other, does not the blood of our fathers and of us their children, cry aloud to the Lord of Sabaoth against you, for the cruelties and murders with which you have, and do continue to afflict us. But it is time for me to close my remarks on the suburbs, just to enter more fully into the interior of this system of cruelty and oppression.

Scott L. Malcomson

Scott L. Malcomson (1961–) is a writer and critic who has been a foreign correspondent on several continents (Europe, Asia, and South America). His sojourn in the Far East resulted in his first book, *Tuturani: A Political Journey in the Pacific Islands* (1990).

The following excerpt is from "We Can Be as Separate as the Fingers: Segregation from the American Revolution to the Gilded Age," a chapter in *One Drop of Blood: The American Misadventure of Race* (2000). Malcomson traces the laws and mores that created social institutions segregated by race.

We Can Be as Separate as the Fingers

Segregation from the American Revolution to the Gilded Age

It was, to be sure, a shared sort of madness. The earliest record of blacks in America wanting to separate themselves along racial lines appeared in 1773, when four slaves in Boston petitioned the legislature for help in returning to Africa. "We are willing," they wrote, "to submit to such regulations and laws, as may be made relative to us, until we leave the province, which we determine to do, as soon as we can, from our joynt labours, procure money to transport ourselves to some part of the Coast of Africa, where we propose a settlement." This was desperation. "Some part of the Coast of Africa" suggests that the men felt they belonged among black people—that their skin color held an importance beyond that of a state, tribe, or lineage. This was not the opinion of people who actually lived on the coast of Africa, unless they were entirely caught up in the slave trade. And the Boston men did not want to go to Africa in order to be caught up, again, in the slave business.

The basic idea of getting away from white people, however, had deep roots. There had been two black escapee states in Brazil in the early and middle seventeenth century. The Cimarrons on the Central American isthmus had also set a powerful example. Following the success of Francis Drake and others at forming black-white alliances, Spain made a treaty with one important Cimarron group, recognizing its sovereignty (and ending its cooperation with the English). Escapees, most famously in Jamaica, had formed durable, if economically marginal, communities.

The fundamental desire seems to have been for freedom, not for any type of racial mission. Because blackness was so much a creation of white power, an escape into blackness might well have been nonsensical. Rather, one would have wanted to escape into a full humanity. In America the Revolutionary environment raised hopes enormously, as whites were quick to realize, and the abolitionist surge after 1776 would have encouraged confidence in a new, multiracial (or nonracial), free America. However, it was evident by 1787, with slavery becoming fixed in the Constitution, that blacks would not be accorded full humanity among white people. In that pivotal year eight black men met in Philadelphia to found the Free African Society, the first significant independent black racial organization. Within months some of the eight joined with others in the first recorded nonviolent action against unequal segregation. At St. George's Methodist Episcopal Church in Philadelphia, a group of blacks arrived one Sunday morning and, at the moment a prayer began, took their seats as usual, then knelt to pray. As they prayed, white men came to them and said they should move to the rear. The worshippers asked to be left alone at least until the prayer had ended. The agitated whites insisted. It must have been such a distracted and chaotic prayer. When it was done, the black worshippers quietly stood and walked out. This act began the process of establishing a separate black church denomination in America. The first black school was founded in that year, in New York City, and by this time some free blacks had already begun separate Masonic lodges and mutual-aid organizations.

Also in 1787, the year of our Constitution, Britain established Sierra Leone as an African home for returning slaves—and Prince Hall led the first large-scale call by American blacks for a return to Africa. Hall, who had organized the first black Masonic lodge in Boston in 1775 and, like thousands of blacks, fought for the Revolution, spoke for seventy-three "African blacks" in telling the Massachusetts General Court of the "disagreeable and disadvantageous circumstances" characteristic of free black life in New England. These "and other considerations which we need not here particularly mention induce us to return to Africa, our native country, which warm climate is more natural and agreeable to us; and for which the God of nature has formed us; and where we shall live among our equals and be more comfortable and happy, than we can be in our present situation." Prince Hall also demanded equal educational opportunity for blacks in Boston. The coincidence of these two ideas—racial equality in America and a return to Africa—implies that as a free black person one felt oneself to be not only a partial American but a provisional one, dependent on future developments. This is a bizarre social status on its face, but, of course, many whites had exactly the same conception of how blacks fit, or didn't fit, into the new society whites considered their own.

As it happened, the early peaceful efforts at racial self-determination coincided with violent ones: the revolt of Haiti's blacks (slave and free) against France and the planter class, and Gabriel Prosser's uprising in Virginia. The Haitian revolution had several stages, beginning in the 1780s and culminating in full independence in 1804. Prosser's revolt, in 1800, was briefer and unsuccessful. Prosser had amassed a core group of a few dozen, whose plan was to take Richmond and go on to make Virginia an independent black state with a white minority. Apparently, several thousand slaves were ready to rise up, but when the attackers assembled, two slaves informed on them. A huge thunderstorm followed, washing out a key bridge. Prosser postponed the invasion, but it was too late to go unnoticed back to the plantations, for the rebels had already been betrayed. Prosser and more than thirty of his men were hanged.

At their trial one of the rebels said, "I have nothing more to offer than what General Washington would have had to offer, had he been taken by the British and put to trial by them. I have adventured my life in endeavouring to obtain the liberty of my countrymen." The rhetoric of American liberation had returned to hit its white beneficiaries with a vengeance. A contributor to a Virginia newspaper commented, following Prosser's revolt: "Liberty and equality have brought the evil upon us. A doctrine which, however intelligible, and admissible, in a land of freemen, is not only unintelligible and inadmissible, but dangerous and extremely wicked in this country, where every white man is a master, and every black man is a slave. This doctrine, in this country, and in every country like this (as the horrors of St. Domingo [Haiti] have already proved), cannot fail of producing either a general insurrection, or a general emancipation." The writer pointed out that whites

5

habitually spoke of liberty and equality even when their slaves could hear, as, for example, at dinnertime when they were serving. "What else then could we expect than what has happened?"

The uprisings in Haiti and Virginia, a surge in private manumissions, and Northern abolition combined to focus in white minds the notion that blacks were united as blacks. As a race, blacks were widely thought to spend much of their mental time imagining a day when they could kill whites and take over the country. Whites attributed to blacks a racial mission. They reacted to it, on one hand, by tightening slave codes and, on the other, by restricting the movement of free blacks. It also became standard white opinion around this time that blacks of whatever condition should not be educated, as a little knowledge would probably take them a long way toward demanding equality. Antiblack laws were extremely common throughout the young republic, not only in the South and the states bordering it but in, for example, the antislavery state of Massachusetts. Within one roughly twenty-four hour period Massachusetts had both proscribed the slave trade and restricted free blacks. The two could be, and often were, part of the same impulse. One could easily be antislavery and antiblack.

White separatism created black separatism, and the solidifying of both coincided with the creation of our nation. Neither race, at this point, appears to have assigned much positive meaning to its racial identity. As we have seen, whites did not desire to be white as such. Their principal wish as whites was not to be black. Similarly, free blacks in the immediate post-Revolutionary period probably did not want to be black. They did not write on the particular excellence of blackness. Blackness was a condition forced upon them. But having noticed, particularly in the Northern states recently freed of slavery, that whites in the new republic were determined to maintain their superiority, black leaders decided to make the best of blackness by organizing themselves along racial lines.

Around 1810 a free black-Indian sea captain in Massachusetts, Paul Cuffe, began thinking of ways to start a trade in black immigrants to Africa. (Prince Hall had died in 1807, his back-to-Africa dreams unrealized.) In 1811 Cuffe visited Sierra Leone and met in England with its backers, the African Institution. Upon return home, he helped organize tiny African Institutions among free blacks in Baltimore, Philadelphia, and New York, as sources for the trade. The work was meant to help Africa itself: Cuffe believed American blacks would, with their Christian faith, uplift the presumably non-Christian Africans they met.

Cuffe had bad luck with his timing. Britain and America were at war by 1812, and Sierra Leone was British. Cuffe petitioned Congress for permission to trade with the enemy. The bill was widely debated; it passed the Senate and went to the House, where one white Cuffe ally argued that immigration of free blacks to Africa would help remove "a part of our population which we could well spare." But the voting went seventy-two to sixty-five against. In early 1816, with the war over, Cuffe did land thirty-eight blacks in Sierra Leone. The British took the colonists but refused, under the terms of the recent peace treaty, to trade with Cuffe. In all, the captain lost about four thousand dollars.

Nevertheless, Cuffe's initiative stirred interest in colonization—at least, among whites, for example, Reverend Robert Finley, who had corresponded with Cuffe. The times were rife with benevolence. A reinvigorated Protestantism had spawned countless societies aimed at the improvement of just about everything. This was the field of action for any ambitious clergyman, and Robert Finley had ambition. He had married well—to the foster daughter of New Jersey's Elias Boudinot, the same Boudinot who took such an interest in Cherokees. The Boudinot connection gave Finley access to men of wealth and distinction. In 1816, casting about for a benevolent cause, Finley hit on African colonization. It would benefit America by helping the country "be cleared of" free blacks and those freed slaves who were no longer needed or wanted. Colonization would benefit Africa by giving that continent some "partially civilized and Christianized" newcomers, who might there achieve an equality not possible for them in America.

Finley first took his idea to the synods of New York and New Jersey, then to a small group of interested people in Princeton. New Jersey whites had watched the state's free black population nearly quadruple in thirty years; this was one source of the Princetonians' interest. Finley argued that having free blacks in the neighborhood was "unfavorable to our industry and morals" and might lead to "intermixture." His proposed colonization society would be directed from Washington, under congressional auspices, and would be national in scope, because racial slavery, "the great violation of the laws of nature," was a national crime requiring a national "atoning sacrifice" for the "injuries done to humanity by our ancestors." Africa's bosom had begun "to warm with hope and her heart to beat with expectation and desire," as she was "panting for the return of her absent sons and daughters."

Finley went to Washington and immediately enlisted the aid of Elias Boudinot Caldwell, his wife's brother, who had taken on the name of his foster father. Caldwell was chief clerk of the Supreme Court—the Court met in his home after the British burned the Capitol in 1814. He knew all the justices, of course, as well as Daniel Webster, Henry Clay, John C. Calhoun, Lafayette, and other notables. Caldwell brought in his good friend Francis Scott Key, an able attorney as well as author of "The Star-Spangled Banner." Finley, Caldwell, and Key knew everyone in Washington and formed the activist core of the nascent American Colonization Society.

Henry Clay, the Speaker of the House, presided over their first hopeful meeting. "Can there be a nobler cause," he asked, "than that which, whilst it proposed to rid our country of a useless and pernicious, if not dangerous part of its population, contemplates the spreading of the arts of civilized life, and the possible redemption from ignorance and barbarism of a benighted quarter of the globe!" Evidently, blacks, who were useless and dangerous in the United States, would become propagators of civilization once they crossed the Atlantic.

Elias Boudinot Caldwell emphasized that, because of prejudice, blacks could never be equal in America, so they should leave. Educating them was a fool's errand: "the more you cultivate their minds, the more miserable you make them." Caldwell, like Clay and like John Randolph of Roanoke, who spoke later, urged that the slavery question be avoided. On that basis, the American Society for Colonizing the Free People of Color in the United States came into being. It united many of the most distinguished men of the nation; the secretary of the treasury quickly joined, as did the future president Andrew Jackson.

The colonizationist movement would gain support in nearly every corner of white American society between 1817 and 1835. Some saw it as a step to abolition, others did not. But all agreed that being rid of free blacks was an excellent notion.

Of the Revolutionary generation, Jefferson, Madison, Monroe, and Samuel Adams had approved the idea; so would Supreme Court justice John Marshall and former justice Bushrod Washington, the presidents of Yale, Columbia, Princeton, and Harvard, politicians such as Clay, Webster, Stephen Douglas, Millard Fillmore, and the future abolitionist leaders Gerrit Smith and William Lloyd Garrison. Dozens of auxiliary societies sprang up across the country. Fourteen state legislatures would eventually give their official endorsement to black removal. Clergymen of various faiths preached colonization as a social reform; the voluntary removal of free blacks to Africa became a special subject of Fourth of July sermons, when collections for it were taken. White American opinion could hardly have been more unanimous. Everywhere, the free black population was increasing, perceived to increase, or expected to increase. Everywhere, whites did not want free blacks near them. And everywhere that the subject was discussed, whites agreed that blacks could never be equal because white prejudice would not allow them to be. Virginia's position in the 1790s had become the national position.

White Americans widely perceived colonization of blacks, by this time numbering several million, to be moderate and rational, a practical compromise. It could bring about a gradual emancipation of slaves by their masters without needlessly upsetting the latter. It would separate two antagonistic populations, enabling both to pursue self-determination alone. Colonization sought a middle course between abolitionism and continued slavery. The first would simply split the Union; the second would gradually destroy the soul. Colonizationists also expected racial slavery to wither away as free labor, in line with population increase, became cheaper. Given this trend, thoughtful men believed black removal to be a timely measure for easing the black race and slave labor out of the picture.

That such an absurd scheme as colonizing three million or so people would appear as the sensible solution to America's racial problems indicates just how much race had unhinged the American mind by about 1820. Many white Americans felt themselves to be under increasing psychological torment because slavery reflected so poorly on them. Some found relief in an argument favored by Thomas Jefferson: that slavery and the presence of blacks in America were not their fault. These had been the fault of Britain, or of one's unwise ancestors, or of a colonialist greed since eliminated by the self-improving men of the nineteenth century. The present white generation, including slave owners, was blameless. Once the physical reminder of the guilty past—black people—had been removed, so too would that past itself, and America would start fresh, much as it would have in 1787 except for the persistence of slavery. Additional solace could be found in the emerging belief that blacks really were different by nature, a scientifically distinct set of people, probably inferior but in any case best kept separate. This belief, of course, needed its companion, that whiteness was a category of nature, an important one, with positive qualities. Each of these three beliefs grew in power from the 1820s onward.

Free blacks, too, were tormented. In some ways, they lived in the same psychological trap as whites did. Most of them, or their ancestors, had been slaves, which gave them an inheritance mainly of pain, shame, and self-doubt. However temporarily hopeful they may have been about their prospects in an independent United States, they began to perceive whites as radically and permanently different, a separate race incapable of changing itself. This perception had its twin: that blacks were a race, created more by circumstance than by nature but separate nonetheless, and perhaps with qualities all its own.

Blacks reacted to the American Colonization Society with ambivalence.   20 Reverend Finley met some free blacks in Philadelphia, and Paul Cuffe's black emigrationist friend James Forten, a prosperous sailmaker, wrote to him of the reaction in January 1817: "Indeed, the people of color here was very much frightened. At first they were afraid that all the free people would be compelled to go, particularly in the southern states. We had a large meeting of males at the Rev. R. Allen's church the other evening. Three thousand at least attended, and there was not one soul that was in favor of going to Africa. They think that the slaveholders want to get rid of them so as to make their property more secure. However, it appears to me that if the Father of all Mercies is in this interesting subject (for it appeared that they all think that something must and ought to be done, but do not know where nor how to begin), the way will be made straight and clear . . . My opinion is that they will never become a people until they come out from amongst the white people." The meeting passed resolutions decrying "the unmerited stigma . . . cast upon the reputation of the free people of color." They did not want to visit "the savage wilds of Africa." America was their home, and their racial fate as free men and women could not be unlinked from that of slaves: "We will never separate ourselves voluntarily from the slave population of this country."

The last sentiment is especially important. Free blacks as blacks were expressing a racial solidarity with slaves, a gesture of profound generosity. It represented a historical depth—a refusal to abandon the past—that must have been nearly incomprehensible to many white minds. Why find in yourself a part that is enslaved? Why dwell upon such suffering? Why not forget as best you can this regrettable slavery business and start over?

The Philadelphia resolutions also rejected Africa, seeing the black part of that continent as backward and inferior. The blackness of these Philadelphia men was not African but a racial condition shared by freeman and slave in the United States (although free-black societies habitually titled themselves African). A group of Richmond free blacks was more receptive to the society's propositions but did not want to go to Africa. They preferred a colony out West, along the Missouri River, or in some other North American location. After meeting with Philadelphia blacks, Reverend Finley reported: "The more enlightened they were, the more decisively they expressed themselves on the desirability of becoming a separate people." The white preacher was among the more thoroughgoing of early black separatists.

Forten had neatly summarized the situation. One had to do something, but what? The whites would use colonization to force people from their homes to a strange and unknown land where people just happened to be black. Emigration, by removing free blacks and the example of freedom they set, and by providing a safe depository for the troublesome, would simply improve the slaveholders' hold on their slaves. And yet it seemed impossible to Forten that blacks could ever realize their desire (or his desire for them) to become "a people" while living with whites— a people just as whites were a people.

Black colonization involved deep paradoxes. One was that it essentially proposed to blacks that they go to a black place so that they could cease being black— so that they could be human like anyone else. This alludes to a more profound paradox of racial separatism, at least in 1817: it represented an urge to be in a race and yet not to be in a race, to be "race-free."

Ida B. Wells-Barnett

Ida B. Wells-Barnett (1862–1931) was a fearless journalist at the turn of the twentieth century, hell-bent on reporting incidents of lynching to shame America's leaders into corrective action as well as on crusading for women's rights. Her works include *Southern Horrors: Lynch Law in All Its Phases (1892)* and *A Red Record: Tabulated Statistics and Alleged Causes of Lynchings in the United States, 1892–1893–1894* (1895).

In this excerpt from Chapter 1 of *A Red Record,* collected in *On Lynchings* (1969), Barnett debunks the rationale for lynchings.

A Red Record

The Case Stated

The student of American sociology will find the year 1894 marked by a pronounced awakening of the public conscience to a system of anarchy and outlawry which had grown during a series of ten years to be so common, that scenes of unusual brutality failed to have any visible effect upon the humane sentiments of the people of our land.

Beginning with the emancipation of the Negro, the inevitable result of unbribled power exercised for two and a half centuries, by the white man over the Negro, began to show itself in acts of conscienceless outlawry. During the slave regime, the Southern white man owned the Negro body and soul. It was to his interest to dwarf the soul and preserve the body. Vested with unlimited power over his slave, to subject him to any and all kinds of physical punishment, the white man was still restrained from such punishment as tended to injure the slave by abating his physical powers and thereby reducing his financial worth. While slaves were scourged mercilessly, and in countless cases inhumanly treated in other respects, still the white owner rarely permitted his anger to go so far as to take a life, which would entail upon him a loss of several hundred dollars. The slave was rarely killed, he was too valuable; it was easier and quite as effective, for discipline or revenge, to sell him "Down South."

But Emancipation came and the vested interests of the white man in the Negro's body were lost. The white man had no right to scourge the emancipated Negro, still less had he a right to kill him. But the Southern white people had been educated so long in that school of practice, in which might makes right, that they disdained to draw strict lines of action in dealing with the Negro. In slave times the Negro was kept subservient and submissive by the frequency and severity of the scourging, but, with freedom, a new system of intimidation came into vogue; the Negro was not only whipped and scourged; he was killed.

Not all nor nearly all of the murders done by white men, during the past thirty years in the South, have come to light, but the statistics as gathered and preserved by white men, and which have not been questioned, show that during these years more than ten thousand Negroes have been killed in cold blood, without the formality of judicial trial and legal execution. And yet, as evidence of the absolute impunity with which the white man dares to kill a Negro, the same record shows that during all these years, and for all these murders only three white men have been tried, convicted, and executed. As no white man has been lynched for the murder of colored people, these three executions are the only instances of the death penalty being visited upon white men for murdering Negroes.

Naturally enough the commission of these crimes began to tell upon the public conscience, and the Southern white man, as a tribute to the nineteenth century civilization, was in a manner compelled to give excuses for his barbarism. His excuses have adapted themselves to the emergency, and are aptly outlined by that greatest of all Negroes, Frederick Douglass, in an article of recent date, in which he shows that there have been three distinct eras of Southern barbarism, to account for which three distinct excuses have been made.

The first excuse given to the civilized world for the murder of unoffending Negroes was the necessity of the white man to repress and stamp out alleged "race riots." For years immediately succeeding the war there was an appalling slaughter of colored people, and the wires usually conveyed to northern people and the world the intelligence, first, that an insurrection was being planned by Negroes, which, a few hours later, would prove to have been vigorously resisted by white men, and controlled with a resulting loss of several killed and wounded. It was always a remarkable feature in these insurrections and riots that only Negroes were killed during the rioting, and that all the white men escaped unharmed.

From 1865 to 1872, hundreds of colored men and women were mercilessly murdered and the almost invariable reason assigned was that they met their death by being alleged participants in an insurrection or riot. But this story at last wore itself out. No insurrection ever materialized; no Negro rioter was ever apprehended and proven guilty, and no dynamite ever recorded the black man's protest against oppression and wrong. It was too much to ask thoughtful people to believe this transparent story, and the southern white people at last made up their minds that some other excuse must be had.

Then came the second excuse, which had its birth during the turbulent times of Reconstruction. By an amendment to the Constitution the Negro was given the right of franchise, and, theoretically at least, his ballot became his invaluable emblem of citizenship. In a government "of the people, for the people, and by the people," the Negro's vote became an important factor in all matters of state and national politics. But this did not last long. The Southern white man would not consider that the Negro had any right which a white man was bound to respect, and the idea of a republican form of government in the southern states grew into general contempt. It was maintained that "This is a white man's government," and regardless of numbers the white man should rule. "No Negro domination" became the new legend on the sanguinary banner of the sunny South, and under it rode the Ku Klux Klan, the Regulators, and the lawless mobs, which for any cause chose to murder one man or a dozen as suited their purpose best. It was a long, gory campaign; the blood chills and the heart almost loses faith in Christianity when one thinks of Yazoo, Hamburg, Edgefield, Copiah, and the countless massacres of defenseless Negroes, whose only crime was the attempt to exercise their right to vote.

But it was a bootless strife for colored people. The government which had made the Negro a citizen found itself unable to protect him. It gave him the right to vote, but denied him the protection which should have maintained that right. Scourged from his home; hunted through the swamps; hung by midnight raiders, and openly murdered in the light of day, the Negro clung to his right of franchise with a heroism which would have wrung admiration from the hearts of savages. He believed that in that small white ballot there was a subtle something which stood for manhood as well as citizenship, and thousands of brave black men went to their graves, exemplifying the one by dying for the other.

The white man's victory soon became complete by fraud, violence, intimida- 10
tion and murder. The franchise vouchsafed to the Negro grew to be a "barren ide-
ality," and regardless of numbers, the colored people found themselves voiceless in the councils of those whose duty it was to rule. With no longer the fear of "Negro Domination" before their eyes, the white man's second excuse became valueless. With the Southern governments all subverted and the Negro actually eliminated from all participation in state and national elections, there could be no longer an excuse for killing Negroes to prevent "Negro Domination."

Brutality still continued; Negroes were whipped, scourged, exiled, shot and hung whenever and wherever it pleased the white man so to treat them, and as the civilized world with increasing persistency held the white people of the South to account for its outlawry, the murderers invented the third excuse—that Negroes had to be killed to avenge their assaults upon women. There could be framed no possible excuse more harmful to the Negro and more unanswerable if true in its sufficiency for the white man.

Humanity abhors the assailant of womanhood, and this charge upon the Negro at once placed him beyond the pale of human sympathy. With such unanimity, earnestness and apparent candor was this charge made and reiterated that the world has accepted the story that the Negro is a monster which the Southern white man has painted him. And today, the Christian world feels, that while lynching is a crime, and lawlessness and anarchy the certain precursors of a nation's fall, it can not by word or deed, extend sympathy or help to a race of outlaws, who might mistake their plea for justice and deem it an excuse for their continued wrongs.

The Negro has suffered much and is willing to suffer more. He recognizes that the wrongs of two centuries can not be righted in a day, and he tries to bear his burden with patience for today and be hopeful for tomorrow. But there comes a time when the veriest worm will turn, and the Negro feels today that after all the work he has done, all the sacrifices he has made, and all the suffering he has endured, if he did not, now, defend his name and manhood from this vile accusation, he would be unworthy even of the contempt of mankind. It is to this charge he now feels he must make answer.

If the Southern people in defense of their lawlessness, would tell the truth and admit that colored men and women are lynched for almost any offense, from murder to a misdemeanor, there would not now be the necessity for this defense. But when they intentionally, maliciously and constantly belie the record and bolster up these falsehoods by the words of legislators, preachers, governors and bishops, then the Negro must give to the world his side of the awful story.

A word as to the charge itself. In considering the third reason assigned by the Southern white people for the butchery of blacks, the question must be asked, what the white man means when he charges the black man with rape. Does he mean the crime which the statutes of the civilized states describe as such? Not by any means. With the Southern white man, any mesalliance existing between a white woman and a colored man is a sufficient foundation for the charge of rape. The Southern white man says that it is impossible for a voluntary alliance to exist between a white woman and a colored man, and therefore, the fact of an alliance is a proof of force. In numerous instances where colored men have been lynched on the charge of rape, it was positively known at the time of lynching, and indisputably proven after the victim's death, that the relationship sustained between the man and woman was voluntary and clandestine, and that in no court of law could even the charge of assault have been successfully maintained.

It was for the assertion of this fact, in the defense of her own race, that the writer hereof became an exile; her property destroyed and her return to her home forbidden under penalty of death, for writing the following editorial which was printed in her paper, the Free Speech, in Memphis, Tenn., May 21, 1892:

"Eight Negroes lynched since last issue of the 'Free Speech' one at Little Rock, Ark., last Saturday morning where the citizens broke (?) into the penitentiary and got their man; three near Anniston, Ala., one near New Orleans; and three at Clarksville, Ga., the last three for killing a white man, and five on the same old racket—the new alarm about raping white women. The same programme of hanging, then shooting bullets into the lifeless bodies was carried out to the letter. Nobody in this section of the country believes the old threadbare lie that Negro men rape white women. If Southern white men are not careful, they will over-reach themselves and public sentiment will have a reaction; a conclusion will then be reached which will be very damaging to the moral reputation of their women."

But threats cannot suppress the truth, and while the Negro suffers the soul deformity, resultant from two and a half centuries of slavery, he is no more guilty of this vilest of all vile charges than the white man who would blacken his name.

During all the years of slavery, no such charge was ever made, not even during the dark days of the rebellion, when the white man, following the fortunes of war went to do battle for the maintenance of slavery. While the master was away fighting to forge the fetters upon the slave, he left his wife and children with no protectors save the Negroes themselves. And yet during those years of trust and peril, no Negro proved recreant to his trust and no white man returned to a home that had been despoiled.

Likewise during the period of alleged "insurrection," and alarming "race riots," it never occurred to the white man, that his wife and children were in danger of assault. Nor in the Reconstruction era, when the hue and cry was against "Negro Domination," was there ever a thought that the domination would ever contaminate a fireside or strike to death the virtue of womanhood. It must appear strange indeed, to every thoughtful and candid man, that more than a quarter of a century elapsed before the Negro began to show signs of such infamous degeneration.

In his remarkable apology for lynching, Bishop Haygood, of Georgia, says: "No race, not the most savage, tolerates the rape of woman, but it may be said without reflection upon any other people that the Southern people are now and always have been most sensitive concerning the honor of their women—their mothers, wives, sisters and daughters." It is not the purpose of this defense to say one word against the white women of the South. Such need not be said, but it is their misfortune that the chivalrous white men of that section, in order to escape the deserved execration of the civilized world, should shield themselves by their cowardly and infamously false excuse, and call into question that very honor about which their distinguished priestly apologist claims they are most sensitive. To justify their own barbarism they assume a chivalry which they do not possess. True chivalry respects all womanhood, and no one who reads the record, as it is written in the faces of the million mulattoes in the South, will for a minute conceive that the southern white man had a very chivalrous regard for the honor due the women of his own race or respect for the womanhood which circumstances placed in his power. That chivalry which is "most sensitive concerning the honor of women" can hope for but little respect from the civilized world, when it confines itself entirely to the women who happen to be white. Virtue knows no color line, and the chivalry which depends upon complexion of skin and texture of hair can command no honest respect.

When emancipation came to the Negroes, there arose in the northern part of the United States an almost divine sentiment among the noblest, purest and best white women of the North, who felt called to a mission to educate and Christianize the millions of southern ex-slaves. From every nook and corner of the North, brave young white women answered that call and left their cultured homes, their happy associations and their lives of ease, and with heroic determination went to the South to carry light and truth to the benighted blacks. It was a heroism no less than that which calls for volunteers for India, Africa and the Isles of the sea. To educate their unfortunate charges; to teach them the Christian virtues and to inspire in them the moral sentiments manifest in their own lives, these young women braved dangers whose record reads more like fiction than fact. They became social outlaws in the South. The peculiar sensitiveness of the Southern white men for women never shed its protecting influence about them. No friendly word from their own race cheered them in their work; no hospitable doors gave them the companionship like that from which they had come. No chivalrous white man doffed his hat in honor or respect. They were "Nigger teachers"—unpardonable offenders in the social ethics of the South, and were insulted, persecuted and ostracized, not by Negroes, but by the white manhood which boasts of its chivalry toward women.

And yet these Northern women worked on, year after year, unselfishly, with a heroism which amounted almost to martyrdom. Threading their way through dense forests, working in the schoolhouse, in the cabin and in the church, thrown at all times and in all places among the unfortunate and lowly Negroes, whom they had come to find and to serve, these Northern women, thousands and thousands of them, have spent more than a quarter of a century in giving to the colored people their splendid lessons for home and heart and soul. Without protection, save that which innocence gives to every good woman, they went about their work, fearing no assault and suffering none. Their chivalrous protectors were hundreds of miles away in their Northern homes, and yet they never feared any "great dark faced mobs," they dared night or day to "go beyond their own roof trees." They never complained of assaults, and no mob was ever called into existence to avenge crimes against them. Before the world adjudges the Negro a moral monster, a vicious assailant of womanhood and a menace to the sacred precincts of home, the colored people ask the consideration of the silent record of gratitude, respect, protection and devotion of the millions of the race in the South, to the thousands of Northern white women who have served as teachers and missionaries since the war.

The Negro may not have known what chivalry was, but he knew enough to preserve inviolate the womanhood of the South which was entrusted to his hands during the war. The finer sensibilities of his soul may have been crushed out by years of slavery, but his heart was full of gratitude to the white women of the North, who blessed his home and inspired his soul in all these years of freedom. Faithful to his trust in both of these instances, he should now have the impartial ear of the civilized world, when he dares to speak for himself as against the infamy wherewith he stands charged.

It is his regret, that, in his own defense, he must disclose to the world that de-   25 gree of dehumanizing brutality which fixes upon America the blot of a national crime. Whatever faults and failings other nations may have in their dealings with their own subjects or with other people, no other civilized nation stands condemned before the world with a series of crimes so peculiarly national. It becomes a painful duty of the Negro to reproduce a record which shows that a large portion of the American people avow anarchy, condone murder and defy the contempt of civilization.

These pages are written in no spirit of vindictiveness, for all who give the subject consideration must concede that far too serious is the condition of that civilized government in which the spirit of unrestrained outlawry constantly increases in violence, and casts its blight over a continually growing area of territory. We plead not for the colored people alone, but for all victims of the terrible injustice which puts men and women to death without form of law. During the year 1894, there were 132 persons executed in the United States by due form of law, while in the same year, 197 persons were put to death by mobs who gave the victims no opportunity to make a lawful defense. No comment need be made upon a condition of public sentiment responsible for such alarming results.

The purpose of the pages which follow shall be to give the record which has been made, not by colored men, but that which is the result of compilations made by white men, of reports sent over the civilized world by white men in the South. Out of their own mouths shall the murderers be condemned. For a number of years the *Chicago Tribune*, admittedly one of the leading journals of America, has made a specialty of the compilation of statistics touching upon lynching. The data compiled by that journal and published to the world January 1st, 1894, up to the present time has not been disputed. In order to be safe from the charge of exaggeration, the incidents hereinafter reported have been confined to those vouched for by the *Tribune*.

Derrick Bell

Derrick Bell (1930–) has had a distinguished career as a lawyer in the federal government and civil rights agencies as well as a law professor at Harvard University, the University of Oregon, and New York University. In addition to publications on law, such as *Shades of Brown: New Perspectives on School Desegregation* (1980) and *Race, Racism and American Law* (1992), Bell has written several literary works to posit his views on race and American society. These works include *Faces at the Bottom of the Well: The Permanence of Racism* (1992); *Confronting Authority: Reflections of an Ardent Protester* (1994); *Gospel Choirs: Psalms of Survival in an Alien Land Called Home* (1996), for which he was awarded the American Book Award; and *Afrolantica Legacies* (1998).

The following selection is Chapter Four of *And We Are Not Saved: The Elusive Quest for Racial Justice* (1987), in which Bell discusses school desegregation practices while narrating a story about African American children who vanish.

Neither Separate Schools Nor Mixed Schools
The Chronicle of the Sacrificed Black Schoolchildren

All the black school-age children were gone. They had simply disappeared. No one in authority could tell the frantic parents more than they already knew. It had been one of those early September days that retain the warmth of summer after shedding that season's oppressive humidity. Prodded perhaps by the moderate weather, the pall of hateful racial invective that had enveloped the long desegregation battle lifted on what was to be the first day of a new school year. It was as well implementation day for the new desegregation plan, the result of prolonged, court-supervised negotiations. Plaintiffs' lawyers had insisted on what one called a "full measure" of racial balance, while the school board and the white community resisted, often bitterly, every departure from the previous school structure.

Now it seemed all for nothing. The black students, every one of them, had vanished on the way to school. Children who had left home on foot never appeared. Buses that had pulled away from their last stop loaded with black children had arrived at schools empty, as had the cars driven by parents or car pools. Even parents taking young children by the hand for their first day in kindergarten, or in pre-school, had looked down and found their hands empty, the children suddenly gone.

You can imagine the response. The media barrage, the parents' anger and grief, the suspects arrested and released, politicians' demands for action, analysts' assessments, and then the inevitably receding hullabaloo. Predictable statements were made, predictable actions taken, but there were no answers, no leads, no black children.

Give them credit. At first, the white people, both in town and around the country, were generous in their support and sincere in the sympathy they extended   5 to the black parents. It was some time before there was any public mention of what, early on, many had whispered privately: that while the loss was tragic, perhaps it was all for the best. Except in scruffy white neighborhoods, these "all for the best" rationales were never downgraded to "good riddance."

Eventually they might have been. After all, statistics showed the life chances for most of the poor children were not bright. School dropouts at an early age; no skills; no jobs; too early parenthood; too much exposure to crime, alcohol, drugs. And the city had resisted meaningful school desegregation for so long that it was now possible to learn from the experience of other districts that integrating the schools would not automatically insulate poor black children from the risks of ghetto life.

Even after delaying school desegregation for several years, the decision to proceed this fall with the now-unneeded plan had been bitterly opposed by many white parents who feared that "their schools" would have to have a 50 percent enrollment of black children to enable the school system to achieve an equal racial balance, the primary goal of the desegregation plan and its civil rights sponsors. So high a percentage of black children, these parents claimed, would destroy academic standards, generate discipline problems, and place white children in physical danger. But under all the specifics lay the resentment and sense of lost status. Their schools would no longer be mainly white—a racial status whites equated with school quality, even when the schools were far from academically impressive.

Black parents had differed about the value of sending their children to what had been considered white schools. Few of these parents were happy that their children were scheduled, under the desegregation plan, to do most of the bus riding—often to schools located substantial distances from their homes. Some parents felt that it was the only way to secure a quality education because whites would never give black schools a fair share of school funds, and as some black parents observed: "Green follows white."

Other black parents, particularly those whose children were enrolled in the W. E. B. DuBois School—an all-black, outstanding educational facility with a national reputation—were unhappy. DuBois's parents had intervened in the suit to oppose the desegregation plan as it applied to their school. Their petition read:

> This school is the fruit of our frustration. It is as well a monument of love for our children. Our persistence built the DuBois School over the system's opposition. It is a harbor of learning for our children, and a model of black excellence for the nation. We urge that our school be emulated and not emasculated. The admission of whites will alter and undermine the fragile balance that enables the effective schooling black children need to survive societal hostility.
>
> We want our children to attend the DuBois School. Coercing their attendance at so-called desegregated schools will deny, not ensure, their right to an equal educational opportunity. The board cannot remedy the wrongs done in the past by an assignment policy that is a constitutional evil no less harmful than requiring black children to attend segregated schools. The remedy for inferior black schools sought by others from the courts we have achieved for ourselves. Do not take away our educational victory and leave us "rights" we neither need nor want.

The DuBois School's petition was opposed by the school board and plaintiffs'   10
civil rights lawyers, and denied by the district court. Under the desegregation plan,
two-thirds of the DuBois students were to be transferred to white schools located at
the end of long bus rides, to be replaced by white children whose parents volun-
teered to enroll them in an outstanding school.

In fact, DuBois School patrons were more fortunate than many parents whose
children were enrolled in black schools that were slowly improving but lacked the
DuBois School's showy academic performance. Most of these schools were slated
for closure or conversion into warehouses or other administrative use. Under a variety of rationales, the board failed to reassign any of the principals of the closed
black schools to similar positions in integrated schools.

Schools in white areas that would have been closed because of declining enrollment gained a reprieve under the school-desegregation plan. The older schools
were extensively rehabilitated, and the school board obtained approval for several
new schools, all to be built in mainly white areas—the board said—the better to ensure that they would remain academically stable and racially integrated.

Then, in the wake of the black students' disappearance, came a new
shock. The public school superintendent called a special press conference to
make the announcement. More than 55 percent of the public school population had been black students, and because state funding of the schools was
based on average daily attendance figures, the school system faced a serious
deficit during the current year.

There were, the superintendent explained, several additional components to
the system's financial crisis:

TEACHER SALARIES. Insisting that desegregation would bring special stresses   15
and strains, the teacher's union had won substantial pay raises, as well as expensive
in-service training programs. A whole corps of teacher aides had been hired and
trained to assist school faculties with their administrative chores. Many newly hired
teachers and all the aides would have to be released.

SCHOOL BUSES. To enable transportation of students required by the desegregation plan, the board had ordered one hundred buses and hired an equal number of new drivers. The buses, the superintendent reported, could be returned.
Many had made only one trip; but the new drivers, mechanics, service personnel,
and many of the existing drivers would have to be laid off.

SCHOOL CONSTRUCTION. Contracts for rehabilitation of old schools and for
planning and building new schools had placed the board millions of dollars in
debt. The superintendent said that hundreds of otherwise idle construction workers were to have been employed, as well as architectural firms and landscape de-
signers. Additional millions had been earmarked for equipment and furniture suppliers, book publishers, and curriculum specialists. Some of these contracts could
be canceled but not without substantial damage to the local economy.

LOST FEDERAL FUNDS. After desegregation had been ordered by the courts,
the board applied for and received commitments for several million dollars in federal desegregation funds. These grants were now canceled.

LOST STATE FUNDS. Under the court order, the state was obligated to subsidize costs of desegregation; and, the superintendent admitted, these appropriations, as well as the federal grants, had been designated to do "double duty": that is, while furthering school-desegregation efforts, the money would also improve the quality of education throughout the system by hiring both sufficient new teachers to lower the teacher-pupil ratio, and guidance counselors and other advisory personnel.

TAX RATES. Conceding that the board had won several increases in local [20] tax rates during the desegregation process, the superintendent warned that, unless approval was obtained for a doubling of the current rate, the public schools would not survive.

ANNEXATIONS. Over the last several years, the city had annexed several unincorporated areas in order to bring hundreds of additional white students into the public school system and slow the steady increase in the percentage of black students. Now the costs of serving these students added greatly to the financially strapped system.

ATTORNEY FEES. Civil rights attorneys had come under heavy criticism after it was announced that the court had awarded them $300,000 in attorney fees for their handling of the case, stretching back over the prior five years. Now the superintendent conceded that the board had paid a local law firm over $2,000,000 for defending the board in court for the same period.

Following the school superintendent's sobering statement, the mayor met with city officials and prepared an equally lengthy list of economic gains that would have taken place had the school-desegregation order gone into effect. The president of the local chamber of commerce did the same. The message was clear. While the desegregation debate had focused on whether black children would benefit from busing and attendance at racially balanced schools, the figures put beyond dispute the fact that virtually every white person in the city would benefit directly or indirectly from the desegregation plan that most had opposed.

Armed with this information, a large sum was appropriated to conduct a massive search for the missing black children. For a time, hopes were raised, but eventually the search was abandoned. The children were never found, their abductors never apprehended. Gradually, all in the community came to realize the tragedy's lamentable lesson. In the monumental school desegregation struggle, the intended beneficiaries had been forgotten long before they were lost.

A most disturbing story, Geneva! Symbolically, the sacrificed black children in [25] the Chronicle represent literally thousands like themselves who are the casualties of desegregation, their schooling irreparably damaged even though they themselves did not dramatically disappear. It certainly calls into question the real beneficiaries in the thousands of school-desegregation cases that the former Legal Defense Fund director, Jack Greenberg, aptly called the 'trench warfare' of the civil rights movement."

"Why are you taking it so hard?" Geneva asked. "In our discussion following the Chronicle of the Celestial Curia, you cited both Lewis Steel, the civil rights lawyer, and Professor Arthur S. Miller for arguing that the Supreme Court's decision in *Brown* v. *Board of Education* should be seen as furthering the nation's foreign and domestic interests far more than it helped black people gain the critically important citizenship right to equal educational opportunity. In fact, you noted that both the NAACP and the federal government briefs argued the value of ending constitutionally supported racial segregation in our competition with communist governments" (see pages 60–62).

"That's true," I admitted, "but—"

"But what?" Geneva interrupted. "If your self-interest approach is a valid explanation for the change in constitutional interpretation—as you and others insist on viewing the *Brown* decision—then why wouldn't the same self-interest have to be present before that decision could be implemented?"

"I'm not sure many people lacking the intellectual insight of a W. E. B. DuBois recognized the factor of self-interest in the first several years after the *Brown* decision," I replied. "Moreover, the early problem, as I remember it, was that resistance to desegregation was so fierce and came from so many directions that any progress we made in overcoming it was simply accepted as a victory without much thought of *how* we—always the understaffed, underfinanced underdogs—had prevailed. We knew we were in the right, that God was on our side, and all of that, but while we spoke and thought in an atmosphere of 'rights and justice,' our opponents had their eyes on the economic benefits and power relationships all the time. And that difference in priorities meant that the price of black progress was benefits to the other side, benefits that tokenized our gains and sometimes strengthened the relative advantages whites held over us."

"And that," said Geneva, "is precisely the Chronicle's message."   30

"Indeed," I said, "the Chronicle portrays in dramatic terms the thesis of Daniel Monti's *A Semblance of Justice,* which reviews the long history of school desegregation in St. Louis. Professor Monti reports that St. Louis school officials staunchly resisted any liability for segregation in their schools. Then, after court orders were finally entered, the same individuals utilized school-desegregation mandates to achieve educational reforms, including magnet schools, increased funding for training, teacher salaries, research and development, and new school construction."[1]

"Amazing! And probably at the same time, they were calling the civil rights people everything but a child of God."

"Probably," I agreed, "but according to Monti, school officials accomplished all of these gains for the system without giving more than secondary priority to redressing the grievances of blacks. This did not seem to bother the officials who candidly told him that the only sensible way to deliver educational resources to the metropolitan area of St. Louis was through a metropolitan school system, and they also used desegregation to accomplish that end."

"Would Professor Monti be able to build a similar case of school-desegregation benefit for the system rather than for the blacks in other school districts?" Geneva asked.

"I'm afraid he could. Moreover, Monti's book explains how school officials   35 used the school-desegregation controversy to increase their legitimacy as the proper policy-making location for public education—an accomplishment furthered by the fact that civil rights lawyers did not call for the abandonment of the school board, even though it and its predecessors in office were responsible for the discriminatory policies attacked in the courts."

"That is certainly an accurate statement, but I doubt that it is fair," Geneva said. "School boards do not make policy as much as reflect in their policies the wishes of those in their constituencies whom they really represent. The society was willing, albeit reluctantly, to drop school-segregation policies after *Brown*. But that decision did not require nor did the public want to dismantle the structure of public school systems. Even when courts placed absolutely recalcitrant school systems into a form of judicial receivership,[2] there was criticism that the courts had gone too far."

"A real catch-22 that made every step painful," I recalled. "When districts finally admitted more than a token number of black students to previously white schools, the action usually resulted in closing black schools, dismissing black teachers, and demoting (and often degrading) black principals. There was some effort to stem this practice via litigation,[3] but our main emphasis was on desegregating the schools. Black faculty, in all too many cases, became victims of that desegregation."

"I gather," Geneva commented, "that the desegregated schools did not provide educational compensation to black children for the involuntary loss of their former teachers and schools."

"It was tough, though for a long time we kept pointing to the strong kids who made it rather than to all those who did poorly or dropped out of school. But in the early days, the experience, even when there was little overt hostility, was much as reported in Ray Rist's *The Invisible Children* (1978). Rist, a social scientist, followed every day for a full school year a group of young black children bused to an upper-class, mainly white school.[4] The principal's policy was to 'treat all the kids just alike.' This evenhanded policy meant—in practice—that the handful of black children from the ghetto were expected to perform and behave no differently than did the white children from comfortable suburbs in this mainly white school where the curriculum, texts, and teaching approaches were designed for the middle-class white kids. As you can imagine, the results of this evenhanded integration were disastrous."

"Do you think," Geneva asked, "that we could have avoided some of the tragedy   40
if educators had been more involved in planning the litigation that led to *Brown*?"

"That's what our former associate Robert L. Carter, who played a major role in planning school-desegregation strategy, seems to think. I'm happy to report that, unlike many of our old colleagues who read any criticism of desegregation strategy as a personal attack, Bob Carter, now a federal judge, has remained objective about his role. In a thoughtful article, he wrote that, if he were preparing *Brown* today, 'instead of looking principally to the social scientists to demonstrate the adverse consequences of segregation, [he] would seek to recruit educators to formulate a concrete definition of the meaning of equality in education.'"[5]

"Interesting—but how did he intend to use the definition effectively?"

"Carter said that he would have based his argument on that definition, and tried 'to persuade the Court that equal education in its constitutional dimensions must, at the very least, conform to the contours of equal education as defined by the educators.'"[6]

"Perhaps," Geneva said, "Carter's approach would have enabled us to avoid some of the pitfalls, but it is lawyer's conceit to think that one tactical approach rather than another will overcome society's strong resistance to a particular racial reform as opposed to gaining a favorable outcome in a case."

I smiled. "Knowing Bob Carter as well as we both do, I'd love to hear his re-   45
sponse to your observation."

"Don't misunderstand me. Judge Carter's point is well taken. We civil rights
lawyers attacked segregation in the public schools because it was the weak link in
the 'separate but equal' chain. Our attack worked. But to equate integration with
the effective education black children need—well, that was a mistake."

"Again, Geneva," I said, with some annoyance, "that's easy for you to say—but
remember how many devices school boards and their lawyers worked out to convey
the sense of compliance with *Brown,* while in fact the schools remained segregated.
'Pupil assignment plans' (requiring black parents to run an administrative gauntlet
of forms and requirements),[7] 'grade-a-year' plans (which maintained the pace of
desegregation at a glacial rate),[8] 'freedom-of-choice' plans (which relied on community pressures and coercion to limit the number of blacks who dared choose
white schools),[9] and on and on. Unraveling the seemingly neutral procedures contained in these plans to get at their segregation-maintaining intent proved a challenge for both civil rights lawyers and for many federal judges who were ostracized
and abused for carrying out the *Brown* mandate."[10]

"I remember how difficult it was," Geneva acknowledged, "but, for the life of
me, I can't understand how you allowed school-board resistance to trap you into relying on racial balance as the only acceptable remedy for segregated schools. If you
ask me, it was the civil rights lawyers' personal commitment to racial integration
that trapped them into a strategy that could not succeed."

"Criticism based on hindsight is easy," I said heatedly, "but what would you,
Geneva, had you been around, have recommended as an alternative strategy?"

"I see that, unlike your friend and mentor, Judge Carter, you are a bit sensitive   50
about criticism of your legal tactics. Or," she added, with a wry smile, "is your apparent anger really advocacy at work?"

"I'll ignore that, Ms. Know-it-all," I sputtered. "But let's assume that, instead of
refusing to clarify its mandate to desegregate the public schools 'with all deliberate
speed'[11]—a refusal that, in effect, gave the South ten years of delay—the Supreme
Court in 1955, in addition to sensing the strong opposition to desegregation, had
recognized that the separation of students by race was actually not an end in itself
but a convenient means of perpetuating the primary aim: the dominance of whites
over blacks in every important aspect of life."

"Fine!" Geneva said, "but where would they have gained that insight? Probably
not from most of you who were convinced that, once we got the damned Jim Crow
signs removed, the racial-integration millennium would roll in with the next tide."

"Please stop rubbing it in! We did what we felt was right at the time, and I
haven't heard of an alternative that had a better chance of success, given the hostility of the climate."

"Well, I don't agree that a better desegregation policy was beyond the reach
of intelligent people whose minds were not clogged with integrationist dreams. For
example—if we recognize that the real motivation for segregation was white domination of public education—suppose the Court had issued the following orders:

1. Even though we encourage voluntary desegregation, we will not order racially   55
   integrated assignments of students or staff for ten years.

2. Even though 'separate but equal' no longer meets the constitutional equal-protection standard, we will require immediate equalization of all facilities and resources.
3. Blacks must be represented on school boards and other policy-making bodies in proportions equal to those of black students in each school district.

"The third point would have been intended to give blacks meaningful access to decision making—a prerequisite to full equality still unattained in many predominantly black school systems. For example, an 'equal representation' rule might have helped protect the thousands of black teachers and principals who were dismissed by school systems during the desegregation process."

"In other words," I asked, "under this 'educational policy' approach, the courts would have given priority to desegregating not the students but the money and the control?"

"Exactly. And rather than beat our heads against the wall seeking pupil-desegregation orders the courts were unwilling to enter or enforce, we could have organized parents and communities to ensure effective implementation for the equal-funding and equal-representation mandates."

"How can you be sure that black parents—as well as some of their integration-crazed lawyers—would not have become demoralized by the ten-year delay and simply done nothing until the courts were willing to take direct action on pupil desegregation?"

"The proof," Geneva answered quickly, "is in the number of black schools like DuBois in the Chronicle where neither personnel nor parents have accepted the argument that black schools must be inferior. Even in the pre-*Brown* era, some black educators, without equal resources and with whites controlling school-board policy, managed to create learning environments that encouraged excellence, motivated ambition, and taught the skills and self-assurance that have produced scores of successful blacks in business and the professions.[12] The educational sociologist Professor Sara Lightfoot, in her *The Good High School,* provides an impressive report of an all-black high school in Atlanta, Georgia—George Washington Carver—and the policies that enabled it to gain a reputation for academic quality."[13]

"It does happen," I conceded, "but good schools in a hostile environment are always fragile, subject to constant stress and continuing challenge. Look what happened to the DuBois School in the Chronicle. Despite the fact that it was effective and the pride of the black community, and that blacks wanted to send their children to its schools, it was sacrificed to school desegregation."

"By the way," Geneva asked, somewhat sarcastically, "had you been the judge in the Sacrificed Black Schoolchildren Chronicle, how would you have ruled on the DuBois School parents' petition?"

"It was a moving petition, I will admit, but—"

Geneva was on her feet. "Oh no you don't! You are not going to sit there and tell me that you would have denied their petition, disavowed the justice of their cause, and dismissed their claim?"

"The problem," I observed in my most measured tones, "is that you black women get so emotionally involved in tactical matters that you fail to see that some must pay a price so that all may advance"—and then I ducked as Geneva rose with a vase in her hand.

But then she smiled and placed it back on the table. "Thought you would taunt me into forgetting my question, did you? *Black woman, emotional*—my foot! Now, Mr. Professor, I am waiting for your answer. What about the black parents' petition to save the DuBois School?"

"I'm shocked," I said in mock horror, "that you'd ever resort to violence over a simple jest and even think I'd resort to trickery to evade an answer on so important a question. A question of that magnitude would require a court, particularly a district court, to check the case law carefully for binding precedents. And, in fact, the DuBois School situation is much like the facts in a case brought by black parents in Chicago whose children had been assigned by lottery away from their integrated neighborhood schools because the percentage of nonwhites in those schools exceeded 60 percent, a figure the board feared would trigger white flight."[14]

"Surely, the district court told the board to amend its plan to reflect better the   70 wishes of the black parents?"

"I'm afraid not. The court did insist that the schools to which the black children were assigned be integrated, and then approved the amended plan. And let me hasten to add that other courts facing similar issues have reached similar results.[15] So, you see, if the issues in the Chronicle suit are viewed primarily from a doctrinal viewpoint, it is a difficult case."

Geneva sighed. "It sounds like you want to play law professor rather than judge. Can you justify the Chicago decision in the next few minutes?"

"It shouldn't be hard. The board's lottery scheme involves an obvious racial classification. That is, when the percentage of nonwhites reaches 60 percent, the number of students—selected by race—exceeding that percentage will be selected by lottery for assignment to other integrated schools farther from their homes. Ordinarily, racial classifications of that type are deemed by courts inherently 'suspect' and can survive judicial scrutiny only if justified by a 'compelling state interest' and if there's a close connection or 'fit' between the classification and the compelling interest to be served."

"And," Geneva anticipated me, "the Chicago school board maintained that stable racial integration is the compelling state interest and that the lottery plan is closely tailored to achieve that interest with the least possible harm."

"Well, they will use that argument if their primary argument is rejected.   75 Basically, they'll contend that their lottery plan involves a benign racial classification. Since race is being used to further an appropriate goal—integrated schools—only an intermediate level of scrutiny is required."

"What is benign about excluding students from the schools they want to attend solely on the basis of their race?"

"The board might respond, 'Look, Miss, you civil rights types got us into this school-desegregation business. Now we've looked at the "white flight" studies, and if we do nothing to change the balance of these schools, they'll soon be all black, and you folks will be black in court screaming that the board allowed the schools to become all black. We don't want that to happen, but we can't force whites to go to the public schools. So, as the percentage of nonwhites increases, we must reassign some of the black kids. Do you have a better plan?'"

"I doubt," said Geneva, "that any court would base its approval on grounds that the society's racism required them to withhold a group's rights."

"I wouldn't bet any serious money on that doubt. One court wrote: 'Although white fears about the admission of minority students are ugly, those fears cannot be disregarded without imperiling integration across the entire system. . . . The exodus of white children from the public schools would disadvantage the entire minority community and nullify this voluntary desegregation effort.'"[16]

"And would you feel bound by these decisions?"   80

"Given your likely reaction, I hesitate to say this, but I think both courts reached the only decision they could for the reason pointed out in the decision I just quoted. While my sympathies are with the black parents, the school board plans are the only way to maintain racial balance."

"That, of course," Geneva chided, "is precisely the problem with equating the 'equal educational opportunity' right established in the *Brown* decision with racial balance. The racial balance goal can be met only in schools where whites are in a majority and retain control. The quality of schooling black children receive is determined by what whites (they of the group who caused the harm in the first place) are willing to provide—which, as we should not be surprised to learn, is not very much."

"And you, Geneva? Let's just suppose that you were on the bench, sitting there without the vaunted power of your Curia friends, and with all the restraints of legal doctrine that bind a judge. How would you rule on the DuBois School parents' petition?"

Geneva's eyes flashed. "I cannot imagine anyone offering me or my accepting a judgeship, but were I somehow to find myself up there in a black robe instead of a Curia gold one, I sure as hell would not dismiss their petition out of hand, either because there was precedent for such action or because both the plaintiffs and the defendants urged me to do it. In fact, a petition like that filed by both a sizable and an articulate portion of the plaintiff class should put any judge on notice that the plaintiffs' class-action suit does not represent all the plaintiffs."

"In defense of the judge," I interjected, "these petitions by portions of the   85 class do not come to light until long after the suit is filed and at a time when formal intervention would be both difficult and unfair to the parties."

"If *I* were the judge, I would hope to employ either judicial imagination or some good old mother wit in the situation."

"Such as?"

"Such as calling for testimony from the petitioners and perhaps holding a nonbinding referendum in the affected community regarding the plan."

"I fear you'd expose yourself to criticism for turning the judicial process into a popularity contest."

"I would not be afraid of criticism, and I think black parents—and likely some   90 white parents as well—would welcome an opportunity to engage in a discussion that has been taken over by the lawyers weighing inappropriate legal standards to reach unjust results."

"You're a tough woman!"

"I assume that *tough* is intended as a grudging compliment and not as a synonym for *evil*, which I would take as an affront. Howsomever," she continued, smiling at her "down home" expression, "my action would not be a precedent. As you know—but likely do not approve—several courts have become more sensitive over time to the fact that the plaintiffs' class in school desegregation is not a monolith, particularly on the issue of relief. Moreover, a few courts have come to recognize both the importance of the educational potential in desegregation remedies, and the fact that racial balance is not synonymous with, and may be antithetical to, effective education for black children. As a result of their tardy but still welcome awakening, a few courts have responded to black parents' preference for relief intended to make the schools more educationally effective rather than simply more racially balanced."[17]

"It's unwise," I cautioned, "to read those decisions for more than they're worth."

"Spoken like the law teacher you are!" Geneva replied, in friendly disdain. "You tell me how I should 'read' the 1981 *Dallas* school-case decision rejecting a civil rights request that a mainly black subdivision of the district be broken up in order to maximize desegregation with neighboring subdistricts that were mainly white.[18] The black subdistrict, like the DuBois School parents, intervened in the case and put on testimony that convinced the district court of the wide difference of opinion within the minority community on the issue of relief.[19] Based on that testimony, the court observed: 'Minorities have begun to question whether busing is "educationally advantageous, irrelevant, or even disadvantageous."' To illustrate his concern, the judge's lengthy opinion referred to what I consider a classic statement by the school-board president, one of three minorities on the board, who had said:

> I don't think that additional busing is even the issue. . . . It has never been the issue. . . . The issue is whether we are going to educate the children and youth. . . . I think that the whole question around the whole busing issue just loses sight of why we are here and what the schools are about now. I think it was a noble idea in 1954 . . . but what I envisioned and I'm sure what other black parents envisioned in 1954 just never happened.[20]

"The witness could extend that comment to cover virtually every aspect of civil rights," Geneva added. "Now, given our general agreement that the Chronicle's message is tragic, how can we use its insight to formulate more effective civil rights strategies in the future?"

"Well, Geneva, my feeling is that while whites continue to use their power to allocate to themselves the best educational resources, and to honor our pleas for justice only when there is further profit for the system, it will be difficult to gain more than limited benefits—whether in racial balance or in improved resources."

"Of course," Geneva said, "neither strategy will be easy! But if the issue and the goal are as the Dallas witness suggested—'whether or not we are going to educate the children and the youth'—then you simply have to agree, first, that racial balance and integration—what the witness called 'a noble idea in 1954'—is of very limited value today; and, second, that our priority must be to gain educationally effective schools for our children."

Geneva's eyes were bright, her black skin had a warm glow, and perspiration was trickling down her forehead. She caught me staring as she looked for her handkerchief. We both laughed.

"Friend," she asked, "if white folks ever decided to straighten up and do right, what would we black folks have to talk about?"

"Lord only knows," I answered. "Take our debate over school policy. It has been going on for two hundred years. In 1787, Prince Hall, the black Revolutionary War veteran and community leader, urged the Massachusetts legislature to provide funds for an 'African' school because, in his words, 'we . . . must fear for our rising offspring to see them in ignorance in a land of gospel light.'[21] That petition was urging separate schools for black children who, while admitted to the public schools in Boston, were treated so poorly that their parents withdrew them."

"I bet your forebears were critical of Hall's action and urged black parents to return their children for more insults and mistreatment."

"Listen, Geneva, I'm not going to swell the ranks of the multitudes of black folks in Boston who claim their forebears were never slaves. Suffice it to say that I'd be proud to be a descendant of such a prophetic critic for, after the black community built a school for themselves which later the school committee assumed responsibility for, parents were soon complaining that the school-master was an incompetent teacher and guilty of 'improper familiarities' with female students—all of which charges the school committee ignored. The result was a suit to desegregate the schools—which the black parents lost in 1850."[22]

"Yes," Geneva agreed, "but the legislature came to the rescue of that nineteenth-century school-integration movement and, a few years later, voted to desegregate the Boston schools. The blacks were likely overjoyed, but they should have listened to one Thomas P. Smith, whom I would like to adopt as an ancestor. On Christmas Eve in 1849, Brother Smith spoke to the 'Colored Citizens of Boston' urging them not to abolish the colored schools. He warned that if the schools were desegregated, black children would have to be assigned to white schools, where the space would be inadequate, necessitating the construction of new schools which would again be all black. Sure enough, within a dozen years, the Boston public schools were totally segregated."[23]

"Despite the Boston setbacks, though, black people continued over the succeeding decades to file dozens of suits either to desegregate the schools or to gain equal facilities in the black schools."[24]

"All that proves," Geneva responded, "is that some truths come hard. In his 1849 speech, Thomas Smith argued that the black school was in good condition, and added that 'the order and discipline of the scholars, their cheerfulness and spirit, are unsurpassed by any school in the city.' Smith said further that if the black school was abolished at the request of blacks, the inference would be drawn that 'when equally taught and equally comfortable, we are ashamed of ourselves, and feel disgraced by being together; but the proverb says, "Respect yourself ere others respect you."'"[25]

"Well, Geneva, I don't think Mr. Smith really understood how the segregation he supported undermined the self-respect he espoused."

"You sound like one of the civil rights stalwarts who castigated W. E. B. DuBois when he said much the same thing in the 1930s. He had serious misgivings about the massive school-desegregation litigation campaign the NAACP was contemplating. In urging a more flexible strategy, Dr. DuBois advised that blacks need neither segregated schools nor mixed schools. What they need is education."[26]

"With all due respect to Dr. DuBois who, as you know, is one of my heroes, I think he was begging the question. We agree our children need education. The issue debated over two centuries is how blacks can best obtain it in a still-resistive society."

"Like too many black folks," Geneva scolded, "you spend more time doing homage to his memory than reading his words. DuBois argued that the priority for blacks should be the educational goal rather than the means of achieving that goal. He also suggested that effective schooling for black children might be possible even though the socializing aspects of integrated classrooms were not available."

"Geneva, we've heard it all before, but the NAACP did proceed with its   110
school-desegregation campaign. After years of trying, they won, and the *Brown* decision settled the matter of our approach to quality schooling for black children—desegregated schools."

"You sound as though the schools were *in fact* desegregated, as though you are still committed to 'the noble idea of 1954.' You need to start paying tardy heed to your hero. What Dr. DuBois said over half a century ago is still pertinent to all the black parents in this damned country who care more about their children's schooling than about their long-lost noble dreams. Listen!

> A mixed school with poor and unsympathetic teachers, with hostile public opinion, and no teaching of truth concerning black folk, is bad. A segregated school with ignorant placeholders, inadequate equipment, poor salaries, and wretched housing, is equally bad. Other things being equal, the mixed school is the broader, more natural basis for the education of all youth. It gives wider contacts; it inspires greater self-confidence; and suppresses the inferiority complex. But other things seldom are equal, and in that case, Sympathy, Knowledge, and Truth, outweigh all that the mixed school can offer."[27]

"The man was a powerful writer," I acknowledged. "Black kids with his ability would make it whatever the school they attended."

"True, but no group produces more than a few persons of Dr. DuBois's caliber. Most children will benefit from good schooling and will suffer if their educations are poor. They are the real subjects of our debate, the real victims of our mistakes, the innocent sacrifices to our continued refusal to face up to our real problem as black people in a white land."

"I thought our real problem was education, Geneva."

"Nonsense. If that were so, you and I would not encounter the discrimination   115
we and even the best educated of us continue to experience. And statistics would not continue to report that, on average, white high school dropouts earn more than blacks who have finished high school, white high school grads earn more than blacks who have finished college, and so on, and on."[28]

"Are you suggesting that the attainment of 'equal educational opportunity' must await a time when we are at least moving in the direction of 'equal economic opportunity'?"

"In a country where individual rights were created to protect wealth, we simply must find a means to prime the economic pump for black people, particularly those of us living at the poverty level."

"That statement," I warned, "will win you several awards from conservative groups who oppose further 'benefits' for blacks and urge that they roll up their sleeves and make it the way immigrants from Europe did several generations ago—and the way some Hispanic and Asian groups seem to be doing today."[29]

"I don't care who agrees with me," Geneva said militantly. "Those conservatives are right about the need for blacks to get into jobs and off welfare. And, whatever their handicaps, Hispanics and Asians are not burdened with the legacy of slavery and segregation in a land of freedom that, over time, has undermined the sense of self-worth for many black people. Nor will these immigrants face, at least initially, obstacles based on the deeply held belief that blacks *should* be on the bottom. Furthermore, white ethnics were helped up the socio-economic ladder by several rungs that have seldom, if ever, been available to blacks."

"A point Professor Martin Kilson made quite well," I said, "reminding us that the white ethnics' experience with upward mobility required no special individualism as far as obtaining government assistance: [120]

> Jews, Italians, Irish, Slavs, Greeks, and other white ethnic groups exploited every conceivable opportunity, including extensive corruption, to bring government—the public purse and public authority—into the balance, providing capital for construction firms and new technological industries, city and state colleges and technical institutes, educational grants and loans, among other government benefits."[30]

Geneva clapped her hands. "Well stated! But it leaves open the question of how those blacks for whom civil rights statutes are mostly meaningless will get a start at a time when unskilled jobs hardly pay a living wage, and manufacturing is leaving the country for so-called off-shore sites where employees can be hired for very low wages."

"You ask the question as though you have an answer."

"Not an answer—but a way of testing the viability of such an economic answer. Bear with me, friend, for the next Chronicle."

ENDNOTES

1. Daniel Monti, *A Semblance of Justice: St. Louis School Desegregation and Order in Urban America* (1985).

2. See, for example, *Morgan v. Kerrigan,* 409 F. Supp. 1141, 1151 (D. Mass. 1976) (placing the South Boston High School in receivership to insure compliance with desegregation orders); *Turner v. Goolsby,* 255 F. Supp. 724, 730–35 (S.D. Ga. 1966).

3. See, for example, *Chambers v. Hendersonville City Bd. of Educ.,* 364 F.2d 189 (4th Circuit 1966); *McCurdy v. Bd. of Public Instruction,* 509 F.2d 540 (5th Circuit 1975); *Williams v. Albemarle City Bd. of Educ.,* 508 F.2d 1242 (4th Circuit 1974). But despite dozens of suits in which black teachers won reinstatement and back pay after being terminated during the desegregation process, literally thousands of black teachers and administrators lost their jobs as Southern school boards complied with desegregation orders. See amicus curiae brief prepared by the *National Education Association for United States v. Georgia,* No. 30,338 (5th Circuit 1971).

4. Ray Rist, *The Invisible Children: School Integration in American Society* (1978).

5. Robert L. Carter, "A Reassessment of *Brown v. Board,*" in D. Bell, ed., *Shades of Brown: New Perspectives on School Desegregation* (1980), pp. 21–27.

6. Ibid., p. 27.

7. See, for example, *Covington* v. *Edwards,* 264 F.2d 780 (4th Circuit 1959), *cert. denied,* 361 U.S. 840 (1959) (pupil-placement law validated and procedures established required to be followed).

8. *Kelley* v. *Board of Educ.,* 270 F.2d 209 (6th Circuit 1959), *cert. denied,* 361 U.S. 924 (1959).

9. *Green* v. *County School Bd. of New Kent Co.,* 391 U.S. 430 (1968) (after several years of approving such plans, they were held not valid unless they work to effectuate a desegregated school system).

10. See, for example, A. Miller, *A "Capacity for Outrage": The Judicial Odyssey of J. Skelly Wright* (1984), pp. 48–88; J. Bass, *Civil Rights Lawyers on the Bench* (1981); J. Peltason, *Fifty Eight Lonely Men* (1961).

11. *Brown* v. *Board of Education,* 349 U.S. 294, 301 (1955).

12. See Faustine C. Jones-Wilson, *A Traditional Model of Educational Excellence: Dunbar High School of Little Rock, Arkansas* (1981); Thomas Sowell, "Black Excellence—The Case of Dunbar High School," *Public Interest* 35 (1974): 3; Thomas Sowell, "Patterns of Black Excellence," *Public Interest* 43 (1976): 26.

13. Sara Lightfoot, *The Good High School* (1983), pp. 29–55.

14. *Johnson* v. *Chicago Board of Educ.,* 604 F.2d 504 (7th Circuit 1979).

15. See, for example, *Parent Ass'n of Andrew Jackson High School* v. *Ambach,* 598 F.2d 705 (2d Circuit 1979) (approving a limit, inspired by "white flight," on the number of black students permitted to transfer from an all-black school to neighboring less-segregated schools).

16. Ibid., p. 720.

17. See, for example, *Milliken* v. *Bradley II,* 433 U.S. 267 (1977) (federal courts can order remedial educational programs as a part of a school-desegregation decree where such relief, in response to the constitutional violation, is designed to as nearly as possible restore victims of the discriminatory conduct to the position they would have occupied in the absence of such conduct, and takes into account the interests of state and local authorities in managing their own affairs, consistent with the Constitution).

18. *Tasby* v. *Wright,* 520 F. Supp. 683 (Northern District of Texas 1981).

19. Ibid., p. 689. The court described the intervenors as a "broad-based minority community group composed of parents, patrons and taxpayers with children in the [schools], as well as representatives from a number of civic, political and ecumenical associations in the black community" (p. 689).

20. Ibid., pp. 732–33.

21. Prince Hall, "Negroes Ask for Equal Educational Facilities" (1787), in H. Aptheker, ed., *A Documentary History of the Negro People in the United States* (1951), p. 19.

22. *Roberts* v. *City of Boston,* 59 Mass. (5 Cush.) 198 (1850) (the school committee's segregation policy was deemed reasonable; and as to plaintiff's charge that segregated schools breed racial prejudice, the court observed that feelings of prejudice by whites were rooted deep in community opinion and feelings, and would influence white actions as effectually in an integrated as in a separate school).

23. Arthur White, "The Black Leadership Class and Education in Antebellum Boston," *Journal of Negro Education* 42 (1973): 504, 513, 514.

24. For a collection of the cases, see Derrick Bell, *Race, Racism and American Law* (2d ed. 1980), pp. 568–74.

25. White, "Black Leadership Class," p. 514.

26. W. E. B. DuBois, "Does the Negro Need Separate Schools?" *Journal of Negro Education* 4 (1935): 328. The essay is reprinted in J. Lester, ed., *The Seventh Son: The Thought and Writings of W. E. B. DuBois* (1971), vol. II, p. 408.

27. Ibid., p. 335.

28. See, for example, Olsen, "Employment Discrimination Litigation: New Priorities in the Struggle for Black Equality," *Harvard Civil Rights–Civil Liberties Law Review* 6 (1970): 20, 24–25.

29. See, for example, Charles Murray, *Losing Ground* (1984). Such views have been challenged vigorously; see, for example, Bernard Anderson, "The Case for Social Policy," in National Urban League, *The State of Black America* (1986), p. 153.

30. Martin Kilson, "Whither Integration," *American Scholar* 45 (1976): 360, 372.

Sonia Sanchez

Sonia Sanchez (1934–) is one of the principal writers of the Black Arts Movement of the 1960s who redefined blackness for America. Sanchez is a social activist. With fiery rhetoric, this wordsmith documents the importance of family, relationships, and community in her varied writings. She retired from a distinguished teaching career at Temple University in 2000. Her opus includes the following poetry collections: *Homecoming: Poems* (1969), *I've Been a Woman: New and Selected Poems* (1979), *Under a Soprano Sky* (1987), *Wounded in the House of a Friend* (1995), *Does Your House Have Lions?* (1995), *Like the Singing Coming Off the Drums: Love Poems* (1998), and *Shake Loose My Skin* (1999). She was awarded the American Book Award in 1985 for *homegirls and handgrenades* (1984).

In the following poem from *Under the Soprano Sky* (1987), Sanchez presents graphic images of the destruction of a Philadelphia neighborhood in 1985 as a result of a clash between residents and city officials.

elegy

(for MOVE* and Philadelphia)

1.

philadelphia	1
a disguised southern city	
squatting in the eastern pass of	
colleges cathedrals and cowboys.	
philadelphia. a phalanx of parsons	5
and auctioneers	
modern gladiators	
erasing the delirium of death from their shields	
while houses burn out of control.	

---

*MOVE: a Philadelphia-based back-to-nature group whose headquarters was bombed by the police on May 13, 1985, killing men, women and children. An entire city block was destroyed by fire.

2.

c'mon girl hurry on down to osage st   10
they're roasting in the fire
smell the dreadlocks and blk/skins
roasting in the fire.

c'mon newsmen and tvmen
hurryondown to osage st and   15
when you have chloroformed the city
and after you have stitched up your words
hurry on downtown for sanctuary
in taverns and corporations

and the blood is not yet dry.   20

3.

how does one scream in thunder?

4.

they are combing the morning for shadows
and screams tongue-tied without faces
look. over there. one eye
escaping from its skin   25
and our heartbeats slowdown to a drawl
and the kingfisher calls out from his downtown capital
And the pinstriped general reenlists
his tongue for combat
and the police come like twin seasons of drought and flood.   30
they're combing the city for lifeliberty and
the pursuit of happiness.

5.

how does one city scream in thunder?

6.

hide us O lord
deliver us from our nakedness.   35
exile us from our laughter
give us this day our rest from seduction
peeling us down to our veins.

and the tower was like no other.   amen.
and the streets escaped under the   40
cover of darkness   amen.
and the voices called out from

their wounds   amen.
and the fire circumsized the city   amen.

7.

who anointeth this city with napalm?   (i say)   45
who giveth this city in holy infanticide?

8.

beyond the mornings and afternoons
and deaths detonating the city.
beyond the tourist roadhouses
trading in lobotomies   50
there is a glimpse of earth
this prodigal earth
beyond edicts and commandments
commissioned by puritans
there are people   55
navigating the breath of hurricanes.
beyond concerts and football
and mummers strutting their
sequined processionals.
there is this earth. this country. this city.   60
this people.
collecting skeletons from waiting rooms
lying in wait. for honor and peace.
one day.

Kenneth Meeks

Kenneth Meeks is the managing editor of *Black Enterprise*. He was a contributing author to *Brotherman: The Odyssey of Black Men in America* (1996). Meeks spent several years gathering evidence and anecdotal stories for his research, culminating in *Driving While Black: Highways, Shopping Malls, Taxicabs, Sidewalks: How to Fight Back If You Are a Victim of Racial Profiling* (2000).

This excerpt is from Chapter 7, "Shopping in a Group While Black."

Shopping in a Group While Black
A Coach's Story

Howie Evans was the basketball coach for the University of Maryland at Eastern Shore in 1985. That year he and his team were on a three-game exhibition tour in South Carolina. When they arrived in Columbia on Thanksgiving Day for their second game, the team unpacked their bags, put on their warm-up uniforms, and stretched their legs. They were hungry from their travels. The National Urban League's local chapter had a planned Thanksgiving Day dinner for the basketball team, but until then they needed something to eat.

Normally, the coach wouldn't allow his players to roam around the city. It takes away the strength in their legs. But on this particular day he bent the rules. It was an exhibition game, so he let his team out. They picked a mall about a quarter of a mile from the hotel.

Evans immediately spotted trouble when the team stepped into the shopping mall. Two security guards who had been sitting nearby went into action. Evans didn't say anything to his team about the guards behind them, but he remained mindful. As the team meandered into the center of the mall, they split into little cliques. A few disappeared into clothing stores, another went into a music store, and a few more just window-shopped. Evans himself went into a Radio Shack to buy some batteries. He never expected to see the two guards placing six of his players against the wall.

"What's going on?" Evans asked as he walked up on the scene.

The taller guard, who had sergeant stripes sewn into his uniform, answered.   5
"They stole something from one of the stores."

"What did you see them take?"

The sergeant paused to eyeball Evans. "Who are you?"

"I'm their coach," Evans answered. He pulled out his identification. "Did you see them take anything?"

"No," the sergeant answered, "but somebody told us they did."

"Show me who told you they saw my team steal something. I want to know   10
what he saw."

"We can't do that. He's not here."

Antennas went up. "What? You're going to search these young men based on something somebody told you, and—by your own admission—he's not even here in the mall?"

"I'm doing my job."

Evans took a deep breath and chose his words carefully. "You know, I watched you guys when we first came in here. You were sitting by the door, and when we got about fifty feet away from you, you got up and started following us. We've only been in here twenty minutes, and already you've accused us of stealing something. Why were you following us in the first place?"

The sergeant fumbled for an answer.   15

"I'm not going to let you search these kids out here in public," Evans continued confidently. "If you want to search them, you're going to have to take us down to the police station."

"I'll have to call them," the sergeant explained, almost as if he hoped the idea would make Evans stand down.

"So call them. If you don't, I will."

The sergeant detained the six players against the wall while Evans huddled with the rest of his team. Spectators watched from the wings.

"Look at these guys. What are they doing now?" a black woman whispered.   20

It broke Evans's heart that black people were walking away shaking their heads in embarrassment because they assumed that these young black men had done something wrong. The team promised him that no one had stolen anything and that it was all a setup. In fact, a black security guard was called to the scene— Evans now believes to justify that no one was being a racist—but after a few minutes of sizing up the situation, he threw his hands in the air in disgust.

"You guys are harassing them," the black guard said and walked away.

"We need you to stay here," the sergeant commanded.

"Give me a break."

But the sergeant wasn't hearing it.   25

While everyone waited for the police to arrive, Evans found a pay phone and called the local chapter of the NAACP. He explained his situation and asked them to send an attorney down to the scene. His second phone call was to the local black newspaper. He informed one of the editors of what was happening to his players. It was mere coincidence that a reporter for a local mainstream newspaper was in the mall at the time. Evans and the young reporter discussed everything.

In the meantime the sergeant let the six kids relax with the rest of the team, but he wanted everyone in a group.

"Don't panic," Evans told his team.

Evans suddenly saw the situation escalate into a potentially dangerous one. He had reasons to keep his team calm. Most of his players were young freshmen and sophomores who had never been on a collegiate road trip before. And for most of them this was their first time away from home on Thanksgiving.

On the other hand, the team was up against an out-and-out Southern racist   30 with a gun. The sergeant stood about six feet and two hundred pounds, walking among the posse of the basketball players with an overbearing attitude and his hand continuously touching his gun. As Evans saw it, the sergeant was trying to impress the other guard by showing that he could take on these young black athletes, that he was someone who was used to grabbing black kids and throwing them up against the wall on a regular basis.

Evans kept a level head and remained very professional. He never raised his voice, just maintained a dignified degree of intelligence and poise. "Are you trying to intimidate us by walking around us with your hand on your gun? Don't you think that's dangerous?"

"I have the safety catch on," he answered.

"I would hope so," Evans said. "But doesn't that present a very intimidating presence, you walking around with your hand on your gun? These kids aren't going anywhere. They will move only if I tell them to move. If I told these kids to get up and run out, they would. But then you'd probably shoot one of them in the back. Right?"

A call blared over the walkie-talkie. The police were here. The sergeant met with the police and the manager of the mall, a man in his late twenties or early thirties, separately while Evans waited with his team.

Finally the manager walked over to Evans. "My guy said that they stole   35 something."

"You know the only reason your guys stopped these kids was because they're black. Look at all these other kids in the mall; no one stopped them. These kids are college kids, and they're wearing identifying uniforms, so why would they go into a store and steal something with all this ID on? They don't even have pockets."

But the manager wasn't convinced.

"Your guy also didn't tell you that the person who told him these kids stole something isn't in the mall either. And your guy didn't see them steal anything."

The manager listened carefully, then walked away to confer with his team. "Stay here."

They took a long time.   40

"So what are you guys going to do?" Evans finally asked as he approached them. "You are accusing these guys of something simply based on who they are. As soon as my lawyer comes—I have an attorney on the way—we're willing to go to the police station, where you can search these kids. But if you search them here, I'm going to bring a lawsuit against you."

"You have a lawyer?" Everyone was surprised. "Just wait for us over there. We'll be there when we're done."

Evans remembers overhearing one of them calling him a wise guy and saying, "They always bring up this we-stopped-them-because-they-were-black stuff."

From a distance Evans could see that the police officers, who were also white, were concerned. "You guys had better handle this. We're leaving."

The policemen left before the NAACP attorney arrived. And as Evans filled in the   45
details for the attorney, the sergeant's case seemed to crumble. Close to two hours after the team walked into the mall, the manager finally had little choice but to let them go.

"Perhaps you wouldn't have a problem, Coach, if you didn't have all these kids coming into the mall at the same time."

"What are you talking about? What am I supposed to do? Bring them in two at a time, go back and bring in two more? This is a team. Would you say that to anybody else? I think you owe us an apology."

"Don't get stressed, Coach," said the attorney from the NAACP. "They're always stopping our kids at this mall."

Neither Howie Evans nor his team ever received a formal apology from the city of Columbia, South Carolina, the manager of the mall, or the security agency hired to patrol it.

Lieutenant Arthur Doyle

Lieutenant Arthur Doyle (1943–) retired from the New York City Police Department after serving 29 years. This excerpt, "From the Inside Looking Out," is his observations of police brutality from *Police Brutality: An Anthology* (2000), edited by Jill Nelson.

From the Inside Looking Out

Twenty-Nine Years in the New York Police Department

It was an ambition of mine going back to high school to join the police department. My family lived on 115th Street and Lenox Avenue, and I was born in Harlem in 1943. My father was a laborer, working at Fordham University. My mom was a housewife. When I was about seven, we moved to the South Bronx, where I went to Prospect Junior High School and then Morris High School. I graduated in 1960, a few years after General Colin Powell.

As a youngster, I was sort of a joiner. I joined the Police Athletic League (PAL), where they had sports I could engage in. An officer from the Forty-first Precinct, a patrolman named Officer Thomas, coordinated PAL. He was African American, one of the few such cops around then. He encouraged me to consider joining the police force.

Basically, I saw cops making things right. No people appreciate the selling of drugs in their neighborhood. Not that that was a big problem in the 1950s in the South Bronx, but I saw police act on things like that. It wasn't that I had any relatives or friends who were police; I simply felt it was something I could do.

I graduated from high school when I was seventeen, and two weeks after that I was on my way to a four-year enlistment in the Marine Corps. Although I liked the Marine Corps, I didn't forget my thoughts about becoming a police officer. In 1963, home on leave, I decided to take the examination.

Right away, I ran into problems. I passed the written part of the exam, and I   5
asked for and received a ninety-six-hour pass from my base down South to come up and take the physical exam. I'd been in the Marine Corps, a pretty tough outfit, and was in good shape, so I wasn't worried about the physical. I thought I'd done pretty well. But the department told me I had failed. The reason? I was missing a tooth. That's something that occurs in my family; some of us are missing teeth. It hardly seemed like a reason to deny me entrance to the police force, though.

I took this rejection letter back to the base dentist, a U.S. Navy captain, and he read it. He examined my teeth and got very upset at the rejection I had received. He said, "Your teeth are excellent. They are good enough that if you had applied to the Naval Academy, you would be accepted without question." The captain wrote a letter to the Department of Personnel in the city. It was a pretty strong letter, mentioning my record in the Marine Corps. The next thing I knew, I got another letter, saying I was accepted and on the list.

Months later, at the graduation ceremony from the Police Academy, I turned to smile at another officer, a White man, standing right next to me. He smiled back. His teeth were all rotten—falling-out rotten.

That was my first experience with recruitment discrimination. I got another one right afterward, involving my own family.

My brother-in-law, who had moved to New York City from Tuskegee, Alabama, was very interested in joining the police department as well. At that time, I was already actively recruiting African Americans to join. My brother-in-law took the exam and did very well, too. But the department investigated him thoroughly. He had never known his father. He had been raised by his grandparents back in Alabama. The police personnel officials told him he had to go back to Tuskegee, find three people who knew his father, and have them write letters attesting to his father's good character. My brother-in-law was humiliated and frustrated. There was no way he could get those letters. So he just went to work for the post office instead.

Those kinds of rejections frustrate people when they occur at ages like nine-   10
teen, twenty, or twenty-one. Most of them are not going to fight back. The department seemed to have ways to frustrate people it didn't really want. In my police

class of five hundred, there was a handful of other Blacks. I found that several had similar stories. One had been put through a tough hearing about a distant relative he knew nothing about, who had been arrested many years earlier. This sort of thing didn't happen with other officers.

It was obvious that minority recruitment was not really a goal in the department. Somebody should have prevented that dental rejection. Someone should have circumvented the demand that my brother-in-law find people in Tuskegee to vouch for his father's character. For my part, I was humiliated. But where would I go to confront the problem? To whom would I talk about it?

My initial assignment was to the Forty-fourth Precinct in the South Bronx, near where I grew up. The first real lesson I learned was that the police department has both a formal and an informal leadership structure. Most people pay greater attention to the informal structure, where leaders have their own rules. In the police department, the informal leaders may be other cops and not necessarily ranking officers. They are the ones who lay down the rules.

One rule I learned was that any suspect who assaulted a police officer in any way was never supposed to be able to walk into the station house on his own. He was supposed to be beaten so badly that he couldn't walk. If you did bring a prisoner in who had assaulted you or another officer and he was still standing, you were admonished by your colleagues, sometimes by supervisors.

This happened to me several times. It led to some bad feelings. I refused to accept prisoners who had been beaten while handcuffed. I made it clear I wouldn't tolerate that in my presence. It was really not a humane or manly thing to do. But it was not uncommon to see officers take advantage of the fact that they were police officers and abuse that power, because that's what the informal leadership structure demanded.

For a while, I worked with youth gangs in the Bronx. There was one particularly tough kid. He was part African American, part White; they called him Red. This kid had a long criminal history and had assaulted police officers in the past. It was indicated he was involved in a double homicide.   15

My partner and I accosted Red on the sidewalk. We arrested him, and he came along with us without a problem. We walked him into the precinct. Within minutes I was called aside by another cop. "Hey, why is this kid walking in?" this cop asked.

"Because he is my prisoner and that is not my thing," I replied. He backed off, but I could see he didn't like it. At other times, if I saw someone else beating a prisoner, I stopped him. They didn't like it, but I insisted.

A similar unwritten law covered chases as well. If an officer had to chase someone, by car or on foot, the person would invariably be beaten when captured. After a long chase, the officers would be pumped up, angry. They would want revenge for having put their lives in danger. That was the case in the Rodney King situation. It was taken to the extreme.

At the trial in Los Angeles, we all saw that video for days on end, and the officers were found not guilty. The system came to their defense. They weren't portrayed as bad cops, within either the law enforcement community or the larger community. Analysts argued that the force used was within departmental guidelines, even though the whole world had seen this man, lying prostrate on the ground, hit over and over and over again. Those cops were out of control. Although a supervisor was present, they were still completely out of control. One needs a supervisor on the scene who keeps his cool, who holds the officers back. Why have a sixty-five-mile-per-hour chase down crowded streets, with the risk of injuring innocent people, over a traffic incident? Better to call off the chase.

But the system came to their defense.　　20

The informal leadership structure that I've described almost demanded that kind of response. Officers were more or less encouraged to be abusive, as long as they stayed within certain parameters. If they did, the system would give them the benefit of the doubt. Even if they went outside those parameters, the system would still come to their aid.

In my first few years on the force, we were often called out to handle civil disturbances. The Harlem riots erupted the same day that I was discharged from the Marine Corps in 1964, and there were frequent incidents in the ensuing weeks and months, some in Harlem, some in the Bronx. They almost always followed the same sort of scenario: unnecessary force, indiscriminate use of the nightstick, unnecessary brutality. The goal was supposed to be to stop the riot or the disturbance and to arrest those who were actively participating. Not to wantonly corral people, or corner them. When you cornered people, you invariably had a group of cops on one side and angry people on the other who defended themselves. At those times, it looked as if it was just one mob chasing another mob.

Later on in the 1960s, I was assigned to a lot of anti-Vietnam War demonstrations. I was also assigned to Columbia University in 1968, where a group of students had taken over a building. The police were called in to clear it. I saw these officers wildly clubbing these kids. I was surprised. That these were White kids offers another clue to the nature of brutality: race does not necessarily have to be a part of it. The only crime of the White students was to have taken over and occupied a building at a prestigious school. Even though there was some provocation—some things were thrown out of windows, and I think a student jumped from a window onto a cop—that sort of response was not necessary. The retaliation, the violence, far outweighed the provocation. I believe this happened because most cops thought the system would protect them if they went overboard.

I learned a different sort of lesson on the job as well, one that drove home to me the need for greater minority recruitment in the police force. Many times, my presence alone at the scene of a confrontation was enough to ease tensions. Having a Black officer as a witness on the scene seemed to discourage officers from abusing people. I think they couldn't be sure whether or not I would report it, and they may have been reluctant to go out of control.

That was particularly true on the few occasions we would encounter interra-　　25 cial couples walking in the city. White officers I worked with became highly perturbed at that sight.

There was a White man whom I generally liked and considered a good cop. Once when we were working as partners, he spotted an interracial couple walking down the street. He was behind the wheel and, without saying a word about what he was doing, he proceeded to drive around the block three times, slowing up each time we came abreast of the couple and glaring at them. At one point, the young Black man hugged the White woman he was with. He bent her back—almost as in a Hollywood swoon. I thought perhaps he had noticed us and was determined to make the point that no one was going to interfere with him. My partner became so outraged that he punched the car dashboard over and over. But he didn't do anything. I have absolutely no doubt that had I not been there he would have gotten out of the car, approached this man, and goaded him into some sort of confrontation.

Partly because I was from the community and had shown a rapport with kids, I was named to a youth aide position in the Bronx. Everyone called it the youth squad. It was a citywide unit, with each division having its own, separate youth squad. We would patrol juvenile delinquents. Our job was to get to know the kids. If there was a graffiti problem, if cars were being broken into, or if juveniles were committing certain other crimes, we would patrol those areas and investigate.

It was during that period that I endured one of the most humiliating personal experiences. I remember it was a very hot August afternoon—hot in the way only the South Bronx can be. The streets were baking. To top it off, the city was in the midst of a water shortage. It was my responsibility, as a youth patrol officer, to drive around with another officer and someone from the city's Department of Water Supply and turn hydrants off. We were on Union Avenue, where the kids had turned on a lot of hydrants. The other officer, a White man, turned to the city official, who was also White, and said, "Let's get them all off. Turn them all off. I want to make life as miserable for these bastards as I possibly can."

I guess he forgot I was even there in the same car with him. Or he didn't care. The man from the water supply department looked at me. I could tell he was embarrassed. Here I was, a Black officer who had grown up in the South Bronx, a boy who had relied on these hydrants himself for relief in hot summer weather, and here was this guy making a comment like that right in front of me.

I was steaming, but tried not to show it. I quickly reminded him that the   30 European Americans on the Lower East Side and in other parts of the city also lived in tenements and projects and also turned hydrants on. He didn't say a word—he just sat there, looking at those kids as though he hated them. I thought, "If this officer can express that kind of hostility with a Black officer in the car, you can imagine what goes on in other places." He and I both had youth squad assignments, where one of the requirements was supposed to be that you had an interest in young people.

There were other incidents like this, not as dramatic or venomous, but they let me know what some of my colleagues really thought. One day when I was headed out on patrol, I realized I had left my wallet at home. I was in a plainclothes unit then and lived on Olinville Avenue, not that far from the station house. I asked the two officers I was working with to drive with me to my home so that I could get my wallet. They did, and when I came back out, one of the officers looked up at the building and asked me, "How can you live in a building with all these Jews?" That was a shock to me. I thought, "If he can make a comment like that to me, I wonder what he is saying about Blacks and Latinos behind my back?" It was a wonderful building, and we had wonderful neighbors, much like those where we live now.

Other things that happened also disturbed me. There would be disparaging remarks on the police radio. Racist graffiti in the station house. Photographs of wanted posters with the names of Black suspects scratched out and the name of a Black officer written in. There were racial jokes, ethnic jokes.

During a locker room bull session with other cops while I was in the youth squad, I made a comment about being Black on the police force. I said that I had spent four years in the South with the Marine Corps from 1960 to 1964—and it was really the pre-Civil Rights South—and I still felt more comfortable with those White Marines than I did with my White colleagues in the New York City Police Department. I still feel that way today. In the Marine Corps, you might once in a while hear something like, "I'm just not used to taking no orders from no colored folks." But that was more comical than anything else, and we would all laugh.

The atmosphere in the squad must have been bad, because we had an old-timer, a lieutenant, who called me into his office. He asked me whether I felt uncomfortable in the squad and wanted a transfer. He was aware of the level of racism that was prevalent there. But I said no, I wanted to stick it out.

The majority of cops were good, hardworking, conscientious individuals.   35 They cared, and they wanted to do a good job. But there were enough bad cops— not one rotten apple, but several rotten apples—to give law enforcement the taint it had received.

Johnnie Cochran

Johnnie Cochran (1949–) is one of the top criminal defense lawyers in the United States. He has served on both sides of the bench while focusing on the problems of unlawful conduct by law enforcement officials. While an assistant Los Angeles County district attorney from 1978 to 1980, Cochran supervised investigations into shootings by police officers. Since the 1980s, he has successfully litigated many cases involving wrongful death and police brutality. As a result of his firm's winning million-dollar jury awards for families of persons who died as a result of the chokehold used by the LAPD, the practice was stopped. Cochran penned his autobiography, *Journey to Justice,* in 1996, followed by *A Lawyer's Life* (2002), in which he discusses his legal career.

In the following chapter of his autobiography, "My Brother's Keeper," Cochran reveals his frustration in losing a case in 1970 in which his client, Geronimo Pratt, a Black Panther, was charged with a double homicide. Cochran vows not to forget Pratt. A postscript is that, in 1997, through the efforts of Cochran and others, Pratt was freed and awarded $4.5 million in restitution (1.75 million from the FBI and 2.75 million from the city of Los Angeles).

My Brother's Keeper

Honest criminal defense lawyers will tell you that they live in terror of innocent clients, if only because the overwhelming majority of criminal cases end in a conviction of one sort or another.

The defense attorney's constitutional duty is to make sure that the state proves his or her client's guilt according to the procedural rules and beyond a reasonable doubt. By fulfilling that obligation, the defense lawyer becomes the guardian of due process, which is what really holds the ever-nascent tyranny of even the most democratic state at bay and prevents the rule of law from degenerating into mob rule.

But when your client is innocent, that constitutional obligation is joined by a profound moral and human duty. Defense of the innocent is an obligation more intimate and individual than even a physician bears. Unchecked disease, after all, destroys only the body; injustice unimpeded can maim its victim's very soul.

In the months following the Panthers' trial, I would have that axiom burned so deeply into me that, even today, I feel as if it is inscribed directly on my heart.

The Panther verdict came down just two days before Christmas 1971. The season's glad tidings were all the more welcome that year.   5

At the time, another lawyer, Frank A. Evans, Jr., and I owned a supper club in South Los Angeles called "There." With its mahogany-paneled walls, warm lighting, topflight chef, and congenial bar, the club soon became a popular hangout for local sports celebrities. Muhammad Ali was a frequent visitor, though as a devout Muslim, he did not drink. The opportunity to rub elbows with sports stars, along with courteous, professional service, which I'd learned to recognize in my catering days, quickly made There a favorite spot among the city's growing black middle class. It would be years before diet and discipline became synonymous in the American mind, and our kitchen was very much a creature of its time. A typical Sunday brunch at There, for example, would, in the words of our menu, "start with our King Crab Cocktail Supreme, move on to a tureen of soup du jour, followed by prime rib of beef au jus, roasted according to an old English recipe in our specially designed ovens, and finish with cheese cake in a hot Cherries Jubilee Sauce. To accompany your meal, we suggest a bottle of cabernet sauvignon." My cholesterol level notwithstanding, that still sounds pretty good.

I always gave a Christmas party for my friends and professional associates at the club, and that year we also invited the jurors who had decided the Panther case. It was a memorable and emotional evening for all of us, our pleasure in each other's company deepened by the spirit of that blessed season with its promise of "peace on earth to men of goodwill." More than any of the reams of favorable publicity I received after the verdict, I still treasure the note those twelve jurors sent me:

"Dear Mr. Cochran," it read. "We would like to thank you for the lovely party you gave in our honor. Everyone had a wonderful time and it was just great to meet all the attorneys personally after our months together in court. We thank you and wish you our best in future cases." It was signed, "Jurors of Dept. 101."

So, as 1972 began, I felt an almost intoxicating sense of confidence and optimism. My colleagues and I had emerged victorious from the longest conspiracy trial in California history, and I personally had won the last ten murder cases that had come my way. I was hot. So I wasn't really surprised when I received a call from Geronimo Pratt, who had remained in custody after the verdict because he was also facing murder, robbery, and assault with a deadly weapon charges as the result of another incident.

Pratt and I had become close during the Panther trial. We were two very   10
different men with two very different backgrounds from which we had derived

two very different ideas about how to change America for the better. But we shared two other things that were more important—an abiding belief that America had to change and a deep, almost affectionate respect for each other. Pratt already had a lawyer, a fine Pasadena attorney named Charles Hollopeter. I pointed that out to Geronimo when he called my office from the jail one afternoon early in 1972.

"I like Hollopeter," he said. "But I want you to be my lawyer, too. I want you to be on my case. I saw the way you were with Willie Stafford. I saw you argue for him. I want you to argue for me like that. I love the way you argue, Cochran."

He was flattering; I was intrigued. Hollopeter and I conferred, and it was clear that we'd have no trouble working together on the case. A few days later, the judge—Kathleen Parker—appointed me. I didn't know it at the time, but I had just crossed over into a twilight zone of deceit, dishonesty, betrayal, and official corruption whose darkest corners have yet to be illuminated.

The crimes with which Pratt was charged were chilling, brutal, and simpleminded. On December 18, 1968, the police alleged, Geronimo and another black man had gone to a public tennis court in Santa Monica's Lincoln Park. There, they allegedly accosted a young white couple, Caroline Olsen, a twenty-seven-year-old schoolteacher, and her thirty-five-year-old husband, Kenneth. The robbers, who were armed, ordered the victims to lie facedown on the court. They then shot Mrs. Olsen once in the back and her husband five times. All of the wounds were inflicted by the same .45 caliber semiautomatic pistol. The robbers took eighteen dollars from Caroline Olsen's purse before fleeing the scene. Eleven days later, Mrs. Olsen died. Her husband, through some miracle, recovered.

In a lineup staged two years after the shooting, Olsen identified Pratt as one of his assailants. Later, during one of the most damning moments of Pratt's trial, Kenneth Olsen would point to my client from the witness stand and say: "That's the man who murdered my wife!"

Pratt, the authorities charged, was linked to these crimes by one critical piece of evidence and a witness whose testimony would corroborate the surviving victim's testimony. The evidence was a .45 caliber handgun that had been seized from a house frequented by the Panthers following the 1969 killings of Carter and Huggins. According to tests performed on the weapon, its chamber mechanism produced distinctive markings similar to those found on empty cartridges recovered at the tennis court. However, the far more definitive rifling left on bullets fired through the recovered .45's barrel did not match the marks on slugs extracted from the victim's bodies. That was crucial, since every rifle or pistol barrel leaves a unique signature on the bullets that pass through it. The police claimed, though, that their key witness could explain that discrepancy, as well as much more.

That witness was himself a former Black Panther, a middle-aged hairdresser and former Los Angeles county sheriff's deputy named Julius Butler. In the wake of the Carter and Huggins murders, both Butler and Pratt had sought the leadership of the party's L.A. chapter. When Pratt won, he expelled Butler because, as he later told me, "I never did trust that guy." Despite their bitter differences, which made it highly unlikely that Pratt ever would have confided in Butler, Julius testified that Pratt had confessed the tennis court shootings to him. He also said Pratt told him he had removed and destroyed the barrel of the gun used in the crimes.

Those were the facts on which the prosecution's case against Geronimo Pratt turned. They would have made any defense attorney's job difficult. What Hollopeter and I didn't know was that there were other, illegally hidden facts that made Pratt's conviction inevitable.

Unbeknownst to us, during the late 1960s, FBI director J. Edgar Hoover had ordered the bureau to undertake a covert "Counter Intelligence Program" (COIN-TELPRO, for short) to spy on, infiltrate, and disrupt dissident political groups. Hoover launched COINTELPRO on August 8, 1967. Hoover, a staunch foe of the civil rights movement, earlier had targeted Dr. King, Roy Wilkins, Whitney Young, Stokely Carmichael, H. Rap Brown, Elijah Muhammad, and other established leaders. The program's other goals were to "prevent the coalition of militant black nationalist groups" and to "prevent the rise of a black messiah who could unify, and electrify, the movement."

Publicly, Hoover had kept his lifelong racism as deep a secret as his homosexuality. But, as we now know from documents obtained under the Freedom of Information Act, he was obsessed with the Black Panthers and ordered his lieutenants to take whatever measures were necessary to "neutralize" the party and its leaders. Pratt, with his military experience and decorations for bravery under fire, was one of COINTELPRO's particular targets.

Agents spied on him almost constantly. Though we did not know it at the time, the FBI had wiretap records that showed Pratt making phone calls from Oakland just three hours before the tennis court shootings hundreds of miles south in Santa Monica. [20]

We did not know that Julius Butler was a confidential informant not only for the FBI but also for the Los Angeles County district attorney's office, a fact that was hidden from us by the prosecutor, Deputy D.A. Richard Kalustian, with whom I had attended Loyola Law School.

We could have impeached Butler's testimony if we had known he was a government informant. The number of government witnesses who perjured themselves in this case was unprecedented. Of course, we did not know they were doing this at the time. There was much more that we would eventually learn.

We knew nothing about the COINTELPRO's Ghetto Informant Program, which was started in October 1967 as a community surveillance measure. A network of informants was recruited from black areas to inform on real and suspected militants, community organizers, even "owners and clientele of African American bookstores." The government wanted to gauge "changes in the attitude of the Negro community toward the white community." We learned much later that FBI field agents were required to have a specified number of black informants. Hoover terminated the informant program along with the COINTELPRO initiative in 1971 following a break-in at an FBI field office, in which an antiwar group seized documents that revealed the intent and scope of the clandestine plan. The materials were later leaked to the press and to Congress.

We also did not know that, during the trial, the FBI tapped my office phone and that, according to an appellate court which later reviewed the case, the bureau maintained "an informant within the defense environs." To this day, that particular quisling's name is unknown to us.

We did not know that, shortly after the crimes, Kenneth Olsen had been   25
shown a photographic lineup and had unhesitatingly identified a man named
Ronald Perkins as the killer. Perkins, however, was in police custody at the time of
the crimes. Mr. Olsen also had told police that his wife's murderer was less than six
feet tall and wore a safari-style jacket. Two years later, when the police created the
new fifteen-man photo lineup out of which Kenneth Olsen finally identified Pratt,
my client's picture was the only one to depict a man under six feet and wearing a sa-
fari jacket. All this was known to Kalustian. The original photo lineup, by the way,
has disappeared, the only time in my experience such evidence has been lost in a
murder investigation.

With all that hidden from us, I began the trial with my habitual optimism. If
anything, my spirits were higher than usual. Barely two months before, my hero
and mentor Leo Branton had come out of retirement to win another controversial
black activist, Angela Davis, an acquittal on murder, kidnapping, and criminal conspiracy charges growing out of a 1970 jailbreak. I had carefully studied Leo's masterful tactics in that case, particularly his use of new scientific data demonstrating
that stress and racial differences dramatically reduce the reliability of eyewitness
identifications. I thought such research might show our own jury how Kenneth
Olsen, through no fault of his own, was mistaken when he pointed to Pratt as his
wife's killer.

In a criminal trial, the prosecution puts its case on first, followed by the defense, and then the prosecution's rebuttal witnesses. The surviving victim's testimony was the centerpiece of the state's case against Pratt, and I still recall talking to
my client in the county jail's attorney room the night after Mr. Olsen identified him
as the murderer in front of our jury.

"I didn't kill this woman, Cochran," he said to me for what must have been
the one hundredth time. "I wouldn't do that. It's not my style. This whole case is
about something else."

"Oh, man," I wearily sighed for what must have been the two hundredth time.
"What is this about except this crime? You are innocent, but you're really being
paranoid."

"You'll see," Pratt replied flatly. "They're after me, and they're going to do   30
whatever it takes to get me, Cochran. Even paranoid people have real enemies, you
know."

I didn't even bother to grimace over that old joke. I just packed up my things
and headed home to prepare for the next day's testimony. As much as I liked and
respected Geronimo Pratt, I refused to follow him into his never-never land of official plots and governmental conspiracies. Time to get back to work, I thought as I
walked back to my car. Time to rejoin the real world. I had faith in the rule of law
as applied by our criminal justice system under the norms ordained by the
Constitution. I did not believe that an agency of the United States government
would conduct its business with all the foul underhandedness of the Borgia court. I
trusted in the integrity of my old classmate, Richard Kalustian. He was a stand-up
guy; we wore the same school tie.

Geronimo Pratt and I were about to learn which of us was living in a dream
world.

In the midst of the prosecution's case, we won one important skirmish. Five days after being ousted from the Panthers, Julius Butler had written a letter recounting Pratt's alleged confession. He sealed it in an envelope and gave it to a Los Angeles police officer named Dwayne Rice. Butler asked Rice—whose snitch he sometimes was—to hold the letter as "insurance," to be opened only if something untoward happened to him. The letter, which ultimately led to Pratt's arrest, had come to light during an investigation into an internal police matter. What did not emerge until years later was that as Rice concluded that initial meeting with Butler on a public street, he was confronted by waiting FBI agents, who demanded a copy of the letter. How they knew what was in the sealed envelope remains a matter of speculation.

I fought hard to keep the letter out of evidence, and Judge Parker agreed it was inadmissible. I wanted Butler on the witness stand, where the jury could judge his credibility for themselves. On Monday, June 19, 1972, Julius Butler, then thirty-nine, was sworn in as a witness. He told the court that the night of Caroline Olsen's murder, Pratt had come to his West Adams beauty shop and told him, "I'm going on a mission." Butler testified that Pratt wanted him to tell the other Panthers if he didn't return. Geronimo came back later that same night, Butler testified, looking "very nervous." "He said he had shot some people in Santa Monica, but didn't know whether he had killed them," Butler alleged.

The day after the shooting, according to Butler, Pratt returned to the shop   35
with a newspaper containing a story about the attack on the Olsens. Butler swore that Pratt pointed to the article and said, "That's what I was talking about." Under prodding from Kalustian, Butler also claimed to recall that Pratt told him "that he had done the shooting because the other guy couldn't shoot" at the helpless couple. It was at that time, Butler alleged, that Pratt told him he had destroyed the barrel of the handgun used in the crime.

On cross-examination, I showed Butler all the consideration he deserved. He bobbed; he weaved. He twisted, turned, evaded, whined, wheedled, and temporized. The only direct, unequivocal response he gave was one we now know to be a lie.

"Are you now or have you ever been an informant for the Federal Bureau of Investigation or any other law enforcement agency?" I demanded.

"No," Butler said emphatically. "Never."

I looked over at our jury—nine whites and three African Americans. Some of them gazed at Butler with perplexity, some with outright loathing. None of them looked very happy. I looked over at my old classmate Dick Kalustian, who knew Butler was lying through his teeth. He looked straight ahead and never flinched. What he knew then—and what we know now—was that Butler had informed thirty-three times to the FBI and had been listed as a confidential informant by Kalustian's own office on January 27, 1972, nearly six months before Pratt's trial began.

We opened our defense by going straight to the heart of the prosecution's   40
case—poor Mr. Olsen's moving testimony. To demonstrate its unreliability, we called as a witness a pioneering psychologist, Dr. Robert Buckhout, whose laboratory research had convincingly demonstrated that eyewitness accounts, particularly those of stressful events, almost always were inaccurate. That was particularly true, his research showed, when the accounts involved identification of people of another race.

There was something, after all, I told the jurors, to the "traditional American myth that white men can't tell one black man from another"—not if he's a black man the white man sees for a handful of seconds during a brutal crime that occurred four years before. Buckhout, in fact, testified that in his "scientific opinion," Mr. Olsen would have been incapable of accurately recalling individual facial features glimpsed that long ago under such traumatic circumstances.

At our request, Kathleen Cleaver returned from her self-imposed exile in Algeria. She testified that she had seen Pratt frequently during the two weeks before Christmas 1968 while both were in the San Francisco Bay Area at Black Panther Party meetings. She could not swear, however, that she saw him at the precise time of the murder since so much time had passed. Other party members, who might have corroborated her testimony, refused to testify for Pratt because they were members of the Huey Newton faction. We, of course, did not know that the FBI's wiretap records would have supported her account. We also now know that the bureau's operatives followed Pratt almost constantly from early in 1968 through December 18, 1968, the day of the crimes. The logs of that surveillance, like so many other state and federal documents related to his case, are mysteriously missing.

Pratt was an effective witness on his own behalf. He looked directly at the jurors when he flatly denied murdering Caroline Olsen and callously shooting her husband. From across the courtroom, you could sense his soldier's contempt for the cowards who had. He gave a credible account of his own whereabouts when the crimes were committed, and he denied ever confessing to Julius Butler. In fact, he chuckled slightly when he said he always "had been a little suspicious of Julius" and never would have confided in him on a serious matter.

Any defense attorney will tell you that there is nothing more nerve-racking than having your client on the witness stand. Kalustian used a textbook cross-examination technique. First he'd walk toward the witness, then move back toward the jury. He'd stand facing them, letting them read his facial reactions to Pratt's responses while under attack. This created a type of split-screen effect. On one screen, the jury saw the prosecutor's face, on the other the defendant's. Each told a different story. The jury got to see both the point and the counterpoint of the hard-line questioning. Nonverbal signals said a lot. For a defense attorney, this is the moment when you can measure the jury's degree of sympathy toward your client. But Pratt testified so credibly and weathered Kalustian's cross-examination so well that our confidence surged. But "pride goeth before a fall," and we made a mistake.

Kenneth Olsen initially had described his assailant as a "clean-shaven black man." Geronimo Pratt has always worn a neatly trimmed mustache and goatee. Late in the trial, Pratt's brother Chuck, who had gone to UCLA with me, produced a Polaroid snapshot he said he had taken the same month as the murder. It showed Chuck's young son sitting in the lap of his bearded Uncle Geronimo.

"Are you sure it was taken in December?" I asked.

He was sure. I took his word and checked no further. I should have. The photograph was admitted in evidence, and Kalustian had his opportunity. The final rebuttal witness he called was an employee of the Polaroid film company, who examined the numerical code on the back of the snapshot and testified that it proved conclusively that the film was manufactured in May of 1969. Kalustian was able to wrap up his case by leaving the jury with the impression that we had tried to put something over on them. I learned an invaluable lesson—at Geronimo Pratt's expense.

After deliberating six days, the jury informed Judge Parker that they were "hopelessly deadlocked." I asked for a mistrial, but Parker insisted the panel continue its deliberations. We did not know it at the time, but they were split ten-two for conviction. Neither of the holdouts was an African American. Two days later, a single juror was still holding out. Finally, on Friday, July 29, on the tenth day of deliberation, the jury sent out a note that they had reached a verdict.

We all stood to receive their decision. While Alice Nishikawa, the court clerk, read the first verdict—"guilty" of first-degree murder—Pratt swore under his breath, shrugged off my cautionary hand, and blurted out: "You're wrong. I didn't kill that woman. You racist dogs. I'm not going to sit here and listen to the rest of this." Judge Parker ordered Pratt removed from the courtroom. After a brief interval, he returned to waive his right to be present while the rest of the verdicts—all guilty—were read.

"I told you, Cochran," he said to me as we parted that day. "They're going to do whatever it takes to get me."   50

I went home that night as dejected as I have ever been. In my mind, I replayed the philosophical debates Geronimo Pratt and I had waged virtually from the time we met. In a way, our differing points of view mirrored the split that divided black families and friends across America in those days. I was very much a man of Dr. Martin Luther King's school. I believed then, as I still do, in the moral imperative of nonviolence. I believed then, as I still do, that courageous people, working within the system, can arouse the popular conscience against injustice. Geronimo Pratt held to the school of Malcolm X and the other militant theorists of his generation. He believed that the gates of justice never would yield to anything but a battering ram propelled by forceful hands. I believed then, as I still do, in the essential goodness of my fellow human beings. Geronimo Pratt, who had seen war in the villages on a foreign shore and in the city streets of his native land, could not tear his eyes from his fellow man's capacity to do evil. Somehow that night, I felt I had let our side of this great argument—my side and Dr. King's—down.

There is an insult in the African American community that dates back to Du Bois's day: "You're not black enough." That night, as I measured myself against Geronimo Pratt, I wondered about myself. "Two-ness," again. It was a bleak moment. Like many of its kind, it marked the end of one phase of my education. I never again would unhesitatingly trust my client's fate to the system's basic fairness. I had learned that prosecutors and law enforcement officials, convinced of their own righteousness, would do anything to make the system yield the "right result." I had learned that during that journey to justice on which I had embarked all those years ago in the kitchen on West Twenty-eighth Street, I would encounter not only the courage of saints but also the treachery of Judas. I had learned that if I was going to be the lawyer I had always wanted to be, I would have to be tougher, more skeptical, and, most of all, braver in the pursuit of truth.

Never again would I accept anything as it appeared at first glance without delving deeper beneath the surface and then deeper still. Never again would I accept the "official version" of anything. That's what the loss of the Geronimo Pratt case taught me: a healthier kind of paranoia.

Geronimo Pratt paid the tuition for all those lessons of mine. That is, in part, why I have labored through all these long years to win his freedom. That is why I have never forgotten him. But through the years, our conversations have deepened along with our friendship. We are brothers, in fact; we have both moved a long way and no longer are so far apart.

Today, I owe Geronimo Pratt not only a debt of justice but one of love.   55 Together, we both have learned just how wise Dr. King was when he taught us: "If you don't stand for something, you'll fall for anything."

Mary Fisher

Mary Fisher is an investigative reporter for *The Gentlemen's Quarterly.* In the following essay from the December 1993 issue, Fisher discusses the plethora of investigations of African American politicians by the U.S. Department of Justice in the 1980s and 1990s.

The Witch-Hunt

His name was Robert Moussallem, and he had an incredible story to tell.

In October 1988, he drove, as directed, to a building in downtown Birmingham, Alabama, where the private meeting was to take place. He entered a large office. Half a dozen IRS and FBI agents introduced themselves. They were on to Moussallem's tax scam, they said, because he had made the mistake of bribing an undercover IRS agent. As the agents spoke, Moussallem noticed a large photo of Mayor Richard Arrington with the word "CORRUPTION" written above it. He found that curious. It didn't go along with the common view of Arrington, the city's first black mayor, who was in the first year of his third term. By most accounts, he was as clean as they come.

The reason for the meeting soon became clear. Moussallem had a "golden opportunity" to work himself out of the hole, an agent said, if he would cooperate in a sting operation. He expressed interest. In a second meeting, they disclosed the details: He was to lure Arrington and other black Birmingham officials into accepting bribes in a phony land deal.

"They [the blacks] all are a bunch of dopeheads," one of the agents told Moussallem. The local United States attorney's office, working in tandem with some of the same federal agents now meeting with Moussallem, had investigated Arrington three years before, bugging his office phones and following him continuously. The mayor knew nothing of it. Federal agents aborted their efforts when it became clear Arrington had no propensity for corruption. Still, even without probable cause, they were going ahead with this sting effort, called Operation Bowtye.

Facing a four-year prison term were he convicted, Moussallem readily ac-   5
cepted the government's offer. He knew Arrington, having campaigned for the
mayor during the 1983 reelection, which meant he could get in to see the mayor
without causing suspicion. Over the next several months, he wore a wire when he
visited Arrington, while IRS and FBI agents in a van parked across the street listened to every word. Arrington wouldn't bite. Moussallem kept trying. Still nothing. He began tape-recording his telephone conversations with government officials, sensing they might try to renege on his immunity deal.

Fearing betrayal, he decided to go to Washington, D.C., and tell his story to a
reporter. He would expose Operation Bowtye, name the agents involved and detail the lengths they went to in trying to bring down Arrington. But first, he went
to the mayor's house and told him everything. Arrington was stunned to learn that
he had been the focus of such an elaborate government investigation. Days later,
Moussallem's suspicions were borne out when he was indicted.

During the week leading up to his trip to the capital, Moussallem told friends
he feared for his life. He gave his tapes to one of them—in case, he said, anything
happened to him. Two days before his scheduled train departure, something did.
Moussallem was killed when a blast from a high-powered shotgun blew off most of
his face.

The mysterious incident tore off more than a man's face. Though extreme in
its outcome, the story behind Moussallem's undercover efforts to topple Richard
Arrington confirmed for many black leaders what they had already suspected.
Arrington's ordeal, they felt, was part of a pattern of federal scrutiny—sometimes
without probable cause—that has targeted black elected officials at all levels of government, a phenomenon that accelerated and peaked during the Reagan and
Bush administrations.

Like Arrington, scores of other black American politicians have been the tar-
gets of government probes, especially during the 1980s. Among them were Georgia
State Legislator Julian Bond; Maryland State Senator Clarence Mitchell III; Federal
Judge Alcee Hastings; Congressmen Ron Dellums, Floyd Flake, Harold Ford,
Mervyn Dymally, John Conyers, Charles Rangel, William Clay and William Gray;
and Mayors Andrew Young, Maynard Jackson, Tom Bradley, Coleman Young, David
Dinkins, Harold Washington and, of course, Marion Barry.

These men were the objects of such tactics as surveillance, buggings, wiretaps,   10
IRS audits, compromised informants, media leaks and grand-jury manipulations.
While these tactics led to one spectacular conviction—that of Washington, D.C.,
Mayor Barry—most of the probes of the 1980s were eventually dropped, and of
those that did go to trial, most ended in acquittals, suggesting they had been
launched and continued despite flimsy evidence.

"We know the problem occurred, [based on] the sheer numbers," says
Washington, D.C., attorney Abbe Lowell, who helped defend Congressman Harold
Ford and State Senator Mitchell against federal prosecution. According to *The
Washington Post*, of the 465 political-corruption probes initiated between 1983 and
1988, 14 percent targeted black officials, though they made up only 3 percent of all
U.S. officeholders.

A pattern is also suggested in the House of Representatives, where roughly
half of the then twenty-six members of the Congressional Black Caucus were the

target of federal investigations and/or indictments between 1981 and 1993. For the numbers to be equal for white representatives, 204 of the 409 white House members would have been subjected to the same scrutiny during that time, yet according to Justice Department figures, only 15 actually were.

The reason for the disparity, depending on whom you talk to, ranges from absolute coincidence to blatant conspiracy. The truth appears to lie somewhere in between.

A partial explanation is that this trend is the consequence of another, more positive one—simply, that more black politicians were elected in the Eighties. In 1965, when the Voting Rights Act passed, there were 280 black elected officials nationwide. In 1980, there were 6,500. Like their white counterparts, many of these officials got caught up in the aftermath of Watergate, when the conduct of officeholders became a fixation of the media and of Justice Department lawyers. That the Watergate prosecutors had become famous seemed to inspire their successors.

Black leaders also considered the scrutiny to be part of a predictable backlash   15
to their having acquired political power. "A substantial core of the Old Guard views [black electoral gains] with alarm," says Edward Dennis Jr., a fifteen-year veteran of the Justice Department who headed the criminal division in 1988. But just as important was the political factor: The black officeholders tended to be Democrats, and they were surging into office at a time when the Justice Department had become heavily influenced by the interests of the Republican-controlled Executive Branch. Even as the Republicans called for less government and reduced domestic spending, the department's budget grew from $2.3 billion, in 1981, to $9.3 billion, in 1993, and the number of department lawyers and assistant U.S. attorneys nearly doubled, to 7,880.

In 1982, black officials received an indication that something more sinister than mere politics might be at work. An FBI operative in Atlanta testified in a federal trial about an unofficial FBI policy called *Frühmenschen,* a German word meaning "primitive man." "The purpose of the policy," the operative stated in an affidavit, "was the routine investigation without probable cause of prominent black elected and appointed officials in major metropolitan areas throughout the United States."

Some who heard about *Frühmenschen* dismissed it as an aging legacy of J. Edgar Hoover. But to black leaders such as Maryland State Senator Clarence Mitchell III (a respected politician whose career ended after he had been investigated more than a dozen times and finally, in 1988, was convicted and sentenced to eighteen months in prison for alleged influence-peddling), news of the disclosure merely confirmed their suspicions. "I believe these indictments are designed to remove blacks from office," Mitchell says today.

The idea that some officials of the federal government might have it in for blacks has some basis in history. The Justice Department and the FBI, its investigating arm, have had a schizophrenic, sometimes bitter relationship with black Americans. While Justice Department officials protected the rights of blacks to vote and to integrate schools, buses and lunch counters, they also knew of and tolerated Hoover's counterintelligence efforts to discredit Martin Luther King Jr. and other civil-rights leaders. Hoover based his racist practices on his perception of black leaders' "inherent inferiority and threat to the social order," Kenneth O'Reilly wrote in *Racial Matters: The FBI's Secret File on Black America, 1960–1972.*

In 1983, black politicians had proof that racism was still alive in some corridors of the federal government. The well-publicized case of Donald Rochon, a black FBI agent who endured years of harassment by white agents, exposed what he called an "internal war within the bureau over racism." His case was resolved when the FBI agreed to a landmark $1 million settlement.

Given this track record, why, many black leaders ask, should they not assume the existence of institutional racism?   20

As it turns out, something more banal than outright racism seemed to drive many of these investigations. In the Eighties, politics, as well as ambition, intersected with the remnants of bigotry. And, this time, the government officials who black leaders had to worry about most were the unfettered federal prosecutors, in increased numbers.

When Attorney General Ed Meese ran the Justice Department, from 1985 to mid-1988, he armed the new generation of prosecutors with enormously expanded power. "The prosecutor's investigating, charging, convicting and sentencing powers have escalated," wrote Bennett Gershman, a law professor at New York City's Pace University, in a 1992 law-review article. Control in the courtroom, he added, tilted so far in favor of the government and away from defendants that it made "the adversary system almost obsolete."

Meese's successor, Richard Thornburgh, took it a step farther when he gave a select group of federal prosecutors—the ninety-three U.S. attorneys—so much autonomy that they were virtually immune to ethical restraints, Gershman concluded.

These chief prosecutors in each of the U.S. court districts influence the nature of fairness in their community's federal courts. They also decide which federal cases to bring to trial in their area, and have control over the department's most potent weapons—search warrants, grand juries, wiretaps.

Recommended by U.S. senators and appointed by the president, these prosecutors occupy an inherently conflicted position. While responsible for dispensing   25
justice, they are also political appointees who can count on keeping their job for only four years. Unlike career government prosecutors, who make up most of the ranks of the Justice Department, U.S. attorneys come to their job with limited or no government experience.

Thornburgh's hands-off policy came out of his own experience. A former U.S. attorney himself, Thornburgh "had always felt hamstrung by the bureaucracy in Washington," says Joseph diGenova, a former U.S. attorney for the District of Columbia.

"Thornburgh had an attitude problem that U.S. attorneys can't do anything wrong," he says. "And of course the evidence is quite the contrary. When you give an army of new prosecutors tremendous new power, there has to be serious oversight and review. And under Thornburgh, there was tremendous reluctance to do that."

In an interview with me, Thornburgh acknowledges that he "was more sympathetic to U.S. attorneys" than his predecessors but flatly denies the lack-of-supervision charge, citing his key role during the Ford administration in creating the department's Office of Public Integrity, which reviews political-corruption cases just prior to indictments' being handed down. He concedes, however, that the unit generally does not get involved at the earlier investigative stage. And this, many black leaders feel, is the core of the problem, as local U.S. attorneys, working in tandem with FBI and IRS agents, can initiate investigations of elected officials as they see fit, without approval from Main Justice.

In June 1989, Thornburgh went too far, many observers felt, when he issued his infamous "Thornburgh memorandum," which sent shock waves through the legal defense community. To reduce restraints on government prosecutors, Thornburgh stated in the memo, they should be allowed to meet with targets of criminal investigations without the targets' lawyer being present. While admitting that this "technically is subverting the attorney-client relationship, I felt there ought to be ways in which prosecutors could talk to defendants about their willingness to cooperate with the government," Thornburgh says.

"Thornburgh's attitude was 'We're the good guys. Let's go get the bad guys and   30
fuck the rules,'" says Joseph F. Lawless, a Pennsylvania lawyer and author of the book *Prosecutorial Misconduct* who has defended several targets of federal indictments. "The Constitution under the Reagan and Bush people was reduced to a cliché."

It was during this free-rein era that many of the investigations of black politicians were launched. In most instances, it seems outright racism wasn't behind the scrutiny. "It's much more a product of ambition than race," claims Carl Rauh, a Washington, D.C., attorney whose firm is representing Clark Clifford in the BCCI scandal. In an effort to advance their career with heavy conviction rates on all types of cases, some U.S. attorneys bent the rules and "went forward on weak cases that should never have been brought to trial," Rauh says. "And then along the way, they lost objectivity about the evidence."

The pattern of harassment derives directly from what Steve Ross, a former counsel in the U.S. House of Representatives, calls a "profile" that federal prosecutors and agents go by when initiating political-corruption cases. "The way things work out, if you're black, you're more likely to be indicted," says Ross.

The profile establishes certain characteristics—most having to do with a politician's financial status—that suggest a greater susceptibility to corruption. "You're more likely to be targeted if you're a Democrat and from the House [as most blacks in Congress are]," says Ross. "People from the House live closer to the financial edge, while the average net worth of senators and Republican officeholders is higher."

Other aspects of the profile are the result of unavoidable realities in the life of many black politicians. Many, like Julian Bond and Clarence Mitchell, came to political office after an earlier life of activism, rather than one of corporate success or accumulated wealth. To make ends meet and conduct their campaigns, black candidates, more than white ones, work at outside businesses, which, says Abbe Lowell, "increases the chances that a conflict of interest, or the appearance of a conflict, will arise."

In their zeal to make headlines before they had to leave their job, some U.S.   35
prosecutors capitalized on the remnants of racism in initiating these investigations. They knew lingering stereotypes, even if only unconscious ones, still influence those who count most in the courtroom—the predominantly white jurors—"many of whom are more willing to assign guilt to a black defendant," says Lowell.

Then, too, the successful prosecution of Marion Barry on drug charges in the late Eighties seemed to suggest to some ambitious U.S. attorneys that there were probably more cases where his came from.

"Marion had his weaknesses," a former colleague says. "But the question you have to ask is, would they have carried on an investigation for that long [nine years] or spent that kind of money—something over $10 million—to get a white official?"

With a new administration, black leaders are becoming increasingly vocal about the situation. "It's unconscionable," says Mitchell, the driving force behind the newly created Center for the Study of Harassment of African Americans, in Washington, D.C. "There's currently no effective vehicle to challenge these government lawyers. But we're determined to change that."

The government's investigation of Richard Arrington lasted twenty years, and it began as many probes of black officials do: without his knowledge and shortly after his first election to political office. His case is worth reviewing in detail because it encapsulates the questionable and invasive tactics employed against black politicians over the years.

In 1972, after Arrington won a Birmingham city-council seat, the FBI put him under surveillance as part of its infamous counterintelligence program, COINTEL-PRO. Rooted in the social upheaval of the Sixties, the covert program sought to neutralize black-nationalist, antiwar and civil-rights groups by intimidating and discrediting their leaders. A 1968 internal FBI memo advised agents "to take an enthusiastic and imaginative approach to this new endeavor and the Bureau will be pleased to entertain any suggestions or techniques you may recommend." 40

In the early Seventies, the FBI labeled Arrington a "Key Black Extremist" who was "anti-government and prone to terrorism," presumably because of his public denunciations of police brutality against blacks, which, Arrington said, was "still rampant" in Birmingham, despite the departure of the notorious police commissioner Bull Connor, in 1963. These allegations came to light as a result of Freedom of Information Act disclosures made to Arrington's office.

When Arrington's friends ultimately learned of how he'd been designated a radical, they roared. "It was a joke," says Donald Watkins, Arrington's chief counsel. "If anything, he was too moderate."

By 1979, when Arrington was elected Birmingham's first black mayor, COINTELPRO had ceased operating. Under Jimmy Carter's Justice Department, hearings into COINTELPRO's activities determined that many had been illegal, having violated the civil rights of those under investigation. "The conspiracy was impelled by a commingling of racial and political motives," a U.S. court of appeals concluded.

Still, Arrington continued to be a target. On the basis of allegations from disgruntled former bodyguards of the mayor's—who claimed that Arrington had taken bribes—U.S. Attorney Frank Donaldson, a Reagan appointee, and Assistant U.S. Attorney Bill Barnett became fixated on indicting Arrington.

But in November 1985, Cecil Moses, an FBI supervisor, informed Donaldson that "there is no probable cause at this point to believe that any laws have been violated." 45

That finding did not, however, deter the federal agents. In 1987, they began a third investigation—Operation Bowtye—designed to entrap Arrington and other black politicians in Birmingham. Six FBI agents, some brought in from Atlanta, were assigned to the task. For more than a year, they kept Arrington under surveillance. They bugged five of his office telephones. They hid out in vans, took photos of cars parked outside places Arrington frequented and wrote down license-plate numbers.

When their efforts again produced nothing incriminating, the agents enlisted Moussallem.

The agents "told me exactly what I had to do to get full immunity from prosecution," Moussallem said in an affidavit four months before he was killed. "The agents said they wanted me to set the mayor up, but to do it under their direction."

It was a complicated, costly plan. The federal agents directed Moussallem to buy an office building that had recently been refused a rezoning request by the Birmingham city council. When Moussallem visited one black councilman, he laid $60,000 cash on a table. The councilman became "confused and irritated" and ordered Moussallem to leave.

At this point, when all his attempts to bribe black council members and the   50
mayor had failed, Moussallem became increasingly distrustful of the agents. Running in the circles he did, Moussallem had a healthy case of paranoia and so began tape-recording his phone conversations with the agents and lawyers—proof that he actually had an arrangement with the government.

On an April evening in 1989, in his boldest move of all, Moussallem went to Arrington and told all. Arrington was so startled by the news, he could hardly speak. Moussallem said he was ready to expose the agents, but he feared for his life.

Before leaving, Moussallem told the mayor the clincher. He had information about a situation in Atlanta that offered proof that Arrington was not alone in his experience. An FBI operative, Hirsch Friedman, had testified in an affidavit for use in a bribery trial that the bureau had an unofficial policy of selectively targeting black officials. Friedman related that his former contact, Agent John McAvoy, had referred to the policy as *Frühmenschen* and that "the basis for this policy was the assumption by the FBI that Black officials were intellectually and socially incapable of governing major governmental organizations and institutions."

The motive behind Friedman's daring disclosures becomes clear the moment I meet him. He rolls into the Atlanta restaurant in a wheelchair. Then he hobbles to the table on crutches. Friedman, a large, friendly man who now practices law, lost most of his left leg and right ankle when he went to start his car one morning, in 1982, and it exploded.

A bomb had been placed under the car's transmission—probably, Friedman believes, by organized-crime members who believed (mistakenly) that he was investigating them. Friedman feels that McAvoy, who had been the best man at his wedding, knew of the Mob's intentions but didn't warn him. "The reason for the attempted murder came out of my relationship with the FBI," he says.

Friedman retaliated doubly by suing the FBI and also by coming forward with   55
the *Frühmenschen* information, which he presented during the 1988 bribery trial of former Atlanta Public Safety Commissioner Reginald Eaves. Eaves, it seems, had been one focus of the so-called "Blue Eyes, Green Eyes and Brown Eyes" FBI investigation that had targeted three black Atlanta officials. Going by their eye color, they were, respectively, top-ranking police official Eldrin Bell, Mayor Maynard Jackson and Eaves. Eaves was convicted. Jackson and Bell were not indicted.

"McAvoy is an old Hooverite," Friedman says. "He's an embarrassment to the FBI." (Repeated phone calls made to McAvoy went unanswered.) "Some of these guys think that if a black comes in, and they wait long enough, they'll catch him. If they want to get someone, they will. If not one way, then another."

Armed with the startling revelations from Moussallem, Arrington fought back. "The only way I was able to make a case against the government was to document everything and mobilize public opinion," he says. "They like to work in the dark. But as soon as we learned something, we went public with it."

Arrington's lawyers documented Moussallem's experiences in an affidavit and then released the provocative document to the local media. As a precaution, Moussallem gave his friend the tapes of his conversations with the agents. The lawyers' report, including Moussallem's story, was inserted into the *Congressional Record* by Alabama Senator Howell Heflin.

Next, Arrington confronted U.S. Attorney Donaldson with his knowledge of Moussallem's efforts. At that point, an all-out war ensued, which came to an end only this past August. "Donaldson repeatedly denied that the mayor was under investigation and said no indictment was planned," mayoral special counsel Watkins says. "I may have said he wasn't under investigation, because he wasn't," says Donaldson. "But I never said an indictment wasn't planned." As far as Moussallem was concerned, "he was a twice-convicted felon. His credibility was zero."

In the summer of 1989, a number of sympathetic IRS and FBI agents secretly contacted Watkins and began supplying him with information of "what Donaldson and Barnett were planning," says Watkins. "They had a sense of outrage because of how Arrington was being hounded. They told me Barnett wanted to get Arrington, whether it took one year or ten." Asked now about the federal agents who supposedly helped Arrington, Donaldson says, "It sounds like some sort of fabrication to me. An awful lot of poppycock came out of city hall during those days." 60

The mayor, the sympathetic agents said, could expect a grand-jury probe, designed to bring indictments against some of the contractors and suppliers doing business with the city, whom federal prosecutors could then squeeze for information on Arrington. (The agents who helped Arrington would not talk to me, even on the telephone, fearing our conversation would be taped and that their recorded voice could then be used to reveal their identity.)

That was finally too much. Arrington complained directly to Attorney General Thornburgh. He, however, declined to meet with Arrington and today remains adamant that black officials are not targets of selective prosecution. "It's a matter of perception," Thornburgh says. "Black citizens in this country have had a tough row to hoe. I think they're more likely to perceive that the system works against them than other American citizens."

Next, Arrington asked for help from the Senate Judiciary Committee, which turned the matter over to the Justice Department's Office of Professional Responsibility, which reviews misconduct complaints. OPR began an investigation.

Thornburgh was having his own troubles at the time, some of them concerning the way he had handled an investigation involving another black elected official—Congressman William Gray of Pennsylvania. A Justice Department leak of a probe into alleged financial irregularities on the part of an accountant of Gray's caused an outcry on Capitol Hill, with Democrats charging that the information had been deliberately leaked to CBS News in an effort to undermine Gray's campaign for a House leadership position. No charges were ever brought against the congressman, but after the incident, he left politics in disgust and now heads the United Negro College Fund.

Thornburgh terminated the investigation into the leak, according to former   65
Deputy Attorney General Don Ayer, when it "raised questions about the roles of two
of his close aides." Ayer's assertions, Thornburgh says, "are totally wrong. I was incensed over the leaks in that investigation and, frankly, was sympathetic to Bill Gray.
There's no one who's been stronger in condemning leaks than I have."

In 1991, Ayer resigned from the department in protest over what he calls
Thornburgh's "ethical breach." He blames Thornburgh for the Justice Department's
tarnished image from that time, particularly because the attorney general "did not inspire public confidence. He used the department as a tool for a political mission."

Three months after Arrington complained to Washington, Moussallem met his
fate. A bail bondsman Moussallem was visiting claims he was showing Moussallem a
shotgun when it went off. The bondsman, a convicted felon who had bragged about
being an FBI operative, said it was an accident. "We do not subscribe to the accident
theory," says attorney Watkins.

Many found it odd, for example, that the bondsman had a gun in the first
place, since a condition of his parole forbade it. "And how was it that the same
FBI agents he had worked with on my case were already at the scene even before our police got there?" Arrington wonders. (Authorities charged the bondsman with illegal possession of a gun and with criminally negligent homicide.)
One possible explanation for the quick arrival of the FBI agents was that
Moussallem had been convicted of the tax charges, was awaiting sentencing and
may have been under observation.

Several months later, as insiders had predicted, Donaldson and Barnett con-
vened a grand jury that produced tax-fraud indictments of two people who'd done
business with the city of Birmingham. Their punishment would be lenient—if they
would testify "to alleged wrongdoing by Mayor Arrington," a government document said. As the probe widened, federal prosecutors subpoenaed Arrington's business records to look for evidence of kickbacks, but the mayor refused to turn them
over. On his way to jail for contempt, Arrington, with thousands of supporters,
marched through the streets in chains. (He spent one night in a federal prison and
was released.)

"What you had in Birmingham was a page right out of Marion Barry's book,"   70
explains Donaldson. "The strategy they both employed was to denigrate the U.S. attorney's office and build public opinion against the prosecution."

In a development that Arrington claims was strategically timed, reporters
learned that he was an unindicted coconspirator in one of the tax-fraud cases from
a document Barnett made public but which, says Arrington, is typically kept under
seal. "That was too much," Arrington says today. "I hadn't even been charged with
anything. We asked OPR to remove Barnett from office." Donaldson today defends
Barnett's disclosure: "It was a public document."

OPR's investigation, however, "found no unprofessional conduct on the part
of Donaldson or Barnett," says David Bobzien, the former OPR attorney who investigated Arrington's complaints. "We were also convinced that no policy [of harass-
ment], either by the name *Frühmenschen* or any other, ever existed. We interviewed
Agent McAvoy's former partner [Hirsch Friedman], who explained that the word
derived from John Batth's novel *Giles Goat-Boy* and that it referred to a mythical
African nation. From there, some agents in Detroit used it as a code word in the

late Sixties so as not to offend blacks, because at that time they weren't sure what to call them—whether 'blacks' or 'Negroes.'" Bobzien did acknowledge that part of the feud between Arrington's camp and federal agents may have had to do with Barnett's temperament: "Barnett was very aggressive and abrasive. He rubbed them the wrong way."

Few were surprised by OPR's conclusions. Though created to police its own lawyers, the office, by virtue of being part of the institution, "has taken on pro-government values," says attorney Lawless. "It's like asking cops to police other cops. It's not going to happen."

This past August, the government's twenty-year pursuit of Arrington seemed to come to an end as the Justice Department withdrew his name as an unindicted coconspirator. But Arrington says he can never be sure it's really over: "I was naive, and now I'm paranoid."

Two hundred miles south of Birmingham, another black official—Thomas Figures—became paranoid about the federal government after he testified against his boss, Jefferson Beauregard Sessions III, the Republican-appointed U.S. attorney in Mobile. A former assistant U.S. attorney, Figures had worked for Sessions, a third-generation southerner who Figures believed was "openly insensitive to blacks." In 1986, Reagan nominated Sessions to a coveted position—federal judge. Figures, along with several black activists, traveled to Washington to try to block Session's confirmation.

Speaking before the Senate Judiciary Committee, Figures cited several racist notions allegedly expressed by Sessions, which contributed to the committee's re-jecting his nomination. Figures became a "marked man," he believes, the day he went before the committee. Ten weeks before the Republicans left office, Figures was indicted by a federal grand jury.

He maintained he was innocent of the charge: offering a bribe to a federal witness, who also intended to testify against one of Figures's clients.

Lingering racial prejudices in Alabama had often made Figures's younger brother, Michael, wonder why he himself had never been brought up on charges, considering his popularity and his high visibility as an Alabama state senator. "I've actually had people who've been in trouble with the law tell me that at points dur-ing interrogations, federal agents [FBI and DEA] asked if they had anything on me or my brother," he says.

Jurors acquitted Thomas Figures this past March—the same month Sessions left the U.S. attorney's post to make room for his Democratic replacement.

While the investigations of Arrington and Figures were traditional corruption probes, the high-profile cases of Congressmen Floyd Flake and Harold Ford typi-fied a new classification created by federal prosecutors in the Eighties—life-style cases. "In Ford's case, the perception was that he had a life-style he wasn't entitled to," says former House counsel Steve Ross.

A popular Memphis Democrat from a prominent family, Ford was elected to the House of Representatives in 1974. He was, and remains, Tennessee's only black congressman.

"What they did to poor Harold Ford is a crime," says Clarence Mitchell. "He went through ten years of hell, and it destroyed his family." Ford's legal saga took him through six investigations, ninety courtroom appearances by his lawyers, two trials, one hung jury, an appeal to the U.S. Supreme Court and a racially tinged jury-selection process that finally prompted the Clinton Justice Department to override the local U.S. attorney and intercede on the congressman's behalf.

Ford's legal problems started the night he was elected. "We caught Republicans in the basement [of the county building], hiding my votes. A maid saw them and told us. We found ballots in the trash can. From that point on, they tried to indict me," he says. The source of his troubles, he believes, were two assistant U.S. attorneys who came in under Richard Nixon. Ford also came into political power when Tennessee's black-voter registration began to spell defeat for many Republicans statewide.

In 1981, federal agents opened a sixth investigation, focusing on Ford's family-run funeral-home business. The FBI surreptitiously set up an office next to his in Memphis. Agents followed him in unmarked cars and monitored his house.

In 1987, federal prosecutors indicted Ford (and three codefendants) on nineteen counts of conspiracy and bank fraud, alleging he had accepted more than $1 million in false bank loans from two Knoxville brothers in exchange for political favors. Ford maintained the loans had been legitimate business transactions. Although he lived in, and had been investigated in, Memphis, a predominantly black city, prosecutors traveled to Knoxville, whose population at the time was 93 percent white, to convene the grand jury. 85

The trial, which took place in Memphis, lasted three months, ending in a deadlocked eight-to-four jury vote, split along racial lines, that favored Ford's acquittal. But the case didn't end there. Government lawyers decided to retry the congressman, and all hell broke loose when they again "went shopping," he says, this time picking a jury—eleven whites and one black—from predominantly white Jackson, seventy-five miles from Memphis.

In February 1993, Ford's lawyers and the Congressional Black Caucus complained bitterly to President Clinton's Justice Department transition team. Acting Attorney General Stuart Gerson overruled the local prosecutors and backed the Ford defense team's motion to scrap the Jackson jury and pick a new one in Memphis. One of the prosecutors—Republican-appointed U.S. Attorney Edward Bryant—quit in protest. "Gerson knew the Justice Department should have dropped the charges from Day One," Ford says.

The judge denied the motion for a new jury, and the trial proceeded in Memphis, with one black and eleven white jurors. On April 9, the jury acquitted Ford of all charges.

"My case was as much about politics as race," he says. "The Reagan forces are the most to blame for it. We started getting these meanspirited U.S. attorneys coming in. They were given the latitude they needed to do something like this. Look what the government spent on my case alone. Close to $40 million, I'm told. And four full-time FBI agents were on my case for six years. The FBI has too much power. I respect the FBI, but they can fabricate lies and get away with it. Had I not kept a paper trail, they would have sent me to jail."

The ten-year ordeal, Ford says, "was pure hell. It hurt my wife and my kids. My son turned to alcohol. He was 14 when I was indicted and that's when he started drinking." Ford still owes more than $1.5 million in legal bills and harbors the suspicion that his phones may still be tapped, though, he says, "I'm not a criminal, so I have nothing to hide." 90

There was dancing in the streets outside another federal courthouse—the one in Brooklyn—and tears in the eyes of the Reverend Floyd Flake when government lawyers finally moved to dismiss the charges against the popular congressman, in April 1991. Like Harold Ford, Flake first drew attention to himself because of his life style, not because of any criminal impropriety. A dapper dresser, Flake drove a Mercedes (with a Lincoln Town Car also at his disposal) and made a good living as the pastor of the Jamaica, Queens-based Allen A.M.E. Church. The son of a janitor, Reverend Flake built the faltering institution into the most powerful black congregation in the borough, with 6,000 members, 700 employees and a $20 million budget. "I should have guessed what was coming," Flake says. "The presumption of innocence is not the starting point for many of these government agents. They assume that a black man could not manage this much money and build such a big organization without stealing some."

Based on the allegations of one woman—an assistant who'd been fired by Flake—federal officials began investigating the congressman in 1987, a year after he'd been elected to the House. In August 1990, U.S. Attorney Andrew Maloney won an indictment against Flake, then 46, on seventeen counts of tax evasion and embezzlement. His wife, M. Elaine, the administrator of the congregation's church school, was charged in nine of the counts. If convicted, they faced twenty years in prison. The Flakes contended they had done nothing improper.

In his role as House counsel, Steve Ross met with Flake and his lawyers before the indictment came down; he later told a reporter that "the government rarely brought tax cases such as the one they contemplated against Flake."

"We go where the evidence takes us," Maloney said after seeking the indictment against Flake. "With the numbers involved, this case would have been brought against any public official."

"I doubt that very seriously," Flake says now. "I don't think this case would have been brought against anyone, unless they had demonstrated the ability to bring out the vote for themselves, independent of the Establishment. What happened to me has been a reality for anyone who has been able to organize blacks in any meaningful way." 95

The case began to fall apart at the beginning of the trial, as even the prosecution's witnesses voiced their respect for the Flakes. Three weeks into the trial, the case ended in an embarrassing defeat for Maloney's office when the judge pinpointed a weakness in the case—a question over a ministerial fund—that had existed all along.

In the end, even when charges are dropped or a jury votes to acquit, there is damage suffered from being a target of a federal investigation. "It steals a degree of our credibility," says Flake.

"A very dangerous thing happened during those years," attorney Lawless says. "Rather than seeing the results of a crime, prosecutors seemed to be targeting individuals whom they wanted to make defendants. They lost sight of something—that their goal is justice—and that's tragic. They just wanted to convict, and felt the ends justified the means."

The solution to the problem, black officials say, lies in rooting out Reagan-Bush "true believers." Another answer: restraining U.S. attorneys and FBI agents. "The Justice Department is not a corrupt institution," Carl Rauh points out. "It just didn't hold the reins right enough on some of its agents and prosecutors."

The most important change, though, from which all other changes would fol-   100
low, must come from the highest levels of the Justice Department. If the official
word on this situation reflected the attitude of the department's chief spokesperson—Public Affairs Director Carl Stern, a former NBC-TV correspondent—black
leaders would be up against a brick wall.

"I told you I don't appreciate your efforts to drag the department into race
politics," Stern replied as he angrily dismissed my request to interview Attorney
General Janet Reno. Nor would he allow my written questions to be brought to
Reno's attention.

But in April, black leaders asked for a meeting with Reno to discuss the problem. Unlike Stern, Reno is reportedly receptive to exploring the issue and has
agreed to meet with black leaders early next year. After Commerce Secretary Ron
Brown became the target of a federal investigation this summer, Reno's involvement became even more imperative, says Clarence Mitchell. The way the investigation of Brown has been handled, with leaks to the media about unsubstantiated allegations of influence-peddling, leads Mitchell and others to conclude that "it's
happening all over again, to Ron."

Encouraged by Reno's receptivity, black leaders are counting on what one former colleague calls the attorney general's "strongly defined sense of justice" to re-
vamp the venerable institution and return it, once again, to a department of justice.

Carl Rowan

Carl Rowan (1925–2000) was best known as a political commentator for his
The Rowan Report on national radio, his political columns in national
newspapers, and his regular appearances on the television public affairs
programs *Inside Washington* and *Meet the Press*. He also had a distinguished
career with the U.S. Department of State and served as U.S. Ambassador to
Finland, 1963–64. His publications include *South of Freedom* (1952), *Go South
to Sorrow* (1957), *Wait Till Next Year: The Life Story of Jackie Robinson* (1960),
his autobiography, *Breaking Barriers: A Memoir* (1991), and *The Coming Race
War in America: A Wake-Up Call* (1996).

One of the concluding chapters of Rowan's *Dream Makers, Dream Breakers:
The World of Thurgood Marshall* (1993) gives the reader insight into the
confirmation hearings for Clarence Thomas, his supporters, and his detractors.

The Clarence Thomas Fiasco

While Justice Marshall knew that he could not pass public comment on anyone
whom President Bush nominated to succeed him, no one in America
watched with greater interest and concern than Marshall, just four days after his retirement, when Bush walked out of his seaside retreat in Kennebunkport, Maine,
with Clarence Thomas at his side.

Bush announced that after a private conversation, in which he said he imposed no litmus test about abortion or any other issue before the Court, he had decided to nominate Thomas to become the 106th justice of the nation's highest Court—and the second black person to serve there.

"I believe he'll be a great justice. He's the best person for this position," Bush said. "I have followed this man's career for some time, and he has excelled in everything that he has attempted. He is a delightful and warm, intelligent person, who has great empathy and a wonderful sense of humor. He's also a fiercely independent thinker with an excellent legal mind who believes passionately in equal opportunity for all Americans.

"Judge Thomas is a model for all Americans, and he's earned the right to sit on this nation's highest court."

Thomas fought back tears as he responded: "As a child I could not dare 5 dream that I would ever see the Supreme Court, not to mention be nominated to it. In my view, only in America could this have been possible."

"Only in America . . ." That line, when uttered by a black person, ensures that only the most unpatriotic of whites could possibly rise in opposition. Here was the quintessential George Bush, trying always to be all things to all men, hoping Thomas would get the blessings of independent black Democrats and conservative whites.

But a lot of Americans did protest. Arthur Kropp, president of People for the American Way, said the nomination was troubling. Thomas was anti-affirmative action, hostile in almost all respects to the Civil Rights Movement. John Jacob, president of the National Urban League, offered some mumbo-jumbo doubts that Thomas would ever hear "voices from the walls" of Marshall's office charging him with protecting "minority and disadvantaged people." NAACP leader Hooks had warned Bush that if he nominated someone who was unacceptable to the civil rights community he would face "the mother of all confirmation battles."

Meanwhile, the press was emphasizing Thomas's previous poverty rather than his political and social views. "FROM POVERTY TO U.S. BENCH" was emblazoned on the front page of the *New York Times*. "SELF-MADE CONSERVATIVE," heralded the *Washington Post*.

Marshall, who even in retirement would be asked to participate in some important federal court cases, was muzzled. Thousands of black "leaders" were paralyzed by the dilemma of campaigning against a black right-winger when they assumed that if Thomas were rejected, Bush would choose a white right-winger more hostile to America's minorities.

Marshall saw Thomas in terms of the issues and causes that had dominated 10 his life. Such as affirmative action, which Marshall had fought for as a way of giving long-cheated minorities, women, everyone, a fair grasp at the American dream. Thomas had derided affirmative action as "a narcotic of dependency." Marshall would shake his head in wonderment that a black man who grew up poor in Jim Crow Georgia, and who had benefited from a thousand affirmative actions by nuns and others, and who had attended Yale Law School on a racial quota, could suddenly find affirmative action so destructive of the characters of black people.

Over forty years I had heard Marshall curse, in a hundred ways, "the goddamn black sellouts." I had no doubt what he was saying about Thomas.

Marshall had warned in his retirement press conference that Bush might use race as a cover to "do the wrong thing." He was suggesting that in nominating a black conservative, Thomas, to replace him, Bush was dividing and disarming blacks, liberals, moderates, who would find it difficult to oppose filling the seat with another black person, no matter what his ideology. Marshall knew that it was a deft political move by the president.

But not all black Americans were conned by Thomas's color. Professor Derrick Bell of Harvard said he was "appalled" and "insulted" by the nomination. Other prominent blacks said that Thomas would do more damage to the hopes and dreams of black people than any white conservative that Bush could have named, because Thomas would give "cover" to the Court's white ultraconservatives, who would be able to say, "Me a racist? Clarence Thomas voted with me." On the other hand, one black talk-show host in Washington expressed the view of millions of black people: "Any black person on the Supreme Court is better for us than any white person."

Blacks who opposed Thomas wished fervently that Marshall could thunder, in his inimitable way, "What is this crap about a black sellout being better for the suffering people of America than an Earl Warren or a Bill Brennan?" But this time they knew that Marshall's "no comment" binge was based on good common sense, not on cantankerousness. Still, Marshall could have given some guts to the National Urban League, which had chickened out into a neutral position. He could have emboldened Benjamin Hooks, the executive director of the NAACP, who waffled and wrung his hands over the fact that some branches had publicly adopted the line that "any black on the Court is better" and had announced support for Thomas. But Marshall couldn't give the backbone speech that black Americans needed—such as his defense of integration in Texas.

So the NAACP floundered in semiparalysis, which was painful to the old   15 NAACP legal warhorse, Thurgood. The Congressional Black Caucus, and some women's groups, came out forcefully against the confirmation of Thomas. But the delegates to the NAACP annual convention in Houston were sent home with only a timid promise that Hooks and others would "talk to Judge Thomas" and see where he really stood. Marshall noted privately the ludicrousness of the NAACP pretending that while no one else in the world could get Thomas to speak out on any issue of importance, it expected him to bare his soul to Hooks. The NAACP was engaging in the kind of cop-out that Marshall had never seen in all his years of fighting within that organization.

On June 2, 1992, the *Baltimore Sun* published an astonishing article about how one of its black reporters, Arch Parsons, had maneuvered to immobilize Hooks and pass word to President Bush that he could nominate Thomas without fear that Hooks would "leap to judgment."

Parsons, at age sixty-six, had left the *Sun* in a retirement agreement. He admitted that he was a friend of Thomas's, that he wanted a black person to replace Marshall, and that he relayed to the White House a Hooks pledge that he and the NAACP would not "be part of a lynch mob." "Lynch" would become the critical word in Thomas's confirmation hearings.

The *Baltimore Sun* said it would have fired Parsons had it known that he was writing its stories about Thomas while secretly plumping for his confirmation.

Parsons, in the pathetic midnight of his journalistic career, said he had engaged in an egregious conflict of interest. The about-to-retire Hooks protested furiously that he had done nothing wrong.

Here was one of the most sordid moments in the history of the NAACP. Here was an indelible blot on the record of Hooks. A generation later the black, brown, yellow, aged, poor, of America would ask whether, deliberately or as a dupe, Hooks had become a party to the sabotaging of Thurgood Marshall's dreams.

While Marshall could not speak out against Thomas, some of us knew that we could. I said on television that "if you sprinkled some flour on Thomas's face you might think you were listening to David Duke," the former Ku Klux Klan leader. That brought me a rebuke from Vice President Quayle, who was quickly silenced when Duke declared that on issues such as welfare and affirmative action his views were the same as Thomas's.

I received a barrage of mail from blacks and whites who thought I was myopic not to see that if Thomas were rejected, Bush would nominate someone more distasteful. I replied, "You don't swallow a dose of arsenic because you fear that someone will give you strychnine tomorrow. You fight off the arsenic to live for another day, when you might also reject the strychnine."

Still, Thomas rolled along breezily toward confirmation. The American Bar Association on August 28 rated him "qualified" for the Supreme Court. Most nominees in the past two decades had received "well qualified" ratings, the top endorsement. Two of the fifteen members of the ABA's Standing Committee on the Federal Judiciary found Thomas "not qualified." No nominee receiving "not qualified" votes had been seated on the Supreme Court for at least twenty years, according to the ABA and the Senate Judiciary Committee.

But Thomas's blackness made him different from Haynsworth, Carswell, Bork, and other rejected nominees. Some southern senators, seeing ambivalence in black America, felt that they did not dare to vote against a black man, however obnoxious he seemed to them.

On September 10, confirmation hearings began in the Senate Judiciary Committee. Thomas professed not to have a view on anything of consequence. He could not recall ever in his life expressing a view about *Roe v. Wade*, the historic case that said women have a constitutional right to an abortion! Marshall, like most of America, was incredulous.

The hearings concluded on September 20, with Thomas still an enigma to the committee and the nation, and it seemed to his opponents that there was no way to block his confirmation.

But another scenario was being played out in secret, according to *Congressional Quarterly* magazine. It said that the Alliance for Justice, a liberal group that had led the fight to block Bork from a Supreme Court seat, had received a tip in August that one of Thomas's former employees had alleged that Thomas had harassed her sexually. This tip was passed to Senate staffers, who contacted the alleged victim, University of Oklahoma law professor Anita Hill. James J. Brudney, an aide to Senator Howard Metzenbaum of Ohio, listened to Hill's charges and relayed them to Metzenbaum, who passed them along to the full Judiciary Committee staff, which was controlled by Senator Joseph Biden, a Delaware Democrat.

20

25

After an internal Judiciary Committee war in which Republicans Strom Thurmond, Marshall's longtime nemesis; Orrin Hatch, Mr. Unctuous of Utah; and Arlen Specter of Pennsylvania did all they could to protect Thomas, the committee decided to hold hearings into Hill's charges of sexual harassment. This produced startling, galvanizing testimony of a nature never before seen and heard on American television.

Hill said that while in Thomas's office he told her that he had found pubic hairs on his Coke can, and implied that he was an expert at cunnilingus. She said he boasted to her of his sexual prowess and the size of his penis, and suggested she ought to see porno movies, especially one featuring "Long Dong Silver," a male freak who, as legend has it, had a penis so long he could tie it into a knot. Most humiliating, she said, was Thomas's discussing with her "pornography involving these women with large breasts who engaged in a variety of sex with different people or animals."

Hill testified that Thomas liked to discuss with her "specific sex acts and frequency of sex," which she took as an invitation for her to have sex with him.

Senator Specter was the prime inquisitioner, who tried to shake Hill's story. He implied in many ways that there was something irrational, queer, and scheming about the accuser. Anita Hill stood up to him so brilliantly that a nation glued to its TV sets knew that only Thomas could save himself.

The nominee was also brilliant, first in disarming the committee by declaring "unequivocally, uncategorically, that I deny each and all allegations against me today that suggested in any way that I had conversations of a sexual nature or about pornographic material with Anita Hill, that I ever attempted to date her, that I ever had any personal sexual interest in her, or that I in any way ever harassed her."

Thomas then intimidated the committee with a declaration that he would not discuss his personal life. This meant that no senator was to ask him if he ever rented pornographic movies, especially ones featuring Long Dong Silver, or films featuring big-breasted women engaging in sex acts with animals. It was striking that no senator, not even a Democrat, dared to ask Thomas about his movie-watching habits.

That critical evening of October 11 Thomas went on the attack, saying:

> I think that this hearing today is a travesty. I think that it is disgusting. I think that this hearing should never occur in America. This is a case in which this sleaze, this dirt, was searched for by staffers of members of this committee, was then leaked to the media, and this committee and this body validated it and displayed it at prime time over our entire nation.
>
> How would any member on this committee, any person in this room or any person in this country like sleaze said about him or her in this fashion? Or this dirt dredged up and this gossip and these lies displayed in this manner, how would any person like it?
>
> The Supreme Court is not worth it. No job is worth it. I am not here for that. I am here for my name, my family, my life and my integrity. I think something is dreadfully wrong with this country when any person, any person in this free country, would be subjected to this.
>
> And from my standpoint, as a black American, it is a high-tech lynching for uppity blacks who in any way deign to think for themselves, to do for

themselves, to have different ideas, and it is a message that unless you kowtow to an old order, this is what will happen to you. You will be lynched, destroyed, caricatured by a committee of the U.S. Senate rather than hung from a tree.

What a bitter twist of fate. This black man who had, in hustling the favors of Bush and the right-wingers who currently controlled America, and who had disparaged and ridiculed Thurgood Marshall, Walter White, James Weldon Johnson, Roy Wilkins, and others who wiped out lynching, was now crying "lynching" to justify his confirmation. This child of Georgia poverty who had, in modest success, exhorted blacks never to fall back on cries of "racism," was shouting "racist lynching" in the most galling of ways.

Black Americans who considered Thomas a consummate con man knew that   35
they were right.

But the key senators on the Judiciary Committee, Dennis DeConcini and Specter, were loath to risk being called "high-tech lynchers."

On September 27, in a 7 to 7 vote on party lines, except for Democrat DeConcini of Arizona supporting Thomas, the committee failed to recommend the confirmation of Thomas. Normally, this tie vote would have been the end of the line, because no Supreme Court nominee had been seated since the 1950s without a favorable vote in the Judiciary Committee. But Biden allowed the Thomas nomination to go to the full floor. There it would not be a party-line vote. The "support a local boy" syndrome was at work. More powerful was the fact that black votes had given Senate seats to southern Democrats John B. Breaux of Louisiana, Wyche Fowler, Jr., of Georgia, Richard C. Shelby of Alabama, and Bennett Johnston of Louisiana; and that these men believed polls indicating that their black constituents wanted Thomas confirmed. Senator Sam Nunn of Georgia, like Fowler, didn't have the guts to stand against a black Georgian, however obnoxious he might be. Then there was Charles S. Robb of Virginia, who himself was agonizing over charges of sexual misconduct, and who voted for another suffering "soul brother." There is no logic to explain why David Boren of Oklahoma, Jim Exon of Nebraska, and Alan Dixon of Illinois voted for Thomas. It is noteworthy that Illinois voters promptly dumped Dixon.

Only two Republicans dared to cross Bush and vote to reject Thomas— James M. Jeffords of Vermont and Bob Packwood of Oregon. Nancy Kassebaum of Kansas was under great pressure to vote against Thomas; the other female senator, Barbara Mikulski, the Maryland Democrat, did vote against him. Kassebaum put party loyalty first. "Some women suggest that I should judge this nomination not as a senator but as a woman," she said. "I reject that. Throughout my years here I have taken pride in the fact that I am a U.S. senator, not a 'woman senator.'"

These sordid Senate hearings taught Americans a lot. They revealed the confusions in black America that Marshall had spent half a century trying to erase—his rush to Denison, Texas, to stop blacks from swallowing "separate but equal," his constant decrying of black hustlers who were selling out the most basic of black aspirations for jobs of no power and no ultimate consequence in the American social equation.

The hearings enabled women and minorities to see Senator Alan Simpson,   40
the Wyoming Republican, at his eloquent worst—which was incredibly bad. The

cameras prodded him into warning Anita Hill that if she detailed charges of sexual harassment against Thomas she would be "caught in the maw," that her career would be ruined, her family disgraced.

Every woman ever harassed sexually, or raped, has known the possible humiliating and costly consequences of making public charges, but to have a senator on the Judiciary Committee lay this reality out as a threat was shocking and dismaying to millions of Americans, female and male.

Then there was the shameful performance of Specter, who faced re-election and clearly was trying to regain the support of Republican right-wingers in Pennsylvania. He showboated, telling Professor Hill that "this is not an adversarial proceeding," and then rushed to call her a "perjurer."

The Hill appearance provoked most members of the Judiciary Committee to behave like sexist asses, who rushed to initiate a stupid, then half-abandoned Senate probe to try to find out who leaked the existence of the Hill charges that turned the Thomas hearings into such an agonizing test of their characters.

On October 15, 1991, after one of the wildest television spectacles, one of the nastiest plunges into sexual prurience in the nation's history—at least up till the William Kennedy Smith Palm Beach rape trial—the Senate voted 52 to 48 to confirm Thomas. This was the closest Supreme Court confirmation in more than a century, and the second closest ever.

The reaction to Thomas's confirmation was divided about as closely as the   45
Senate vote. President Bush said that Thomas demonstrated that "he is a man of honesty, dedication and commitment to the Constitution and the rule of law." Thomas's chief sponsor in the Senate, Senator John Danforth of Missouri, a Republican, predicted, "Clarence Thomas is going to surprise a lot of people. He is going to be the people's justice."

On the other side, Democratic senator Harry Reid of Nevada, who had pledged to vote for Thomas before the hearings but reversed himself in the final showdown, explained, "From a political standpoint I badly wanted to vote for Clarence Thomas. However, my conscience wouldn't let me do it. I thought she [Anita Hill] was telling the truth." Democratic senator Robert C. Byrd of West Virginia said that he had written a speech supporting Thomas, but changed his mind after seeing Hill, "who did not flinch, who showed no nervousness, who spoke calmly throughout."

The gut-wrenching internal tug-of-war that many senators experienced was reflected by Kassebaum. While voting for Thomas, she acknowledged that he would "live under a cloud of suspicion he can never fully escape."

Two of the nation's most influential newspapers responded to the final vote with let's-get-on-with-business editorials. The *Washington Post* said, "[Thomas's] contributions can only be enhanced if it turns out that his reluctance to be specific about his judicial thinking during his confirmation hearings reflects a determination to think through anew the questions that come to him on the court." The *New York Times* expressed hope that "everyone involved in this brutal divisive battle will work toward restoring comity and good will."

Political division was reflected by men and women in the street. *Washington Post* reporters who spoke with local residents after the final Senate vote found "some visibly disgusted and outraged. Others . . . pleased and relieved."

If public and official opinion was split about Thomas himself, there was una-   50
nimity on two related issues: women's rights emerged as a winner, the confirmation
process a loser.

In an open letter to Anita Hill on its editorial page, the *New York Times* said,
"You simply spoke the truth as you saw it, and in so doing, exposed a dark subject
whose power all women know and countless men have begun to grasp. For bearing
witness to that, what you have earned is their thanks."

No such appreciation was heard from any quarter for the confirmation
process. President Bush termed the hearings "a messy situation," adding, "I was
troubled thinking of my little grandchildren, hearing some of the specific sexual allegations." Bush only heard testimony about pubic hairs on Coke cans. The issue of
justice eluded him. Several senators called the procedure "flawed" and "perverted."
Several, along with historians, law professors, and others, urged that the process be
changed. There had been too much personal posturing by Biden, Specter, Hatch.
A bunch of old white men acted as if they had no idea what sexual harassment was
all about.

Knowing Marshall and his wife, Cissy, as well as I did, I could surmise that they
found ironic, though unwelcome, satisfaction in the grilling of Thomas on his
"nonviews" regarding *Roe,* and his confrontation with Anita Hill. Marshall would
surely see that that sordid Senate episode was doing more for women's rights than
all the arguments he had made, the tirades he had uttered in the conference room,
the dissents that had sometimes become splenetic. The Thomas hearings had awakened the women of America, had made them stand up for the rights that he had
defended judicially for a quarter century. Anita Hill had become a catalyst for
changing America in areas that were dear to him.

As Thurgood and Cissy watched, with most of America, the lurid, dismaying
confirmation hearings, they could not imagine how far their impact would reach.
Bush's insistence on putting Thomas in his seat created the political "year of the
woman." All of a sudden, ten women Democrats and one female Republican were
nominated to run for seats in the U.S. Senate, where only two out of one hundred
members were women. One hundred and six women campaigned for election to
the House of Representatives. In November 1992 Carol Moseley Braun of Illinois
was elected as the first black woman ever in the United States Senate. California
made history by electing two women—Diane Feinstein and Barbara Boxer—to represent that state in the Senate. We now have six women in the Senate, triple the highest number ever. Virginia elected its first woman to the House of Representatives.
"Womanpower," thanks to Anita Hill, has become a critical part of a sea change in
American politics.

America was wrought up over the issue of abortion in ways that Marshall   55
could not have hoped for before.

I had at first assumed that Marshall would consider the Thomas hearings, the
result, the fallout, part of a great American tragedy. He had in one moment of sudden candor said, when the vote confirming Thomas was final, "We've gone from
chicken salad to chicken shit." But by the summer of 1992 it was clear that the overall results included some mixed blessings.

No Supreme Court justice had ever taken office under such sordid, humiliating circumstances. Hundreds of cartoonists portrayed Thomas as a sex maniac, a

porno plague who would lie on the floor of the Supreme Court conference room and look up the robe of Justice O'Connor. The question arose as to whether a black justice so humiliated could ever have any moral force for liberty and justice on a Court that was sinking into the depths of harshly insensitive conservatism. The answer was clear that this strange black man, Thomas, had no desire or intention of influencing the Court in the ways of Thurgood Marshall.

Still, millions of Americans, including powerful members of the judiciary, hoped and prayed that once secure in a lifetime post on the Supreme Court, Thomas would remember the racial insults and deprivations of his Georgia beginnings, would understand the sufferings and dreams of his sister and other blacks working at poverty wages, would ask why his young black brothers get arrested and imprisoned in such disproportion in America, and say to the white far right: "Gotcha, didn't I?"

An eminent black federal senior judge, A. Leon Higginbotham, Jr., of the Third Circuit Court of Appeals in Philadelphia, took the extraordinary step of writing Thomas "An Open Letter . . . from a Federal Judicial Colleague," urging him to let his roots temper his rulings.

This letter by Higginbotham, sixty-four, to Thomas, forty-four, is emotional, sometimes angry, often condescending, but it is worth quoting at some length for those who seek to understand the world of Thurgood Marshall. On November 29, 1991, Higginbotham wrote:

Dear Justice Thomas:

At first I thought that I should write you privately—the way one normally corresponds with a colleague or friend. I still feel ambivalent about making this letter public but I do so because your appointment is profoundly important to this country and the world, and because all Americans need to understand the issues you will face. . . .

. . . You can become an exemplar of fairness and the rational interpretation of the Constitution, or you can become an archetype of inequality and the retrogressive evaluation of human rights. The choice as to whether you will build a decisional record of true greatness or of mere mediocrity is yours. . . . You must reflect more deeply on legal history than you ever have before. You are no longer privileged to offer flashy one-liners to delight the conservative establishment. . . .

During the time when civil rights organizations were challenging the Reagan administration, I was frankly dismayed by some of your responses to and denigrations of these organizations. . . . If that is still your assessment of these civil rights organizations or their leaders, I suggest, Justice Thomas, that you should ask yourself every day what would have happened to you if there had never been a Charles Hamilton Houston, a William Henry Hastie, a Thurgood Marshall, and that small cadre of other lawyers associated with them who laid the groundwork for success in the twentieth-century racial civil rights cases? . . . If there had never been an effective NAACP, isn't it highly probable that you might still be in Pin Point, Georgia, working as a laborer as some of your relatives did for decades? . . .

In my lifetime, I have seen African Americans denied the right to vote, the opportunities to a proper education, to work and to live where they choose. I have seen and *known* racial segregation and discrimination. But I have also seen the decision in *Brown* rendered. I have seen the first African American sit on the Supreme Court. And I have seen brave and courageous people, black and white, give their lives for the civil rights cause. . . . I wonder whether their magnificent achievements are in jeopardy. I wonder whether (and how far) the majority of the Supreme Court will continue to retreat from protecting the rights of the poor, women, the disadvantaged, minorities, and the powerless. And if, tragically, a majority of the court continues to retreat, I wonder whether you, Justice Thomas, an African American, will be part of that majority.

No one would be happier than I if the record you will establish on the Supreme Court in years to come demonstrates that my apprehensions were unfounded. You were born into injustice, tempered by the hard reality of what it means to be poor and black in America, and especially to be poor because you are black. You have found a door newly cracked open and you have escaped. I trust that you shall not forget that many who preceded you and many who follow you have found, and will find, the door of equal opportunity slammed in their faces through no fault of their own. And I also know that time and the tides of history often call out of men and women qualities that even they did not know lay within them. And so, with hope to balance my apprehensions, I wish you well as a thoughtful and worthy successor to Justice Marshall in the ever ongoing struggle to assure equal justice under law for all persons.

> Sincerely,
> A. Leon Higginbotham, Jr.

Thomas telephoned Higginbotham upon receipt of the letter for what each described only as an "amicable" conversation. But black conservatives assailed Higginbotham for "moral conceit" and "a long, ugly, cheap attack." Conservative legal activist Clint Bolick, the Arch Parsons contact who passed word to Bush that Hooks would not "rush to judgment," told the *Washington Post* that he "found the entire [Higginbotham] article extremely patronizing."

At the bottom of the fallout is the fact that Higginbotham's letter had no noticeable influence on Thomas, whose first votes as a justice made it clear that he was everything Marshall, Higginbotham, and millions of other Americans feared he would be—and much worse.

First it became clear that Thomas had lied his way into confirmation.

A crucial issue during confirmation hearings was whether Thomas, who benefited from an affirmative action (in fact, quota) program at Yale Law School would vote to outlaw such programs for minorities and women who now needed them so desperately. Thomas gave the Senate Judiciary Committee a dose of double-talk, leaving every senator in doubt about how he would rule on affirmative action.

Then *Legal Times,* a weekly newspaper in Washington, D.C., published a story asserting that Thomas already had written the majority opinion in a 2 to 1 decision of the Court of Appeals for the District of Columbia declaring that it was unconstitutional for the Federal Communications Commission to give women preferences in the awarding of some broadcast licenses. *Legal Times* suggested that the release of this opinion was being held up to conceal Thomas's real views about affirmative action. 65

Some disturbed Senate supporters of Thomas asked him point-blank if the *Legal Times* story was true. "No," Thomas replied. The decision, in *Lamprecht v. FCC*, was released after confirmation, showing that Thomas had written exactly what *Legal Times* said.

More nauseating than this was Thomas's deceitful testimony about the rights of the accused and the constitutional protections of criminals. Time and again during the hearings he faked great compassion for young men ensnared in the criminal justice system. He told, with Hollywood emotion, how he had looked out his window at prisoners arriving in vans and said to himself, "There but for the grace of God, go I."

Once seated on the Court, Thomas got a chance to apply a little of the grace of God and the justice of the Eighth Amendment to Louisiana prisoner Keith Hudson, who was shackled and beaten by two guards who split his lip, loosened his teeth, and broke his dental plate. Justice Sandra Day O'Connor and six other justices concluded that this was cruel and unusual punishment, which the Eighth Amendment forbids.

Thomas wrote a dissent suggesting that Hudson's complaint was akin to gripes about prison food, and that the Court majority was stretching the scope of the Bill of Rights. Confirmation "compassion" had turned to cruelty.   70

A major fear expressed during confirmation hearings was that this momentarily enigmatic black man would help to make the Supreme Court an instrument for wiping out the major civil rights gains Marshall had shepherded to reality during the previous forty years. Sure enough, when some southern whites finagled to strip power away from black elected officials, the Justice Department said the whites had violated the Voting Rights Act. But Thomas and a Court majority ruled that rooking the black officials was constitutional.

A few who voted to confirm Thomas began to see the ever-growing damage that they had done. But they watched knowing that their decisions were, for all practical purposes, irreversible.

Thomas's vote in the case of the beating of prisoner Keith Hudson provoked the *New York Times* to assail him editorially, in a headline, as "THE YOUNGEST, CRUELEST JUSTICE." The *Times* called Thomas's dissent a "crashing disappointment" because "He might well serve until the year 2030 or beyond . . . he could attract enough support from future appointees to move the Court still further to the right."

Perhaps the ten Democrats, Arlen Specter, Nancy Kassebaum, and others who voted for Thomas out of political cowardice, cynicism, or bad judgment are finding that for all Americans the "chicken salad" days of Thurgood Marshall are over, and the chicken shit has come home to roost.

Media Resources

Home of the Brave [1949]. Directed by Mark Robson. 85 minutes. Independent. Lone African American soldier in Army patrol unit experiences mental problems following death of his best friend, with flashbacks to racist incidents.

To Kill a Mockingbird [1962]. Directed by Robert Mulligan. 129 minutes. Universal. Harper Lee's Pulitzer Prize autobiographical novel adapted to film is about a small-town Alabama lawyer who defends an African American accused of rape.

Ida B. Wells: A Passion for Justice [1989]. Produced by William Greaves and Louise Archambault. 58 minutes. WGBH Educational Foundation. Film is a biography of the African American journalist and her campaign against lynching.

A Time to Kill [1996]. Directed by Joel Schumacher. 150 minutes. Warner. A black father's revenge on men who raped and severely beat his daughter leads him to murder them.

Fires in the Mirror [1996]. Directed by George C. Wolfe. 90 minutes. California Newsreel. Dramatic recording of racial upheaval following the death of an African American child and rabbinical student in Brooklyn, N.Y., in 1991.

Amistad [1997]. Directed by Steven Spielberg. 155 minutes. DreamWorks. The story of Africans on a slave ship, *Amistad*, who revolted and won their freedom in an American court.

America in Black and White: Racial Profiling and Law Enforcement [1998]. Produced by ABC News. 44 minutes. Films for the Humanities and Sciences. Ted Koppel and Michel McQueen investigate this issue, interviewing victims, the police, a law professor, and a prosecutor.

Beloved [1998]. Directed by Jonathan Demme. 171 minutes. Touchstone. The film is an adaptation of Toni Morrison's novel about a slave mother's bolt for freedom with her four children.

The Green Mile [1999]. Directed by Frank Darabont. 181 minutes. Warner Brothers. In this adaptation of the Stephen King novel, prison guards learn that an African American prisoner, convicted of the heinous murder of two white girls, is innocent, but they still execute him.

The Life of a Black Cop [1999]. 22 minutes. Films for the Humanities and Sciences. Department harassment ensues when a policeman reports police brutality.

CHAPTER 5

The Mirror Has Many Faces

There are many ways to address the images and myths surrounding African Americans. If we approach "blackness" from the definitions of black, we consistently come away with negative feelings and attitudes. Dehumanizing propaganda has been connected to African American ethnicity historically. However, we can celebrate the strength of character, the purpose, the conviction with which African Americans have resisted, survived, and risen above the onslaught of negative pressures and demands. As a result, we look at heroes and "sheroes" for balance. We celebrate the fortitude, consistency, resilience, and beauty of those who have striven to make the lives of African American people meaningful.

Donald Bogle's "Black Beginnings: From *Uncle Tom's Cabin* to *The Birth of a Nation*" is the frame selection for Chapter 5, "The Mirror Has Many Faces." Bogle records the various stereotypes of African American character as depicted by white authors in the nineteenth and early twentieth centuries. In the next selection, James Baldwin, aware of the pervasiveness of prejudice in American society, exhorts his nephew not to be cowed but to garner strength from his ancestors. Ted Joans and Mari Evans celebrate the African American man and woman, respectively, in their poems, and John Gwatley records comments about the role color plays in the African American community. Johnetta Cole labels the community a subculture and describes its lifestyles and components. Michael Eric Dyson comments on the effects of *The Bill Cosby Show*, which dominated television ratings in the 1980s, in changing viewers' perceptions about the black middle class. Finally, Jewelle Gomez analyzes the portrayal of the black gay community in twentieth-century film.

Negative images and myths that black people internalize can affect their psychological well-being. The promulgation of negative, distorted images and myths about the African American community can distort relationships within and without. This chapter is devoted to sharing both the negative and the positive perspective in order to provide a context in which new choices and new images can be made in the twenty-first century.

Donald Bogle

Donald Bogle has written several incisive books on the depiction of the African American in film and television. He teaches at the University of Pennsylvania and the New York University's Tisch School of the Arts. His works include *Toms, Coons, Mulattoes, Mammies & Bucks: An Interpretive History of Blacks in Films* (1973), *Blacks in American Film and Television: An Encyclopedia* (1989), *Brown Sugar: Eighty Years of America's Black Female Superstars* (1985), *Dorothy Dandridge: A Biography* (1996), and *Primetime Blues: African Americans on Network Television* (2001).

The following selection is Chapter 1 of *Toms, Coons, Mulattoes, Mammies & Bucks: An Interpretive History of Blacks in Films,* in which Bogle describes the black stereotypes depicted in American movies.

Black Beginnings

From Uncle Tom's Cabin *to* The Birth of a Nation

In the beginning, there was an Uncle Tom. A former mechanic photographed him in a motion picture that ran no longer than twelve minutes. And a new dimension was added to American movies.

The year was 1903. The mechanic-turned-movie-director was Edwin S. Porter. The twelve-minute motion picture was *Uncle Tom's Cabin.* And the new dimension was Uncle Tom himself. He was the American movies' first black character. The great paradox was that in actuality Tom was not black at all. Instead he was portrayed by a nameless, slightly overweight white actor made up in blackface. But the use of whites in black roles was then a common practice, a tradition carried over from the stage and maintained during the early days of silent films. Still, the first Negro character had arrived in films, and he had done so at a time when the motion-picture industry itself was virtually nonexistent. The movies were without stars or studios or sound. There were no great directors or writers. And the community of Hollywood had not yet come into being.

After the tom's debut, there appeared a variety of black presences bearing the fanciful names of the coon, the tragic mulatto, the mammy, and the brutal black buck. All were character types used for the same effect: to entertain by stressing Negro inferiority. Fun was poked at the American Negro by presenting him as either a nitwit or a childlike lackey. None of the types was meant to do great harm, although at various times individual ones did. All were merely filmic reproductions of black stereotypes that had existed since the days of slavery and were already popularized in American life and arts. The movies, which catered to public tastes, borrowed profusely from all the other popular art forms. Whenever dealing with black characters, they simply adapted the old familiar stereotypes, often further distorting them.

In the early days when all the black characters were still portrayed by white actors in blackface, there was nothing but the old character types. They sat like square boxes on a shelf. A white actor walked by, selected a box, and used it as a base for a very square, rigidly defined performance. Later, when real black actors played the roles and found themselves wedged into these categories, the history became one of actors battling against the types to create rich, stimulating, diverse characters. At various points the tom, the coon, the tragic mulatto, the mammy, and the brutal black buck were brought to life respectively by Bill "Bojangles" Robinson, Stepin Fetchit, Nina Mae McKinney, Hattie McDaniel, and Walter Long (actually a white actor who portrayed a black villain in *The Birth of a Nation*), and later "modernized" by such performers as Sidney Poitier, Sammy Davis, Jr., Dorothy Dandridge, Ethel Waters, and Jim Brown. Later such performers as Richard Pryor, Eddie Murphy, Lonette McKee, Whoopi Goldberg, and Danny Glover also found themselves struggling to turn old stereotypes inside out. Often it seemed as if the mark of the actor was the manner in which he individualized the mythic type or towered above it. The types were to prove deadly for some actors and inconsequential for others. But try as any actor may to forget the typecasting, the familiar types have most always been present in American black movies. The early silent period of motion picture remains important, not because there were any great black performances—there weren't—but because the five basic types—the boxes sitting on the shelf—that were to dominate black character for the next half century were first introduced then.

▨ The Tom

Porter's tom was the first in a long line of socially acceptable Good Negro characters. Always as toms are chased, harassed, hounded, flogged, enslaved, and insulted, they keep the faith, n'er turn against their white massas, and remain hearty, submissive, stoic, generous, selfless, and oh-so-very kind. Thus they endear themselves to white audiences and emerge as heroes of sorts.   5

Two early toms appeared in the shorts *Confederate Spy* (c. 1910) and *For Massa's Sake* (1911). In the former, dear old Uncle Daniel is a Negro spy for the South. He dies before a Northern firing squad, but he is content, happy that he "did it for massa's sake and little massa." In *For Massa's Sake* a former slave is so attached to his erstwhile master that he sells himself back into slavery to help the master through a period of financial difficulties.

During the silent period, there were also remakes of the Harriet Beecher Stowe novel in which the tale of the good Christian slave was again made the meat of melodrama. The first remakes in 1909 and 1913 had little in style or treatment to distinguish them. But a fourth version, directed by William Robert Daly in 1914, distinguished itself and the tom tradition by starring the Negro stage actor Sam Lucas in the title role. Lucas became the first black man to play a leading role in a movie. Later in 1927, when Universal Pictures filmed *Uncle Tom's Cabin,* the handsome Negro actor James B. Lowe was signed for the leading role. Harry Pollard directed the Universal feature. Twelve years earlier, Pollard had filmed a version of the Stowe classic in which he portrayed the Christian slave in blackface. But for this new venture Negro Lowe was selected to fit in with the "realistic" demands of the times. Congratulating itself on its liberalism, Universal sent out press releases about its good colored star:

> James B. Lowe has made history. A history that reflects only credit to the Negro race, not only because he has given the "Uncle Tom" character a new slant, but because of his exemplary conduct with the Universal company. They look upon Lowe at the Universal Studio as a living black god. . . . Of the directors, critics, artists, and actors who have seen James Lowe work at the studio there are none who will not say he is the most suited of all men for the part of "Tom." Those who are religious say that a heavenly power brought him to Universal and all predict a most marvelous future and worldwide reputation for James B. Lowe.

Although a "heavenly power" may have been with actor Lowe, it had little effect on his interpretation of the role. Tom still came off as a genial darky, furnished with new color but no new sentiments. Yet to Lowe's credit, he did his tomming with such an arresting effectiveness that he was sent to England on a promotional tour to bally-hoo the picture, thus becoming the first black actor to be publicized by his studio. The film also introduced the massive baptism scene, which later became a Hollywood favorite. Curiously, in 1958 this version of *Uncle Tom's Cabin,* although silent, was reissued with an added prologue by Raymond Massey. Because it arrived just when the sit-ins were erupting in the South, many wondered if by reissuing this film Universal Studios hoped to remind the restless black masses of an earlier, less turbulent period, when obeying one's master was the answer to every black man's problems.

▓ The Coon

Although tom was to outdistance every other type and dominate American hearth and home, he had serious competition from a group of coons. They appeared in a series of black films presenting the Negro as amusement object and black buffoon. They lacked the single-mindedness of tom. There were the pure coon and two variants of his type: the pickaninny and the uncle remus.

The pickaninny was the first of the coon types to make its screen debut. It   10
gave the Negro child actor his place in the black pantheon. Generally, he was a harmless, little screwball creation whose eyes popped, whose hair stood on end with the least excitement, and whose antics were pleasant and diverting. Thomas Alva Edison proved to be a pioneer in the exploitation and exploration of this type when he presented *Ten Pickaninnies* in 1904, a forerunner of the Hal Roach *Our Gang* series. During his camera experiments in 1893, Edison had photographed some blacks as "interesting side effects." In *Ten Pickaninnies,* the side effects moved to the forefront of the action as a group of nameless Negro children romped and ran about while being referred to as snowballs, cherubs, coons, bad chillun, inky kids, smoky kids, black lambs, cute ebonies, and chubbie ebonies. In due time, the pickaninnies were to be called by other names. In the 1920s and the 1930s, such child actors as Sunshine Sammy, Farina, Stymie, and Buckwheat picked up the pick-aninny mantle and carried it to new summits. In all the versions of *Uncle Tom's Cabin,* the slave child Topsy was presented as a lively pickaninny, used solely for comic relief. When the 1927 version of *Uncle Tom's Cabin* opened, the character was

singled out by one critic who wrote: "Topsy is played by Mona Ray, a wonderfully bright youngster who seems to have the comedy of her part in extraordinary fashion . . . her eyes roll back and forth in alarm. She also evinces no liking for her plight when she is found by Miss Ophelia while dabbing powder on her ebony countenance." In her day, the character Topsy was clownish and droll and became such a film favorite that she starred in *Topsy and Eva* (1927), in which her far-fetched meanderings and her pickaninnying won mass audience approval.

Shortly after Edison introduced the pickaninny in 1904, the pure coon made its way onto the screen in *Wooing and Wedding of a Coon* (1905). This short depicted a honeymooning black couple as stumbling and stuttering idiots. Later the coon appeared in *The Masher* (1907), which was about a self-styled white ladies' man who is rebuffed by all the women he pursues. When he meets a mysterious veiled woman who responds to his passes, the hero thinks he has arrived at his blue heaven. And so finding success, he removes the veil only to discover that his mystery lady love is *colored!* Without further ado, he takes off. He may have been looking for a blue heaven, but he certainly did not want a black one.

Before its death, the coon developed into the most blatantly degrading of all black stereotypes. The pure coons emerged as no-account niggers, those unreliable, crazy, lazy, subhuman creatures good for nothing more than eating watermelons, stealing chickens, shooting craps, or butchering the English language. A character named Rastus was just such a figure.

How Rastus Got His Turkey (c. 1910) was the first of a series of slapstick comedies centering on the antics of a Negro called Rastus. Here Rastus tries to steal a turkey for his Thanksgiving dinner. Next came *Rastus in Zululand,* about a darky who dreams of going to Zululand in the heart of Africa. There he wins the affections of the chief's daughter. He is willing to flirt with the girl, but when asked to marry her, in true unreliable, no-account nigger fashion, he refuses, expressing a wish for death rather than matrimony. The savage chief (from the beginning, all Africans are savages) nearly grants that wish, too. *Rastus and Chicken, Pickaninnies and Watermelon,* and *Chicken Thief* were other shorts in the series, all appearing during 1910 and 1911. In some respects, this series and its central character simply paved the way for the greatest coon of all time, Stepin Fetchit.

The final member of the coon triumvirate is the uncle remus. Harmless and congenial, he is a first cousin to the tom, yet he distinguishes himself by his quaint, naïve, and comic philosophizing. During the silent period he was only hinted at. He did not come into full flower until the 1930s and 1940s with films such as *The Green Pastures* (1936) and *Song of the South* (1946). Remus's mirth, like tom's contentment and the coon's antics, has always been used to indicate the black man's satisfaction with the system and his place in it.

■ The Tragic Mulatto

The third figure of the black pantheon and the one that proved itself a moviemaker's darling is the tragic mulatto. One of the type's earliest appearances was in *The Debt* (1912), a two-reeler about the Old South. A white man's wife and his black mistress bear him children at the same time. Growing up together, the white   15 son and the mulatto daughter fall in love and decide to marry, only to have their re-lationship revealed to them at the crucial moment. Their lives are thus ruined not only because they are brother and sister but also—and here was the catch—because the girl has a drop of black blood!

In *Humanity's Cause, In Slavery Days,* and *The Octoroon,* all made around 1913, explored the plight of a fair-skinned mulatto attempting to pass for white. Usually the mulatto is made likable—even sympathetic (because of her white blood, no doubt)—and the audience believes that the girl's life could have been productive and happy had she not been a "victim of divided racial inheritance."

■ The Mammy

Mammy, the fourth black type, is so closely related to the comic coons that she is usually relegated to their ranks. Mammy is distinguished, however, by her sex and her fierce independence. She is usually big, fat, and cantankerous. She made her debut around 1914 when audiences were treated to a blackface version of *Lysistrata.* The comedy, titled *Coon Town Suffragettes,* dealt with a group of bossy mammy wash-erwomen who organize a militant movement to keep their good-for-nothing hus-bands at home. Aristophanes would no doubt have risen from his grave with right-eous indignation. But the militancy of the washerwomen served as a primer for the mammy roles Hattie McDaniel was to perfect in the 1930s.

Mammy's offshoot is the aunt jemima, sometimes derogatorily referred to as a "handkerchief head." Often aunt jemimas are toms blessed with religion or mam-mies who wedge themselves into the dominant white culture. Generally they are sweet, jolly, and good-tempered—a bit more polite than mammy and certainly never as headstrong. The maids in the Mae West films of the 1930s fit snugly into this category.

■ The Brutal Black Buck and *The Birth of a Nation*

D. W. Griffith's *The Birth of a Nation* (1915) was the motion picture to introduce the final mythic type, the brutal black buck. This extraordinary, multidimensional movie was also the first feature film to deal with a black theme and at the same time to articulate fully the entire pantheon of black gods and goddesses. Griffith pre-sented all the types with such force and power that his film touched off a wave of controversy and was denounced as the most slanderous anti-Negro movie ever released.

In almost every way, *The Birth of a Nation* was a stupendous undertaking, un-like any film that had preceded it. Up to then American movies had been two- or three-reel affairs, shorts running no longer than ten or fifteen minutes, crudely and casually filmed. But *The Birth of a Nation* was rehearsed for six weeks, filmed in nine, later edited in three months, and finally released as a record-breaking hundred-thousand-dollar spectacle, twelve reels in length and over three hours in running time. It altered the entire course and concept of American moviemaking, developing the close-up, cross-cutting, rapid-fire editing, the iris, the split-screen shot, and realistic and impressionistic lighting. Creating sequences and images yet to be surpassed, the film's magnitude and epic grandeur swept audiences off their feet. At a private White House screening President Woodrow Wilson exclaimed, "It's like writing history with lightning!" *The Birth of a Nation,* however, not only vividly re-created history, but revealed its director's philosophical concept of the universe and his personal racial bigotry. For D. W. Griffith there was a moral order at work in the universe. If that order were ever thrown out of whack, he believed chaos would ensue. Griffith's thesis was sound, relatively exciting, and even classic in a purely Shakespearean sense. But in articulating his thesis, Griffith seemed to be saying that things were in order only when whites were in control and when the American Negro was kept in his place. In the end, Griffith's "lofty" statement—and the film's subject matter—transformed *The Birth of a Nation* into a hotly debated and bitterly cursed motion picture.

It told the story of the Old South, the Civil War, the Reconstruction period, and the emergence of the Ku Klux Klan. Basing his film on Thomas Dixon's novel *The Clansman* (also the original title of the film), Griffith focused on a good, decent "little" family, the Camerons of Piedmont, South Carolina. Before the war, the family lives in an idyllic "quaintly way that is to be no more." Dr. Cameron and his sons are gentle, benevolent "fathers" to their childlike servants. The slaves themselves could be no happier. In the fields they contentedly pick cotton. In their quarters they dance and sing for their master. In the Big House Mammy joyously goes about her chores. All is in order. Everyone knows his place. Then the Civil War breaks out, and the old order cracks.

The war years take their toll. In Piedmont, the Cameron family is terrorized by a troop of Negro raiders, and all the South undergoes "ruin, devastation, rapine, and pillage." Then comes Reconstruction. Carpetbaggers and uppity niggers from the North move into Piedmont, exploiting and corrupting the former slaves, unleashing the sadism and bestiality innate in the Negro, turning the once congenial darkies into renegades, and using them to "crush the white South under the heel of the black South." "Lawlessness runs riot!" says one title card. The old slaves have quit work to dance. They roam the streets, shoving whites off sidewalks. They take over the political polls and disenfranchise the whites. A black political victory culminates in an orgiastic street celebration. Blacks dance, sing, drink, rejoice. Later they conduct a black Congressional session, itself a mockery of Old South ideals, in which the freed Negro legislators are depicted as lustful, arrogant, and idiotic. They bite on chicken legs and drink whiskey from bottles while sprawling with bare feet upon their desks. During the Congressional meeting, the stench created by the barefoot Congressmen becomes so great that they pass as their first act a ruling that every member must keep his shoes on during legislative meetings! Matters in *The Birth of a Nation* reach a heady climax later when the renegade black Gus sets out to rape the younger Cameron daughter. Rather than submit, the Pet Sister flees from him and throws herself from a cliff—into the "opal gates of death." Then the mulatto Silas Lynch attempts to force the white Elsie Stoneman to marry him. Finally, when all looks hopelessly lost, there emerges a group of good, upright Southern white men, members of an "invisible empire," who, while wearing white sheets and hoods, battle the blacks in a direct confrontation. Led by Ben Cameron in a rousing stampede, they magnificently defeat the black rebels! Defenders of white womanhood, white honor, and white glory, they restore to the South everything it has lost, including its white supremacy. Thus we have the birth of a nation. And the birth of the Ku Klux Klan.

The plot machinations of the Griffith epic may today resound with melodramatic absurdities, but the action, the actors, and the direction did not. The final ride of the Klan was an impressive piece of film propaganda, superbly lit and brilliantly edited. Indeed it was so stirring that audiences screamed in delight, cheering for the white heroes and booing, hissing, and cursing the black militants. *The Birth of a Nation* remains significant not only because of its artistry but also because of its wide-ranging influence. One can detect in this single film the trends and sentiments that were to run through almost every black film made for a long time afterward. Later film makers were to pick up Griffith's ideas—his very images—but were to keep them "nicely" toned down in order not to offend audiences.

Griffith used three varieties of blacks. The first were the "faithful souls," a mammy and an uncle tom, who remain with the Cameron family throughout and staunchly defend them from the rebels. By means of these characters, as well as the pickaninny slaves seen dancing, singing, and clowning in their quarters, director Griffith propagated the myth of slave contentment and made it appear as if slavery had elevated the Negro from his bestial instincts. At heart, Griffith's "faithful souls" were shamelessly naïve representations of the Negro as Child or the Negro as Watered-Down Noble Savage. But these characters were to make their way through scores of other Civil War epics, and they were to leave their mark on the characterizations of Clarence Muse in *Huckleberry Finn* (1931) and *Broadway Bill* (1934) and of Bill Robinson in *The Little Colonel* (1935) and *The Littlest Rebel* (1935).

Griffith's second variety were the brutal black bucks. Just as the coon stereotype could be broken into subgroups, the brutal black buck type could likewise be divided into two categories: the black brutes and the black bucks. Differences between the two are minimal. The black brute was a barbaric black out to raise havoc. Audiences could assume that his physical violence served as an outlet for a man who was sexually repressed. In *The Birth of a Nation,* the black brutes, subhuman and feral, are the nameless characters setting out on a rampage full of black rage. They flog the Camerons' faithful servant. They shove and assault white men of the town. They flaunt placards demanding "equal marriage." These characters figured prominently in the Black Congress sequence, and their film descendants were to appear years later as the rebellious slaves of *So Red the Rose* (1935), as the revolutionaries of *Uptight* (1969), and as the militants of *Putney Swope* (1969).

But it was the pure black bucks that were Griffith's really great archetypal figures. Bucks are always big, baadddd niggers, oversexed and savage, violent and frenzied as they lust for white flesh. No greater sin hath any black man. Both Lynch, the mulatto, and Gus, the renegade, fall into this category. Among other things, these two characters revealed the tie between sex and racism in America. Griffith played on the myth of the Negro's high-powered sexuality, then articulated the great white fear that every black man longs for a white woman. Underlying the fear was the assumption that the white woman was the ultimate in female desirability, herself a symbol of white pride, power, and beauty. Consequently, when Lillian Gish, the frailest, purest of all screen heroines, was attacked by the character Lynch—when he put his

25

big black arms around this pale blond beauty—audiences literally panicked. Here was the classic battle of good and evil, innocence and corruption. It was a master stroke and a brilliant use of contrast, one that drew its audience into the film emotionally.* But in uncovering the attraction of black to white, Griffith failed to reveal the political implications. Traditionally, certain black males have been drawn to white women because these women are power symbols, an ideal of the oppressor. But Griffith attributed the attraction to an animalism innate in the Negro male. Thus the black bucks of the film are psychopaths, one always panting and salivating, the other forever stiffening his body as if the mere presence of a white woman in the same room could bring him to a sexual climax. Griffith played hard on the bestiality of his black villainous bucks and used it to arouse hatred.

Closely aligned to the bucks and brutes of *The Birth of a Nation* is the mulatto character, Lydia. She is presented as the mistress of the white abolitionist carpetbagger, Senator Stoneman. Through Lydia, Griffith explored the possibilities of the dark, sinister half-breed as a tragic leading lady. Although merely a supporting character, Lydia is the only black role to suggest even remotely genuine mental anguish. She hates whites. She refuses to be treated as an inferior. She wants power. Throughout, she anguishes over her predicament as a black woman in a hostile white world.

Lydia is also the film's only passionate female. Griffith was the first important movie director to divide his black women into categories based on their individual colors. Both Lydia and Mammy are played by white actresses in blackface. But Mammy is darker. She is representative of the all-black woman, overweight, middle-aged, and so dark, so thoroughly black, that it is preposterous even to suggest that she be a sex object. Instead she was desexed. This tradition of the desexed, overweight, dowdy *dark* black woman was continued in films throughout the 1930s and 1940s. Vestiges of it popped up as late as the 1960s with Claudia McNeil in *A Raisin in the Sun* (1961) and Beah Richards in *Hurry Sundown* (1967). A dark black actress was considered for no role but that of a mammy or an aunt jemima. On the other hand, the part-black woman—the light-skinned Negress—was given a chance at lead parts and was graced with a modicum of sex appeal. Every sexy black woman who appeared afterward in movies was to be a "cinnamon-colored gal" with Caucasian features. The mulatto came closest to the white ideal. Whether conscious or not, Griffith's division of the black woman into color categories survived in movies the way many set values continue long after they are discredited. In fact, it was said in 1958 and 1970 that one reason why such actresses as Eartha Kitt in *Anna Lucasta* and Lola Falana in *The Liberation of L. B. Jones* failed to emerge as important screen love goddesses was that they were too dark.

Influential and detrimental as the Griffith blacks were to be for later generations, they were not meekly accepted in 1915. *The Birth of a Nation's* blackfaced bad-

---

*Lillian Gish's comments in the January 1937 issue of *Stage* verify the fact that Griffith was well aware of this contrast and that he used it to arouse his audience. Said Gish: "At first I was not cast to play in *The Clansman*. My sister and I had been the last to join the company and we naturally supposed . . . that the main assignments would go to the older members. But one day while we were rehearsing the scene where the colored man picks up the Northern girl gorilla-fashion, my hair, which was very blond, fell far below my waist and Griffith, seeing the contrast in the two figures, assigned me to play Elsie Stoneman (who was to have been Mae Marsh)."

dies aroused a rash of hostilities. At the film's New York première, the NAACP picketed the theater, calling the movie racist propaganda. Later the Chicago and Boston branches of the NAACP led massive demonstrations against its presentation. Other civil rights and religious organizations were quick to protest. Race riots broke out in a number of cities. Newspaper editorials and speeches censured the film. Black critics such as Laurence Reddick said it glorified the Ku Klux Klan, and Reddick added that the film's immense success was at least one factor contributing to the great and growing popularity the organization enjoyed during this period. In the South, the film was often advertised as calculated to "work audiences into a frenzy . . . it will make you hate." In some regions, the ad campaign may have been effective, for in 1915 lynchings in the United States reached their highest peak since 1908. Ultimately, *The Birth of a Nation* was banned in five states and nineteen cities.

The anger and fury did not die in 1915 either. The film was reissued at regular intervals in later years. At each reopening, outraged moviegoers, both black and white, vehemently opposed its showing. In 1921, *The Birth of a Nation* was attacked as a part of a "Southern campaign to stimulate the Ku Klux Klan"—which it had already done. The Museum of Modern Art temporarily shelved the picture in 1946. Because of "the potency of its anti-Negro bias . . . " read the Museum's press announcement, "exhibiting it at this time of heightened social tensions cannot be justified." The 1947 revival of the movie by the Dixie Film Exchange was blasted by the Civil Rights Congress, and the NAACP picketed New York's Republic Theatre where it was to be shown. "It brings race hatred to New York City," said NAACP Secretary Walter White, "and we don't want it here." The Progressive Labor Party led demonstrations against the film during the following year. In 1950, there were renewed outcries when word leaked out that a Hollywood company was to remake the movie in sound. The remake plans were quickly aborted, as were the 1959 proposals to present it on television.

Throughout the years, D. W. Griffith defended himself as a mere filmmaker with no political or ideological view in mind. Surprised and apparently genuinely hurt when called a racist, Griffith made speeches across the country, wrote letters to the press, accused the NAACP and its supporters of trying to bring about screen censorship, and even went so far as to issue a pamphlet titled "The Rise and Fall of Free Speech in America," all in an effort to squelch the controversy. As late as 1947, one year before his death and some thirty-two years after the movie's release, D. W. Griffith still maintained that his film was not an attack on the American Negro.

The Birth of a Nation has become one of the highest grossing movies of all time. (The amount it has earned has never been fully tabulated.) Eyeing its profits, a number of Hollywood producers undertook projects with similar anti-Negro themes. *Broken Chains* (c. 1916) and *Free and Equal* (filmed in 1915 but not released until 1925) were prominent imitations. The former failed miserably. The latter's release was held up for some ten years while the producer waited for the furor to cool down. For one thing was certain after *The Birth of a Nation:* never again could the Negro be depicted in the guise of an out-and-out villain. This treatment was too touchy and too controversial. Griffith's film had succeeded because of its director's artistry and technical virtuosity, but no studio dared risk it again. Consequently, blacks in Hollywood films were cast almost exclusively in comic roles. And thus even the great comic tradition of the Negro in the American film has its roots in the Griffith spectacle. Finally, many of Hollywood's hang-ups and hesitations in pre-senting sensual black men on screen resulted, in part, from the reactions to the Griffith spectacle. So strong was his presentation, and so controversial its reception, that movie companies ignored and avoided such a type of black character for fear of raising new hostilities. Not until more than a half century later, when Melvin Van Peebles' *Sweet Sweetback's Baadasssss Song* (1971) appeared, did sexually assertive black males make their way back to the screen. Afterward, when the box-office success of that film indicated that audiences could at long last accept such a type, the screen was bombarded with an array of buck heroes in such films as *Shaft* (1971), *Super Fly* (1972), *Slaughter* (1972), and *Melinda* (1972).

With *The Birth of a Nation* in 1915, all the major black screen types had been introduced. Literal and unimaginative as some types might now appear, the naïve and cinematically untutored audiences of the early part of the century responded to the character types as if they were the real thing.

As far as the audiences were concerned, the toms, the coons, the mulattoes, the mammies, and the bucks embodied all the aspects and facets of the black experience itself. The audience's deep-set prejudice against any "foreigners" accounts for the typing of all minorities in all American films. But no minority was so relentlessly or fiercely typed as the black man. Audiences rejected even subtle modifications of the black caricatures. When Jack Johnson became the first black heavyweight champion of the world in 1908, filmed sequences of him knocking out white Tommy Burns so disturbed the "racial pride" of white America that they were banned for fear of race riots. Thereafter, black boxers in films were invariably defeated by their white opponents. Similarly, when the first film versions of *Uncle Tom's Cabin* were released in the South, advertisements announced that the black characters were portrayed by white actors. Even at this stage, the evolving film industry feared offending its dominant white audience.

Once the basic mythic types were introduced, a number of things occurred. Specific black themes soon emerged. (The Old South theme proved to be a great favorite.) And the basic types came and went in various guises. Guises long confused many movie viewers. They were (and remain) deceptive, and they have traditionally been used by the film industry to camouflage the familiar types. If a black appeared as a butler, audiences thought of him as merely a servant. What they failed to note was the variety of servants. There were tom servants (faithful and submissive), coon servants (lazy and unreliable), and mammy servants, just to name a few. What has to be remembered is that the servant's uniform was the guise certain types wore during a given period. That way Hollywood could give its audience the same product (the types themselves) but with new packaging (the guise).

With the Griffith spectacle, audiences saw the first of the guises. The brutes, the bucks, and the tragic mulatto all wore the guise of villains. Afterward, during the 1920s, audiences saw their toms and coons dressed in the guise of plantation jesters. In the 1930s, all the types were dressed in servants' uniforms. In the early 1940s, they sported entertainers' costumes. In the late 1940s and the 1950s, they donned the gear of troubled problem people. In the 1960s, they appeared as angry militants. Because the guises were always changing, audiences were sometimes tricked into believing the depictions of the American Negro were altered, too. But at heart beneath the various guises, there lurked the familiar types.

James Baldwin

James Baldwin (1924–1987) was an internationally acclaimed novelist and essayist who captivated readers with his searing depictions of American life, particularly regarding race relations and black family life. A young minister of an evangelical church while in high school, he immortalized the experience in *Go Tell It on the Mountain* (1953). Stymied by the racism in his native land, Baldwin chose to live in France after 1948 as an expatriate. His other writings include the following novels: *Giovanni's Room* (1956), *Another Country* (1962), *Tell Me How Long the Train's Been Gone* (1968), *If Beale Street Could Talk* (1974), and *Just Above My Head* (1979). His nonfiction includes *Notes of a Native Son* (1953), *Nobody Knows My Name: More Notes of a Native Son* (1961), *The Fire Next Time* (1963), *No Name in the Street* (1972), *The Devil Finds Work* (1976), *The Evidence of Things Not Seen* (1985), and *The Price of a Ticket: Collected Nonfiction, 1948–1985* (1985). Baldwin's awards include the Eugene F. Saxton Fellowship (1945), Rosenwald Fellowship (1948), Guggenheim Fellowship (1954), Ford Foundation Grant (1959), Foreign Drama Critics Award (1964) for *Blues for Mr. Charlie,* and an American Book Award nomination in 1980 for *Just Above My Head.* In France, Baldwin was named a Commander of the Legion of Honor in 1986.

The following is an excerpt from *The Fire Next Time* (1963) in which Baldwin exhorts his nephew to triumph over the corrosive effects of racism.

My Dungeon Shook

Letter to My Nephew on the One Hundredth Anniversary of the Emancipation

Dear James:

I have begun this letter five times and torn it up five times. I keep seeing your face, which is also the face of your father and my brother. Like him, you are tough, dark, vulnerable, moody—with a very definite tendency to sound truculent because you want no one to think you are soft. You may be like your grandfather in this. I don't know, but certainly both you and your father resemble him very much physically. Well, he is dead, he never saw you, and he had a terrible life; he was defeated long before he died because, at the bottom of his heart, he really believed what white people said about him. This is one of the reasons that he became so holy. I am sure that your father has told you something about all that. Neither you nor your father exhibit any tendency towards holiness: you really *are* of another era, part of what happened when the Negro left the land and came into what the late E. Franklin Frazier called "the cities of destruction." You can only be destroyed by believing that you really are what the white world calls a *nigger.* I tell you this because I love you, and please don't you ever forget it.

I have known both of you all your lives, have carried your Daddy in my arms and on my shoulders, kissed and spanked him and watched him learn to walk. I don't know if you've known anybody from that far back; if you've loved anybody that long, first as an infant, then as a child, then as a man, you gain a strange perspective on time and human pain and effort. Other people cannot see what I see whenever I look into your father's face, for behind your father's face as it is today are all those other faces which were his. Let him laugh and I see a cellar your father does not remember and a house he does not remember and I hear in his present laughter his laughter as a child. Let him curse and I remember him falling down the cellar steps, and howling, and I remember, with pain, his tears, which my hand or your grandmother's so easily wiped away. But no one's hand can wipe away those tears he sheds invisibly today, which one hears in his laughter and in his speech and in his songs. I know what the world has done to my brother and how narrowly he has survived it. And I know, which is much worse, and this is the crime of which I accuse my country and my countrymen, and for which neither I nor time nor history will ever forgive them, that they have destroyed and are destroying hundreds of thousands of lives and do not know it and do not want to know it. One can be, indeed one must strive to become, tough and philosophical concerning destruction and death, for this is what most of mankind has been best at since we have heard of man. (But remember: *most* of mankind is not *all* of mankind.) But it is not permissible that the authors of devastation should also be innocent. It is the innocence which constitutes the crime.

Now, my dear namesake, these innocent and well-meaning people, your countrymen, have caused you to be born under conditions not very far removed from those described for us by Charles Dickens in the London of more than a hundred years ago. (I hear the chorus of the innocents screaming, "No! This is not true! How *bitter* you are!"—but I am writing this letter to *you,* to try to tell you something about how to handle *them,* for most of them do not yet really know that you exist. I *know* the conditions under which you were born, for I was there. Your countrymen were *not* there, and haven't made it yet. Your grandmother was also there, and no one has ever accused her of being bitter. I suggest that the innocents check with her. She isn't hard to find. Your countrymen don't know that *she* exists, either, though she has been working for them all their lives.)

Well, you were born, here you came, something like fifteen years ago; and though your father and mother and grandmother, looking about the streets through which they were carrying you, staring at the walls into which they brought you, had every reason to be heavyhearted, yet they were not. For here you were, Big James, named for me—you were a big baby, I was not—here you were: to be loved. To be loved, baby, hard, at once, and forever, to strengthen you against the loveless world. Remember that: I know how black it looks today, for you. It looked bad that day, too; yes, we were trembling. We have not stopped trembling yet, but if we had not loved each other none of us would have survived. And now you must survive because we love you, and for the sake of your children and your children's children.

This innocent country set you down in a ghetto in which, in fact, it intended that you should perish. Let me spell out precisely what I mean by that, for the heart of the matter is here and the root of my dispute with my country. You were born where you were born and faced the future that you faced because you were black and *for no other reason.* The limits of your ambition were, thus, expected to be set for-

5

ever. You were born into a society which spelled out with brutal clarity, and in as many ways as possible, that you were a worthless human being. You were not expected to aspire to excellence: you were expected to make peace with mediocrity. Wherever you have turned, James, in your short time on this earth, you have been told where you could go and what you could do (and *how* you could do it) and where you could live and whom you could marry. I know your countrymen do not agree with me about this, and I hear them saying, "You exaggerate." They do not know Harlem, and I do. So do you. Take no one's word for anything, including mine—but trust your experience. Know whence you came. If you know whence you came, there is really no limit to where you can go. The details and symbols of your life have been deliberately constructed to make you believe what white people say about you. Please try to remember that what they believe, as well as what they do and cause you to endure, does not testify to your inferiority but to their inhumanity and fear. Please try to be clear, dear James, through the storm which rages about your youthful head today, about the reality which lies behind the words *acceptance* and *integration*. There is no reason for you to try to become like white people and there is no basis whatever for their impertinent assumption that *they* must accept *you*. The really terrible thing, old buddy, is that *you* must accept *them*. And I mean that very seriously. You must accept them and accept them with love. For these innocent people have no other hope. They are, in effect, still trapped in a history which they do not understand; and until they understand it, they cannot be released from it. They have had to believe for many years, and for innumerable reasons, that black men are inferior to white men. Many of them, indeed, know better, but, as you will discover, people find it very difficult to act on what they know. To act is to be committed, and to be committed is to be in danger. In this case, the danger, in the minds of most white Americans, is the loss of their identity. Try to imagine how you would feel if you woke up one morning to find the sun shining and all the stars aflame. You would be frightened because it is out of the order of nature. Any upheaval in the universe is terrifying because it so profoundly attacks one's sense of one's own reality. Well, the black man has functioned in the white man's world as a fixed star, as an immovable pillar: and as he moves out of his place, heaven and earth are shaken to their foundations. You, don't be afraid. I said that it was intended that you should perish in the ghetto, perish by never being allowed to go behind the white man's definitions, by never being allowed to spell your proper name. You have, and many of us have, defeated this intention; and, by a terrible law, a terrible paradox, those innocents who believed that your imprisonment made them safe are losing their grasp of reality. But these men are your brothers— your lost, younger brothers. And if the word *integration* means anything, this is what it means: that we, with love, shall force our brothers to see themselves as they are, to cease fleeing from reality and begin to change it. For this is your home, my friend; do not be driven from it; great men have done great things here, and will again, and we can make America what America must become. It will be hard, James, but you come from sturdy, peasant stock, men who picked cotton and dammed rivers and built railroads, and, in the teeth of the most terrifying odds, achieved an unassailable and monumental dignity. You come from a long line of great poets, some of the greatest poets since Homer. One of them said, *The very time I thought I was lost, My dungeon shook and my chains fell off.*

You know, and I know, that the country is celebrating one hundred years of freedom one hundred years too soon. We cannot be free until they are free. God bless you, James, and Godspeed.

Your uncle,
James

Ted Joans

Ted Joans (1928–) is a poet, former jazz musician, surrealist painter, and world traveler. He became an expatriate in the 1960s and currently resides in Mali. His works include *Beat Poems* (1957), *Funky Jazz Poems* (1957), *All of Ted Joans and No More: Poems and Collages* (1960), *Black Pow Wow: Jazz Poems* (1969), *A Black Manifesto in Jazz Poetry and Prose* (1971), *Afrodisia: New Poems* [and illustrator] (1971), *Spectrophilia: Poems, Collages* (1973), *Vergriffen: Oder, Blitzlieb Poems* (1979), and *Teducation: Selected Poems, 1949–1999* (1999).

The following poem appears in *You Better Believe It* (1973, edited by Paul Breman). The speaker asserts himself as a proud black man who refuses to be called "boy."

Je suis un homme

I am a man   I am a homo sapiens   I have never banged
   any one in the tail nor has anyone banged me
   I AM A MAN i am no homosexual

I am a man   I have hair on my face like Christ
   I am a terror and nightmare to razor blade   5
   salesmen I am a man I wear my beard proudly
   as your mother wears her permanent pubic hair

I am a man   I differ from other men because they're
   not me, I am the ONE, I am the real man and I'm
   authentic as hell, ask any anthropologist, they   10
   can give you diluvial egocentric facts about me
   and the tree from which I grew

I am a man   I am erotically in love with six women,
   one black, one white, one yellow, one brown, one
   pink, one purple and I have technicolored sex   15
   with all six each dawn at the dark entrance of
   the colored waiting room

I am a man   I wear my clothes until I outgrow them
I don't support the fashions I am neither fat
nor skinny tall nor short I am just a rightsized   20
hipster who is out to destroy bigotry and old
styled ignorance

I am a man   I am as healthy as the cum, I wear a
wrinkled scrotum, I read poetry in the girl
schools of America and I still refuse to read for   25
no bread or circumcise my tool again

I am a man   I sleep sideways and I am more fluent in
a bed I can make a Victorian Hen moist and I can
love across the sea from the Halls of Montezuma
to the shores of Tripoli   30

I am a man   I believe only in the poets musicians
painters sculptors and hipsters and I continue to
use deodorant between my fingers and toes and I
shall remain an individual in the United States of
ununited ideas of democracy   35

I am a man   I write sensual surrealist letters to
young virgins and my best female companions who
I continue to tell: women, Use ye not Tampax but
make a Lipton Tea bag scene for double duty.

I am a man   I say to you the square Swingeth with me   40
and ye too will learneth to dig

I am a man   my ideas are more important than the Naacp
and White Citizens Council
All men must be free now and this moment the chains
should be broken   45

I am a man   I have read the Gettysburg address but I
prefer the Ginsberg address and I continue the fight
for freedom of everything except physical harm to
my fellow man and never to stand in his way toward
happiness   50

I am a man   I introduced democracy to Lil abner

I am a man   I kissed André Breton on Rue Bonaparte in
Paris and kissed Kaldis in front of the American
Express in Athens and Peter Orlovsky in the New
Years Eve dawn of New York, but I am still a man   55

I am a man   I saw maumau kicking santa claus underneath
   Washington's Squarepark's arch last night and it was
   then that I knew kangaroo shoes just don't fit
   aardvarks and there should be a neon vagina on the
   statue of liberty   60

I am a man   I know damn well what side the bread is
   buttered on and where to plant contagious freedom
   ideas into the oppressed people of the world
   through jazz poetry, jazz painting and jazz music

I am a man   I have a head on my shoulder and her name   65
   is your neighbor nextdoor

I am a man   I advocate the right for men to continue
   pee standing and that all women should cop a squat
   anywhere in a handbag or parking lot

I am a man   I have taken baths and showers all my life   70
   I can not stand the dirt that you have in the corner
   of your fisheyes nor can I tolerate the grime under
   your fingernails and please remove that body of
   yours out of my way and take your foot off of my
   neck and that filthy hand out of my hardworking   75
   pocket

I am a man   I am not lecherous like you and those that
   have joined the day-in-day-out rat race to get
   involved in the eternal payments for so called
   pleasures   80

I am a man   America I am a man I have had babies call
   me daddio I am a man I am a man I have held the
   hand of Elizabeth Taylor and the hand of Charlie
   Parker and the hand of Kwame Nkrumah and the hand
   of my mother who told me at the age of twelve that   85
   I was a man so dig me American don't call me BOY!!!

Mari Evans

Mari Evans (1923–) is a champion of black pride in her poetry, plays, and
essays. Her opus includes poetry volumes: *I Am a Black Woman* (1970),
Nightstar: 1973–1978 (1981), *A Dark and Splendid Mass* (1992); criticism:
Black Women Writers 1950–1980: A Critical Evaluation (1984, editor); and

plays: *River of My Song* (1977) and *Eyes* (1979). Evans was a John Hay Whitney fellow (1965), MacDowell fellow (1975), and Yaddo Writers Colony fellow (1984). She was awarded the Builders Award by Third World Press in 1977 and the Black Arts Celebration Poetry Award in 1981.

The following is the title poem of her poetry volume *I Am a Black Woman* (1970). The speaker celebrates the fortitude and virtues of the black woman.

I Am a Black Woman

I am a black woman
the music of my song
some sweet arpeggio of tears
is written in a minor key
and I   5
can be heard humming in the night
Can be heard
        humming
in the night

I saw my mate leap screaming to the sea   10
and I/with these hands/cupped the lifebreath
from my issue in the canebrake
I lost Nat's swinging body in a rain of tears
and heard my son scream all the way from Anzio
for Peace he never knew. . . . I   15
learned Da Nang and Pork Chop Hill
in anguish
Now my nostrils know the gas
and these trigger tire/d fingers
seek the softness in my warrior's beard   20

I
am a black woman
tall as a cypress
strong
beyond all definition still   25
defying place
and time
and circumstance
   assailed
      impervious   30
        indestructible
Look
  on me and be
renewed

John Langston Gwaltney

John Langston Gwaltney (1928–) is an anthropologist who has done fieldwork in North America and West Africa. His works include *The Thrice Shy: Cultural Accommodations to Blindness and Other Disasters in a Mexican Village* (1970) and *Role of Expectation of Blindness in an Oaxaca Village* (1970).

The following is an excerpt from *Drylongso: A Self-Portrait of Black America* (1993) in which two women interviewed by Gwaltney give their opinions about colorism, intraracial prejudice.

The Many Shades of Black
Angela McArthur

One reason the whole thing is so hard to deal with is that nobody really talks about it.

At twenty, Angela McArthur is even less reconciled to not being able to take the world on faith than most black people I know. Her shyness and suspiciousness are consequently more readily detectable. When a doctor told her that she was made to bear children, she promptly switched physicians. That was a year ago and she still occasionally wonders if she acted justly with the first medical man. Her neighbors' judgment is that she is a good, sensible, pretty girl who is prone to take too much time with people who "can't mean anyone else any good because they are messing themselves up." The last impression Miss McArthur would want to leave almost anyone with is contempt or callousness on her part. She does not wish anyone to think her vain because she is very pretty or pompous because she is formally well educated. So she tends to keep silent, even suffering the unmerited abuse of fools and opportunists.

Miss McArthur is a capable amateur viola player who generally underestimates both her technical capacity and her familiarity with the score. Her sister, Deborah, says, "Angela just lets people and things get to her too much." "Sometimes I wish I had one of those hearts like a rock cast in the sea," Miss McArthur told me once, after having sustained one of her sister's exhortations to toughness. Her most discerning neighbors know, however, that her heart is everything it ought to be and in the right place. A woman who later became a major contributor and participant in this research warned Miss McArthur to think long and well before granting me an interview in her home. In a world where would-be burglars are posing as salesmen, repairmen and census takers, in communities where the ringing of the phone may be a prelude to breaking and entering, this admonition is entirely understandable. All three of us laughed about this later, but it is a kind of insurance to be the sort of person who will hear and weigh the counsel of discreet and discerning people. Miss McArthur is that kind of person.

I have never been asked to pass an opinion on anything by anybody! I wouldn't mind giving my opinions. I guess I would really like to do this, but nobody ever asked me. I would like to see if people felt the same way about things that I do, but I guess I'd be afraid to go up to somebody and ask them how they feel about something. I guess we're all suspicious. It's too bad that it's like that. Miss Lula is a

different kind of person. She will tell you what she thinks if you ask her and sometimes even if you don't! But she's not mean and she has good sense. You know how
I met her? She just came up to me one day and said, "I don't know your name,
daughter, and what I'm going to tell you you might say is none of my business if
you're a fool, but I'm going to tell you what I have to say anyway because if you were
my granddaughter I would hope somebody would have sense enough to tell you."
Now, she was right about the things she told me and I thanked her because she
went out of her way to try to help me.

I didn't do anything wrong or anything like that. You see, I was going out with
this man and I thought he was one kind of person and he was really not like I
thought he was at all. Miss Lula told me the truth about him and some other people I kind of half knew around here. Now, I thank her for that because I was not trying to get in with those people. I really didn't know that they were doing things that
could get them in bad trouble and me with them if I had not found out about
them. Sometimes I'm not too smart about that kind of thing. I mean, I just used to
take people for what they said they were if everything seemed to match—I mean, if
they looked like what they said they were. I tried—I guess I still do try—to be
friendly with people. You know how people can just look at you and say, "I know
where he's coming from," or "I know her type." Well, I never liked that. I always was
taught that you should be nice to any person who was nice to you. This man told
me that he was a student and he dressed and talked like I thought a student might
and he had this white friend who was also like what I guess I thought a student
should be like. They did a lot of things that I didn't approve of. But, you see, I did-
n't know that they were doing these things. They were selling dope and they were
taking things from people's apartments, but I didn't know that until Miss Lula told
me about that. I liked to listen to them talk.

One day Kasavubu told me that he really liked me and he gave me a big tran-
sistor, so I asked him how much it was because I didn't want to take a thing like that
from any man. He wouldn't tell me and said it was a gift because he liked me very
much. I think he really did. I know I did like him, but I didn't like the things Miss
Lula said he was doing. So I asked him if he really did do those things. He said no,
but I could tell that he was lying. He said that I was just trying to put him down because he was black—I mean, dark. That didn't make any difference to me and I
think he knew that, but I'm not really sure about that. But I hate to be accused of
something like that because I know that there are people like that and I really hate
it. I never did anything like that because I never thought that way. I'm really not
that kind of person.

That's not a very nice thing about us, is it? It's true that most of us don't take
dope and are not muggers and go to work all the time, I mean every day, but there
are some things we do—I mean some ways that we think or that some of us think—
you can't really say how many of us think this way, but a lot of people do think in a
very wrong way about color. Now, I don't know if you want people to talk about that,
but it is there. I think there are more black people who are not thinking right
about color than there are who are taking or selling dope.

You know, when I was a little girl we would be reading about the Egyptians or
some other people and I would wonder what it would be like to be that kind of person way back then. So I would pretend to be an Egyptian girl. I'll be twenty-one on

the fifth of June and I still do that sometimes. I have five sisters and I pretended to have a brother for so long that I almost think I do have one sometimes. I used to pretend to have a brother, but I could never get so far out as to pretend to *be* a brother. I never could pretend that I was something really very different than I am. If I pretended to be an Egyptian, I could only pretend to be an Egyptian girl. Or if I was in typing class I might think—you know, pretend—that I was a girl astronaut or maybe a cowgirl. But I could never pretend to be white or male or something without life, like a machine. I used to watch little boys making noises like they were trucks or tanks or something, and that always used to seem very funny.

My sister, Debbie, tried to make me pretend that I was a dead patient. My mother was a nurse, so we always played these hospital and doctor and scientist games. Debbie tried to make me pretend to be a dead person and it just was too much for me. That was the only time I ever fought with my sister, Debbie, or any of the others. You just have to know Debbie! She is one of these people who will not take no for an answer! I tried to do it, but it really did scare me, so I told her no good. But she said she was going to make me do it and then she would do it. But I didn't care who else did it, I just thought it was crazy to pretend to be dead, so I wouldn't lie down, and she pushed me down and I guess that was it. I was the youngest, so they pretty generally let me have my way, but we were like stairsteps, so none of us really had much more sense than the others.

Anyway, we all beat up Debbie because of that and my mother got the word 10 from her friend Miss Chapple, who had a hard time minding her own business. Miss Emily told us to stop. Miss Emily Chapple was one of the ladies who sort of looked out for us. But Debbie wouldn't play anything else and the thing just kept starting up again. Debbie said it was my fault and that she was going to kill me. She said this under her breath, but my father asked her to say it so he could hear what she had said and, Debbie-like, she repeated it. So my mother, who was ironing her uniform, said, "All right, you want to kill something, do you, miss? I'll shore God see that you get a chance!"

So my mother didn't go to the supermarket to get the chicken we generally had on weekends. She took Debbie with her to this chicken market and brought back this turkey and it was alive. So my mother said, "All right, Miss Dracula, do your thing!" Well, you see, Debbie didn't even know how to begin to kill this turkey, and when my mother said she was going to untie the turkey and let Debbie deal with it, well, Debbie just couldn't stand that. So she ran out of the house and we tried to stop her, but my father said, "Leave her alone." Debbie came back after about an hour and my mother said, "The turkey is right where you left it. Now, Bad Bertha, you choose: Either you kill *it* or I am going to half kill you!" Debbie didn't kill the turkey, so my mother was as good as her word and beat Debbie.

But Debbie was still mad at me, you know. She was the kind of person who always held a grudge the longest. I guess Debbie is what people would call evil. She was always very different from the rest of us. I don't mean that she looked different; she didn't, because we all look pretty much alike. Debbie is a twin, but she is probably most different from Marva. Actually, Debbie likes to fight with people, and she is the only one of us who is really like that.

But getting back to this color thing, I think it is the most important thing that we have to fight. You know that you said that your ideas about color might not be like—well, it might not be how people who can see think about colors. Well, I think you should know—I mean, if you don't know—that people who see colors don't always see them as they really are. When you said that about pinkish skin that people think of as white, you were really close to the truth. If I tell white people who are darker than I am that I am black, they will see me as being darker than I am and darker than they are. I heard what Mr. Chester said about you and I guess he wanted to see what you would do if he said that. He likes to shock people sometimes, maybe because he has been shocked so much himself. But you should know that your skin is not really black. I mean, there would be nothing wrong if it were, but really, it isn't. I mean, your skin is dark, but it isn't the color of anything that people would really call black. My skin is not really the color of anything that any sensible person would really think was white. I mean that my skin doesn't look anything like snow or milk and your skin doesn't look like my coat. So I just want to start by making it clear. It isn't that one color is not as nice as another, not only that, but that we don't even see straight when we talk about colors and we say things that we don't really mean. Each color looks different depending on what it is coloring. It's like you said about the textures and temperatures of things that you feel. I used to work in a hospital, and a lady there who was my supervisor liked me until she found out that I was not white. She used to tell me that she envied me my complexion. She called me her peaches-and-cream girl. Well, that's just something people say. Nobody really looks exactly like a shortcake! It's just something people say about a kind of mixture of pinks that you see in some skin.

Sometimes we all take turns spoiling Manman, my cousin, because he's such a nice kid and it really doesn't take much to give him a good time. Then, too, I guess all of us girls like to play mother or something. Anyway, one time Debbie and Marva and I took him to Quebec City, and a little girl ran up to us and said that Manman was a "little gingerbread boy." Well, that's the same thing, you see. Colors remind people of things that have something like the same colors or of ideas, you know, that people have about colors. I think it would be much better if people could start all over again. See, people have gotten colors all mixed up with ideas about what is good or bad or nasty or clean. I mean, people can just look at me and right away they have made up their minds about me. That's why I was surprised—pleasantly, I mean—when you told me that my hand made you think of the color green. I really like that because so many other people have gone through so many changes not to shake hands with me. You know what they say about white people having dead hands or fish hands. You know, my mother said that a lot of her own relatives did not want to eat her cooking because her skin was light. I mean, a lot of people think that light people are all—well, that they are not clean cooks. It works both ways—not the same thing, but every group has these stupid things about color.

My mother used to tell me about the blue veins, and when I was in high school some girls were really interested in that. If the skin is—well, if it is less dark you can see your veins. And this small thing was made so big that it split up friendships and made people hate and envy each other. My father told me about those paper-bag tests and comb tests that you had to pass to get into some of the clubs that they used to have in Louisiana—that's where he came from. I've never been there so that I can remember it, so I don't know if they are still doing this stupid thing now, but I don't think so. They used to put a brown paper bag in the bend of your arm, and if your skin was the same color or lighter, then you could join. Or maybe you could come in and eat or do whatever they did in those clubs. Sometimes there would be a man who would run a comb through your hair, and if it went through easily—you know, if your hair wasn't too curly—then you could get in.

You know the hospital job I told you about? Well, when a girl I knew in high school saw me there, she came up to me and started speaking the way black people from the South speak to me. Well, that's not the way I talk and that's not the way Princess talks, either, but she wanted everybody to know that I was black too. Well, I never told anybody that I *wasn't* black. I got the job because a black lady recommended me for it, and I never tried to be anything but what I am. I never have tried to pass or anything like that. I am the kind of person who speaks to anybody who speaks to me, and Princess should have known that. After all, we lived on the same street for half of our lives and I never did anything like that and Princess knew that, but still she did that! I asked her why and told her when she was going through her act that every girl at that table knew I was black and proud of it, so I asked her what she was trying to prove and she just walked away. Now, she knew that she was wrong about that.

There is another girl, a friend of mine—we went to school together for a long time. Her name was Virginia, but everybody called her Peaches. I don't know how people get that nickname. Anyway, Peaches had—I mean, living in their house was a boy there. They used to say he was a state kid. He lived with them. I mean, Ginny's mother kept these children and the state gave her money to take care of them. This boy, Roy, was very dark and Peaches was not very dark. His real name was Royal, but nobody ever called him that except me. One day he asked me to go to the movies. I went and a couple of days later Peaches and some other girls were teasing me about that. You know, we were just beginning to go out like that, and Peaches said, "Girl, I didn't know you dealt in coal." Well, I felt bad that she said that. Royal found out about it and he got mad with me, I guess. He never spoke to me after that. Now, I had not done anything to him. I liked him because he was very nice. I would never have said anything like that. I'm sure he liked me too. We used to do homework in the library and at my house. He told me how he felt about things, and he wasn't one of these boys who were always fresh. I really thought a great deal of him, but after that thing happened he never spoke to me. I tried to explain what happened, but he just stood there and when I finished he just left; he never opened his mouth. People used to say that he was "too smart"—I mean, that he had too many brains, you know what they say. My mother asked why he didn't come after school any more and I told her.

Some junkies cut him and I went to the hospital to see him, but he wouldn't talk to me. I never knew what he thought. In a way it's very silly, but it was very important to me.

My Uncle Matt used to say this little saying: "Black is evil, yallah so low-down, look here, honey, ain't you glad you brown?" I guess people think that way. I just wouldn't like them to think that way about me. I know that a lot of people feel that way. My Uncle Matt was brown, but I wasn't and I used to feel funny about that. But I'm sure he wasn't trying to make me feel bad. I guess I'm a kind of soft person in a way. I know that my feelings are easily hurt, but really, there are a lot of people who want to hurt—who like to hurt—my feelings. You might say, "Who does she think she is that people should be trying to hurt her feelings all the time?"

One reason the whole thing is so hard to deal with is that nobody really talks   20
about it. Once there was this sort of program—I guess you could call it a kind of
forum—and we were talking about some of the major problems in the country between the black people and the white people, and they asked me to point out one
and I didn't say anything because I didn't know whether to mention the one that is
very important to me. There were a lot of white people there, and some of the
black people would have thought that it was wrong to talk about that when there
were white people there too. We should really do something about it ourselves.

We should treat everybody well if they treat us well, no matter what color they
are. People like Peaches and Princess should be shown up when they do wrong
things like that. People should judge me by what I do to them. I think we should
break up this business of light people marrying only light people and dark people
marrying dark people. People just worry too much about color, and if it's wrong for
white people to do it—I mean, make people's lives miserable for such an unimpor-
tant cause—then it's just as wrong for our people to behave like that.

Celia Delaney

It's sex and color that present the most difficulty, right?

*Miss Celia Delaney is not yet forty, but her life seems fixed in such a way as to suggest early re-
tirement. I have known her for more than half her life. I have never known a less frantic person than she is now. Her current reputation is that of a cool person who has come by that status the hard way. She extracted wisdom from the hectic crash course of the black revolution of
fashion, which almost destroyed her. "I guess I sought my roots everywhere but where they are—
in me," she reflected. "I think awareness made me a kind of prodigal daughter," she mused
while driving me to an interview with an elderly retired teacher.*

*Miss Delaney too is a teacher. She teaches in an exclusively white school and derives sat-
isfaction from her profession, but still regrets the failure of her perilous attempt to instruct children in a school in a black town. She has learned, at great cost to herself, that all things have
their natural limitations. She has come to expect very little of other people and to doubt that
anyone is much better than she is at her best. She counts it an extraordinary stroke of good fortune to be alive and unencumbered, and means to remain that way.*

It's sex and color that present the most difficulty, right? I know I don't *have* to talk
about anything. Just eat your gorgeous, gorgeous cake and listen to Celia, and
she will give you cold milk and good advice. First, if people want to tell you something, let them. If they didn't trust you, they would be the first to know.

My mother and father were both Geechees. I say that now, I knew it then, so I   5
suppose that makes me a Geechee, but the only Geechee trait I have is rice cooking.
I inherited that via my very sedate grandmother and her sisters. My mother was very
pretty, and I am told that she and her brother, my reverend Uncle Isaiah, died in a
fight with some white men who were bent on raping my mother. The truth is, we
never talked much about my mother, but dwelt at great length on my uncle. Most of

the four sisters who sacrificed so much for me are mildly disappointed in me. Some of the values they tried so hard to instill in me are still with me; others I have let go.

I grew up in Charleston and Boston and Queens. I was, I suppose, what you would call a sedity. I was properly finished at Spelman and Radcliffe. I have been a teacher and a social worker. Even without a turban I have some trouble sometimes establishing my charter right with some blacks. That's because it was my particular luck to draw greenish-blue eyes, sort of yellowish hair, and the kind of light-pinkish skin which people mistakenly call white. During my thirty-six years I have been alternately proud, ashamed, reconciled and contented with my physical appearance.

When I was a very young child I remember that the good "mulatto" ladies who took such good care of me placed a high value on low spirits. I was inordinately starched and mercilessly scrubbed and subdued with great vigor. I had to wear wide hats to keep the sun off. I call my aunts mulattoes not because they would ever have called themselves mulattoes but to emphasize that they thought of themselves as members of what they would, and still do (however privately), refer to as the "better-class-of-colored-people." Members of the better-class-of-colored-people are fond of their blow hair, their fine features, their soft voices and their yearning for the finer things of life. I took piano and violin lessons because they were among the finer things of life—in spite of my astounding unmusicality. I was always dressed as if I were going to a party, but it was not until much later in my life that I experienced the feeling of having gone to a party and come home and taken my shoes off. As a child I always had the feeling of having gone to a great deal of trouble to do something which I had no great desire to do. I don't mean that I was especially unhappy; it's just that I was always expecting something more exciting to happen.

I always thought that food should taste a little bit better than it did to me. I can remember that ice water was one of the few things which did not disappoint me. On those rare occasions on which this genteel child was permitted the luxury of working up a sweat, ice water always tasted exactly as I wanted it to taste. If ice water failed to meet my expectations, I always knew why, and remembering to cover a strong-smelling food I had left uncovered or filling the water bottle earlier the next time would always restore ice water to its sparkling best. As a very young girl I can remember wishing that people could be understood and restored as easily.

Everything in our house was quiet and deliberate. Moving fast or randomly or being late were things I could just barely imagine. Looking back on it, I don't think there was a tremendous difference between me and my starched, carefully posed dolls, which I never liked much anyway. My aunts regarded spontaneity, full enjoyment and virtuosity as foreign to the character of the better-class-of-colored-people. Although they lived by these things, just like all the rest of us did, in a kind of subdued fashion they discouraged this in me. A dark-brown skin, bad hair and coarse—you understand, "coarse" means African—features were also things which the better-class-of-colored-people would do well to avoid. But these serious handicaps could be overlooked if the unfortunate offenders, or victims (we were never sure about that), had money and behavior. There were several dark-brown clergymen and medical types who established regular and grateful relations with the poorer female members of the better-class-of-colored-people.

I don't know how I was being fashioned or even that I was being molded. Assumptions which I now blush at were once taken for self-evident gospel. Like most everybody I know, I never thought much about my life. I was a terrible phony, but I didn't know it. I can remember having certain friends whose principal use—that's right, use—was as velvet against which I could display my better-class-of-colored-people hair and skin. My friend Astrid's dark-brown better-class father made up for his physical shortcomings by giving his daughter a name which was as white as he wished he could have made her. Astrid needed me because she needed someone to amuse and astonish, and I needed her because the jewel I then imagined myself to be required an Ethiop's ear. Now, when I say that I blush at my past behavior, I mean just that. But there was a time when I was shamefully exultant at being able to rattle off such phrases as "Was my face red" and "I blushed all over." I thought of myself as precious for all the wrong reasons, and most people I knew seemed to share my opinion of my purely external merits.

I really don't think most black people are much saner than I was. The insanity   10
takes different forms, but color is something most of us are quite irrational about. It's hopelessly confused with sexuality and God knows what else.

I don't know how valid a physical anthropological observation it is, but it seems to me that pale black girls mature later. Anyway, I can remember the anxiety expressed by my aunts about my breasts, or the absence of those vital organs. I was rubbed with everything from coconut oil to goose grease and lard, with the general aim of bringing out my breasts. That is what they called it—"bringing out the breasts." Now it seems to me that one of those home stimulators came very close to overdoing it, but even at fifteen I can remember saying, deep inside myself, of course, "Maybe I'm flat, but I'm yellow." You see, I knew I was not white. I called myself yellow because I could not bring myself to say "yaller," even to myself.

I distinguished between us and them. Most white people I know are darker than I am. Even when I was most firm in my allegiance to my better-class-of-colored-people values, there was still the black-versus-white thing. I was far from a black nationalist then. My aunts had taught me that the better-class-of-colored-people had a responsibility to lead the less fortunate of our race. They didn't only mean poor black people, but darker black people, who, despite their unfortunate dark-brown-ness, had many things going for them—they were honest, clean, resourceful and strong. Actually, we lived among people of all colors. We told each other jokes about white people and black people, but I can't remember any jokes about yellow people versus dark brown people. These crazy things I and my relatives thought about dark brown people then was a part of the whole thing.

You know that dark brown people have their insanities also. Astrid Haley's dark brown father would resort to almost any stratagem to avoid eating any food in the house of the most proper members of the better-class-of-colored-people. He shared the prejudice which so many dark people have about paler black people—you know, "Yaller's so low-down," as they say in the street. Both Astrid and I were under strict orders not to play with certain black kids. This off-limits group were, of course, the people we were most interested in. This group consisted of all kinds of black people. Some of those who were out looked like Astrid and some like me.

Astrid has married a German and her father will not have anything to do with her. Her father will not have anything to do with his grandchildren. Now, it is important to remember that these grandchildren look just like he would have liked Astrid to look. He says he considers his daughter to be dead, and he has acted as if she had died for eight years now. Astrid's husband is darker than I am, but her father is my most faithful correspondent! Astrid's little sister used to call both Astrid and me black whenever she was sufficiently provoked, and we spent a lot of time provoking her because she was a little sister.

Color is just one thing we blacks are unreasonable about. I call this mishmash crazy, but it is not the kind of madness which prevents us from being saner than any other people I know. Black people in America really have no choice about sticking together. Much of my own insanity about color was a part of my own provincialism, like many other prejudices of mine. For all our color hang-ups, we are a great deal saner than white people about it. We don't kill each other about color, although we have much more color diversity than white people do. I don't think color in itself is very important; it's only when it gets to be the formal excuse for other things that we think much about it. When you ask me what color something is, especially in comparison with something else, it is very difficult to give anything like an objective answer. Color is not objectively important; it's very important to ordinary daily behavior, though.

15

Johnetta B. Cole

Johnetta B. Cole (1936–), a noted anthropologist, was the first female president of Spelman College (1987–1997) and continues her interest in education as president at Bennett College in Greensboro, North Carolina. Her works include the edited volumes *Anthropology for the Eighties: Introductory Readings* (1982), *All-American Women: Lines That Divide, Ties That Bind* (1986), and *Anthropology for the Nineties: Introductory Readings* (1988). Cole's other books include *Conversations: Straight Talk with America's Sister President* (1993) and *Dream the Boldest Dreams: And Other Lessons of Life* (1997).

In the following essay from the June 1970 issue of *The Black Scholar,* Cole analyzes the African American community as a subculture with unique mores and lifestyles.

Culture

Negro, Black, and Nigger

One of the many offshoots of the Black Liberation movement is an increased awareness of being black. Black Americans are turning attention to the complexities and glories of Afro-American history, probing the psychology of being black, and seeking the boundaries of black subculture. However, anthropological attention to black subculture remains sparse. When anthropologists, along with sociologists and psychologists, have turned specifically to the study of black subculture, their conclusions (and indeed the very selection of problems) are most often cast in terms of social and cultural pathology or psychological stress: the problem of matrifocality, the dirty dozens as an example of severe role conflict among males, alcoholism and crime in the ghetto.

This paper presents a very basic and exploratory statement on black subculture,

- suggesting components of that subculture,
- identifying soul and style as major expressions in black subculture, and
- describing several life styles.

The data for this paper are drawn from the meager literature, my current research among black university students, and the observations and insights which stem from my own black experience.

This discussion assumes the existence of a black subculture, an assumption held only recently by most scholars. Following the tradition established by E. Franklin Frazier, Charles S. Johnson, Robert Park, and others, the dominant opinion for many years was that the way of life of black folk is no more than an imitation, and a poor one at that, of the mainstream values and actions of white America. Discussions of this position inevitably begin with vivid descriptions of how black Americans were torn from the shores of their African homeland, stripped of their cultural heritage and processed through the severities of slavery. An alternative explanation, best exemplified in the works of Melville J. Herskovits, argues the retention of African cultural traits. Most anthropologists do not accept Herskovits' position, however, on grounds that he over-weighted the influence of Africanisms on Afro-American culture. Whereas we can document certain African retentions in music, folklore, and to some extent in religion, it is difficult and often impossible to establish the persistence of African traits in other areas of black subculture. Regardless of the difficulty in establishing Africanisms, it is not therefore warranted to conclude that the subculture of black folks is simply a passive receptor for general American traits.

When a people share a learned set of values/attitudes and behavior patterns   5 which are distinctive to them, they possess a culture; when the distinctive patterns are restricted to certain areas, while other patterns are drawn from a mainstream pool, a people possess a subculture. In this sense, black Americans do form a subculture. The term which will be used to describe this way of life is "nigger culture," popular epithet for "Negro culture."

The subculture of black America has three sets of components: those drawn from mainstream America, those which are shared, in varying proportions, with all oppressed peoples, and those which appear to be peculiar to blacks. We might note a few examples of each. Black Americans share, with mainstream America, many traits of material culture, (cars, house types, clothing); values (emphasis on technology and materialism); and behavior patterns (watching TV and voting in terms of interest groups).

Black Americans also share a number of cultural traits with all individuals who are oppressed—Catholics in Northern Ireland, Native Americans, Jews, Chinese Americans. One of these traits is what I call the "minority sense." When a Jew enters a room of gentiles, a Chicano a room of Anglos, a black a room of whites, there is a common reaction, namely, the minority member will attempt to sense out where there is severe hostility and bigotry. Minority subculture teaches that one must detect or at least attempt to detect hostile attitudes and behavior in the interest of self-protection—from protection of one's pride and self-esteem to protection of one's life. All oppressed peoples also share degrees of what I call the "denial urge." This is the condemnation of one's status and by extension of one's *self*. It leads 200,000 Asian women each year to undergo operations to reduce the slant of their eyes, it leads Jews to have their noses bobbed, and blacks to suffer through bleaching creams and hair straighteners.

The last set of components of black American subculture, and the ones to which we turn special attention in this paper, are those which we can identify as the essence of blackness. Throughout the literature in anthropology, we do not identify bits of culture which are absolutely confined to a single people. It is in the combination of traits that we see the distinctiveness of a given people; it is in the subtleties associated with universal attributes, the emphasis on certain themes by which we define a people. Using these same requirements with respect to black America, it is suggested here that the consistent and important themes in black American life are soul and style. When blacks refer to "nigger culture," they often very explicitly speak of soul and style: the way blacks get happy (possessed) in sanctified churches, that's soul; the movement of a black woman's hips when she dances, that's soul; the way a brother bops into a room, especially when he is clean (that is, dressed sharply), that's style; the way a black woman will speak of going to the beauty parlor to get her "kitchen touched up," that's in order to style; the way a young black man says, "I got to go take care of business," that's soul and style. We might focus in more closely on each of these themes.

There is probably no term which is more often used by black folks, and so seldom defined, as soul. By implication, blacks view it as the essence of "nigger culture," the one attribute which is possessed exclusively, or almost exclusively, by Afro-Americans. The explanation is not that it is a genetic phenomenon, but simply that being black in the United States teaches one how to live, feel, and express soul. Anthropologists have only rarely attempted to objectively define soul, and seldom have they recorded folk definitions. On the basis of the limited literature, my own involvement in black communities, and research, currently, among black students, I suggest that soul consists of at least the following three notions:

- One, soul is long suffering. It is the look of weariness on the faces of black folk, weariness with racism and poverty; it is the pathos in a black mother's cry of "Oh Lord, have mercy"; it is the constant presence of the blues. Black Americans cannot claim a monopoly on being long suffering. What is implied, however, is that the type of suffering, the "brand" of weariness which black folks have endured (largely because blacks are so highly and so systematically used as a source of power for white Americans), is what constitutes one part of soul. 10

- Soul, secondly, is deep emotion. It's the plea, often heard in black churches, "help me Jesus"; it is what a black man feels and expresses when he says, "I just ain't gonna take no more"; it's what James Brown and Aretha Franklin feel and instill in others. A variation on this notion of soul as deep emotion is found in most of the stereotypes which black Americans have of themselves; for blacks (no less than whites) feel that they are better dancers, singers and lovers than whites, because while white Americans perform these acts mechanically, blacks engage in them with deep emotion.

- Finally, soul is the ability to feel oneness with all black people. It is the know-ing smile as two blacks, perfect strangers, exchange a glance in the middle of a crowded urban street; it is shucking "the man" (i.e., putting on a white person) while winking at an observing brother or sister; it is the way all black people are tied together because of shared experiences, like being called nigger. Soul then is the theme in black America which minimizes differences in class and political con-sciousness among Afro-Americans, for it is oneness.

The second major theme in black subculture is style, a theme no less difficult to define and no less important than soul. Style, to define again by example, is when a brother is wearing his gators (alligator shoes), fine vines (clothes), a slick do (process), in the old days, or an "uptight" natural today; style is having a heavy rap (verbal display), like the preacher, the young militant and the pimp (three strong and admired characters in black communities); style is driving an Eldorado; style is standing on a street corner looking cool, hip and ready; style is digging on Yusef Latef rather than Johnny Cash; style is the way a black man looks at a woman and says, "Come here with your bad self."

According to the students among whom I work, what constitutes style is the com-bination of ease and class; among black folks it is the ability to look rich when you are poor, the ability to appear loose when you're uncomfortable or tense; the ability to ap-pear distinctive among many. Style, unlike soul, is not viewed as exclusively black (the students with whom I work say that Ché Guevera had style). Sitting Bull sure had style when he faced Custer and Peter Fonda had it in *Easy Rider.* However, there are clearly black versions of style. The male black students with whom I work feel that Fonda showed style on his chopper, but the black version of style must be in a car (a "hog"). Blackness is best expressed, they argue, when style combines with soul.

All black people, of course, do not express black subculture in the same way. Variation among the members of this subculture is often overlooked, however, in the anthropological literature. The data on black subculture is overwhelmingly that of the street life style—smoking dope, pimping, hustling, and rapping. We have yet to record the variety in the life styles of black people. Again, this paper can only be suggestive, resting on the meager literature, my own limited research, and my per-sonal experiences. Four life styles in nigger culture are the street, down-home, mil-itant and upward bound. Obviously, these are not suggested as rigidly defined and exclusive life styles. Black folk, like any folk, do not live in categories.

The street life style is the cool world, centering around hustling. It is basically the urban world of American blacks. It is here that we see the greatest development of stylized talking, sounding, signifying, shucking and jiving, copping a plea and whupping game (Kochman). This is the world which is best described in the "ethno-graphies" written by black folk themselves: *The Autobiography of Malcolm X, Manchild in the Promised Land* (Claude Brown), *Pimp, the Story of My Life* (Iceberg Slim), *His Eye is on the Sparrow* (Ethel Waters). This is the world of severe poverty for many, hope-lessness for most, cool for a few. This life style can be described in many ways, but here I choose to use the medium of a short story from the *Liberator* magazine.

15

While sitting round in back of the drugstore having our usual taste of Molly Pitcher dark port, our most pleasant conversation was bodily interrupted by the noisy, yelling, arm-waving approach of Little Willie upon the scene. His eyes were mere slits, heavily weighted down by the mellow smoke—light green marijuana. Having the jug in hand and clearly in the sight of Willie, I expected the first four words out of his mouth to be, 'Save me the corner,' but instead he pleasantly surprised me by screaming, 'Big Time is in the poolroom, baby!' Big Time, the magic name that made every young potential pimp, hustler, gamer, mack man, booster or player tremble with excitement, for he represented all the things that they hoped to imitate or possibly even emulate someday. Big Time was it. He was *in*, baby—really what was happening. All you had to do was name it and have the proper amount of collateral and Big Time would score for you, or turn you on to someone in the position to do so. He was sharp, cool, untouchable. To quote Brother Cassius, he was 'the greatest.' Sharp? This man was really sharp. From his nylon underwear to his two-hundred-dollar imported mohair suit. Cool? No one ever heard him speak above a whisper. Always calm. Never, I mean never in a hurry. Slow and steady. Always seeming to know his next move in advance. Untouchable? He was always a mile further ahead, a pound heavier or a foot taller than anyone he associated with. Like on a pedestal, but always in touch spiritually, you dig?

Down-home life style is the traditional way of black folks. It is basically rural and southern. It centers in the kitchens of black homes, in the church halls for suppers, in the fraternal orders. "Down-home" is a common expression among black Americans, indicating one's point of origin, down south, or the simple, decent way of life. Let me characterize this life style by reading excerpts from the journal of a student, Pamela Smith, in my anthropology/black studies course. She wrote of her first visit south and she entitled it, "Down-home."

The street my grandparents lived on was unpaved, because they lived in the black section of town. The house was kind of shabby but gave off some type of radiant warmth. What really appealed to me was the porch. It had a swing and rocking chair. I found the porch was one of the main facets of the house. If any company came over, it seemed that most of the entertaining was done on the porch. Especially in the evening, the family would gather on the porch to get what little relief they could from the heat . . .

Breakfast at my grandmother's was comparatively big but couldn't compare to what cousin Rosa cooked. My cousin Rosa would start breakfast very early; one usually ate around six-thirty in her home. She would have fresh eggs, homemade biscuits, bacon and ham from their smoke house, homemade applesauce, grits, beans, pork chops, sometimes fish, all sorts of homemade jams, fresh milk, and potato fritters. God, one could hardly move after breakfast. It was puzzling to me why my grandmother didn't have such an enormous breakfast. I found that the reason was cousin Rosa's family worked in the fields and needed a heavy meal to sustain them until lunch . . .

I thought that going to church once a Sunday was enough but my grandma informed me that we were going to get "religion" (we were Catholics and so after mass) . . . we went to the Baptist church . . . After preaching the minister informed the congregation that next Sunday there was to be a dinner in the church to help raise money, and that any women willing to help were to stay after service . . .

Another thing one did not do while down home was to call an elderly lady by her last name, I remember the lady across the street was a Mrs. Brown and I would constantly call her this until one kid confronted me and said 'ain't you got any culture, her name is Miss Ann.' And naturally I wanted culture so I called her Miss Ann.

The militant life style is the political world, centered today on college campuses, in high school Black Student Unions and in the urban black ghettos. This is the life style of the cultural and revolutionary nationalists—of LeRoi Jones, Ron Karenga, Robert Williams, Eldridge Cleaver and Bobby Seale. Although this life style appears to be new, a product of the 1960's, there have been American blacks of this life style since black folks came to the new world. Gabriel, Denmark Vesey, Nat Turner, Marcus Garvey, and Fredrick Douglass are but the most famous of the early militants. This life style is infused with the urgency of changing the plight of black folks; it is the constant search for relief from oppression. To offer only a taste of the fervor of this life style, let me read the opening passage of a speech which Bobby Seale delivered in 1968. The speech was entitled, "Free Huey."

Brothers and Sisters, tonight I want to have the chance to tell you in large mass something about Brother Huey P. Newton: a black man who first introduced me to what black nationalism was all about; a black man that I've been closely associated with for the last three years in the organizing of a black people's party on a level that dealt with black people's problems. To explain to you who Brother Huey P. Newton is in his soul, I've got to explain to you also your soul, your needs, your political desires and needs, because that is Huey's soul . . .

Now look, the Black Panther Party is a revolutionary party. Revolution means that we got to get down to the nitty gritty and change this situation that we're in and don't miss any nits or any grits—that's very very important. (We've got to work at it.) All the time.

Upward bound life style is the life style which E. Franklin Frazier characterized in his book, *Black Bourgeoisie*. It is the way that many blacks call high giddy or bourgy. It centers in the "better neighborhoods," in the so-called integrated churches and clubs. It is the way of the black middle class, the teachers, accountants, and other professionals who are trying to move on up. This life style has never been captured more pointedly than in the ironic tone of LeRoi Jones' poem, entitled, *Black Bourgeoisie*:

> has a gold tooth, sits long hours
> on a stool, thinking about money.
> sees white skin in a secret room
> rummages his senses for sense
> dreams about Lincoln(s)
> conks his daughter's hair
> sends his coon to school
> works very hard
> grins politely in restaurants
> has a good word to say

never says it
does not hate ofays
hates, instead, himself
him black self.

In this exploratory paper, we have looked at some of the dimensions of nigger American culture. We can reach but one conclusion from the very tentative data presented on the components of black subculture, the expressions of soul and style and the variation in life styles. That conclusion is that we need an anthropology of black subculture. Or, to put it in the idiom, when it comes to nigger culture, somebody ain't been takin' care of business.

Michael Eric Dyson

Michael Eric Dyson (1958–) is a Baptist minister, widely published author, and print and radio commentator. He is the Avalon Foundation Professor in the Humanities at the University of Pennsylvania. He was the Ida B. Wells-Barnett Professor and Professor of Religious Studies at DePaul University and has taught at the Chicago Theological Seminary, the University of North Carolina, and Columbia and Brown universities. Dyson's most recent biographical book is *Holler If You Hear Me: Searching for Tupac Shakur* (2002). His other books include *Reflecting Black: African-American Culture Criticism* (1993), which won the Gustavus Myers Center for Human Rights Award, and *Making Malcolm: The Myth and Meaning of Malcolm X* (1994), which both the *New York Times* and the *Philadelphia Inquirer* named Notable Book of 1994.

The following is an excerpt from "Bill Cosby and the Politics of Race," Chapter 6 in *Reflecting Black: African-American Cultural Criticism* (1993). Dyson commends Cosby for the depiction of an affluent African American family on the award-winning television show *The Cosby Show* but decries the absence of programming about the poor and many social ills besetting black America.

Bill Cosby and the Politics of Race

Bill Cosby is a formidable national icon. He is a powerful symbol of the graceful confluence of talent, wealth, and industry that are the American Dream. His television series, "The Cosby Show," has singlehandedly revived the situation comedy, spawning numerous imitations within the genre, surely the sincerest form of media flattery. His show has even spun off the highly successful "A Different World," a sitcom about contemporary black college life, second only to "The Cosby Show" in ratings and popularity. As if that weren't enough, "The Cosby Show" is now in syndication, with the prospect of generating almost a billion dollars in revenue.

Cosby's philanthropic gestures, too, have matched his larger-than-life television persona. He and his wife Camille's recent gifts to black colleges and universities, totaling almost 25 million dollars, have both aided the beleaguered black academy and generated renewed interest in black charitable activity. At Harlem's famed Apollo Theatre, Cosby raised more than one hundred thousand dollars for Jesse Jackson's 1988 presidential campaign. And at the beginning of the Tawana Brawley case, Cosby and Essence Communications' chief executive Ed Lewis offered a twenty-five-thousand-dollar reward, in part to signal their disdain for all forms of violence.

It is somewhat ironic, then, that until almost the last season of "The Cosby Show," there was continuing controversy about its treatment of the issue of race. From the very beginning, the Cosby series has been shadowed by persistent questions growing out of the politics of racial definition: Is "The Cosby Show" really black enough? Does "The Cosby Show" accurately reflect most African-American families, or should it attempt to do so? Shouldn't "The Cosby Show" confront the menacing specter of the black underclass and address a few of its attendant problems, such as poverty and unemployment? And so on.

The answers to these questions are not so simple, because they involve larger issues of how one defines racial identity and the role of television in catalyzing or anesthetizing social conscience. Needless to say, however, "The Cosby Show" does not exist in a sociohistorical vacuum, either in film and television history or in the larger history of American culture.

Part of the pressure on Cosby (fair or not) results from the paucity of mass media images that positively portray African-Americans. Most black American characters in early film were celluloid enfleshments of stereotypes existing in the minds of white directors, reinforcing notions of black character and culture that prevailed in society at large. Whole categories of black personality were socially constructed and then visually depicted, including the coon, the buck, the clown, the mammy, the darky, the spook, the shiftless shine, and the shuffling Negro.

The history of television has not improved much on this sad state of affairs. In most cases, TV has merely updated conventional film practices with newfangled glosses on old character types, such as with Amos 'n Andy and Rochester (Jack Benny's valet, played by Eddie Anderson). Even when there has been growth in representing black characters, television has often presented problematic versions of racial progress. With the likes of George Jefferson, J. J. "Kid Dyn-o-mite," and Arnold or Webster, blacks were either high-class variations on the theme of clown, or filling another social slot as a stereotypical slum dweller, or beneficiaries of white patrons-cum-adoptive parents, whose largesse brought domestic stability and upward mobility to chosen black children. Each of these options simply served to reinforce the narrow range of options open to black actors, to reinscribe the stereotype-creating practices of white directors and writers in the construction of black characters on television, and to downplay the increasing diversity and robust complexity of African-American culture.

Cosby's series is a marked departure from racial stereotyping, a leap made possible in large part by the social transformation of race relations under the aegis of the civil rights movement. The role of innovator not alien to him, Cosby was the first black to appear in a regular role in a television series, starring opposite Robert Culp for three years in "I Spy." "The Cosby Show" has shattered narrow conceptions of African-American identity and culture, presenting an intact, two-parent, upper-middle-class black family. Indeed, "The Cosby Show" has assumed authoritative status in popular culture, establishing the Cosby viewpoint on many matters as an authentic lens on the American Weltanschauung. Cosby's television brood, the Huxtables, now occupy privileged territory within the folklore of American family relations. The show, in many respects, is a televisual compendium of received wisdom about adults and adolescents where Spock and McLuhan easily embrace. Cliff, an obstetrician, and Clair, a lawyer, are an exemplary dual-career couple. They smoothly meld tradition and change into a formula of tender devotion and tough love, blending parental authority and adolescent autonomy in perfect measure.

Despite all of this, or perhaps because of it, the question persists: Is the Huxtable family "authentically black"? Such a question raises the ire of Cosby and his show's consultant, well-known Harvard psychiatrist Alvin Poussaint. First of all, such a question presumes a monolithic conception of racial identity and a narrow view of the diversity of black culture. Poussaint, in an October 1988 issue of *Ebony*, comments:

> As opportunities for Blacks expand, it is reasonable to expect that certain styles and actions, which might have typified past Black behavior, will change and vary widely in the future. . . . The Huxtable family is helping to dispel old stereotypes and to move its audience toward more realistic perceptions. Like Whites, Blacks on television should be portrayed in a full spectrum of roles and cultural styles, and no one should challenge the existence of such an array of styles within a pluralistic society.

Both Cosby and Poussaint have argued that no other sitcom is expected to address the issue of racism, and that it is unfair to hold "The Cosby Show" responsible for such racial and cultural didacticism. "No one asks whether 'Three's Company' is going to deal with racism," Cosby has remarked. Furthermore, they argue that the sitcom, designed to entertain, is not well suited to handle such weighty matters as racism, and an attempt to do so would only compromise the possible impact of addressing such an important social issue in a more responsible fashion. Poussaint writes, "The sitcom formula also limits the range of what are considered appropriate story lines; audiences tune in to be entertained, not to be confronted with social problems. Critical social disorders, like racism, violence and drug abuse, rarely lend themselves to comic treatment; trying to deal with them on a sitcom could trivialize issues that deserve serious, thoughtful treatment."

Cosby's and Poussaint's arguments are certainly on target when they suggest   10
the difficulty of addressing (especially with integrity) social problems such as racism. But it is certainly not impossible. In fact, one encouraging sign derives from the very success of "The Cosby Show" in addressing other tough social issues. For instance, "The Cosby Show" has consistently addressed the issue of sexism, creatively and comically showing how it should be debunked and resisted. There have been many humorously insightful encounters between Clair and her Princeton-educated son-in-law Elvin, a bona fide chauvinist. Cliff and Clair have continually attempted to counsel Elvin away from his anachronistic patriarchal proclivities, cajoling him, for example, about the folly of gender-conscious division of domestic labor.

Also, Cliff has occasionally confronted the issue of misdirected machismo, promoting a fuller meaning of manhood and a richer understanding of fatherhood. He has influenced the husbands of clients who thought the responsibility of child rearing was "woman's work." Cosby has said that in deciding to make his character an obstetrician, besides wanting to make women feel comfortable about giving birth, he wanted

> to talk to their husbands and put a few messages out every now and then. . . . That fathering a child isn't about being a macho man, and if you think it is, you're making a terrible mistake. It's about becoming a parent. . . . In one episode last season, a new husband comes into Cliff's office and says, "I'm the man, the head of the household. Women should be kept barefoot and pregnant." Cliff tells the guy that being a parent has nothing to do with that kind of concept of manhood. And he really straightens him out by telling him that neither he nor his wife will be in charge of the house—their children will.

And Cliff is often seen in the kitchen preparing meals for the family.

Such positive images of responsible male participation in all aspects of life on Cosby's show reflect a real-life concern and no mean influence on such matters, as attested to by his best-selling book *Fatherhood,* and his new book on marriage. Thus, "The Cosby Show" has shown how a complex social issue such as sexism can be addressed in humorous ways, producing socially responsible entertainment. The juxtaposition of comedy and conscience is not impossible, nor does it necessarily cost ratings.

Of course, as Cosby and Poussaint maintain, other sitcoms are not pressed about addressing issues of race. One implication of their point suggests that other shows should shoulder responsibility for addressing crucial social concerns. And that is right. Similar to what occurs in American culture, real progress in race relations is not made until white persons introduce norms of social equality within their own communities, workplaces, and homes, not simply waiting for a black spokesperson to deliver that message. Other sitcoms and dramatic series, therefore, must reflect a heightened degree of social awareness in regard to many issues, including race, sex, and class.

But that doesn't mean that "The Cosby Show" shouldn't touch such issues, even within the context of a half-hour sitcom. One of the most useful aspects of Cosby's dismantling of racial mythology and stereotyping is that it has permitted America to view black folk as *human beings.* The Cosby show has shown that much of what concerns human beings transcends race, such as issues of parenting, family relations, work, play, and love. This fact does not, however, negate the reality that some issues and concerns affect particular groups in more harmful ways than other groups. The fact that black people continue to be burdened with racial stereotyping in the workplace, for example, cannot be avoided, even as Cosby clarifies the ways in which black folk are just human beings. The two insights must not be considered mutually exclusive.

Cosby has amassed a good deal of moral authority and cultural capital and has captured the attention of millions of Americans who may have otherwise not tuned in or who would have categorized "The Cosby Show" as "just another black sitcom." Thus, he is in a unique position to show that concern for issues of race need not be merely the concerns of black folk, but can, and should, be the concern

15

of human beings. To the degree, then, that his show is about an upper-middle-class family that "happens to be black," his show, like others, bears part of the responsibility of dealing with social issues, which he has proven can be effectively done without sacrificing his large viewing audience or humorous effect.

"The Cosby Show" can also indicate that being concerned about issues of race as black American human beings is legitimate and healthy and should not be avoided. It must communicate the reality that despite the upward social mobility experienced by an increasing number of black people, racism continues to plague African-Americans, although in new and different ways. For instance, while the architecture of legal segregation has been largely dismantled, the undeniable persistence of inequitable socioeconomic conditions for many limits the range of opportunities to the educated upper and middle classes. And even among those blacks who make substantial economic and social progress, the subtlety of racist ideologies, social practices, and cultural expressions means that racism's hibernation in slippery presuppositions, ambiguous attitudes, and equivocal behavior (which have the benefit of appearing neutral, but which actually endorse racist thought or deed) must be exposed and repudiated. To a captive white audience, Cosby's message could create useful awareness about the subversive shift in the ways racism persists and continues to manifest itself.

It is certainly healthy for Cosby not to be obsessed with race consciousness, which would indicate that black life is lived only in response to white racism, that black culture is merely reactive and is incapable of forming visions of life beyond the reach of race. That is not the same, however, as acknowledging that race continues to determine social relations and influence employment opportunities. Even obstetricians, lawyers, and upper-middle-class black children are not exempt from the prospect of racial tensions of some sort.

More pointedly, issues of race, sex, and class could be handled in a way that avoids the banal stereotyping that prevails elsewhere on television. Cosby's show has a responsibility to address these issues precisely because he has created cultural space for the legitimate existence of upper-middle-class blacks on television. The progressive vision of his show as exhibited in its insightful handling of the issue of sexism, then, creates the reasonable expectation of addressing such matters. Thus, the very skillful debunking of racial stereotypes that is generated by his show, and not the insistence that "black shows should do black stuff," is the reason Cosby's show must at least in some form address the problems of race and class.

"The Cosby Show" reflects the increasing diversity of African-American life, including the continuous upward social mobility by blacks, which provides access to new employment opportunities heretofore closed and expands the black middle class. Such mobility and expansion insures the development of new styles of existence for blacks that radically alter and impact African-American culture. Cosby's show is a legitimate expression of one aspect of that diversity. Another aspect is the intraracial class division and differentiation introduced as a result of this diversification of African-American life.

"The Cosby Show" is, therefore, also emblematic of the developing gulfs between black Americans who occupy varying social and class slots in American life and is a symbol of the gap between the upper and under classes. As I have argued [20] before, black track from the ghetto, which mimicked earlier patterns of white flight from the inner city, has resulted in severe class changes in many black communities. A sense of social isolation has also resulted as upper-middle-class blacks leave and those left behind experience loss of economic support, role models, and social continuity and cultural contact with more well-to-do blacks.

Cosby is certainly not expected to answer the enormously complex problem of the underclass and its relationship to the black middle and upper middle classes, a problem that social scientists continue to heatedly debate. But what is certain is that the silence and invisibility of the underclass in American life, and in television, except in threatening, stereotypical, or negative ways, continues to reinforce the belief that *all* occupants of the underclass are black and are active participants in illegal criminal behavior. Cosby's silence on the underclass and their complete invisibility on his show are therefore troubling. Cosby could go a long way toward helping America to see that many occupants of the underclass are conscientious people who are victimized, often by socioeconomic forces beyond their immediate control. "The Cosby Show" could certainly brush the fringes of the problem and at least give passing acknowledgment to the crisis that so many Americans who are black live with. Some indication of the existence of less fortunate blacks—some visiting relative whose situation is desperate, some deserving youth whose intellectual brilliance is not matched by material resources—could *both* alert America to the vicious effects of poverty on well-meaning people and send the message that the other side of the American Dream for many is the American Nightmare.

It is perhaps this lack of acknowledgment of the underside of the American Dream, the avoidance of its division of blacks by class, that is the most unfortunate feature of the Huxtable opulence. Cosby defends against linking the authenticity of the Huxtable representation of black life to the apparently contradictory luxury and comfort the family lives in when he says, "To say that they are not black enough is a denial of the American dream and the American way of life. My point is that this is an American family—an *American* family—and if you want to live like they do, and you're willing to work, the opportunity is there." But surely Cosby knows better than this. Such a statement leads us to believe that Cosby is unaware that there are millions of people, the so-called working poor, who travail in exemplary assiduity daily, but who nonetheless fall beneath the poverty level. Surely Cosby understands that Martin Luther King indicated in 1967, less than a year before his death, that he had lived long enough to see his American Dream turn into an American Nightmare on the streets of too many northern cities, and that King died in the midst of a campaign that accentuated the structurally denied opportunities for the poor across racial and ethnic lines.

Such a statement about opportunity provokes even closer scrutiny of the trajectory of Cosby's career, which has made him a cultural icon. He has risen to such phenomenal stature precisely because he embodies so much of the power of the ideology of Americanism: an individual who, despite a poor beginning, overcame problems of race and class in order to become a great stand-up comedian, actor, and spokesperson for several companies, including Jell-O, E. F. Hutton, Ford, and Coke. Cosby's career, too, is a lesson about how the management and commodification of staggering talent leads to even more staggering success, which is then recycled in the production of American fantasies about duplicating or somehow participating in that success.

Cosby's career also reveals the consolidation of the hegemonic relationship among television, the generating and shaping of consumptive desires and appetites for material goods, and the dissemination and perpetuation of the myths of universal access to the American dream. Inevitably, too, his career entails some contradictions that attest to the powerful ability of that success to transform, for good and ill, one's perspective. For instance, in his dissertation, cited by Daniel Okrent in the February 1987 *New England Monthly,* Cosby stated: "Each day advertisers bombard millions of viewers with their products to satisfy all the sensory needs, both internal and external. This mesmerized audience chases one fad after . . . another in the effort to 'build a . . . healthier, happier, [more] beautiful you.'" Cosby's subsequent endorsements as the most highly esteemed pitchman in American culture speak volumes about the price of progress.

We must certainly celebrate material progress, social advancement, educational attainment, and professional development, but not at the expense of remembering that for too long access to the higher reaches of the American Dream has been based on structural factors like race, class, and gender. This awareness, then, must inform the African-American construction of television images, characters, and families. Black folk, like Cosby, who are influential in television must, like the rest of us, engage in a self-criticism that perennially scrutinizes the values and visions that contribute to the development of lifestyles, the adoption of beliefs, or the formation of social conscience, especially as they are represented on TV.   25

Perhaps the greatest lesson from "The Cosby Show" is that being concerned about issues that transcend race and therefore display our humanity is fine, but that does not mean we should buy into a vacuous, bland universality that stigmatizes diversity, punishes difference, and destroys dissimilarities. As we painfully learned in the past, we cannot be thrown into the pot and melted down into one phenomenon called The American Experience. Although Cosby unquestionably runs up against the limits of the televisual medium, which seeks the lowest common denominator in human experience as a basis of blurring the differences between peoples and cultures and which seeks to maintain present power relations, systems of distributing wealth, and ways of assigning cultural authority, his show should teach us how to display the diversity of African-American life without compromising conscience, or consciousness, about those closed out of the American dream.

Similar to Spike Lee, but with a much different aesthetic feel, Cosby presents a black universe as the norm, feeling no need to announce the imposition of African-American perspectives, since they are assumed. But it is probably the case that many upper-middle-class black folk continue to talk about the racism of American culture, whether discussing its diminishing impact, its paralyzing persistence, or its prayed-for demise. Cosby has certainly shown us that we need not construct the whole house of our life experience from the raw material of our racial identity and that black folk are interested in issues that transcend race. However, such coming-of-age progress should not lead to zero-sum social concern, so that to be cognizant of race-transcending issues *replaces* or cancels out concern, for example, about the black poor or issues that generate intraracial conflict. "The Cosby Show" is an important advance in the fight to portray the profound complexity and rich diversity of black life on the small screen, because it shows a side of African-American life that is rarely seen on television. But "The Cosby Show" (and other TV sitcoms and drama series) must be pushed to encompass and attend to parts of that diversity that, although badly misrepresented under the plague of past stereotyping, must be addressed within the worldview that Cosby has the power and talent to present.

Jewelle Gomez

Jewelle Gomez (1944–) has written extensively on issues affecting the gay community. Her works include *Flamingoes & Bears: Poems* (1986), *The Gilda Stories: A Novel* (1991), *Forty-Three Septembers: Essays* (1993), *Oral Tradition: Selected Poems Old & New* (1995), *Swords of the Rainbow* (1996, edited with Eric Garber), *Best Lesbian Erotica* (1997, edited with Tristan Taormino), and *Don't Explain: Short Fiction* (1998).

The following excerpt is from "Black Lesbians: Passing, Stereotypes, and Transformation," an essay in *Dangerous Liaisons: Blacks, Gays and the Struggle* (1999, edited by Eric Brandt). Gomez discusses the depiction of African American lesbians in films.

Black Lesbians
Passing, Stereotypes, and Transformation

When I piece together the snippets of images and ideas that help form the picture of myself that I carry in my head it's as if I'm wrestling with a tornado. Imagine the special effect that experts conjure up in the movies: houses, cars, cows, books, kitchen table conversations all swirl around whole, until, released by the gale, they smash to the ground and I have to reassemble them. It's a cataclysmic process experienced, I think, by many people of color, especially of my generation. Growing up with television news coverage of the civil rights and black power movements, the newly recovered history of black Americans, my father's tales of life as a black man, and the pieces of grandmother's youth on an Indian reservation mingled with all the mainstream books, movies and television shows. These were the competing elements I wrangled into manageable reference points for grounding.

Because I knew, even as an adolescent, that I wanted to be a writer, it's not surprising that I absorbed many aspects of the arts almost as fully as I did personal experience. Released in 1959, *Imitation of Life* raised my first real questions about how we decide who we are—even before I was consciously aware of political movements, analyzing family history or embracing the quest for identity. This remake of an earlier adaptation of the Fannie Hurst novel had a powerful impact on me partly because I was such a media baby and because it featured the young stars who appeared in all the banal teen movies I also watched—Troy Donahue, Sandra Dee, Susan Kohner. But most important was its unexpected emotional impact—it threw me into confusion about race, identity, and loyalty.

The story is of a black girl, Peola, who chooses to pass for white, denying her community and humiliating her dark-skinned mother. For me, as an adolescent child in a mixed-race family (before the term was in vogue), some of whose members were also light-skinned, watching the film evoked dread and sorrow. At the moment when the daughter (played by a black actress in the 1934 film and by a white actress in this later version) denies her heritage my stomach clenched in fear as if I were watching her step out of a twenty story window, a decision that could never be rescinded. The presumed advantages of faux whiteness didn't seem worth the loss of family to me; and the deep shame of disavowing one's heritage shook me to the core. But the allure of masquerading as "the other" was also a compelling mystery.

I didn't know then how common stories about blacks passing as white were, even in my own family. Later, in college, when I read work from the writers of the 1920s I realized that "passing" had a long and complicated history in African American society, and, I imagine in all oppressed communities.

The "passing" novel of the early 1900s was a popular genre written by black writers as well as white. In Nella Larson's classic novel, *Quicksand,* her light-skinned protagonist, Helga, is a schoolteacher who scurries out of the sun to avoid becoming darker. Yet she chafes under the self-hatred of the black middle class which is manifested in their proscriptions: "Dark complected people shouldn't wear yellow, or red or green.[1] She escapes to Chicago where she lives in ambivalence and bitterness. In another novel, *Passing,* Larson's protagonist, Claire, marries a white professional and lives as a white woman and, like Helga, cuts herself off from her history and the community that had been her support.

"Passing" novels were thought to help invest white readers in the lives of the light-skinned, educated black protagonists and thereby gain sympathy for the plight of black people in general. That strategy—convincing white people that black people were exactly like them—had some success for the civil rights movement but at the same time its usefulness was limited in an evolving political arena. Its focus on external effects served to short-circuit black exploration of our identities as unique individuals with variations within the group of class, gender, sexual orientation. We formed our own personal mythology of who black people were, which was almost as narrow and misleading as the stereotypes that white people clung to.

During the 1960s, I managed to never mention my sexual desire in any personal conversation with friends. I could feel the expectations pressing in on me. Oblique references made it clear that no contemporary African queen was ever queer. But even a decade earlier, Fanon had written: "If one wants to understand the racial situation psychoanalytically, not from a universal viewpoint but as it is experienced from individual consciousnesses, considerable importance must be given to sexual phenomenon."[2]

Today, the "passing" novel has been gone for more than half a century and the "passing" strategy has lost currency in the black political arena. It is almost that long since Fanon suggested the examination of "sexual phenomenon" within the context of race. Yet African Americans are still walking around the edge of the room, trying to ignore the elephant sitting in the middle. I think many would prefer me to "pass" in the black community. For some African Americans, I can be a lesbian in what they imagine as my "dark, secret world," but when I'm in "the community," the message to me is: don't bring "that mess." Asking me to pass as a heterosexual, to not call myself a dyke is a demand for self-hatred and delusion equal to saying black people shouldn't wear "yellow or red or green." It is a demand for a lie I was able to tell by not telling in my youth. Today, the question of a lie feels more significant. Adrienne Rich wrote some years ago that "Truthfulness has never been considered important for women, as long as we have remained faithful to men, or chaste."[3] I think both women and people of color have been rewarded for lying too long. By pretending to be less than we are, we've avoided punitive notice, unfair restrictions, and overt aggression. Girls pretend not to be as smart as boys so they can be dating material; black people pretend not to know "nuthin' 'bout birthing babies." Each poses, a lie and a protection; each lie a brick shoring up the status quo, blocking my view to myself. My ongoing engagement with eliminating the layers of illusion and to coalesce the parts that are me is too important to ever concede to such a demand. And each word that some consider a label, I see as a door—a door which opens onto more aspects of me. As Mary Helen Washington says in discussing Nella Larson's classic novel *Quicksand,* "Passing is an obscene form of salvation.[4] Just as a black woman passing for white is required to "deny everything about her past," a black lesbian who passes for heterosexual is required to deny everything about her present.

Recently, I had an experience in a black-owned bookstore in the Bay Area that I'm sure is repeated regularly across the country in all types of establishments. I was browsing the shelves with the comforting camaraderie and laughter of the black cashier and two black patrons in the background. The discussion roamed freely then turned to the topic of the "rights" that gay people were "demanding." The three were united in their disdain for gay people's very basic civic concerns. Without thinking, the people I'd thought of as "family" only moments before were repeating the same bigotry I'd heard from radical conservatives. They were refusing to recognize any validity in another's desire to be equal before the law, even though that had been the cornerstone of the Civil Rights Movement. It was as if the previous fifty years had never happened and the idea of struggle for civil recognition was anti-American.

I stood among the shelves, stock-still, feeling like the proverbial deer in headlights. If I moved, or indicated I was listening, they would know I was a lesbian! They would do something ugly. I was the elephant in the room—invisible, passing, lying—until the conversation turned to another topic. Then I reshelved the book I was holding and didn't return to the store for many months. As I slipped out of the store, I understood that I'd missed an opportunity to challenge their misinformation, but there was something disturbing about hearing such callous dismissal from black people in a bookstore who only moments before had felt so close. I wanted to shout at them, words Barbara Smith had written: "The oppression that affects Black gay people, female and male, is pervasive, constant, and not abstract. Some of us die from it."[5]

As I walked away I tried to calm my anger and humiliation. But the reality of how easily they erased who I was kept cutting into me. It was a reminder to me that

10

in my twenty years of writing and presenting my work in the United States, Canada, and Europe, I've only been invited to read in a black-owned bookstore once. If I knew it intellectually before, that day I knew in my heart that it's true: those closest to you can cause the most hurt.

I didn't know what to say to the people in the bookstore, maybe because the work it would have taken to make them see me was more than I could handle in one visit. But the encounter made it clearer still that my image of who I am has no substance without all the elements swirling around inside me. Even if black people would so easily reject me, I would never cast them out of my blood. It is for me alone to decide which face I see in the mirror.

In the mid-1970s, a white woman interviewing me for a job asked me who I would choose to play me if Hollywood was making a movie. She couldn't know how complex a question that was. Finding an image to represent me is a trip back into the maelstrom. Although I'd been an avid fan of popular culture, growing up I knew that I wasn't reflected in the movies or on television. Peola, who'd settled for an "imitation of life," certainly wasn't me. But who could be? The question was both intriguing and frustrating.

I'd always liked Ernestine Wade, the actress who played the much-maligned Sapphire on television's "Amos and Andy." Even then I knew that for a black woman to be independent she would have to risk having her name become synonymous with being a bitch. But I didn't think I'd be mentioning Sapphire to a prospective white employer.

I was a major fan of movie queen Dorothy Dandridge, but the tragedy that 　15 remained part of her mystique didn't really fit me. And I never could quite see myself as a sarong-wearing siren.

I finally chose Diana Sands, who'd played the sister in the film version of "Raisin in the Sun." She easily embodied the character's outspoken intelligence and determination, qualities I wanted to believe were mine. Searching for the suitable personality to fit my idea of myself was a great exercise for me but turned out to be useless as an interview tool: my future employer had no idea who Diana Sands was.

Twenty years later if I were asked to make a casting choice I have a wider field to examine, but again who would I pick? Angela Bassett? Too thin and buffed. Vanessa Williams? Too ethereal. Alfre Woodard? Interesting possibility. But I doubted any of them would ever allow themselves to be filmed with their hair natural, not straightened, much less play a lesbian.

In almost every case, when I encountered the images of black women, the subtleties of who we might be were almost completely unexamined—in the media, in the public consciousness, and in the black community. And the particulars of who black lesbians might be are not even a question in the larger world.

Lesbians, usually white in movies and books, are generally presented as a bundle of tics and quirks that reflect the heterosexual world's fear and ambivalence. As a teenager, I looked for myself in all of them. The icy Lakey of Mary McCarthy's novel, *The Group* (produced as a film in 1966), the pathetic Martha of *The Children's Hour* (1962), the predatory Jo in the film version of *Walk on the Wild Side* (1962) were all one-dimensional concoctions designed to intrigue and repulse. For years the stereotypical lesbian was the only image I could find with which to identify.

It wasn't until much later that I understood that one way to maintain lesbian invisibility is, paradoxically, to create exaggerations or stereotypes that obliterate the reality. The same had been done with African Americans and most other ethnic Americans over the years: Steppin' Fetchit, Aunt Jemima, Charlie Chan, the Frito Bandito helped more than one generation of Americans overlook the real people behind the laugh. When we say that something frightening gives us the "willies" most of us don't remember that the term is derived from the actor Willie Best who perfected a comic character who embodied fear, especially of ghosts. His eye-rolling, stuttering, lazy character was featured in Hollywood movies during the 1930s and in them was often the butt of racial jokes from stars like Bob Hope. But Best's brilliant parody became the stereotype that, lacking solid alternative images, came to stand for all black men. The same can be said for every mammy/maid stock character since *Gone with the Wind*. The reality of who we are as black people is subsumed under the one-dimensional distortions that are standard in mass culture. It has been much the same for lesbians although they haven't been such a standard part of the core consciousness. . . .

When the three people in that black bookstore dismissed equal rights for gays, they didn't picture me or any of the characters created by Audre Lorde or Cheryl Dunye. They imagined the caricature of lesbians that is repeatedly reinforced by popular culture in films like *Set It Off*. I wouldn't argue against the artistic freedom that results in such archaic portrayals. I can only be grateful that there are alternative places for young lesbians of color to now look for their reflection and at the same time feel very sad that mainstream culture—black and white—still needs the comfort of such distorted information.

In retrospect, what made me flee from my brothers and sisters in that store was more than anger and humiliation; it was exhaustion. After a lifetime commitment to human rights, I feel almost the same about educating black people about their heterosexism as I do about educating white people about their racism. It's time for them to check themselves.

In an essay written by Cheryl Clarke in 1983, she says: "It is ironic that the Black Power Movement could transform the consciousness of an entire generation of black people regarding black self-determination and, at the same time, fail so miserably in understanding the sexual politics of the movement and of black people across the board." The underlying tone of Clarke's essay reveals a similar weariness with confronting the lagging black community that I feel continually. It is also a sentiment sadly echoed more than a decade later by the editors of *Afrekete*, the first anthology with the words "black lesbian" on its cover. Published in 1995, it takes its name from a mythic character in Audre Lorde's Zami. In the introduction, the editors comment: "We did not contemplate too long the specter of political debate that the writing would meet. We take on these debates every day in everything we do. It is tiring. It mutes our passion."[6] There always comes a turning point in a struggle, when the focus shifts, the power dynamic changes. I feel that happening in my pursuit of approval from the black community. The energy I've put into recognizing myself as a whole person has come to mean more than my disappointment at their failure to transform themselves.

For years I had hoped for growth and change in the black community so that the one-dimensional, male-dominated mythology of who we are did not continue to represent all that we could be. But the discourse of black politics and culture flows through the generations with the same male voice—from Baraka and Bullins to Gates, Lee and Als. Even when it is queer or queer friendly, it's a voice comfortable with leaving black women in the background or speaking for black women and letting black lesbians remain invisible.

Maybe in moving from the East to the West Coast in mid-life I got to see   25 things from a different perspective. Unlike in New York, African Americans are not the primary voice for progressive social change in California. The larger Asian American and Spanish-speaking communities have varying strategies and philosophies they employ—not to mention their different histories. Because we are a part of the Pacific Rim, there is a more global orientation to the activism. Discussions about ethnic concerns are presumed to be connected to the environment, gender parity, and economic class.

But, whatever the reasons, in the struggle for social change, it is I, in fact, who have been transformed. I see a larger picture of human rights than the civil rights or black power movements showed me. Those movements were only the first door I walked through. Learning the extent and complexity of oppression on a global as well as local level has necessitated walking through many more doors than I ever would have suspected in the 1960s.

When I work with my writing students or relate to my young cousins and nieces and nephews, I insist that they see these doors. I could be the "unmarried aunt" but I prefer to be "the dyke aunt"—much more interesting and more accurate. And if it causes a storm, better the maelstrom I know than the one caused by unspoken secrets. One of my greatest joys was telling my ten-year-old niece that I was a lesbian and seeing the understanding fill her eyes. Whatever she'd heard in her school or with her friends was forever changed by my ability to be that image she had been unable to find for herself. Her affection for me and my partner, because my family made room for that experience, is the radical social change I've been looking for. She is the community I need for my context, my support.

When I talk to her and other young people I want them to be willing to go out into the storm, no matter how uncertain the outcome. I pass on to them Audre Lorde's words: "I speak without concern for the accusations/that I am too much or too little woman/that I am too black or too white/or too much myself . . . "[7]

ENDNOTES

1. Nella Larson, *Quicksand* (New York: A. A. Knopf, 1928), 191.
2. Frantz Fanon, *Black Skin, White Masks* (New York: Grove Press, 1967), 160.
3. Adrienne Rich, *On Lies, Secrets, and Silence* (New York: W.W. Norton, 1979), 188.
4. Mary Helen Washington, ed., *Invented Lives* (New York: Doubleday, 1987), 164.
5. Barbara Smith, ed., *Home Girls* (New York: Kitchen Table Women of Color Press, 1983), xlvii.
6. Audre Lorde, *Zami: A New Spelling of My Name* (Watsonville, Calif.: The Crossing Press, 1982), xi.
7. Audre Lorde, *Undersong: Chosen Poems Old and New* (New York: W.W. Norton & Co., 1992), 110.

Media Resources

The Birth of a Nation [1915]. Directed by D. W. Griffith. 195 minutes. Epoch. An adaptation of Dixon's *The Clansman* and *The Leopard's Spots,* this film depicts a proslave Southerner's perspective on the status of the African American before and after the Civil War.

Bill Cosby on Prejudice [1971]. Directed by Bill Cosby and Tom Massman. 24 minutes. Pyramid Film & Video. In satiric monologue, the comedian discusses racial stereotypes.

The Color Purple [1985]. Directed by Stephen Spielberg. 154 minutes. Warner Brothers. Adaptation of Pulitzer prize novel by Alice Walker that caused controversy because of its depiction of an African American wife beater and lesbianism.

Race Against Prime Time [1985]. Directed by David Shulman. 58 minutes. California Newsreel. This study reveals how news personnel report activities in African American communities.

Ethnic Notions [1986]. Produced by Marlon Riggs. 58 minutes. California Newsreel. Riggs chronicles racist images and stereotypes of African Americans in American culture.

Coming to America [1988]. Directed by John Landis. 116 minutes. Paramount. Stereotypes about African Americans are showcased when an African prince comes to the United States to find a bride.

Boyz N the Hood [1991]. Directed by John Singleton. 112 minutes. Columbia. In South Central Los Angeles three African American teenage boys come of age.

Color Adjustment: Blacks in Prime Time TV [1991]. Directed by Marlon Riggs. 88 minutes. California Newsreel. How African Americans are depicted on television from *Amos 'n' Andy* to *The Cosby Show* is the subject of this documentary.

Jungle Fever [1991]. Directed by Spike Lee. 131 minutes. Universal. Interracial dating causes family dissension in African American and Italian American households.

Separate But Equal [1991]. Directed by George Stevens. 194 minutes. Republic Pictures. This dramatization of the U. S. Supreme Court hearing of *Brown* v. *Board of Education* pits Thurgood Marshall (Sidney Poitier) against John W. Davis (Burt Lancaster).

A Question of Color [1993]. Directed by Kathe Sandler. 56 minutes. California Newsreel. This documentary explores colorism regarding appearance.

The Inkwell [1994]. Directed by Matty Rich. 120 minutes. Touchstone. An idyllic summer is the setting for middle-class African American teenagers on Martha's Vineyard during 1976.

Black Is—Black Ain't: A Personal Journey Through Black Identity [1995]. Directed by Marlon Riggs. 87 minutes. California Newsreel. Riggs addresses the myriad definitions of blackness in interviews with African Americans, dealing with color, class, gender, and language.

Waiting to Exhale [1995]. Directed by Forest Whitaker. 123 minutes. Twentieth Century Fox. Middle-class African American women tackle love and marriage while adhering to the strong bonds of sisterhood.

Skin Deep: The Science of Race [1995]. Produced by the Canadian Broadcasting Corporation. 60 minutes. Filmakers Library. The documentary explores whether a scientific basis exists regarding race or whether color and physical features are the determinants.

All God's Children [1996]. Directed by Dr. Dee Mosbacher, Frances Reid, and Dr. Sylvia Rhue. 26 minutes. The Cinema Guild, Inc. How the African American church has accepted the gay and lesbian members therein, as well as its commitment to equal rights and social justice, is the subject of this film.

Get on the Bus [1996]. Directed by Spike Lee. 120 minutes. Columbia. A chartered busload of African American men talk on their way to the Million Man March.

I Shall Not Be Removed: The Life of Marlon Riggs [1996]. Directed by Karen Everett. 58 minutes. California Newsreel. This film is a biography of the African American filmmaker who produced films about the African American gay community.

The Mirror Lied [1999]. Directed by Jennifer Haskin-O'Reggio. 27 minutes. Filmakers Library. How the younger sister of the film director reacts to the dictates of beauty imposed by white American society.

The Brothers [2001]. Directed by Gary Hadwick. 101 minutes. Columbia. Middle-class African American men deal with the vagaries of love and marriage.

CHAPTER 6

One Family, One Blood

In American culture we emphasize the individual, but the African American worldview is essentially communal. Even with the shifts in American life, African Americans have retained core values that are largely a part of their Africanicity. The immediate and extended family are important members of the family, and several generations living in one household is a mainstay of African American life. Further, "family" titles, such as "Aunt," "Uncle," "play mother," "play sister or brother," "adopted mother, daughter, or son," may be attached to friends of the family. Church members may be referred to as "Brother" or "Sister." These persons are considered members of the family and will be as important for support as blood kinship. The reliance on the community for both financial and social support is a matter of history closely tied to the slave experience in America, as well as to the communal life in African society. However, the ravages of slavery and the residual lifestyles created in its aftermath have created multiple problems for the African American family.

This chapter begins with an excerpt from John W. Blassingame's book *The Slave Community* (1972), which frames the discussion on family life by others. Blassingame discusses the development of family patterns in Latin America and the southern states of America before 1865. Identifying the family as the most important survival mechanism for slaves, he goes on to discuss love, marriage, courtship, morals, and the hardships faced by families who could not protect their women or their young. Following the historical essay is Frank Banks's brief description of courtship practices from the *Journal of American Folklore*. Banks's data is based on a discussion he held with "Uncle Gilbert," an elderly slave who instructed young men in courtship matters. This description echoes Blassingame's description of the theme of marriage and courtship on the plantation.

Another theme in this chapter has to do with women's work. The selection "Laura Smalley" is an interview with a former slave who shares her insights on many

253

topics, including breeding, child care, debt, and sharecropping. Nearly 50 years later, Elizabeth Clark-Lewis interviews women from the rural South concerning their work and the jobs they label "men's work" and therefore shun. Their comments mirror concerns voiced about antebellum practices. Farai Chideya offers yet another perspective on African American women and work in *Don't Believe the Hype: Fighting Cultural Misinformation about African Americans.* In the excerpt from this book, Chideya explodes the myths and stereotypes about black women and their relationship to work, one being that they are "welfare queens."

Another important strand in this chapter has to do with family connections. The next two selections focus on, Etheridge Knight (1970), a contemporary prisoner who speaks to us from his prison cell, remembering his ancestry and reciting his relationship to family pictures on his wall, and Joseph Beam (1986), who explores issues of parenting for gay men who adopt. In both pieces there is clearly a desire for connection to family. Anna Mulrine writes in 1997 about the shift in Northern-born African Americans' desire to return to their Southern homesteads to connect with family through family reunions.

The final two pieces in this chapter recite ways African American families can survive and thrive. Marian Wright Edelman's "A Family Legacy," from *The Measure of Our Success: A Letter to My Children and Yours* (1992), relates how her South Carolina home, parents, and community thrived on a tradition of service, shared child rearing, and extended community expectations and pride. Her saying, "Service is the rent we pay for living," provides insight to the importance placed on this activity. The chapter concludes with Morehouse College's Conference on African American Fathers. Here men and women, mothers and fathers, blacks and whites, liberals and conservatives gathered because they shared a concern over father absence. The result of the conference was a statement and ten recommendations for giving children the strong and positive relationships with their fathers that they deserve.

The guidance of elders has sustained the African American community since the assault on family during slavery. Over time, African American families have strengthened traditions and mores regarding family. This chapter provides a historical perspective on the many ways that African Americans have experienced issues of family and ends with suggestions for its survival.

John W. Blassingame

John W. Blassingame (1940–2000) was the founder and general editor of The Frederick Douglass Papers project. After earning his B.A. from Fort Valley State College and his M.A. from Howard University, Blassingame studied with C. Vann Woodward at Yale University and received his Ph.D. in 1971. He taught in the history and African and African American Studies departments, and chaired the African American Studies department at Yale during the 1980s. Many of today's leading scholars in African American Studies were his students. Blassingame's best-known publication is *The Slave Community: Plantation Life in the Antebellum South* (1972), a monumental work on the historiography of the American slave experience.

This third chapter from *The Slave Community* introduces issues of love, courtship, marriage, and child rearing and the hardships resulting from the inability to protect the family.

The Slave Family

O, where has mother gone, papa?
What makes you look so sad?
Why sit you here alone, papa?
Has anyone made you mad?
O, tell me, dear papa.
Has master punished you again?
Shall I go bring the salt, papa,
To rub your back and cure the pain?
—W. H. ROBINSON

The Southern plantation was unique in the New World because it permitted the development of a monogamous slave family. In sharp contrast to the South, the general imbalance in the sex ratio among Latin American slaves severely restricted the development of monogamous mating arrangements. For example, in 1860 there were 156 males for every 100 female slaves in Cuba. The German traveler Alexander Humboldt found that there was only 1 female to every 4 male slaves on most Cuban sugar estates and in the San Juan de los Remedios region there was only 1 female to every 19 males. One Cuban plantation that Humboldt visited had 700 males and no female slaves. The imbalance in the sex ratio among Latin American slaves was partly a result of the planter's initial lack of interest in reproducing the slave population and his preference for importing more males than females from Africa. For instance, in the Brazilian coffee-growing country of Vassouras, Stanley Stein found that between 1820 and 1880 70 per cent of the African-born slaves were males. Robert Conrad's analysis of ship manifests in the 1830s and 1840s showed that 4 out of every 5 Africans imported into Brazil were males. Whatever the cause, the great disparity in the sex ratio restricted the development of monogamous family patterns among Latin American slaves.[1]

The physical basis for the monogamous slave family appears clearly in the sex ratio among slaves in the Southern states. The number of females to every 100 male slaves in the United States was 95.1 in 1820, 98.3 in 1830, 99.5 in 1840, 99.9 in 1850, and 99.3 in 1860. When the sex ratio is broken down by ages, there were 99.8 and 99.1 females for every 100 male slaves over 15 years of age in 1850 and 1860 respectively. The excess of males over female slaves was very slight in the South in comparison to the disparity in Latin America. For example, in 1860 only one Southern state, Missouri, had as many as 109 males to every 100 female slaves. In actuality, the sex ratio among slaves was more nearly equal in most Southern states than among whites. In 1860, in the Southern states, there were 106 white males for every 100 white females; in six states there were more than 110 white males for every 100 white females.[2]

Since childhood is the most crucial era in the development of personality, and parents play so large a role in determining behavioral patterns, attitudes, ideals, and values, the slave family must be analyzed in order to understand slave life. The family, while it had no legal existence in slavery, was in actuality one of the most important survival mechanisms for the slave. In his family he found companionship, love, sexual gratification, sympathetic understanding of his sufferings; he learned how to avoid punishment, to cooperate with other blacks, and to maintain his self-esteem. However frequently the family was broken, it was primarily responsible for the slave's ability to survive on the plantation without becoming totally dependent on and submissive to his master. The important thing was not that the family was not recognized legally or that masters frequently encouraged monogamous mating arrangements in the quarters only when it was convenient to do so, but rather that some form of family life did exist among slaves.

While the form of family life in the quarters differed radically from that among free Negroes and whites, this does not mean that the institution was unable to perform many of the traditional functions of the family. The rearing of children was one of the most important of these functions. Since slave parents were primarily responsible for training their children, they could cushion the shock of bondage for them, help them to understand their situation, teach them values different from those their masters tried to instill in them, and give them a referent for self-esteem other than their master.

If he was lucky, the slave belonged to a master who tried to foster the development of strong family ties in the quarters. Although the slaveholders sometimes encouraged monogamous mating arrangements because of their religious views, they generally did it to make it easier to discipline their slaves. A black man, they reasoned, who loved his wife and his children was less likely to be rebellious or to run away than would a "single" slave. The simple threat of being separated from his family was generally sufficient to subdue the most rebellious "married" slave. Besides, there was less likelihood of fights between slaves when monogamous mating arrangements existed.[3]

A number of planters attempted to promote sexual morality in the quarters, punished slaves for licentiousness and adultery, and recognized the male as the head of the family. On William J. Minor's plantations, slaves had to give a month's notice before their "marriage" or "divorce."[4] One planter asserted in 1836 that he particularly enjoined upon his slaves, "the observance of their marriage contracts. In no instance do I suffer any of them to violate these ties; except where I would consider myself justified in doing so."[5] Hugh Davis of Alabama also sought to promote morality on his plantation. He informed his overseer that "all violations of the right of husband and wife and such other immorality will meet with chastisement[.] From 10 to 50 stripes is the general measure of punishment for stated offenses according to their grade."[6]

White churches (when slaves attended them) sometimes helped to promote morality in the quarters by excommunicating adulterers and preaching homilies on fidelity.[7] For instance, in Liberty County, Georgia, white ministers systematically instructed slaves about their religious duties. R. Q. Mallard, one of the missionaries to the slaves, asserted that slave marriages were

> gladly celebrated by the white pastor or colored minister. . . . We hesitate not to say that the marriages thus contracted were, by the slaves themselves and their masters, generally regarded quite as sacred as marriages solem-

nized with legal license of the courts; and the obligations as commonly observed as among the same class anywhere. There were as many faithful husbands and wives, we believe, as are to be found among the working white population in any land.[8]

Most planters were far less successful or interested in promoting morality in the quarters than those in Liberty County. The typical experience was related by a Mississippi planter: "As to their habits of amalgamation and intercourse, I know of no means whereby to regulate them, or to restrain them; I attempted it for many years by preaching virtue and decency, encouraging marriages, and by punishing, with some severity, departures from marital obligations; but it was all in vain."[9] It is obvious that most slaveholders did not care about the sexual customs of their slaves as long as there was no bickering and fighting. As a result, planters were generally more interested in encouraging monogamy because it was conducive to discipline than because of any interest in encouraging morality in the quarters. According to one planter, "the general rule of the plantation recognized the relation of man and wife and compelled not virtue perhaps, but monogamy."[10] Many of the plantations were so large that it was impossible for masters to supervise both the labor and the sex life of their slaves. Sexual morality, often imperfectly taught (or violated by whites with impunity), drifted down through a heavy veil of ignorance to the quarters. Consequently, for a majority of slaves, sex was a natural urge frequently fulfilled in casual liaisons. William Wells Brown's mother, for example, had seven children fathered by seven different men, black and white.[11]

The white man's lust for black women was one of the most serious impediments to the development of morality. The white man's pursuit of black women frequently destroyed any possibility that comely black girls could remain chaste for long. Few slave parents could protect their pretty daughters from the sexual advances of white men. This was particularly true when the slaves belonged to a white bachelor or lived near white bachelors. Lucius Holsey's white father, for instance, never married but instead chose successive lovers from among the female slaves on his plantation.[12]

The black autobiographers testified that many white men considered every slave cabin as a house of ill-fame. Often through "gifts," but usually through force, white overseers and planters obtained the sexual favors of black women. Generally speaking, the women were literally forced to offer themselves "willingly" and receive a trinket for their compliance rather than a flogging for their refusal and resistance. Frederick Douglass declared that the "slave woman is at the mercy of the fathers, sons or brothers of her master."[13] Many of the black autobiographers recounted stories of slave women being forced to submit to white men: Henry Bibb's master forced one slave girl to be his son's concubine; M. F. Jamison's overseer raped a pretty slave girl; and Solomon Northup's owner forced one slave, "Patsey," to be his sexual partner. Slave traders frequently engaged in the same kind of practices. Moses Roper, who once helped a slave trader, declared that the traders often had intercourse with the most beautiful black women they purchased. When Henry Bibb and his wife were sold to a trader in Louisville, Kentucky, the trader forced Bibb's wife to become a prostitute.[14]

A number of white men sought more than fleeting relationships with black women. Frequently they purchased comely black women for their concubines. In many cases the master loved his black concubine and treated her as his wife. Jacob Stroyer declared that the white groom on his master's plantation shared his cabin with his black lover and their two daughters. (One of the girls married a white man after the Civil War.) Two of the black autobiographers, Jermain Loguen and John Mercer Langston, lived in such households. Langston's father was a wealthy Virginia planter, Ralph Quarles, who wanted to abolish slavery. Ostracized by his neighbors because of his abolitionist views, Quarles restricted himself almost solely to the company of his slaves. He took Langston's mother, Lucy, as his concubine, made her mistress of his household, and had four children by her. Eventually he freed her and the children. Langston declared that his father treated him "tenderly and affectionately." Early each morning he would rise and tutor his children, and when the boys reached a certain age, he sent them to school in Ohio. Upon the marriage of his daughter to a slave, Quarles purchased and freed her husband and gave them a plantation and some slaves. At his death in 1834, Quarles freed some of his slaves and willed all of his property to his three sons.[15]

Miscegenation often led to complications in the South. Sometimes, white men loved their black concubines more than they did their white wives. Consequently, the white women sued for, and obtained, divorce. Henry Watson asserted that the wife of a Natchez, Mississippi, slave trader divorced him because of his concubine. White women were frequently infuriated by their husband's infidelities in the quarters and took revenge on the black women involved. When Moses Roper was born, for example, his mistress tried to kill him when she discovered that her husband was Roper's father. To prevent this, the man sold Roper and his mother.

On innumerable occasions white women also had assignations with black slaves. The evidence from Virginia divorce petitions is conclusive on this point: a Norfolk white man asserted in 1835 that his wife had "lived for the last six or seven years and continues to live in open adultery with a negro man. . . ." A Nansemond County white man declared in 1840 that his wife had given birth to a mulatto child and that she had "recently been engaged in illicit intercourse with a negro man at my own house and on my own bed." In many cases the sexual relations between Negro men and white women went undetected because the children resulting from such unions were light enough to pass for white. For example, one Virginian testified that when his white wife gave birth to a mulatto he "did not at first doubt [it] to be his, notwithstanding its darkness of color, and its unusual appearance." One white woman in eighteenth-century Virginia who had a mulatto child convinced her husband that the child was dark because someone had cast a spell on her. (He believed the story for eighteen years.)[16]

Regardless of the actions of the planters, the courtship pattern in the quarters differed, in many respects, from that of whites. An imperfect understanding of the unnatural puritanical code of their masters freed blacks from the insuperable guilt complexes that enslaved nineteenth-century white Americans in regard to sex. Besides, they argued, they could gain nothing from observing this part of the American creed when whites considered them outside the rest of it. Consequently, freed from social restraints, young slave men pursued their black paramours with a reckless abandon which was often the envy of their white masters.

Sexual conquest became a highly respected avenue to status in the quarters.[15] The slave caroused with black damsels on his own plantation and slipped away, with or without a pass, to other estates until he was smitten by love. He persistently pursued the one of his choice often over a long period of courtship. He flattered her, exaggerated his prowess, and tried to demonstrate his ambition and especially his ability to provide for her. If he won her affections, he often had to obtain the consent of her parents. This was almost always required in the few cases where slave men married free women. In some cases the slaves were engaged for as much as a year before their union was consummated. In the interim, the prospective husband prepared a cabin and furniture for his family, and the prospective wife collected utensils she would need to establish a household.[17]

Love is no small matter for any man; for a slave it represented one of the major crises in his life. Many slaves vowed early in life never to marry and face separation from loved ones. If they had to marry, the slave men were practically unanimous in their desire to marry women from another plantation. They did not want to marry a woman from their own and be forced to watch as she was beaten, insulted, raped, overworked, or starved without being able to protect her. John Anderson declared that when he was contemplating marriage: "I did not want to marry a girl belonging to my own place, because I knew I could not bear to see her ill-treated."[18] Henry Bibb felt the same way. He contended: "If my wife must be exposed to the insults and licentious passions of wicked slavedrivers and overseers; if she must bear the stripes of the lash laid on by an unmerciful tyrant; if this is to be done with impunity, which is frequently done by slaveholders and their abettors, Heaven forbid that I should be compelled to witness the sight."[19] Most of the slaves tried every stratagem to avoid being placed in this position. Moses Grandy summed up the general view when he wrote: "no colored man wishes to live at the house where his wife lives, for he has to endure the continual misery of seeing her flogged and abused, without daring to say a word in her defence."[20]

Unfortunately for most slaves, the master had the final word in regard to their marriage partners. Most slaveholders, feeling that the children their male slaves had by women belonging to other planters was so much seed spewed on the ground, insisted that they marry women on their own estates. Such a practice placed all of the slave's interests under the control of the master and gave the slave fewer excuses to leave the estate. Some masters brought both of the prospective mates together and inquired if they understood the seriousness of their undertaking. If they belonged to different masters it was often more difficult for them to obtain the consent of either one. But, if both the lovers persistently spurned prospective partners on their own plantations, the planters, by mutual agreement, might resolve the controversy. Wealthy masters frequently purchased the female slave and thereby won the loyalty of the male. If the matter could not be resolved by the planters, the love might be consummated in spite of their objections. The marriage ceremony in most cases consisted of the slaves' simply getting the master's permission and moving into a cabin together. The masters of domestic servants either had the local white minister or the black plantation preacher perform the marriage ceremony and then gave a sumptuous feast in their own parlors to the slave guests. Afterwards, the slaves had long dances in the quarters in honor of the couple.[21]

In spite of the loose morality in the quarters, in spite of the fact that some men had two wives simultaneously, there was a great deal of respect for the monogamous family. Whether the result of religious teachings, the requirements of the master, or the deep affection between mates, many slaves had only one partner. Henry Box Brown, for instance, refused his master's order to take another mate after his wife was sold because he felt marriage "was a sacred institution binding upon me." Affection, not morality, was apparently the most important factor which kept partners together. This emerges most clearly in the lamentations and resentments which pervade the autobiographies over the separation of family members. Frequently when their mates were sold, slaves ran away in an effort to find them. The fear of causing disaffection forced planters to recognize the strength of the monogamous family; they frequently sold a slave in the neighborhood of his mate when they moved their slaves farther South. Because they were denied all the protection which the law afforded, slaves had an almost mythological respect for legal marriage. Henry Bibb believed that "there are no class of people in the United States who so highly appreciate the legality of marriage as those persons who have been held and treated as property."[22] In no class of American autobiographies is more stress laid upon the importance of stable family life than in the autobiographies of former slaves.

After marriage, the slave faced almost insurmountable odds in his efforts to build a strong stable family. First, and most important of all, his authority was restricted by his master. Any decision of his regarding his family could be countermanded by his master. The master determined when both he and his wife would go to work, when or whether his wife cooked his meals, and was often the final arbiter in family disputes. In enforcing discipline, some masters whipped both man and wife when they had loud arguments or fights. Some planters punished males by refusing to let them visit their mates when they lived on other plantations. In any event, these slaves could only visit their mates with their master's permission. When the slave lived on the same plantation with his mate, he could rarely escape frequent demonstrations of his powerlessness. The master, and not the slave, furnished the cabin, clothes, and the minimal food for his wife and children. Under such a regime slave fathers often had little or no authority.[23]

The most serious impediment to the man's acquisition of status in his family was his inability to protect his wife from the sexual advances of whites and the physical abuse of his master. Instead, according to Austin Steward, slave husbands had to "submit without a murmur" when their wives were flogged.[24] Sometimes, in spite of the odds, the men tried to protect their mates. W. H. Robinson's father once told him that he "lay in the woods eleven months for trying to prevent your mother from being whipped."[25] The black male frequently could do little to protect his wife from the sexual advances of whites. Most whites, however, realized that a liaison with a slave's wife could be dangerous. Occasionally, slaves killed white men for such acts. Generally, however, the women had no choice but to submit to the sexual advances of white men.[26] Henry Bibb wrote that "a poor slave's wife can never be. . . true to her husband contrary to the will of her master. She can neither be pure nor virtuous, contrary to the will of her master. She dare not refuse to be reduced to a state of adultery at the will of her master. . . ."[27]

By all odds, the most brutal aspect of slavery was the separation of families. This was a haunting fear which made all of the slave's days miserable. In spite of the fact that probably a majority of the planters tried to prevent family separations in order to maintain plantation discipline, practically all of the black autobiographers were touched by the tragedy. Death occurred too frequently in the master's house, creditors were too relentless in collecting their debts, the planter's reserves ran out too often, and the master longed too much for expensive items for the slave to escape the clutches of the slave trader. Nothing demonstrated his powerlessness as much as the slave's inability to prevent the forceable sale of his wife and children.[28]

The best objective evidence available concerning the separation of mates by planters appears in the marriage certificates of former slaves preserved by the Union army and the Freedmen's Bureau in Tennessee (Dyer, Gibson, Wilson, and Shelby counties), Louisiana (Concordia Parish), and Mississippi (Adams County) from 1864 to 1866. Although these records contain the best material available on the actions of masters in regard to the slave family, they must be used with caution. In the first place, the number of unbroken unions may be exaggerated: those blacks who had retained the strongest sense of family would be most likely to come to the posts to be married. Second, multiple separations by masters were apparently understated (often old slaves simply noted how they were separated from their *last* mate). Third, it was sometimes impossible to determine from the army records whether a childless couple had been united in slavery.

The data concerning the 2,888 slave unions are summarized in Table 1.

The most difficult problem involved in analyzing the slave family is defining the term "unbroken." Since the most important characteristic of the slave union which differentiated it from legal marriage was the right the master had to separate mates, this factor must be isolated, and separations caused by death, war-related activities, and personal choice treated as unions "unbroken by masters." Through this technique, we can arrive at an approximation of the role of masters in dissolving slave families. This is not to argue, of course, that casual separations and high mortality rates did not lead to instability in these families. In fact, the dissolution of 50 per cent of the unions was directly attributable to these causes. However intimately related they are to family instability, neither of these factors involved the deliberate intervention of the master for the purpose of separating mates.

It seems logical to treat couples separated by war and death as unbroken unions, since many of them had cohabited together for decades before impersonal forces caused their dissolution. If couples separated by death are dropped from the sample, 66 per cent of the remaining unions were dissolved by masters in Mississippi, 50 per cent in Louisiana, and 43 per cent in Tennessee. This, however, 25

TABLE 1: Slave families[29]

Unions	Mississippi		Tennessee		Louisiana		Totals	
	No.	Per Cent	No.	Per Cent	No.	Per Cent	No.	Per Cent
Totals	1225	—	1123	—	540	—	2888	—
Unbroken	78	6.3	226	20.1	90	16.6	394	13.6
Broken	1147	93.7	897	79.9	450	83.3	2494	86.3
by: Master	477	39.0	302	26.8	158	29.2	937	32.4
Personal choice	145	11.9	106	9.4	58	10.7	309	10.6
Death	509	41.5	418	37.2	226	41.8	1153	39.9
War	16	1.3	71	6.3	8	1.4	95	3.2

would seem unfair, because it penalizes the planters for events over which they had little control. The issue here is not family stability (which involves an analysis of a number of complex factors) but the extent to which masters deliberately separated their "married" slaves. It is obvious, when all of the factors contributing to dissolution are added together, that the slave family was an extremely precarious institution. Even so, the high mortality rate among slaves was apparently more important in this than any other single factor. In a strict sociological sense, only 13.6 per cent of the unions were unbroken.

The callous attitudes frequently held by planters toward slave unions are revealed clearly in the statistics: 32.4 per cent of the unions were dissolved by masters. An overwhelming majority of the couples were separated before they reached their sixth anniversary. The heartlessness of the planters is revealed more clearly in their separation of slaves who had lived together for decades. Several instances of this appeared in Louisiana: Hosea Bidell was separated from his mate of twenty-five years; Valentine Miner from his after thirty years; and, in the most horrifying case of them all, Lucy Robinson was separated from her mate after living with him for forty-three years. Although such separations made the slave family one of the most unstable institutions imaginable, it should be emphasized that there were numerous unions which lasted for several decades. Those enduring for twenty or thirty years were not uncommon, and a few recorded in Tennessee lasted for more than forty years. If only the actions of masters are considered, 67.6 per cent of the slave unions were unbroken. In other words, in spite of their callous attitudes, masters did not separate a majority of the slave couples.

Many slaves were lucky enough to have masters who refused to intercede in family affairs. In order to relieve themselves of responsibility, many planters gave slave parents complete control of their children. Some masters did not punish slave children but instead asked their parents to do so. On Charles Ball's plantation the overseer did nothing to undermine the authority black males had in their families even when they beat their wives.[30] On large plantations and in cities the slaves were so rarely under the constant surveillance of their masters that there the black male faced no obstacle (other than his mate) in exercising authority in his family. While living in Baltimore, for instance, Noah Davis declared that he had "the entire control" of his family.[31]

There were several avenues open to the slave in his effort to gain status in his family. Whenever possible, men added delicacies to their family's monotonous fare of corn meal, fat pork, and molasses by hunting and fishing. If the planter permitted the family to cultivate a garden plot or to raise hogs, the husband led his wife in this family undertaking. The husband could also demonstrate his importance in the family unit by making furniture for the cabin or building partitions between cabins which contained more than one family. The slave who did such things for his family gained not only the approbation of his wife, but he also gained status in the quarters.[32] According to William Green, in the view of the slaves when one tried to provide for his family in this manner: "the man who does this is a great man amongst them."[33] Sometimes, by extra work, slave men earned enough money to buy sugar and coffee for the family or to surprise their wives with scarves or dresses. Often, when masters did not provide adequate clothing for their slaves, black men bought clothes for their children and wives.

Masters, not the black men, determined how much care and attention slave women received when they were pregnant and the treatment that infants received. During her pregnancy a slave wife usually continued her back-breaking labor until a few weeks before her child was born. Solicitous of the health of the new child, the slave owner generally freed the mother of labor for a few days and often for weeks to nurse the infant. If he were especially interested in rearing slave children (and most masters were), he established a definite routine for nursing the child. The mother either carried the infant to the field with her or returned to the cabin at intervals during the day to nurse it.

The routine of the plantation prevented the lavishing of care upon the infant. In this regard, Frederick Douglass, who did not remember seeing his mother until he was seven years old, asserted: "The domestic hearth, with its holy lessons and precious endearments, is abolished in the case of a slave-mother and her children."[34] On many plantations women did not have enough time to prepare breakfast in the morning and were generally too tired to make much of a meal or to give much attention to their children after a long day's labor. Booker T. Washington's experience was typical: "My mother . . . had little time to give to the training of her children during the day. She snatched a few moments for our care in the early morning before her work began, and at night after the day's work was done."[35] At a very early stage the child was placed in the plantation nursery under the care of old women or placed in the hands of his elder siblings. In either case, he was neglected. Fed irregularly or improperly, young black children suffered from a variety of ills. Treated by densely ignorant mothers or little more enlightened planters, they died in droves.[36]

If he survived infancy, the slave child partook, in bountiful measure for a while, of many of the joys of childhood. One important reason for this was the large size of most slave families. Some of the black autobiographers enjoyed the exquisite pleasure of being the youngest child. Sibling rivalry was apparently minimal. Slave parents, in spite of their own sufferings, lavished love on their children. Fathers regaled their children with fascinating stories and songs and won their affections with little gifts. These were all the more important if the father lived on another plantation. The two weekly visits of the father then took on all the aspects of minor celebrations. They were truly this for Elizabeth Keckley, for her father was only allowed to visit his family at Easter and Christmas time. Grandparents, as for all children, loomed large in the life of the slave child. Grandmothers frequently prepared little tidbits for the children, and grandfathers often told them stories about their lives in Africa.

Often assigned as playmates to their young masters, Negro children played in promiscuous equality with white children. Together they roamed the plantation or went hunting, fishing, berry picking, or raiding watermelon and potato patches. Indeed, at first, bondage weighed lightly on the shoulders of the black child.[37] Lunsford Lane, in reflecting on his childhood on a North Carolina plantation, wrote: "I knew no difference between myself and the white children, nor did they seem to know any in turn. Sometime my master would come out and give a biscuit to me and another to one of his white boys; but I did not perceive the difference between us."[38]

The pleasures of early childhood and the equality of playmates which transcended color sometimes obscured the young slave's vision of bondage. During this period many of the young blacks had no idea they were slaves. J. Vance Lewis wrote that on a Louisiana plantation during his early childhood: "As a barefoot boy my stay upon the farm had been pleasant. I played among the wild flowers and wandered, in high glee, over hill and hollow, enchanted with the beauty of nature, and knew not that I was a slave, and son of a slave." Sam Aleckson, though in less lyrical terms, declared the same thing. Until he was ten years old, he asserted, "it had never dawned on me that my condition was not as good as that of any boy in the country." Frederick Douglass reported that during his childhood, "it was a long time before I knew myself to be a *slave*." This was true, he said, because "the first seven or eight years of the slave-boy's life are about as full of sweet content as those of the most favored and petted *white* children of the slaveholder . . . freed from all restraint, the slave-boy can be, in his life and conduct, a genuine boy, doing whatever his boyish nature suggests. . . ."[39]

The planters frequently contributed directly to the idyllic existence of the young slaves. Many of the black autobiographers were the favorites of their masters, who, in a number of cases, were their fathers. In such an event, the child would be fondled, taken on horseback rides, or rewarded with numerous gifts and acts of kindness. William Grimes recalled that his master "was very fond of me, and always treated me kindly." Other slaves declared that their masters were indulgent and often gave them sweets and sometimes protected them from parental wrath. Amanda Smith's childhood was typical of this experience. She declared: "I was a good deal spoiled for a little darkey. If I wanted a piece of bread, and it was not buttered, and sugared on both sides, I wouldn't have it; and when mother would get out of patience with me, and go for a switch, I would run to my old mistress and wrap myself up in her apron, and I was safe. And oh! how I loved her for that."[40]

Most of the slaves, of course, did not have such idyllic childhoods. While J. Vance Lewis recalled that his master's son "was as true a friend as I ever had," the memories of many slaves were clouded with tales of brutal treatment from their little white playmates who were often spurred on by their masters. Others were cuffed about by the planters and flogged for daring to visit the plantation house. Thomas Jones summed up the experience of many slaves when he declared: "I was born a slave. . . . I was made to feel, in my boyhood's first experience, that I was inferior and degraded, and that I must pass through life in a dependent and suffering condition."[41]

Those who were lucky enough to avoid Jones's experience in early childhood knew what he felt by the time they reached their teens. Many began working irregularly at light tasks before they were ten. After that age they usually started working in the fields. Such labor was the first, and irreparable, break in the childhood equality in black-white relations. Lunsford Lane's reaction illustrates the impact of this change:

> When I began to work, I discovered the difference between myself and my master's white children. They began to order me about, and were told to do so by my master and mistress. . . . Indeed all things now made me *feel*, what I had before known only in words, that *I was a slave*. Deep was this feeling, and it preyed upon my heart like a never dying worm. I saw no prospect that my condition would ever be changed.[42]

Most black children learned vicariously what slavery was long before this point. They were often terrified by the violent punishment meted out to the black men around them. The beginning of Jermain Loguen's sense of insecurity and brutal awareness of what he was, for example, occurred when he saw a vicious white planter murder a slave and was cautioned to silence by his mother. The shock of seeing their parents flogged was an early reminder to many black children of what slavery was.[43] When young William Wells Brown saw his mother flogged for being late going to the fields he recalled that "the cold chills ran over me, and I wept aloud."[44] The flogging Charles Ball's mother received when he was four years old still retained its "painful vividness" to him forty-seven years later.

In the face of all of the restrictions, slave parents made every effort humanly possible to shield their children from abuse and teach them how to survive in bondage. One of the most important lessons for the child was learning to hold his tongue around white folks. This was especially true on those plantations where the masters tried to get the children to spy on their parents.[45] Sam Aleckson pointed out that as a child he "was taught to say nothing," about the conversations in the quarters. Frequently mothers had to be severe with their children to prevent them from breaking this important rule. Elijah P. Marrs, for example, declared: "Mothers were necessarily compelled to be severe on their children to keep them from talking too much. Many a poor mother has been whipped nearly to death on account of their children telling white children things. . . ."[46]

Many of the slave parents tried to inculcate a sense of morality in their children. The children were taught to be honest and to lead Christian lives.[47] The Reverend Lucius Holsey gave his "intensely religious" mother credit for the moral lessons he had learned as a boy. Henry Box Brown's mother taught him "not to steal, and not to lie, and to behave myself in other respects." Strict and pious parents not only taught religious principles to their children, they also taught them not to rebel against their masters. William Webb asserted that his mother "taught me there was a Supreme Being, that would take care of me in all my trials; she taught me not to rebel against the men that were treating me like some dumb brute, making me work and refusing to let me learn."[48] Learning to accept personal abuse and the punishment of loved ones passively was one of the most difficult lessons for the slave child. Young Austin Steward indicated this when he recounted how he felt upon observing a white man flogging his sister:

> The God of heaven only knows the conflict of feeling I then endured; He alone witnessed the tumult of my heart, at this outrage of manhood and kindred affection. God knows that my will was good enough to have wrung his neck; or to have drained from his heartless system its last drop of blood! And yet I was obliged to turn a deaf ear to her cries for assistance, which to this day ring in my ears. Strong and athletic as I was, no hand of mine could be raised in her defence, but at the peril of both our lives.[49]

The lessons the slave child learned about conformity were complex and contradictory. Recognizing the overwhelming power of the whites, parents taught children obedience as a means of avoiding pain, suffering, and death. At the same

40

time, they did not teach unconditional submission. Instead, children were often taught to fight their masters and overseers to protect their relatives. For instance, W. H. Robinson's father once told him: "I want you to die in defense of your mother. . . ."[50] On many occasions the children saw their parents disobey and sometimes fight their master. Listening to stories of runaways and seeing slaves interact in the quarters, the slave child had many models of behavior. In fact, he saw his parents playing two contradictory roles. In the quarters, for example, where he saw his parents most often, his father acted like a man, castigating whites for their mistreatment of him, being a leader, protector, and provider. On the few occasions when the child saw him at work the father was obedient and submissive to his master. Sometimes children internalized both the true personality traits and the contradictory behavioral patterns of their parents. Since, however, their parents' submission was on a shallow level of convenience directed toward avoiding pain, it was less important as a model of behavior than the personality traits they exhibited in the quarters.

When a young slave received his first flogging he was usually so angry that he either wanted to run away or to seek revenge. His parents, upon hearing this, tried to dissuade him, advised him of ways to avoid future punishment, or attempted to raise his hopes.[51] After receiving his first flogging, for example, Jacob Stroyer vowed to fight the next time he was attacked. His father argued against such action, saying: "'the best thing for us to do is to pray much over it, for I believe that the time will come when this boy with the rest of the children will be free, though we may not live to see it.'" His father's comments on freedom, according to Stroyer, "were of great comfort to me, and my heart swelled with the hope of the future, which made every moment seem an hour to me."[52]

The degree to which slaves were able to give their children hope in the midst of adversity is reflected in the attitudes the black autobiographers held toward their parents. Fathers were loved and respected because of their physical strength, courage, and compassion. Austin Steward described his father as "a kind, affectionate husband and a fond, indulgent parent." James Watkins admired his father because he was "a clever, shrewd man." James Mars stood in awe of his father who "was a man of considerable muscular strength, and was not easily frightened into obedience." Although they were not always perfect male models, most slave fathers had the respect of their children. Viewing the little things that they did to make life more pleasant for their children, Charles Ball asserted: "Poor as the slave is, and dependent at all times upon the arbitrary will of his master, or yet more fickle caprice of the overseer, his children look up to him in his little cabin, as their protector and supporter."[53]

Slave mothers, were, of course, held in even greater esteem by their children. Frequently small children fought overseers who were flogging their mothers. Even when they had an opportunity to escape from bondage, many slaves refused to leave their mothers. As a young slave, William Wells Brown did not run away because he "could not bear the idea" of leaving his mother. He felt that he, "after she had undergone and suffered so much for me would be proving recreant to the duty which I owed to her."[54]

The love the slaves had for their parents reveals clearly the importance of the family. Although it was weak, although it was frequently broken, the slave family provided an important buffer, a refuge from the rigors of slavery. While the slave father could rarely protect the members of his family from abuse, he could often gain their love and respect in other ways. In his family, the slave not only learned how to avoid the blows of the master, but also drew on the love and sympathy of its members to raise his spirits. The family was, in short, an important survival mechanism.

ENDNOTES

1. Philip D. Curtin, "Epidemiology and the Slave Trade," *Political Science Quarterly* LXXXIII (June 1968), 190–216; Stanley J. Stein, *Vassouras: A Brazilian Coffee County: 1850–1900* (Cambridge, Mass., 1957); Alexander Humboldt, *Personal Narrative of Travels to the Equinoctial Regions of the New Continent, During the Years 1799–1804* (7 vols., London, 1829), VII, 276–79; Alexander Humboldt, *The Island of Cuba* (New York, 1856), 189, 203–16, 249; Carl Degler, *Neither Black nor White* (New York, 1971), 36–39.

2. *Eighth Census of the United States,* I, 594–95; *Compendium of the Seventh Census* (Washington, 1854), 87, 91. For earlier surveys of the slave family, see: Bobby F. Jones, "A Cultural Middle Passage: Slave Marriage and Family in the Ante-Bellum South" (Ph.D., University of North Carolina, 1965); Orville W. Taylor, *Negro Slavery in Arkansas* (Durham, 1958), 189–202; J. Winston Coleman, *Slavery Times in Kentucky* (Chapel Hill, 1940), 57–61; E. Franklin Frazier, *The Negro Family in the United States* (Chicago, 1948); E. Franklin Frazier, "The Negro Slave Family," *Journal of Negro History* XV (April 1930), 198–259.

3. William Wells Brown, *Narrative of William W. Brown, A Fugitive Slave* (Boston, 1847), 21–26, 80–90; James Watkins, *Narrative of The Life of James Watkins* (Bolton, England, 1852), 18–21; I. E. Lowery, *Life on the Old Plantation in Ante-Bellum Days: Or A Story Based on Facts* (Columbia, S.C., 1911), 42; William O'Neal, *Life and History of William O'Neal* (St. Louis, 1896), 33–41; James L. Smith, *Autobiography of James L. Smith* (Norwich, Connecticut, 1881), 1–9.

4. J. Carlyle Sitterson, "The William J. Minor Plantations: a Study in Ante-Bellum Absentee Ownership," *Journal of Southern History* IX (Feb. 1943), 59–74; L. Tibbetts to "Sister," Jan. 23, 1853, John C. Tibbetts Correspondence, Jan. 4, 1862. Priscilla Bond Diary, Memoranda Book No. 9, Alexandre DeClouet Papers, Louisiana State University Archives; Philip H. Jones, "Reminiscences of Days Before and After the Civil War," Southern Historical Collection, University of North Carolina; Mathilda Houston, *Hesperos* (2 vols., London, 1850), II, 157–59.

5. *Southern Agriculturalist* IX (Dec. 1836), 626.

6. Weymouth T. Jordan, "The Management Rules of an Alabama Black Belt Plantation, 1848–1862," *Agricultural History* XVIII (Jan. 1944), 64.

7. Mary W. Highsaw, "A History of Zion Community in Maury County, 1806–1860," *Tennessee Historical Quarterly* V (June 1946), 111–40; William H. Gehrke, "Negro Slavery Among the Germans in North Carolina," *North Carolina Historical Review* XIV (Oct. 1937), 304–24.

8. R. Q. Mallard, *Plantation Life Before Emancipation* (Richmond, 1892), 49.

9. *DeBow's Review* X (June 1851), 623.

10. John W. DuBose, "Recollections of the Plantations," *Alabama Historical Quarterly* I (Spring 1930), 66.

11. Brown, *Narrative,* 1–15; William Grimes, *Life of William Grimes, The Runaway Slave, Brought Down to The Present Time* (New Haven, 1855), 5–14.

12. Grimes, *Life,* 5–14; Annie L. Burton, *Memories of Childhood's Slavery Days* (Boston, 1909), 3–9; Harriet Martineau, *Retrospect of Western Travel* (3 vols., London, 1838), II, 146–48; Thomas Anburey, *Travels Through the Interior Parts of America* (London, 1789), 385; John Davis, *Travels in the United States of America 1798 to 1802* (2 vols., Boston, 1910), I, 70, II, 141;

Robert Sutcliff, *Travels in Some Parts of North America in the Years 1804, 1805 and 1806* (York, England, 1811), 53, 101; Victor Tixier, *Travels on the Osage Prairies* (Norman, Oklahoma, 1940), 97.

13. Frederick Douglass, *My Bondage and My Freedom* (New York, 1968 [1855]), 60.

14. Henry Bibb, *Narrative of the Life and Adventures of Henry Bibb, An American Slave* (New York, 1849), 98–99, 112–16; Moses Roper, *A Narrative of the Adventures And Escape of Moses Roper From American Slavery* (London, 1840), 24, 63–66; Bethany Veney, *The Narrative of Bethany Veney, A Slave Woman* (Worcester, Mass., 1889), 26.

15. Israel Campbell, *An Autobiography* (Philadelphia, 1861), 228–35; John Mercer Langston, *From the Virginia Plantation To The National Capital* (Hartford, Conn., 1894), 1–36; Jermain Wesley Loguen, *The Rev. J. W. Loguen, As A Slave And As A Freedman* (Syracuse, New York, 1859), 19–37; Jacob Stroyer, *My Life in the South* (Salem, 1890), 30–37.

16. James H. Johnston, *Race Relations in Virginia and Miscegenation in the South, 1776–1860* (Amherst, Mass., 1970), 253–56.

17. Brown, *Narrative*, 88–90; Solomon Northup, *Twelve Years A Slave* (London, 1853), 191–222; Stroyer, *My Life*, 15–20.

18. John Anderson, *The Story of the Life of John Anderson, A Fugitive Slave* (London, 1863), 129.

19. Bibb, *Adventures*, 42.

20. Moses Grandy, *Narrative of the Life of Moses Grandy* (London, 1843), 25.

21. John Brown, *Slave Life in Georgia* (London, 1855), 31–44; Lunsford Lane, *The Narrative of Lunsford Lane* (Boston, 1848), 9–16; Thomas Jones, *The Experiences of Thomas Jones, Who Was A Slave For Forty-Three Years* (Boston, 1850), 29–36; W. H. Robinson, *From Log Cabin To The Pulpit* (Eau Claire, Wis., 1913), 152–63; Charles Sealsfield, *The Americans As They Are* (London, 1828), 133; Tixier, *Travels*, 47; Amelia Murray, *Letters From the United States, Cuba and Canada* (New York, 1856), 224, 351.

22. Henry Box Brown. *Narrative of Henry Box Brown* (Boston, 1851), 57; Bibb, *Adventures*, 152.

23. Douglass, *Bondage*, 51.

24. Austin Steward, *Twenty-Two Years A Slave, and Forty Years A Freeman* (Rochester, N.Y., 1861), 18.

25. Robinson, *Pulpit*, 25.

26. Northup, *Twelve Years*, 176–90, 223–62; Loguen, *Freedman*, 19–25, 38–52; Henry Watson, *Narrative of Henry Watson, A Fugitive Slave* (Boston, 1848), 5–17; Bibb, *Adventures*, 112–18.

27. Bibb, *Adventures*, 191–92.

28. Charles Ball, *Slavery in the United States: A Narrative of the Life and Adventures of Charles Ball* (Lewiston, Pa., 1836), 15–22, 258–300; Elkanah Watson, *Men and Times of the Revolution* (New York, 1857), 69; Henry B. Whipple, *Bishop Whipple's Southern Diary* (Minneapolis, 1937), 69, 88–89; John O'Connor, *Wanderings of a Vagabond* (New York, 1873), 110.

29. Compiled from "Marriage Certificates," Bureau of Refugees, Freedmen and Abandoned Lands, Record Group 105, National Archives; see also: Amelia Murray, *Letters*, 271, 303–4; Carl D. Arfwedson, *The United States and Canada in 1832 and 1834* (2 vols., London, 1834), I, 405–6; Charles Lyell, *A Second Visit to the United States of North America* (2 vols., New York, 1850), I, 209–10.

30. J. Brown, *Slave Life*, 62–68; J. Anderson, *Story*, 8–20; Northrup, *Twelve Years*, 176–90.

31. Noah Davis, *A Narrative of the Life of Rev. Noah Davis, A Colored Man* (Baltimore, 1859), n.p.

32. Ball, *Slavery*, 168–205; Grandy, *Narrative*, 52–64.

33. William Green, *Narrative of Events In The Life of William Green* (Springfield, 1853), 9.

34. Douglass, *Bondage*, 48.

35. Booker T. Washington, *Up From Slavery* (Cambridge, 1928), 4.

36. John Thompson, *The Life of John Thompson, A Fugitive Slave* (Worcester, Mass., 1856), 13–19; J. Smith, *Autobiography*, 33; Allen Parker, *Recollections of Slavery Times* (Worcester, Mass., 1895), 32–40.

37. R. Anderson, *From Slavery*, 3–8; Stroyer, *My Life*, 15–20; Lucy Ann Delaney, *From the Darkness Cometh The Light Or Struggles For Freedom* (St. Louis, Mo., n.d.), 13; Thomas L. Johnson, *Twenty-Eight Years A Slave: Or The Story of My Life in Three Continents* (London, 1909), 2.

38. Lane, *Narrative*, 6.

39. J. Vance Lewis, *Out of the Ditch* (Houston, Texas, 1910), 8; Sam Aleckson, *Before the War and After the Union* (Boston, 1929), 113; Douglass, *Bondage*, 38, 40–41.

40. Grimes, *Life*, 8; Amanda Smith, *An Autobiography* (Chicago, 1893), 22.

41. Lewis, *Ditch*, 9; Jones, *Experience*, 5.

42. Lane, *Narrative*, 7–8.

43. Loguen, *Freedman*, 38–52, 109–22; Watson, *Narrative*, 5–17; Thompson, *Life*, 13–19; Douglass, *Bondage*, 91.

44. W. W. Brown, *Narrative*, 16.

45. Grandy, *Narrative*, 7–18; Ball, *Slavery*, 74–94; Stroyer, *My Life*, 9–14.

46. Aleckson, *Union*, 67; Elijah P. Marrs, *Life and History* (Louisville, Ky., 1855), 11.

47. Aleckson, *Union*, 17–21; Davis, *Colored Man*, 9–17; Stroyer, *My Life*, 24–29; Veney, *Woman*, 7–13.

48. H. B. Brown, *Narrative*, 16; William Webb, *The History of William Webb* (Detroit, 1873), 3.

49. Steward, *Twenty-Two Years*, 97.

50. Robinson, *Pulpit*, 25.

51. J. H. Banks, *A Narrative of Events Of The Life of J. H. Banks* (Liverpool, 1861), 20.

52. Stroyer, *My Life*, 23.

53. Steward, *Twenty-Two Years*, 126; Watkins, *Narrative*, 7; James Mars, *Life of James Mars, A Slave Born and Sold in Connecticut* (Hartford, 1864), 3; Ball, *Slavery*, 211.

54. W. W. Brown, *Narrative*, 31–32.

Frank D. Banks

Frank D. Banks was born in the nineteenth century. Banks wrote about various memories of encounters with slaves and former slaves in the *Journal of American Folklore.*

In this 1894 selection, Banks shares his memory of a conversation with Uncle Gilbert regarding habits of courtship among slaves.

Plantation Courtship*

The American slave's life was a desert of suffering certainly, but in it there were oases whose shades and springs yielded comforts whose delights were all the keener for their infrequency.

He had his holidays and his social seasons, and there were hours when, his day's task done, he poured his story of admiration and love into the ears of some

---

*Paper read before the Hampton (Va.) Folk-Lore Society, April 30, 1894.

dusky maiden whose presence brought to him a joy as sweet, perhaps sweeter, than that which his smart young master felt in the society of the free woman whom he loved and honored.

The slave girl had to be won as surely as did her fair young mistress, and her black fellow in slavery who aspired to her hand had to prove his worthiness to receive it.

Instances were not a few where the black knight laid down his life in defence of the honor of his lady-love, but of course milder proofs of worthiness were the rule.

Among the slaves there were regular forms of "courtship," and almost every large plantation had an experienced old slave who instructed young gallants in the way in which they should go in the delicate matter of winning the girls of their choice.

I have distinct recollection of "Uncle Gilbert," a bald, little, dark man, who carried his spectacles on his forehead the most of the time.

"Uncle Gilbert" was the shoemaker on a plantation where there were a hundred slaves, whose good young master, "Pete," allowed them to receive company Sundays and some evenings in the week from all the surrounding neighborhood.

What gay times there were on that plantation in the days befo' de wah!

"Uncle Gilbert" was very learned in the art of "courtship," and it was to his shop the slave lads went for instruction in "courtship's words and ways."

The old man had served a half dozen masters, had won and buried as many wives and had travelled much. It was therefore conceded by the people of all the neighborhood that nobody thereabouts was a greater authority on wooing than he.

"Uncle Gilbert" held the very generally accepted opinion that "courtin' is a mighty ticklish bizness," and that he who would "git a gal wuth havin' mus' know how to talk fur her."

I never had the honor of being one of "the old man's" pupils, being too young when I knew him to make inquiry along the courtship line, but I tracked many young men to Uncle Gilbert's shop in the interest of general gossip.

The courtship idea, of course, belongs to people of every clime and race. People only differ in expressing it.

The American slave's courtship words and forms are the result of his attempt at imitating the gushingly elegant manners and speech of his master.

Uncle Gilbert's rule of courtship was that a "young man mus' tes' an' prove a gal befo' offerin' her his han'. Ef er gal gives a man as good anser as he gives her queston, den she is all right in min'. Ef she can look him squar in de face when she talks to him, den she kin be trusted; and ef her patches is on straight, an' her close clean, den she is gwine ter keep de house straight and yer britches mended. Sich er ooman is wuth havin'."

Guy Bailey, Natalie Maynor, and Patricia Cukor-Avila

Guy Bailey (1950–) is Provost and Vice President for Academic Affairs at the University of Texas at San Antonio. Bailey has served as the head of the English department at Memphis State University and has taught at Texas A & M

University and Oklahoma State University. He was also the Dean of the College of Liberal Arts at the University of Nevada, Las Vegas. His research focuses on varieties of American English, mainly on language variation and change. He is also co-editor of *Language Variety in the South* (1986), *The Emergence of Black English* (1991), and *African-American English: Structure, History and Use* (1998).

Natalie Maynor is Professor of English at Mississippi State University. She earned a Ph.D. from the University of Tennessee, Knoxville, in 1978; her dissertation is *Joseph Beaumont's Psyche in the Seventeenth-Century Context*.

Patricia Cukor-Avila obtained her Ph.D. from the University of Michigan in 1995, where she wrote her dissertation, *The Evolution of AAVE in a Rural Texas Community: an Ethnolinguistic Study*.

The following text, collected by John Henry Faulk in 1941, is housed at the American Folklife Society in the Library of Congress. Laura Smalley was a former slave who talks about the work of black women slaves, providing insights into these women's experiences and their impact on African American families.

Laura Smalley

INFORMANT: Ten' to all the children, ten' to the children. Jus' like, you know, you bring a whole lot of children you know, an' put them down, you know, at one house. Well there somebody have to look over them you know an' ten' to them, that-a-way. Just a house full of little children. And if one act bad, you know they'd whip him, they'd whip him too, the ol' woman. An' if the ol' woman didn' ten' to the children they'd whip, they'd whip her too, you know, to make her ten' to the children, she wasn' doing nothing. Well she wasn' a cripply woman like me you know. She wasn' no ol' cripply woman, satisfied she wasn' no ol' cripply woman like me. An' they'd whip her. An' they had trays, I don' know whether you see a tray. Wooden tray, dug out you know, oh about that, that long. An' all of them, you know, would get aroun' that tray with spoons. An' just eat. I can recollect that 'cause I ate out of the tray. With spoons you know, and eat, such as like mush or soup or something like that. They'd feed them you know 'fore twelve o'clock. An' all them children get aroun' there and just eat, eat, eat, eat out of that thing. An' that ol' woman, you know, she would ten' to them. Her name Aunt T. Yeah I know that woman, ol' woman, name Aunt T. An' she [FW *interrupts*]

FIELDWORKER: Just like slopping hogs, wasn't it? [INF *interrupts*]

INF: Yes ma'am. An' they had a regular nurse, you know. Nurse, you never did see old missus with the baby, never no time. They had a regular nurse. I's like, you know, you'd hire somebody to nurse, but be a grown woman nurse, ten' to that baby. An' you'd keep him in the, never did, never did carry it to old missus, without it was hungry, night or day. Not without it was hungry. They carry it there to her. You ten' to that baby. That baby slep' with the ol' nurses an' all.

FW: Huh.

INF: Yes sir. Slep' with them. Didn't have nothing to do. Carry that baby an', uh, an' uh, sit there until uh, he'd till, uh, he'd nurse. An' then after he'd nurse, you know, then you carry it back, ten' to it. She didn' have to, jus', she ten' to it you know an' give it to you. You go give it to her an' nurse it, don' care how col' it is, an' you carry that baby back on in that bed, that room where you was. An' I know [FW *interrupts*]

FW: Well did the mistress nurse the baby, or did she have?

INF: She, she nurse from the breast.

FW: Uh huh.

INF: But see see, she'd nurse this baby that, that he would be hungry. Well this here nurse would bring it to her. An' let her nurse it, an' then when she'd nurse she'd han' it right back, night or day . . .

FW2:   Tell me about the business of, of, uh, taking, carrying some of the Negroes, the good hands, you know, and good women, good men going off and breeding them like cattle. Do you remember anything about that?

INF: No'm. I didn' know any, you see, they wouldn' let children know of that, you know. But I heard it after. After that they'd do that. But see, when we was coming up they wouldn' let us know nothing 'bout like that. But they say that was sure so. You know, jus' like a big fine looking woman, big fine looking man, you know, old boss wants, you know, children from them, you know. They just fasten them up in the house or somewhere, you know, and go on off and leave them in there. Wan' to breed them like they was hogs or horses something like that I say. . . .

FW: Have you ever been down in the Brazos Bottoms any?

INF: Me? Yes sir. I stayed down in the Brazos Bottom. Leas' I didn' say stay right down in it, but then see I worked down there. I worked down there a-cropping there. An' when I moved over here, I jus' move out of the bottom, working on it, right on the banks of the river. Yes sir.

FW: Bet you ya'll made some crops down there.

INF: Yes sir. Couldn', I couldn' uh go close to the river on accoun' of, you know, afraid the horses would get scared, look down in the river an' run off with me. An' I use' to plow. Yeah, I would work down there in that Brazos Bottom.

FW: On whose place was you working, at P.'s?

INF: No, I, I'd been working on P.'s, but I working then on, on uh, the B. place. They call it the B. place. Uh, orphan, you know, uh, orphan children I call it. They had will it to orphan children. Then, they call it the B. place, had willed it to the orphan children, schools, you know. An' that's where I worked, 'bout four or five years. Down there on the B. place.

FW: Well, they're claiming some parts of the Bottoms they won't let the folks leave the place they living on. Colored folks. You know just make them stay there and work year after year, to pay their debt.

INF: Yes well, well, that must be some, way down in the Bottom somewhere. Well that uh, down there on the uh, B. place, they, some places was. They'd let you go jus' as far in debt as you wan' to go you know. An' then see, uh, uh, they,

they know your crop wasn' gonna, gonna clear it you know, an' then, then so next year you'd have to stay an' work out your debt. If you didn', you know, they'd take all your horses, cows an' everything away from you.

FW2: And leave you with nothing.   20

INF: Yeah, leave you with nothing. You see, tha's why they, they keep them there, you know, that way. So they, you know, they could get everything they had if they didn' work. And wouldn' wait for some of them. They jus' take an' give everything they had up, and go on off. Give everything up. They see you is going, sure enough, they'd beg you to stay, you know. Another year, get anything you wanted, any kin' of money. But now you gonna stay there next year 'cause your crop ain' gonna clear it, you know, ain' gonna clear it. They'd let you stay. An' feed you to the highest. An' I have children like this girl here, jus' any kind of dress she wanted, they'd let you take it up. But now when the crop come, they take every bit of that crop. You wouldn't have nothing to live on, uh, uh, live on, you know, nex' year till, nex' year come. Well, they open account right there before Christmas, you know, get jus' what you wanted. Tha's the way they'd do, in places over there. But they was sure fine white folks over there, where they work at. . . .

Etheridge Knight

Etheridge Knight (1931–1991) enlisted in the Army at seventeen and served from 1947 to 1951 as a medical technician. He got hooked on drugs in the service after being wounded. Convicted of robbery to support his narcotics habit in 1960, Knight served a 10 to 25-year indeterminate sentence in Indiana State Prison until 1968. He started a career as a poet while in prison, sending out poetry to publishers. He corresponded with and received visits from such established African American literary figures as Gwendolyn Brooks and Dudley Randall, who published his first book, *Poems from Prison* (1968), one year before Knight was released from prison. Knight became a member of the Black Arts Movement during the Black Power Era. His other works include *Black Voices from Prison* (1970), *Belly Song and Other Poems* (1973), *Born of a Woman: New and Selected Poems* (1980), and *The Essential Etheridge Knight* (1986). Knight was nominated for a Pulitzer Prize and National Book Award for *Belly Song* in 1973. He received an NEH grant in 1972 and was a Guggenheim Fellow in 1974.

The following poem, "The Idea of Ancestry," comes from the *Poems from Prison* collection. In it, a convict praises the extended family whose pictures adorn his jail cell.

The Idea of Ancestry

1

Taped to the wall of my cell are 47 pictures: 47 black
faces: my father, mother, grandmothers (1 dead), grand
fathers (both dead), brothers, sisters, uncles, aunts,

cousins (1st & 2nd), nieces, and nephews. They stare
across the space at me sprawling on my bunk. I know   5
their dark eyes, they know mine. I know their style,
they know mine. I am all of them, they are all of me;
they are farmers, I am a thief, I am me, they are thee.

I have at one time or another been in love with my mother,
1 grandmother, 2 sisters, 2 aunts (1 went to the asylum),   10
and 5 cousins. I am now in love with a 7 yr old niece
(she sends me letters written in large block print, and
her picture is the only one that smiles at me).

I have the same name as 1 grandfather, 3 cousins, 3 nephews,
and 1 uncle. The uncle disappeared when he was 15, just took 15
off and caught a freight (they say). He's discussed each year
when the family has a reunion, he causes uneasiness in
the clan, he is an empty space. My father's mother, who is 93
and who keeps the Family Bible with everybody's birth dates
(and death dates) in it, always mentions him. There is no   20
place in her Bible for "whereabouts unknown."

2

Each Fall the graves of my grandfathers call me, the brown
hills and red gullies of mississippi send out their electric
messages, galvanizing my genes. Last yr/like a salmon quitting
the cold ocean—leaping and bucking up his birthstream/I   25
hitchhiked my way from L. A. with 16 caps in my pocket and a
monkey on my back, and I almost kicked it with the kinfolks.
I walked barefooted in my grandmother's backyard/I smelled
    the old
land and the woods/I sipped cornwhiskey from fruit jars with the 30
    men/
I flirted with the women/I had a ball till the caps ran out
and my habit came down. That night I looked at my grand
    mother
and split/my guts were screaming for junk/but I was almost   35
contented/I had almost caught up with me.
(The next day in Memphis I cracked a croaker's crib for a fix.)

This yr there is a gray stone wall damming my stream, and
    when
the falling leaves stir my genes, I pace my cell or flop on my   40
    bunk
and stare at 47 black faces across the space. I am all of them,
they are all of me, I am me, they are thee, and I have no sons
to float in the space between.

Joseph Beam

Joseph Beam (1954–1988) was committed to getting African American gay men and lesbians to organize politically. Heavily involved in the National Coalition of Black Gays, he was also interested in black gay male solidarity. His groundbreaking book *In the Life* (1986) was the first black gay anthology published. *Brother to Brother: New Writings by Black Gay Men,* edited by Essex Hemphill and Joseph Beam (1991), was published following Beam's death.

In this chapter from *In the Life,* Beam interviews a gay black man who adopted a child.

Color Him Father

An Interview

Sometimes during idle chit-chat, as we recount the events of an evening out, we say: the kids were too fierce, or the children wore me out, I forget that we are not talking about young people, but our peers. I have only recently realized and felt the absence in my life of "real children" who question everything and approach the simplest things with an excitement I have difficulty mustering. As a gay man, the choices I have to fill this need to nurture children and have them be a significant part of my life are myriad. I may choose big brother surrogating, fatherhood, childcare work, or adoption. "Bernard," an articulate man in his mid-forties, who lives in the Powelton Village section of Philadelphia, chose adoption. He shares his story:

Well, I decided to adopt a child for the main reason that my family is in the South. I come from a family of five brothers and sisters who are all very close. We are close to our parents, and there are a large number of nieces and nephews. I was the youngest and single one up until I was thirty-four or thirty-five and missed that kind of family connection. Since marriage was not an option I'd chosen to take, adoption seemed to be a more viable choice.

I had worked with kids in the classroom at that point for about 12 years, so I was pretty familiar with and very much attached to kids. I spent a lot of time, weekends and holidays with my children from school, and spent most summers with kids at camp. So there was that attachment to children, that need to be with them, do for them, and get back from them a great deal. So adoption seemed to be a logical kind of choice to me.

I didn't identify myself as a gay man when I approached the adoption agency. In fact, I went back to them for a second child, so my relationship with them lasted for four or five years. The question of my sexuality never arose, and if it had I'm not sure what I would have done. This is a real issue. Openly gay men, I think, would be rejected. If not formally, then for all practical purposes they would be, because their applications would simply be frozen by most agencies.

I considered many things before choosing to adopt: what kind of future can I offer a child; how will this affect my social life and relationships with friends. I also thought about how I would deal with my sexuality with my prospective adopted children. I was committed from the outset to discussing it openly with them when I felt they were ready. So when the time did arrive it was not a trauma for me, as I think it could have been had I not prepared. I had even discussed my plan with a professional and he concurred with my position.

My older son, who is 16, has had some problems with my gayness; my younger son, who is 12, has not. But my older son is the more troubled of the two, the more scarred of the two as a result of rejection by his natural mother. So his acceptance of me is very much a part of the kinds of problems he is going through. The younger son, very naturally, is accepting.

Their friends seem to like me very much and are comfortable with me. I have always been the one neighborhood father who was always available to take the boys swimming or to a scout meeting. I have always been a parent who attended the home and school meetings. And I'm *always* the one available during the summer for drinks of water and emergency phone calls.

Both my friends and family have been very supportive from the beginning. They were supportive when I originated the idea, very supportive during the early stages, and have continued to be supportive. Except for my father, who also had some problems handling my sexuality as well.

Over the years, I have noticed a difference between friendships that were basically social and those that were more personal and intimate. The former kind of friend has fallen by the wayside, while my really close friends have adjusted to me, because it's more difficult for me to make certain kinds of adjustments. The close friends have continued to be "aunts" and "uncles" to the boys and are very special to them.

I don't have a lover and I'm not sure I want that kind of loving relationship. I've been involved with one man during the course of the boys' presence and it did not pose any problems. But I didn't allow the relationship to overpower my life. The relationship was adjusted to my life and I think this can cause a problem. It has with other gay fathers that I know, and in one particular instance, destroyed both relationships because there was such a great degree of jealousy. Now whether that is greater or lesser than what would have occurred in a heterosexual relationship—I don't know.

My sexuality is only a product of with whom I go to bed; it does not *pervade* my life 24 hours a day. And *that* to me is a mistake that many people seem to make. It's like immersing oneself in any subculture—total Blackness or whatever. There's an obvious danger: I think one can lose perspective.

I've had my good times and I've gone to the parties. I did all that! And had an enormous amount of fun doing so! I would never undo or deprecate how much I enjoyed those years, but that's behind me, that was a different stage.

I'm a parent now. Parenting and being gay is not different than parenting and being heterosexual. Just as I don't think that single parenting is that different than parenting as a couple. I think to some extent that the highs and lows, as a gay parent, might be higher and lower, but basically there is no real difference. A single parent or gay parent must be resourceful in terms of community, planning things for the kids, exposing things to the kids, because there's only one of you, and you've got the responsibility of the cooking, cleaning, shopping, checking homework, washing, ironing, and all that sort of stuff. So you've got to be well organized or you become bogged down in the whole thing and it becomes a chore.

Do I want my sons to be gay? Oh—I want them to be whatever is natural for them and when talking with them have made this very clear. You have a choice to make, that I didn't have and you may not either—but be whatever it is that is natural for you to be.

The interview with "Bernard" took place in August 1984 and originally appeared in the Philadelphia Gay News *(10/25/84), as part of an interview trilogy called "Speaking for Ourselves." I attempted to contact him in May and June 1985 in hopes of having an expanded version to appear in this anthology. I called his phone number in another state, where I was told by a member of his family that he had died. Because I was uncertain (whether) he was out to his family, I gave my condolences and hung up. I later found out that he had suffered a heart attack. His older son is living with a family member; the younger son is being placed through an adoption agency.*

Elizabeth Clark-Lewis

Elizabeth Clark-Lewis is a historian, genealogist, and professor at Howard University. As director of Howard's Public History Program, she offers courses on museums and archives, oral history, and historic preservation, including a seminar in the field. She also teaches about genealogical research, family history, and genealogy. She has published books and articles on these subjects, among them *This Work Had a' End: The Transition from Live-In to Day Work* (1985), *First Freed: Emancipation in the District of Columbia* (1998), and *Living In, Living Out: African American Domestics in Washington, D.C.* (1994, paperback 1996). She is a winner of the Letitia Brown Prize in Women's History.

In this excerpt from *Living In, Living Out,* "A Woman Just Wouldn't," Clark-Lewis interviews women who talk about the ways that African American women attempted to combat the negative stereotypes extending from slavery by making careful distinctions between men's and women's labor. They also discuss the impact of these stereotypes on their daughters.

A Woman Just Wouldn't

African American women have always constituted an important labor sector in the rural South. During slavery, white owners fully exploited women who worked as field laborers, household laborers, breeders, and objects of white male sexuality. This legacy of social and occupational exploitation had a powerful impact on the societal perceptions of African American women. Conveniently overlooking its instrumental role in determining women slaves' lives, Southern white society considered female slave agricultural workers debased, degraded, and masculinized because they had entered a traditionally male labor environment. This view resulted in the social judgment that women who worked in the fields were unworthy of preferential treatment, or of the title "lady."[1]

In the aftermath of slavery, African American women fought to destroy the vestiges of slavery's denigration and devaluation of their own labor and social status. They felt keenly the burden of the negative stereotypes that they were sexually loose, masculine, dirty, and undignified. To combat the personal stigma of their purported masculinity, women were careful to distinguish their labor from that of men. Eula Montgomery remembered clear differences for women's work in her Alabama hometown:

> It was the same but different. Women could do anything. But generally they didn't do some things. A woman wouldn't just pick up and hunt game. Or do too much building on a house or trapping game—like that. They be the ones to help in a home or field; maid work, I mean, for jobs out in places like Nixburg and Cottage Grove [Alabama]. If they were alone, like a widow, a brother, cousin—some man'd do for them. If not, they made do or just try to do some things themselves.

Isetta Peters spoke about her difficult childhood as the eldest of ten children. Born north of Hickory, South Carolina, to a tenant farm family, she revealed that the women were busy

> doing . . . mostly home things. Cooking, cleaning, caring for young or old in a house. Then they'd do field work and garden. Now when I was young you'd never see a woman hunt. After we moved to North Carolina, I never saw a woman do butchering. They'd never do fixing on a wagon or maybe smithing. Some did if they had to now. I once saw Miss Daisy Lucas's horse throw a shoe. Now she'd just delivered a baby. She went back and put the horseshoe on. Herself. But generally real heavy work would be done by a man or a boy with some size on him—fourteen, fifteen, like that.

On the Arkansas farm where Frances Pollard grew up, some jobs were handled by both sexes, but child care followed a particular pattern:

> Anybody did what was to be done. Boys had to help wash; girls did field work and carried some of the wood for a fire. Everybody'd just put in and did in Back Gate [Arkansas].
> If it was a young family this is what—down home—people would do. Your aunt, big cousin, somebody in the family would keep you while Ma worked. Now my Aunt Til kept us [and everybody around there so that the adults] could work. . . . No man would do that—just keeping children. If they was his or other people's—he'd not go place-to-place keeping people's childrens so they could work.

A blushing Velma Davis recalled only one job she was never allowed to perform in Virginia:

> One thing would ruin a girl for life—having children and all [cause infertility]. So, I know a woman or girl never did only one thing. We never went into the ice house to get ice. My father, uncle, or brother went in to get ice. There you wouldn't go . . . not handling ice no matter when, and we had ice the whole year too. My uncle or father would get it off the pond below the house, put it in the ice house in blocks and it'd be there in July. But I never could touch or handle ice.

She also remembered an incident that clearly showed what jobs were women's and not to be performed by men or boys:

> Now on the farm, about five minutes to or quarter to twelve, they say, Velma, go ring the bell. My aunt and mother was preparing the food and they told me to ring the bell. Now I was the oldest girl, and I had to go out there and take a piece of iron and bang on an old piece of railroad tie. Don't you know, wherever they was on the farm they'd hear that bell and they'd come first thing . . . water the horses, feed the horses, and come in an eat. Once my cousin did it and he was in trouble. He got told straight that was not a job a boy or man ever did.

If women rarely performed "men's work" at home, their hard labor both within and outside the home sometimes took a toll on their relationship with their children and with their family in general. All of the women proclaimed that whereas their fathers were often playful and attentive, their mothers were more austere and showed little or no affection toward them. From the time they could walk, life for their mothers had been synonymous with hard labor. Cassie Hackney, thoughtful and mentally clear in spite of a body weakened by a recent illness, has an angular, dark brown face. She remembered her mother as a stern woman who rarely smiled. Exchanges of tender feelings, words, or moments were not a part of her experience of the mother-child relationship. As she recalled her early years in Ashe County, North Carolina, her deeply wrinkled face registered pain: "My mother never played with her children like a mother is supposed to do. She never did. To her we were there to work and mind grown people. We said so little right to her. At most we said, 'Ma,' and better had said that carefully!"

Cassie Hackney's mother, Odella Ingraham, had worked on the nearby farm of a family as a live-in cook and nursemaid for a white lady named Miss Jennie. During the periods that she was separated from the home, her mother-in-law, Ida Jacobs, took care of the children and managed the family's small tenant farm. The birth of twins Mary Louise and Cassie had complicated Ida's life; and Cassie Hackney insisted that Odella particularly disliked the twins because, becoming too much for Ida to handle, she had to leave her live-in job and return home to help raise them.

Another twin, Marie Jefferies Stone (she and her twin brother were the twenty-third and twenty-fourth children of Peter and Eliza Jefferies), vividly recalled that her mother "never stopped working. She always had so many things to do, and even more things than that for you to do." Marie's mother, Eliza, had the primary responsibility for rearing the children, cleaning the farmhouse, cooking, doing laundry, sewing, and cultivating the family garden—while "being pregnant every year for twenty-three years, when you count the miscarriages and babies that died!" Eliza Jefferies was an industrious farm wife who sold eggs, fresh vegetables, and hand-sewn clothing and took in laundry to supplement her husband's small income. Marie recalled her mother working "when we got up and long after she'd put the children to bed." Her mother possessed a perpetually severe and uncompromising countenance. Marie Stone, always buoyant and sociable, laughed as she admitted knowing very little about her mother's employment outside the home before she was born. Marie was often told that her mother worked outside the home, "by the week until her fourth child was born." She was able to work as far away as Brightwood, Virginia, because her mother-in-law watched her young children. Eliza Jefferies believed in strict discipline for all her children, but she was hardest on her daughters: "My mother was strict, but with the girls she had no sympathy at all. To me she was a person who always felt nothing in life was worth looking at." Although Marie never stated that her mother was unduly harsh to her children, she did express a strong regret that she did not have a more intimate and caring relationship with her.[2]

Many women sounded a similar note of regret. Fannie King, for example, remarked that when mothers in rural Mississippi spoke, it was only "to give you directions: how to work, when to work, and what more to do when you did all that! That's the most she ever said to us. Period!" Despite her mother's consternation, however, Cassie Hackney remembered growing up surrounded by the laughter of her eight brothers and sisters on the farm of their caretaker, Miss Edith Moore. Miss Moore took special pride in the twins because they were born in the same month as her own youngest daughter's only surviving set of twins, and she personally prided herself on how well the Hackney twins "got on and grew up so nicely—from the first." Cassie Hackney described Miss Moore's home as "a place where I had real fun. When I think of good times down home—that's the place where I remember. We'd play around and have fun. We'd go behind the house or down near the spring and just laugh, tell jokes, and have a good time." But that ended quickly when "somebody'd miss you and call you to do what you come here for . . . work." As early as age four, Cassie "helped with the wash, picked the small plants in the garden, and helped to mind the babies." She carried clean wash and rinse water and fed the chickens.

By the age of seven, Marie Stone was considered "nearly trained up." Every morning, when she got up from the large bed she shared with her four sisters, she walked to the opposite side of the large living room/dining room/kitchen to "wash off in the tin pail of clean water." After washing off and eating a breakfast "of mostly molasses and cornmeal," she would begin to clear the table and wash the dishes. Then she would make the "girls'" bed and tote in the water for washing clothes. After washing, she might work in the garden, or in the field with her grandmother. After morning chores, she would help with the main meal for the day: "Supper was a soup or stew with a piece of meat in it for taste, some meal bread, and that was about all. Every so often you'd have some fish in the dinner. Not often. Mostly just a piece of fat meat."

After helping serve supper, she would pick berries in summer or sort dry beans in the winter. All year soap was made, starch mixed, and food was processed by canning or drying. She also helped fold the clothes her mother ironed. There might be wood to be brought into the house, ashes to be sorted and saved for soap, and freshly ironed clothes to be delivered to nearby farms in Culpeper County, Virginia. Animals had to be tended. Four younger children had to be changed and fed. Floors needed sweeping. In the evening, after dinner, each of the smaller children had to be bathed before bed. More wood had to be carried in for the morning breakfast, and often garden food had to be shelled, washed, and placed in water to soak for the next day's meals.

By age nine, Marie could cook, clean, and care for the entire interior of a house and mash "wrinkles out of most pieces sent by whites to be laundered and returned." Outside, she could wash, boil, and hang clothes out to dry. In the field she could plant, weed, and harvest most crops. All of the women were fully introduced to the responsibilities of farm life before the few short years they would attend the poor, segregated schools in the rural South.

Velma Davis, who spent all of her childhood at the rear of the white landowner's house in Nelson County, Virginia, had been born prematurely and the "first child come a girl." Her father was close to her and often treated her "like a boy—with a lot of talk and play from morning on as we worked." As a small child, she remembered she woke up in the morning and walked to the main kitchen in the "big house" to eat breakfast. Her mother and two aunts would serve the children breakfast. Then she would wash, scald, dry, and put away the dishes and sweep the porch and floors with a homemade broom. Every other day was wash day, and she would fill up all the water pails, tin and wooden tubs, and, in the yard, a "big old wash pot where they heated the water."

"Mama made a fire," Velma said, "and we carried the hot water and poured that in the tubs as they washed, using soap they made with lye. The clothes had to be washed, boiled, taken out of the boiling water, put in the first rinse water, the second rinse water, and then the bluing water." On the days there was no washing to be done she had to clean up the "lock room" (pantry): "The flour was there—barrels—big barrels—wooden barrels full of flour. And one barrel full of meal. My uncles and father was farmers who worked hard, and they wanted to make sure that lock room was cleaned right." Then she made all the beds in the big house, "except the owner of the farm's bed [Mr. Mitchell]. His bed had to be just so. My mother made that one—it had to look just as smooth as this couch." The children were then sent to the field— to carry water from the spring to those who had been working there since before the children had awakened. In the late morning, the children picked vegetables or fruit from the groves on the farms. She closed her eyes as she envisioned her past: 10

> There were two or three gardens to be worked each and every day God sent. My mother and aunt prepared the meal for everyone on the farm. It would be maybe a piece of meat with vegetables and hot bread. A little more on Sunday, a slice of sweetcake maybe. The men would break and go back to work by two o'clock. The women would do sewing on each day and ironing on the days they didn't wash.
>
> Each day my cousin Richard and I would go out and bring the cows in. We'd get the cows in, wash our hands, and milk the cow. And some old grown person would come along and tell us to get back and strip the cow good—go back and strip her good—get all the milk out.

Then she would go to Piney River, Virginia, carrying milk, butter, eggs, and vegetables from their garden. And when she returned, she'd have money—"just about the only money my whole family'd see." And this she did every other day. What was she doing at night?

> Sitting down shelling green peas or stringing green beans to take to the market. And we churned. What you talking about? Me and my cousin churned. Just soon as we finished that milk and butter, they'd put in some more. And we had to churn that too. We'd be having our fireside chat with Mr. Mitchell 'bout then, while we did our handwork—picking beans, cleaning potatoes, or whatever we was told. And, like I said—other than church, his words was the law. Now he didn't meddle with church.

ENDNOTES

1. Bell Hooks, *Ain't I a Woman: Black Women and Feminism* (Boston, Mass.: South End Press, 1981), 48–49, 62; Joe M. Richardson, *The Negro in Reconstruction in Florida* (Tallahassee: Florida State University Press, 1965), 63; Paula Giddings, *When And Where I Enter: The Impact of Black Women on Race and Sex in America* (New York: W. Morrow, 1984), 60–66, 185; and Leon Litwack, *Been in the Storm* (New York: Knopf, 1979), 244–45. On the Southern idealization of "the white Lady" and femininity, see Kathleen M. Blee, *Women of the Klan: Racism and Gender in the 1920's* (Berkeley and Los Angeles: University of California Press, 1991), 41–48; Glenna Matthews, *Just A Housewife: The Rise and Fall of Domesticity in America* (New York: Oxford University Press, 1987), 193–94; Jane Flax, "Postmodernism and Gender Relations in Feminist Theory," *Signs* 12 (Summer 1987): 621–43; Phyllis Marynick Palmer, "White Women/Black Women," 151–70; Judith Stacey, "The New Conservative Feminism," *Feminist Studies* 9 (Fall 1983): 559–84; Doris Davenport, "The Pathology of Racism: A Conversation with Third World Wimmin," in *This Bridge Called My Back: Writings by Radical Women of Color,* ed. Cherríe Moraga and Gloria Anzaldua (Watertown, Mass.: Persephone Press, 1981), 88; Jacquelyn Dowd Hall, "'The Mind That Burns in Each Body': Women, Rape, and Racial Violence"; Barbara Omolade, "Hearts of Darkness," in *Powers of Desire: The Politics of Sexuality,* ed. Ann Snitow, Christine Stansell, and Sharon Thompson (New York: Monthly Review Press, 1983), 328–49, 350–67; and Sara Ruddick, "Material Thinking," *Feminist Studies* 6 (Summer 1980): 342–67. For nineteenth-century beliefs in leisured ladyhood, Faye Dudden, *Serving Women: Household Service in Nineteenth-Century America* (Middletown, Conn.: Wesleyan University Press, 1983). Dudden shows how the mistress-servant relationship evolved and that servants enabled middle-class women to lead feminist movements. See also Minrose C. Gwin, *Black and White Women of the Old South: The Peculiar Sisterhood in American Literature* (Knoxville: University of Tennessee Press, 1985), 4–14, 46; Rosemary Daniell, *Fatal Flowers: On Sin, Sex, and Suicide in the Deep South* (New York: Avon Books, 1984), 17; Catherine Clinton, *Plantation Mistress,* x–xv, 6–15, 202–4; and Lawrence N. Powell, *New Masters: Northern Planters During the Civil War and Reconstruction* (New Haven, Conn.: Yale University Press, 1980), 218.

2. This regret was one expressed by many other young women during the Victorian period of the late nineteenth century. But the distance she experienced was in many ways determined by the cultural, economic, and social constraints of her family's situation.

Farai Chideya

Farai Chideya (1969–), who received her B.A. from Harvard University, is a journalist and author. She has worked as a researcher and reporter for *Newsweek,* 1990–1994; assignment editor for MTV News, 1994–1996; political analyst for CNN, 1996–1997; ABC News correspondent, 1997–1999; host of *Pure Oxygen* for Oxygen Media, 1999–; and syndicated columnist for the *Los Angeles Times* since 2000. She also runs a website titled *Pop and Politics,* reflecting current events and American diversity. She frequently does political commentary on BET News and the CNN, MSNBC, and Fox networks. Chideya's *Don't Believe the Hype: Fighting Cultural Misinformation about African Americans* (1995) shattered stereotypes about African Americans.

In "The Myth of the Welfare Queen," Chapter 4 from *Don't Believe the Hype,* Chideya explores the stereotype of the black woman as welfare mother.

The Myth of the Welfare Queen

Some women on welfare are more concerned by the feeding of their drug habit than by the gut instinct to feed their children.
          —A STATEMENT BY CONGRESSWOMAN NANCY JOHNSON OF CONNECTICUT.[1]

Smith is a walking statistic: a single welfare mother of five who dropped out of high school at seventeen, pregnant with her first child.
          —FROM AN ARTICLE IN THE NEW YORK NEWSPAPER *NEWSDAY.*[2]

Just as black men are stereotyped as criminals, black women in the American media are typecast as welfare mothers. America's newspapers are filled with images of slovenly, ne'er-do-well women and their multitudes of children—families who are nearly always African-American. Yet this image is startlingly at odds with the majority of families receiving Aid to Families with Dependent Children (AFDC), or welfare. Although the welfare crisis is very real, it is nothing like the social and financial armageddon described by its critics. In fact, most women who are forced to rely for a time on welfare work for a living most of the time, and the AFDC program is less than one percent of the entire federal budget.

The stereotype of the "welfare queen" has a clear racial component. Although nearly all of the women pictured in stories on welfare are black, blacks and non-Hispanic whites constitute a virtually equal number of women receiving assistance. (When the figures are broken down by race alone and not ethnicity, as they are in many census listings, whites constitute the solid majority of those on welfare.) So why the pervasive stereotyping? One problem is geography—another is journalistic myopia. White women on welfare tend to live in the suburbs and in rural areas, farther from reporters' eyes. Even when articles and broadcasts state that women on welfare are of all races, they often slip up on visuals. An April 12, 1992 segment of "This Week with David Brinkley" paid lip service to the issue of race by stating: "Most welfare recipients are white, not black; most live in the suburbs, not the inner city; and the notion that they live high is nonsense. . . . Nevertheless, the image of 'welfare queens' getting a free ride on society's back persists." Then the segment proceeded to illustrate welfare with repeated images of inner-city blacks. Politicians regularly rely on welfare as an explanation for all urban ills. In 1992, White House chief of staff Marlon Fitzwater said that the "Great Society" programs begun in the sixties (which include everything from Head Start to welfare) were a cause of the Los Angeles riots.[3]

Welfare is an easy target for both racial and non-racial smears because it has come to symbolize a sort of anti-American Dream, a complete lack of work ethic and responsibility. Americans see welfare as giving money to people who are somehow unworthy or undeserving. One *New York Times*/CBS News poll asked people about assistance for the poor: two-thirds said there was too little. But when those polled were asked about welfare, only 23 percent said the amount of assistance was too little.[4] In fact, the typical woman on welfare is someone who has worked and will work most of her life, has only one or two children, and uses welfare as a fallback when she's unemployed.

▓ Top Twenty Facts: The Real Face of Welfare

RACE

1. The population of families on AFDC covers all races. Thirty-nine percent of the families receiving welfare are black; 38 percent are non-Hispanic white; 17 percent are Hispanic, and 3 percent are Asian.
2. In a strict racial breakdown, the majority of welfare recipients are white.[5]
3. Hispanic origin is an ethnicity and not a race. Some Hispanic-Americans choose not to mark a race on census forms; 90 percent of those who do designate a race select white.

OVERALL NUMBERS

4. In 1991, there were 4,374,708 families on welfare.[6]
5. In the midst of the recession, in 1992 the welfare rolls topped a record five million families.[7]

FAMILY SIZE

6. The average family on welfare consists of a woman and two young children.[8]
7. Over 40 percent of families on AFDC have only one child, as opposed to less than 4 percent with five or more children.[9]
8. Over 60 percent of children who receive welfare are five years old or less.[10]
9. Men are 11 percent of the adults on welfare.[11]
10. Fifty-three percent of children on welfare come from families where the parents never married; 33 percent come from broken marriages.[12]

TEEN MOTHERS

11. Over two-thirds of women on welfare are between the ages of twenty and thirty-four. Less than 9 percent are teenagers; less than 2 percent are under the age of 18.[13]

DURATION OF BENEFITS

12. Families receiving welfare have been on assistance for an average of twenty-two months.[14]
13. Over half of families have been on the rolls for two years or less, and only 20 percent of families have been on welfare for more than five years.[15]

BENEFITS RECEIVED

14. The average payment for a family of three was a mere $388 per month or $4,656 per year—less than half of the $10,860 poverty level.[16]
15. The average monthly income for AFDC households of three (which includes all types of benefits plus any earned income) was $456—still just half of poverty-level income for a family of three.[17]

16. Eight percent of families on AFDC also earned income, averaging $330 per month.[18]

17. Some surveys have shown that many women on welfare do work in the under- [20] ground economy—baby-sitting children, sewing, working off the books. Currently, women who work legally have their welfare checks reduced by the same amount as their earnings, providing little incentive to find employment. And those who work off the books are considered welfare cheats, even if their income is meager. The federal officials orchestrating welfare reform are considering ways to encourage poor women, even those who earn sub-poverty incomes, to enter or stay in the workforce.[19]

18. In 1972, a woman with income totaling three-fourths of the poverty level could have supplemented her earnings with AFDC in most states. Today, she can no longer get assistance.[20]

HOUSING

19. The vast majority of families receiving welfare live in private housing and receive no rent subsidies. Less than 10 percent live in public housing.[21]

CHILD POVERTY

20. The U.S. child poverty rate is twice that in Canada, and four times that of most Western European nations.[22]

ENDNOTES

1. Jason DeParle, "Plan for Welfare Limits Questioned about Its Own," *New York Times* (11/17/93).

2. D. J. Hill, "Proud but Often Powerless, Wyandanch Residents Try to Stabilize Their Community," *New York Newsday* (9/23/90).

3. Michael Wines, "White House Links Riots to Welfare," *New York Times* (5/5/92).

4. Robin Toner, "Politics of Welfare: Focusing on the Problems," *New York Times* (7/5/92).

5. U.S. Department of Health and Human Services, *Characteristics and Financial Circumstances of AFDC Recipients: Fiscal Year 1991* (1993).

6. Ibid, p. 5.

7. DeParle, "Plan for Welfare Limits Questioned About Its Own."

8. *Characteristics and Financial Circumstances of AFDC Recipients: Fiscal Year 1991*, pp. 1–4.

9. Ibid.

10. Ibid., p. 1.

11. Ibid., p. 2.

12. Ibid., p. 1.

13. Ibid., p. 42.

14. Ibid., pp. 1–4.

15. Ibid.

16. Ibid., pp. 2–3, 9; and U.S. Department of Commerce, table on poverty threshold, 1991 figures, *The Statistical Abstract of the United States: 1993*, p. 441.

17. Ibid.

18. Ibid.

19. Associated Press, "A New View on Welfare, Work," *Chicago Tribune* (7/9/93).

20. Isaac Shapiro and Robert Greenstein, "Selective Prosperity: Increasing Income Disparities Since 1977," (Washington, D.C.: The Center on Budget and Policy Priorities, July 1991).

21. *Characteristics and Financial Circumstances of AFDC Recipients: Fiscal Year 1991*, pp. 1–4.

22. Shapiro and Greenstein, "Selective Prosperity: Increasing Income Disparities Since 1977."

Anna Mulrine

Anna Mulrine, in the following article, "In Praise of Black Family Reunions," counters the stereotype of dysfunctional extended African American families by showing one of the family traditions that is very alive today.

In Praise of Black Family Reunions

The black family reunion is a peculiarly American phenomenon, made necessary by itinerant forebears. In Bowie, Md., recently, the Walcott family stood hand in hand as Aunt Lucille recited the blessing. Her prayer of thanks for strong parents ended with a command: "Now go love each other." That's what the 12 children of Jack and Edna Walcott (ranging in age from 50 to 72), 47 grandchildren, and 50-plus great-grandchildren came to do, from Zambia, England, Canada, Texas, Alabama, and New York. Among the oldest generation at the reunion, it was the most Walcotts who had been in one place since the youngest left their birth home in Guyana, South America, 37 years ago.

While black families have been having reunions for over 50 years, most have been initiated only in the last generation. Until the 1960s, many African Americans who lived in Northern cities regarded their Southern homesteads as oppressive places they needed to leave behind, spiritually as well as physically. But as the abolition of Jim Crow laws ended the humiliation of riding in the back of the bus on the journey home, and as black student leaders pressed for black-studies programs, black churches in the South began to lead members in a search for their heritage. African-Americans who had left for the North in the 1940s and '50s were drawn to seek the Southern roots and families they had left behind. In 1977, Alex Haley's *Roots* aired on television and harnessed the medium's power to stir those quests. Partly as a result, there's been a reversal of an old pattern: For nearly a generation, more black Americans have moved to the South than have left.

Counting Blessings

More reunions have been happening every year as well. Genealogy is a middle-class pursuit, among whites and others as well as blacks; reunions are dependent on family success. For blacks especially, reunions are a chance to assert that they have a history different from the stereotype of black families broken down.

But at the heart of the reunion movement is a conviction that while families should count their blessings, they must also share them to keep other parts of the family from crumbling. And as reunions progress to greater levels of organization—first with family newsletters, then family chapters, eventually with family officers and bylaws—families seek ways to leverage their prosperity. Reunions begin to look like conferences, with discussions about fund-raisers for scholarships and plans for credit unions to support small-business initiatives.

Perhaps because black family reunions seem to exist outside politics, African American organizations like the Urban League and the National Association for the Advancement of Colored People have not included the reunion movement on their agendas. Instead, the enterprising turn of reunions has attracted the interest of corporations like Coca-Cola and Coors Brewing, which are keen to tap the market of middle-class blacks. This week, however, the National Council of Negro Women will launch its 11th annual Black Family Reunion Celebration in Atlanta, in recognition that the concerns of major black organizations are those of the families that gather in reunions: identity, self-help, empowerment.

At the Walcott family reunion, cousins in matching reunion T-shirts stood knee to knee to see if they had the same bowlegs. Brothers and sisters lined up to talk to a sister who, nearly 30 years ago, left the United States for Zambia. They were self-energizing, buffered for the moment from the strains of outside forces. The Walcott family is following a path well worn by other blacks. As they vote about how to use money they have pooled, elect family leaders, and debate the merits of reconstituting themselves as something even more purposeful than a family, black families are creating parts that might be models for a larger whole.

Marian Wright Edelman

Marian Wright Edelman (1939–) is a lawyer, activist, and children's rights advocate. She obtained her B.A. from Spelman College in 1960 and her LL.B. from Yale Law School in 1963. She is the founding president of the Children's Defense Fund, created in 1973. She has worked in numerous capacities, including staff attorney for the Legal Defense & Education Fund, 1963–1964, and director, 1964–1968; partner in the Washington Research Project of the Southern Center for Public Policy, 1968–1973; director of the Center for Law & Education, Harvard University, 1971–1973. Her honors are numerous, including the *Black Enterprise* magazine Professional Achievement Award (1980); the Leadership Award from the National Women's Political Caucus (1980); Black Women's Forum Award (1980); Columbia Teachers College Medal, Barnard College (1984); MacArthur Foundation Prize Fellowship (1985); Albert Schweitzer Humanitarian Prize (1998); the Heinz Award (1994); and the Presidential Medal of Freedom (2000).

In the chapter "A Family Legacy" from *The Measure of Our Success: A Letter to My Children and Yours* (1992), Edelman shares her family's tradition of service and helping those in their community.

A Family Legacy

South Carolina is my home state and I am the aunt, granddaughter, daughter, and sister of Baptist ministers. Service was as essential a part of my upbringing as eating and sleeping and going to school. The church was a hub of Black children's social existence, and caring Black adults were buffers against the segregated and hostile outside world that told us we weren't important. But our parents said it wasn't so, our teachers said it wasn't so, and our preachers said it wasn't so. The message of my racially segregated childhood was clear: let no man or woman look down on you, and look down on no man or woman.

We couldn't play in public playgrounds or sit at drugstore lunch counters and order a Coke, so Daddy built a playground and canteen behind the church. In fact, whenever he saw a need, he tried to respond. There were no Black homes for the aged in Bennettsville, so he began one across the street for which he and Mama and we children cooked and served and cleaned. And we children learned that it was our responsibility to take care of elderly family members and neighbors, and that everyone was our neighbor. My mother carried on the home after Daddy died, and my brother Julian has carried it on to this day behind our church since our mother's death in 1984.

Finding another child in my room or a pair of my shoes gone was far from unusual, and twelve foster children followed my sister and me and three brothers as we left home.

Child-rearing and parental work were inseparable. I went everywhere with my parents and was under the watchful eye of members of the congregation and community who were my extended parents. They kept me when my parents went out of town, they reported on and chided me when I strayed from the straight and narrow of community expectations, and they basked in and supported my achievements when I did well. Doing well, they made clear, meant high academic achievement, playing piano in Sunday school or singing or participating in other church activities, being helpful to somebody, displaying good manners (which is nothing more than consideration toward others), and reading. My sister Olive reminded me recently that the only time our father would not give us a chore ("Can't you find something constructive to do?" was his most common refrain) was when we were reading. So we all read a lot! We learned early what our parents and extended community "parents" valued. Children were taught—not by sermonizing, but by personal example—that nothing was too lowly to do. I remember a debate my parents had when I was eight or nine as to whether I was too young to go with my older brother, Harry, to help clean the bed and bedsores of a very sick, poor woman. I went and learned just how much the smallest helping hands and kindness can mean to a person in need.

The ugly external voices of my small-town, segregated childhood (as a very young child I remember standing and hearing former South Carolina Senator James Byrnes railing on the local courthouse lawn about how Black children would never go to school with whites) were tempered by the internal voices of parental and community expectation and pride. My father and I waited anxiously for the *Brown v. Board of Education* decision in 1954. We talked about it and what it would mean for my future and for the future of millions of other Black children. He died

5

the week before *Brown* was decided. But I and other children lucky enough to have caring and courageous parents and other adult role models were able, in later years, to walk through the new and heavy doors that *Brown* slowly and painfully opened—doors that some are trying to close again today.

The adults in our churches and community made children feel valued and important. They took time and paid attention to us. They struggled to find ways to keep us busy. And while life was often hard and resources scarce, we always knew who we were and that the measure of our worth was inside our heads and hearts and not outside in our possessions or on our backs. We were told that the world had a lot of problems; that Black people had an extra lot of problems, but that we were able and obligated to struggle and change them; that being poor was no excuse for not achieving; and that extra intellectual and material gifts brought with them the privilege and responsibility of sharing with others less fortunate. In sum, we learned that service is the rent we pay for living. It is the very purpose of life and not something you do in your spare time.

Morehouse Research Institute

Morehouse Research Institute is located at Morehouse College, Atlanta, Georgia. Following the publication of his book *Fatherless America* (1995), David Blankenhorn, Director of the American Values Institute, has spoken out on issues concerning African American fatherhood. In 1999 he organized a national conference on the topic, attracting men and women from many walks of life. The conference participants produced a statement entitled *Turning the Corner on Father Absence in Black America* in collaboration with the American Values Institute, which aims to provide intellectual support for a national fatherhood movement. This document was endorsed by 50 leading (mostly African American) academics, intellectuals, and civic leaders.

The following excerpt is from the conference report, *Turning the Corner on Father Absence in Black America*. The discussion therein ends decades of silence and denial regarding the role and importance of African American fathers. It concludes with 10 recommendations for reversing the trend of father absence among African American families.

Turning the Corner on Father Absence in Black America
About the Morehouse Conference

This project largely stems from conversations that began in 1996 and 1997 involving Obie Clayton of the Morehouse Research Institute, Ron Mincy of the Ford Foundation, David Blankenhorn of the Institute for American Values, and others. From these discussions, three questions emerged. First, what are the best ways to support the growing fatherhood movement in the African American community—a movement that is relatively ignored by the national media, but which is transforming the lives of many young, poorly educated fathers? Second, is it time for the nation's prominent African American scholars and leading experts on the African American family to come together to assist this movement? And finally, is it possible for this movement to make common cause—intellectually, morally, and organizationally—with a broad spectrum of other fatherhood and civic leaders?

The result of these deliberations was the Morehouse Conference on African American Fathers, held at Morehouse College in Atlanta on November 4–6, 1998, co-sponsored by the Morehouse Research Institute and the Institute for American Values and funded in part by the Ford Foundation.

In the eyes of the sponsors, and for many of the participants, the Morehouse Conference was an important moment. The group did not agree on everything, but it did agree unequivocally that African American children deserve strong and positive relationships with their fathers and that reversing the trend of father absence must rise to the top of the agenda for African Americans and for the nation. We agreed that both the economic structures, the cultural values, and the private and public sector policies that discourage many Black men from becoming active in their children's lives demand urgent attention.

This Statement is an outgrowth of the Morehouse Conference. It includes   5
among its signatories men and women who were a part of the Morehouse Conference and others who are part of the continuing conversation about how best to respond to the challenge of father absence in the African American community.

What Unites Us

> Are Black fathers necessary? You know, I'm old and I'm tired, and there are some things that I just don't want to debate anymore. One of them is whether African American children need fathers. Another is whether marriage matters. Does marriage matter? You bet it does. Are Black fathers necessary? Damn straight we are.

With these words, the Pulitzer Prize–winning columnist William Raspberry struck the key note of a conference on African American fathers held in the fall of 1998 at historic Morehouse College. Mr. Raspberry's words reflect the resounding consensus of the diverse group of scholars, activists, and advocates who journeyed to Atlanta from cities across the United States to focus on the challenges facing African American fathers and their families on the eve of a new millennium.

We gathered together because of our shared concern about the national trend of father absence that is affecting nearly all races and ethnic groups in the United States, and because of our particular concern about father absence in the African American community.

We gathered together because we believe that among the most urgent problems facing the African American community, and the entire nation, is the reality that 70 percent of African American children are born to unmarried mothers, and that at least 80 percent of all African American children can now expect to spend at least a significant part of their childhood years living apart from their fathers.[1]

We gathered together because of evidence showing that children of all races and ethnic groups who grow up without their fathers in their lives face higher risks of problems that can keep them from leading healthy, caring, and productive lives.

We gathered knowing in our hearts that the estrangement of fathers from their children is wrong, that children need both their fathers and their mothers, and that neither the African American community, nor the nation as a whole, can truly prosper unless and until we reverse the alarming trend of father absence.

We gathered together inspired by the strength, courage, and determination of the countless African American men who are heroic models of responsible fatherhood. We acknowledge the many and varied barriers, including racial discrimination, economic and educational disadvantages, and negative cultural attitudes and influences, that undermine the possibility of responsible fatherhood for many African American men. We are committed to overcoming all of these barriers.

We are men. Many of us are fathers. We are women. Many of us are mothers. We are sons and we are daughters. We are black and we are white. There are liberals, conservatives, and independents among us. Some of us work daily on the front lines of the fatherhood movement. Others are a part of efforts aimed at strengthening the institution of marriage. Some of us represent communities of faith. Others come from academia. Some of us are advocates for children and families. Others are community activists.

We differ in approach and emphasis. But we are united in our belief that fathers are necessary, and that African American children, no less than other children, need and deserve the loving, nurturing, and sustained presence of their fathers in their lives.

We gathered together because of our commitment to one overarching goal: We seek to promote the well-being of African American children by lifting the burden of father absence from the African American community, so that as many children as possible will enjoy the love, nurture, protection, guidance, and support of their fathers.

This is what unites us. This is our shared mission.

A Shared Vision

We agree on the vital importance of fathers as equal partners with mothers in the raising of children.

Although we differ on the relative weight to be given to economic, cultural, and private and public policy factors in shaping the lives of African American fathers, we agree that each of these factors is at work, and that comprehensive strategies are needed to confront the crisis of father absence in the African American community.

Although we differ on how to enhance marriage, we do agree that a key goal of the fatherhood movement must be to encourage both enhanced marriageability *and* healthy marriages.

We agree that strategies to promote responsible fatherhood must address the diverse needs of families, including fragile families formed by out-of-wedlock births to disadvantaged parents.[2]

We agree that there are profound spiritual dimensions to this crisis, and that in   20
order to make the way for nurturing relationships between fathers and their children, much healing must be done between fathers and mothers, men and women.

We agree that to address this crisis there is much to be done by the African
American community, and much to be done by the larger society, including
government.

We agree that inaction by any segment of the larger society cannot excuse inaction by the African American community.

■ A Call to Action

We call upon all African American fathers who are not actively and lovingly involved
in their children's lives, to turn their hearts toward their little ones, and to work toward healing their relationships with their children and with the mothers of their
children.

We call upon the Black church to make the healing and restoration of African
American families a major focus of its work, and to take a leadership role in re–
uniting fathers and children, and mothers and fathers—wherever possible, through
marriage.

We call upon the leaders of all African American civil rights, fraternal, profes-   25
sional, philanthropic, social, and civic organizations to put the issue of re-uniting
fathers with their children at the very top of their agendas for at least the next
decade, and to forge creative partnerships with the many African American leaders
now at the forefront of the fatherhood movement.

We call upon all African American leaders to bring to this movement the same
energy and dedication, the same passion and fearlessness, and the same creativity
and courage that was summoned to wage the struggle for basic civil rights.

And we call upon our national, state, and municipal leaders to put the full
weight of government resources at all levels, for at least the next decade, behind
partnerships designed to re-unite fathers with their children and to strengthen
families.

■ Why Fathers Matter

Father absence is not a uniquely African American problem. It is an American problem that crosses racial, ethnic, and class lines. All across the United States, fathers
are quietly disappearing from the lives of children. For many years, this subtle and
growing form of child neglect has been tolerated in communities throughout the
country, among rich, poor, and middle class alike, and in nearly every ethnic
group. Driven by growing rates of out-of-wedlock births, separation, and divorce,
this trend is robbing millions of our nation's children of the spiritual, emotional,
and material support of their fathers.

Tonight, about four of every ten children in the United States will go to sleep
in homes where their fathers do not live. Before they reach the age of eighteen,
more than half of America's children are likely to spend at least a significant portion of their childhoods living apart from their fathers.[3]

Growing numbers of children in our nation live in family and community envi-   30
ronments that might be called "radically fatherless." For example, in 1990, nearly 3
million children—about one of every twenty children in our country—were living
in father-absent homes in neighborhoods in which a majority of families with children were headed by single mothers. About 4.5 million U.S. children that year
resided in predominantly fatherless neighborhoods, in which more than half of all
families with children were headed by single mothers. Of these 4.5 million at-risk
children, nearly 80 percent were African American.[4]

Although the proportion of children with absent fathers is growing fastest
among whites, the problem of father absence is especially acute in the African
American community. Of all Black babies born in 1996, approximately 70 percent
were born to unmarried mothers. On average, a Black child born in the early 1950s
would eventually spend about four years (or about 22 percent of childhood) living
in a one-parent home. But for Black children born in the early 1980s, that figure,
according to one estimate, would nearly triple, to almost 11 years or about 60 percent of childhood.[5]

These trends pose significant threats to African American children, to the
African American community, and to our nation.

There is compelling evidence that children raised by single parents generally
do not fare as well as children raised by two married parents. After years of careful
study, including analyses of four large national databases, and controlling for race,
income, and education, Sara McLanahan and Gary Sandefur recently concluded
that, "The evidence is quite clear: children who grow up in a household with only
one biological parent are worse off, on average, than children who grow up in a
household with both of their biological parents, regardless of the parents' race or
educational background, regardless of whether the parents are married when the
child is born, and regardless of whether the resident parent remarries."[6]

Controlling for parental education, occupation, family income, welfare receipt,
parenting styles, time spent with children, children's age, gender, and race, Lingxin
Hao of Johns Hopkins University finds that "the net effects of non-intact family
structure on child development outcomes are negative and strong."[7]

Again, controlling for race, neighborhood characteristics, and mother's edu-   35
cation and cognitive ability, boys raised in single-parent homes are twice as likely
(and boys raised in step-families three times as likely) to commit a crime leading to
incarceration.[8] A child growing up without both parents also faces a greater risk
that he or she will be a victim of a crime, especially child abuse.[9]

Compared to children with both parents at home, children who live apart from
their fathers are five times as likely to be poor.[10] Children who live apart from their
fathers are also much more likely to do poorly in school and twice as likely to drop
out of school.[11]

Beyond the statistics is the pain of real children—boys and girls, young men
and young women, who bear, and often pass on to their own children, the pains of
father hunger. There are the boys and young men who, without the protection and
guidance of fathers, struggle each day to figure out what it means to be a man, im-
provising for themselves expedient, and too often violent and self-destructive,
codes of manhood.[12] There are the little girls and young women who, facing life
without the first men who should have loved them and stayed with them, struggle

to develop a sense of their own love-worthiness, often offering sex in exchange for what they hope will be love.[13]

We can no longer afford to deny the vital importance of the father-child bond. Nor can we any longer deny the struggles of Black women raising children without the help of fathers, nor the suffering of Black men living at the margins of family life and society. When fathers are absent, children suffer—one child at a time, one family at a time. And that suffering reverberates throughout our society.

▓ The Global Trend

As Sylvia Ann Hewlett and Cornel West have put it, "Biologically speaking, the link between mother and child is incontrovertible. Fatherhood, in contrast, is inherently uncertain, which is why societies have tried so hard to connect children to their fathers."[14]

Yet, as many countries have progressed materially and technologically, their commitment to teaching and enforcing the norms that connect children to fathers, and keep the father-child bond intact, has weakened dramatically.[15]

The nearly universal understanding of marriage as an indispensable social institution that binds men to their families is breaking down. Marriage has come to be seen less as a way of life meant to guide intimacy and define commitments, especially to children, and more as a vehicle for fulfilling the psychological needs of adults. And in the Western world, from the Scandinavian countries to Canada and the United States, rates of out-of-wedlock births and divorce have skyrocketed.

A dramatic confluence of events, many of which promote individualism more than obligation, has led to an abandonment of the norms that once taught men a sense of responsibility to their children.

Nowadays, little stigma is attached to having a child out of wedlock. Divorces are common. With the easy availability of birth control and abortion, and the decline in the practice of "shotgun" marriages, sexual behavior is no longer inextricably linked with child-bearing and marriage. With the large scale entry of women into the workforce and women's increasing independence, as well as economic changes that have meant stagnating wages and growing economic insecurity for many men, the male's role as provider has become less significant. Perhaps most importantly, with these changes has come a devaluing of the role of fathers: a growing sense that fathers are not as important, not as necessary, as mothers.

For these reasons, fatherhood as an institution is disintegrating in many modern societies. The set of social expectations, codes, and laws that once kept most fathers connected to their families are loosening, and fathers the world over, rich and poor alike, are increasingly disengaging from their children and from the mothers of their children.

▓ Challenges to African American Fatherhood

Economic, cultural, and policy changes that have devalued fatherhood in the West in general and in the United States in particular, have hit the African American community especially hard. For example, as the Harvard sociologist (and participant in the Morehouse Conference) William Julius Wilson and others have pointed out, basic structural changes in the U.S. economy have increasingly disadvantaged lower-skilled workers, thus undermining the marriageability of many young African American men.

"For the first time in the 20th century," notes Wilson, "most adult males in many inner city-ghetto neighborhoods are not working in a typical week. The disappearance of work has adversely affected not only individuals, families, and neighborhoods, but the social life of the city at large as well." Furthermore, "The problems of joblessness and social dislocation in the inner city are, in part, related to the processes in the global economy that have contributed to greater inequality and insecurity among American workers in general, and of the failure of U.S. social policies to adjust these processes."[16]

For African American men, moreover, the effects of these global trends are exacerbated by a series of racially specific historical events that began with slavery and include the legacies of slavery, as well as the racism and economic discrimination that are an intrinsic part of American society and the African American experience.

The legacy of slavery is tragically relevant to the issue of Black fatherhood, for the conditions of slavery in the United States provided exactly the opposite of what is required in order to preserve the fragile bond between father and child. By law, the male slave could fulfill none of the duties of husband and father. The institution of slavery created a subculture where all the societal norms, mores, expectations, and laws, instead of helping to connect men to their offspring, forcibly severed the bonds between fathers and their children.

▓ The Great Upheaval

This legacy makes all the more heroic the many Black men throughout American history who, with so many forces arrayed against them, stood tall to fulfill their responsibilities as fathers.

Even in the face of concerted and persistent discrimination, including economic discrimination, and the harsh inequalities of Jim Crow, many Black families maintained two-parent households well into the 1960s, when rates of out-of-wedlock births began to escalate dramatically. In 1960, 22 percent of all Black babies were born to unmarried mothers. By 1996, that figure had jumped to 70 percent.

Many factors contributed to this dramatic change. The 1960s ushered in great social, cultural, and economic upheavals that had a profound impact on fatherhood in the United States generally and among African Americans particularly. Shifting occupational structures (from manufacturing to services), stagnating real wages, and the declining relative demand for low-skilled labor undermined the economic status of many Black men. Welfare policies that focused on helping mothers and children, to the exclusion of fathers, had the practical effect of keeping or driving men out of the home and away from children. Housing discrimination that facilitated the movement of whites out of the cities while hampering the mobility of African Americans, the increasing suburbanization of employment, inadequate urban school systems, and the growing incarceration of Black men, fueled in large measure by the war on drugs, also played crucial roles in undercutting opportunities for many Black men.

In 1960, there were 70 employed civilian Black men for every hundred Black women. But by 1990, the figure had dropped to 40.[17] Between the 1960s and 1990s, the percent of Black female-headed households rose dramatically as Black male unemployment and underemployment also increased. In the absence of genuine opportunities, and in the face of persistent poverty, more and more young Black males dropped out of both the labor force *and* family life.[18] All of these trends, moreover, occurred within the context of a growing societal belief that fathers, when all is said and done, are non-essential.

The institution of fatherhood is sensitive to social, economic, cultural and policy changes. African American fatherhood is especially sensitive to such changes because it never had the full support of American society. As the value of fatherhood has declined in the larger American culture, and social and economic conditions have grown more unfavorable for many fathers, the bonds holding many African American families together have frayed severely, separating more and more fathers from their children.

■ Culture, Economics, *and* Policy

We believe that the fatherhood movement within the African American community must include *both* aggressive steps to improve public and private sector policies as they affect fathers and to open up greater economic opportunities for African American men, *and* equally aggressive steps to promote changes in norms and expectations that support marriage and strengthen the father-child bond.

Some of us see the principal cause of father absence among African Americans as the lack of adequate economic opportunities. We argue that the economic conditions affecting a great number of African American men make it nearly impossible for them to be adequate providers, and that this inability to provide is the root cause of father absence for African American children. We are encouraged by a recent study from the National Bureau of Economic Research showing a positive link between greater employment opportunities for young Black men and declining crime rates. These and similar findings support arguments advanced by William Julius Wilson, John Sibley Butler of the University of Texas (a participant in the Morehouse Conference), and others suggesting that young African American men "would benefit especially from consistent and full employment."[19] We argue in favor of government and private sector action that creates jobs, provides social services and job training, and facilitates access to places of work, all of which would enhance the marriageability of Black men.

Others of us believe that the problem of father absence in the African American community cannot be explained solely or even primarily by reference to economic structures, especially given the high and growing rates of father absence outside of the ranks of the African American community and outside the ranks of the poor. We believe that father absence in the Black community is caused in large part by damaging and historically rooted cultural patterns that promote behaviors leading to high rates of out-of-wedlock births, low rates of marriage, and conflictual relationships between Black men and Black women. We argue for cultural changes within the community and in the larger society that would encourage personal responsibility and healthy marriages and discourage out-of-wedlock births and divorce.

Despite our differences, as a group we agree that it is difficult to disentangle cultural values from the effects of economics and policy. We agree that the forces driving father absence in the African American community are complex and mutually reinforcing, and that economics and cultural values, as well as public and private sector policies, play key roles in the crisis of father absence in the African American community.

As William Julius Wilson recently noted, "In the inner-city ghetto, not only have the norms in support of husband-wife families and against out-of-wedlock births become weaker as a result of the general trend in society, they have also gradually disintegrated because of the sharp rise in joblessness and declining real incomes in the inner city over the past several decades, especially from the mid 1970s to 1995. The weakening of social sanctions has had the greatest impact on the jobless, but it has also affected many who are employed, especially those whose jobs are not very secure or stable and/or those who are experiencing declining real incomes. The declining marriage rates among inner-city Black parents is a function not simply of increased economic marginality, or of changing attitudes toward sex and marriage, but of the interaction between the two."[20] This point is also reinforced by Elijah Anderson of the University of Pennsylvania (a participant in the Morehouse Conference) and author of *Code of the Street,* who notes that very few young men in the inner city have the opportunity to see older men in their neighborhood going to work and building strong families. According to Anderson, when "a critical mass of jobless people are concentrated in the inner city community, various factors come together and conspire to produce an almost intractable result. In these circumstances alienation thrives and little that is conventional retains legitimacy."[21]

Cultural values, economics, and public policy are never entirely distinct realms. They are inextricably linked aspects of the human experience. Public and private policies can encourage or discourage behavior. The economy is influenced by—and promotes—certain cultural values. People's lives are partly shaped by the economic conditions and circumstances in which they find themselves. Economic conditions can uplift—or debase—people and the communities in which they live. But it is equally true that people's values can help them respond to those conditions in ways that are either self-defeating or self-empowering.

We believe that we must address, with equal force, *all* the factors that would keep fathers from building caring and nurturing relationships with their children.

Strategies for action must address economic and private and public policy factors that particularly affect the Black community. They must also address cultural shifts affecting the United States in general, and the cultural and behavioral patterns that affect the African American community in particular.

■ Marriage *and* Marriageability

In nearly every culture, marriage has been the main institution which binds men to their families. Through the institution of marriage, societies have legitimized the masculine role, connected men to women and to future generations, and held men accountable to their children and to their family responsibilities.

When marriage fails or fails to form, when mothers and fathers do not commit to one another, nurturing fatherhood typically dwindles away. Over time, unmarried and divorced fathers tend to disengage from their children—both emotionally and financially. This is true for fathers of all races and classes. Although one study suggests that unmarried Black fathers are more likely to spend time with their children than are unwed white and Hispanic fathers, the evidence is quite strong that over time single fathers of all races tend to separate from their children and families, and that marriage significantly increases the likelihood that a child will grow up being nurtured by his or her father.[22]

We believe that a key goal of the fatherhood movement within the African American community must be strengthened relationships between mothers and fathers that lead, wherever possible, to strong, healthy marriages. We believe also that strategies to promote fatherhood must take into account the diverse conditions of contemporary father absence, strengthening the father-child bond at all stages of a relationship between a father and a mother. As a group, we believe that the fatherhood movement must promote both marriage *and* marriageability.

Some of us see father absence in the African American community as rooted mainly in norms and behavior patterns that devalue marriage, weaken the male-female bond, and tolerate high rates of out-of-wedlock births and divorce. We argue that we cannot rebuild fatherhood outside of marriage and that marriage must be the primary line of defense in the struggle to re-unite fathers and children. We believe that efforts to reverse the trend of father absence in the African American community must focus on increasing dramatically the proportion of children living with their two parents, committed to one another in marriage.

From this perspective, moreover, marriage itself promotes economic achievement in men. Some studies suggest that marriage alone increases men's earnings. Husbands, in general, earn at least ten percent more than similar single men, and in some cases married men earn as much as 40 percent more. Accordingly, marriage should be promoted as a social institution that not only maximizes emotional benefits, but also one that by itself can have a substantial positive effect on the economic condition of fathers and families.[23]

Some of us take the position that marriage cannot be the first line of defense for promoting responsible fatherhood in the African American community. We argue that poor employment prospects make Black men less marriageable and that low marriage rates are largely a consequence of limited economic opportunities. As William Julius Wilson has pointed out, employed single Black fathers ages 18–31 in Chicago's inner-city neighborhoods are eight times more likely to marry eventually than their jobless counterparts.[24] Because Black men have lower employment rates and lower earnings than white men, they are less able to provide for a family and therefore less likely to be able to marry. In addition, educational differences between Black men and Black women, along with Black women's comparatively improved employment prospects and earnings, make Black women less dependent on the earnings of men, giving them more freedom in the choice of whether or not to marry.

For some of us, then, promotion of a "marriage first" strategy fails to take account of the decreased marriageability of Black men. It also discounts the suffering of many mothers and children who have lived through abusive marriages, and pays insufficient attention to other practical realities that make marriage the wrong answer for many couples. We do not condone childbirth outside of marriage. But we support strategies that take into account the current reality of high rates of nonmarital births. We argue that families must be nurtured and strengthened as we find them. For example, until recently, it was assumed that in most cases children born outside of marriage are born to couples in which the father is essentially absent. But a recent study shows that nearly half of poor children born out of wedlock are born to cohabiting couples or to couples where the father visits the child weekly. Accordingly, many of these fathers are not absent from their children's lives, yet our national policies assume that they are absent and make few attempts to strengthen the attachment of these fathers to their children and to the mothers of their children.[25]

Despite our different points of view, as a group we strongly favor efforts to strengthen relationships between parents in ways that help fathers connect to their children. One important goal of these efforts is to help move as many unmarried couples as possible toward healthy, nurturing marriages. We are therefore in agreement that a loving marriage, founded on principles of equal regard between husband and wife, is the ideal way to raise children, and that African American children no less than other children deserve the care of their two married parents.

Marriage is already an important, though frequently unrealized, goal for many young, low-income African Americans. One recent study of fragile families—parents who are young, poor and unwed—finds that about half of these parents are living together at the time of the birth of their child. The great majority say they are romantically involved. More than half say that either it is "almost certain" that they will get married or that there is a "good chance" that they will get married.[26] We must build upon this foundation. We should not ignore or destroy this natural human desire for intimacy and a stable family life, but instead do everything we can to nourish and support it.

As a group, we support a "marriage matters" and "marriage wherever possible" set of strategies. We believe that marriage should be held up as the preferred way to raise children and that fatherhood programs, wherever possible, should promote the benefits of marriage and help fathers and mothers move toward stable, nurturing marriages. Strong marriages are connected to cultural values as well as economics and policy. For example, men's sense of personal worth as well as their sense of value to their families are tied in powerful ways to their role as breadwinners—their ability to provide materially for their children. For this reason, increased economic opportunities for African American men must be a part of any movement that seeks to re-unite fathers and children and promote marriage.

But marriage and marriageability are also deeply connected to the quality of the relationships between adult males and females.

Much has been written in popular fiction and non-fiction about the state of gender relations between Black men and Black women.[27] Recent demographic data and social survey data reveal wide gaps in the socio-economic conditions, and also in the basic attitudes and behavior patterns separating Black men from Black women.[28] Ethnographic data analyzed by William Julius Wilson reveal that "the relationships between inner-city black men and women, whether in a marital or non-marital situation, are often fractious and antagonistic."[29] The conclusion is inescapable: there is a crisis in gender relations in the Black community. This is a painful reality. But acknowledging the crisis points to a vital strategy for reversing the trend of father absence. We believe that efforts to promote fatherhood and marriage in the African American community must include urgent and concerted work aimed at gender reconciliation: the healing of relationships between men and women.

▓ The Spiritual Dimensions of Father Absence in Black America

There are profound spiritual aspects to the problem of father absence in the African American community. It is tied to a spiritual brokenness that is, in turn, linked to economic, political, cultural, and social patterns that are partly rooted in slavery and continuing adversities.

The institution of slavery stripped African American fatherhood of much of its sacred character. Continuing racism, economic discrimination, and public and private sector policies that have divided families have adversely affected relationships between Black men and Black women. These painful influences have adversely affected the raising of Black children. They have harmed marriages and thwarted the formation of families. It is time now to take the time to recover, as fully as possible, what has been lost.

In the words of the Reverend Frederick J. Streets, Chaplain of Yale University, 75 "We need a kind of excavation of our spiritual and emotional troubles for the purpose of dealing with them creatively and releasing us from the power they have to influence our behavior, both on the conscious and the unconscious levels."[30]

Dr. Bernard Franklin, Vice President of the National Fathering Center (and a participant in the Morehouse Conference) notes that, "Part of the untold story is that the brutal pain injected by slavery has gone unforgiven in the lives of many African American men . . . Carrying around bitterness and anger is like carrying a sack of cement. It weighs men down and makes their journey exasperating. They are left with no energy for parenting and for caring for their families . . . Thus the bitter root of judgment has become so ingrained in many families that men who are born into these families become alcoholic, lethargic, unable or unwilling to support their wives, violent, and, generally, men without hope. Far more descends through our physical inheritance than we suspect."[31]

Since the arrival of the first Africans on these shores, African Americans have been called upon in their time and place to make a way out of no way. The Black community has the highest measurable level of religiosity of any group in the United States.[32] What has made the difference in every generation and what will make the difference now on the eve of the 21st century is the community's faith in God.

The crisis of father absence poses a profound challenge to the Black church. The church's challenge is to rise to this most vital mission of helping the African American community to heal through ministries of forgiveness and reconciliation.

And because the church is affected by the same forces affecting all African Americans, it, too, must take time to heal, even as it goes forth to help heal others.

The struggle for inward renewal within the African American community has 80 been postponed for too long. It is time to enter a new century on a path to wholeness, for the sake of our children.

▓ Ten Recommendations

Reversing the trend of father absence both nationally and among African Americans in particular will require long-term efforts aimed at all the political, economic, social and cultural forces that are separating fathers from their children.

1. *We urge African American fathers and mothers to recognize their obligations to each other and to work to build stronger parenting partnerships for the benefit of their children.* We applaud all fathers who play active and loving roles in the lives of their children, and we encourage them to serve as mentors to other fathers and to young men. To fathers who are not now actively involved in nurturing their children, we urge you to become a part of one of the growing number of programs focused on re-uniting fathers and children and on improving relationships between fathers and mothers. We especially hope that older African American fathers, who by virtue of their dedication can serve as models of responsible fatherhood, will call on and help younger African American men to reject what Elijah Anderson terms the "code of the street," and to embrace responsibility to self, family, and community. As Anderson reminds us, "The old heads are the saving grace of the community . . . by telling people to be responsible, they are affirming that something can be done, that there is hope for the future."[33]

We urge mothers to be open to building partnerships that enable fathers to establish strong, loving relationships with their children. For too long, there has been a widespread assumption that if fathers do not provide financially for their children, there is little else that they can do. Children need their fathers as nurturers and protectors as well. Sometimes, mothers who are estranged from the fathers of their children will say or do things that, intentionally or not, alienate children from their fathers. This behavior can not only damage children's relationships with their father, but also damage their emotional development and their abilities to form healthy relationships with others.

2. *We urge the Black church to help build a powerful new movement aimed at gender and family healing.* This movement should include the following aspects: initiatives designed to improve the quality of relationships between Black men and Black women; programs aimed at preparing men and women for marriage, including helping men and women to deal with their relationships with their own families of origin; programs aimed at improving relationships between parents and children; rites of passage programs that challenge the code of the street by preparing young men and young women for responsible manhood and womanhood, and responsible motherhood and fatherhood; and ministries aimed at helping incarcerated fathers re-unite and establish healthy relationships with their children. We urge the Black church to work in partnership with other communities of faith and with organizations at the forefront of the fatherhood movement, and to collaborate with colleges, universities, public health agencies, and mental health agencies for the promotion of family health and well-being.

3. *We urge churches and other organizations to support families by taking a much more active role in the education of Black children through the development of alternative community-based and values-oriented educational systems.* The larger society should encourage these initiatives by supporting charter school legislation, increasing scholarship fund assistance for alternative schools, and, where feasible, providing vouchers so that needy parents can send their children to any public school, regardless of location.

4. *We urge civil rights organizations and professional, civic, fraternal and philanthropic groups within the African American community to make the issue of re-uniting fathers and*

*children a top priority for at least the next decade through programs of advocacy, family recon-
ciliation, and community mobilization.* We call upon these organizations to work in
partnership with leaders of the fatherhood movement and the Black church to
build a critical mass of community-based programs aimed at strengthening Black
families, with special emphasis on improving relationships between men and
women, and between parents and children.

5. *We urge all media organizations, especially Black media, to use their power for at least the
next decade to promote positive images of men and fatherhood in Black America.* The media
does influence behavior, for better or for worse. We urge all media outlets, particularly those serving the Black community, to use their creative talents to develop programs and public service campaigns that promote the ideals of responsible fatherhood and motherhood, strong marriages, and healthy family life.

6. *We call upon the United States Congress to pass, and the President to sign, legislation this
fiscal year authorizing at least $2 billion over the next five years to support community-based
fatherhood programs aimed at reversing the trend of father absence in our nation.* These programs should focus on three objectives. First, increasing the attachment of fathers
to their children. Second, increasing the spiritual, educational, social, and economic contributions that fathers make to their children. And third, fostering both
marriage and marriageability, especially for young, poorly educated, low-income
men. We particularly urge support for programs that emphasize the development
of the "whole man," combining an intensive focus on economic and social opportunity, including access to social services, employment readiness skills, job training,
and job placement, with an equally intensive focus on values and attitudes, including spiritual development, the importance of the marriage commitment, and the
importance of good parenting habits and skills for both custodial and non-custodial
fathers. Both the Clinton/Gore Administration and leading members of Congress
from both parties have expressed initial support for this type of federal initiative.
We urge them to act now.

7. *We call upon the federal-state Child Support Enforcement Program to institute basic reforms to encourage fathers' active participation in the lives of their children by promoting self-
sufficiency for fathers, encouraging marriage, and engaging faith-based and other community
organizations in promoting responsible fatherhood.*

- We urge the federal-state Child Support Enforcement Program to reexamine 90
  its policies toward low-income non-custodial parents with respect to the size
  of initial orders, arrearage policies, and modification of orders when earnings
  of the non-custodial parent change. Most importantly, the program should
  seek to insure that child support payments primarily benefit the children,
  and are not solely used to reimburse government for welfare costs.

- We urge the federal-state Child Support Enforcement Program, operating under revised federal guidelines, to create a number of experimental or demonstration projects in which child support enforcement becomes an active partner with the fatherhood movement. Specifically, under this arrangement, child
  support enforcement agencies could choose, on a case by case basis, and draw-
  ing on lessons learned from programs such as Parents Fair Share and Children

First, to permit delinquent fathers to participate in community-based fatherhood programs as an alternative to incarceration or other punitive measures. These pilot projects would help today's fatherhood movement to reach out to those fathers who are willing to commit themselves to straightening out their lives, paying child support, respecting and working with the mothers of their children, and their children. In this way, for the first time, the child support enforcement program could become an ally of the fatherhood movement.

8. *We urge government at all levels, the business community, and the entire civil society to take concerted action for at least the next decade to reverse inequities in the treatment of fathers in public and private sector policy and to improve the economic prospects and marriageability of poor men, including, but not limited to, the following initiatives:*

- Reforming the Earned Income Tax Credit to eliminate its substantial marriage penalty.

- Allowing more fathers, including unmarried fathers paying child support and spending time with their children, to receive the Earned Income Tax Credit, structuring any reforms so that they do not weaken incentives to marriage.

- Reforming federal laws to allow states to extend child care and medical benefits for transitions off welfare through marriage as well as through work.

- Reforming housing policies to promote family formation, for example, by developing pilot projects within public housing to allow fathers of welfare families to live in public housing with their families without a rental surcharge for up to 18 months.

- Increased public and private sector support to develop employment and entrepreneurship opportunities in urban areas.

- Increased public and private sector support for job training, job skills development, and transportation to jobs in suburban areas.

- Greater economic development opportunities in urban areas through private investment.

9. *We urge the criminal justice system at all levels of government to develop creative strategies aimed at reconnecting fathers and children where there is a desire to do so on the part of family members.* Although African Americans comprise 12 percent of the U.S. population, they account for nearly 30 percent of arrests and over half of all prisoners. Today, about 5 million men—a group of men who are "majority minority"—are at least partly under the control of the criminal justice system, either due to incarceration or as a result of being on parole. Many of these men are fathers. By definition, they are absent fathers. On any given day, there are in our nation approximately 1,300,000 minor sons and daughters of incarcerated men. These children are especially at risk.[34] To help stop what in too many cases becomes a generational cycle of involvement with the criminal justice system, special efforts should be made to reconnect these children to their fathers whenever possible.

10. *We urge every governmental or community-based program that has a relationship with unwed parents to help connect interested parents with faith-based marriage education and marriage mentoring programs.* Why? Because marriage matters and because we know

that many young people want to marry but need support in order to build healthy marriages and families.

ENDNOTES

1. "Report of Final Natality Statistics, 1996," *Monthly Vital Statistics Report* 46, no. 11, Supplement (Washington, D.C.: U.S. Department of Health and Human Services, June 30, 1998): 46; Sandra Hoffreth, "Updating Children's Life Course," *Journal of Marriage and the Family* 47 (February 1985): 93–115; Written correspondence from Larry L. Bumpass, May 12, 1999. See also Teresa Castro Martin and Larry L. Bumpass, "Recent Trends in Marital Disruption," *Demography* 26, no. 1 (February 1989): 37–51.

2. For a definition of fragile families see, Ronald B. Miney and Hillard Pouney, "There Must Be 50 Ways to Start a Family," in Wade F. Horn, David Blankenhorn, and Mitchell B. Pearlstein, *The Fatherhood Movement: A Call to Action*, (Lanham, MD: Lexington Books, 1999), pps. 83–104.

3. David Blankenhorn, *Fatherless America: Confronting Our Most Urgent Social Problem*, (New York, Basic Books, 1995) pps. 1, 18–19; See also Sara McLanahan and Gary Sandefur, *Growing Up With A Single Parent: What Hurts, What Helps* (Cambridge, MA: Harvard University Press, 1994), pps. 2, 3.

4. *Kids Count Data Book: 1995* (Baltimore, MD: Annie E. Casey Foundation, 1995), p. 5. The figure on the proportion of these at-risk children who are African American was provided by the Annie E. Casey Foundation.

5. Hofferth, *op. cit.*

6. McLanahan and Sandefur, p. 1. Until fairly recently, some scholars have argued that what appear in some studies to be the negative effects of father absence are in fact more likely to be the negative effects of other, presumably more potent variables, such as low income, racism, or neighborhood conditions. But today, a large and growing body of careful scholarly research—complete with "controls" for a wide variety of factors, including race, income, residential instability, urban location, parents' education, the child's cognitive ability, child support payments, and others—is showing as clearly as the social sciences can show anything that father absence itself is a leading cause of harmful outcomes for children in all dimensions of their lives. Urie Bronfenbrenner, one of the nation's most respected family scholars, briefly sums up the weight of scholarly evidence by stating that, "controlling for associated factors such as low income, children growing up in such [father-absent] households are at greater risk for experiencing a variety of behavioral and educational problems, including extremes of hyperactivity or withdrawal, lack of attentiveness in the classroom, difficulty in deferring gratification, impaired academic achievement, school misbehavior, absenteeism, dropping out, involvement in socially alienated peer groups, and, especially, the so-called 'teenage syndrome' of behaviors that tend to hang together—smoking, drinking, early and frequent sexual experience, a cynical attitude toward work, adolescent pregnancy, and, in the more extreme cases, drugs, suicide, vandalism, violence, and criminal acts." See Urie Bronfenbrenner, "Discovering What Families Do," in David Blankenhorn, Steven Bayme, and Jean Bethke Elshtain (eds.), *Rebuilding the Nest: A New Commitment to the American Family* (Milwaukee: Family Service America, 1990), p. 34. For a similar overview, see Ronald J. Angel and Jacqueline L. Angel, *Painful Inheritance: Health and the New Generation of Fatherless Children* (Madison: University of Wisconsin Press, 1993), p. 118, *passim*.

7. Lingxin Hao, "Family Structure, Parental Input, and Child Development," Paper presented to the Population Association of America (March 1997): 27–28.

8. Cynthia C. Harper and Sara S. McLanahan, "Father Absence and Youth Incarceration," Paper presented at the annual meeting of the American Sociological Association (San Francisco, August 1998). For similar findings, see William S. Comanor and Llad Phillips, "The Impact of Family Structure on Delinquency," Working Paper in Economics no. 7-95R,

University of California at Santa Barbara Economics Department (February 1998); and Ross Matsueda and Karen Hemier, "Race, Family Structure and Delinquency: A Test of Differential Association and Social Control Theories," *American Sociological Review* 52, no. 6 (1987): 826–840.

9. Martin Daly and Margo Wilson, "Evolutionary Psychology and Marital Conflict: The Relevance of Stepchildren," in David M. Buss and Neil Malamuth (eds.), *Sex, Power, Conflict: Evolutionary and Feminist Perspectives* (New York: Oxford University Press, 1996), pps. 9–28.

10. McLanahan and Sandefur, p. 23.

11. *Ibid.*, pps. 41, 44–46.

12. See Elijah Anderson, "Caught in the Welfare Web," *Crisis,* March 1994; and Anderson, *Code of the Street* (New York: W.W. Norton, 1999). See also Frank Pittman, *Man Enough: Fathers, Sons, and the Search for Masculinity* (New York: G.P. Putnam's Sons, 1993).

13. See Seymour Fisher, *Sexual Images of the Self* (Hillsdale, N.J.: Lawrence Erlbaum, 1989), pps. 43–44, 46; Judith S. Wallerstein, "The Long-Term Effects of Divorce on Children: A Review," *Journal of the American Academy of Child Adolescent Psychiatry* 30, no. 3 (May 1991); and Judith Musick, *Young, Poor, and Pregnant: The Psychology of Teenage Motherhood* (New Haven: Yale University Press, 1993).

14. Sylvia Ann Hewlett and Cornel West, *The War Against Parents: What We Can Do For America's Beleaguered Moms and Dads* (Boston: Houghton Mifflin, 1998), p. 160.

15. See David Popenoe, "Challenging the Culture of Fatherlessness," in Wade Horn, David Blankenhorn, and Mitchell Pearlstein (eds.), *The Fatherhood Movement: A Call to Action,* (Lanham, MD: Lexington Books, 1999); David Popenoe, *Disturbing the Nest: Family Change and Decline in Modern Societies* (New York: Aldine de Gruyter, 1988); and William J. Goode, *World Changes in Divorce Patterns* (New Haven: Yale University Press, 1993). See also Francis Fukuyama, "The Great Disruption: Human Nature and the Reconstruction of Social Order," *The Atlantic Monthly,* May 1999, p. 72.

16. William Julius Wilson, *When Work Disappears: The World of the New Urban Poor* (New York: Knopf, 1996), p. xiii. See also Doris Wilkinson, "Afro-American Women and Their Families," *Marriage and Family Review* 7 (Fall 1984): 125–142.

17. Hewlett and West, p. 174.

18. Hewlett and West, pps. 76–77.

19. Richard B. Freeman and William M. Rodgers III, "Area Economic Conditions and the Labor Market Outcomes of Young Men in the 1990s Expansion," Working Paper 7073 (Washington, D.C.: National Bureau of Economic Research, April 1999): 3. See also Obie Clayton, "Old Problems and Shifting Challenges: Preparing African American Fathers for the 21st Century Labor Market," Paper presented at a closed session of the U.S. Department of Labor, 1995 (revised May 1998); Douglas S. Massey and Nancy A. Denton, "Trends in the Residential Segregation of Blacks, Hispanics, and Asians," *American Sociological Review* 52 no. 6 (1987): 802–825; Ronald F. Ferguson, "Shifting Challenges: Fifty Years of Economic Change Toward Black-White Earnings Equality," *Daedalus,* Winter 1995.

20. William Julius Wilson, "Fatherhood and Welfare Reform," Paper presented at a conference on "The Politics of Fatherhood," Howard University, March 23, 1999, p. 3.

21. Anderson, *Code of the Street,* p. 320.

22. R. I. Lerman, "National Profile of Young, Unwed Fathers," in R. I. Lerman and T. J. Ooms (eds.), *Young, Unwed Fathers: Changing Roles and Emerging Policies* (Philadelphia, Pa.: Temple University Press, 1993); Steven Nock, *Marriage and Men's Lives,* (New York: Oxford University Press, 1998); Anu Rangarajan and Philip Gleason, "Young Unwed Fathers of AFDC Children: Do They Provide Support?," *Demography* 35, no. 2 (May 1998): 175–186; Frank Furstenberg and Kathleen Mullan Harris, "The Disappearing American Father? Divorce and the Waning Significance of Biological Parenthood," in Scott J. South and Stewart E. Tolnay (eds.), *The Changing American Family: Sociological and Demographic Perspectives* (Boulder, Colo.: Westview Press, 1992); and Eleanor E. Maccoby and Robert H. Mnookin,

Dividing the Child: Social and Legal Dilemmas of Custody (Cambridge, Mass.: Harvard University Press, 1992).

23. See Jeffrey S. Gray, "The Fall in Men's Return to Marriage," *Journal of Human Resources* 32, no. 3 (1997): 481–503; Kermit Daniel, "The Marriage Premium," in M. Tommasi and K. Lerulli (eds.), *The New Economics of Human Behavior* (Cambridge: Cambridge University Press, 1995), pps. 113–125; and Sanders Korenman and David Neumark, "Does Marriage Really Make Men More Productive?", *Journal of Human Resources* 26, no. 2 (1991): 282–307.

24. Wilson, *When Work Disappears*, p. 96.

25. Data from Elaine Sorenson, *The National Survey of America's Families*, 1997.

26. Preliminary data from Sara S. McLanahan and Irwin Garfinkel, *The Fragile Families and Child Wellbeing Study*, April 1999.

27. See, for example, Terry MacMillan, *Waiting to Exhale* (New York: Viking Press, 1992); Derek S. Hopson and Darlene Powell Hopson, *Friends, Lovers, and Soulmates: A Guide to Better Relationships Between Black Men and Women* (New York: Fireside/Simon & Schuster, 1994); Ernest H. Johnson, *Brothers on the Mend: Understanding and Healing Anger for African American Men and Women,* (New York: Pocket Books, 1998).

28. Orlando Patterson, *Rituals of Blood: Consequences of Slavery in Two American Centuries* (Washington, D.C.: Civitas, 1998), pps. 3–167.

29. Wilson, "Fatherhood and Welfare Reform."

30. Telephone interview with Rev. Dr. Frederick J. Streets, May 6, 1999.

31. E. Bernard Franklin, "Fatherhood in the African American Church," in Don E. Eberly (ed.), *The Faith Factor in Fatherhood,* (Lanham, Md.: Rappaport, Littlefield, forthcoming).

32. See Robert Joseph Taylor, Linda M. Chatters, Rukmalie Jayakody and Jeffrey S. Levin, "Black and White Differences in Religious Participation: A Multi-Sample Comparison," *Journal for the Scientific Study of Religion* 35 (1996): 403–410; Wade C. Roof and William McKinney, *American Mainline Religion: Its Changing Shape and Future* (New Brunswick, N.J.: Rutgers University Press, 1987).

33. Anderson, *Code of the Street*, p. 324.

34. Telephone interview with Dr. John DiIulio, May 9, 1999. See also, "Families of Adult Prisoners," in *Prison Fellowship Bulletin,* December 1993.

Media Resources

Film

Scar of Shame [1927]. Directed by Frank Peregini. 68 minutes. Colored Players Film Corp. This is a melodrama about the effects of class and caste on the marriage of a concert pianist and a poor, lower-class young woman.

Cabin in the Sky [1943]. Directed by Vincent Minnelli. 98 minutes. MGM (Metro-Goldwyn-Mayer). The film depicts how the power of prayer, faith, and love can change life.

Cooley High [1975]. Directed by Michael Schultz. 107 minutes. American International Pictures. This film was the foundation for the television show *What's Happening?* It depicts a Chicago high school and surrounding community.

Sounder [1975]. Written by Lonne Elder III and directed by Martin Ritt. 105 minutes. Fox Studios. This film is about an African American sharecropper family in the 1930s.

Roots [1977]. Directed by Marvin J. Chomsky, John Erman, David Greene, Gilbert Moses. Warner Brothers. This is a saga of African American life, based on Alex Haley's family history.

Roll of Thunder, Hear My Cry [1978]. Directed by Jack Smight. Television. The story recounts the struggles of a poor black Mississippi family in the 1930s and their attempt to hold on to their family's piece of land despite the machinations of white bigots all around them.

The Color Purple [1985]. Directed by Steven Spielberg. 152 minutes. Warner Brothers. This is a masterful adaptation of Alice Walker's Pulitzer prize–winning novel about a southern black girl's rise from tragedy to personal triumph through the course of her lifetime.

Sankofa [1994]. Video/C 6503. Directed by Haile Gerima. 124 minutes. Mypheduh Films. The film depicts a woman's journey to the past in order to appreciate her heritage.

Once Upon a Time . . . When We Were Colored [1996]. Directed by Tim Reid. 115 minutes. BET Pictures. A narrator tells the story of his childhood years in a tightly knit African American community in the Deep South under racial segregation.

Rosewood [1997]. Directed by John Singletary. 141 minutes. Warner Brothers. It re-creates the story of a shameful event in American history, the race riot of whites against blacks in a 1923 Florida community.

Soul Food [1997]. Directed by George Tillman Jr. 114 minutes. 20th Century Fox. This is a drama glorifying a family relationship and the importance of food in keeping the family together.

The Wood [1999]. Directed by Rick Famuyiwa. 90 minutes. Paramount Pictures. This film retells a semiautobiography of three young men who grew up in Inglewood, California in middle-class families with middle-class values.

TELEVISION

Amos 'n' Andy [1951–1953]. Directed by Charles Barton. ML Productions. 30 minutes. These stories were mostly centered on the Kingfish's schemes to get rich, often by duping his lodge brothers. It was the first television series to employ an all-black cast.

The Cosby Show [1984–1992]. NBC. 30-minute segments. These stories about a middle-class African American family living in Brooklyn, New York, corrected some and created other stereotypes about the family experience.

CHAPTER 7

We Come This Far by Faith

M ost individuals have some experience or experiences that give them pause to examine their belief system. One indisputable facet of the African American worldview is that spiritual and secular experiences are interconnected. Basically, every experience is a spiritual one. That sense of spirituality is usually maintained through community, whether in the church or temple. These religious settings provide social, political, and economic power for African Americans. For example, the black church has been an endless source of political activism. Regardless of whether they participate in a formalized act of religious faith, African Americans search for the answers to their spiritual well-being.

This chapter begins with a historical essay by Stacey Close, who examines the Africanness of religion among the enslaved community. He describes the important place that the elderly hold as they sustain the community's religious life, whether through Christianity, conjuring, or Islam. This trio of spiritual practices, taken up variously by the other authors in this chapter, exemplifies the importance of faith in men, women, and children.

The traditional spiritual "Steal Away" is revealed to have multiple meanings and purposes. The transmission of this song in the fields served to signal a variety of transitions from a call to freedom to a call to lay down troubles. However, another kind of "calling" was described in the 1836 journal written by Jarena Lee sharing her summons to preach. In the process, she reveals some of the workings of the African Methodist Episcopal (A.M.E.) church, the first African American church founded for freed blacks in the eighteenth century. This journal illuminates the strong belief in prayer and conversion, which closely mirrors the discussion in the opening Stacey Close essay.

In his reaction to the founding of the A.M.E., Christian Methodist Episcopal, A.M.E. Zion, and other churches, Frederick Douglass in 1848 decried the separation of religious organizations and schools exclusively for coloreds. He saw that practice as a pernicious prejudice against black-skinned humanity. Likewise, Cheryl Townsend Gilkes in 1977 expresses similar concerns about the exclusion of women in many of the church's official rituals. The Sanctified Church has served as the exception to that rule because it elevates black women to the status of visible heroines—spiritual and professional role models. James Tinney writes about the establishment of the black gay church growing out of the history of Christianity. Like the development of the A.M.E. church and other denominations created out of the desire to have equal participation and leadership, the black gay church is a part of the emerging black gay culture. One wonders how Frederick Douglass would respond to the further bifurcation of religious organizations.

Close's discussion of religions also lays the groundwork for examining the practice of Islam by African Americans. He introduces the idea that Africans continued to embrace Islam during slavery. An excerpt from the 1964 autobiography of Malcolm X explores the problems, misgivings, and enlightenment Malcolm X experienced as he became involved with orthodox Muslims during his trip to Mecca. Alice Walker's "Roselily" reveals the thoughts of a woman during her marriage ceremony to a Muslim man. In the short story, she contemplates her life and the changes she will experience in Chicago as a Muslim woman. Monica Rhor, in a newspaper article written in 2000, describes the growing prevalence of Islam among African Americans and Latinos. With about 80,000 Muslims in Philadelphia alone, she states today about 75 percent are African American.

Certainly a clear retention of African culture referred to by Stacey Close was that of conjuring. Although it is no longer referred to by that name, there is continued evidence of traditional African religious and cultural practices. From the traditional religious practices adopted from the Akans of Ghana, West Africa, to the West African–derived Yoruba social structure and religious practices in Oyotunji, South Carolina described by Mikelle Smith Omari in 1991, African Americans maintain African culture through artistic forms and religious experiences.

The final reading in this chapter comes from Susan L. Taylor's introduction to her book *In the Spirit* (1993). She reveals her own "calling" to embrace the power within. She refers to it as the power of positive thinking for those looking for peace and solutions. Taylor calls it life-affirming thought and encourages all to "Have Faith."

And so we have it. "We Come this Far by Faith," the title of this chapter, leads us to the indisputable fact that the church, temple, and shrine have been the center of social and political power and social change, from Nat Turner to Jesse Jackson, from Sojourner Truth to Minister Ava Muhammad. The readings in this chapter express the collective spiritual search from the past to the present. Continued, unbroken faith reveals a framework of activism, positivism, change, and stability in the African American community regardless of individual religious practices.

Stacey K. Close

Stacey K. Close (1966–) received an M.A. from Ohio State University in 1990. His thesis was "The Role and Status of Elderly Male Slaves in the Plantation South." Close's book, *Elderly Slaves of the Plantation South,* was published in 1997.

This excerpt, "Sending Up Some Timber: Elderly Slaves and Religious Leadership in the Antebellum Slave Community," comes from *Black Religious Leadership from the Slave Community to the Million Man March* (1998),edited by Felton O. Best. In it Close introduces readers to the antebellum practices of Christianity, conjuring, and the Muslim faith.

Sending Up Some Timber
Elderly Slaves and Religious Leadership in the Antebellum Slave Community

Henry's Hymn

Come ye that love the Lord
And let your joys be known
Join in a song of sweet accord
And thus surround the throne
Let those refuse to sing
Who never Knew the Lord
But servants of the heavenly king
should speak their joys abroad
The God that rules on high
And all the earth surveys
He rides upon the storm sky
And calms the roaling sea.[1]

The baptist hymnal used for devotional ceremonies during the antebellum period contained the above hymn, "Come Ye That Love The Lord." This hymn and others reverberated in common meter and short meter from churches in the South. Such hymns sent up timbers of hope and joy for enslaved people. Sending up timber was the process by which enslaved people prepared themselves for the afterlife. The hymns echoed the powerful importance of an omnipotent God in the lives of enslaved people. Consequently, African American churchgoers sang such hymns with tremendous pride. Slave owners sometimes recognized such fondness in their records. Shirley Jackson ("Black Slave Drivers") argued that the recording of Henry's favorite hymn was a testimony to the fondness the slave owning Pettigrew Family had for their old driver.[2] Indeed, it may have been; however, the hymn is also a powerful testament to Henry's religious beliefs.

Along with the family, religion proved to be a major stabilizing factor for enslaved people in the "Old South." Religion led by African Americans offered a challenge to that proposed by slave owners. A portion of that challenge can be found in the Africanness of religion among the enslaved community. In the traditional African religions, the living have a direct link to the dead through the spirits of the ancestors. The old people hold a special role because they are viewed as approaching the time of this spiritual power sooner than others. Floyd M. Wylie argues that "a case could be made for the dropping away of the cultural traditions were it not for the fact that young Africans from their earliest days were inculcated with these values" about ancestors.[3]

The elderly were in all likelihood no more religious than other slaves; however, the acquiescence of younger people to the leadership of older, experienced people resulted because of cultural traditions. Religious leadership in the slave quarters provided elderly slaves with their greatest opportunity for influence over other slaves. It was often from the grandparents that children acquired their religious beliefs. Younger enslaved people respected the aged for being old as well as for being religious leaders. Elderly enslaved men and women proved pivotal in sustaining the religious lives of people in the enslaved community.

The African Americans of the antebellum South religiously practiced not only Christianity but also conjuring and the Muslim faith. This Christianity was an African American form of Christianity. Slave owners' version of Christianity involved using religion to control enslaved people. While some owners were effective in establishing Christianity as a controlling entity, such efforts in regards to conjuring did not materialize quite as often. Conjuring came from the Yoruba of Africa, and the older slaves used it to control and influence younger slaves. Conjuring was used by the "old root doctors" to stop masters from whipping slaves and to bring luck, good or bad.

The white Southerners often made the assertions that they were pious 5 Christians. Such individuals were quite approving of African American preachers, some of whom were elderly. On Pierce Butler's Georgia plantation, Old Cooper London served as an influential Christian leader in the enslaved community. London taught the African American community the rights and wrongs in a religious sense. In moments of grief, London provided words of comfort for bereaved family members of Shadrach. London eulogized Shadrach (a slave) with remarks from the American Episcopalian prayer book as well as adding several extemporaneous phrases of his own. London proved to be an acceptable religious leader to members of the African American community along with Butler and overseer, Roswell King. On an Alabama plantation, the Methodist preacher was the slave Uncle Sam. In a building near his house, Uncle Sam would gather all the children on Sunday morning to teach them their duty to God and man.[4] Eliza Frances Andrews of Georgia recalled:

> Old Uncle Lewis, the old gray haired slave who has done nothing for years but live at his ease, was coddled and believed in by the whole family as its religious leader on the plantation. The children called him not Uncle Lewis but Uncle as if he had really been kin to them. Uncle Alex (Andrew's Uncle) had such faith in him that during his last illness he would send for the old

man to talk and pray with him . . . A special place was always reserved for him at family prayer and Uncle Lewis was often called upon to lead devotions. I was brought up with a firm belief in him as in the Bible itself.[5]

Ex-slave Katie Dudley Baumont also related that elderly male slaves were important in religious life. The slave owner of Baumont allowed the enslaved community to establish a church of their own. Baumont recalled that "We had a church about three quarters of a mile down the road." Africanness existed in the religion of enslaved people, African people challenged mainstream Southern religion. Remarkably, the challenge emerged from within a group of uneducated people. Much of what the leaders learned had to be memorized over the years. Reverend William Spotswood White remembered Old Uncle Jack as the pious Christian leader in Virginia. Jack could not read or write; yet his knowledge of religious matters resulted from his conversing and sharing his views with other knowledgeable persons.[6]

The Christianity in the slave community developed into an African American version of Christianity. The services contained call and response music and the ring shout, which were brought over from Africa. John Blassingame reports that a great portion of the religious music, methods, scale, dancing, patting of feet, clapping of hands, and pantomiming came from Africa.[7] "Call and response was vital to the progression of the sermon"; the spirit uplifted the congregation to ecstatic response to sermons.[8] Slaves strongly related to the teachings in the Old Testament, which they had often heard. They connected their station in life to that of the Israelites during the times of Moses.[9] This belief gave African American slaves a feeling that freedom would one day succeed. Moses Grandy recalled that, during his days as a slave in North Carolina, aged slaves and others would often go out into the rain and raise their hands to the heavens during violent rainstorms, while whites hovered beneath the sheets to be safe from the lightning.[10]

The African American version of religion not only provided an avenue to pray for freedom, it also granted slaves religious freedom. Erskine Clarke says in *Wrestlin' Jacob* that the slaves of Charles Colock Jones accepted Christianity as a buffer against the use of guards, guns, and bayonets.[11] Frederick Douglass received religious advice from Uncle Charles Lawson. Lawson served as his trusted counselor, and unknown to his master he even predicted that Douglass had some special calling.

The slave preacher, regardless of age, had to be sure not to preach a gospel of freedom that whites might overhear. Sarah Ford (ex-slave) reported that Uncle Lew spoke to an audience about unity and equality of whites and blacks. The owner moved Uncle Lew into the fields because of his statements.[12] An old preacher, Uncle Tom Ewing, once spoke the words "freed indeed, free from work, free from the white folks, free from everything" in the presence of his owner and found himself threatened with not being allowed to preach. Consequently, Tom never used the words again.[13]

Elderly religious leaders also found other areas in which their knowledge of religious matters might benefit the plantation economy. The ritual elder, Leonard Haynes (originally from Abodoo on the Gold Coast of Ghana) used his religious power to ensure bountiful crops. During planting and harvest periods, Haynes

10

"performed a religious dance of the first fruit," a ritual that insured excellent crops for the plantation.[14] Haynes' ritual masked those found on the African continent.

There was also a Muslim religious influence among the slaves. A planter on the Georgia coast had a head man, Bu Allah, who was described as being an African of superior intelligence and character. Bu Allah reared his children in the Muslim faith. Three times a day, he would spread his sheepskin prayer rug to the East and pray to Allah. Bu Allah lived to be a very old man and when buried, his Koran and prayer rug were buried along with him. On a visit to the Hopeton plantation, Sir Charles Lyell met Old Tom, an African of Foulah origin who still adhered to his Muslim religion. Tom was not as influential religiously as Bu Allah because most of his offspring declined the Muslim faith and adopted Christianity.[15]

Conjuring was a religion to slaves, and the conjurer held a special role in the slave community. Religion defined in this paper is the belief in supernatural or superhuman forces. Conjuring certainly fits within this definition, even though some slaves considered it superstition. Conjurers were part of a group of significant others, who, unknown to the master, commanded respect in the slave community. Conjurers had "distinct features such as 'red eyes and blue gums,' unusual dress, and the accoutrements of the trade—a crooked cane, charms, and conjure bag. . . ."[16] Conjuring involved using roots or incantations to bring harm or good luck to slaves down in the quarters. As noted in the *American Slave*, "the lore of conjure men whom negroes looked up to and respected and feared as the equivalent of witches, wizards, and magicians came from African forefathers."[17] Old slave conjurers and persons with medical expertise passed their knowledge down to younger slaves, and not always exclusively to males. Gus Smith remembered that his grandfather passed his knowledge on to one of Smith's female relatives.[18] James Parker's grandfather not only taught him to read but gave him systematic religious instruction in the signs.[19]

Conjuring or fortune telling strongly influenced the slave community. It provided a source of protection beyond the family. One old slave promised that his potions would provide protection from the master's whippings. The charm did not always work. Julia Henderson of Augusta, Georgia, remembered that "old hoodoo man promised no whippings for slaves who chewed on a piece of root, his conjuring failed and as a result he received a good cursing from a slave by the name of Tom for its failure."[20]

Henry Bibb had somewhat better results in his negotiations with an old conjurer to get immunity from being flogged: "It worked the first occasion that he left the plantation without permission. On the second occasion he was flogged by his master."[21] Bibb had not learned his lesson about conjuring, so he decided to go to another conjurer. This old conjurer told him that the other slave was a quack and if Bibb paid him money, the old man would tell him how to keep from being flogged. Even with the new potion, Bibb was treated no better.[22]

Nicey Kinney, an ex-slave from Georgia, believed that an old witch-man conjured her into marrying Jordan Jackson. A fortune teller told her how the conjuring was done. Kinney said that she preferred not to marry Jordan: "He could not get me to pay attention to him, so he went and got a conjure man to put a spell on me."[23]

An excellent example of the influence that old conjurers wielded is provided by Ellen Belts. Belts recalled that an old man had cursed a group of children who had thrown rocks at him along the road. The man warned a young boy to cease or he would be cursed with death. Kinney and her family members were horrified the next morning as the boy died upon the kitchen floor. Kinney recalled that "nobody ever bother that old man no more, for he sure lay an evil finger on you."[24]

Frank, a seventy year old fortune teller, resided on the plantation where the fugitive William Wells Brown lived during his enslavement. Uncle Frank was a favorite with the young ladies, who would flock to him in great numbers to get their fortunes told.[25] Although Brown says that he was not a believer in soothsaying, he was at a loss to know how so many of Uncle Frank's predictions came true. Most important to Brown was the fact that his eventual freedom was among the conjurer's many predictions that came about. Brown states that this alone was worth the twenty-five cents he paid the old man.[26]

One old conjurer was believed by ex-slave William Adams to have the power to pass his hands over a wound and heal the wound. The old man miraculously healed a deep cut on a mule's leg. "He came over and passed his hand over the cut. Before long, the bleeding stopped. . . ."[27]

In some cases, the old conjurers wielded a certain amount of influence over masters. For example, one slaveholder overheard an old conjurer predicting the misfortune that was supposedly to befall an overseer. The overseer had angered the old man in some way, and because of this the old man was going to seek his revenge by riding the back of the overseer. The slaveholder stated that "the old man was a conjurer and his wife was a witch. One night the conjurer touched his son with a stick and together they went to ride the backs of the overseer and his son."[28]

Old female slaves also proved quite adept at swaying religious practices in the slave community. On the Sea Islands in 1864, Laura Towne encountered Maum Katie, an African woman, who remembered worshipping her own gods in Africa. Over a century old, she was a spiritual mother, a fortune teller, prophetess, and a woman of tremendous influence over other slaves.[29] "The interpretation of dreams and strange occurrences brought the real world closer to the supernatural realm and offered spiritual guidance to the ill, the troubled, and the lovelorn."[30] Although Katie worked on the plantation for a number of years, she still adhered to cherished beliefs from Africa. In this way, Katie resisted in part the culture of her owner. On the Whitehall Plantation of Richard James Arnold, Mum Kate led and influenced the plantation slaves with her ability to recall with great precision biblical lessons from the text of the plantation minister.[31] At the Beaufort Church in South Carolina, elders both male and female exercised religious control over other slaves by inspecting not only reports of death but also the propensity of members of society to backslide.

Although many of the slave preachers were men, the women both old and young were the primary conveyers of spirit possession and the ecstatic Christian religion of the slave community. The female slaves were often the first members of the slave community to shout and praise God.[32] In *Voices from Slavery,* an ex-slave indicated that his "grandmother was a powerful Christian woman, and she did love to sing and shout." The master had her locked up in the loom room because the grandmother would begin shouting so loud and make so much noise that people in the church could not hear the minister. Later, the woman would "wander off from de gallery and go downstairs and try to go down to de white folkses aisles." This behavior continued, and the owner could never stop her from shouting and wandering around the meeting house, after she became aged.[33]

20

On numerous plantations, the enslaved population appointed old women who cared for children to teach the children their prayers, catechisms, and a few hymns in the evenings.[34] Women, particularly old women, had a stronger propensity to practice their religion more openly than men.

Testimonial services emphasized the power of old enslaved women within the Christian faith on other members of the slave quarters. Women usually led the slave community in this religious practice. "Religious testimony was so important that slaves reduced prayers to formulas and taught them to young converts."[35] During these testimonial services, younger slaves learned from old women "old cherished ways of saying and doing things for the edification of their fellow negroes on the slave plantations of the United States."[36] African American women continued to lead most African American evangelical churches in testifying, even after slavery.

Such ecstatic behavior profoundly affected slave children. Some slave children believed that their grandmothers' prayers might produce freedom. Ex-slave Amanda Smith recalled hearing her grandmother pray that God would deliver her grandchildren from bondage. This charge for freedom came along with a desire for Smith and her siblings to have better masters and mistresses.[37]

Some elderly slave women resorted to using religion to gain control of a slave plantation from a white overseer. Old Sinda passed as prophetess among her fellow slaves on the Butler Plantation in Georgia. Sinda acquired so much authority over the rest of the slaves that her prediction of the end of the world became resistance that caused a halt to all work by slaves on the Butler Plantation. Her assertion took such a massive hold upon the African American population that the rice and cotton fields were threatened with an indefinite fallow because of this strike on the part of the workers. The overseer warned the rest of the people that he believed that Sinda was mistaken in her prediction and if her prophecy proved false she would be punished. Nevertheless, King had no choice but to wait until the appointed time for the appearance of the prophecy because Sinda had greater influence than King over the rest of the workers during the time of her prophecy. Obviously, Sinda's prophecy failed to occur; consequently, King severely flogged her for causing upheaval on the plantation.[38]

Old Julie, a conjure woman, rivaled the mystical abilities of Sinda. Shortly after the Civil War, freedmen recounted the exploits of Julie. The freedmen recalled that Julie caused much death and maiming on the plantation. As a result the owner responded by selling Old Julie. This sale proved quite difficult. Although the owner personally escorted Julie to a steamboat to carry her far from her home, witnesses reported that the old woman miraculously used her powers and forced the steamboat to reverse its course. To his chagrin, the plantation owner found the boat anchored the next morning at its previous point of exit. This momentous feat supposedly compelled the owner not to part with Julie.[39] The actions of Julie are extremely suspect; however, the fact that the slaves remembered her with such awe is a testament to the power of conjuring within the slave community. An ex-slave in *Weevils in the Wheat* recalled an old woman who instilled fear in a white owner because of her mystical ability. "Ole Aunt Crissy was another slave what was [a] caution. She was, ole she was, ..."[40] "Aunt Crissy was a smart talkin' woman . . . Ole master got sore, but he ain't never said nothin' Aunt Crissy."[41] This old woman used her influence as a conjurer to usurp the authority of the white owner, thus increasing her power within the slave community.

In some instances, the Muslim faith supplanted the influence of Christianity and conjuring in the lives of older women. Such was the case with the ancestors of ex-slave Katie Brown. Brown recalled that her grandmother staunchly adhered to the Muslim faith during a time in which most slave families were more receptive to Christianity. Katie's grandmother made a "funny flat cake she call 'saraka.' She make um same day ebry yeah, an it big day. Wen dey finish, she call us in all duh chillun, an put in hans lill, flat cake an we eats its."[42] Brown stated that her grandmother and grandfather carefully fasted and feasted in recognition of specific Muslim holidays.

The slave community admired and respected old female slaves because of their staunch religiosity and other actions. They generally were well thought of by the younger slaves and slave children. Frederick Douglass's assessment of the respect granted to old slaves in *My Bondage and My Freedom* certainly applied to treatment of old female slaves on other plantations.[43] Douglass stated that there was "rigid enforcement of the respect to elders."[44] The young slaves who resided on the plantation with Maum Katie showed a similar kind of deference to the old spiritual mother that Douglass spoke of in *My Bondage and My Freedom*.[45]

Although more old male slaves served as preachers than did elderly female slaves, the old slave women of the plantation South were among the most vocal and open practitioners of the ecstatic form of African American Christianity. Together with old men, elderly women prayed and shouted numerous slaves to near convulsions. Within the realm of the conjurers, the abilities of old slave women reached heights that were unparalleled by the best male conjurers young or old. Women like Old Sinda at times controlled entire plantations, including the white overseers. Along with old male slaves, elderly women sent out timber of freedom and hope for younger people through religious avenues. While many of these individuals no longer performed extensive labor, their presence established a religious leadership that served to keep the "African American community" alive. In addition, religious leadership provided the elderly with a feeling of belonging. This feeling of belonging established a traditional respected place for elderly African Americans in the antebellum South that transcended time.

ENDNOTES

1. Shirley M. Jackson, "Black Slave Drivers in the Southern United States" (Ph.D. diss.: Bowling Green State University, 1977), 134.

2. Ibid.

3. Floyd M. Wylie, "Attitudes Toward Aging and the Aged Among Black Americans: Some Historical Perspectives," *Aging and Human Development* (1971), 68; W. Andrew Achenbaum, *Old Age in the New Land* (Baltimore: Johns Hopkins University Press, 1978), 2–3, 193; Pollard, 229; Ibid; Achenbaum, 2–3; see also Southern Historical Collection, Kelvin Grove Plantation Book, Chapel Hill: University of North Carolina; U.B. Phillips, *American Negro Slavery* (Gloucester, Massachusetts: Peter Smith, 1959), 360; Deborah White, *Ar'n't I a Woman?* (New York: W.W. Norton, 1985), 130; see also Southern Historical Collection, James Hamilton Couper Papers, Chapel Hill: University of North Carolina; Ibid., Kelvin Grove Plantation Book, Ibid.; Ibid., Kollock Plantation Book, Ibid.; Manuscripts Department, University of Virginia Library, Huger Family Papers, Charlottesville: University of Virginia. The plantation listings make reference to the ages of several elderly female slaves on the Huger Plantation near Savannah in 1860 and 1861. The Huger Plantation at Murry Hill contained 87 slaves, 37 males and 50 females. No men were listed in a separate category as old; however, Phillis, Sabrina, Lucy, and Linda were listed as old women. In

1861, Hester is listed as Old Hester, who works in the house. In addition, Sally, Judy, Charlotte, and Granny Phillis have been added to Huger's list of old women making the total of elderly women at 8. Southerners, both white and African American, had some concept of elderly. Some people used the terms aunt and uncle to mean elderly. However, a definition of elderly, even during the antebellum period, was not absolutely clear. W. Andrew Achenbaum stated in *Old Age in the New Land* (1978) that some people considered the elderly to be those people of 50 years of age or older, while others considered those people 60 years of age or older as elderly. In "Aging and Slavery: A Gerontological Perspective," Pollard argued that there are certain inherent problems in defining old age for the purpose of determining attitudes. Pollard held that "old age defied the magical significance that we today attach to the 65th birthday." For the purpose of this study, elderly slaves are those 50 years of age or older. After the slave had reached the age of 50, masters believed the work capacity and monetary value of the slave would decline so drastically that in a short time the worker would be valueless as far as the slave market was concerned. In *Ar'n't I A Woman?*, Deborah G. White stated that women referred to as aunt or granny were "either middle-aged or elderly but odds were that they had also had children and some grannies were past childbearing." Slave narratives, autobiographies, and plantation records often make no mention of the actual age of the old slaves; however, they do identify elderly slaves by using such terms as "old," "aged," and "bent."

4. Katherine M. Jones, *The Plantation South* (Indianapolis: The Bobbs-Merrill Co., 1957), 268; Frances Kemble, *Journal of a Residence on a Georgian Plantation* (New York: Alfred A. Knopf, 1961), 190–91; Frederick Douglass, *Life and Times of Frederick Douglass* (Hartford: Connecticut Park Publishing Company, 1881), 90–92.

5. Eliza Frances Andrews, *The War Time Journal of a Georgia Girl 1864–65* (New York: D. Appleton and Company, 1961), 202.

6. William Spotswood White, *The African Preacher: An Authentic Narrative* (Philadelphia: Presbyterian Board of Education, 1849), 47.

7. John Blassingame, *Slave Community* (New York: Oxford University Press, 1979), 33.

8. Ibid., 237.

9. Albert J. Raboteau, *Slave Religion* (Oxford: Oxford University Press, 1978), 66–67; Blassingame, 22, 138.

10. James Oakes, *The Ruling Race* (New York: Vintage Books, 1983), 116.

11. Erskine Clarke, *Wrestlin' Jacob: A Portrait of Religion in the Old South* (Atlanta: John Knox Press, 1979), 58.

12. Raboteau, 232.

13. Ibid.

14. William Charles Suttles, Jr., "A Trace of Soul: The Religion of Negro Slaves on the Plantations of North America" (Ph.D. diss.: Univ. of Michigan, 1979), 49.

15. Caroline Couper Lovell, *Golden Isles* (Boston: Little, Brown, and Company, 1932), 103–4; Sir Charles Lyell, *A Second Visit to the United States of North America* (London: John Murray, 1850), 359.

16. Ibid., 276.

17. George P. Rawick, ed., *The American Slave: The Georgia Narratives* (Greenwood, Ct.: Westport Publishing, vol. 3, suppl. series part 1), 232.

18. Norman Yetman, ed., *Voices from Slavery* (New York: Holt Rinehart and Winston, 1970), 287.

19. Thomas L. Webber, *Deep Like Rivers* (New York: W.W. Norton Co., 1978), 175.

20. Rawick, ed., *The American Slave: The Georgia Narratives* (vol. 3, suppl. series part 1), 75.

21. Gilbert Osofsky, ed., *Puttin' On Ole Massa* (New York: Arno Press, 1969), 70–1.

22. Ibid., 71.

23. B. A. Botkin, ed., *Lay My Burden Down* (Chicago: University of Chicago Press, 1958), 83.

24. Ibid., 128.

25. Osofsky, ed., *Puttin' On Ole Massa*, 215.

26. Ibid.

27. Botkin, ed., 37.

28. Blassingame, 113.

29. *Letters and Diary of Laura M. Towne, 1862–1884,* ed. Rupert S. Holland (Cambridge, Mass.: Riverside Press, 1912), 144–45.

30. Finkelman, ed., *Articles on American Slavery: Women and the Family in Slavery* (New York: Garland Publishing, Inc., 1989), 217.

31. Charles Hoffman and Tess Hoffman, *North by South: The Two Lives of Richard James Arnold* (Athens: The University of Georgia Press, 1988), 53.

32. Margaret Washington Creel, *The Peculiar People: Slave Religion and Community-Culture Among the Gullahs* (New York and London: New York University Press, 1988), 231–32. The middle aged and elderly women were the practitioners and leaders of much of the spirit possession in the religion of the slave community.

33. Norman R. Yetman, ed., 64.

34. Albert Raboteau, *Slave Religion,* 176.

35. Harry P. Owens, ed., *Perspectives and Irony in American Slavery,* (Jackson: University Press of Mississippi, 1976), John Blassingame, "Status and Social Structure in the Slave Community: Evidence from New Sources" (1976), 145.

36. William Charles Suttles, Jr., "A Trace of Soul: The Religion of Negro Slaves on the Plantations" (Ph.D. diss.: University of Michigan, 1979), 44.

37. Amanda Smith, *The Story of the Lord's Dealings with Mrs. Amanda Smith: An Autobiography* (Chicago: Meyer & Brother, Publishers, 1893), 19–24, 27.

38. Frances Ann Kemble, *Journal of Residence on a Georgian Plantation* (Chicago: Afro-Am Press, 1969), 84.

39. Lawrence Levine, *Black Culture and Black Consciousness* (Oxford: Oxford University Press, 1977), 71.

40. Charles L. Perdue, et. al., *Weevils in the Wheat* (Charlottesville: University Press of Virginia, 1976), 183.

41. Ibid.

42. Charles Joyner, *Remember Me: Slave Life in Coastal Georgia* (Atlanta: Georgia Humanities Council, 1989), 41.

43. Frederick Douglass, *My Bondage and My Freedom* (New York: Arno Press, 1968), 69.

44. Ibid., 70.

45. Letters of Laura M. Towne, 144–45.

Gwendolyn Sims Warren

Gwendolyn Sims Warren has performed with the Metropolitan Opera and throughout Europe. Warren is a minister of music at the Allen African Methodist Episcopal Church in Queens, New York.

In this short 1997 essay based on the traditional spiritual "Steal Away" from *Ev'ry Time I Feel the Spirit: 101 Best-Loved Psalms, Gospel Hymns, and Spiritual Songs of the African-American Church,* Warren recites some history of the spiritual and its connection to revolts like Nat Turner's.

Steal Away

Traditional Spiritual

2. *Green trees a-bending,*
   Poor sinner stands a-trembling:
   The trumpet sounds within-a my soul;
   I ain't got long to stay here!

3. *My Lord, He calls me;*
   He calls me by the lightning;
   The trumpet sounds within-a my soul;
   I ain't got long to stay here!

In its brief verses, "Steal Away" spoke to the slave community with resonance. While the slave masters' preachers most often limited their sermons to the propaganda that sustained slavocracy, the slaves stole themselves and their spirits away to their secret hush harbors or even to freedom in the North via the Underground Railroad. "When [we] go round singin' 'Steal Away to Jesus,'" recalled one slave named Wash Wilson, "dat mean dere gwine be 'ligious meetin' dat night." The first phrase of the song could be hummed by a leader to another person who would hum the song in turn to someone else. The signal would be softly given all day until everyone was notified, and the slave master would never know what was going on. "De masters . . . didn't like dem 'ligious meetin's, so us natcherly slips off at night, down in de bottoms or somewhere. Sometimes us sing and also pray all night," Wilson added. Believers were also looking to steal away to be with Jesus in eternity.

It's clear from the testimony of fugitive and freed slaves that slave holders considered any evidence of an "invisible" church subversive or at least threatening. It's no wonder, since the songs and services were used in so many ways to communicate among the folk. Slave revolt leader Nat Turner, a preacher in Virginia, reportedly used this song to call his co-conspirators together. Slave holder responses to the discovery of services varied. Some might do no more than send someone to warn worshippers to stop the noise or else answer to abusive, violent patrollers. Others went so far as to flog the preacher "until his back pickled," then flog his listeners until they were forced to tell who else was there. An utmost punishment was meted out to a preacher in Georgia. This preacher, named George, disregarded his so-called master's threat of five hundred lashes if he continued preaching to his slave community. George escaped across the Savannah River to Greenville, South Carolina, in an attempt to avoid the whip. On the way, however, he ended up striking with a rifle a white man who had tried to shoot him. George was captured and jailed, and his master came to claim him, but was unable to do so. The authorities instead gave George's master $550 as payment for George's life. Then, in a wooden pen in front of a huge, forced assemblage of other enslaved African-Americans, Greenville officials burned George alive.

Jarena Lee

Jarena Lee was born February 11, 1783, in Cape May, New Jersey. Widowed at age 44 in 1827, Mrs. Lee traveled 2,325 miles—much on foot, the rest by wagon, ferryboat, and carriage—delivering 178 sermons. She preached hundreds of sermons before every conceivable audience in Great Britain. Her book, *The Life and Religious Experience of Jarena Lee, a Coloured Lady, Giving an Account of Her Call to Preach the Gospel,* was originally published in 1849.

In "The Subject of My Call to Preach Renewed," Lee relates her religious fervor and ability to pray and preach the gospel.

The Subject of My Call to Preach Renewed

It was now eight years since I had made application to be permitted to preach the gospel, during which time I had only been allowed to exhort, and even this privilege but seldom. This subject now was renewed afresh in my mind; it was as a fire shut up in my bones. About thirteen months passed on, while under this renewed impression. During this time, I had solicited of the Rev. Bishop Richard Allen, who at this time had become Bishop of the African Episcopal Methodists in America, to be permitted the liberty of holding prayer meetings in my own hired house, and of exhorting as I found liberty, which was granted me. By this means, my mind was relieved, as the house was soon filled when the hour appointed for prayer had arrived.

I cannot but relate in this place, before I proceed further with the above subject, the singular conversion of a very wicked young man. He was a coloured man, who had generally attended our meetings, but not for any good purpose; but rather to disturb and to ridicule our denomination. He openly and uniformly declared that he neither believed in religion, nor wanted anything to do with it. He was of a Gallio disposition, and took the lead among the young people of colour. But after a while he fell sick, and lay about three months in a state of ill health; his disease was consumption. Toward the close of his days, his sister who was a member of the society, came and desired me to go and see her brother, as she had no hopes of his recovery; perhaps the Lord might break into his mind. I went alone, and found him very low. I soon commenced to inquire respecting his state of feeling, and how he found his mind. His answer was, "O tolerable well," with an air of great indifference. I asked him if I should pray for him. He answered in a sluggish and careless manner, "O yes, if you have time." I then sung a hymn, kneeled down and prayed for him, and then went my way.

Three days after this, I went again to visit the young man. At this time there went with me two of the sisters in Christ. We found the Rev. Mr. Cornish, of our denomination, labouring with him. But he said he received but little satisfaction from him. Pretty soon, however, brother Cornish took his leave; when myself, with the other two sisters, one of which was an elderly woman named Jane Hutt, the other was younger, both coloured, commenced conversing with him, respecting his eternal interest, and of his hopes of a happy eternity, if any he had. He said but little; we then kneeled down together and besought the Lord in his behalf, praying that if mercy were not clear gone forever, to shed a ray of softening grace upon the hardness of his heart. He appeared now to be somewhat more tender, and we thought we could perceive some tokens of conviction, as he wished us to visit him again, in a tone of voice not quite as indifferent as he had hitherto manifested.

But two days had elapsed after this visit, when his sister came for me in haste, saying, that she believed her brother was then dying, and that he had *sent* for me. I immediately called on Jane Hutt, who was still among us as a mother in Israel, to go with me. When we arrived there, we found him sitting up in his bed, very restless and uneasy, but he soon laid down again. He now wished me to come to him, by the side of his bed. I asked him how he was. He said, "Very ill;" and added, "Pray for me, quick?" We now perceived his time in this world to be short. I took up the hymn-book and opened to a hymn suitable to his case, and commenced to sing.

But there seemed to be a *horror* in the room—a darkness of a mental kind, which was felt by us all; there being five persons, except the sick young man and his nurse. We had sung but one verse, when they all gave over singing, on account of this unearthly sensation, but myself. I continued to sing on alone, but in a dull and heavy manner, though looking up to God all the while for help. Suddenly, I felt a spring of energy awake in my heart, when darkness gave way in some degree. It was but a glimmer from above. When the hymn was finished, we all kneeled down to pray for him. While calling on the name of the Lord, to have mercy on his soul, and to grant him repentance unto life, it came suddenly into my mind never to rise from my knees until God should hear prayer in his behalf, until he should convert and save his soul.

Now, while I thus continued importuning heaven, as I felt I was led, a ray of light, more abundant, broke forth among us. There appeared to my view, though my eyes were closed, the Saviour in full stature, nailed to the cross, just over the head of the young man, against the ceiling of the room. I cried out, brother look up, the Saviour is come, he will pardon you, your sins he will forgive. My sorrow for the soul of the young man was gone; I could no longer pray—joy and rapture made it impossible. We rose up from our knees, when lo, his eyes were gazing with ecstasy upward; over his face there was an expression of joy; his lips were clothed in a sweet and holy smile; but no sound came from his tongue; it was heard in its stillness of bliss, full of hope and immortality. Thus, as I held him by the hand his happy and purified soul soared away, without a sign or a groan, to its eternal rest.

I now closed his eyes, straightened out his limbs, and left him to be dressed for the grave. But as for me, I was filled with the power of the Holy Ghost—the very room seemed filled with glory. His sister and all that were in the room rejoiced, nothing doubting but he had entered into Paradise; and I believe I shall see him at the last and great day, safe on the shores of salvation.

But to return to the subject of my call to preach. Soon after this, as above related, the Rev. Richard Williams was to preach at Bethel Church, where I with others were assembled. He entered the pulpit, gave out the hymn, which was sung, and then addressed the throne of grace; took his text, passed through the exordium, and commenced to expound it. The text he took is in Jonah, 2d chap. 9th verse,— "Salvation is of the Lord." But as he proceeded to explain, he seemed to have lost the spirit; when in the same instant, I sprang, as by an altogether supernatural impulse, to my feet, when I was aided from above to give an exhortation on the very text which my brother Williams had taken.

I told them that I was like Jonah; for it had been then nearly eight years since the Lord had called me to preach his gospel to the fallen sons and daughters of Adam's race, but that I had lingered like him, and delayed to go at the bidding of the Lord, and warn those who are as deeply guilty as were the people of Ninevah.

During the exhortation, God made manifest his power in a manner sufficient to show the world that I was called to labour according to my ability, and the grace given unto me, in the vineyard of the good husbandman.

I now sat down, scarcely knowing what I had done, being frightened. I imagined, that for this indecorum, as I feared it might be called, I should be expelled from the church. But instead of this, the Bishop rose up in the assembly, and related that I had called upon him eight years before, asking to be permitted to preach, and that he had put me off; but that he now as much believed that I was called to that work, as any of the preachers present. These remarks greatly strengthened me, so that my fears of having given an offence, and made myself liable as an offender, subsided, giving place to a sweet serenity, a holy job of a peculiar kind, untasted in my bosom until then.

The next Sabbath day, while sitting under the word of the gospel, I felt moved to attempt to speak to the people in a public manner, but I could not bring my mind to attempt it in the church. I said, Lord, anywhere but here. Accordingly, there was a house not far off which was pointed out to me, to this I went. It was the house of a sister belonging to the same society with myself. Her name was Anderson. I told her I had come to hold a meeting in her house, if she would call in her neighbours. With this request she immediately complied. My congregation consisted of but five persons. I commenced by reading and singing a hymn, when I dropped to my knees by the side of a table to pray. When I arose I found my hand resting on the Bible, which I had not noticed till that moment. It now occurred to me to take a text. I opened the Scripture, as it happened, at the 141st Psalm, fixing my eye on the 3rd verse, which reads: "Set a watch, O Lord, before my mouth, keep the door of my lips." My sermon, such as it was, I applied wholly to myself, and added an exhortation. Two of my congregation wept much, as the fruit of my labour this time. In closing I said to the few, that if any one would open a door, I would hold a meeting the next sixth-day evening; when one answered that her house was at my service. Accordingly I went, and God made manifest his power among the people. Some wept, while others shouted for joy. One whole seat of females, by the power of God, as the rushing of a wind, were all bowed to the floor at once, and screamed out. Also a sick man and woman in one house, the Lord convicted them both; one lived, and the other died. God wrought a judgment—some were well at night, and died in the morning. At this place I continued to hold meetings about six months. During that time I kept house with my little son, who was very sickly. About this time I had a call to preach at a place about thirty miles distant, among the Methodists, with whom I remained one week, and during the whole time, not a thought of my little son came into my mind; it was hid from me, lest I should have been diverted from the work I had to, to look after my son. Here by the instrumentality of a poor coloured woman, the Lord poured forth his spirit among the people. Though, as I was told, there were lawyers, doctors, and magistrates present, to hear me speak, yet there was mourning and crying among sinners, for the Lord scattered fire among them of his own kindling. The Lord gave his handmaiden power to speak for his great name, for he arrested the hearts of the people, and caused a shaking amongst the multitude, for God was in the midst.

I now returned home, found all well; no harm had come to my child, although I left it very sick. Friends had taken care of it which was of the Lord. I now began to think seriously of breaking up housekeeping, and forsaking all to preach the everlasting Gospel. I felt a strong desire to return to the place of my nativity, at Cape May, after an absence of about fourteen years. To this place, where the heaviest cross was to be met with, the Lord sent me, as Saul of Tarsus was sent to Jerusalem, to preach the same gospel which he had neglected and despised before his conversion. I went by water, and on my passage was much distressed by sea sickness, so much so that I expected to have died, but such was not the will of the Lord respecting me. After I had disembarked, I proceeded on as opportunities offered, toward where my mother lived. When within ten miles of that place, I appointed an evening meeting. There were a goodly number came out to hear. The Lord was pleased to give me light and liberty among the people. After meeting, there came an elderly lady to me and said, she believed the Lord had sent me among them; she then appointed me another meeting there two weeks from that night. The next day I hastened forward to the place of my mother, who was happy to see me, and the happiness was mutual between us. With her I left my poor sickly boy, while I departed to do my Master's will. In this neighborhood I had an uncle, who was a Methodist, and who gladly threw open his door for meetings to be held there. At the first meeting which I held at my uncle's house, there was, with others who had come from curiosity to hear the coloured woman preacher, an old man, who was a deist, and who said he did not believe the coloured people had any souls—he was sure they had none. He took a seat very near where I was standing, and boldly tried to look me out of countenance. But as I laboured on in the best manner I was able, looking to God all the while, though it seemed to me I had but little liberty, yet there went an arrow from the bent bow of the gospel, and fastened in his till then obdurate heart. After I had done speaking, he went out, and called the people around him, said that my preaching might seem a small thing, yet he believed I had the worth of souls at heart. This language was different from what it was a little time before, as he now seemed to admit that coloured people had souls, whose good I had in view, his remark must have been without meaning. He now came into the house, and in the most friendly manner shook hands with me, saying, he hoped God had spared him to some good purpose. This man was a great slave holder, and had been very cruel; thinking nothing of knocking down a slave with a fence stake, or whatever might come to hand. From this time it was said of him that he became greatly altered in his ways for the better. At that time he was about seventy years old, his head as white as snow; but whether he became a converted man or not, I never heard.

The week following, I had an invitation to hold a meeting at the Court House of the County, when I spoke from the 53d chap. of Isaiah, 3d verse. It was a solemn time, and the Lord attended the word; I had life and liberty, though there were people there of various denominations. Here again I saw the aged slaveholder, who notwithstanding his age, walked about three miles to hear me. This day I spoke twice, and walked six miles to the place appointed. There was a magistrate present, who showed his friendship, by saying in a friendly manner, that he had heard of me: he handed me a hymn-book, pointing to a hymn which he had selected. When the meeting was over, he invited me to preach in a schoolhouse in his neighbourhood, about three miles distant from where I then was. During this meeting one backslider was reclaimed. This day I walked six miles, and preached twice to large congregations, both in the morning and evening. The Lord was with me, glory be to his holy name. I next went six miles and held a meeting in a coloured friend's house, at eleven o'clock in the morning, and preached to a well behaved congregation of both coloured and white. After service I again walked back, which was in all twelve miles in the same day. This was on Sabbath, or as I sometimes call it, seventh-day; for after my conversion I preferred the plain language of the Quakers: On fourth-day, after this, in compliance with an invitation received by note, from the same magistrate who had heard me at the above place, I preached to a large congregation, where we had a precious time: much weeping was heard among the people. The same gentleman, now at the close of the meeting, gave out another appointment at the same place, that day week. Here again I had liberty, there was a move among the people. Ten years from that time, in the neighbourhood of Cape May, I held a prayer meeting in a school house, which was then the regular place of preaching for the Episcopal Methodists; after service, there came a white lady of the first distinction, a member of the Methodist Society, and told me that at the same school house, ten years before, under my preaching, the Lord first awakened her. She rejoiced much to see me, and invited me home with her, where I staid till the next day. This was bread cast on the waters, seen after many days.

From this place I next went to Dennis Creek meeting house, where at the invitation of an elder, I spoke to a large congregation of various and conflicting sentiments, when a wonderful shock of God's power was felt, shown everywhere by groans, by sighs, and loud and happy amens. I felt as if aided from above. My tongue was cut loose, the stammerer spoke freely; the love of God, and of his service, burned with a vehement flame within me—his name was glorified among the people.

But here I feel myself constrained to give over, as from the smallness of this pamphlet I cannot go through with the whole of my journal, as it would probably make a volume of two hundred pages; which, if the Lord be willing, may at some future day be published. But for the satisfaction of such as may follow after me, when I am no more, I have recorded how the Lord called me to his work, and how he has kept me from falling from grace, as I feared I should. In all things he has proved himself a God of truth to me; and in his service I am now as much determined to spend and be spent, as at the very first. My ardour for the progress of his cause abates not a whit, so far as I am able to judge, though I am now something more than fifty years of age.

As to the nature of uncommon impressions, which the reader cannot but have noticed, and possibly sneered at in the course of these pages, they may be accounted for in this way: It is known that the blind have the sense of hearing in a manner much more acute than those who can see: also their sense of feeling is exceedingly fine, and is found to detect any roughness on the smoothest surface, where those who can see can find none. So it may be with such as I am, who has never had more than three months schooling; and wishing to know much of the way and law of God, have therefore watched the more closely the operations of the Spirit, and have in consequence been led thereby. But let it be remarked that I have never found that Spirit to lead me contrary to the Scriptures of truth, as I understand them. "For as many as are led by the Spirit of God are the sons of God."— Rom. viii. 14.

I have now only to say, May the blessing of the Father, and of the Son, and of the Holy Ghost, accompany the reading of this poor effort to speak well of his name, wherever it may be read. AMEN.

Frederick Douglass

Frederick Douglass (1817–1895), esteemed freedom fighter and statesman, was known for his leadership in the Abolitionist Movement. He wrote and spoke about segregation and racism in American culture decades prior to the Civil War. Douglass was a spokesperson for the American Anti-Slavery Society. His speeches against slavery won him fame and recognition. He published his autobiography *The Narrative of the Life of Frederick Douglass, An American Slave* in 1845 and an antislavery newspaper, *The North Star.* Douglass's political career included being the District of Columbia Counsel under President Lincoln, U.S. Marshall for the District of Columbia under President Hayes, the Recorder of Deeds under Presidents Garfield and Cleveland, and Minister to Haiti and Santo Domingo under President Harrison. Throughout his life, Douglass advocated civil liberties for African Americans and is revered today for his unswerving commitment to equal rights.

In "Black Churches and Segregation," published in *The North Star,* March 10, 1848, Douglass takes to task separation of the races in church or school.

Black Churches and Segregation

One of the greatest evils resulting from separate religious organizations for the exclusive use of colored persons is the countenance and support which they give to exclusive colored schools. The very existence of the former is an argument in favor of the latter. If there be any good reason for a colored church, the same will hold good in regard to a colored school, and indeed to every other institution founded on complexion. Negro pews in the church; negro boxes in the theatre; negro cars on the railroad; negro berths in the steamboat; negro churches and negro schools in the community are all the pernicious fruit of a wicked, unnatural, and blasphemous prejudice against our God-given complexion; and as such stand directly in the way of our progress and equality. The axe must be laid at the root of the tree. This whole system of things is false, foul, and infernal, and should receive our most earnest and unceasing reprobation. The evils of separate colored schools are obvious to the common sense of all. Their very tendency is to produce feelings of superiority in the minds of white children, and a sense of inferiority in those of colored children; thus producing pride on the one hand, and servility on the other, and making those who would be the best of friends the worst of enemies. As we have frequently urged on the platform and elsewhere, prejudice is not the creature of birth, but of education. When a boy in the streets of Baltimore, we were never objected to by our white playfellows on account of our color. When the hat was tossed up for a choice of partners in the play, we were selected as readily as any other boy, and were esteemed as highly as any. No one ever objected to our complexion. We could run as fast, jump as far, throw the ball as direct and true, and catch it with as much dexterity and skill as the white boys; and were esteemed for what we could do. And such, in our judgment, would be the case here at the North, but for the many influences tending to a separation of white from colored children. We shall, however, have more to say on this subject at another time; for it is one which ought to receive speedy and thorough attention, not only in this community, but throughout the Union.

Another reason against colored churches originates in the character and qualifications of the men almost universally and necessarily employed as their teachers and pastors. With few exceptions, colored ministers have not the mental qualifications to instruct and improve their congregations; and instead of advancing they retard the intellectual progress of the people. Some of the most popular colored preachers in this country are men unable to write their own names; and many of them are unable to read without spelling half their words. Colored churches form a field for this class of "would-be ministers;" and their existence is one great reason of the ignorance and mental inactivity, and general want of enterprise among us as a class. We have heard them denounce what they called "letter killeth but the spirit giveth life: and that all we should care about is to get to heaven when we die." Of course the effect of such teachers and teaching is to establish the conviction, that "ignorance is bliss, and it is folly to be wise." A virtue is made of ignorance, and sound is preferred to sense. In point of elevation and improvement, wicked as are the white churches, and corrupt as are their white ministers, colored persons would have gained much more by remaining in them, than they have done by coming out from them; and they might ere this, in the northern States, at least have obtained equal rights in every department of the church, had they remained in them and contended for their rights. The example set by a few colored men in New England, with respect to the unjust and odious distinctions formerly practiced there in the use of railroad cars, is worthy of imitation in the churches. We have frequently gone into cars intended only for white passengers, and allowed ourself to be beaten and dragged out by the servants and conductors, as a means of distinctly asserting the equal rights of colored persons in the use of those cars. And what has been the result of such conduct on our part! Why this—the whole system of compelling colored persons to ride in separate cars from others has been totally abolished. The railroad companies became ashamed of their proscription, and abandoned it. Colored men are now treated with the utmost kindness and equality on the same roads where five years ago, they were insulted and degraded. We should like to see the same course pursued toward white churches. Colored members should go in and take seats, without regard to their complexion, and allow themselves to be dragged out by the ministers, elders, and deacons. Such a course would very soon settle the question, and in the right way. It would compel the church to develop her character in such a manner as either to secure the rights of her colored members, or to secure her own destruction. We shall practice on this principle, and in every instance give white religious worshippers the trouble of removing us from among them, or the pain of enduring our dark appearance.

Another evil of colored churches is their expensiveness. Colored people are scattered over the country in small numbers, and are generally poor; and to be compelled to build churches for themselves, and hire their own minister, is by no means a trifling hardship. The minister and his family must be supported, though the members have scarcely the means of living, to say nothing of the means of educating and improving the minds of their children. We have known of churches composed of a dozen good colored women and as many men; the former gaining their living over the washtub, and the latter obtaining theirs by daily toil; at the same time supporting a minister and his family at an expense of from two to three hundred dollars a year.

Cheryl Townsend Gilkes

Cheryl Townsend Gilkes (1947–) received her B.A. in 1970 from Northeastern University, her M.A. in 1973, and her Ph.D. in 1979 from Harvard University's Divinity School. She has been a research associate, visiting lecturer, faculty fellow, and associate minister with the Bunting Institute of Radcliffe College and the Union Baptist Church. At Boston University, she became an Assistant Professor of Sociology in 1978. She has been secretary of the Cambridge Civic Unity Community (1978–) and Assistant Dean of the Congress of Christian Education, United Baptist Convention of Massachusetts, Rhode Island, and New Hampshire (1986–).

In this 1977 article, "Together and in Harness: Women's Traditions in the Sanctified Church," Gilkes discusses the Sanctified Church as one institution that has uplifted women, giving them a powerful, respected voice as church leaders and educators.

Together and in Harness
Women's Traditions in the Sanctified Church

All human communities contain enterprising and historically aware members who struggle to maintain the cherished values, statuses, roles, activities, and organizations of earlier generations that serve to structure the group's presentation of self and, therefore, constitute tradition. Within the black community in the United States, women have been some of the most enterprising agents of tradition. Since sociologists have seriously neglected study of tradition, women, and black people, black women's traditions in community institutions represent the most under-developed topic of social inquiry.

Black women and men have perceived racial oppression to be the most pervasive source of their individual and group suffering, but it has not been the sole catalyst for their collective action. In addition to mounting organized responses to problems of political subordination, economic exploitation, and social exclusion, black people have constructed a historical community that has provided a context for traditions, distinctive ethnic identity, and group consciousness. When pressure to abandon tradition has come from outside the black community, maintaining tradition has become a matter of political resistance, even though this struggle may take place in parts of the community that typically avoid confrontation with the dominant culture. For example, religion and religious activity have been the most important spheres for the creation and maintenance of tradition. Black women have invested considerable amounts of time, energy, and economic resources in the growth and development of religious organizations.

Recognition of the variety of strong traditions that black women have established in the religious and secular affairs of their community has been obscured by sociologists' exclusive focus on family roles and on black women's deviation from patriarchal expectations in a sexist and racist society. The tendency to view black churches only as agencies of sociopolitical change led by black male pastors also obscures the central and critical roles of black women. Throughout all varieties of black religious activity, women represent from 75 to 90 percent of the participants; yet there is little documentation or analysis of their role in the development of this oldest and most autonomous aspect of black community life.[1] This article examines the place and importance of black women and their traditions within one segment of the black religious experience, the Sanctified Church.

The Sanctified Church, a significant but misunderstood segment of a very pluralistic black church, comprises those independent denominations and congregations formed by black people in the post-Reconstruction South and their direct organizational descendents. In contrast to those Baptist and Methodist denominations organized before the Civil War, the Sanctified Church represents the black religious institutions that arose in response to and largely in conflict with postbellum changes in worship traditions within the black community. Although these congregations and denominations were part of the Holiness and Pentecostal movements of the late nineteenth and early twentieth centuries, the label "Sanctified Church" emerged within the black community to distinguish congregations of "the Saints" from those of other black Christians. This label not only acknowledges the sense of ethnic kinship and consciousness underlying the black religious experience but also designates the part of the black religious experience to which a Saint belongs without having to go through the sometimes dizzying maze of organizational histories involving at least twenty-five denominations.

The importance of the Sanctified Church lies in its relationship to black history, its normative impact on the larger black religious experience, and its respect for and positive redefinition of black women's historical experience. When black people were first making choices about their cultural strategies as free women and men, the Sanctified Church rejected a cultural and organizational model that uncritically imitated Euro-American patriarchy. In the face of cultural assaults that used the economic and sexual exploitation of black women as a rationale for their denigration, the Sanctified Church elevated black women to the status of visible heroines—spiritual and professional role models for their churches. At a time when Baptist and Methodist denominations relegated Christian education to the structural margins of their organizations, the Sanctified Church professionalized this activity, and women were able to use their roles as educators and the "educated" as a source of power and career opportunity. At a time when employment opportunities for black women were the worst possible, the Sanctified Church presented "professional" role models for black working women to emulate. Higher education and work were identified as legitimate means of upward mobility for black women, and they were encouraged to achieve economic power through white-collar employment. As a consequence, the women's growing economic power helped to maintain their collective autonomy and reinforced their heroic role in the church. Finally, taking their cue from the feminist infrastructure of the black women's racial uplift movement, churchwomen created an institutional basis for women's

5

self-consciousness. The result was an alternative model of power and leadership within the most authoritarian and least democratic of formal organizations—the episcopally governed church. These religious organizations transformed the negative and contradictory experiences of black women into an aspect of community life that maintained tradition and fostered social and individual change.

Within the Sanctified Church, black women have created for themselves a variety of roles, careers, and organizations with great influence but with variable access to structural authority. Their activities and their consciousness represent a part of the black religious experience that underscores both the dynamic and unsettled nature of gender relations in the wider black community and the historical centrality of gender as a public issue within it. Although the women in the Sanctified Church have worked within structures that range from egalitarian to purely patriarchal, they have neither ceased nor relaxed their efforts to improve their status and opportunities within these organizations. In a variety of ways, their efforts are related to those of women in other black religious and secular organizations.

Women's experience in the Sanctified Church has been part of the larger historical role of black women, a role that emphasizes independence, self-reliance, strength, and autonomy and that contradicts the dominant culture's expectations and demands of women.[2] Like many of the black community's activities of the late nineteenth and early twentieth centuries, the rise of the Sanctified Church contained a gender-conscious response to the problems of racial oppression. Concern about the status and role of women was reflected in one among a number of cultural debates within the post-Reconstruction black community. In a response to black women's suffering and role demands in the context of violent racial oppression, the Sanctified Church took account of at least four specific aspects of their history when developing churchwomen's roles: the devaluation of black women by dominant culture, the education of black women and their recruitment as educators of "the Race" during the late nineteenth and early twentieth centuries, the "relative" economic independence of black women through sustained participation in the labor force, and the autonomous political organization of black women between 1892 and 1940.[3] . . .

The Sanctified Church and its women's traditions are an important resource for the entire range of the black religious experience. Churchmen cannot ignore the written tradition of women's achievement, and they ignore the oral tradition of cooperative protest with great difficulty. In denominations that do not ordain women, female members point to their tremendous records of service and continue the conflict over their role in the church. If and when these denominations change their stance—and there are a variety of reasons to be pessimistic about this prospect—ordained women will have a greater impact than they now do as unordained evangelists. As has been the case in the area of music, the Sanctified Church continues to have normative impact on the larger black experience greater than would be expected from its actual number of members, and that number is growing.

A major problem exists concerning the values of churchmen, which range from a commitment to patriarchy, domination, and hierarchy to a belief in male-female cooperation and mutual influence. The history of the Sanctified Church demonstrates that both sets of values exist in the world of black men. In the

Sanctified Church and beyond, many black men want to achieve the pure patriarchy they have never truly experienced. The functional necessity of women to the very survival of congregations, convocations, and denominations opposes such a tendency. James Tinney suggests that some black men absent themselves from churches precisely because of authoritarian male domination.[4] However, such male resistance to religious patriarchy is undermined by the dominant culture's persistent denigration of black women as matriarchs who are too assertive, powerful, and aggressive. Such labeling feeds a sexist backlash within the black community that encourages a rejection of the model of womanhood black women represent and deepens intragroup hostilities.[5]

Thus it has become fashionable since the civil rights movement to dismiss the achievements of black women in church, community, and society at large as a mere consequence of economic necessity. Unfortunately, many black men perceived the message of the 1960s to be, "If you will be sexist, we white men won't be racist". Such ideological assaults led to attempts to enforce European or dominant culture patriarchy where it had been effectively resisted.

The disestablishment of sexism in the dominant culture remains a threat to many black males who perceive the traditional model of gender relations as a component of the goal of assimilation. In order to persist in this thinking, such men must reject as unseemly and inappropriate any institutional record that suggests a tradition of heroism by black women. They must refuse to transform their observations of women's church and community roles and of the historical records of the churches into an internalized norm of egalitarian gender relationships. The saving grace for black women in the Sanctified Church is that, even in a context of structural subordination, they do control the record books and therefore the written record of their role. As long as women are involved in this process of cultural interpretation, there exists a strong egalitarian potential within the Sanctified Church. Additionally, black women do have their allies among pastors who have never adopted or who have abolished the separate lectern or "double pulpit" and among sympathetic bishops who will ordain them to take a charge outside the church (e.g., military chaplaincies) or to begin new churches.

Racial oppression and its gender-specific racist ideologies still invade the black experience. Black women who do not conform to patriarchal traditions have been particularly victimized. Unless black women's image in the dominant culture changes radically, their struggles against racial oppression must proceed both inside and outside the black community; they will continue to be tied to internal struggles to maintain what power they now have in the face of embarrassed black male opposition, as well as to the external struggles with white racism. As long as racism limits opportunities for black men, black women will continue to express some ambivalence about competing with black men inside the black community and will also strive to avoid direct confrontation and overt conflict. As long as racism and patriarchy operate as combined forces in the oppression of black women and men, black women will not abandon those institutions that are responsive to the shared aspects of the problems. The history of formal and informal organization within the black community suggests that the cooperative and egalitarian model of male-female leadership would be the preferred outcome. Black women's traditions in the Sanctified Church yield great hope for the transformation of structures that alienate and trivialize women's experiences. In the meantime, black women will maintain their solidarity and organizational strength—"stuck together [holding] the church in harness"—until deliverance comes.

ENDNOTES

1. Teressa Hoover, "Black Women and the Churches: Triple Jeopardy," in *Black Theology: A Documentary History*, ed. Gayraud Wilmore and James Cone (Maryknoll, N.Y.: Orbis Books, 1979), pp. 377–88; James Tinney, "The Religious Experience of Black Men," in *The Black Male*, ed. Lawrence E. Gary (Beverly Hills, Calif.: Sage Publications, 1981), pp. 269–76. See also Pearl Williams-Jones, "A Minority Report: Black Pentecostal Women," *Spirit: A Journal of Issues Incident to Black Pentecostalism* 1, no. 2 (1977): 31–44.

2. Bonnie Thornton Dill, "The Dialectics of Black Womanhood," *Signs: Journal of Women in Culture and Society* 4, no. 3 (Spring 1979): 543–55.

3. On the dominant culture's devaluation of black women, see Bell Hooks, *Ain't I a Woman: Black Women and Feminism* (Boston: South End Press, 1981). On the role of black women in education, see Linda Perkins, "Black Women and Racial 'Uplift' Prior to Emancipation," in *The Black Woman Cross-Culturally*, ed. Filomena Chioma Steady (Cambridge, Mass.: Schenkman Publishing Co., 1981), pp. 317–34; Angela Y. Davis, *Women, Race and Class* (New York: Random House, 1981); and Gerda Lerner, ed., *Black Women in White America: A Documentary History* (New York: Random House, 1971). On the "relative" economic independence of black women, see Dill; and Davis. On the political organization of black women, see Perkins; Davis; and Cheryl Townsend Gilkes, "Living and Working in a World of Trouble: The Emergent Career of the Black Woman Community Worker" (Ph.D. diss., Northeastern University, 1978).

4. Tinney, "The Religious Experience of Black Men" (n. 1 above).

5. Dill (n. 2 above); Pauli Murray, "The Liberation of Black Women," in *Voices of the New Feminism*, ed. Mary L. Thompson (Boston: Beacon Press, 1970), and "Jim Crow and Jane Crow," in Lerner, ed. (n. 3 above), pp. 592–99; Hooks (n. 3 above).

Malcolm X and Alex Haley

Malcolm X (1925–1965) was a Muslim leader whose extraordinary life is recorded in *The Autobiography of Malcolm X* (1965), which he related to Alex Haley. Until the last year of his life, he was the chief spokesman for Elijah Muhammad, the founder of the Nation of Islam and one of the most electric leaders of the Black Liberation Movement of the late 1950s and early 1960s. He stirred the passions of many when he described white people as "devils" who had exploited black people throughout history, and, for years, he scorned the Civil Rights Movement led by the Reverend Martin Luther King, Jr., calling the latter's goal of a fully integrated society a "sham" that was intended to "lull" African Americans to sleep. In 1964, Malcolm X left the Nation of Islam, after discovering that Elijah Muhammad had apparently violated the strict moral code of Muslims. He went on a religious pilgrimage to Mecca, where he was so touched by the warmth and friendliness shown to him by Muslims of all colors that he changed his views about racism. After he came back to the

United States to build a new organization to fight for the rights of African Americans, he expounded on his belief that blacks and whites of goodwill could coexist in brotherhood.

Alex Haley (1921–1992), a journalist and writer, first gained national attention as the collaborator-editor of *The Autobiography of Malcolm X*. His highly acclaimed work *Roots: The Saga of an American Family* (1976) won a Pulitzer Prize. It blended fact with fiction and was loosely based on his African roots. Haley had spent 12 years researching his ancestry, tracing it to Kunta Kinte, a slave who was brought to the United States from Gambia in 1767. The book was the basis of a phenomenally successful television miniseries (1977), for which he received a special Pulitzer Prize and the Spingarn Medal. A sequel, *Queen* (1993), also appeared as a book and television miniseries.

In the following excerpt from Chapter 17 of *The Autobiography of Malcolm X*, Malcolm X describes his experience in Mecca and his resulting enlightenment.

Mecca

The pilgrimage to Mecca, known as Hajj, is a religious obligation that every orthodox Muslim fulfills, if humanly able, at least once in his or her lifetime.

The Holy Quran says it, "Pilgrimage to the Ka'ba is a duty men owe to God; those who are able, make the journey."

Allah said: "And proclaim the pilgrimage among men; they will come to you on foot and upon each lean camel, they will come from every deep ravine."

At one or another college or university, usually in the informal gatherings after I had spoken, perhaps a dozen generally white-complexioned people would come up to me, identifying themselves as Arabian, Middle Eastern or North African Muslims who happened to be visiting, studying, or living in the United States. They had said to me that, my white-indicting statements notwithstanding, they felt that I was sincere in considering myself a Muslim—and they felt that if I was exposed to what they always called "true Islam," I would "understand it, and embrace it." Automatically, as a follower of Elijah Muhammad, I had bridled whenever this was said.

But in the privacy of my own thoughts after several of these experiences, I did question myself: if one was sincere in professing a religion, why should he balk at broadening his knowledge of that religion?   5

Once in a conversation I broached this with Wallace Muhammad, Elijah Muhammad's son. He said that yes, certainly, a Muslim should seek to learn all that he could about Islam. I had always had a high opinion of Wallace Muhammad's opinion.

Those orthodox Muslims whom I had met, one after another, had urged me to meet and talk with a Dr. Mahmoud Youssef Shawarbi. He was described to me as an eminent, learned Muslim, a University of Cairo graduate, a University of London Ph.D., a lecturer on Islam, a United Nations advisor and the author of many books. He was a full professor of the University of Cairo, on leave from there to be in New York as the Director of the Federation of Islamic Associations in the United States and Canada. Several times, driving in that part of town, I had resisted the impulse to drop in at the F.I.A. building, a brownstone at 1 Riverside Drive. Then one day Dr. Shawarbi and I were introduced by a newspaperman.

He was cordial. He said he had followed me in the press; I said I had been told of him, and we talked for fifteen or twenty minutes. We both had to leave to make appointments we had, when he dropped on me something whose logic never would get out of my head. He said, "No man has believed perfectly until he wishes for his brother what he wishes for himself."

Then, there was my sister Ella herself. I couldn't get over what she had done. I've said before, this is a *strong*, big, black, Georgia-born woman. Her domineering ways had gotten her put out of the Nation of Islam's Boston Mosque Eleven; they took her back, then she left on her own. Ella had started studying under Boston orthodox Muslims, then she founded a school where Arabic was taught! *She* couldn't speak it; she hired teachers who did. That's Ella! She deals in real estate, and *she* was saving up to make the pilgrimage. Nearly all night, we talked in her living room. She told me there was no question about it; it was more important that I go. I thought about Ella the whole flight back to New York. A *strong* woman. She had broken the spirits of three husbands, more driving and dynamic than all of them combined. She had played a very significant role in my life. No other woman ever was strong enough to point me in directions; I pointed women in directions. I had brought Ella into Islam, and now she was financing me to Mecca.

Allah always gives you signs, when you are with Him, that He is with you.   10

When I applied for a visa to Mecca at the Saudi Arabian Consulate, the Saudi Ambassador told me that no Muslim converted in America could have a visa for the Hajj pilgrimage without the signed approval of Dr. Mahmoud Shawarbi. But that was only the beginning of the sign from Allah. When I telephoned Dr. Shawarbi, he registered astonishment. "I was just going to get in touch with you," he said. "By all means come right over."

When I got to his office, Dr. Shawarbi handed me the signed letter approving me to make the Hajj in Mecca, and then a book. It was *The Eternal Message of Muhammad* by Abd ar-Rahman Azzam. . . .

The literal meaning of Hajj in Arabic is to set out toward a definite objective. In Islamic law, it means to set out for Ka'ba, the Sacred House, and to fulfill the pilgrimage rites. The Cairo airport was where scores of Hajj groups were becoming *Muhrim,* pilgrims, upon entering the state of Ihram, the assumption of a spiritual and physical state of consecration. Upon advice, I arranged to leave in Cairo all of my luggage and four cameras, one a movie camera. I had bought in Cairo a small valise, just big enough to carry one suit, shirt, a pair of underwear sets and a pair of shoes into Arabia. Driving to the airport with our Hajj group, I began to get nervous, knowing that from there in, it was going to be watching others who knew what they were doing, and trying to do what they did.

Entering the state of Ihram, we took off our clothes and put on two white towels. One, the *Izar,* was folded around the loins. The other, the *Rida,* was thrown over the neck and shoulders, leaving the right shoulder and arm bare. A pair of simple sandals, the *na'l,* left the ankle-bones bare. Over the *Izar* waist-wrapper, a money belt was worn, and a bag, something like a woman's big handbag, with a long strap, was for carrying the passport and other valuable papers, such as the letter I had from Dr. Shawarbi.

Every one of the thousands at the airport, about to leave for Jedda, was   15
dressed this way. You could be a king or a peasant and no one would know. Some
powerful personages, who were discreetly pointed out to me, had on the same
thing I had on. Once thus dressed, we all had begun intermittently calling out
"Labbayka! Labbayka!" (Here I come, O Lord!) The airport sounded with the din of
Muhrim expressing their intention to perform the journey of the Hajj.

Planeloads of pilgrims were taking off every few minutes, but the airport was
jammed with more, and their friends and relatives waiting to see them off. Those
not going were asking others to pray for them at Mecca. We were on our plane, in
the air, when I learned for the first time that, with the crush, there was not supposed
to have been space for me, but strings had been pulled, and someone had been put
off because they didn't want to disappoint an American Muslim. I felt mingled
emotions of regret that I had inconvenienced and discomfited whoever was
bumped off the plane for me, and, with that, an utter humility and gratefulness
that I had been paid such an honor and respect.

Packed in the plane were white, black, brown, red, and yellow people, blue
eyes and blond hair, and my kinky red hair—all together, brothers! All honoring
the same God Allah, all in turn giving equal honor to each other.

From some in our group, the word was spreading from seat to seat that I was a
Muslim from America. Faces turned, smiling toward me in greeting. A box lunch
was passed out and as we ate that, the word that a Muslim from America was aboard
got up into the cockpit.

The captain of the plane came back to meet me. He was an Egyptian, his complexion was darker than mine; he could have walked in Harlem and no one would
have given him a second glance. He was delighted to meet an American Muslim.
When he invited me to visit the cockpit, I jumped at the chance.

The co-pilot was darker than he was. I can't tell you the feeling it gave me. I   20
had never seen a black man flying a jet. That instrument panel: no one ever could
know what all of those dials meant! Both of the pilots were smiling at me, treating
me with the same honor and respect I had received ever since I left America. I
stood there looking through the glass at the sky ahead of us. In America, I had rid-
den in more planes than probably any other Negro, and I never had been invited
up into the cockpit. And there I was, with two Muslim seatmates, one from Egypt,
the other from Arabia, all of us bound for Mecca, with me up in the pilots' cabin.
Brother, I *knew* Allah was with me.

Alice Walker

Alice Walker (1944–) is a social activist and acclaimed writer whose novels,
short stories, and poems are noted for their insightful treatment of African
American culture, particularly that of women. She is also known for her critical
essays on such women writers as Flannery O'Connor and Zora Neale Hurston.
Walker's first book of poetry, *Once,* appeared in 1968, and her first novel, *The
Third Life of Grange Copeland* (1970), a narrative that spans 60 years and three
generations, followed two years later. A second volume of poetry,
Revolutionary Petunias and Other Poems, and her first collection of short

stories, *In Love and Trouble: Stories of Black Women,* both appeared in 1973. The latter bears witness to sexist violence and abuse in the African American community. After moving to New York, Walker completed *Meridian* (1976), a novel describing the coming of age of several civil rights workers in the 1960s.

Walker's most popular novel, *The Color Purple* (1982), won a Pulitzer Prize and was adapted into a film by Steven Spielberg in 1985. Through letters between two sisters, we bear witness to the cruel, segregated world of the Deep South and the growing up and self-realization of an African American woman between 1909 and 1947. Later works include *In Search of Our Mother's Gardens: Womanist Prose* (1983), *The Temple of My Familiar* (1989), *Possessing the Secret of Joy* (1992), *By the Light of My Father's Smile* (1998), and *The Way Forward Is with a Broken Heart* (2000).

This following entry, "Roselily," comes from *In Love and Trouble: Stories of Black Women.* A single mother reflects during her wedding ceremony about the changes she will face by marrying a Muslim man.

Roselily

Dearly Beloved,

She dreams; dragging herself across the world. A small girl in her mother's white robe and veil, knee raised waist high through a bowl of quicksand soup. The man who stands beside her is against this standing on the front porch of her house, being married to the sound of cars whizzing by on highway 61.

we are gathered here

Like cotton to be weighed. Her fingers at the last minute busily removing dry leaves and twigs. Aware it is a superficial sweep. She knows he blames Mississippi for the respectful way the men turn their heads up in the yard, the women stand waiting and knowledgeable, their children held from mischief by teachings from the wrong God. He glares beyond them to the occupants of the cars, white faces glued to promises beyond a country wedding, noses thrust forward like dogs on a track. For him they usurp the wedding.

in the sight of God

Yes, open house. That is what country black folks like. She dreams she does not already have three children. A squeeze around the flowers in her hands chokes off three and four and five years of breath. Instantly she is ashamed and frightened in her superstition. She looks for the first time at the preacher, forces humility into her eyes, as if she believes he is, in fact, a man of God. She can imagine God, a small black boy, timidly pulling the preacher's coattail.

to join this man and this woman

She thinks of ropes, chains, handcuffs, his religion. His place of worship. Where she will be required to sit apart with covered head. In Chicago, a word she hears when thinking of smoke, from his description of what a cinder was, which they never had in Panther Burn. She sees hovering over the heads of the clean neighbors in her front yard black specks falling, clinging, from the sky. But in Chicago. Respect, a chance to build. Her children at last from underneath the detrimental wheel. A chance to be on top. What a relief, she thinks. What a vision, a view, from up so high.

in holy matrimony.

Her fourth child she gave away to the child's father who had some money. Certainly a good job. Had gone to Harvard. Was a good man but weak because good language meant so much to him he could not live with Roselily. Could not abide TV in the living room, five beds in three rooms, no Bach except from four to six on Sunday afternoons. No chess at all. She does not forget to worry about her son among his father's people. She wonders if the New England climate will agree with him. If he will ever come down to Mississippi, as his father did, to try to right the country's wrongs. She wonders if he will be stronger than his father. His father cried off and on throughout her pregnancy. Went to skin and bones. Suffered nightmares, retching and falling out of bed. Tried to kill himself. Later told his wife he found the right baby through friends. Vouched for, the sterling qualities that would make up his character.

  It is not her nature to blame. Still, she is not entirely thankful. She supposes New England, the North, to be quite different from what she knows. It seems right somehow to her that people who move there to live return home completely changed. She thinks of the air, the smoke, the cinders. Imagines cinders big as hailstones; heavy, weighing on the people. Wonders how this pressure finds its way into the veins, roping the springs of laughter.

If there's anybody here that knows a reason why

But of course they know no reason why beyond what they daily have come to know. She thinks of the man who will be her husband, feels shut away from him because of the stiff severity of his plain black suit. His religion. A lifetime of black and white. Of veils. Covered head. It is as if her children are already gone from her. Not dead, but exalted on a pedestal, a stalk that has no roots. She wonders how to make new roots. It is beyond her. She wonders what one does with memories in a brand-new life. This had seemed easy, until she thought of it. "The reasons why . . . the people who" . . . she thinks, and does not wonder where the thought is from.

these two should not be joined

She thinks of her mother, who is dead. Dead, but still her mother. Joined. This is confusing. Of her father. A gray old man who sold wild mink, rabbit, fox skins to Sears, Roebuck. He stands in the yard, like a man waiting for a train. Her young sisters stand behind her in smooth green dresses, with flowers in their hands and hair. They giggle, she feels, at the absurdity of the wedding. They are ready for something new. She thinks the man beside her should marry one of them. She feels old. Yoked. An arm seems to reach out from behind her and snatch her backward. She thinks of cemeteries and the long sleep of grandparents mingling in the dirt. She believes that she believes in ghosts. In the soil giving back what it takes.

together,

In the city. He sees her in a new way. This she knows, and is grateful. But is it new enough? She cannot always be a bride and virgin, wearing robes and veil. Even now her body itches to be free of satin and voile, organdy and lily of the valley. Memories crash against her. Memories of being bare to the sun. She wonders what it will be like. Not to have to go to a job. Not to work in a sewing plant. Not to worry about learning to sew straight seams in workingmen's overalls, jeans, and dress pants. Her place will be in the home, he has said, repeatedly, promising her rest she had prayed for. But now she wonders. When she is rested, what will she do? They will make babies—she thinks practically about her fine brown body, his strong black one. They will be inevitable. Her hands will be full. Full of what? Babies. She is not comforted.

let him speak

She wishes she had asked him to explain more of what he meant. But she was impatient. Impatient to be done with sewing. With doing everything for three children, alone. Impatient to leave the girls she had known since childhood, their children growing up, their husbands hanging around her, already old, seedy. Nothing about them that she wanted, or needed. The fathers of her children driving by, waving, not waving; reminders of times she would just as soon forget. Impatient to see the South Side, where they would live and build and be respectable and respected and free. Her husband would free her. A romantic hush. Proposal. Promises. A new life! Respectable, reclaimed, renewed. Free! In robe and veil. 10

or forever hold

She does not even know if she loves him. She loves his sobriety. His refusal to sing just because he knows the tune. She loves his pride. His blackness and his gray car. She loves his understanding of her *condition.* She thinks she loves the effort he will make to redo her into what he truly wants. His love of her makes her completely conscious of how unloved she was before. This is something; though it makes her unbearably sad. Melancholy. She blinks her eyes. Remembers she is finally being married, like other girls. Like other girls, women? Something strains upward behind her eyes. She thinks of the something as a rat trapped, cornered, scurrying to and fro in her head, peering through the windows of her eyes. She wants to live for once. But doesn't know quite what that means. Wonders if she has ever done it. If she ever will. The preacher is odious to her. She wants to strike him out of the way, out of her light, with the back of her hand. It seems to her he has always been standing in front of her, barring her way.

his peace.

The rest she does not hear. She feels a kiss, passionate, rousing, within the general pandemonium. Cars drive up blowing their horns. Firecrackers go off. Dogs come from under the house and begin to yelp and bark. Her husband's hand is like the clasp of an iron gate. People congratulate. Her children press against her. They look with awe and distaste mixed with hope at their new father. He stands curiously apart, in spite of the people crowding about to grasp his free hand. He smiles at them all but his eyes are as if turned inward. He knows they cannot understand that he is not a Christian. He will not explain himself. He feels different, he looks it.

The old women thought he was like one of their sons except that he had somehow got away from them. Still a son, not a son. Changed.

She thinks how it will be later in the night in the silvery gray car. How they will spin through the darkness of Mississippi and in the morning be in Chicago, Illinois. She thinks of Lincoln, the president. That is all she knows about the place. She feels ignorant, *wrong*, backward. She presses her worried fingers into his palm. He is standing in front of her. In the crush of well-wishing people, he does not look back.

James S. Tinney

James S. Tinney, a Howard University journalism professor, died in 1988. Having first received widespread attention as a 14-year-old preacher in Kansas City, Missouri, he wrote many articles on Rev. William Seymour, a black minister whom he credited with founding the Pentecostal Church in America. After dissolving his marriage in 1962 with an announcement that he was gay, Tinney moved from Missouri to Washington, D.C., and earned advanced degrees in political science at Howard University.

Tinney's "Why a Black Gay Church?" appears in *In The Life* (1986, edited by Joseph Beam). He addresses supporting a black gay church for the same reasons that separate black churches and mostly white gay churches exist.

Why a Black Gay Church?

The Support of History: Black gay churches exist for the same reasons that separate Black churches and separate, mostly white, gay churches exist. Historically, the Christian church has often been fluid and dynamic enough to include many different types of congregations and denominations, many of which appeal to certain needs that are not met in other churches. In fact, sociologists know that denominations themselves reflect certain economic class characteristics—reflected in differences in liturgy and beliefs—even among persons of the same race. Among whites, for instance, the Episcopal church is a church of the upper classes (even though it has some middle-class congregations), while the Primitive Baptist church is a church of the mostly rural poor.

On the other hand, other churches have come into existence precisely because the Christian church was not fluid and dynamic enough to be comfortable with pluralism. Black churches as a whole were created because white churches excluded Blacks from equal participation and leadership. Early in American history, Christianity officially taught that Black people were created without souls and could not be saved. In fact, the baptism of slaves was finally permitted only after Christian slave-holders became convinced that baptism would not legally alter the slaves' inferior socio-political status. (The word "Christian" is being used here to mean "formal, structural and institutional Christianity" rather than "genuine conversion or faithfulness to the truth as taught by Christ.")

The first independent Black denomination—the African Methodist Episcopal Church—came into being because even free Blacks, who were not slaves, were not permitted to kneel at the altar and receive Holy Communion at the same time whites did. Even after independent Black Baptist and Methodist churches originated, white laws did not permit Black churches to own their own property (even in the North) or to have Black pastors over them or to even worship in Black churches (in the South) unless a white person was present.

Even today, Black denominations have been reluctant to merge with white ones, and separate Black caucuses exist in every major white denomination, and new Black congregations are being formed even under white denominations, because white churches still do not permit Black Christians the freedom to worship using Afro-American traditions in liturgy, and do not permit access to governing positions of authority over whites, and do not encourage Black liberation theology to be taught or proclaimed from the pulpit, and do not even understand or recognize the special gifts—as well as special needs—that Black Christians possess.

White gay churches have, within the past 10 years or more, come into existence under circumstances related to the oppression of sexual identity that parallel the circumstances related to oppression of Black identity. Unfortunately, however, many Black lesbians and gays find the same racial oppressiveness in these white gay churches that Blacks generally experience in predominantly white churches of whatever label.   5

Black gay churches should be supported because, on the one hand, they represent the pluralism that America and American Christianity are supposed to represent; and on the other hand, they represent the same desire for freedom, access, encouragement, understanding, and recognition that Blacks find impossible in most white churches, and that white gays find impossible in most "straight" churches.

The Development of Community

Black gay churches are being created spontaneously as a result of the search for, and the formation of, a sense of community. Since the sixties, there has been a growing emphasis on the wholeness and self-determination of the Black community wherever it is located. This has meant a visibly increased sense of loyalty to Black institutions and Black social cohesiveness. Similarly, since the seventies, there has been a growing emphasis on the existence of the gay community in whatever city it is found. This has meant growing support for lesbian and gay institutions.

Yet Black lesbians and gays have often found themselves "caught in the middle" (so to speak) since the "two-ness" of identity (to use a term of W. E. B. DuBois) reflected in being both Black and gay was not wholly approved in either the Black or gay communities. To maintain comfortability in the Black community, particularly in those places that cultivate Black culture and Black solidarity, many have felt a need to downplay their homosexuality. As the Rev. Renee McCoy, pastor of the Black gay Harlem Metropolitan Community Church, has said, "If Black lesbians and gay men are willing to check their sexuality at the door of the church, and come bearing gifts of talent, there are relatively few problems." And in order to maintain comfortability in the gay community, others have felt a need to downplay their Blackness.

This should not be. But the facts remain; and the pressures coming from both sides have necessitated the formation of a distinctly Black *and* gay community. Even without those pressures, an identifiable Black gay community would undoubtedly have still come into existence, simply because of the uniqueness in talents, gifts, sensitivity, experience, dress, and behavior that is inherently a part of being both Black *and* gay—both as a manifestation of God's creation and our own creation.

The Black gay community—and the Black gay church which is an integral   10
part of that community and that culture (as all churches are inseparable from some community and some culture)—are therefore not the result of some conspiratorial "invasion" of the Black community by white gays, or even the result of some "separatist" invasion of the gay community by Black extremists. Black gay churches are part and parcel of the newly emerging Black gay culture which is so inevitable.

Furthermore, Black gay churches are reflections of a valid and vital sense of growing commonality and unity and community among Black gay Christians. They both exhibit and promote a sense of fellowship and mission. Non-gay Black Christians should support them because they are reaching out with the message of Christ to a gay community that has been alienated from Christ and from "straight" churches. White gay Christians should support them because they are countering the many anti-gay myths in the Black community—and in the Black Christian community—that white gays cannot possibly reach.

Mikelle Smith Omari-Tunkara

Mikelle Smith Omari-Tunkara is a professor of art history at the University of Arizona, specializing in African American art. She earned her Ph.D. from the University of California, Los Angeles, in 1984, where she wrote her dissertation, "Cultural Confluence in Candomble Nago Socio-Historical Study of Art and Aesthetics in an Afro-Brazilian Religion." Omari-Tunkara's writings include "Solutions: Afro-Brazilian Women, Their Power, and Their Art" (1988), "The Role of the Gods in Afro-Brazilian Ancestral Ritual" (1989), "Creativity in Adversity: Afro-Bahian Women, Power and Art" (1990), "Completing the Circle: Notes of African Art, Society, and Religion in Oyotunji" (1991), and *Manipulating the Sacred: Yoruba Art, Ritual, and Resistance in Brazil* (2002).

In "Completing the Circle," Omari-Tunkara describes a town in South Carolina modeled on a Yoruba village as an alternative traditional religious experience in America.

Completing the Circle

Notes on African Art, Society, and Religion in Oyotunji, South Carolina

In Oyotunji, South Carolina, West African-derived social structures, religious practices, and their closely related artistic forms are dynamic agents that not only promulgate the maintenance of "traditional"[1] African culture in "modern" America, but also act as significant multivalent symbols of resistance against what the residents of this community perceive to be a racial and socioeconomic hegemony that dehumanizes and oppresses many African Americans.[2] In this respect, African "traditional" art forms and religions have been combined in Oyotunji to "invent" (Wagner 1981) an alternative New World "African" culture that contrasts provocatively with the increasing Westernization of African cultures on the continent itself.[3] Because Oyotunji is the only African cultural outpost in the New World that cannot be traced to survivals of slave cultures,[4] it can be said to complete the African cognitive and cultural circle in the Diaspora.

Calling themselves the "Yoruba," the residents of Oyotunji are a group of African Americans who made conscious choices to subscribe to social structures, behavior patterns, and beliefs based on West African models. These conceptual frames of reference are primarily Yoruba, but they also incorporate Dahomean, Egyptian, Asante, and other eclectic African borrowings as they suit specific purposes. Knowledge of West African cultural elements was (and still is) largely attained through an intensive study of the available literature written by African, African-American, Anglo-American, and European scholars. Intellectual knowledge supplemented with practical experience gained from rare trips to Africa provided Oyotunji with the requisite patterns concerning religious practices and procedures, art, architecture, marriage, social behavior, economics, and political structure. To this cultural mixture were added elements from Euroamerica (e.g., astrology, numerology) and from Cuba (devotional candles and flowers, altar construction, the Ojo Agunwa throne day, and certain other initiation procedures). In view of these factors, the "Yoruba" of Oyotunji can be considered to constitute a society[5] characterized by a distinctive, syncretic, neo-Yoruba culture.

Oyotunji is known variously as the "kingdom," the "village," or the "African village". Its name, meaning "Oyo rises again," refers to the ancient and powerful political seat of the Yoruba of Nigeria, and the community is perceived as the re-creation of the spiritual essence of that kingdom on American soil. Located in Beaufort County, near Sheldon, South Carolina, close to the crossroads of routes 17 and 21, Oyotunji is considered to be the spiritual center of the "Yoruba" in the United States. It was founded in 1970 by its king, Oba Efuntola Oseijeman Adefunmi I, formerly Walter Serge (Roy) King, who was a dancer and commercial artist from Detroit. Other offshoot communities of the "Yoruba" are located in Los Angeles, Miami, Philadelphia, Gary (Indiana), Chicago, Savannah, and Washington, D.C.

The Oba of Oyotunji was "crowned" by his constituency in 1972 after his return from Nigeria, where he had just been initiated as a *babalawo,* or priest of Ifa. His names themselves reflect the African cultural eclecticism that characterizes Oyotunji. Efuntola refers to his initiation as a priest of Obatala, the Yoruba god of creation who molded bodies from clay; in Yoruba, Efun means white chalk, and Ola means wealth. Oseijeman, meaning "savior of the people," is a chiefly name common among the Akan of Ghana. The name Adefunmi reflects the Yoruba custom of including *ade* (crown) in the names of all members of the royal lineage; Funmi ("for me") alludes to the fact that the Oba "invented" the "kingdom" and created for himself the right to rule, or wear a crown. In accordance with Yoruba tradition, the Oba of Oyotunji is commonly referred to as Kabiyesi.

The village is located on a ten-acre land tract in a relatively isolated, essentially agricultural area. Kabiyesi Adefunmi attributes his decision to locate in South Carolina to several reasons, foremost among which is the South Carolina origin of earlier generations of his family, and his effort to gain contact with his "roots." The second deciding factor was the underlying "Africanity" of the general populace, expressed most strikingly in the pervasive Pentecostal religion with its stress on "possession/trances" of the "Holy Ghost," and strong beliefs in Dr. Buzzard and other "root doctors" who cure with herbs, potions, and "magic spells." These "African" behaviors and practices make South Carolina residents generally more tolerant of the related "Yoruba" village practices, and in fact, many of them go regularly to the village for aid, advice, and divination. . . .[6]

The traditional Yoruba religion (Isin Orisa) as practiced in West Africa dominates the synthesis of gods honored in Oyotunji and is combined with Santeria, Haitian Vodun, and the version of Yoruba religion (Lucumi) practiced in Cuba.[7] In Oyotunji, the *orisa* are believed to be personifications of electromagnetic energy found in nature, and are aligned with numerological and astrological forces.[8] Oludumare is the supreme energy and originator of life, and the *orisa* are regarded as the intermediaries of Oludumare. Orunmila, equated with the sun, is the god of divination. Olokun, associated with the planet Neptune and Pisces, is the god of wealth and the sea. He is also the generic god of the souls of all descendants of Africans, and the patron deity of African peoples.

Obatala, the creator god who fashioned man from earth, has the greatest number of devotees in Oyotunji. Obatala is regarded as the patron deity of the kingdom because the Oba was initiated as a *babalosha* (priest) of Obatala in Cuba. Obatala is associated with the planet Jupiter and is considered astrologically connected with Sagittarius.

Sango, the *orisa* of thunder and also a former king of old Oyo, is governed by Uranus and equated with Aquarius. Osun, goddess of love, fertility, sex, and beauty, and one of the wives of Sango, is associated with the number 5. Yemoja, who is the mother of all the *orisa*, is the patroness of Gelede, and a moon goddess associated with Cancer and the number 4. Ogun, god of iron and force, is associated with Mars, Aries, and the number 3.

Esu-Elegba, the trickster *orisa* who is regarded as the youngest of all the gods, is associated with Mercury, Virgo, Gemini, and the numbers 1, 3, 11, and 21. Esu is also seen as the god of luck, and his image is found at every shrine and compound in Oyotunji, as well as at a major shrine near the palace entrance. This *orisa*, whose domain is the crossroads, is believed to possess the power to open roads and remove obstacles as well as to close roads.

Oya, the goddess of winds and death, is governed by Pluto and is associated with Scorpio. Damballa Wedo (the rainbow serpent), the worship of whom was brought from Cuba by the Oba and linked to the Dahomean pantheon of Vodun, represents all African Americans who died during the "middle passage" and slavery.

Each of the *orisa* has a separate temple with one priest or priestess in charge, although there may be others associated with the temple. Each temple complex is composed of a main shrine to the patron *orisa*, a shrine to the deity's Esu-Elegba, an *igbodu* (where novices are housed during initiation), and a shrine to all the deceased priests and priestesses of the deity, all arranged around a large, central courtyard for dancing and public rituals.

Socioreligious rank in Oyotunji seems to be allocated on the basis of seniority of initiation and extensiveness of training. Priests function as doctors as well as psychologists and are in charge of esoteric and detailed religious knowledge concerning the *orisa* they serve. Most of the villagers interviewed in 1977 were "read" at least once a day by one of the priests or priestesses. In addition to traditional Yoruba rituals, curing procedures, and divination, the process incorporates palmistry, numerology, tarot, and astrology. The priesthoods of the various *orisa* are usually responsible for the discipline of devotees as well as their education in traditional Yoruba history, rituals, songs, dances, chants, food taboos, and proper care of the deities.

Oyotunji must be viewed not only as an educated, organized general manifestation of "African" resistance to mainstream Euroamerican society, but more specifically as a part of a global phenomenon of maintenance of traditional Yoruba religion and culture in the Diaspora, although in this instance the connections are intellectual rather than distinctly hereditary, as is the case in, say, Bahia, Brazil. Most important, Oyotunji is the only African cultural community in the New World that has no links to survivals of slave cultures. Thus in my view, it completes the African cognitive and cultural circle in the Diaspora.

REFERENCES CITED

Bascom, William. 1969, *Ifa Divination: Communication Between Gods and Men in West Africa.* Bloomington: University of Indiana Press.

Hunt, Carl. 1979. "Oyo Tunji." Ph.D. dissertation, University of Virginia.

Semmes, Clovis S. 1981. "Foundations of an Afrocentric Social Science," *Journal of Black Studies* 12, 13–17.

Wagner, Roy. 1981. *The Invention of Culture,* Rev. ed. Chicago and London: University of Chicago Press.

ENDNOTES

1. The validity and usefulness of the term "traditional" have been much debated but not satisfactorily resolved by historians of African art in recent decades. As used here, it refers to an identifiable indigenous corpus of conventions that have remained little modified even in colonial- or postcolonial-contact situations.

2. All of the forty individuals I interviewed during the combined 1977 and 1989 research periods expressed this view, registered through dissatisfaction with the mainstream American status quo. Most residents I talked with were college educated (at least one had earned a master's degree) and were fully aware that they were dropping out of the dominant society, frequently against their extended family's wishes.

3. Roy Wagner's theses in *The Invention of Culture* (1981) that cultures all over the world maintain a dialectic between convention and invention, and that all cultures are constantly invented and reinvented by both culture bearers and culture recorders, bear important theoretical ramifications for a clearer understanding of Oyotunjians (generally regarded as an anomaly in the African Diaspora) as conscious creative cultural "actors." These ideas are most convincingly articulated in the chapters "The Power of Invention" (pp. 35–70) and "The Invention of Society" (pp. 103–32).

Oyotunji presents an interesting contrast to contemporary West Africa with its dialectic of movements toward modernism or Westernism, and counter-movements toward the traditional.

4. This situation contrasts with those found in Brazil and Cuba, where direct and indirect historical links to slavery can be traced. Although the term "survivals" has received a great deal of bad press in the literature, it is my view that the true essence and positive value

of the term can only be appreciated if understanding is attempted from the culture bearer's point of view. In this context, the emphasis is placed on the idea of tenacious adherence to African beliefs and behaviors despite often overwhelming adversity from the dominant European-oriented culture. The concept of survival is seen by informants as being closely related to the concept of resistance.

5. "Society in this instance is conceived and operated (from 'within') as a set of (differentiating) devices for eliciting consistency and similarity, and its most basic distinctions are the ones that 'put the world together.'" (Wagner 1981:121).

6. I have observed a number of consultations with Merindinlogun (sixteen cowries) divination in 1977 and 1989 and been told of its divinations and "roots readings" performed for local residents as well as those who regularly come from Savannah, Charleston, and other nearby areas.

7. A significant reason for this amalgamation is that the Oba, who is the Chief Priest, was initiated in both Cuba (as a babalosha) and Absakura, Nigeria (as a babalawo, or Ifa priest).

8. This appears to be an insertion of the American concern with astrology that was popular when the village was founded.

Monica Rhor

Monica Rhor was a staff writer for the *Philadelphia Inquirer* when this article was published in 2000. She is currently on the staff of the *Miami Herald* and writes for the *Bradenton & East Manatee Herald* in Florida.

She wrote "For U.S. Blacks, an Ancient Faith, a Renewed Hope" on October 14, 2000, to examine the growth of Islam among African Americans, particularly in the Philadelphia metropolitan area.

For U.S. Blacks, an Ancient Faith, a Renewed Hope

A sign in the barbershop window advertises 10-dollar haircuts and five-dollar shape-ups. Hip-hop music muscles through the air. The swivel-chair banter flows fast and furious.

But Makkah Deen, at the corner of G Street and Westmoreland Avenue in the hardscrabble Kensington neighborhood of Philadelphia, is more than a barbershop. And many of the young men who slip through its doors are seeking more than a quick trim.

They rush past mirrored walls and head to the basement, where, in a makeshift musallah (prayer room), they remove their shoes and kneel in devotion to Allah. Some are searching for a better way of life, others for peace, but all hope to find the answer through Islam.

"It speaks to our young people in a way that society does not," said Abdul Jalil Hassan, 23, of Kensington, who owns Makkah Deen. "Allah had a way for me. He helped me see a brighter view. So I wanted to do the same for the younger brothers."

An increasing number of African Americans and Latinos are turning to Islam, the nation's fastest-growing religion, according to the American Muslim Council. More than 40 percent of the estimated 5 million to 8 million Muslims in the United States are African American. Philadelphia's Muslim community numbers about 80,000, and about 75 percent are African American.

Islam teaches that Allah revealed his scripture, the Quran, to the Prophet Muhammad in the seventh century. Its five religious pillars are a profession of faith, daily prayer, fasting, zakat (a religious tax), and hajj (a one-time pilgrimage to Mecca).

Muslims subscribe to a code of conduct that forbids the use of alcohol or drugs and extramarital sex. For many of the young men finding their way to Islam, that strict framework is a contrast for lives lacking discipline and rules.

Kensington resident Nasr Haqq, 14, grew up seeing his father practicing Islam and became a Muslim himself just three years ago after reading about the religion and asking questions of his father and other elders.

"I love the religion," said Haqq, who wears a white crocheted kufi (skullcap) in public. "I used to get smart with people, but I don't act bad like that anymore."

He curbs his behavior, he said, by "trying to stay in the books," meaning the   10
Quran. And his enthusiasm for Islam—and the visible way that it has helped change his attitude—has spread to some of his friends. Haneef Dyches, 18, a Kensington High School student, said he was impressed by the discipline that Haqq seemed to get from Islam and converted three months ago.

"I was out of control," admitted Dyches, who was raised as a Christian but said he felt an immediate connection with Islam. "I used to get high, sell drugs, smoke weed. But now I've calmed down."

Hassan opened his musallah six months ago, just after his own conversion, to provide a gathering place in Kensington, where the Muslim community is just taking root.

But in other Philadelphia neighborhoods and in African American communities across the United States, Islam has long been a part of the culture. Many Africans brought here as slaves were believed to be Muslim. In the late 1960s, during the black-identity movement, those historical roots were rediscovered and many African Americans embraced Islam.

Perhaps the best-known convert was Malcolm X, who became Malik El-Shabazz,   15
a traditional Muslim, near the end of his life. By then, he had renounced the Nation of Islam, which had modified the teachings of orthodox Islam to preach black nationalism.

The Nation of Islam, which claims about 100,000 members in the United States, has a history linked to black separatism. But orthodox Islam—second only to Christianity in adherents throughout the world—affirms the oneness of mankind and teaches that Allah has no color.

"Some things about Christianity didn't feel right," said Jihaad Abu Aqiyb, 23, of Kensington, who converted at 16. "With Islam, my eyes blew open. Everything matched up perfectly. I felt full."

In Islam, said Aqiyb, who is Latino, "all groups are welcomed with open arms—white, Latino, African American."

Hassan, also raised as a Christian, said Islam provided him a clear sense of direction to a life that had seemed to be rambling.

"So many of us end up lost in the system, lost in society," said Hassan, who   20
married his girlfriend, also a convert, a week after his shahadah (profession of faith). "But Allah has a way for us."

In Arabic, the Islamic way of life is called deen. For observant Muslims, it means weaving the tenets of Islam into everyday life.

Over the last 30 years, deen has become increasingly visible in African American communities. In West Philadelphia, dozens of shops sell prayer rugs, Islamic books, kimars and hijabs (head scarves and veils worn by Muslim women), and kufis (worn by Muslim men).

Across the city, restaurants and grocery stores offer pizza, cheesesteaks and barbecue made with halal meat. Muslims, forbidden from eating pork, can eat the meat of only those animals slaughtered in accordance with Islamic law.

A growing number of Philadelphia schools, meanwhile, are accommodating Muslim students by setting aside spaces for salat (prayer) or allowing them, with parental permission, to leave Friday-afternoon classes for congregational prayers.

Shahid Abdullah, 12, a sixth grader at the Al-Aqsa Islamic School on Germantown Avenue, has noticed that even his Catholic friends now use the Islamic greeting As-salaam Aleikum ("Peace be unto you").   25

Wakil Shakur, 13, an eighth grader at Al-Aqsa, said his non-Muslim friends and relatives accept his religion without question.

Both boys, like most of the African American students at Al-Aqsa, are second-generation Muslims. African Americans make up 75 percent of the 270 students at the school, whose student body once consisted primarily of Arab immigrants. Shakur said he welcomed the rules of Islam.

"It teaches you to respect others and respect yourself," he said. "If I wasn't Muslim, I'd probably be drawn to the bad stuff, not the good."

Jihaad Abu Aqiyb, who often stops by Makkah Deen to pray, said he was headed in the wrong direction before he discovered Islam through his younger brother.

"My idol was Scarface at one time," he said, referring to the violent drug lord   30 portrayed by Al Pacino in a film by that name. "All I cared about was money and the material things."

With Islam, everything fell into place, he said. He liked the faith's emphasis on family responsibility and its admonitions against getting caught up in material wealth. He married at 16 and got an apartment, a job, and new discipline to his life.

But it came at a price: His mother criticized his appearance, his beard, and his loose-fitting clothing, and other relatives continued to serve pork products and other non-halal food.

Despite the initial hostility, Aqiyb said, he has had no second thoughts.

"I've become more understanding, more caring," he said. "There's more love in my heart. My heart is not dark anymore."

Susan Taylor ▪

Susan Taylor (1946–) is senior vice president and editorial director of *Essence* magazine in New York City. She started at *Essence* as a freelance beauty editor and, by 1981, had worked her way up to the top editorial job. Since she took over, the magazine's circulation has grown from 600,000 to over 1 million. One of the most popular *Essence* features is her column "In the Spirit," in which she often writes about incidents from her private life to make a point about the importance of self-reliance, discipline, and faith. She has authored *In the Spirit: The Inspirational Writings of Susan L. Taylor* (1993) and *Lessons in Living* (1995). She is also the coeditor, with her husband, of an anthology entitled *Confirmation: The Spiritual Wisdom That Has Shaped Our Lives* (1997). Taylor was recently inducted into the American Society of Magazine Editors' Hall of Fame.

In the following excerpt from the Introduction to *In the Spirit,* Taylor expresses the "new age" focus on positive affirmations and faith.

Coming to Faith

That day of transformation seems so long ago. It was a cold, rainy Sunday morning in November, and I was having difficulty breathing. I'd been short of breath for several days and had awakened that morning with a pain in my chest. It felt as though a heavy weight were pressing against my heart. I thought I was having a heart attack. I called and asked my baby's father to come get her and take me to the hospital for a chest X-ray.

So many things seemed to be happening at once. I was 24 years old, newly separated and living on my own with my year-old daughter, Shana-Nequai. I'd been hired, for $500 a month, as a freelance beauty editor at the new magazine *Essence.* Money was tight: The monthly rent on my new apartment was $368, and I had car payments, utilities bills and other living expenses to cover.

I had been worrying a lot: My car was broken, my rent was due, the holidays were just around the corner, and I had $3 in my wallet and no backup in the bank. That past summer I had started a new company, Nequai Cosmetics, which was doing well, but I had lost my business because the inventory was in my husband's beauty salon, and I had no safe way to get it out.

That memorable Sunday I sat in the emergency room with people who, like me, had no health insurance and had been waiting for hours to be examined, tested and given some relief. My mood brightened when the young physician assured me that I wasn't dying: my heart seemed fine and he could detect no medical problems. But he did say that I seemed overly anxious and needed to relax.

But how could I relax when the earth was shifting under my feet? This was no *little* funk I was in. I felt depressed and hopeless. I couldn't imagine any bright tomorrows. I had been working hard since high school, had saved my money and built my company, and suddenly I had nothing to show for it. When I left my volatile marriage, I went from middle-class wife to poor single mother overnight.

It was late afternoon when I finally left the hospital and stepped into the crisp fall air. It had stopped raining, and I decided to walk home, from Manhattan to The Bronx. I needed to save the carfare and use the time to think.

I was feeling so alone. I had no money, no man. All my troubles were on my mind: How was I going to feed my baby? Pay the rent? Did I really even *want* to make it through the night? I was gripped by fear.

As I was walking up Broadway, I passed a church, and something drew me through the big brass doors into the evening service. A powerful force was guiding me. I hadn't been to church in years, and I had been raised always to "dress" to go to worship. But there I was sitting in a back pew wearing jeans and a leather jacket.

That night I heard a sermon that would change my life. The preacher said that our minds could change our world. That no matter what our troubles, if we could put them aside for a moment, focus on possible solutions and imagine a joyous future, we would find a peace within, and positive experiences would begin to unfold.

I had grown up Catholic and had gone to Catholic schools. I had read my catechism each day and attended church seven days a week at times. I believed that God was in heaven, that there was power in the statues of the saints, in the cross that hung in the center of the church, in the wafer placed on my tongue when I took communion. I thought the nuns and the priest had a direct line to God. Never once had I heard that there was power within *me*.

The minister's talk about the power of positive thinking and looking within for peace and solutions seemed simplistic, rather like hocus-pocus. But I was clinging to the edge, not sure I even had the will to hold on. What did I have to lose?

I decided to try it. I gathered up some of the small pamphlets in the church vestibule. Little did I know I was taking the first step toward replacing my fears with faith. I was breaking a negative cycle that had so engulfed me that I couldn't see life's beauty. It was the beginning of my realization that our thoughts create our reality.

I felt lighter as I headed home over the bridge that crosses the Harlem River. I felt that tremendous weight lifting from my heart. All the next week I worked to keep my commitment to try to think positively. Instead of mourning the things that I felt were missing in my life—happiness, my new business, a love relationship—I began counting my many blessings. Throughout the day I would pause and give thanks for my life—for breath and health and the fact that I was here. I thanked God for my healthy child, for the part-time job that was keeping a roof over our heads. I gave thanks that I still had my mother and my good friends.

Within days I forgot that I'd been depressed. The shortness of breath and pressure in my chest disappeared. And within weeks I was offered another part-time job, teaching at Ophelia DeVore's modeling school. Several months later, Marcia Ann Gillespie became editor-in-chief of *Essence* and offered me a full-time position as the fashion and beauty editor, and my salary doubled. I began to see clearly how focusing on my blessings instead of my woes increased the many good things in my life.

My positive thoughts, prayers and affirmations didn't cause God to treat me more kindly and make changes in my life. Rather, the positive, life-affirming thoughts and words changed me. They lifted my faith. Now I was focused on the beauty of life, on my talents and strengths—on the power of God within me. I began to step into the world expecting good things to happen. I was learning that, depending on my positive or negative energy, I have the power to attract either good or bad things.

The wisdom of the minister's words is still unfolding for me: Having faith means being active, not sitting back bemoaning life and waiting for a change to come. It means loving ourselves, believing in ourselves and using the transforming power of God to move our lives forward. The Reverend Alfred Miller's words were simple. The truth is always simple, but living it is not easy.

If I'd had a man or felt any sweetness in my life that Sunday morning, I would have lingered in bed. If not for the pain in my chest, I wouldn't have gone to the hospital. If I'd had money, I would have taken a taxi or gotten my car repaired and driven past that church as I had many a Sunday. I would have missed that important sermon. I might have missed renewing my life.

During these difficult times, the most revolutionary thing we can do is to have faith—to hold a positive vision of what we want for ourselves and for our children and to put the energy behind that vision and make it a reality. Our enemy is not the system or those who foster it. Our enemy is fear—fear that blinds us to truth, fear that keeps us ensnarled in anger and disempowered by grief. Fear keeps us focused on what we don't want rather than on what we need to lead us toward a harmonious, healthful way of living.

With faith we are never alone. We realize that we have within us everything we need to overcome any of life's challenges. There have been countless times since that Sunday when I have felt the earth shake beneath me. This is what is happening to our people today, and to people throughout the world. It's but one of the many ways in which the Holy Spirit speaks to us and encourages us to make changes. At times it seems as if our face must hit the ground before we listen, before we heed our inner wisdom.

We are a spiritual people. I have faith that these hard times are awakening us   20
to a new unity and a reaffirmation of purpose. Faith played a large part in the lives of our elders—and that should tell us something. Their faith sustained them. We must never become too sophisticated to believe. Our parents and grandparents were strong women and men, sensitive and sensible. Despite the many forces arrayed against them, they moved the race forward. They took us higher. Faith gave them the inner security to know that they would find their way, even when they couldn't see the light. Keeping the faith is part of our legacy. We are a people who created astronomy, mathematics, medicine. We created art, built empires. We have suffered dispersion and barbaric oppression. We have endured and survived. We have come too far not to go the distance.

Let us continue to be champions of faith, not just when it's easy but also when we're in crisis. Let us keep our expectations and our vision high. Whatever we focus on is what we are moving toward. By directing our minds we direct our lives. It is our Creator's wish to give us life in abundance. My monthly editorials in *Essence* and the essays in this book are dedicated to helping us remember that truth.

Media Resources

Hallelujah [1929]. Directed by King Vidor. MGM. This was Hollywood's second successful black musical, following *Hearts in Dixie*. Showcasing black musical talents, King Vidor's film reflects technical advancements made in film during the early history of sound.

God's Stepchildren [1938]. Directed by Oscar Micheaux. Micheaux Pictures. 105 minutes. Film dramatizes the issues of passing and intraracial hierarchies.

The Blood of Jesus [1941]. Directed by Spencer Williams. Amegro Films. 68 minutes. This film provides an important representation of black religious music and doctrine.

Buck and the Preacher [1972]. Directed by Sidney Poitier. Columbia Pictures. 102 minutes. This western depicts the lives of former slaves and their use of obeah as they moved across the West.

Let the Church Say Amen [1973]. Directed by St. Clair Bourne. First Run/Icarus Films. 67 minutes. The viewer explores the effects of the black church on the community through the experiences of a seminary student.

Voices of the Gods [1984]. Directed by Al Santana, independent filmmaker. 60 minutes. The film makes a comparison between the Yoruba, Akan, and Christian religious practices.

Zajota and the Boogie Spirit [1989]. Directed by Ayoka Chenzira. Red Carnelian Films. This animated short chronicles black empowerment through music and dance from precontact Africa to contemporary America.

Cycles [1989]. Directed by Zeinabu Irene Davis. Women Make Movies. 17 minutes. This short film reveals a woman's biological and metaphysical cycles.

To Sleep with Anger [1990]. Directed by Charles Burnett. British Film Institute. 102 minutes. Characters in this film experience good times and bad times resulting from the use of metaphysical spiritual practices.

Sankofa [1994]. Directed by Haile Gerima. Mypheduh Films. 124 minutes. Video/C 6503. The film depicts a woman's journey to the past in order to appreciate her heritage. It illustrates the power of religious belief in the slaveholding islands.

Beloved [1998]. Directed by Jonathan Demme. Touchstone Pictures. 172 minutes. Video/C 82. This film is based on the Pulitzer Prize–winning novel by Toni Morrison, in which a slave is visited by the spirit of her deceased daughter.

Achievements in American Black History: Black Religion. 40 minutes. Video/C 82. This series traces the history of black religion from its African origins. It includes discussion of the roots of black religion in tribal life and beliefs, its adoption of the white church framework, and its spiritual, social, and political influence in America.

The African Burial Ground: An American Discovery [1994]. Directed by David Kutz. Kutz Television, Inc. 116 minutes. Video/C 5182. This film explores the history and archeological excavation of a burial ground for African slaves discovered in lower Manhattan Island, New York, during construction of a federal office building in the summer of 1991. The burial ground has provided additional information on the role of African Americans in colonial American life.

All God's Children [1996]. Directed by Dee Mosbacher. Woman Vision Productions. 26 minutes. Video/C 6200. The black church embraces African American lesbians and gay men as dedicated members of its spiritual family with commentary by prominent political and religious leaders in the black community.

CREDITS

Aikens, C. "The Struggle of Curt Flood," *Black Scholar,* November 1971, pp. 10–15. Reprinted by permission of The Black Scholar; **Allen, W.F.** "The Negro Dialect." Reprinted with permission from the December 14, 1865 issue of *The Nation;* **Anokye, Akua Duku.** "A Case for Orality in the Classroom," *The Clearing House,* Vol. 70, No. 5 (May/June 1997), pp. 229–231. Reprinted with permission of the Helen Dwight Reid Educational Foundation. Published by Heldref Publications, 1319-18th Street, NW, Washington, D.C. 20036-1802. Copyright © 1997; **Anonymous.** "Turning the Corner on Father Absence in Black America," a statement from the Morehouse Conference on African American Fathers. Reprinted by permission of the Morehouse Research Institute and Institute for American Values, 1999; **Anonymous.** Linguistic Society of America Resolution on the Oakland "Ebonics" Issue. Chicago, Illinois. January 3, 1997. Reprinted by permission of the Linguistic Society of America; **Anonymous.** "Objecting to the Negro Dialect," *Literary Digest,* Vol. 53 (November 11, 1916), p. 1253; **Bailey, Guy, Natalie Maynor, and Patricia Cukor-Avila, eds.** "Laura Smalley," *The Emergence of Black English: Text and Commentary.* Amsterdam: John Benjamins Publishing Company, 1991, pp. 61–78. Reprinted by permission; **Baldwin, James.** "My Dungeon Shook: Letter to My Nephew on the One Hundredth Anniversary of the Emancipation," © 1962, 1963 by James Baldwin was originally published in *The Progressive.* Collected in *The Fire Next Time,* published by Vintage Books. Reprinted by arrangement with the James Baldwin Estate; **Banks, Frank D.** "Plantation Courtship," *Journal of American Folklore,* Vol. VII, 1894, pp. 147–149. Reprinted by permission of the American Folklore Society; **Wells-Barnett, Ida B.** "A Red Record," *On Lynchings: Southern Horrors, a Red Record Mob Rule in New Orleans.* NY: Arno Press and The New York Times, 1969, pp. 7–15. Reprinted by permission of Ayer Company Publishers; **Beam, Joseph.** "Color Him Father: An Interview," *In the Life.* Boston: Alyson Publications, Inc., 1986, pp. 153–156. Reprinted by permission; **Bell, Derrick.** "Neither Separate Schools Nor Mixed Schools," *Faces at the Bottom of the Well: The Permanence of Racism.* NY: Basic Books, Inc., 1992, pp. 102–122. Copyright © 1992 by Basic Books, Inc. Reprinted by permission of Basic Books, a member of Perseus Books, L.L.C.; **Blassingame, John W.** "The Slave Family," *The Slave Community: Plantation Life in the Antebellum South.* NY: Oxford University Press, 1972, pp. 77–103. Reprinted by permission; **Bogle, Donald.** From *Toms, Coons, Mulattoes, Mammies, & Bucks: An Interpretive History of Blacks in American Films.* NY: Continuum, 1993, pp. 3–18. © 1993 The Continuum International Publishing Group. Reprinted with permission of the publisher; **Brown, William Wells.** *The Narrative of William W. Brown.* Boston: Boston Anti-Slavery Society, 1847. Pp. 21–22; **Bunche, Ralph.** "What Is Race?" *A World View of Race.* Port Washington, NY: Kennikat Press, Inc., 1936, pp. 1–24; **Cahn, Susan K.** "Cinderellas of Sport: Black Women in Track and Field." Reprinted with permission of The Free Press, a Division of Simon & Schuster, Inc., from *Coming on Strong: Gender and Sexuality in Twentieth-Century Women's Sport.* Copyright © 1994 by Susan K. Cahn; **Chideya, Farai.** "The Myth of the Welfare Queen," from *Don't Believe the Hype: Fighting Cultural Misinformation About African-Americans.* NY: Plume, 1995, pp. 35–45. Copyright © 1995 by Farai Chideya. Used by permission of Dutton Signet, a division of Penguin Putnam Inc.; **Close, Stacey K.** "Sending Up Some Timber: Elderly Slaves and Religious Leadership in the Antebellum Slave Community," *Black Religious Leadership from the Slave Community to the Million Man March: Flames of Fire.* Ed. Felton O. Best. Lewiston: Edwin Mellon Press, 1998, pp. 61–90. Reprinted by permission; **Cochran, Jr., Johnnie L. with Tim Cochran.** "My Brother's Keeper," from *Journey to Justice.* Copyright © 1996 by Johnnie L. Cochran, Jr. Used by permission of Ballantine Books, a division of Random House, Inc.; **Cole, Johnetta B.** "Culture: Negro, Black and Nigger," *The Black Scholar,* June 1970, pp. 40–44. Reprinted by permission of The Black Scholar; **Conrad, Mark.** "Blue-Collar Law and Basketball," *Basketball Jones: America Above the Rim.* Ed. Todd Boyd and Kenneth L.

Shropshire. NY: NY University Press, 2000, pp. 90–102. Permission granted courtesy of New York University Press; **Cullen, Countee.** "Incident," *Color.* NY: Harper & Brothers, 1925. Copyrights held by Amistad Research Center administered by Thompson and Thompson, New York, NY. Reprinted by permission; **Derricotte, Toi.** From *The Black Notebooks: An Interior Journey.* NY: W.W. Norton & Company, 1997, pp. 25–27. Copyright © 1997 by Toi Derricotte. Used by permission of W.W. Norton & Company, Inc.; **Douglass, Frederick.** "Black Churches and Segregation," *Frederick Douglass: The Narrative and Selected Writings.* Ed. Michael Meyer. NY: The Modern Library, 1984, pp. 269–272; **Doyle, Lieutenant Arthur.** "From the Inside Looking Out," from *Police Brutality: An Anthology.* Ed. By Jill Nelson. NY: W.W. Norton & Company, 2000, pp. 171–178. Copyright © 2000 by Jill Nelson. Used by permission of W.W. Norton & Company, Inc.; **Du Bois, W.E.B.** "Of Our Spiritual Strivings," *The Souls of Black Folk.* NY: The Library of America, 1986, pp. 7–15; **Dyson, Michael Eric.** "Bill Cosby and the Politics of Race," *Reflecting Black: African-American Cultural Criticism.* Minneapolis, MN: University of Minnesota Press, 1993, pp. 78–87. Reprinted by permission of the author; **Edelman, Marian Wright.** "A Family Legacy," *The Measure of Our Success: A Letter to My Children and Yours.* Boston: Beacon Press, 1992, pp. 3–11. Reprinted by permission; **Edwards, Harry.** "Crisis of Black Athletes on the Eve of the 21st Century," *Society,* Vol. 37, no. 3 (Mar/April 2000), pp. 9–13. Copyright © 2000 by Transaction Publishers. Reprinted by permission of Transaction Publishers; **Entine, Jon.** "More Brains or More . . . " from *Taboo: Why Black Athletes Dominate Sports and Why We're Afraid to Talk About It.* Copyright © 1999 by Jon Entine. Reprinted by permission of Public Affairs, a member of Perseus Books, LLC; **Evans, Mari.** "I Am a Black Woman," *I Am a Black Woman.* NY: William Morrow and Company, 1970, pp. 11–12. Reprinted by permission of the author; **Brice-Finch, Jacqueline.** "Ebonics: When Is Dialect Acceptable English?" *The Clearing House,* Vol. 70, No. 5 (May/June 1997), pp. 228–229. Reprinted with permission of the Helen Dwight Reid Educational Foundation. Published by Heldref Publications, 1319-18th Street, NW, Washington, D.C. 20036-1802. Copyright © 1997; **Fischer, Mary A.** "The Witch-Hunt: It Was Not Paranoia That Made Black Politicians Believe They Were Being Set Up by Their Own Justice Department," *Gentlemen's Quarterly,* December 1993, pp. 242–252. Reprinted by permission of the author; **Fish, Stanley.** "Reverse Racism or How the Pot Got to Call the Kettle Black," *Atlantic Monthly,* 272:5 (November 1993), pp. 128, 130–2, and 135–6. © 1993 by Stanley Fish, as first published in The Atlantic Monthly. Reprinted by permission of the author; **Gilkes, Cheryl Townsend.** Excerpts from "Together and in Harness: Women's Traditions in the Sanctified Church," *Black Women in America: Social Science Perspectives.* Eds. Micheline R. Malson, et al. Chicago: The University of Chicago Press, 1977, pp. 223–26, 242–44. Reprinted by permission of The University of Chicago Press and Cheryl Townsend Gilkes; **Gilyard, Keith.** "A Legacy of Healing: Words, African Americans, and Power," *Let's Flip the Script.* Detroit: Wayne State University Press, 1996, pp. 99–111. Reprinted by permission of the Wayne State University Press; **Gomez, Jewelle.** "Black Lesbians: Passing, Stereotypes and Transformation," *Dangerous Liaisons: Blacks, Gays and the Struggle.* Ed. Eric Brandt. NY: The New Press, 1999, pp. 161–177. Reprinted by permission of the author; **Hughes, Langston.** "Who's Passing for Who?" From *Short Stories.* Copyright © 1996 by Ramona Bass and Arnold Rampersad. Reprinted by permission of Hill and Wang, a division of Farrar, Straus, and Giroux, LLC; **Hurston, Zora Neale.** "Pa Henry's Prayer," *Mules and Men.* NY: Harper Perennial, 1990, pp. 25–26. Reprinted by permission of Harper Collins Publishers Inc.; **Jackson, Emma D.** "The N Word: A History of Pain, A New Generation Converge Over a Painful Word," *Sandusky Register,* December 15, 1999, pp. A1 & 9. Reprinted by permission; **Joans, Ted.** "Je Suis Un Homme," *You Better Believe It.* Ed. Paul Breman. Harmondsworth, Middlesex, England: Penguin Books, 1973, pp. 229–232. Reprinted by permission of the author; **Johnson, James Weldon.** From *Black Manhattan.* NY: Alfred A. Knopf, Inc., 1930, pp. 58–73; **Jones, Leroi.** "Primitive Blues and Primitive Jazz," *Blues People.* NY: William Morrow & Company, 1963, pp. 60–70. Copyright © 1963 by Leroi Jones. Reprinted by permission of Harper Collins Publishers Inc.; **King, Peter.** "Scorecard: The NFL's Black Eye," *Sports Illustrated,* February 7, 2000, p. 29. Copyright © 2000, Time Inc. Reprinted courtesy of Sports Illustrated. All rights reserved; **Knight, Etheridge.** "The Idea of Ancestry," *Black Voices From Prison.* NY: Pathfinder Press, Inc., 1970, pp. 86–87. Copyright © 1970 by Pathfinder Press. Reprinted by permission; **Lee, Jarena.** "The Subject of My Call to Preach Renewed," from *Sisters of the Spirit.* Ed. William L. Andrews. Bloomington: Indiana University Press, 1986, pp. 42–48. Reprinted with permission from Indiana University Press; **Clark-Lewis, Elizabeth.** "A Woman Just Wouldn't," from *Living In and Living Out: African American Domestics in Washington, D.C., 1910–1940.* Copyright © 1994 by the Smithsonian Institution. Used by permission of the publisher; **Malcomson, Scott L.** Excerpt from "We Can Be As Separate As The Fingers: Segregation from the American Revolution to the Gilded Age," *One Drop of Blood: The American Misadventure of Race.* Copyright

INDEX

Aikens, Charles, 94
Allen, W. F., 47
Anokye, Akua Duku, 72

Bailey, Guy, 270
Baldwin, James, 216
Banks, Frank D., 269
Baraka, Amiri, 56
Beam, Joseph, 275
Bell, Derrick, 148
Bill Cosby and the Politics of Race, 237
Black Beginnings: From Uncle Tom's Cabin
    to The Birth of a Nation, 206
Black Churches and Segregation, 327
*Black Identity: Shades of Beauty
    and Pride*, 24
*Black Lesbians: Passing, Stereotypes,
    and Transformation*, 244
Black Manhattan, 91
Black Notebooks, The, 22
Black Power, 20
Blassingame, John W., 254
Blue-Collar Law and Basketball, 100
Bogle, Donald, 206
Brice-Finch, Jacqueline, 70
Brown, William Wells, 89
Bunche, Ralph, 8

Cahn, Susan, 111
Case for Orality in the Classroom, A, 72
Chideya, Farai, 282
*'Cinderellas' of Sport: Black Women
    in Track and Field*, 111
Clarence Thomas Fiasco, The, 193
Clark-Lewis, Elizabeth, 277
Close, Stacey K., 311
Cochran, Johnnie, 173
Cole, Johnnetta B., 231
Color Him Father: An Interview, 275
Coming to Faith, 349
*Completing the Circle: Notes on African Art,
    Society, and Religion in Oyotunji, South
    Carolina*, 342
Conference on College Composition
    and Communication (CCCC), 75

*Confronting and Changing Images and
    Representations of Black Womanhood
    in Rap Music*, 81
Conrad, Mark, 100
*Crisis of Black Athletes on the Eve of
    the 21st Century*, 119
Cukor-Avila, Patricia, 271
Cullen, Countee, 56
Culture: Negro, Black, and Nigger, 231

*David Walker's Appeal in Four Articles,
    Preamble*, 132
Derricotte, Toi, 22
*Do We Need a National Language
    Policy?* 75
Douglass, Frederick, 327
Doyle, Arthur, 168
Dropping the 'One Drop' Rule, 37
DuBois, W.E.B., 2
Dyson, Michael Eric, 237

*Ebonics: When Is Dialect Acceptable
    English?* 70
Edelman, Marian Wright, 287
Edwards, Harry, 119
elegy, 163
Entine, Jon, 115
*Ethics of Living Jim Crow, The: An
    Autobiographical Sketch*, 13

Family Legacy, A, 287
Fish, Stanley, 30
Fisher, Mary, 181
*For U.S. Blacks, an Ancient Faith,
    a Renewed Hope*, 346
From African to African American, 43
*From the Inside Looking Out: Twenty-Nine
    Years in the New York Police
    Department*, 168

Gilkes, Cheryl Townsend, 329
Gilyard, Keith, 59
Gomez, Jewelle, 244
Gwaltney, John Langston, 223

Haley, Alex, 334
Hall, Ronald E., 24
Hoop Roots, 125
Hughes, Langston, 16
Hurston, Zora Neale, 54

I Am a Black Woman, 222
Idea of Ancestry, The, 273
In Praise of Black Family Reunions, 286
Incident, 56

Jackson, Emma D., 76
Je suis un homme, 219
Joans, Ted, 219
Johnson, James Weldon, 91

King, Peter, 114
Knight, Etheridge, 273

"Laura Smalley," 271
Lee, Jarena, 321
Legacy of Healing, A, 60
Linguistic Society of America Resolution on the Oakland 'Ebonics' Issue, 69
Linguistic Society of America, 69
Literary Digest, 52

Malcomson, Scott L., 135
Many Shades of Black, The, 223
Mari Evans, 221
Maynor, Natalie, 271
McBride, James, 19
Mecca, 333
Meeks, Kenneth, 165
More Brains or More . . . , 115
Morehouse Research Institute, 289
Mulrine, Anna, 286
My Brother's Keeper, 173
My Dungeon Shook: Letter to My Nephew on the One Hundredth Anniversary of the Emancipation, 216
Myth of the Welfare Queen, The, 282

N-Word, The, 76
Narrative of William W. Brown, The: From Slave to Abolitionist, 90
Negro Dialect, The, 47
Neither Separate Schools nor Mixed Schools: The Chronicle of the Sacrificed Black Schoolchildren, 148
NFL's Black Eye, The, 114

Objecting to the Negro Dialect, 52
Of Our Spiritual Strivings, 2
Omari-Tunkara, Mikelle Smith, 342

Pa Henry's Prayer, 54
Plantation Courtship, 269
Pough, Gwen, 81
Primitive Blues and Primitive Jazz, 57

Race-Holding, 27
Red Record, A: The Case Restated, 142
Reising, Robert W., 75
Reverse Racism, or How the Pot Got to Call the Kettle Black, 31
Rhor, Monica, 346
Robbing the Cradle, 109
Roselily, 337
Rowan, Carl, 193
Russell, Kathy, 24

Sanchez, Sonia, 163
Sending Up Some Timber: Elderly Slaves and Religious Leadership in the Antebellum Slave Community, 311
Shopping in a Group While Black, 165
Slave Family, The, 254
Smitherman, Geneva, 43
Steal Away: Traditional Spiritual, 320
Steele, Shelby, 27
Struggle of Curt Flood, The, 95
Students' Right to Their Own Language, The, 75
Subject of My Call to Preach Renewed, The, 322

Taylor, Susan, 348
Tinney, James S., 340
Together and in Harness: Women's Traditions in the Sanctified Church, 329
Turning the Corner on Father Absence in Black America: About the Morehouse Conference, 289

Walker, Alice, 336
Walker, David, 132
Warren, Gwedolyn Sims, 318
We Can Be as Separate as the Fingers: Segregation from the American Revolution to the Gilded Age, 136
Wells-Barnett, Ida B., 142
What Is Race? 8
Who's Passing for Who? 16
Why a Black Gay Church? 340
Wideman, John Edgar, 125
Will, George F., 37
Williams, Dennis A., 109
Wilson, Midge, 24
Witch-Hunt, The, 181
Woman Just Wouldn't, A, 277
Wright, Richard, 12

X, Malcolm, 333